THE TIMES
Guide to the House of Commons May 1979

Times Books

Published by Times Books Limited, 18 Ogle Street, London W1P 7LG

Copyright © Times Newspapers Limited 1979

ISBN 0 7230 0225 8

Printed in Great Britain by Tonbridge Printers Limited

Contents

Her Majesty's Government

The Cabinet

Prime Minister and First Lord of the Treasury
Mrs Margaret Thatcher

Secretary of State for the Home Department
Mr William Whitelaw

Lord Chancellor
Lord Hailsham of St Marylebone

Secretary of State for Foreign and Commonwealth Affairs and Minister of Overseas Development
Lord Carrington

Chancellor of the Exchequer
Sir Geoffrey Howe

Secretary of State for Industry
Sir Keith Joseph

Secretary of State for Defence
Mr Francis Pym

Lord President of the Council and Leader of the House of Lords
Lord Soames

Secretary of State for Employment
Mr James Prior

Lord Privy Seal
Sir Ian Gilmour

Minister of Agriculture, Fisheries and Food
Mr Peter Walker

Secretary of State for the Environment
Mr Michael Heseltine

Secretary of State for Scotland
Mr George Younger

Secretary of State for Wales
Mr Nicholas Edwards

Secretary of State for Northern Ireland
Mr Humphrey Atkins

Secretary of State for Social Services
Mr Patrick Jenkin

Chancellor of the Duchy of Lancaster, Leader of the House of Commons and Minister for the Arts
Mr Norman St John-Stevas

Secretary of State for Trade
Mr John Nott

Secretary of State for Energy
Mr David Howell

Secretary of State for Education and Science
Mr Mark Carlisle

Chief Secretary to the Treasury
Mr John Biffen

Paymaster General
Mr Angus Maude

Ministers not in the Cabinet

Minister of Transport
Mr Norman Fowler

Parliamentary Secretary to the Treasury and Government Chief Whip in the Commons
Mr Michael Jopling

Minister of State for Consumer Affairs (at Department of Trade)
Mrs Sally Oppenheim

Minister of State for Foreign and Commonwealth Affairs
Mr Douglas Hurd

Minister of State for Foreign and Commonwealth Affairs
Mr Nicholas Ridley

Minister of State for Foreign and Commonwealth Affairs
Mr Peter Blaker

Minister of State for Foreign and Commonwealth Affairs (Overseas Development)
Mr Neil Marten

Financial Secretary to the Treasury
Mr Nigel Lawson

Minister of State, Treasury
Mr Peter Rees

Minister of State, Treasury
Lord Cockfield

Minister of State for Housing (at Department of the Environment)
Mr John Stanley

Minister of State, Civil Service Department
Mr Paul Channon

Minister of State for Local Government (at Department of the Environment)
Mr Tom King

Minister of State, Home Office
Mr Timothy Raison

Minister of State, Home Office
Mr Leon Brittan

Minister of State for Energy
Mr Hamish Gray

Minister of State for Defence
Lord Strathcona

Minister of State for Industry
Mr Adam Butler

Minister of State for Industry
Viscount Trenchard

Minister of State for Northern Ireland
Mr Michael Alison

Minister of State for Northern Ireland
Mr Hugh Rossi

Minister of State for Scotland
The Earl of Mansfield

Minister of State for Agriculture, Fisheries and Food
Earl Ferrers

Minister of State for Agriculture, Fisheries and Food
Mr Alick Buchanan-Smith

Minister of State for Trade
Mr Cecil Parkinson

Minister of State for Employment
The Earl of Gowrie

Minister of State for Health
Dr Gerard Vaughan

Minister of State for Social Security (Disabled)
Mr Reginald Prentice

Minister of State for Education and Science
Lady Young

LAW OFFICERS
Attorney General
Sir Michael Havers

Lord Advocate
Mr James Mackay

Solicitor General
Sir Ian Percival

Solicitor General for Scotland
Mr Nicholas Fairbairn

Departments and Ministers

AGRICULTURE

Minister
Mr Peter Walker

Ministers of State
Earl Ferrers
Mr Alick Buchanan-Smith

Parliamentary Secretary
Mr Jerry Wiggin

CIVIL SERVICE

Minister
The Prime Minister

Lord President of the Council, (responsible for day-to-day administration)
Lord Soames

Minister of State
Mr Paul Channon

DEFENCE

Secretary of State
Mr Francis Pym

Minister of State
Lord Strathcona

Under Secretary of Defence for the Royal Navy
Mr Keith Speed

Under Secretary of Defence for the Army
Mr Barney Hayhoe

Under Secretary of Defence for the RAF
Mr Geoffrey Pattie

DUCHY OF LANCASTER

Chancellor (Leader of the House of Commons and Minister for the Arts)
Mr Norman St John-Stevas

EDUCATION AND SCIENCE

Secretary of State
Mr Mark Carlisle

5

Minister of State
Lady Young

Under Secretaries of State
Mr Rhodes Boyson
Mr Neil Macfarlane

EMPLOYMENT

Secretary of State
Mr James Prior

Minister of State
The Earl of Gowrie

Under Secretaries of State
Mr James Lester
Mr Patrick Mayhew

ENERGY

Secretary of State
Mr David Howell

Minister of State
Mr Hamish Gray

Under Secretaries of State
Mr Norman Lamont
Mr John Moore

ENVIRONMENT

Secretary of State
Mr Michael Heseltine

Ministers of State
Mr Tom King (Local government)
Mr John Stanley (Housing)

Under Secretaries of State
Mr Marcus Fox
Mr Geoffrey Finsberg
Lord Bellwin
Mr Hector Monro (Sport)

FOREIGN AND COMMONWEALTH OFFICE

Secretary of State
Lord Carrington

Lord Privy Seal (principal spokesman in the House of Commons)
Sir Ian Gilmour

Ministers of State
Mr Douglas Hurd
Mr Nicholas Ridley
Mr Peter Blaker
Mr Neil Marten (Overseas Development)

Under Secretary of State
Mr Richard Luce

HEALTH AND SOCIAL SECURITY

Secretary of State for Social Services
Mr Patrick Jenkin

Ministers of State
Dr Gerard Vaughan (Health)
Mr Reginald Prentice (Social Security and Disabled)

Under Secretaries of State
Sir George Young
Mrs Lynda Chalker

HOME OFFICE

Home Secretary
Mr William Whitelaw

Ministers of State
Mr Timothy Raison
Mr Leon Brittan

Under Secretary of State
Lord Belstead

INDUSTRY

Secretary of State
Sir Keith Joseph

Ministers of State
Mr Adam Butler
Viscount Trenchard

Under Secretaries of State
Mr Michael Marshall
Mr David Mitchell

LORD CHANCELLOR

Lord Hailsham of St Marylebone

LORD PRIVY SEAL (and principal Foreign and Commonwealth Office spokesman in the House of Commons)
Sir Ian Gilmour

NORTHERN IRELAND OFFICE

Secretary of State
Mr Humphrey Atkins

Ministers of State
Mr Michael Alison
Mr Hugh Rossi

Under Secretaries of State
Lord Elton
Mr Philip Goodhart
Mr Giles Shaw

PAYMASTER GENERAL
Mr Angus Maude

PRIVY COUNCIL OFFICE
Lord President of the Council (and Leader of the House of Lords)
Lord Soames

SCOTTISH OFFICE
Secretary of State
Mr George Younger

Minister of State
The Earl of Mansfield

Under Secretaries of State
Mr Alexander Fletcher
Mr Russell Fairgrieve
Mr Malcolm Rifkind

TRADE
Secretary of State
Mr John Nott

Minister of State for Consumer Affairs
Mrs Sally Oppenheim

Minister of State
Mr Cecil Parkinson

Under Secretaries of State
Mr Norman Tebbit
Mr Reginald Eyre

TRANSPORT
Minister
Mr Norman Fowler

Parliamentary Secretary
Mr Kenneth Clarke

TREASURY
Prime Minister and First Lord of the Treasury
Mrs Margaret Thatcher

Chancellor of the Exchequer
Sir Geoffrey Howe

Chief Secretary to the Treasury
Mr John Biffen

Parliamentary Secretary and Government Chief Whip in the House of Commons
Mr Michael Jopling

Ministers of State
Mr Peter Rees
Lord Cockfield

Financial Secretary
Mr Nigel Lawson

Lords Commissioners (Government whips)
Mr Carol Mather
Mr Peter Morrison
Lord James Douglas-Hamilton
Mr John MacGregor
Mr David Waddington

Assistant whips
Mr Robert Boscawen
Mr John Cope
Mr Antony Newton
Mr John Wakeham
Mr Peter Brooke

WALES
Secretary of State
Mr Nicholas Edwards

Under Secretaries of State
Mr Michael Roberts
Mr Wyn Roberts

HER MAJESTY'S HOUSEHOLD
Treasurer (Government Deputy Chief Whip in the House of Commons)
Mr John Stradling Thomas

Comptroller
Mr Spencer Le Marchant

Vice-Chamberlain
Mr Anthony Berry

Captain, Gentlemen-at-Arms (Government Chief Whip in the House of Lords)
Lord Denham

Captain, Yeomen of the Guard (Government Deputy Chief Whip in the House of Lords)
Lord Sandys

Lords-in-Waiting
Lord Mowbray and Stourton
Viscount Long
Lord Lyell
Lord Cullen of Ashbourne
Lord Trefgarne

Second Church Estates Commissioner
Mr William van Straubenzee

The House of Commons

In this list of members returned to the House of Commons at the General Election on May 3, 1979, a † denotes new members. The abbreviations used to designate political parties are: C – Conservative; Lab – Labour; Lab & Co-op – Labour and Co-operative; L – Liberal; Off UU – Official Ulster Unionist; Dem U – Democratic Unionist; Scot Nat – Scottish National; Pl Cymru – Plaid Cymru; SDLP – Social Democratic and Labour Party; UU – Ulster Unionist; UUUP – United Ulster Unionist Party; Ind – Independent.

A

ABSE, Leo: *Pontypool*	Lab
†ADAMS, Allen: *Paisley*	Lab
ADLEY, Robert: *Christchurch and Lymington*	C
AITKEN, Jonathan: *Thanet, East*	C
†ALEXANDER, Richard: *Newark*	C
ALISON, Michael: *Barkston Ash*	C
ALLAUN, Frank: *Salford, East*	Lab
ALTON, David: *Liverpool, Edge Hill*	L
AMERY, Julian: *Brighton, Pavilion*	C
†ANCRAM, Michael: *Edinburgh, South*	C
ANDERSON, Donald: *Swansea, East*	Lab
ARCHER, Peter: *Warley, West*	Lab
ARMSTRONG, Ernest: *Durham, North-West*	Lab
ARNOLD, Tom: *Hazel Grove*	C
ASHLEY, Jack: *Stoke-on-Trent, South*	Lab
ASHTON, Joe: *Bassetlaw*	Lab
†ASPINWALL, Jack: *Kingswood*	C
ATKINS, Humphrey: *Spelthorne*	C
†ATKINS, Robert: *Preston, North*	C
ATKINSON, David: *Bournemouth, East*	C
ATKINSON, Norman: *Haringey, Tottenham*	Lab

B

BAGIER, Gordon: *Sunderland, South*	Lab
BAKER, Kenneth: *City of Westminster, St Marylebone*	C
†BAKER, Nicholas: *Dorset, North*	C
BANKS, Robert: *Harrogate*	C
BARNETT, Guy: *Greenwich*	Lab

BARNETT, Joel: *Heywood and Royton* — Lab
†BEAUMONT-DARK, Anthony: *Birmingham, Selly Oak* — C
BEITH, Alan: *Berwick-upon-Tweed* — L
BELL, Ronald: *Beaconsfield* — C
BENDALL, Vivian: Redbridge, *Ilford, North* — C
BENN, Anthony Wedgwood: *Bristol, South-East* — Lab
BENNETT, Andrew: *Stockport, North* — Lab
BENNETT, Sir Frederic: *Torbay* — C
†BENYON, Thomas: *Abingdon* — C
BENYON, William: *Buckingham* — C
BERRY, Anthony: *Enfield, Southgate* — C
†BEST, Keith: *Anglesey* — C
†BEVAN, David: *Birmingham, Yardley* — C
BIDWELL, Sydney: *Ealing, Southall* — Lab
BIFFEN, John: *Oswestry* — C
BIGGS-DAVISON, John: *Epping Forest* — C
†BLACKBURN, John: *Dudley, West* — C
BLAKER, Peter: *Blackpool, South* — C
BODY, Richard: *Holland with Boston* — C
†BONSOR, Sir Nicholas: *Nantwich* — C
BOOTH, Albert: *Barrow-in-Furness* — Lab
BOOTHROYD, Miss Betty: *West Bromwich, West* — Lab
BOSCAWEN, Robert: *Wells* — C
BOTTOMLEY, Arthur: *Teesside, Middlesbrough* — Lab
BOTTOMLEY, Peter: *Greenwich, Woolwich, West* — C
BOWDEN, Andrew: *Brighton, Kemptown* — C
BOYSON, Rhodes: *Brent, North* — C
BRADFORD, Rev. Robert: *Belfast, South* — Off UU
BRADLEY, Tom: *Leicester, East* — Lab
BRAINE, Sir Bernard: *Essex, South-East* — C
BRAY, Jeremy: *Motherwell and Wishaw* — Lab
†BRIGHT, Graham: *Luton, East* — C
†BRINTON, Timothy: *Gravesend* — C
BRITTAN, Leon: *Cleveland and Whitby* — C
BROCKLEBANK-FOWLER, Christopher: *Norfolk, North-West* — C
BROOKE, Peter: *City of London and Westminster, South* — C
BROTHERTON, Michael: *Louth* — C
BROWN, Hugh: *Glasgow, Provan* — Lab
†BROWN, Michael: *Brigg and Scunthorpe* — C
BROWN, Robert: *Newcastle upon Tyne, West* — Lab
BROWN, Ronald W: *Hackney, South and Shoreditch* — Lab
†BROWN, Ronald: *Edinburgh, Leith* — Lab
†BROWNE, John: *Winchester* — C
†BRUCE-GARDYNE, John: *Knutsford* — C
BRYAN, Sir Paul: *Howden* — C
BUCHAN, Norman: *Renfrewshire, West* — Lab

BUCHANAN-SMITH, Alick: *Angus, North and Mearns*   C
BUCK, Anthony: *Colchester*   C
BUDGEN, Nicholas: *Wolverhampton, South-West*   C
BULMER, Esmond: *Kidderminster*   C
BURDEN, Frederick: *Gillingham*   C
†BUTCHER, John: *Coventry, South-West*   C
BUTLER, Adam: *Bosworth*   C

C

†CADBURY, Jocelyn: *Birmingham, Northfield*   C
CALLAGHAN, James: *Cardiff, South-East*   Lab
CALLAGHAN, James: *Middleton and Prestwich*   Lab
CAMPBELL, Ian: *Dunbartonshire, West*   Lab
†CAMPBELL-SAVOURS, Dale: *Workington*   Lab
CANAVAN, Dennis: *Stirlingshire, West*   Lab
CANT, Robert: *Stoke-on-Trent, Central*   Lab
†CARLISLE, John: *Luton, West*   C
†CARLISLE, Kenneth: *Lincoln*   C
CARLISLE, Mark: *Runcorn*   C
CARMICHAEL, Neil: *Glasgow, Kelvingrove*   Lab
CARTER-JONES, Lewis: *Eccles*   Lab
CARTWRIGHT, John: *Greenwich, Woolwich, East*   Lab
CHALKER, Mrs Lynda: *Wallasey*   C
CHANNON, Paul: *Southend, West*   C
†CHAPMAN, Sydney: *Barnet, Chipping Barnet*   C
CHURCHILL, Winston: *Stretford*   C
CLARK, Alan: *Plymouth, Sutton*   C
†CLARK, David: *South Shields*   Lab
CLARK, William: *Croydon, South*   C
CLARKE, Kenneth: *Rushcliffe*   C
CLEGG, Walter: *North Fylde*   C
†COCKERAM, Eric: *Ludlow*   C
COCKS, Michael: *Bristol, South*   Lab
COHEN, Stanley: *Leeds, South-East*   Lab
COLEMAN, Donald: *Neath*   Lab
†COLVIN, Michael: *Bristol, North-West*   C
CONCANNON, Dennis: *Mansfield*   Lab
CONLAN, Bernard: *Gateshead, East*   Lab
COOK, Robin: *Edinburgh, Central*   Lab
COPE, John: *Gloucestershire, South*   C
CORMACK, Patrick: *Staffordshire South-West*   C
CORRIE, John: *Ayrshire, North and Bute*   C
COSTAIN, Albert: *Folkestone and Hythe*   C
COWANS, Harry: *Newcastle upon Tyne, Central*   Lab
COX, Thomas: *Wandsworth, Tooting*   Lab
CRAIGEN, James: *Glasgow, Maryhill*   Lab & Co-op
†CRANBOURNE, Viscount: *Dorset, South*   C

CRAWSHAW, Richard: *Liverpool, Toxteth* — Lab
CRITCHLEY, Julian: *Aldershot* — C
CROUCH, David: *Canterbury* — C
CROWTHER, Stanley: *Rotherham* — Lab
CRYER, Robert: *Keighley* — Lab
†CUNLIFFE, Lawrence: *Leigh* — Lab
CUNNINGHAM, George: *Islington, South and Finsbury* — Lab
CUNNINGHAM, John: *Whitehaven* — Lab

D

DALYELL, Tam: *West Lothian* — Lab
DAVIDSON, Arthur: *Accrington* — Lab
DAVIES, Denzil: *Llanelli* — Lab
†DAVIES, Hudson: *Caerphilly* — Lab
DAVIES, Ifor: *Gower* — Lab
DAVIS, Clinton: *Hackney, Central* — Lab
†DAVIS, Terence: *Birmingham, Stechford* — Lab
DEAKINS, Eric: *Waltham Forest, Walthamstow* — Lab
DEAN, Joseph: *Leeds, West* — Lab
DEAN, Paul: *Somerset, North* — C
DEMPSEY, James: *Coatbridge and Airdrie* — Lab
DEWAR, Donald: *Glasgow, Garscadden* — Lab
†DICKENS, Geoffrey: *Huddersfield, West* — C
†DIXON, Donald: *Jarrow* — Lab
†DOBSON, Frank: *Camden, Holborn and St Pancras, South* — Lab
DODSWORTH, Geoffrey: *Hertfordshire, South-West* — C
DORMAND, John: *Easington* — Lab
†DORRELL, Stephen: *Loughborough* — C
†DOUGLAS, Richard: *Dunfermline* — Lab & Co-op
DOUGLAS-HAMILTON, Lord James: *Edinburgh, West* — C
DOUGLAS-MANN, Bruce: *Merton, Mitcham and Morden* — Lab
†DOVER, Denshore: *Chorley* — C
†DUBS, Alfred: *Wandsworth, Battersea, South* — Lab
DU CANN, Edward: *Taunton* — C
DUFFY, Patrick: *Sheffield, Attercliffe* — Lab
DUNLOP, John: *Ulster, Mid* — UUUP
DUNN, James: *Liverpool, Kirkdale* — Lab
†DUNN, John: *Dartford* — C
DUNNETT, Jack: *Nottingham, East* — Lab
DUNWOODY, Mrs Gwyneth: *Crewe* — Lab
DURANT, Anthony: *Reading, North* — C
DYKES, Hugh: *Harrow, East* — C

E

EADIE, Alexander: *Midlothian*	Lab
†EASTON, Kenneth: *Manchester, Blackley*	Lab
EDEN, Sir John: *Bournemouth, West*	C
EDWARDS, Nicholas: *Pembroke*	C
EDWARDS, Robert: *Wolverhampton, South-East*	Lab & Co-op
†EGGAR, Timothy: *Enfield, North*	C
ELLIOTT, Sir William: *Newcastle upon Tyne, North*	C
†ELLIS, Raymond: *Derbyshire, North-East*	Lab
ELLIS, Thomas: *Wrexham*	Lab
EMERY, Peter: *Honiton*	C
ENGLISH, Michael: *Nottingham, West*	Lab
ENNALS, David: *Norwich, North*	Lab
EVANS, Ioan: *Aberdare*	Lab & Co-op
EVANS, John: *Newton*	Lab
EWING, Harry: *Stirling, Falkirk and Grangemouth*	Lab
EYRE, Reginald: *Birmingham, Hall Green*	C

F

FAIRBAIRN, Nicholas: *Kinross and West Perthshire*	C
FAIRGRIEVE, Russell: *Aberdeenshire, West*	C
†FAITH, Mrs Irene: *Belper*	C
FARR, John: *Harborough*	C
FAULDS, Andrew: *Warley, East*	Lab
FELL, Anthony: *Yarmouth*	C
†FENNER, Mrs Peggy: *Rochester and Chatham*	C
†FIELD, Frank: *Birkenhead*	Lab
FINSBERG, Geoffrey: *Camden, Hampstead*	C
FISHER, Sir Nigel: *Kingston upon Thames, Surbiton*	C
FITCH, Alan: *Wigan*	Lab
FITT, Gerard: *Belfast, West*	SDLP
FLANNERY, Martin: *Sheffield, Hillsborough*	Lab
FLETCHER, Alex: *Edinburgh, North*	C
FLETCHER, Edward: *Darlington, Lab*	Lab
FLETCHER, Raymond: *Ilkeston*	Lab
FLETCHER-COOKE, Charles: *Darwen*	C
FOOKES, Miss Janet: *Plymouth, Drake*	C
FOOT, Michael: *Ebbw Vale*	Lab
FORD, Benjamin: *Bradford, North*	Lab
FORMAN, Nigel: *Sutton, Carshalton*	C
FORRESTER, John: *Stoke-on-Trent, North*	Lab
†FOSTER, Derek: *Bishop Auckland*	Lab
†FOULKES, George: *Ayrshire, South*	Lab & Co-op
FOWLER, Norman: *Sutton Coldfield*	C

Fox, Marcus: *Shipley*   C
FRASER, Hugh: *Stafford and Stone*   C
FRASER, John: *Lambeth, Norwood*   Lab
†FRASER, Peter: *Angus, South*   C
FREESON, Reginald: *Brent, East*   Lab
FREUD, Clement: *Isle of Ely*   L
FRY, Peter: *Wellingborough*   C

G

GALBRAITH, Thomas: *Glasgow, Hillhead*   C
GARDINER, George: *Reigate*   C
GARDNER, Edward: *South Fylde*   C
†GAREL-JONES, William: *Watford*   C
GARRETT, Edward: *Wallsend*   Lab
GARRETT, John: *Norwich, South*   Lab
GEORGE, Bruce: *Walsall, South*   Lab
GILBERT, John: *Dudley, East*   Lab
GILMOUR, Sir Ian: *Chesham and Amersham*   C
GINSBURG, David: *Dewsbury*   Lab
GLYN, Dr Alan: *Windsor and Maidenhead*   C
GOLDING, John: *Newcastle-under-Lyme*   Lab
GOODHART, Philip: *Bromley, Beckenham*   C
GOODHEW, Victor: *St Albans*   C
GOODLAD, Alistair: *Northwich*   C
GORST, John: *Barnet, Hendon, North*   C
GOURLAY, Harry: *Kirkcaldy*   Lab
Gow, Ian: *Eastbourne*   C
GOWER, Sir Raymond: *Barry*   C
GRAHAM, Edward: *Enfield, Edmonton*   Lab & Co-op
GRANT, Anthony: *Harrow, Central*   C
GRANT, George: *Morpeth*   Lab
GRANT, John: *Islington, Central*   Lab
GRAY, Hamish: *Ross and Cromarty*   C
†GREENWAY, Harry: *Ealing, North*   C
GRIEVE, Percy: *Solihull*   C
GRIFFITHS, Eldon: *Bury St Edmunds*   C
†GRIFFITHS, Peter: *Portsmouth, North*   C
GRIMOND, Jo: *Orkney and Shetland*   L
GRIST, Ian: *Cardiff, North*   C
GRYLLS, Michael: *Surrey, North-West*   C
†GUMMER, Selwyn: *Eye*   C

H

HAMILTON, Archibald: *Epsom and Ewell*   C
HAMILTON, James: *Bothwell*   Lab
HAMILTON, Michael: *Salisbury*   C
HAMILTON, William: *Fife, Central*   Lab

HAMPSON, Keith: *Ripon*   C
HANNAM, John: *Exeter*   C
HARDY, Peter: *Rother Valley*   Lab
HARRISON, Walter: *Wakefield*   Lab
HART, Mrs Judith: *Lanark*   Lab
HASELHURST, Alan: *Saffron Walden*   C
HASTINGS, Stephen: *Bedfordshire, Mid*   C
HATTERSLEY, Roy: *Birmingham, Sparkbrook*   Lab
HAVERS, Sir Michael: *Merton, Wimbledon*   C
HAWKINS, Paul: *Norfolk, South-West*   C
†HAWKSLEY, Warren: *Wrekin, The*   C
HAYHOE, Barney: *Hounslow, Brentford and Isleworth*   C
†HAYNES, Frank: *Ashfield*   Lab
HEALEY, Denis: *Leeds, East*   Lab
HEATH, Edward: *Bexley, Sidcup*   C
†HEDDLE, John: *Lichfield and Tamworth*   C
HEFFER, Eric: *Liverpool, Walton*   Lab
†HENDERSON, Barry: *Fife, East*   C
HESELTINE, Michael: *Henley*   C
HICKS, Robert: *Bodmin*   C
HIGGINS, Terence: *Worthing*   C
†HILL, James: *Southampton, Test*   C
†HOGG, Douglas: *Grantham*   C
†HOGG, Norman: *Dunbartonshire, East*   Lab
HOLLAND, Philip: *Carlton*   C
†HOLLAND, Stuart: *Lambeth, Vauxhall*   Lab
†HOMEWOOD, William: *Kettering*   Lab
HOOLEY, Frank: *Sheffield, Heeley*   Lab
†HOOSON, Tom: *Brecon and Radnor*   C
HORAM, John: *Gateshead, West*   Lab
HORDERN, Peter: *Horsham and Crawley*   C
HOWE, Sir Geoffrey: *Surrey, East*   C
HOWELL, David: *Guildford*   C
HOWELL, Denis: *Birmingham, Small Heath*   Lab
HOWELL, Ralph: *Norfolk, North*   C
HOWELLS, Geraint: *Cardigan*   L
HUCKFIELD, Leslie: *Nuneaton*   Lab
HUGHES, Mark: *Durham*   Lab
HUGHES, Robert: *Aberdeen, North*   Lab
HUGHES, Roy: *Newport*   Lab
HUNT, David: *Wirral*   C
HUNT, John: *Bromley, Ravensbourne*   C
HURD, Douglas: *Oxon, Mid*   C

I

IRVINE, Godman: *Rye*   C
IRVING, Charles: *Cheltenham*   C

J

JAMES, Robert Rhodes: *Cambridge*	C
JANNER, Greville: *Leicester, West*	Lab
JAY, Douglas: *Wandsworth, Battersea, North*	Lab
JENKIN, Patrick: *Redbridge, Wanstead and Woodford*	C
JESSEL, Toby: *Richmond upon Thames, Twickenham*	C
JOHN, Brynmor: *Pontypridd*	Lab
JOHNSON, James: *Kingston upon Hull, West*	Lab
JOHNSON, Walter: *Derby, South*	Lab
JOHNSON SMITH, Geoffrey: *East Grinstead*	C
JOHNSTON, Russell: *Inverness*	L
JONES, Alec: *Rhondda*	Lab
JONES, Barry: *Flint, East*	Lab
JONES, Daniel: *Burnley*	Lab
JOPLING, Michael: *Westmorland*	C
JOSEPH, Sir Keith: *Leeds, North-East*	C

K

KABERRY, Sir Donald: *Leeds, North-West*	C
KAUFMAN, Gerald: *Manchester, Ardwick*	Lab
KELLETT-BOWMAN, Mrs Elaine: *Lancaster*	C
KERR, Russell: *Hounslow, Feltham and Heston*	Lab
KERSHAW, Anthony: *Stroud*	C
KILFEDDER, James: *Down, North*	UU
KILROY-SILK, Robert: *Ormskirk*	Lab
KIMBALL, Marcus: *Gainsborough*	C
KING, Tom: *Bridgwater*	C
KINNOCK, Neil: *Bedwellty*	Lab
KITSON, Sir Timothy: *Richmond, Yorks*	C
KNIGHT, Mrs Jill: *Birmingham, Edgbaston*	C
KNOX, David: *Leek*	C

L

LAMBIE, David: *Ayrshire, Central*	Lab
LAMBURN, Harry: *Southwark, Peckham*	Lab
LAMOND, James: *Oldham, East*	Lab
LAMONT, Norman: *Kingston upon Thames*	C
†LANG, Ian: *Galloway*	C
LANGFORD-HOLT, Sir John: *Shrewsbury*	C
LATHAM, Michael: *Melton*	C
LAWRENCE, Ivan: *Burton*	C
LAWSON, Nigel: *Blaby*	C
LEADBITTER, Edward: *Hartlepool*	Lab
†LEE, John: *Nelson and Colne*	C
†LEIGHTON, Ronald: *Newham, North-East*	Lab

LE MARCHANT, Spencer: *High Peak*   C
†LENNOX-BOYD, Mark: *Morecambe and Lonsdale*   C
LESTER, James: *Beeston*   C
LESTOR, Miss Joan: *Eton and Slough*   Lab
LEVER, Harold: *Manchester, Central*   Lab
LEWIS, Arthur: *Newham, North-West*   Lab
LEWIS, Kenneth: *Rutland and Stamford*   C
LEWIS, Ronald: *Carlisle*   Lab
LLOYD, Ian: *Havant and Waterloo*   C
†LLOYD, Peter: *Fareham*   C
LOFTHOUSE, Geoffrey: *Pontefract and Castleford*   Lab
LOVERIDGE, John: *Havering, Upminster*   C
LUCE, Richard: *Shoreham*   C
†LYELL, Nicholas: *Hemel Hempstead*   C
LYON, Alexander: *York*   Lab
LYONS, Edward: *Bradford, West*   Lab

M

MABON, Dr Dickson: *Greenock and Port Glasgow*   Lab & Co-op
MACFARLANE, Neil: *Sutton and Cheam*   C
MACGREGOR, John: *Norfolk, South*   C
MACLENNAN, Robert: *Caithness and Sutherland*   Lab
McADDEN, Sir Stephen: *Southend, East*   C
McCARTNEY, Hugh: *Dunbartonshire, Central*   Lab
McCRINDLE, Robert: *Brentwood and Ongar*   C
McCUSKER, James: *Armagh*   Off UU
McDONALD, Miss Oonagh: *Thurrock*   Lab
McELHONE, Frank: *Glasgow, Queen's Park*   Lab
McGUIRE, Michael: *Ince*   Lab
McKAY, Allen: *Penistone*   Lab
†McKELVEY, William: *Kilmarnock*   Lab
†McMAHON, Andrew: *Glasgow, Govan*   Lab
McMILLAN, Thomas: *Glasgow, Central*   Lab
McNAIR-WILSON, Michael: *Newbury*   C
McNAIR-WILSON, Patrick: *New Forest*   C
†McNALLY, Tom: *Stockport, South*   Lab
McNAMARA, Kevin: *Kingston upon Hull, Central*   Lab
†McQUADE, John: *Belfast, North*   Dem U
†McQUARRIE, Albert: *Aberdeenshire, East*   C
†McWILLIAM, John: *Blaydon*   Lab
†MACKAY, John: *Argyll*   C
MACKENZIE, Gregor: *Rutherglen*   Lab
MACMILLAN, Maurice: *Farnham*   C
MADEL, David: *Bedfordshire, South*   C
MAGEE, Bryan: *Waltham Forest, Leyton*   Lab

MAGUIRE, Frank: *Fermanagh and South Tyrone*   Ind
†MAJOR, John: *Huntingdonshire*   C
MARKS, Kenneth: *Manchester, Gorton*   Lab
†MARLAND, Paul: *Gloucestershire, West*   C
†MARLOW, Anthony: *Northampton, North*   C
†MARSHALL, David: *Glasgow, Shettleston*   Lab
MARSHALL, Edmund: *Goole*   Lab
MARSHALL, James: *Leicester, South*   Lab
MARSHALL, Michael: *Arundel*   C
MARTEN, Neil: *Banbury*   C
†MARTIN, Michael: *Glasgow, Springburn*   Lab
MASON, Roy: *Barnsley*   Lab
MATES, Michael: *Petersfield*   C
MATHER, Carol: *Esher*   C
MAUDE, Angus: *Stratford-on-Avon*   C
MAWBY, Ray: *Totnes*   C
†MAWHINNEY, Brian: *Peterborough*   C
†MAXTON, John: *Glasgow, Cathcart*   Lab
MAXWELL-HYSLOP, Robin: *Tiverton*   C
MAYHEW, Patrick: *Royal Tunbridge Wells*   C
MAYNARD, Miss Joan: *Sheffield, Brightside*   Lab
MEACHER, Michael: *Oldham, West*   Lab
MELLISH, Robert: *Southwark, Bermondsey*   Lab
†MELLOR, David: *Wandsworth, Putney*   C
MEYER, Sir Anthony: *Flint, West*   C
MIKARDO, Ian: *Tower Hamlets, Bethnal Green
      and Bow*   Lab
MILLAN, Bruce: *Glasgow, Craigton*   Lab
MILLER, Hilary: *Bromsgrove and Redditch*   C
MILLER, Dr Maurice: *East Kilbride*   Lab
†MILLS, Iain: *Meriden*   C
MILLS, Peter: *Devon, West*   C
MISCAMPBELL, Norman: *Blackpool, North*   C
MITCHELL, Austin: *Grimsby*   Lab
MITCHELL, David: *Basingstoke*   C
MITCHELL, Richard: *Southampton, Itchen*   Lab
MOATE, Roger: *Faversham*   C
MOLYNEAUX, James: *Antrim, South*   Off UU
MONRO, Hector: *Dumfries*   C
MONTGOMERY, Fergus: *Altrincham and Sale*   C
MOORE, John: *Croydon, Central*   C
MORGAN, Geraint: *Denbigh*   C
MORRIS, Alfred: *Manchester, Wythenshawe*   Lab & Co-op
MORRIS, Charles: *Manchester, Openshaw*   Lab
MORRIS, John: *Aberavon*   Lab
MORRIS, Michael: *Northampton, South*   C
MORRISON, Charles: *Devizes*   C
MORRISON, Peter: *Chester, City of*   C

Morton, George: *Manchester, Moss Side*	Lab
Moyle, Roland: *Lewisham, East*	Lab
Mudd, David: *Falmouth and Camborne*	C
Mulley, Frederick: *Sheffield, Park*	Lab
†Murphy, Christopher: *Welwyn and Hatfield*	C
†Myles, David: *Banff*	C

N

†Neale, Gerrard: *Cornwall, North*	C
†Needham, Richard: *Chippenham*	C
Nelson, Anthony: *Chichester*	C
Neubert, Michael: *Havering, Romford*	C
Newens, Stanley: *Harlow*	Lab & Co-op
Newton, Antony: *Braintree*	C
Normanton, Tom: *Cheadle*	C
Nott, John: *St Ives*	C

O

Oakes, Gordon: *Widnes*	Lab
Ogden, Eric: *Liverpool, West Derby*	Lab
O'Halloran, Michael: *Islington, North*	Lab
†O'Neil, Martin: *Stirlingshire, East and Clackmannan*	Lab
Onslow, Cranley: *Woking*	C
Oppenheim, Mrs Sally: *Gloucester*	C
Orme, Stanley: *Salford, West*	Lab
Osborn, John: *Sheffield, Hallam*	C
Owen, Dr David: *Plymouth, Devonport*	Lab

P

Page, Graham: *Crosby*	C
Page, John: *Harrow, West*	C
Paisley, Rev Ian: *Antrim, North*	Dem U
Palmer, Arthur: *Bristol, North-East*	Lab & Co-op
Park, George: *Coventry, North-East*	Lab
Parker, John: *Barking, Dagenham*	Lab
Parkinson, Cecil: *Hertfordshire, South*	C
†Parris, Matthew: *Derbyshire, West*	C
Parry, Robert: *Liverpool, Scotland Exchange*	Lab
†Patten, Christopher: *Bath*	C
†Patten, John: *Oxford*	C
Pattie, Geoffrey: *Chertsey and Walton*	C
Pavitt, Laurence: *Brent, South*	Lab & Co-op
†Pawsey, James: *Rugby*	C
Pendry, Thomas: *Stalybridge and Hyde*	Lab

PENHALIGON, David: *Truro*	L
PERCIVAL, Sir Ian: *Southport*	C
PEYTON, John: *Yeovil*	C
PINK, Bonner: *Portsmouth, South*	C
†POLLOCK, Alexander: *Moray and Nairn*	C
†PORTER, Barry: *Bebington and Ellesmere Port*	C
POWELL, Enoch: *Down, South*	Off UU
†POWELL, Raymond: *Ogmore*	Lab
PRENTICE, Reginald: *Daventry*	C
PRESCOTT, John: *Kingston upon Hull, East*	Lab
PRICE, Christopher: *Lewisham, West*	Lab
PRICE, David: *Eastleigh*	C
PRIOR, James: *Lowestoft*	C
†PROCTOR, Harvey: *Basildon*	C
PYM, Francis: *Cambridgeshire*	C

R

†RACE, Reg: *Haringey, Wood Green*	Lab
RADICE, Giles: *Chester-le-Street*	Lab
RAISON, Timothy: *Aylesbury*	C
RATHBONE, John: *Lewes*	C
REES, Merlyn: *Leeds South*	Lab
REES, Peter: *Dover and Deal*	C
REES-DAVIES, William: *Thanet, West*	C
RENTON, Timothy: *Sussex, Mid*	C
RHYS WILLIAMS, Sir Brandon: *Kensington and Chelsea, Kensington*	C
RICHARDSON, Miss Josephine: *Barking*	Lab
RIDLEY, Nicholas: *Cirencester and Tewkesbury*	C
RIDSDALE, Julian: *Harwich*	C
RIFKIND, Malcolm: *Edinburgh, Pentlands*	C
RIPPON, Geoffrey: *Hexham*	C
ROBERTS, Albert: *Normanton*	Lab
†ROBERTS, Allan: *Bootle*	Lab
†ROBERTS, Ernest: *Hackney, North and Stoke Newington*	Lab
ROBERTS, Gwilym: *Cannock*	Lab
ROBERTS, Michael: *Cardiff, North-West*	C
ROBERTS, Wyn: *Conway*	C
ROBERTSON, George: *Hamilton*	Lab
ROBERTSON, John: *Berwick and East Lothian*	Lab
ROBINSON, Geoffrey: *Coventry, North-West*	Lab
†ROBINSON, Peter: *Belfast, East*	Dem U
RODGERS, William: *Teesside, Stockton*	Lab
ROOKER, Jeffrey: *Birmingham, Perry Barr*	Lab
ROPER, John: *Farnworth*	Lab & Co-op
†ROSS, Ernest: *Dundee, West*	Lab

Ross, Stephen: *Isle of Wight* — L
Ross, William: *Londonderry* — Off UU
Rossi, Hugh: *Haringey, Hornsey* — C
Rost, Peter: *Derbyshire, South-East* — C
Rowlands, Edward: *Merthyr Tydfil* — Lab
Royle, Sir Anthony: *Richmond upon Thames, Richmond* — C
Ryman, John: *Blyth* — Lab

S

Sainsbury, Timothy: *Hove* — C
St. John-Stevas, Norman: *Chelmsford* — C
Sandelson, Neville: *Hillingdon, Hayes and Harlington* — Lab
Scott, Nicholas: *Kensington and Chelsea, Chelsea* — C
Sever, John: *Birmingham, Ladywood* — Lab
Shaw, Giles: *Pudsey* — C
Shaw, Michael: *Scarborough* — C
†Sheerman, Barry: *Huddersfield, East* — Lab & Co-op
Sheldon, Robert: *Ashton-under-Lyne* — Lab
Shelton, William: *Lambeth, Streatham* — C
Shepherd, Colin: *Hereford* — C
†Shepherd, Richard: *Aldridge-Brownhills* — C
Shersby, Michael: *Hillingdon, Uxbridge* — C
Shore, Peter: *Tower Hamlets, Stepney and Poplar* — Lab
Short, Mrs Reneé: *Wolverhampton, North-East* — Lab
Silkin, John: *Lewisham, Deptford* — Lab
Silkin, Samuel: *Southwark, Dulwich* — Lab
Silverman, Julius: *Birmingham, Erdington* — Lab
Silvester, Frederick: *Manchester, Withington* — C
Sims, Roger: *Bromley, Chislehurst* — C
Skeet, Trevor: *Bedford* — C
Skinner, Dennis: *Bolsover* — Lab
Smith, Cyril: *Rochdale* — L
Smith, Dudley: *Warwick and Leamington* — C
Smith, John: *Lanarkshire, North* — Lab
Snape, Peter: *West Bromwich, East* — Lab
†Soley, Clive: *Hammersmith, North* — Lab
Spearing, Nigel: *Newham, South* — Lab
Speed, Keith: *Ashford* — C
†Speller, Anthony: *Devon, North* — C
Spence, John: *Thirsk and Malton* — C
Spicer, James: *Dorset, West* — C
Spicer, Michael: *Worcestershire, South* — C
Spriggs, Leslie: *St Helens* — Lab
Sproat, Iain: *Aberdeen, South* — C

†SQUIRE, Robin: *Havering, Hornchurch*	C
STAINTON, Keith: *Sudbury and Woodbridge*	C
STALLARD, Albert: *Camden, St Pancras North*	Lab
STANBROOK, Ivor: *Bromley, Orpington*	C
STANLEY, John: *Tonbridge and Malling*	C
STEEL, David: *Roxburgh, Selkirk and Peebles*	L
STEEN, Anthony: *Liverpool, Wavertree*	C
†STEVENS, Martin: *Hammersmith, Fulham*	C
STEWART, Ian: *Hitchin*	C
STEWART, Donald: *Western Isles*	Scot Nat
†STEWART, Allan: *Renfrewshire, East*	C
STODDART, David: *Swindon*	Lab
STOKES, John: *Halesowen and Stourbridge*	C
STOTT, Roger: *Westhoughton*	Lab
STRADLING THOMAS, John: *Monmouth*	C
STRANG, Gavin: *Edinburgh, East*	Lab
†STRAW, Jack: *Blackburn*	Lab
SUMMERSKILL, Dr Shirley: *Halifax*	Lab

T

TAPSELL, Peter: *Horncastle*	C
TAYLOR, Mrs Ann: *Bolton, West*	Lab
TAYLOR, Robert: *Croydon, North-West*	C
TEBBIT, Norman: *Waltham Forest, Chingford*	C
TEMPLE-MORRIS, Peter: *Leominster*	C
THATCHER, Mrs Margaret: *Barnet, Finchley*	C
THOMAS, Dafydd: *Merioneth*	Pl Cymru
THOMAS, George: *Cardiff, West*	The Speaker
THOMAS, Jeffrey: *Abertillery*	Lab
THOMAS, Mike: *Newcastle upon Tyne, East*	Lab & Co-op
THOMAS, Peter: *Barnet, Hendon, South*	C
†THOMAS, Roger: *Carmarthen*	Lab
†THOMPSON, Derek: *Sowerby*	C
†THORNE, Neil: *Redbridge, Ilford, South*	C
THORNE, Stanley: *Preston, South*	Lab
†THORNTON, George: *Liverpool, Garston*	C
TILLEY, John: *Lambeth, Central*	Lab & Co-op
TINN, James: *Teesside, Redcar*	Lab
TORNEY, Thomas: *Bradford, South*	Lab
†TOWNEND, John: *Bridlington*	C
TOWNSEND, Cyril: *Bexley, Bexleyheath*	C
†TRIPPIER, David: *Rossendale*	C
TROTTER, Neville: *Tynemouth*	C

U

URWIN, Thomas: *Houghton-le-Spring*	Lab

V

VAN STRAUBENZEE, William: *Wokingham*	C
VARLEY, Eric: *Chesterfield*	Lab
VAUGHAN, Dr Gerard: *Reading, South*	C
VIGGERS, Peter: *Gosport*	C

W

WADDINGTON, David: *Clitheroe*	C
WAINWRIGHT, Edwin: *Dearne Valley*	Lab
WAINWRIGHT, Richard: *Colne Valley*	L
WAKEHAM, John: *Maldon*	C
†WALDEGRAVE, William: *Bristol, West*	C
WALKER, Harold: *Doncaster*	Lab
WALKER, Peter: *Worcester*	C
†WALKER, William: *Perth and East Perthshire*	C
WALKER-SMITH, Sir Derek: *Hertfordshire, East*	C
WALL, Patrick: *Haltemprice*	C
†WALLER, Gary: *Brighouse and Spenborough*	C
WALTERS, Dennis: *Westbury*	C
†WARD, John: *Poole*	C
WARREN, Kenneth: *Hastings*	C
WATKINS, David: *Consett*	Lab
†WATSON, John: *Skipton*	C
WEATHERILL, Bernard: *Croydon, North-East*	C
WEETCH, Kenneth: *Ipswich*	Lab
WELLBELOVED, James: *Bexley, Erith and Crayford*	Lab
WELLS, John: *Maidstone*	C
†WELLS, Petrie: *Hertford and Stevenage*	C
†WELSH, Michael: *Don Valley*	Lab
†WHEELER, John: *City of Westminster, Paddington*	C
WHITE, Frank: *Bury and Radcliffe*	Lab
WHITE, James: *Glasgow, Pollok*	Lab
WHITEHEAD, Phillip: *Derby, North*	Lab
WHITELAW, William: *Penrith and the Border*	C
WHITLOCK, William: *Nottingham, North*	Lab
WHITNEY, Raymond: *Wycombe*	C
†WICKENDEN, Keith: *Dorking*	C
WIGGIN, Jerry: *Weston-super-Mare*	C
WIGLEY, Dafydd: *Caernarvon*	Pl Cymru
†WILKINSON, John: *Hillingdon, Ruislip-Northwood*	C
WILLEY, Frederick: *Sunderland, North*	Lab
WILLIAMS, Alan: *Swansea, West*	Lab
†WILLIAMS, David: *Montgomery*	C
WILLIAMS, Sir Thomas: *Warrington*	Lab & Co-op
WILSON, Gordon: *Dundee, East*	Scot Nat
WILSON, Sir Harold: *Huyton*	Lab

Wᴉʟsᴏɴ, William: *Coventry, South-East*	Lab
†Wɪɴɴɪᴄᴋ, David: *Walsall North*	Lab
Wɪɴᴛᴇʀᴛᴏɴ, Nicholas: *Macclesfield*	C
†Wᴏʟғsᴏɴ, Mark: *Sevenoaks*	C
Wᴏᴏᴅᴀʟʟ, Alec: *Hemsworth*	Lab
†Wᴏᴏʟᴍᴇʀ, Kenneth: *Batley and Morley*	Lab
Wʀɪɢɢʟᴇsᴡᴏʀᴛʜ, Ian: *Teesside, Thornaby*	Lab & Co-op
†Wʀɪɢʜᴛ, Mrs Sheila: *Birmingham, Handsworth*	Lab

Y

Yᴏᴜɴɢ, David: *Bolton, East*	Lab
Yᴏᴜɴɢ, Sir George: *Ealing, Acton*	C
Yᴏᴜɴɢᴇʀ, George: *Ayr*	C

In Mr James Callaghan's dissolution honours list issued on June 12, 1979, Mr Harold Lever was made a life peer, thus creating a vacancy in Manchester, Central, where a by-election is to be held.

The General Election, May 1979

In the general election on May 3, 1979, the Conservative Party, under the leadership of Mrs Margaret Thatcher, who thus became Britain's first woman Prime Minister, was returned to power with a majority of 44 over all other parties, excluding the Speaker, and a majority over the Labour Party of 71. The last Parliament was dissolved in April after the Labour Government led by Mr James Callaghan had been defeated in the House of Commons by one vote on a motion of no confidence.

The state of the parties compared with the compositions of the Commons at dissolution and after the general election in October, 1974, was:

	May 1979	Dissolution	Oct 1974
Conservative	339	282	276
Labour	268	306	319
Liberal	11	14	13
Scottish National	2	11	11
Ulster Unionist	5	7	10
Plaid Cymru	2	3	3
Scottish Labour Party	—	2	—
Social Democratic and Labour ..	1	1	1
Democratic Unionist	3	1	—
United Ulster Unionist	1	1	—
Independent Ulster Unionist	1	1	—
Independent	1	1	1
The Speaker	1	1	1
Vacant	—	4	—

Details of the seats that changed hands:
From Labour to Conservative — Aldridge-Brownhills; Anglesey; Basildon; Bebington and Ellesmere Port; Belper; Birmingham, Northfield; Birmingham, Selly Oak; Birmingham, Yardley; Brecon and Radnor; Brigg and Scunthorpe; Brighouse and Spenborough; Bristol, North-West; Chorley; City of Westminster, Paddington; Coventry, South-West; Dartford; Dudley, West; Ealing, North; Enfield, North; Gloucestershire, West; Gravesend; Hammersmith, Fulham; Havering, Hornchurch; Hemel Hempstead; Hertford and Stevenage; Huddersfield, West; Kingswood; Lichfield and Tamworth; Lincoln; Liverpool, Garston; Loughborough; Luton, East; Luton, West; Meriden; Nelson and Colne; Newark; Northampton, North; Oxford; Peterborough; Portsmouth, North; Preston, North; Redbridge, Ilford South; Rochester and Chatham; Rossendale; Rugby; Southampton, Test; Sowerby; Wandsworth, Putney; Watford; Welwyn and Hatfield; Wrekin, The.
From Scottish National to Conservative — Aberdeenshire, East; Angus, South; Argyll; Banffshire; Galloway; Moray and Nairn; Perth and East Perthshire.
From Liberal to Conservative — Cornwall, North; Devon, North; Montgomery.
From Conservative to Labour — Ashfield; Birmingham, Stechford; Glasgow, Cathcart; Newham, North-East; Walsall, North; Workington.
From Scottish Labour to Labour — Ayrshire, South; Paisley.
From Plaid Cymru to Labour — Carmarthen.
From Scottish National to Labour — Dunbartonshire, East; Stirlingshire, East and Clackmannan.
From Official Ulster Unionist to Democratic Unionist — Belfast, East; Belfast, North.

The nation's choice: a Conservative woman Prime Minister

by George Clark

Political Correspondent of *The Times*

Mrs Margaret Thatcher, aged 53, the daughter of a Grantham shopkeeper, grammar schoolgirl, industrial chemist and a barrister specialising in taxation law before she entered politics, went to 10 Downing Street on May 4, 1979, as the nation's first woman Prime Minister on a wave of new popular support for the Conservative Party.

Backing for the Labour Party had remained fairly constant in Scotland and the industrial north of England, but the electors in the Midlands and the south of England had swung decisively to the Conservatives and the vital marginal seats went to the challenging party.

After a hard-fought campaign, the departing Prime Minister, Mr James Callaghan, aged 67, was the first to acknowledge the historic importance of the event.

Magnanimous in defeat, he said: 'I would like to congratulate Mrs Thatcher on becoming Prime Minister. It is a great office, a wonderful privilege to hold it. For a woman to occupy that office is a tremendous moment in the country's history.

'Everybody must wish her well and wish her success in the great responsibilities which fall to her now. She will need health, strength and stamina, and a lot of support.'

Mr Callaghan said it would be churlish for him and his party not to wish the Government well; although they would, of course, work vigorously for the return of another Labour Administration, they would not be a fractious opposition; they would be constructive in their approach.

Mrs Thatcher, nicknamed 'the Iron Lady' by the Russians after her aggressive speech at Kensington two years before on the Soviet military threat, had steadfastly sought to establish that this was a cartoonist phrase, that she was no extremist.

Outside 10 Downing Street, on taking office, she recalled some words of St Francis of Assisi: 'Where there is discord, may we bring harmony. Where there is error, may we bring truth. Where there is doubt, may we bring faith. Where there is despair, may we bring hope.'

In the words of the Conservative election manifesto, it was 'the time for a new beginning'.

During the 1974-79 Parliament, a period of falling living standards, partly due to the world recession in the wake of the oil-price crisis, all three main parties had changed their leaders.

After the election defeats in 1974, there was a strong 'Heath must go' movement within the Conservative Party and the leadership election of 1975 was dramatic. In the first ballot, Mrs Thatcher won 130 votes, Mr Heath, 119, and Mr Hugh Fraser, 16. Shaken by the size of the revolt, Mr Heath resigned the leadership. In the final ballot on February 11, 1975, the voting was: Mrs Thatcher, 146; Mr William Whitelaw, 79; Sir Geoffrey Howe, 19; Mr James Prior, 19; and Mr John Peyton, 11.

Mr Harold Wilson (to become Sir Harold) amazed the world in March, 1976, by resigning the office of Prime Minister. He maintained that he had indicated to H.M. the Queen and others that he intended his departure at that time. After a strong challenge from the Left, Mr Callaghan was elected to the Labour leadership and became Prime Minister. In the final ballot on April 6, 1976, he had 176 votes to Mr Michael Foot's 137.

The Liberal Party went through an embarrassing, troubled period when Mr Jeremy Thorpe's leadership was put in doubt by the accusations made by Mr Norman Scott, a male model. He alleged that he and Mr Thorpe once had a homosexual relationship, a charge strongly denied by Mr Thorpe. But in May, 1976, he resigned. Mr Steel, aged 38, was elected by the party at large in July, 1976. He obtained 12,541 votes to Mr John Pardoe's 7,032.

25

In 1978 Mr Thorpe was charged with conspiring with others to murder Mr Scott. He was able to obtain a postponement of the Old Bailey trial until after the general election, but he was defeated at North Devon, a seat he had held since 1959.

Elected with an overall majority of three on October 10, 1974, Labour soon suffered a series of by-election defeats and Mr Callaghan would have been forced into an election in March, 1977, had he not been able to cobble together the 'Lib-Lab Pact' which gave him, in return for an abandonment of socialistic measures, the reinforcement of 13 Liberal votes in the Commons.

When this support was withdrawn in the autumn of 1978, the Government's future was precarious. After party workers and the trade unions had been prepared for action, Mr Callaghan astonished everyone by announcing he had decided not to go to the country. The Government's fate hung on the goodwill of the minor parties.

It was finally dismissed on March 28 on a classic constitutional issue which had already caused divisions within both main parties. The Conservatives under Mr Heath, and Labour under Mr Wilson, had chosen to appease rather than counter-attack in face of pressure from the Scottish Nationalists for home rule. Both main parties had promised a measure of devolution to Scotland.

Under the new leadership of Mrs Thatcher, the Conservatives reversed the policy and helped to get a proviso written into the Scottish devolution Bill ensuring that if a referendum did not show more than 40 per cent of the electorate backing the establishment of a Scottish assembly, the proposal would not go ahead.

After the referendum on March 1 had failed to produce the required percentage (though there was a majority in favour of an assembly), the Scottish and Welsh nationalists made their future support of the Government dependent on Mr Callaghan and his colleagues forcing through legislation to set up an assembly.

With all the Conservatives against him, and a threatened revolt of 20 or more Labour backbenchers from England and Wales on his hands, Mr Callaghan knew that he could not placate the nationalists.

Now it was possible for Mrs Thatcher to strike the death blow. A no-confidence motion was put. The Liberals, the Scottish Nationalists and eight Ulster Unionists joined in a strange alliance with the Tories, and the Government was out – by one vote.

By wheeling and dealing with politicians in the minor parties, the Government might have staved off defeat for a few more weeks or months, but Mr Callaghan was not prepared to continue on that path, stumbling from one expedient to another. Better to go to the people.

Next day, March 29, after a short Cabinet and an audience of the Queen, Mr Callaghan announced that Parliament would be dissolved on April 7, the election held on May 3, the new Parliament would assemble on May 9, and the Queen would open the new session on May 15.

Bearing in mind its weak voting strength, the Government's record was impressive. Ministers could show that out of 68 commitments in the October, 1974, manifesto, 42 had been carried into effect, and another 10 had been partly achieved.

To cover up dissension in the Labour ranks, Labour had promised a referendum on the question of Britain remaining a member of the European Economic Community. On June 5, 1975, the nation voted. There was a 63.2 per cent turn-out; 67.2 per cent of the voters said the UK should stay in the EEC; 32.8 per cent were against.

The Government had pinned its hopes on bringing down the rate of inflation. In this effort, it had to abandon its promise of a return to free collective bargaining. By July, 1975, it had to put the brakes on. In conjunction with the TUC, a £6 limit was imposed on all pay increases in 1975-76; in Phase II increases were limited to a maximum of 5 per cent; in Phase III, covering 1977-78, the Government asked that the total of pay settlements should not rise by more than a single figure and earnings should not rise by more than 10 per cent, a target not achieved.

For 1978-79, the Government proposed a 5 per cent guideline. The reaction of the TUC and the Labour Party annual conferences showed that there was not the slightest chance of this being accepted.

There was a winter of strikes and disruption which caused great anger and frustration. Some disputes were still rumbling on during the election campaign. Experienced Labour campaigners knew they had been forced into an election at the worst possible time.

When it was all over and he had accepted the verdict of the people, Mr Callaghan confessed sadly: 'Memories of the winter have been too great for many people and undoubtedly that handicapped us. . . . I have a feeling that people voted *against* last winter, rather than *for* the Conservative proposals.'

One of the Conservative Party's party political TV broadcasts concentrated on the winter's troubles, showing mountains of rubbish in the streets of London, pickets outside hospitals, empty shelves in the supermarkets . . . there was no lack of material to stir people's memories. And the message was pumped home: this was chaos produced by trade unions, the unions with whom the Labour Government was supposed to have a special relationship.

In every speech in his campaign, Mr Callaghan admitted that there had been a breakdown in the Government's 'agreement' with the unions. 'It was a great shame, a great pity', he told an audience in Upminster. 'I do not escape responsibility for that. . . . But what we saw this winter was what this society could become if there is a free-for-all wages scramble.'

He assured his audiences that he was convinced that the latest concordat with the TUC, including a pledge to use the strike weapon as the last, not first, resort and to collaborate in bringing the rate of inflation down to 5 per cent in three years, would be honoured. 'Working together', not the confrontation threatened by the Tories, offered the best way forward.

Mrs Thatcher and her campaign advisers, starting a week after Mr Callaghan had begun his tour, concentrated on publicising the Government's 'dismal record' on unemployment, prices, economic growth, taxation, housing, education, defence and law and order.

The Conservative manifesto pledged a future Conservative Government to reducing taxation, reforming trade union law, curbing the flow of immigrants, cutting down public spending (except on the police and the Forces), and drastically reducing Government intervention in industry.

Most controversial was the promise to review the payment of social security payments to the families of strikers to 'ensure that unions bear their fair share of the cost of supporting those of their members who are on strike.' The promised legislation would make secondary picketing illegal, give people the right to seek compensation if they lost a job as a result of the closed shop, and provide Government finance for postal ballots for the election of union officers and on strike decisions.

Mr Denis Healey, the Chancellor of the Exchequer, commented: 'Mrs Thatcher is planning some refinements which even Mr Heath refused to contemplate. If a man is on strike – official or unofficial – she has committed herself, with Mr James Prior's support, to rob his family of up to £9 a week in social security payments.

'That is something no British Government has ever done, even to the family of a murderer. When Tory extremists demanded that the Heath Government should introduce it, it was rejected by none other than Sir Keith Joseph – not because it was wrong, but because it would not work.'

Mrs Thatcher said that the promise to reduce taxation was 'an article of faith.' The whole strategy, she said, was to create extra wealth, produce more goods and services, and increase the size of the national cake. The Conservatives would not make endless promises about improving the social services, she said. 'What Britain can afford will depend on the prosperity we create.'

Everywhere he went, Mr Callaghan was armed with facts and figures about Government aid being given to public and private enterprises in the locality. He put fear into the hearts of many thousands in the industrial areas with his prediction that 'deserts of unemployment' would be created by the Conservatives through the withdrawal of industrial assistance and support for job creation schemes. Mrs Thatcher and her aides dismissed the suggestion that 1,200,000 jobs would be lost as 'scare tactics'.

Mr Heath, the former Conservative Prime Minister, campaigned vigorously. He accused Mr Callaghan of tactics which were 'utterly unscrupulous and immensely damaging to the national interest'. Mr Callaghan had decided to make Europe a scapegoat, blaming foreigners for all his ills because he was unable to fight on the disastrous record of the past five years and was bankrupt of ideas for the next five.

In fact, Mr Callaghan on the hustings did not make much of the Common Market issue. He lauded his ministers' defence of British interests, condemned the workings of the Common Agricultural Policy as 'the economics of the madhouse', and forecast that the Tories would let the Europeans 'walk all over them' when it came to the negotiation of food prices. Dire predictions were made by Labour spokesmen about the effect on prices of the Conservative pledge to devalue the Green Pound within the lifetime of the next Parliament.

At his first rally, in the funereal surroundings of the Apollo Theatre, Glasgow, Mr Callaghan waded into the Scottish Nationalists who had precipitated the 'devolution election' through their marriage of convenience with the Tories. 'Not since Laurel met

Hardy was there a more comical misalliance,' said Mr Callaghan. 'I warned them that they were turkeys voting for Christmas! Now it is up to you to carve them up in the polling booths.'

(This advice seems to have been well taken, since the Nationalists' vote fell from 839,617 to 504,259, and they lost nine of their 11 seats.)

Two days after the Government's defeat, just as MPs were preparing for the election, Mr Airey Neave, MP for Abingdon, head of Mrs Thatcher's private office and shadow Secretary of State for Northern Ireland, was killed by an assassin's bomb that exploded in his car as he was driving out of the House of Commons car park. The self-styled Irish National Liberation Army, a break-away from the IRA, claimed responsibility.

Thereafter, political leaders were given stronger police protection as they went on their walkabouts. The 'Troops Out' movement and other fringe political groups tried to disrupt many of Mr Callaghan's rallies but he took it calmly, often appealing to the stewards, 'Be gentle to them,' as they threw the interrupters out. However, he was angry at Birmingham on April 17, when a heckler complained about British troops torturing people in Northern Ireland. Mr Callaghan retorted: 'I wonder how anyone can have the effrontery to come here, when four policemen have just been slaughtered in Northern Ireland, and make a comment like that. You ought to go and hang your head in shame.'

When Mr Callaghan spoke at Ealing town hall on May 1, the Irish protesters were joined by supporters of the Anti-Nazi League who paraded with posters alleging that one of their number, Mr Blair Peach, a New Zealander, had been killed by the police during a riot at nearby Southall on April 23. The police had to intervene when hundreds of people, many of them coloured, gathered to try to stop a meeting of the National Front and 340 people were arrested. Thirty-five policemen were hurt.

Mr Callaghan said a searching inquiry was being made into the incident. If Labour was returned to power, he said, the Government would examine whether the Public Order Act should be amended to permit the banning of meetings as well as marches of the National Front. But he emphasised the serious impact this might have on the right of free speech.

Mrs Thatcher described the riot as a disgrace to democracy. She said the Conservatives totally condemned the National Front's racial policies and had no sympathy with any extremist groups. The only way to beat the National Front, she said, was 'by the ballot box, not by bricks and bombs.'

(In fact, the NF candidates received only 0·6 per cent of the votes cast at the election.)

Mr David Steel, the Liberal leader, ably assisted by Mr John Pardoe (who lost his seat at North Cornwall), fought a courageous campaign, using a well-equipped bus as his mobile headquarters. The main points in the Liberal manifesto concerned electoral reform, the decentralisation of legislative power from Westminster, complete reform of the tax system, the liberty of the individual and the protection of the environment.

Mr Steel argued that during the 18 months of the Lib-Lab pact there had been stability, a reduction in the rate of inflation, and the Government had been deterred from divisive policies. He appealed to the electors to send more Liberals to Parliament. During the last week of the campaign, having seen developments in various key constituencies, he reckoned that there might be between 20 and 50 Liberal MPs in the new House of Commons as a steadying influence. But events proved him wrong.

Both Mr Steel and Mr Pardoe insisted that the Liberals would not enter into an agreement with any other party unless they received 'copper-bottomed guarantees' that the next election would be on a system of proportional representation. In the end, the Liberals lost three of their 14 seats, and their vote fell from 5,346,704 to 4,313,931.

When it was clear that there would be a decisive victory for the Conservatives, Mr Heath was asked whether he was looking for a position in the Government. He replied that he had always been willing to serve his country when invited. Two days later, when Mrs Thatcher announced the names of her Cabinet, Mr Heath's was not among them.

Mrs Thatcher convinced all her audiences that what the Conservatives said, they meant. And within a week of coming into power, the new Government had carried out the Conservative pledges to increase the pay of the police, in the cause of strengthening the forces of law and order, and of the Services, in line with recommendations of the Armed Forces Review Body. The Government also indicated its support for the modernisation of Nato nuclear weapons as a response to the new missiles developed by the Soviet Union.

In her first Commons speech as Prime Minister, Mrs Thatcher gave a firm commitment that in early legislation the Price Commission would be abolished, freedom would be restored to education authorities over the organisation of schools, trade union law would be reformed, and the Community Land Act repealed.

'Our priorities,' she said, 'are to restore the balance in our economy and to restore the balance between the individual and the State: to promote the freedom of the individual under the rule of law and to defend our interests wherever they are challenged.

'These are the policies that we submitted to the people. The path we now take is the path the people have chosen.'

It was, Mrs Thatcher told the House, 'a watershed election and the result was decisive, with a difference of some 2 million votes between the two major parties, the largest difference since 1935.'

What remained to be shown was whether the Conservative Party, with its clear majority over all other parties of 44 votes, excluding the Speaker, could put into effect policies which would completely transform the British economic and industrial climate, and re-establish the United Kingdom's leading role on the European and world stage.

Table of the Polls

First and last poll results taken during election campaign

Poll	C	Lab	L	Date of Fieldwork
NOP (*Daily Mail*)	48·0	42·0	8·0	April 2–3
	46·0	39·0	12·5	May 1–2
Research Services Ltd (*Observer*)	54·5	33·5	9·0	April 3–4
	49·5	38·0	10·0	April 24–25
Gallup (*Daily Telegraph*)	49·0	38·5	9·0	March 28–April 2
	43·0	41·0	13·5	April 30–May 1
Market and Opinion Research International (*Daily Express*)	51·0	38·0	10·0	April 1–2
	44·4	38·8	13·5	April 29–May 1
Marplan (*The Sun*)	51·0	41·0	6·0	April 17
	45·0	38·5	13·5	May 1
Final Result	43·9	36·9	13·8	May 3

Date election called : March 29

House of Commons
Elected in May, 1979

The parliamentary constituencies of the United Kingdom (England, Scotland, Wales and Northern Ireland) for election to the House of Commons are set out in alphabetical order with those in the Greater London area appearing under the name of the relevant London borough. Outside London, constituencies in cities or towns (for example, Liverpool, Manchester, Glasgow, Cardiff, Belfast, etc) are listed under that city or town. The Teesside seats are listed together. An abbreviated index is at the back of the book.

Abbreviations used to designate the principal political parties contesting the election are: C—Conservative; Lab—Labour; Lab and Co-op—Labour and Co-operative; L—Liberal; Scot Nat—Scottish National Party; Pl Cymru—Plaid Cymru; Off UU—Official Ulster Unionist; Dem U—Democratic Unionist; SDLP—Social Democrat and Labout Party; Nat Front—National Front; WRP—Workers' Revolutionary Party; Ecology— Ecology Party. Abbreviations of minor parties are given at the end of this constituency analysis followed by abbreviations of trade unions and other organizations mentioned in the biographical details.

The percentage of the votes cast for each candidate and the majority in relation to the total poll in each constituency and the swing figures (+ to Conservative and—to Labour) are calculated to the nearest decimal place, as is the percentage turnout.

The electoral register came into effect on February 16, 1979, and the electorate figures for each constituency consist of those eligible to vote when the register came into force plus the relevant proportion of those registered as becoming 18 years of age during the year. The relevant proportion used was 76/364ths—the number of days the register was in force until polling day.

Ministers resign their directorships while holding office.

*Denotes member of the last Parliament.

ABERAVON

Electorate 64,864   1974: 64,667

*Morris, J. (Lab)	31,665
McCarthy, F. (C)	12,692
Cutts, Mrs. S. M. (L)	4,624
Thomas, G. (Pl Cymru)	1,954
Rowden, G. (Comm)	406
Lab majority	18,973

No Change

	1974		1979
Total votes	47251		51,341
Turnout	73·6%		79·2%
Lab	29·683	62·8%	61·7%
C	7,931	16·8%	24·7%
L	5,178	11·0%	9·0%
Pl Cymru	4,032	8·5%	3·8%
WRP	427	0·9%	—
Comm	—	—	0·8%
Lab maj	21,752	46·0%	37·0%
Swing		−1·7%	+4·5%

Mr John Morris, QC, Secretary of State for Wales; 1974-79, was Opposition spokesman on defence, 1970-74; Minister of Defence for Equipment, 1968-70; Parliamentary Secretary, Ministry of Transport, 1966-68; Parliamentary Secretary, Ministry of Power, 1964-66. Elected in 1959. Barrister (Gray's Inn, 1954). B November, 1931; ed University College of Wales, Aberystwyth, Gonville and Caius College, Cambridge, and the Academy of International Law, The Hague. Chairman Welsh Labour group, 1970-71, and Welsh parliamentary party, 1972-73.

Mr Frank McCarthy, BBC sound engineer. B October, 1943; ed St Illtyds College, Cardiff. Member, Cardiff City Council, 1970-74; South Glamorgan County Council, since 1973 (Deputy Leader); Chairman, South Glamorgan Education Committee, ABS.

Mrs Sheila Cutts, teacher and partner in flower farm, contested seat, October, 1974. B November, 1928; ed Exeter University and City of Bath Teacher Training College.

Mr Geraint Thomas, economist, contested seat, October, 1974. B December, 1949; ed Carmarthen Grammar School, Jesus College, Oxford, Hebrew University, Jerusalem. Former Welsh secretary, National Council for Civil Liberties.

Mr Gerald Rowden, aged 25, building worker. Branch secretary, UCATT. Delegate to Mid-Glamorgan Trades Council.

ABERDARE

Electorate 47,500   1974: 48,380

*Evans, I. L. (Lab Co-op)	26,716
Deere, D. (C)	6,453
Richards, P. (Pl Cymru)	3,652
Winter, Mrs M. (Comm)	518
Lab and Co-op majority	20,263

No Change

	1974		1979
Total votes	38251		37,339
Turnout	79·1%		78·6%
Lab & Coop	24,197	63·3%	71·5%
Pl Cymru	8,133	21·3%	9·8%
C	2,775	7·3%	17·3%
L	2,118	5·5%	—
Comm	1,028	2·7%	1·4%
Lab & Co-op maj	16,064	42·0%	54·2%
Swing		−2·2%	+0·9%

Mr Ioan Evans, elected in February, 1974, was Comptroller of the Household (whip), 1968-70; an assistant Government whip, 1966-68. MP for Birmingham, Yardley, 1964-70. B July, 1927; ed Llanelli Grammar School and Swansea University College. Director, International Defence and Aid Fund, 1970-74. Hon Secretary, Welsh Group of Labour MPs, 1974 and since 1977. Chairman, PLP trade group, 1977-78; vice-chairman, disablement group and prices and consumer protection group. Member, Commons Services Committee.

Mr David Deere, partner in family estate agent business. B 1945; ed St John's School, Newton,

Porthcawl. Member, Ogwr Borough Council, since 1973. President, Porthcawl Chamber of Trade, 1975-76.

Mr Philip Richards, barrister, contested Cardiff, North, February and October, 1974. B August, 1946; ed Cardiff High School and Bristol University. TGWU.

Mrs Mary Winter, 33, community work organizer employed by Mid-Glamorgan social services department. Chairman, Welsh Committee of Communist Party.

ABERDEEN, North

Electorate 64,747   1974: 65,230

*Hughes, R. (Lab)	26,771
Adams, G. (C)	7,657
Watt, Miss. M. (Scot Nat)	5,796
McMillan, Miss. L. (L)	4,887
Lab majority	19,114

No Change

	1974		1979
Total votes	45,464		45,111
Turnout	69·7%		69·7%
Lab	23,130	50·9%	59·3%
Scot Nat	13,509	29·7%	12·6%
C	5,125	11·3%	17·0%
L	3,700	8·1%	10·8%
Lab maj	9,621	21·2%	42·3%
Swing		−4·3%	−1·4%

Mr Robert Hughes, Under Secretary, Scottish Office, 1974-75. Engineering draughtsman. Elected in 1970; contested North Angus and Mearns, 1959. B January, 1932; ed Benoni High School, Transvaal and Pietermaritzburg Technical College, Natal. Chairman, Anti-Apartheid Movement. Member, Aberdeen Town Council 1962-1971. Sponsored by AUEW.

Mr Gordon Adams, self-employed technical consultant. B April, 1924; ed Frederick Street School, Aberdeen. Aberdeen district councillor.

Miss Maureen Watt works in insurance. B June, 1951; ed Keith Grammar School and universities of Strathclyde and Birmingham. Assistant secretary, SNP Manpower and Employment Policy Committee.

Miss Lin Macmillan, personnel officer. B March, 1955; ed Leeds Girls High School and Aberdeen University.

ABERDEEN, South

Electorate 65,090   1974: 68,241

*Sproat, I. M. (C)	20,820
Godman, N. A. (Lab)	20,048
Pitt-Watson, Mrs. H. (L)	5,901
Stronach, A. (Scot Nat)	4,361
C majority	772

No Change

	1974		1979
Total Votes	52,084		51,130
Turnout	76·3%		78·6%
C	18,475	35·5%	40·7%
Lab	18,110	34·8%	39·2%
Scot Nat	10,481	20·1%	8·5%
L	5,018	9·6%	11·5%
C maj	365	0·7%	1·5%
Swing		−2·9%	+0·4%

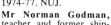

Mr Iain Sproat runs his own group of companies. Won the seat in 1970; contested Rutherglen, by-election and general election, 1964. B November, 1938; ed Winchester and Magdalen College, Oxford. Chairman, Conservative foreign affairs committee Soviet Union and East Europe groups, 1974-77. NUJ.

Mr Norman Godman, teacher and former shipwright. B April, 1937; ed Hull University. TGWU, AUT.

Mrs Helen Pitt-Watson, music teacher, B November, 1921; ed primary school, Dumfries Academy and Edinburgh University. Convenor, Overseas Committee, Presbytery of Aberdeen; member, Overseas Council, Church of Scotland. EIS.

Mr Alexander Stronach, lecturer, contested the seat, February and October, 1974. B June, 1937; ed Inverurie Academy and Robert Gordon's Institute of Technology. Dyce District councillor, 1969-71. Senior partner in electrical engineering company. EIS.

ABERDEENSHIRE, East

Electorate 54,292   1974: 47,736

McQuarrie, A. (C)	16,827
*Henderson, D. (Scot Nat)	16,269
Bonney, N. L. (Lab)	6,201
C majority	558

C gain from Scot Nat

	1974		1979
Total Votes	33,642		39,297
Turnout	70·5%		72·4%
Scot Nat	16,304	48·5%	41·4%
C	11,933	35·5%	42·8%
Lab	3,173	9·4%	15·8%
L	2,232	6·6%	—
Scot Nat maj	—	13·0%	—
C maj	—	—	1·4%
			+0·4%

Mr Albert McQuarrie, professional civil engineer, contested Kilmarnock, 1966, and Caithness and Sutherland, October, 1974. B January 1918; ed Greenock High School and Royal College of Science and Technology. Chairman, Scottish Conservative Party's fisheries consultative committee. Dean of Guild, Town Council, Burgh of Gourock, Renfrewshire.

Mr Douglas Henderson, management consultant, was SNP spokesman on employment 1974-79; whip to the parliamentary party 1974-78. Previously spokesman on finance, trade and industry. Won the seat from Conservatives in February, 1974. B July, 1935; ed Royal High School and Edinburgh University. Senior vice-chairman, SNP, until 1972.

Mr Norman Bonney, university lecturer. B March, 1944; ed Great Yarmouth Grammar School, LSE and University of Chicago. Secretary, Aberdeen City Council Labour Group. AUT.

ABERDEENSHIRE, West

Electorate 67,915   1974: 55,341

*Fairgrieve, T. R. (C)	21,086
Bruce, M. (L)	18,320
Grant, G. (Lab)	7,907
Hulbert, Dr. J. (Scot Nat)	4,260

C majority	2,766

No Change

	1974		1979
Total Votes	42,348		51,573
Turnout	76·5%		75·9%
C	15,111	35·7%	40·9%
L	12,643	29·9%	35·5%
Scot Nat	9,409	22·2%	8·3%
Lab	5,185	12·2%	15·3%
C maj	2,468	5·8%	5·4%
Swing		−2·5%	+1·0%

Mr Russell Fairgrieve became an Under Secretary of State for Scotland in May 1979. An Opposition whip, 1975-77, he became chairman of the Scottish Conservative Party in 1976. Non-executive company director. Elected February, 1974; contested Roxburgh, Selkirk and Peebles, 1970. B May, 1924; ed St Mary's School, Melrose, Sedbergh School, Yorkshire, and Scottish College of Textiles, Galashiels. Member, Galashiels Town Council and Selkirk County Council, 1949-59. ASTMS.

Mr George Grant, scientific officer. B 1951. Grampian regional councillor since 1978. IPCS.

Dr John Hulbert, general practitioner. B March, 1939; ed Madras College, St Andrews and St Andrews and Edinburgh universities.

ABERTILLERY

Electorate 35,602   1974: 36,561

*Thomas, J. (Lab)	21,698
Tuck, R. (C)	4,613
Harries, D. (Pl Cymru)	2,248

Lab majority	17,085

No Change

	1974		1979
Total Votes	27,458		28,559
Turnout	75·1%		80·2%
Lab	20,835	75·9%	76·0%
Pl Cymru	2,480	9·0%	7·9%
C	2,364	8·6%	16·2%
L	1,779	6·5%	
Lab maj	18,355	66·9%	59·8%
Swing		−3·3%	+3·7%

Mr Jeffrey Thomas QC (Gray's Inn, 1957) was elected in 1970; contested Barry, 1957 and 1966. A Recorder of the Crown Court since 1975. B November, 1933; ed Abertillery Grammar School, King's College, London. President, London University Union, 1955-56. Chairman, British Caribbean Association. Member, Council of Justice; executive committee, British Group, IPU; court of governors of University College of Wales, Aberystwyth, National Library of Wales and (ex officio) National Museum of Wales.

Mr Ralph Tuck, security officer. B November, 1921; ed Tredegar Grammar School. Member, national executive, Conservative Trade Unionists; Brynmawr Town Council.

Mr David Harries, lecturer in chemical engineering at the Polytechnic of Wales, Pontypridd. ed Newbridge Grammar School and University College, Swansea, and Lancaster University. Coach to Tredegar Rugby Club.

ABINGDON

Electorate 96,447   1974: 90,451

Benyon, T. (C)	41,211
Popper, A. J. D. (Lab)	18,920
Blair, I. (L)	16,164
Pinder, Miss. R. (Ind)	381

C majority	22,291

No Change

	1974		1979
Total Votes	68,514		76,676
Turnout	75·7%		79·5%
C	31,956	46·6%	53·7%
Lab	21,319	31·1%	24·7%
L	15,239	22·2%	21·1%
Ind	—		0·5%
C maj	10,637	15·5%	29·0%
Swing		−1·5%	+6·7%

Mr Thomas Benyon, founder and director of an insurance broking group and co-founder and director of the Rossminister group of companies. Contested Haringey, Wood Green, October 1974, and Huyton, February, 1974. B 1942; ed Angusfield School, Edinburgh, Wellington School and RMA Sandhurst. Member, Aylesbury Vale District Council, since 1976; Bucks Community Health Council. Vice-chairman, Buckingham Conservative Association. Executive member, National Councils of two charities for the mentally sick and the young and distressed.

Mr Andrew Popper, solicitor. B April, 1951; ed St Paul's School and Oriel College, Oxford. Member, Barnet Borough Council, 1974-78. APEX.

Mr Ian Murray Blair, nuclear physicist. B May, 1936; ed King George V, Southport and Oriel College, Oxford.

ACCRINGTON

Electorate 50,822   1974: 50,820

*Davidson, A. (Lab)	19,576
Cheetham, Mrs. A. (C)	16,282
Holden, R. (L)	3,646
Riley, D. (Nat Front)	508

Lab majority	3,294

No Change

	1974		1979
Total Votes	40,336		40,012
Turnout	79·4%		78·7%
Lab	19,838	49·2%	48·9%
C	13,618	33·8%	40·7%
L	5,704	14·1%	9·1%
Nat Front	1,176	2·9%	1·3%
Lab maj	6,220	15·4%	8·2%
Swing		−1·8%	+3·6%

Mr Arthur Davidson, Par-
liamentary Secretary to the
Law Officers, 1974-79.
Elected in 1966; contested
Preston, North, 1959, and
Blackpool, South, 1955.
Barrister (Middle Temple,
1953). B November, 1928;
ed Liverpool College, King
George V School, South-
port, and Trinity College,
Cambridge. PPS to Solicitor
General, 1968-70 and to
Attorney-General, 1974.
GMWU.

Mrs Anne Cheetham, Company secretary and house-
wife. B 1942; ed Merrow Grange, Guildford and
Weybridge Technical College, Surrey. Ex-chairman,
Manchester City Young Conservatives; governor,
Tyldesley High School for Special Children.

Mr Richard Holden, teacher. B May, 1951; ed
Swansea and Manchester university.

ALDERSHOT

Electorate 86,516   1974: 80,522

*Critchley, J. M. G. (C)	38,014
Westbrook, N. (L)	14,438
Somerville, D. (Lab)	13,698

C majority	23,576

No Change

	1974		1979
Total Votes	58,623		66,150
Turnout	72·8%		76·5%
C	26,463	45·1%	57·5%
L	16,104	27·5%	21·8%
Lab	14,936	25·5%	20·7%
Nat Front	1,120	1·9%	—
C maj	10,359	17·6%	35·7%
Swing		−1·0%	+8·6%

Mr Julian Critchley, writer,
journalist and public affairs
consultant, was returned in
1970; MP for Rochester
and Chatham, 1959-64,
contested seat, 1966. B
December, 1930; ed
Shrewsbury, Sorbonne, and
Pembroke College, Oxford.
Chairman, Bow Group,
1966-67, and Conservative
Party Media Committee
since 1976; vice-chairman,
Conservative Party
Defence Committee. Delegate to WEU and Council

of Europe; chairman, WEU Defence Committee
1975-77.

Mr Nicholas Westbrook, public relations consultant,
contested Plymouth Devonport, October, 1974. B
May, 1948; ed Framlingham College, Suffolk and
Heriot-Watt University.

Mr Dennis Somerville, royalty accountant. B May,
1930; ed North Paddington Central School and Paddington Technical College. Rushmoor councillor,
1974-76. Secretary, Racial Unity Movement.
ASTMS.

ALDRIDGE-BROWNHILLS

Electorate 63,377   1974: 61,731

Shepherd, R. (C)	26,289
*Edge, G. (Lab)	20,621
Aldridge, J. (L)	5,398

C majority	5,668

C gain from Lab

	1974		1979
Total Votes	49,190		52,308
Turnout	79·7%		82·5%
Lab	21,403	43·5%	39·4%
C	18,884	38·4%	50·3%
L	8,693	17·7%	10·3%
Pros Brit	210	0·4%	—
Lab maj	2,519	5·1%	—
C maj	—		10·9%
Swing		−2·2%	+8·0%

Mr Richard Shepherd,
director of a retail food business in London, contested
Nottingham, East, in Feb-
ruary 1974. B December
1942; ed LSE and the
School of Advanced Inter-
national Studies. Under-
writing member of Lloyd's
since 1974. In 1971
appointed member of S.E.
Economic Planning Coun-
cil. Member, Conservative
Group for Europe.

Mr Geoffrey Edge, lecturer at the Open University,
1970-74, was elected, February, 1974. B May 1943;
ed Rowley Regis Grammar School, LSE and Birmingham University. Served on Bletchley Urban Council
and Milton Keynes Borough Council. Member, PLP
industry, education and foreign affairs groups.

Mr John Aldridge, insurance broker. B August, 1944;
ed Moseley Grammar School. Contested Birmingham, Yardley, Feb and Oct 1974. Director, Aldridge
Harrison and Co Ltd.

ALTRINCHAM AND SALE

Electorate 74,547   1974: 73,296

*Montgomery, W. F. (C)	29,873
Pratt, G. (Lab and Co-op)	14,643
Campbell, J. (L)	12,603
Marsh, Miss. C. (Ecology)	796

C majority	15,230

No Change

	1974		1979
Total Votes	55,888		57,915
Turnout	76·2%		77·7%
C	23,910	42·8%	51·6%
Lab	16,998	30·4%	25·3%
L	14,980	26·8%	21·8%
Ecology	—		1·4%
C maj	6,912	12·4%	26·3%
Swing		−3·0%	+6·9%

Mr Fergus Montgomery, teacher, was elected in October, 1947; MP for Brierley Hill from the by-election in 1967 until February, 1974, when he unsuccessfully contested Dudley, West. Represented Newcastle upon Tyne. East, 1959-64; contested Consett, 1955. B November, 1927; ed Jarrow Grammar School and Bede College, Durham. PPS to Mrs

Thatcher as Secretary of State for Education and Science, 1973-74, and as Leader of the Opposition, 1975-76. NAS.

Mr Garth Pratt, research officer. Aged 36.

Mr John Campbell, interior designer. B April, 1953; ed Pangbourne Nautical College, Berks. Contested Wigan, October 1974.

ANGLESEY

Electorate 47,726   1974: 44,026

Best, K. L. (C)	15,100
Morgan, D. E. (Lab)	12,283
Williams, J. L. (Pl Cymru)	7,863
Jones, J. G. (L)	3,500
C majority	2,817

C gain from Lab

	1974		1979
Total Votes	33,514		38,746
Turnout	76·1%		81·2%
Lab	13,947	41·6%	31·7%
C	7,975	23·8%	39·0%
Pl Cymru	6,410	19·1%	20·3%
L	5,182	15·5%	9·0%
Lab maj	5,972	17·8%	
C maj	—	—	7·3%
Swing		−0·7%	+12·5%

Mr Keith Best, barrister, Brighton borough councillor since 1976. B June, 1949; ed Brighton College, Keble College, Oxford. A former Parachute Regiment Captain.

Mr Elystan Morgan was MP for Cardigan, 1966 to February, 1974. Under Secretary Home Office, 1968-70; Opposition spokesman on Wales, 1973-74 and on the Home Office, 1970-73. Solicitor. B December 1932; ed Ardwyn Grammar School, Aberystwyth, and University College of Wales, Aberystwyth. As Plaid Cymru candidate contested Merioneth in 1964 and Wrexham 1959, and the general election and by-election, 1955.

Mr John Williams, lecturer in Welsh at the Normal College, Bangor. Contested seat, 1970. B October, 1924; ed Beaumaris County School and University College, Bangor. Gwynedd county councillor.

Mr John Jones, farmer and local councillor. Aged 63.

ANGUS, North and Mearns

Electorate 43,122   1974: 37,604

*Buchanan-Smith, A. L. (C)	18,302
Murray, I. (Scot Nat)	7,387
McMahon, H. R. (Lab)	6,132
C majority	10,915

No Change

	1974		1979
Total Votes	27,173		31,821
Turnout	72·3%		73·8%
C	11,835	43·6%	57·5%
Scot Nat	9,284	34·2%	23·2%
Lab	3,354	12·3%	19·3%
L	2,700	9·9%	—
C maj	2,551	9·4%	34·3%
Swing		−2·4%	+3·4%

Mr Alick Buchanan-Smith appointed Minister of State for Agriculture, Fisheries and Food in May 1979, was Under-Secretary of State, Scottish Office, 1970-74. Former Opposition spokesman on Scottish affairs, and member of Shadow Cabinet from which he resigned in 1977, over devolution issue. Elected in 1964, contested West Fife, 1959. Farmer. B

April, 1932; ed Edinburgh Academy, Clenalmond, Pembroke College, Cambridge, and Edinburgh University. Member, Select Committee on Agriculture, 1968-69; vice-chairman, Conservative agricultural committee, 1965-66. Director Graigton Golf Co.

Mr Iain Murray, management consultant, contested seat, October, 1974, and Stirling and Falkirk, 1970. B February, 1924; ed Stirling High School and Heriot-Watt College.

Mr Hugh McMahon assistant head teacher. B June, 1938; ed Ardrossan Academy and Glasgow University. Chairman, Socialist Educational Association, Scotland.

ANGUS, South

Electorate 57,513   1974: 52,275

Fraser, P. (C)	20,029
*Welsh, A. (Scot Nat)	19,066
Philip, I. G. (Lab)	4,623
Will, H. (L)	2,218
C majority	963

C gain from Scot Nat

	1974		1979
Total Votes	38,954		45,936
Turnout	74·5%		79·9%
Scot Nat	17,073	43·8%	41·5%
C	15,249	39·1%	43·6%
Lab	4,103	10·5%	10·1%
L	2,529	6·5%	4·8%
Scot Nat mj	1,824	4·7%	
C maj	—		2·1%

Mr Peter Fraser, judge advocate, fought Aberdeen North in October, 1974. B May, 1945; ed Loretto School, Gonville and Caius College, Cambridge, and Edinburgh University. Former lecturer in constitutional law, Heriot-Watt University, 1971-75. Former chairman, Thistle Group.

Mr Andrew Welsh, a teacher, won the seat in

October 1974; contested Dunbartonshire, Central, February, 1974. SNP Chief Whip since 1978-79; SNP spokesman on housing, 1974-78; also a spokesman on the self-employed, small businesses and agriculture. B April, 1944; ed Govan High School and Glasgow University, Stirling District councillor. EIS.

Mr Ian Philip, chartered accounted. B 1937.

Mr Harry Will, area textile sales manager, fought seat, October, 1974. B November 1923; ed Robert Gordon's College, Aberdeen.

ANTRIM, North

Electorate 102,202   1974: 103,737

*Paisley, Rev. I. R. K. (Dem U)	33,941
Burchill, D. J. (Off U.U.)	15,398
Wilson, H. (Alliance)	7,797
Farren, S. N. (SDLP)	4,867
Turnly, J. F. (IIP)	3,689

Dem U majority	18,543

No Change

	1974		1979
Total Votes	59,491		65,692
Turnout	57·3%		64·3%
UUUC	43,186	72·6%	23·4%
Dem U	—		51·7%
Alliance	8,689	14·6%	11·9%
SDLP	7,616	12·8%	7·4%
IIP	—		5·6%
UUUC maj	34,497	58·0%	—
Dem U maj	—	—	28·3%

The Rev Ian Paisley, leader of the Ulster Democratic Unionist Party, won the seat in 1970. Minister of Religion; Moderator of the Free Presbyterian Church, Founded the Protestant Unionist Party and sat as Protestant Unionist MP from 1970-74. B April, 1926; ed Model School, Ballymena, and Ballymena Technical College, South Wales Bible Colleges, and

Reformed Presbyterian Theological College, Belfast. Ordained 1946. He stood (as Prot U) in Bannside against Lord O'Neill of the Maine in the N Ireland general election of 1969 for Stormont, won the seat in the by-election caused by Lord O'Neill's resignation in 1970 and was MP until 1972. Dem U member for North Antrim in Northern Ireland Assembly, 1973-75, and UUUC member in the NI Constitutional Convention, 1975-76. Leader of Opposition, and Chairman Public Accounts Committee in Stormont, 1970-72.

Mr Jeremy Burchill, barrister, represented South Belfast in the Constitutional Convention. Chairman, Ulster Young Unionist Council, member, party's security and housing committee. B 1952; ed Campbell College, Belfast and Queen's University, Belfast.

Mr Hugh Wilson, President of the Alliance Party, is a retired surgeon and was a member of the Northern Ireland Assembly and Convention for North Antrim. Contested Larne, Northern Ireland Assembly election, 1974; Contested North Antrim in 1974 General Election. Member of Larne Council since 1973.

Mr Sean Farren, Lecturer, University of Ulster. Chairman, Central Policy Committee and vice-chairman, SDLP. Member, Coleraine Borough Council. B 1940; ed National University of Ireland.

Mr John Turnly, vice-president, Irish Independence Party, represented North Antrim (SDLP) in Northern Ireland Convention. Member, Larne Borough Council. B 1935; ed Cheltenham College.

ANTRIM, South

Electorate 126,444   1974: 117,834

*Molyneaux, J. H. (Off UU)	50,782
Kinahan, C. H. G. (Alliance)	11,914
Rowan, P. J. (SDLP)	7,432
Kidd, R. (ULP)	1,895
Smyth, K. (Rep Clubs)	1,615

Off UU majority	38,868

No Change

	1974		1979
Total Votes	68,413		73,638
Turnout	58·1%		58·2%
UUUC	48,892	71·5%	
Off U	—		69·0%
Alliance	10,460	15·3%	16·2%
SDLP	9,061	13·2%	10·1%
ULP	—		2·6%
Repub Clubs	—		2·2%
UUUC maj	38,432	56·2%	—
Off U maj	—		52·8%

Mr James Molyneaux is leader of Ulster Unionist MPs. Elected in 1970. Partner in the family firm of letterpress printers. B August, 1920; ed Aldergrove School, co Antrim. Deputy Grand Master, Orange Order. Sovereign Grand Master, Commonwealth Royal Black Institution, 1971. Member, Antrim County Council, 1964-73. Vice-president,

Ulster Unionist Council, 1974. Chairman, Monday Club of Ulster. RAF 1941-46. Vice-chairman, Eastern Special Care Hospital Committee, Chairman, Antrim Division Unionist Association.

Mr Charles Kinahan, company director, Deputy Lieutenant for county Antrim and member of Belfast Harbour Commissioners and Senate of Queen's University Belfast. Represented South Antrim in the N I Convention, contested the seat in February and October 1974. B1915. ed Stowe School.

Mr Patrick Rowan, principal teacher. Member of the Executive of SDLP and contested seat February and October 1974. Member of Civil Rights Movement.

Mr Robert Kidd is a member of Newtonabbey District Council. B 1923; ed public elementary school and technical College.

Mr Kevin Smyth, teacher, is a member of the national executive of the Republican Clubs. B 1950.

ARGYLL

Electorate 43,327   1974: 41,814

Mackay, J. J. (C)	12,191
*MacCormick, I, (Scot Nat)	10,545
Macgregor, M. J. N. (Lab)	5,283
Michie, Mrs. R, (L)	5,113

C majority	1,646

C gain from Scot Nat

	1974		1979
Total Votes	30,106		33,132
Turnout	72·0%		76·1%
Scot Nat	14,967	49·7%	31·8%
C	11,036	36·7%	36·8%
Lab	4,103	13·6%	15·9%
Scot Nat maj	3,931	13·0%	—
C maj	—	—	5·0%
Swing	—	—	−1·1%

Mr John Mackay contested the seat in October, 1974 and Western Isles in February, 1974. Principal teacher of mathematics, Oban High School. B November, 1938; ed Dunoon and Campbeltown Grammar Schools, Glasgow University and Jordanhill College of Education. Chairman, Scottish Conservatives education policy committee; member, Scottish Secondary Teachers Association.

Mr Iain MacCormick, senior history master, Oban High School, gained the seat for the SNP from the Conservatives in February, 1974, having contested it in 1970, SNP spokesman on local government and transport 1974-79. B September, 1939; ed Glasgow High School and Glasgow University, President, Oban branch, SNP.

Mr Malcolm MacGregor, sheep farmer. B January, 1928; ed Oban High School and London University. Contested seat, February and October, 1974.

Mrs Ray Michie, speech therapist. B 1974; ed Aberdeen High School for Girls and Lansdowne House School, Edinburgh.

ARMAGH

Electorate 93,069   1974: 91,060

*McCusker, J. H. (Off UU)	31,668
Mallon, S. (SDLP)	23,545
Calvert, D. (Dem U)	5,634
Moore, T. (Rep Clubs)	2,310
Ramsay, W. (Alliance)	2,074
Off UU majority	8,123

No Change

	1974		1979
Total Votes	62,511		65,231
Turnout	68·6%		70·1%
UUUC	37,518	60·0%	—
Off UU	—		48·5%
SDLP	19,855	31·8%	36·1%
Repub	5,138	8·2%	3·5%
Alliance	—		3·2%
UUUC maj	17,663	28·2%	—
Off U maj	—		12·4%

Mr Harold McCusker won the seat in Febrauty, 1974. Teacher 1961-68; personnel officer 1968-72; production manager, 1968-72. B February, 1940; ed Lurgan College. UUUC whip, 1975. Chairman, Northern Ireland Gas Employers' Board. Member, all party textile group.

Mr Seamus Mallon, teacher. Chairman of the SDLP in Assembly and Assembly representative on party's executive. Contested seat, October 1974. Chairman Mid-Armagh anti-discrimination committee 1963-68; member Northern Ireland Civil Rights Association 1969-72 and vice-chairman Teachers against Internment 1972 B 1939; ed, Christian Brothers' Grammar School, Newry and St. Joseph's College of Education, Belfast.

Mr David Calvert, director of family shirt manufacturing company is a founder member of the Democratic Unionist Party in Co Armagh and a member of Craigavon Borough Council.

Mr Tom Moore, stores clerk is a founder member of Republican Clubs party in Armagh South Down and a member of the national executive. Chairman, Newry and District Trades Union Council, Member, branch and regional committees, T.G.W.U. B 1936.

ARUNDEL

Electorate 91,638   1974: 83,464

*Marshall, R. M. (C)	43,968
Kingsbury, J. R. (L)	13,208
Tizard, J. N. (Lab)	10,509
C majority	30,760

No Change

	1974		1979
Total Votes	60,887		67,685
Turnout	73·0%		73·9%
C	34,215	56·2%	65·5%
L	15,404	25·3%	19·5%
Lab	11,268	18·5%	15·5%
C maj	18,811	30·9%	45·5%
Swing		−1·7%	+5·9%

Mr Michael Marshall became Under Secretary of State for Industry in May 1979. Elected in February 1974; contested The Hartlepools, 1970. Writer and broadcaster. B June 1930; ed Bradfield College, Harvard and Stanford universities. Member, Select Committe on Overseas Development, 1974-76 and on Nationalized Industries, 1976-78. Vice-chairman, Conservative Industry Committee, 1975-78. Joint Chairman, all-party group on the theatre. Chairman, Marshall Consultants Ltd. Member, Equity. Former BBC cricket commentator.

Mr John Kingsbury, teacher, contested seat, February and October, 1974, and Wembley, North, 1970. B May, 1935; ed Chichester High School and Bognor Regis College of Education. Arundel district councillor.

Mr John Tizard, appeals officer with the Spastics Society. B November, 1954; ed Colchester Royal Grammar School and LSE. TGWU.

ASHFIELD

Electorate 77,878   1974: 74,701

Haynes, F. (Lab)	33,116
*Smith, T. (C)	25,319
Flint, H. C. (L)	3,914
Annable, W. (Nat Front)	397
Lab majority	7,797

Lab gain from C

	1974		1979
Total Votes	55,778		62,746
Turnout	74·7%		80·6%
Lab	35,367	63·4%	52·8%
C	12,452	22·3%	40·4%
L	7,959	14·3%	6·2%
Nat Front	—		0·6%
Lab maj	22,915	41·1%	12·4%
Swing		−2·6%	+14·3%

1977 by-election; Total vote: 45,875 (59.7%). C 19,616 (43.1%). Lab 19,352 (42.5%). L 4,380 (9.6%). NF 1,734 (3.8%). SWP 453 (1.0%). C maj 264 (0.6%). C gain from Lab.

Mr Frank Haynes, a miner, has been an NUM branch official for 20 years and a member of the union for 34 years. B March 1926; ed secondary schools in London. Member, Nottinghamshire County Council for 13 years, and district council for 12 years. Chairman, Central Notts Community Health Council. Sponsored by NUM.

Mr Timothy Smith, chartered accountant and company secretary, won the seat at the April 1977 by-election. B October 1974; ed Harrow and St Peter's College, Oxford. President, Oxford University Conservative Association, 1968. Joint Secretary, Conservative Prices and Consumer Protection Committee, 1977-78. Treasurer, Dulwich Conservative Association 1975-76; member, Greater London area Youth Conservative committee, 1972-75. Chairman, United Nations Youth and Student Association, 1975-76.

Mr Hampton Flint, fruiterer, contested seat, April 1977 by-election, and October and February, 1974. B August, 1926. Former president, National Market Traders' Federation, and Mansfield Chamber of Trade and Commerce.

ASHFORD

Electorate 61,460   1974: 58,419

*Speed, K. (C)	26,224
Gilbert, A. A. (Lab)	12,586
Wainman, A. (L)	7,631
McKilliam, K. R. (Nat Front)	678
C majority	13,638

No Change

	1974		1979
Total Votes	43,546		47,119
Turnout	74·5%		76·7%
C	19,294	44·3%	55·7%
Lab	13,269	30·5%	26·7%
L	10,983	25·2%	16·2%
Nat Front	—		1·4%
C maj	6,025	13·8%	29·0%
Swing		−3·4%	+7·6%

Mr Keith Speed, a marketing consultant, became Under Secretary of Defence for the Royal Navy in May, 1979. Opposition spokesman on environment and local government, 1975-79. Elected for this seat in October 1974; MP for Meriden, March 1968 to February 1974. Regular naval officer, 1947-56. Under Secretary for the Environment, 1972-74; assistant Government whip, 1970-72. B March 1934; ed Greenhill School, Evesham, Bedford Modern School, and Royal Naval Colleges, Dartmouth and Greenwich. Served in Conservative Research Department, 1965-68.

Mr Alan Gilbert, master printer. B July, 1938; ed Beverley School. NGA.

Mrs Allison Wainman, journalist. B July, 1940; ed Priory School, Jamaica. Chairman, Bicknor Parish Council.

ASHTON-UNDER-LYNE

Electorate 58,588   1974: 60,393

*Sheldon, R. E. (Lab)	24,535
Fearn, A. (C)	16,156
Taylor, G. (L)	3,699
Jones, D. (Nat Front)	486
Lab majority	8,379

No Change

	1974		1979
Total Votes	43,609		44,876
Turnout	72·2%		76·6%
Lab	23,490	53·9%	54·7%
C	12,763	29·3%	36·0%
L	7,356	16·9%	8·2%
Nat Front	—		1·1%
Lab maj	10,727	24·6%	18·7%
Swing		−3·6%	+2·9%

Mr Robert Sheldon, Financial Secretary to the Treasury in 1975-79; Minister of State, Treasury, 1974-75; Minister of State, Civil Service Department, 1974. Former Opposition spokesman on the Civil Service and machinery of government; member, Fulton Committee on Civil Service, 1966-68. Elected in 1964; contested Manchester, Withington, 1959. Former company director. B September 1923; ed grammar school and technical colleges; external graduate, London University. Chairman, general sub-committee of Commons expenditure committee 1972-74. TGWU.

Mr Alan Fearn, dental surgeon, contested Middleton and Prestwich, October 1974; Accrington, February 1974, and Ashton-under-Lyne, 1970. B July 1924; ed Bury Grammar School, Shrewsbury School and Guy's Hospital. Member, Rochdale Town Council, 1955-60; General Dental Council, Council of British Dental Association.

Mr George Taylor, personnel manager B September, 1926; ed Greenfield Secondary School; Hyde Technical College.

AYLESBURY

Electorate 74,746   1974: 67,729

*Raison, T. H. F. (C)	33,953
Power, J. G. (Lab)	14,091
Cook, M. J. (L)	10,248
C majority	19,862

No Change

	1974		1979
Total Votes	50,376		58,292
Turnout	74·4%		78·0%
C	23,565	46·8%	58·2%
Lab	14,592	29·0%	24·2%
L	12,219	24·3%	17·6%
C maj	8,973	17·8%	34·0%
Swing		−1·4%	+8·1%

Mr Timothy Raison, Minister of State, Home Office, from May, 1979, was chief Opposition spokesman on the environment and member of the Shadow Cabinet, 1974-77; spokesman on prices and consumer affairs, 1974-75 and on social services and education during 1974. Under Secretary for Education and Science, 1973-74. Journalist and magazine publisher.

Elected in 1970. B November 1929; ed Dragon School, Oxford; Eton and Christ Church, Oxford. Senior fellow, Centre for Studies in Social Policy. Director, Private Patients Plan. Member, Richmond upon Thames Borough Council 1967-71.

Mr John Power, storeman. B May, 1938; ed East Oxford Secondary School and Oxford City Technical School. AUEW district president.

Mr Michael Cook, managing director of family motor trade business. B April, 1927; ed Lord Williams Grammar School, Thame. Contested seat in Feb. and Oct. 1974. Member, Aylesbury Vale District and Brill Parish Councils.

AYR

Electorate 54,753   1974: 51,975

*Younger, G. K. H. (C)	18,907
MacDonald, K. (Lab)	16,139
Mabon, R. (L)	4,656
McGill, J. (Scot Nat)	3,998
C majority	2,768

No Change

	1974		1979
Total Votes	41,268		43,700
Turnout	79·4%		79·8%
C	17,487	42·4%	43·3%
Lab & Co-op	14,268	34·6%	36·9%
Scot Nat	6,902	16·7%	9·1%
L	2,611	6·3%	10·7%
C maj	3,219	7·8%	6·4%
Swing		−2·0%	−0·7%

Mr George Younger, who became Secretary of State for Scotland in May, 1979, had been an Opposition spokesman on Scottish Office matters; chief Opposition spokesman on defence and member of Shadow Cabinet, 1975-76; a spokesman on defence, 1974-75. Minister of State for Defence, 1974; Under Secretary for Development, Scottish Office, 1970-73.

Elected in 1964; contested North Lanarkshire, 1959. Scottish Conservative whip, 1965-67. Eldest son of Viscount Younger of Leckie. B September, 1931, ed Cargilfield School, Edinburgh, Winchester College, and New College, Oxford. Governor, Royal Scottish Academy. Director, Tennant Caledonian Breweries Ltd, Glasgow. Chairman, Scottish Conservative Party, 1974-75. Member, Select Committees on Procedure.

Mr Keith MacDonald, bookseller. B 1953. Member, Kyle and Carrick District Council, since 1977.

Mr Richard Mabon, senior scientific officer, fought Ayrshire, South, October, 1974. B July 1927; ed Leith Academy and Heriot-Watt University. IPCS.

Mr John McGill, sales manager. B September, 1934; ed St Joseph's Academy and Kilmarnock Technical College.

AYRSHIRE Central

Electorate 67,288   1974: 59,273

*Lambie, D. (Lab)	27,438
Wilkinson, R. (C)	15,734
MacDonald, I. (Scot Nat)	5,596
Clarkson, I. (L)	4,896
Lab Majority	11,704

No Change

	1974		1979
Total votes	46,994		53,664
Turnout	79·3%		79·8%
Lab	21,188	45·1%	51·1%
C	11,633	24·8%	29·3%
Scot Nat	11,533	24·5%	10·4%
L	2,640	5·6%	9·1%
Lab maj	9,555	20·3%	21·8%
Swing		−3·7%	−0·8%

Mr David Lambie was elected in 1970; contested Ayrshire, North and Bute 1966, 1964 and 1959. Former teacher. B July 1925; ed Ardrossan Academy, Glasgow, and Glasgow and Geneva universities. Former executive member, EIS; chairman, Scottish Labour Party, 1965-66. Member, Select Committee on Parliamentary Commissioner for Administration, since 1974.

Mr Richard Wilkinson, health service administrator; a member of Nalgo and the Conservative trade unionists organization. Member, Strathclyde Regional Council, since 1978. B September, 1947; ed Irvine Royal Academy.

Mr Ian Macdonald runs a dry-cleaning business. B 1934; ed Glasgow Academy and Glasgow University. Former party national organizer, vice-president and executive vice-chairman. Member, national executive committee of SNP.

AYRSHIRE, North and Bute

Electorate 49,931   1974: 49,071

*Corrie, J. A. (C)	17,317
Smith, M. J. (Lab)	13,004
Brown, M. (Scot Nat)	5,272
Giffney, P. (L)	2,280
C majority	4,313

No Change

	1974		1979
Total votes	34,971		37,873
Turnout	71·3%		75·9%
C	13,599	38·9%	45·7%
Lab	10,093	28·9%	34·3%
Scot Nat	9,055	25·9%	13·9%
L	2,224	6·4%	6·0%
C maj	3,506	10·0%	11·4%
Swing		−4·0%	+0·7%

Mr John Corrie, a farmer, was elected in February, 1974. Member European Parliament, 1975-76. Opposition whip 1976-79. B July, 1935; ed George Watson's College, Edinburgh, and Lincoln Agricultural College, New Zealand. Contested Ayrshire Central, 1966, and Lanark, North, 1964. Past President, Scottish Young Conservatives and Kirk-

cudbright Unionist Association. Nuffield Agricultural Scholar, 1972-73.

Mr Matthew Smith, Scottish District officer for Nalgo. B February, 1952; ed Stevenston High School and Ardrossan Academy. Member, Stevenston Town Council. TGWU (ACTS).

Mr Matthew Brown owns engineering firm. B January, 1940; ed Larkhall Academy and Stow College. Chairman, Cunningham District Council.

AYRSHIRE, South

Electorate 50,727   1974: 51,330

Foulkes, G. (Lab and Co-op)	14,271
*Sillars, J. (Scot Lab)	12,750
Young, G. (C)	10,287
Cameron, C. (Scot Nat)	3,233
Lab and Co-op majority	1,521

Lab and Co-op gain from Scot Lab

	1974		1979
Total votes	39,712		40,541
Turnout	77·4%		79·9%
Lab	22,329	56·2%	35·2%
Scot Lab	—		31·4%
Scot Nat	7,851	19·8%	8·0%
C	7,402	18·6%	25·4%
L	2,130	5·4%	—
Lab maj	14,478	36·4%	3·8%
Swing		−3·4%	+13·9%

Mr George Foulkes, Director of Age Concern, Scotland, contested Edinburgh Pentlands in October. 1974, and Edinburgh West, 1970. B January 1942; ed Keith Grammar School, Banffshire, Haberdashers' Aske School and Edinburgh University. Member, Edinburgh Corporation, 1970-75; Lothian Regional Council since 1974 (chairman, education commit-

tee). Chairman, education committee of Convention of Scottish local authorities. Director, St Cuthbert's Co-operative Association. APEX.

Mr James Sillars was returned for Labour at the by-election in March, 1970, but resigned the Labour whip in 1976 over disagreements with Government policy and became a leading figure in forming the Scottish Labour Party. Full-time Labour Party agent in 1964 and 1966 general elections. B October, 1937; ed Newton Park School, Ayr, and Ayr Academy. Former official, Fire Brigades Union, and head of Scottish TUC organization department. Vice-chairman "Yes for Scotland" in 1979 referendum.

Mr Gordon Young, cost accountant. B 1951; ed Greenock Academy; Central College of Commerce and Distribution and Cambridge Technical College.

Mr Colin Cameron, solicitor. B August, 1933; ed Uddingston Grammar School and Glasgow University.

BANBURY

Electorate 72,711   1974: 67,530

*Marten, H. N. (C)	31,137
Hodgson, J. B. (Lab)	16,623
White, M. (L)	8,658
Cherry, I. (Nat Front)	504
C majority	14,514

No Change

	1974		1979
Total votes	51,128		56,922
Turnout	75·7%		78·3%
C	24,210	47·4%	54·7%
Lab	18,019	35·2%	29·2%
L	8,352	16·3%	15·2%
Ind Eng Nat	547	1·1%	—
Nat Front	—		0·9%
C maj	6,191	12·2%	25·2%
Swing		−0·1%	+0·9%

Mr Neil Marten was appointed Minister of State for Foreign and Commonwealth Affairs, with special responsibilities for Overseas Development, in May 1979. A leading opponent of the EEC, he had been a member of the Select Committee on European Secondary Legislation since

1974. Member of the Council of "Get Britain Out" (of EEC) Campaign. Elected in 1959. Parliamentary Secretary, Ministry of Aviation, 1962-64. Director, shipping/aviation company. B December 1916; ed Rossall School and Law Society. Hon Treasurer, Commonwealth Parliamentary Association and of Britain-America Parliamentary Group. Vice-chairman, Conservative Parliamentary foreign and Commonwealth affairs centre, 1968-70. Member, executive, 1922 Committee; and Chairman, all-party Disabled Drivers' Committee since 1968.

Mr James Hodgson, lecturer. B October, 1938; ed Bradfield College and King's College, Newcastle. Member, Fabian Society, National Council for Civil Liberties and NATFHE.

Mr Malcolm White, self employed. Aged 39; ed Worcester College of Higher Education and London University.

BANFFSHIRE

Electorate 32,768   1974: 31,992

Myles, D. J. (C)	10,580
*Watt, H. (Scot Nat)	9,781
Duncan, R. E. (Lab)	3,381
C majority	799

C gain from Scot Nat

	1974		1979
Total votes	23,184		23,742
Turnout	72·5%		72·5%
Scot Nat	10,638	45·9%	41·2%
C	8,787	37·9%	44·6%
L	2,059	8·9%	—
Lab	1,700	7·3%	14·2%
Scot Nat maj	1,851	8·0%	—
C maj	—		3·4%
Swing	—		−0·1%

Mr David Myles, hill farmer and director of an auction company, has served as president of North Angus and Mearns Conservative Association. B May 1925; ed Edzell Primary and Brechin High Schools. Member of several Scottish NFU committees; presently Convenor of Organization and Publicity Committee.

Mr Hamish Watt, SNP spokesman on agriculture, forestry and fisheries, 1974-79. Won the seat in February, 1974; contested it in 1970 and Caithness and Sutherland in 1966 (as a Conservative). Dairy and

sheep farmer and company director. B December, 1925; ed Keith Grammar School and St Andrew's University. Banffshire county councillor. Member, Expenditure Committee 1974-79. NFU (past branch president).

Mr Robert Duncan, a history teacher at Banff Academy. B August, 1948; ed Forres Academy, Aberdeen University.

BARKING, Barking

Electorate 48,289   1974: 50,039

*Richardson, Miss. J. (Lab)	18,111
Roe, Mrs. M. (C)	11,103
Taylor, M. F. (L)	3,679
Newport, I. (Nat Front)	1,021
Barry. J. (Ind Lab)	400
Lab Majority	7,008

No Change

	1974		1979
Total votes	33,708		34,314
Turnout	67·4%		71·1%
Lab	21,546	63·9%	52·8%
C	5,256	15·6%	32·4%
L	5,245	15·6%	10·7%
Nat Front	1,661	4·9%	3·0%
Lab maj	16,290	48·3%	20·4%
Swing		-3·%	+13·9%

Miss Josephine Richardson was elected in February, 1974; contested Harrow, East, 1964; Hornchurch 1959, and Monmouth, 1955 and 1951. B August, 1923; ed Southend High School for Girls. Member, Tribune group of MPs; Select Committee on Nationalized Industries since 1975, and Select Committee on Procedure; Expenditure Committee, 1974-75; executive council, National Council for Civil Liberties. APEX and ASTMS.

Mrs Marion Roe, GLC member for Ilford North, since 1977; deputy chief whip and vice chairman of general management committee. Member, Bromley Borough Council, 1975-78, and of executive council, Orpington Conservative Association, 1975-78.

Mr Martin Taylor, an administrative officer with the ILEA, contested the seat, February and October, 1974. B September, 1945; ed Fairlop Secondary Modern School, Beal Grammar School, and Essex University.

BARKING Dagenham

Electorate 67,990   1974: 70,004

*Parker, J. (Lab)	24,707
Hyams, G. (C)	14,600
Long, M. (L)	5,583
Roberts, J. (Nat Front)	1,553
Connor, D. (Comm)	553
Lab majority	10,107

No Change

	1974		1979
Total votes	45,495		46,996
Turnout	65·0%		69·1%
Lab	29,678	65·2%	52·6%
C	7,684	16·9%	31·1%
L	7,564	16·6%	11·9%
Nat Front	—		3·3%
Comm	569	1·3%	1·2%
Lab maj	21,994	48·3%	21·5%
Swing		-0·3%	+13·4%

Mr John Parker, Father of the House, writer and former publisher, was MP for Romford, 1935-45; returned for Dagenham, 1945; contested Holland with Boston, 1931. Under Secretary, Dominions Office, 1945-46. B July 1906; ed Marlborough and St John's College, Oxford. Former General Secretary, Fabian Society. Member, Procedure Committee, 1964-74. Member, National Trust Executive since 1966 and Historic Buildings Council since 1974, and executive of Inland Waterways Amenities Advisory Council, Chairman, PLP forestry group; vice-chairman PLP Art and Amenities Group. Chairman, British-Yugoslav Parliamentary Group since 1960. TGWU.

Mr Gary Hyams, company director. B November 1949; ed Bancroft's School, Woodford Green.

Mr Mark Long, research laboratory technician, Aged 23.

Mr Dan Connor, 54, union convenor of Fords body plant at Dagenham. Chairman, TGWU automotive group.

BARKSTON ASH

Electorate 91,890   1974: 83,803

*Alison, M. J. H. (C)	40,381
Muir, J. H. (Lab)	21,670
Pughe-Morgan, P. (L)	7,909
Corry, D. (Ecology)	1,829
C majority	18,711

No Change

	1974		1979
Total votes	63,538		71,789
Turnout	75·8%		78·1%
C	30,498	48·0%	56·2%
Lab	20,557	32·4%	30·2%
L	12,483	19·6%	11·0%
Ecology	—	—	2·5%
C maj	9,941	15·6%	26·0%
Swing		-1·8%	+5·2%

Mr Michael Alison, appointed Minister of State for Northern Ireland, in May 1979. An Opposition spokesman on environment 1978-79, and on Home Affairs 1975-78, was elected in 1964. Under Secretary for Health and Social Security, 1970-74. B June 1926; ed Eton, Wadham College, Oxford and Ridley Hall, Cambridge. Member, Commons Expenditure Committee, 1974-75; Kensington Borough Council, 1956-59. Research officer, foreign section of Conservative Research Department. 1958-64.

Mr John Muir, barrister, contested seat in both 1974 elections. B June, 1941; ed Strathclyde and London Universities. APEX and Society of Labour Lawyers.

Mr Philip Pughe-Morgan, health service administrator. Aged 33; ed Lancaster Royal Grammar School and York University.

BARNET, Chipping Barnet

Electorate 58,254   1974: 56,487

Chapman, S. (C)	25,154
Dawe, P. J. (Lab)	11,147
Ive, D. (L)	6,867
Cole, R. (Nat Front)	865

C majority	14,007

No Change

	1974		1979
Total votes	41,547		44,033
Turnout	73·6%		75·6%
C	19,661	47·3%	57·1%
Lab	11,795	28·4%	25·3%
L	8,884	21·4%	15·6%
Nat Front	1,207	2·9%	2·0%
C maj	7,866	18·9%	31·8%
Swing		−1·3%	+6·4%

Mr Sydney Chapman, an architect and town planner, was MP for Birmingham, Handsworth, 1970 until February, 1974. Member, Council of Royal Institute of British Architects, 1972-77. Former secretary, Conservative parliamentary committee on local government and development. Contested Stalybridge and Hyde, 1964. B October, 1935; ed Rugby School and Manchester University. Member, executive committee, National Union of Conservative and Unionist Associations, 1961-70; vice chairman, North West area of Conservative and Unionist Associations. 1966-70. National Chairman, Young Conservatives, 1964-66. Partner in firm of architects and planning consultants. Planning consultant, Home Builders' Federation. Originator of National Tree Planting Year, 1973.

Mr Peter Dawe, teacher. B November, 1947; ed Hardye's School, Dorchester, University College, London, Institute of Education, London. Contested Dorset West, October, 1974. Vice-chairman, West Roding Community Health Council, 1977, member Waltham Forest Community Relations Council. Methodist local preacher. NUT.

Mr David Ive, solicitor. Aged 29; ed Birmingham University.

BARNET, Finchley

Electorate 55,468   1974: 53,933

*Thatcher, Mrs M. H. (C)	20,918
May, R. G. (Lab)	13,040
Paterson, A. (L)	5,254
Verity, W. (Nat Front)	534
Lloyd, Mrs E. (Ind Dem)	86

C majority	7,878

No Change

	1974		1979
Total votes	37,462		39,832
Turnout	69·5%		71·8%
C	16,498	44·0%	52·5%
Lab	12,587	33·6%	32·7%
L	7,384	19·7%	13·2%
Nat Front	993	2·7%	1·3%
Ind Dem	—	—	0·2%
C maj	3,911	10·4%	19·8%
Swing		−2·0%	+4·7%

Mrs Margaret Thatcher the first woman Prime Minister took office on May 4, 1979. She was elected as Leader of the Conservative Party and Leader of the Opposition in February, 1975. Member of the shadow Cabinet and chief Opposition spokesman on the environment 1974-75; Secretary of State for Education and Science, 1970-74. Chief Opposition spokesman on education, 1969-70; previously spokesman on transport, power, treasury matters, housing, and pensions. Member, Shadow Cabinet, 1967-70. Returned for Finchley in 1959; contested Dartford in 1950 and 1951. Parliamentary Secretary, Ministry of Pensions and National Insurance, 1961-64. Barrister (Lincoln's Inn, 1954) and formerly a research chemist. B October, 1926, ed Grantham High School and Somerville College, Oxford, where she was treasurer and president of the University Conservation Association.

Mr Richard May, barrister. B November, 1938; ed Haileybury and Selwyn College, Cambridge. Member, Westminster City Council, 1971-78 and leader of Labour Group, 1974-77. Contested Dorset, South, 1970. APEX.

Mr Anthony Paterson, solicitor. B May, 1951; ed Winchester College and Worcester College, Oxford. Special constable since 1975. Chairman, Finchley community relations group.

BARNET, Hendon North

Electorate 54,036   1974: 50,762

*Gorst, J. M. (C)	20,766
Cooper, F. A. (Lab)	14,374
Perkin, C. (L)	4,113
Franklyn, B. (Nat Front)	638

C majority	6,392

No Change

	1974		1979
Total votes	36,670		39,891
Turnout	72·2%		73·8%
C	16,299	44·4%	52·1%
Lab	14,549	39·7%	36·0%
L	5,822	15·9%	10·3%
Nat Front	—	—	1·6%
C maj	1,750	4·7%	16·1%
Swing		−0·9%	+5·7%

Mr John Gorst, public relations, advertising and communications consultant. Elected in 1970; contested Bodmin, 1966, and Chester-le-Street, 1964. B June, 1928; ed Ardingly College and Corpus Christi College, Cambridge. Director, Cassius Film Productions Ltd, since 1969. Founder and former secretary, Telephone Users' Association. Member, Conservative group for the self-employed.

Mr Frank Cooper, sheet metal worker. B January, 1924; ed Kingston Technical College. Member, Greater London Council and Hillingdon Borough Council. NUSMW.

Mr Christopher Perkin, photographer. B February 1955; ed Addey and Stanhope, and Latymer schools.

BARNET, Hendon South

Electorate 53,954   1974: 51,889

*Thomas, P. J. M. (C)	19,981
Mantle, Mrs W. P. (Lab)	11,231
Palmer M. (L)	5,799
Syer, G. (Ecology)	563
Elder, A. (Nat Front)	290

C majority	8,750

No Change

	1974		1979
Total votes	36,173		37,864
Turnout	69.7%		70.2%
C	16,866	46.6%	52.8%
Lab	11,903	32.9%	29.7%
L	7,404	20.5%	15.3%
Ecology	—	—	1.5%
Nat Front	—	—	0.8%
C maj	4,963	13.7%	23.1%
Swing		−1.5%	+4.7%

Mr Peter Thomas, QC, was a member of the Shadow Cabinet as Chief Opposition spokesman on Wales, 1974-75. Secretary of State for Wales, 1970-74. President, National Union of Conservative and Unionist Associations, 1974-76. Chairman, Conservative Party organization, 1970-72; Minister of State, Foreign Affairs, 1963-64; Under Secretary, Foreign Office, 1961-63; Parliamentary Secretary, Ministry of Labour, 1959-61. Elected for Hendon, South, 1970. MP for Conway, 1951-66. Barrister (Middle Temple, 1947), QC, 1965; Recorder. B July 1920; ed Epworth College, Rhyl and Jesus College, Oxford. Member, Select Committee on Conduct of Members, 1977.

Mrs Wendy Mantle, solicitor. B February, 1940; ed Pontypool Grammar School and St Anne's College, Oxford.

Mr Monroe Palmer, chartered accountant. B November, 1938; ed Orange Hill Grammar School. National treasurer of Liberal Party. Partner in Felton and Palmer, of Wembley.

BARNSLEY

Electorate 77,699   1974: 76,572

*Mason, R. (Lab)	36,276
England, G. (C)	13,654
Whitaker, W. (L)	5,751
Gallagher, B. (TOI)	638
Davis, J. (WRP)	348

Lab majority	22,622

No Change

	1974		1979
Total votes	52,365		56,667
Turnout	68.4%		72.9%
Lab	34,212	65.3%	64.0%
C	9,400	18.0%	24.1%
L	8,753	16.7%	10.1%
TOI	—	—	1.1%
WRP	—	—	0.6%
Lab maj	24,812	47.3%	39.9%
Swing		−1.9%	+3.7%

Mr Roy Mason, Secretary of State for Northern Ireland, 1976-79, was Secretary of State for Defence, 1974-76. Opposition spokesman on trade and civil aviation, 1970-74. Former chairman of the PLP miners' group. President of the Board of Trade, 1969-70; Minister of Power, 1968-69; Postmaster-General, April-June, 1968; Minister of Defence (Equipment), 1967-68; Minister of State, Board of Trade, 1964-67. Returned at a by-election in March, 1953. B April, 1924; ed elementary schools and LSE. Miner, 1938-53. Sponsored by NUM.

Mr George England, barrister. B 1946; ed Barnsley Holgate Grammar School and Sheffield University. Hon secretary (1973-74) and hon treasurer (1975-76), Barnsley Constituency Conservative Association.

Mr Wilfred Whitaker, lecturer, contested Keighley, February, 1974, and Normanton, October, 1974. B January, 1946; ed secondary modern school, Morley Grammar School, Hull University and Huddersfield Polytechnic. NATFHE.

Mr John Davies, aged 32, colliery face worker.

BARROW-IN-FURNESS

Electorate 54,451   1974: 54,541

*Booth, A. E. (Lab)	22,687
Thompson, P. (C)	14,946
Thompson, G. (L)	4,983

Lab majority	7,741

No Change

	1974		1979
Total votes	42,032		42,616
Turnout	77.1%		78.3%
Lab	21,607	51.4%	53.2%
C	14,253	33.9%	35.1%
L	5,788	13.8%	11.7%
Ind	384	0.9%	—
Lab maj	7,534	17.5%	18.1%
Swing		−2.9%	−0.3%

Mr Albert Booth, Secretary of State for Employment, 1976-79; Minister of State for Employment, 1974-76. Chairman, Select Committee on Statutory Instruments, 1970-74. An Opposition spokesman on trade and industry, 1973-74. Elected in 1966; contested Tynemouth, 1964. B May, 1928; ed St Thomas's, Winchester, South Shields Marine School, Rutherford College of Technology. Member, Tynemouth Borough Council, 1952-58; chairman, 1958-63. Sponsored by AUEW (TASS).

Mr Patrick Thompson, schoolmaster, contested Bradford, North, February and October 1974. B October 1935; ed Felsted School, Essex, and Emmanuel College, Cambridge. Chairman, North Norfolk Conservative Association, since 1975. AMA.

Mr Geoffrey Thompson, lecturer and teacher. B September 1924; ed St John's College, York, and Lancaster and Keele universities.

BARRY

Electorate 75,127   1974: 69,992

*Gower, Sir R. (C)	30,720
Stead, P. P. (Lab)	21,928
Berritt, W. N. (L)	6,105
Dixon, A. J. (Pl Cymru)	1,281
Kerton, E. R. (Nat Front)	312
C majority	8,792

No Change

	1974		1979
Total votes	54,374		60,346
Turnout	77·7%		80·3%
C	23,360	43·0%	50·9%
Lab	20,457	37·6%	36·3%
L	8,764	16·1%	10·1%
Pl Cymru	1,793	3·3%	2·1%
Nat Front	—	—	0·5%
C maj	2,903	5·4%	14·6%
Swing		−2·2%	+4·6%

Sir Raymond Gower was elected in 1951; contested Ogmore, 1950. Solicitor. Vice President, National Chamber of Trade. Chairman, *Penray Press and Barry Herald* newspaper, 1955-64. Former director, Nicholson Construction and of other companies. B August, 1916; ed Neath Grammar School; Cardiff High School; University College, Cardiff, and Cardiff School of Law. Vice-chairman, Welsh Conservative MPs since 1974. Treasurer, Welsh Parliamentary Party (all-party). Member, Speaker's conference on electoral reform, 1967-69 and 1971-74.

Mr Peter Stead, university lecturer. B August, 1943; ed Barry and Gowerton Grammar Schools and University College, Swansea. AUT.

Mr William Barritt, chartered accountant. Chairman, Barry Liberal Association. Aged 46.

Mr Andrew Dixon, computer programmer. B August, 1951; ed Penarth Grammar School. Nalgo.

BASILDON

Electorate 103,595   1974: 91,416

Proctor, K. H. (C)	37,919
*Moonman, E. (Lab)	32,739
Auvray, R. (L)	9,280
Sawyer, G. A. (Nat Front)	880
C majority	5,180

C gain from Lab

	1974		1979
Total votes	67,460		80,818
Turnout	73·8%		78·0%
Lab	32,298	47·9%	40·5%
C	21,747	32·2%	46·9%
L	12,816	19·0%	11·5%
Ind Lab	599	0·9%	—
Nat Front	—	—	1·1%
Lab Maj	10,551	15·7%	—
C maj	—	—	6·4%
Swing		−0·7%	+11·0%

Mr Harvey Proctor, assistant secretary to a trade federation, contested Hackney, South and Shoreditch, February and October 1974. B January, 1947; ed High School for Boys, Scarborough, and York University (chairman of University Conservative Association, 1967-69).

Mr Eric Moonman was elected in February, 1974; MP for Billericay, 1966-70 and contested Chigwell and Ongar, 1964. B April, 1929; ed elementary and secondary schools and Manchester and Liverpool universities. Member, Select Committee on Race Relations and Immigration, since 1974. Chairman, all party mental health committee and all party management affairs group. Chairman, PLP new towns and urban affairs subcommittee, 1977-78. Former northern manager, *Daily Mirror.* Sponsored by NGA

Mr Raymond Auvray, senior careers officer. B June, 1948; ed Bideford Grammar School and Reading University. Nalgo.

BASINGSTOKE

Electorate 99,124   1974: 86,782

*Mitchell, D. B. (C)	42,625
Harris, R. W. (Lab)	20,879
Clatworthy, P. (L)	14,605
Packer, Miss B. (Nat Front)	677
C majority	21,746

No Change

	1974		1979
Total votes	67,263		78,786
Turnout	77·5%		79·5%
C	29,038	43·2%	54·1%
Lab	22,826	33·9%	26·5%
L	14,636	21·8%	18·5%
Nat Front	763	1·1%	0·9%
C maj	6,212	9·3%	27·6%
Swing		−0·8%	+9·1%

Mr David Mitchell became an Under Secretary of State for Industry in May, 1979. Elected in 1964; contested St Pancras, North, 1959. Opposition whip, 1965-67. Wine shipper and director of firm of wine merchants. B June, 1928; ed Aldenham. Member, St Pancras Borough Council, 1956-59. Secretary, Conservative parliamentary labour committee, 1968-70; chairman, Conservative parliamentary small businesses committee since 1974; chairman, Small Businesses Bureau.

Mr Robert Harris, comprehensive school teacher, fought Rye, February, 1974, and Guilford, October, 1974. Member, Havering Borough Council. B March, 1945; ed state primary and grammar schools and Durham University. NUT.

Mr Peter Clatworthy, sales manager. B June, 1948; ed Edmonton County Grammar School and St Ignatius College, London. Member, Liberal Party Council. ASTMS.

BASSETLAW

Electorate 73,763   1974: 71,724

*Ashton, J. W. (Lab)	29,426
Harris, D. K. (C)	22,247
Wilkinson, A. (L)	6,913

Lab majority	7,179

No Change

	1974		1979
Total votes	53,386		58,586
Turnout		74·4%	79·4%
Lab	28,663	53·7%	50·2%
C	16,494	30·9%	38·0%
L	7,821	14·6%	11·8%
Chr Pty	408	0·8%	—
Lab maj	12,169	22·8%	12·2%
Swing		−1·4%	+5·3%

Mr Joseph Ashton, a design engineer, was returned at a by-election in October, 1968. Government whip, 1976-77; PPS to Mr Wedgwood Benn, 1974-76. Member, Select Committee on nationalized industries, 1974-76. Weekly political columnist, *Sheffield Star* since 1970 and for other regional and national papers. Columnist in *Labour Weekly*. Broadcaster, Sponsored by AUEW (TASS). B October, 1933; ed High Storrs Grammar School, Sheffield, and Rotherham Technical College.

Mr David Harris, solicitor and director of a public Relations Company, contested the seat in October 1974. B January 1945; ed Worksop College and King's College, London. Commands a Nato Reserve TAVR company.

Mr Anthony Wilkinson, company chairman. B April, 1937; ed Repton. Contested the seat, October 1974.

BATH

Electorate 63,575   1974: 62,304

Patten, C. (C)	23,025
Mayhew, C. P. (L)	13,913
Baber, M. (Lab)	11,407
Grimes, D. (Ecology)	1,082
Mundy, T. (Nat Front)	206

C majority	9,112

No Change

	1974		1979
Total votes	48,979		49,633
Turnout	78·6%		78·1%
C	18,470	37·7%	46·4%
L	16,348	33·4%	28·0%
Lab	14,011	28·6%	23·0%
UDP	150	0·3%	—
Ecology	—	—	2·2%
Nat Front	—	—	0·4%
C maj	2,122	4·3%	18·4%
Swing		−1·9%	+7·1%

Mr Christopher Patten, director of the Conservative Research Department since 1974, contested Lambeth Central in February, 1974. B May, 1944; ed St Benedict's School, Ealing; Balliol College, Oxford. Joined Conservative Research Department 1966. Seconded to Cabinet Office, 1970-72, working on coordination of social policy and in 1972 joined Home Office to set up the Voluntary Service Unit. Personal Assistant and political secretary to Lord Carrington when he was Chairman of the Conservative Party, 1972-74. Former secretary of the Shadow Cabinet.

Mr Christopher Mayhew who contested the seat in October, 1974, took the Liberal whip on July 9 that year. He was Labour Minister of Defence for the Royal Navy from 1964 until he resigned in 1966; party spokesman on foreign affairs from December, 1961 to 1964, and previously on War Office matters. Labour MP for Woolwich, East, 1951-74 and for South Norfolk 1945-50. Under Secretary for Foreign Affairs, 1946-50. B June 1915; ed Haileybury and Christ Church, Oxford; President of the Union, 1937 Writer and television broadcaster. Executive chairman, Middle East International (Publishers) Ltd; and of National Association for Mental Health.

Mr Martin Baber, chartered accountant. B May, 1937; ed Colston School, Bristol. District councillor.

Mr Donald Grimes, security firm's technical supervisor. Aged 35; ed Goldbeaters Secondary Modern School, Edgware.

BATLEY AND MORLEY

Electorate 62,871   1974: 61,894

Woolmer, K. J. (Lab)	22,984
Crone, G. N. A. (C)	17,632
Caywood, C. (L)	4,943
Parkins, D. (Ind)	848
Lord, C. (Ecology)	460

Lab Majority	5,352

No Change

	1974		1979
Total votes	43,038		46,867
Turnout	69·5%		74·5%
Lab	21,179	49·2%	49·0%
C	12,931	30·0%	37·6%
L	8,928	20·7%	10·5%
Ind	—	—	1·8%
Ecology	—	—	1·0%
Lab maj	8,248	19·2%	11·4%
Swing		−2·3%	+3·9%

Mr Kenneth Woolmer, a university lecturer, contested Leeds, North West, 1970. B April, 1940; ed Kettering Grammar School and Leeds University. Member, Leeds County Borough Council 1970-74; West Yorkshire Metropolitan County Council since 1973 (leader of Labour Group and of Council, 1973-74). AUT and GMWU.

Mr Neill Crone, solicitor, fought the seat in both general elections of 1974. B August 1937; ed

Scarborough College and College of Law, Guildford. Chairman, Yorkshire CPC since 1977 and member, CPC National Advisory Committee and Conservative Group for Europe. Hon Secretary, Batley Parish Church parochial church council and of Heavy Woollen Cricket Society.

Mr Christopher Caywood, teacher, contested Bradford, South, October, 1974. B December, 1941; ed Roundhay Grammar School, Leeds and London University.

Mr Clive Lord, probation officer. Aged 44.

BEACONSFIELD

Electorate 67,961   1974: 68,541

*Bell, R. M. (C)	31,938
Glasson, E. L. (Lab)	10,443
Meyer, P. (L)	8,853
Noyes, J. (Nat Front)	548

C majority	21,495

No Change

	1974		1979
Total votes	48,093		51,782
Turnout	70·2%		76·2%
C	23,234	48·3%	61·7%
L	12,606	26·2%	17·1%
Lab	12,253	25·5%	20·2%
Nat Front	—	—	1·1%
C maj	10,628	22·1%	41·5%
Swing		−2·3%	+9·3%

Mr Ronald Bell, QC, was returned in February, 1974; MP for South Buckingham, 1950-74. Contested Caerphilly by-election, 1939. Won Newport by-election in 1945 and lost seat two months later in general election. Barrister (Gray's Inn, 1938); QC, 1966. B April, 1914; ed Cardiff High School and Magdalen College, Oxford. Member, Select Committee on Education, 1968-70; on Statutory Instruments, 1953-74; Select Committee on European Secondary Legislation since 1974.

Mr Edwin Glasson, metallurgist. B August, 1943; ed Ealing College, Ealing Grammar School, Brunel University. ASTMS.

Mr Percy Meyer, account executive, contested Mid-Bedfordshire, February and October, 1974, East Surrey, 1970, and Hornsey, 1966. B December, 1925; ed The Hall School, Hampstead, and Ardingly College, Sussex. Member, Finchley Borough Council, 1962-65.

BEBINGTON AND ELLESMERE PORT

Electorate 91,816   1974: 86,641

Porter, B. (C)	32,488
*Bates, A. (Lab)	32,002
Gilchrist, P. (L)	9,591

C majority	486

C gain from Lab

	1974		1979
Total votes	68,076		74,081
Turnout	78·6%		80·7%
Lab	32,310	47·5%	43·2%
C	25,819	37·9%	43·9%
L	9,947	14·6%	12·9%
Lab maj	6,491	9·6%	
C maj	—		0·7%
Swing		−1·7%	+5·1%

Mr Barry Porter contested Chorley, October, 1974; Newton in February, 1974, and Liverpool, Scotland Exchange, April 1971. Solicitor. B 1939; ed Birkenhead School and University College, Oxford. Member, Birkenhead County Borough Council, 1967-74.

Mr Alfred Bates, a Government whip 1976-79. Elected in February, 1974; contested Northwich, 1970. Mathematics lecturer. B June, 1944; ed Stretford Grammar School, Manchester University, and Corpus Christi, Cambridge. Member, Expenditure Committee, 1975-76; Stretford Borough Council, 1971-74. NUT.

Mr Philip Gilchrist, part-time Liberal Party worker. Aged 27; ed York University and Edge Hill College of Education. Member, Merseyside County Council and Wirral Borough Council.

BEDFORD

Electorate 77,315   1974: 74,143

*Skeet, T. H. H. (C)	31,140
Hyman, N. A. (Lab)	18,727
Gibbons, B. (L)	10,129
Stearns, R. (Nat Front)	813

C majority	12,413

No Change

	1974		1979
Total votes	56,940		60,809
Turnout	76·8%		78·7%
C	24,834	43·6%	51·2%
Lab	20,746	36·4%	30·8%
L	11,360	20·0%	16·7%
Nat Front	—	—	1·3%
C maj	4,088	7·2%	20·4%
Swing		−1·5%	+6·6%

Mr Trevor Skeet won the seat in 1970; MP for Willesden, East, 1959-64; contested Llanelli, 1955, and Stoke Newington and Hackney, North 1951. Barrister (Inner Temple, 1947) and industrial consultant. B January, 1918; ed King's College, Auckland, and University of New Zealand. Vice-chairman, Conservative power and energy committees; chairman, oil sub-committee; chairman, Conservative trade committee. Member, Select Committee on Wealth Tax, 1975-76. Secretary, All-party group on airships. Consultant to Associated Portland Cement Manufacturers Ltd and British Quarrying and Slag Federation.

Mr Nicholas Hyman, lecturer. B November, 1944; ed The Hall School, Hampstead, Charterhouse and London University. Contested Folkestone and Hythe, 1970. ASTMS.

Mr Brian Gibbons, a principal systems accountant. Aged 52. County councillor since 1974.

BEDFORDSHIRE, Mid

Electorate 81,564   1974: 75,171

*Hastings, S. L. E. (C)	37,724
Peacock, F. G. (Lab)	17,140
Smout, C. A. P. (L)	11,467
C majority	20,584

No Change

	1974		1979
Total votes	58,832		66,331
Turnout	78·3%		81·3%
C	26,885	45·7%	56·9%
Lab	17,559	29·8%	25·8%
L	14,388	24·5%	17·3%
C maj	9,326	15·9%	31·1%
Swing		−0·8%	+7·6%

Mr Stephen Hastings was elected at a by-election in November 1970. Chairman, European Supersonic Aviation Ltd. Director, Oxley Development and Dust Suppression Ltd. B May 1920; ed Eton and Sandhurst. Former member, executive, 1922 Committee. Former vice-chairman, horticulture sub-committee and Conservative agriculture committee. Regular Officer in the Scots Guards, 1939-48 being aide-de-camp to the Minister of State in the Middle East, 1943, served with Special Air Service Regiment in Africa, 1944-45, and then in the Special Forces. Assistant military attache, Helsinki, 1950-53. Worked in Foreign Office, 1953-55, and 1955-58 at the Embassy in Paris; with the political office, Middle East Forces Cyprus, 1958-60.

Mr Frederick Peacock, chemist's dispenser. B August, 1927; ed Huntingdon Grammar School. Member Hertfordshire County Council; former member, Hitchin Council. USDAW.

Mr Charles Smout, deputy headmaster, contested Daventry, February, 1974 and South Northants, 1970. B November, 1929; ed Leys School, and Clare College, Cambridge, and Birmingham University.

BEDFORDSHIRE, South

Electorate 73,247   1974: 64,329

*Madel, W. D. (C)	32,988
Gardner, J. (Lab)	16,505
Turner, M. (L)	8,402
Smith, L. A. (Nat Front)	626
C majority	16,483

No Change

	1974		1979
Total votes	50,339		58,521
Turnout	78·3%		79·9%
C	20,794	41·3%	56·4%
Lab	16,351	32·5%	28·2%
L	13,194	26·2%	14·4%
Nat Front	—		1·1%
C maj	4,443	8·8%	28·2%
Swing		−0·8%	+9·7%

Mr David Madel, publishing executive and consultant, won the seat in 1970; contested Erith and Crayford, 1965 by-election and 1966. B August, 1938; ed Uppingham School, Keble College, Oxford. Member, Expenditure Committee. Secretary, Conservative parliamentary home affairs committee, 1972-73. Joint vice-chairman (previously joint secretary), Conservative employment committee since 1974. Advertising executive, Thomson Organization, 1964-70.

Mr John Gardner, an engineer at British Aerospace, Stevenage. B May, 1935; ed Corby Secondary Modern School. ASTMS.

Mr Malcolm Turner, principal systems accountant. County councillor since 1974. Aged 52.

BEDWELLTY

Electorate 50,708   1974: 50,183

*Kinnock, N. G. (Lab)	28,794
Walter, R. (C)	8,358
Richards, T. (Pl Cymru)	2,648
Rout, P. M. (Ecology)	556
Lab Majority	20,436

No Change

	1974		1979
Total votes	38,681		40,356
Turnout	77·1%		79·6%
Lab	27,418	70·9%	71·3%
C	4,556	11·8%	20·7%
L	3,621	9·4%	—
Pl Cymru	3,086	8·0%	6·6%
Ecology	—	—	1·4%
Lab maj	22,862	59·1%	50·6%
Swing		−2·3%	+4·2%

Mr Neil Kinnock was a trade union tutor with the WEA. Returned in 1970. Elected to Labour Party National Executive Committee, October, 1978. B March 1942; ed Lewis School, Pengam, Glamorgan, and University College, Cardiff. Chairman, PLP Wales group. Former member, Select Committees on European secondary legislation and nationalized industries. Member, Tribune Group; unpaid director, Tribune Publications; executive member Anti-apartheid Movement; council member, 'Get Britain Out' of EEC Campaign. Sponsored by TGWU.

Mr Robert Walter, insurance company investment executive. B May, 1948; ed Colston's School, Bristol; Lord Weymouth School, ,Warminster and the University of Aston, Birmingham. Vice-chairman, Westbury CPC Committee, since 1974. Chairman, UK Committee of European Democrat Forum.

Mr Timothy Richards, lecturer. Aged 28; ed University College, Aberystwyth. Member, Cardiff Trades Union Council; vice-chairman, local branch of NATFHE.

Mr Peter Rout, aged 34, driver. Chairman of neighbourhood council.

BEESTON

Electorate 77,802   1974: 74,172

*Lester, J. T. (C)	33,273
Jacob, J. M. (Lab)	23,077
Turner, T. (L)	6,935
C majority	10,196

No Change

	1974		1979
Total votes	59,727		63,285
Turnout	80·5%		81·3%
C	25,095	42·0%	52·6%
Lab & Co-op	24,974	41·8%	36·5%
L	9,658	16·2%	11·0%
C maj	121	0·2%	16·1%
Swing		−2·0%	+7·9%

Mr James Lester, became an Under Secretary of State for Employment in May, 1979. Director of footwear distributing company. Elected in February, 1974. Opposition whip since 1975. B May 1932; ed Nottingham High School. Contested Bassetlaw, 1968 by-election and 1970. Member, Nottinghamshire County Council, 1967-74. Delegate, Council of Europe and WEU, 1974-75.

Mr Joseph Jacob, lecturer in law at LSE. B July, 1943; ed University College, London. Member, Camden Council, 1971-74. Member, ASTMS and AUT, Society of Labour Lawyers, Socialist Medical Association; Socialist Education Association and Fabian Society.

Mr Timothy Turner, management accountant. B May 1939; ed Bancrofts School, Woodford and Durham University. Parish Councillor.

Mr Peter Robinson is general secretary of the Democratic Unionist Party and member of the party's executive committee. Deputy Mayor of Castlereagh Borough Council. B 1949.

Mr William Craig, a solicitor, was returned in February, 1974. B December, 1924; ed Dungannon Royal School, Larne Grammar School, Queen's University, Belfast. Former Leader of the Vanguard Party. Elected to Stormont for Larne in 1960. Chief Whip, Parliament of Northern Ireland, 1962-63; Minister of Home Affairs, 1963-64 and 1966-68; Minister of Health and Local Government, 1964; Minister of Development, 1965-66.

Mr Oliver Napier, solicitor, is leader of the Alliance Party. Member, Northern Ireland Assembly; Minister of Law Reform in power-sharing Executive. Member, East Belfast in the N.I. Convention. Member, Belfast City Council. B 1941; ed. St. Malachy's College and Queen's University, Belfast.

Dr. Norman Agnew, chartered surveyor and chartered structural engineer. Former member, Belfast Corporation secretary and registrar of Belfast City and District Water Commissioners. Fellow of the Royal Society of Health, hon member, British Waterworks Association and Rating and Valuation Association. Ed Quenn's University, Belfast.

Mr George Chambers, primary school vice-principal. B 1939. Member executive, Northern Ireland Labour Party. Labour candidate in local government elections.

BELFAST, East

Electorate 75,481   1974: 79,591

Robinson, P. (Dem U)	15,994
*Craig, W. (Off UU)	15,930
Napier, O. (Alliance)	15,066
Agnew, N. (UPNI)	2,017
Chambers, G. (NI LAB)	1,982
Dem U majority	64

Dem U gain from Off UU

	1974		1979
Total votes	53,426		50,989
Turnout	67·1%		67·6%
Dem U	—	—	31·4%
UUUC	31,594	59·1%	—
Off UU	—	—	31·2%
UPNI	14,417	27·0%	4·0%
NI Lab	7,415	13·9%	3·9%
Alliance	—	—	29·5%
UUUC maj	17,177	32·1%	—
Dem U maj	—	—	0·2%

BELFAST, North

Electorate 65,073   1974: 71,779

McQuade, J. (Dem U)	11,690
Walker, A. C. (Off UU)	10,695
O'Hare, P. (SDLP)	7,823
Dickson, Mrs A. L. (UPNI)	4,220
Cushnahan, J. (Alliance)	4,120
Lynch, S. (Repub Clubs)	1,907
Carr, A. (NI Lab)	1,889
Dem U majority	995

Dem U gain from Off UU

	1974		1979
Total votes	47,310		42,344
Turnout	65·9%		65·1%
Dem U	—	—	27·6%
Off UU	—	—	25·3%
UPNI	—	—	10·0%
Repub Clubs	—	—	4·5%
UUUC	29,622	62·6%	—
SDLP	11,400	24·1%	18·5%
Alliance	3,807	8·0%	9·7%
NI Lab	2,481	5·2%	—
UUUC maj	18,222	38·5%	—
Dem U maj	—	—	2·3%

Mr John McQuade sat as Unionist M.P. for Woodvale in Stormont 1965-1972. Councillor for Court Ward and subsequently Shankill Ward in Belfast Corporation. War service in Burma with Chindits; ed, public elementary school, Belfast.

Mr Cecil Walker, manager of a Belfast company of timber merchants, secretary Shankill Unionist Association. Member Eastern Health and Social Services Board. B 1925; ed Belfast Model School and Methodist College, Belfast.

Mr Paschal O'Hare, solicitor. Alderman, Belfast City Council, vice-chairman of the community services committee and general purposes and finance committee. Supporter of civil rights movement. B 1932.

Mrs Anne Dickson, leader of the Unionist Party of Northern Ireland, succeeded late Lord Faulkner. Only woman member Stormont 1969-72, representing Carrick. Member Northern Ireland Assembly and convention. Chairman, Carrick Division Unionist Association; vice-chairman, Newtownabbey Council. Former Chairman, Northern Ireland Advisory Board for the Salvation Army. Ed Holywood and Richmond Lodge School, Belfast.

Mr John Cushnahan, former teacher and community worker. General secretary, Alliance Party since 1974. Elected to Belfast City Council, 1977. B 1950; ed Queen's University, Belfast.

Mr Seamus Lynch, trade union official. Vice-president, national executive, Republican Clubs and chairman, regional executive. Member, Belfast City Council; member, committee, Irish International Peace Movement. B 1945.

Mr Alan Carr, chairman, Northern Ireland Labour Party since 1977. University lecturer and a regional adminstrator for Open University. B 1948; ed Annadale Grammar School, Belfast and New University of Ulster.

The Rev Robert Bradford, Methodist minister, was elected in February 1974. B 1941; ed Queen's University. Unsuccessful Vanguard candidate in the Northern Ireland Assembly electons. Member, Orange Order and Royal Black Institution.

Mr Basil Glass, a partner in a Belfast law firm. Elected to N I Assembly for South Belfast in 1973, convention member in 1975. In both, was chief whip, the Alliance Parliamentary Party, becoming deputy leader of the party. Contested South Belfast October 1974. Member, Belfast City Council. B 1928; ed Methodist College Belfast and Queen's University, Belfast.

Dr. Alisdair McDonnell stood as National Democratic Party candidate in North Antrim, 1970. Resumed medical studies at University College, Dublin and has held several appointments in Ulster hospitals. Elected to SDLP executive, in 1976. East Belfast representative on Belfast City Council since 1977. B 1951; ed St MacNissi's College and University College, Dublin.

Mr Victor Brennan, Teacher. Member, Belfast City Council since 1977. B 1927, ed Belfast High School and Trinity College, Dublin.

Mr Jeffrey Dudgeon. B 1946; ed Campbell College, Belfast, Magee College, Londonderry, Trinity College, Dublin Secretary Campaign for Labour Integration in Northern Ireland; secretary, the Northern Ireland Gay Rights Association.

BELFAST, West

Electorate 58,884   1974 : 66,279

*Fitt G. (SDLP)	16,480
Passmore T. (Off UU)	8,245
Dickson W. (Dem U)	3.716
Brennan B. (Repub Clubs)	2,284
Cousins J. (Alliance)	2,024
Peters D. (NI Lab)	540

SDLP majority	8,235

No Change

	1974		1979
Total votes	44,526		33,289
Turnout	67·2%		56·5%
SDLP	21,821	49·0%	49·5%
UUUC	16,265	36·5%	—
Repub	3,547	8·0%	6·9%
VPP	2,690	6·0%	—
Marx Len	203	0·5%	—
Off UU	—	—	24·8%
Alliance	—	—	6·1%
NI Lab	—	—	1·6%
SDLP maj	5,556	12·5%	24·7%

Mr Gerard Fitt, leader of the Social Democratic and Labour Party in Northern Ireland, was deputy chief minister of the former Northern Ireland Executive. Won Belfast West from the Ulster Unionists in 1966. B April, 1926; ed Christian Brothers School, Belfast. MP for Dock constituency in Belfast from 1962 until Stormont ceased to function. Member Northern Ireland Assembly 1973-75, deputy chief executive, Northern Ireland Executive, 1974. Served

BELFAST, South

Electorate 68,920   1974: 75,112

*Bradford, Rev. R. J. (Off UU)	28,875
Glass, B. (Alliance)	11,745
McDonnell, Dr A. (SDLP)	3,694
Brennan, V. (UPNI)	1,784
Dudgeon, J. (Lab Integ)	692

Off UU majority	17,130

No Change

	1974		1979
Total votes	50,846		46,790
Turnout	67·7%		67·9%
UUUC	30,116	59·2%	—
Alliance	11,715	23·0%	25·1%
Off UU	—	—	61·7%
UPNI	—	—	3·8%
Lab Integ	—	—	1·5%
Unionist	4,982	9·8%	—
SDLP	2,390	4·7%	7·9%
NI Lab	1,643	3·2%	—
UUUC maj	18,401	36·2%	—
Off UU maj	—	—	36·6%

in Merchant Navy 1941-53. Member, Belfast City Council, 1958-79.

Mr Thomas Passmore, salesman; has been County Grand Master of the City of Belfast Grand Orange Lodge since 1973. Chairman of Woodvale Unionist Association and a Justice of the Peace. B 1931; ed local elementary school.

Mr William Dickson, is a founder member of Democratic Unionist Party. B 1947, ed Kelvin Secondary School, Belfast. Member of Belfast City Council.

Mr Brian Brennan, architect, is a member of the National Executive of the Republican Clubs and spokesman on economic affairs in Northern Ireland. Represents Public Service Alliance on Belfast Trades Council. B 1950.

Mr John Cousins, chief technician in the chemistry department of Queen's University, Belfast. Alliance Party spokesman on housing. B 1949. Alderman of Lisburn Borough Council.

Mr Derek Peters is proprietor of a house decorating business. B 1932. A member of the executive committee of the Northern Ireland Labour Party and Ballynafeigh Housing Association. Served as a radio operator in the Merchant Navy and was treasurer of the Campaign for Nuclear Disarmament in Northern Ireland.

BELPER

Electorate 73,341   1974 : 71,197

Faith Mrs S. (C)	27,193
*MacFarquhar R. L. (Lab)	26,311
Peel M. (L)	7,331
Grand-Scrutton J. (Nat Front)	460

C majority	882

C gain from Lab

	1974		1979
Total votes	58,063		61,295
Turnout	81·6%		83·6%
Lab	27,365	47·1%	42·9%
C	21,681	37·3%	44·4%
L	9,017	15·5%	12·0%
Nat Front	—		0·8%
Lab maj	5,684	9·8%	
C maj	—		1·5%
Swing		−3·2%	+5·6%

Mrs Sheila Faith, dental surgeon and director of family fashion business. Contested Newcastle upon Tyne, Central, in October, 1974. B June 1928; ed Newcastle upon Tyne Central High School and Durham University. Member, Northumberland County Council, 1970-74; Newcastle City Council, 1975-78. Magistrate.

Mr Roderick MacFarquhar, research scholar, freelance broadcaster, author and journalist, was elected February, 1974, B December, 1930; ed Fettes, Oxford and Harvard. Contested Ealing, South, 1966; Meriden by-election, 1968. Member, Select Committee on Wealth Tax, 1975-77; Select Committee on Science and Technology, 1976-79; North Atlantic Assembly, 1974-79; was vice-chairman, PLP Foreign and Commonwealth Group. NUF.

Mr Malcolm Peel, training manager, contested Derby North, October and February 1974. Derby borough councillor, 1973-76. B February 1931; ed Lower School of John Lyon, Harrow, Sheffield University and Magdalene, Cambridge.

BERWICK AND EAST LOTHIAN

Electorate 60,919   1974 : 57,503

*Robertson J. D. H. (Lab)	21,977
Marshall Miss M. (C)	20,304
Glen T. (L)	4,948
Macartney A. (Scot Nat)	3,300

Lab majority	1,673

No Change

	1974		1979
Total votes	47,758		50,529
Turnout	83·1%		82·9%
Lab	20,682	43·3%	43·5%
C	17,942	37·6%	40·2%
Scot Nat	6,323	13·2%	6·5%
L	2,811	5·9%	9·8%
Lab maj	2,740	5·7%	3·3%
Swing		−3·4%	+1·2%

1978 by-election: Total vote 43,290 (71·1%)—Lab 20,530 (47·4%); C 17,418 (40·2%); Scot Nat 3,799 (8·8%); L 1,543 (3·6%)—C majority 3,112 (7·2%).

Mr John Home Robertson retained the seat for Labour in the October, 1978 by-election. Farmer. B December, 1948; ed Ampleforth and West of Scotland Agricultural College. Chairman, Rural Affairs Group, Scottish PLP. Member, Berwickshire District Council, since 1974. NUAAW and NFU.

Miss Margaret Marshall, chartered secretary, contested Lewisham, West, October 1974 and Lambeth, Vauxhall, February 1974. B 1934; ed Laurel Bank School and St Andrew's University.

Mr Allan Macartney, staff tutor with Open University. B February, 1941; ed Elgin Academy and Edinburgh and Glasgow Universities.

BERWICK-UPON-TWEED

Electorate 42,493   1974 : 41,861

*Beith A. J. (L)	19,351
Baker-Cresswell C. A. E. (C)	13,663
Elliott G. M. (Lab)	2,602

L majority	5,688

No Change

	1974		1979
Total votes	34,063		35,616
Turnout	81·4%		83·8%
L	14,684	43·1%	54·3%
C	14,611	42·9%	38·4%
Lab	4,768	14·0%	7·3%
L maj	73	0·2%	15·9%

Mr Alan Beith won the seat in a by-election, 1973, having contested it, 1970. Chief whip since March 1977 and education spokesman, previously spokesman on home affairs and Northern Ireland. Member, procedure and Selection committees. B April, 1943; ed King's School, Macclesfield; Balliol and Nuffield Colleges, Oxford. University lecturer. Member, General Advisory

Council, BBC; former member, Tynedale district council, Hexham rural council, Corbridge Parish Council. AUT.

Mr Charles Baker-Cresswell, farmer, contested the seat October, 1974. Former chairman of constituency Conservative association; co-opted member of Northumberland County Council social services committee. B 1935; ed Winchester.

Mr Michael Elliot, agricultural seed merchant. B January, 1947; ed in Berwick. Member, Berwick Council, since 1976.

BEXLEY, Bexleyheath

Electorate 50,872   1974 : 51,022

*Townsend C. D. (C)	21,888
Blackwell R. (Lab)	13,342
Crowhurst J. (L)	4,782
Wilkens A. (Nat Front)	749
C majority	8,546

No Change

	1974		1979
Total votes	39,693		40,761
Turnout	77·8%		80·1%
C	17,399	43·8%	53·7%
Lab	15,412	38·8%	32·7%
L	6,882	17·3%	11·7%
Nat Front	—		1·8%
C maj	1,987	5·0%	21·0%
Swing		−2·0%	+8·0%

Mr Cyril Townsend was elected in February, 1974. Joint Secretary, Conservative Greater London MPs. Member, Select Committee on Violence in the Family, 1976-77. Chairman of all-party "Freedom for Rudolph Hess" Campaign. Council member, "Friends of Cyprus". B December, 1937; ed Bradfield College, Berkshire, Royal Military Academy. Was employed in Conservative Research Department.

Mr Richard Blackwell, Post Office engineer, sponsored by his union, POEU. B 1947.

Mr John Crowhurst, lecturer in accountancy. B January, 1935; ed St Albans School and Worcester College, Oxford. Member, National Association of Teachers in Further and Higher Education.

BEXLEY, Erith and Crayford

Electorate 61,350   1974 : 60,595

*Wellbeloved A. J. (Lab)	22,450
Blunt S. (C)	19,717
Jamieson Mrs M. (L)	4,512
Hawke O. (Nat Front)	838
Lab majority	2,733

No Change

	1974		1979
Total votes	44,296		47,517
Turnout	73·1%		77·5%
Lab	22,670	51·2%	47·2%
C	14,203	32·1%	41·5%
L	7,423	16·8%	9·5%
Nat front	—	—	1·8%
Lab maj	8,467	19·1%	5·1%
Swing		−2·3%	+6·7%

Mr James Wellbeloved, Under Secretary of State for Defence for the RAF, 1976-79, was elected in 1965 by-election. Commercial consultant. B July, 1926; ed elementary school and South East London Technical College. Member, Erith Borough Council, 1956-65. Former vice-chairman, PLP Defence and Services Group. Former Leader of the Council of the London Borough of Bexley. Opposition whip, 1972-73. Former joint vice-chairman, Manifesto Group.

Mr Simon Blunt, manager with a computer company. B September 1933; ed Michael Hall, Forest Row, Sussex, and Trinity College, Cambridge. Chairman, East Lewisham CPC Committee, 1975.

BEXLEY, Sidcup

Electorate 49,976   1974: 49,564

*Heath, E. R. G. (C)	23,692
Keohane, F. (Lab)	10,236
Vickers, P. (L)	4,908
Webb, A. (Nat. Front)	774
C majority	13,456

No Change

	1974		1979
Total votes	37,628		39,610
Turnout	75·9%		79·3%
C	18,991	50·5%	59·8%
Lab	11,448	30·4%	25·8%
L	6,954	18·5%	12·4%
Ind	174	0·5%	—
Ind	61	0·2%	—
Nat Front	—		2·0%
C maj	7,543	20·1%	34·0%
Swing		−1·6%	+6·9%

Mr Edward Heath resigned as Leader of the Conservative Party and Leader of the Opposition in February, 1975, when he failed to top the first of three ballots for the Conservative leadership. He had been Leader of the Opposition since February, 1974. Prime Minister from 1970-74, he first became Leader of the Opposition and Leader of the Conservative Party on

August 2, 1965, after securing an overall majority over his two rivals in the ballot of Conservative MPs under the Parliamentary Party's new electoral process. After the 1964 general election, he led for the Opposition on Treasury and economic affairs; was appointed chairman of the Party's policy committee and research department. Secretary of State for Industry, Trade and Regional Development, and President of the Board of Trade, October 1963-64. Lord Privy Seal, 1960-63, being the principal Foreign Office spokesman in the Commons, leading the British team in negotiations to join the EEC. Minister of Labour, October 1959-July 1960; Parliamentary Secretary to the Treasury (Chief Whip), 1955-59; Deputy Chief Whip, 1952-55. Elected 1950. B July, 1916; ed Chatham House School, Ramsgate, and Balliol College, Oxford; president of the Union, 1939. Musician; chairman, trustee of London Symphony Orchestra, 1963-70; vice-president Bach Choir since 1970. International yachtsman and author.

Mr Francis Keohane, financial analyst. B April, 1939. Former shipwright apprentice. Mature student at London University (President of Students' Union) TGWU.

Mr Peter Vickers, accountant, is an executive member, London Western General Branch, Apex. B November, 1954; ed, St Joseph's Grammar School, Blackpool.

BIRKENHEAD

Electorate 56,421   1974: 60,400

Field, F. (Lab)	20,803
Gill, P. (C)	14,894
Perkins, R. (L)	5,708
Fletcher, M. (WRP)	306
Lab majority	5,909

No Change

	1974		1979
Total Votes	42,392		41,711
Turnout	70·2%		73·9%
Lab	21,748	51·3%	49·9%
C	12,264	28·9%	35·7%
L	8,380	19·8%	13·7%
WRP	—		0·7%
Lab maj	9,484	22·4%	14·2%
Swing		−3·6%	+4·1%

Mr Frank Field has been director of Child Poverty Action Group and of the Low Pay Unit. Former teacher. Contested South Buckinghamshire in 1966. B July 1942; ed St Clement Danes Grammar School and Hull University.

Mr Mark Fletcher joined the Young Socialists in 1973 and the Workers Revolutionary Party one year later. Took part in the 'Free the Shrewsbury Two' Hull-Liverpool, March, 1974. Aged 21.

BIRMINGHAM, Edgbaston

Electorate 68,645   1974: 70,078

*Knight, Mrs J. C. J. (C)	25,192
Hudson, A. G. (Lab)	15,605
Dugued, J. I. (L)	4,377
Tyler, J. R. (Ecology)	852
Howlett, Miss D. C. (JHC)	297
Dore, B. (SBE)	129
Marshall L. W. (Ind)	112
C majority	9,587

No Change

	1974		1979
Total Votes	44,326		46,564
Turnout	63·3%		67·8%
C	19,483	44·0%	54·1%
Lab	17,073	38·5%	33·5%
L	7,770	17·5%	9·4%
Ecology	—	—	1·8%
JHC	—	—	0·6%
SBE	—	—	0·3%
Ind	—	—	0·2%
C maj	2,410	5·5%	20·6%
Swing		−3·4%	+7·5%

Mrs Jill Knight, vice-chairman, Conservative back bench committee on health and social services since 1972, was elected in 1966; contested Northampton, 1959 and 1964. Housewife, lecturer and broadcaster, B July 1927, ed Fairfield School, O.S.C. Birmingham. Member, Northampton Borough Council, 1956-66. Member, Council of Europe, since

1977, and chairman, Lords and Commons all-party Family and Child Protection Group.

Mr Andrew Hudson, sales supervisor, contested Esher in October, 1974. Member, Haringey Borough Council, 1971-74. B October, 1948; ed Dunsmore School, Rugby and Middlesex Polytechnic. APEX.

Mr James Dugued, personnel and industrial relations manager, Cadbury Schweppes Bournville factory, B February 1948; ed Sidcot School, Winscombe, Somerset.

Mr Jonathan Tyler, lecturer in transport at Birmingham University, fought Walsall, North, by-election, November, 1976. National chairman, Ecology Party, since October, 1977. Aged 29; ed Reading School and Cambridge University.

BIRMINGHAM, Erdington

Electorate 64,341   1974: 65,764

*Silverman, J. (Lab)	20,105
Alden, J. E. C. (C)	19,425
Duffy, H. J. (L)	3,487
Hastilow, F. (Nat Front)	687
Lab majority	680

No Change

	1974		1979
Total Votes	43,075		43,704
Turnout	65·5%		67·9%
Lab	22,160	51·4%	46·0%
C	13,383	31·1%	44·4%
L	6,119	14·2%	8·0%
Nat Front	1,413	3·3%	1·6%
Lab maj	8,777	20·3%	1·6%
Swing		−2·8%	+9·3%

Mr Julius Silverman was returned for this seat in February, 1974. Elected in 1945 to the former Erdington seat, represented Aston 1955-74; contested Moseley, 1935. Barrister (Gray's Inn, 1931). B. December, 1905, ed Leeds Central High School. First employed as a warehouseman but later read for the

Bar. Birmingham City councillor, 1934-1945. Member, Commons Expenditure Committee and Select Committee on European Secondary Legislation, since 1974. ASTMS.

Mr John Alden, taxation accountant, contested the seat, October, 1974. B 1947; ed Westlain Grammar School, Brighton. Member, YC National Advisory Committee, 1975.

Mr Hugh Duffy, insurance inspector. Aged 37.

BIRMINGHAM, Hall Green

Electorate 67,683   1974: 67,043

*Eyre, R. E. (C)	27,072
Stewart, Mrs T. J. (Lab)	17,508
Lockyer, P. M. (L)	4,440
Maylin, R. (Nat Front)	615
C majority	9,564

No Change

	1974		1979
Total Votes	47,046		49,635
Turnout	70·2%		73·3%
C	20,569	43·7%	54·5%
Lab	17,945	38·1%	35·3%
L	8,532	18·1%	8·9%
Nat Front	—		1·2%
C maj	2,624	5·6%	19·2%
Swing		−3·7%	+6·8%

Mr Reginald Eyre appointed Under Secretary of State for Trade in May, 1929, has been a vice-chairman of the Conservative Party, with responsibility for urban areas, since 1975. Under Secretary (Housing and Construction) for Environment 1972-74; Comptroller of HM Household, 1970-72; Lord Commissioner of the Treasury, 1970; Opposition whip, 1966-70. Returned at by-election, May 1965; contested Birmingham, Northfield, 1959. Solicitor and company director. B May, 1924; ed King Edward's Camp Hill School, Birmingham and Emmanuel College, Cambridge. Member, Committee of Selection. Director, Auckland Building Co.

Mrs Theresa Stewart fought the seat in October, 1974. Member, Birmingham City Council, since 1970; West Midlands County Council, 1973-77. B August, 1930; ed Allerton High School, Leeds, and Somerville College, Oxford. APEX.

Mr Peter Lockyer, teacher, Aged 29, ed Milton Keynes College of Education.

BIRMINGHAM, Handsworth

Electorate 45,018   1974: 45,676

Wright, Mrs S. R. R. (Lab)	16,998
Tyler, R. (C)	13,789
Lab majority	3,209

No Change

	1974		1979
Total Votes	30,377		30,787
Turnout	66·5%		68·4%
Lab	15,011	49·4%	55·2%
C	11,115	36·6%	44·8%
L	3,205	10·6%	—
Nat Front	838	2·8	—
Pros Brit	105	0·3%	—
Marx Len	103	0·3%	—
Lab maj	3,896	12·8%	10·4%
Swing		−3·9%	+1·2%

Mrs Sheila Wright, social worker, fought the seat in 1964, 1966, and 1970. B March 1925; ed India, Southampton University and took BSc Lond (External). Member West Midlands County Council; Birmingham City Council 1956-74; Birmingham Regional Hospital Board 1966-74. Member, West Midlands Regional Health Authority (vice chairman 1979). APEX.

Mr Robert Tyler, director of a meat distribution company and meat industry consultant, fought the seat in October, 1974. B May 1926; ed St Phillips Grammar School, Birmingham. Member, Birmingham City Council, 1970-74; Food, Drink and tobacco Industries' Training Board, since 1968. Chairman, Birmingham City Police Crime Prevention Executive Committee since 1975. Past president, National Federation of Meat Traders and President, Birmingham Chamber of Trade, 1969-71. Liveryman, Worshipful Company of Butchers and Freeman, City of London.

BIRMINGHAM, Ladywood

Electorate: 33,989   1974: 40,394

*Sever E. J. (Lab)	13,450
Newhouse A. (C)	5,691
Hardeman K. G. (L)	2,030
Lab majority	7,759

No Change

	1974		1979
Total Votes	22,983		21,171
Turnout	56·9%		62·3%
Lab	14,818	64·5%	63·5%
C	5,079	22·1%	26·9%
L	3,086	13·4%	9·6%
Lab maj	9,739	42·4%	36·6%
Swing		−3·9%	+2·9%

1977 by-election: Total vote 15,484 (42·6%)—Lab 8,227 (53·1%); C 4,402 (28·4%); Nat Front 888 (5·7%); L 765 (4·9%); others 1,202 (7·8%)—Lab majority 3,825 (24·7%).

Mr John Sever retained the seat for Labour in August, 1977, by-election. Contested Birmingham, Edgbaston, 1970. B April, 1943; ed Sparkhill Commercial School, Member, Labour home affairs, foreign affairs and housing groups, Member, Birmingham City Council, since 1970. Member and former branch chairman, Apex.

Mr Anthony Newhouse, solicitor and senior law lecturer, Member, West Midlands Metropolitan County Council, since 1977, East Birmingham Community Health Council, and Council of Management, City of O.S.C. Birmingham Bow Group. B May, 1944; ed Merchant Taylor's School and St Andrew's University. Legal assistant, Board of Inland Revenue, 1970-75. Fought seat in 1977 by-election.

BIRMINGHAM, Northfield

Electorate: 78,873   1974: 77,593

Cadbury J. B. L. (C)	25,304
*Carter R. J. (Lab)	25,100
Lewthwaite R. (L)	4,538
Newman R. A. (Nat Front)	614
Beale J. E. (WRP)	144
C majority	204

C gain from Lab

	1974		1979
Total Votes	52,663		55,700
Turnout	67·9%		70·6%
Lab	27,435	52·1%	45·1%
C	16,838	32·0%	45·4%
L	7,851	14·9%	8·1%
People	359	0·7%	—
Comm	180	0·3%	—
Nat Front	—	—	1·1%
WRP	—	—	0·3%
Lab maj	10,597	20·1%	—
C maj	—	—	0·3%
Swing		−2·5%	+10·2%

Mr Jocelyn Cadbury, production section manager, Cadbury-Schweppes Ltd, fought the seat, October 1974. B March 1946; ed Eton, Trinity College, Cambridge and Manchester Business School. Chairman, Birmingham Bow Group, since 1974; vice-chairman, London Bow Group.

Mr Raymond Carter, Under-Secretary of State, Northern Ireland Office, 1976-79, had held the seat since 1970. Contested Warwick and Leamington, 1968 by-election, and Wokingham, 1966. Electrical engineer. B September, 1935; ed Reading College of Technology and Stafford College of Technology. Member, Select Committee on Wealth Tax, 1974-76; Select Committee on Science and Technology, 1974-76. Sponsored by TGWU.

Mr Roy Lewthwaite, Liberal Party organiser for West Midlands and former teacher, fought the seat in 1964 and Birmingham, Selly Oak, 1966. B September, 1929; ed King Edward VI Grammar School, Birmingham, and College of St Mark and St John, Chelsea.

Mr Joseph Beal, transport driver with Rolls Royce; TGWU shop steward. B 1948.

BIRMINGHAM, Perry Barr

Electorate: 51,794   1974: 52,509

*Rooker J. W. (Lab)	18,674
Kinsey J. R. (C)	18,183
Griffiths Mrs O. L. (L)	1,811
Axon K. A. (Nat Front)	582
Lab majority	491

No Change

	1974		1979
Total Votes	38,521		39,250
Turnout	73·4%		75·8%
Lab	18,291	47·5%	47·6%
C	15,087	39·2%	46·3%
L	4,231	11·0%	4·6%
Nat Front	826	2·1%	1·5%
Pros Brit	86	0·2%	—
Lab maj	3,204	8·3%	1·3%
Swing		−1·7%	+3·5%

Mr Jeffrey Rooker, chartered engineer. Elected in February, 1974. B June, 1941; ed Handsworth Technical School and College, Aston University and Warwick University. Vice-chairman, PLP employment group; secretary, Birmingham Labour Group. Co-opted member, Birmingham Education Committee, 1972-74. Sponsored by ASTMS.

Mr Joseph Kinsey, who is in a retail and wholesale floral and horticultural distribution business, was MP for the seat, 1970 to February 1974; fought seat in October 1974 and Birmingham, Aston, 1966. B August, 1921; ed Birmingham elementary and Church of England School. Member and Alderman, Birmingham City Council, 1955-70.

BIRMINGHAM, Selly Oak

Electorate: 64,631   1974: 62,757

Beaumont-Dark A. M. (C)	23,175
*Litterick T. (Lab)	18,400
Clifford P. (L)	5,452
Bassett G (Nat Front)	401
Crome P. J. (CFPG)	190
C majority	4,775

C gain from Lab

	1974		1979
Total Votes	42,164		47,618
Turnout	67·2%		73·7%
Lab	17,320	41·1%	38·6%
C	16,994	40·3%	48·7%
L	7,850	18·6%	11·4%
Nat Front	—	—	0·8%
CFPG	—	—	0·4%
Lab maj	326	0·8%	—
C maj	—	—	10·1%
Swing		−3·5%	+5·4%

Mr Anthony Beaumont-Dark, economist and investment analyst, is senior partner of his firm and director of various investment companies. Contested Birmingham Aston in 1964 and 1959. B 1932; ed Cedarhurst School, Solihull, Birmingham College of Arts and Birmingham University. Member Birmingham City Council 1957-67 (alderman from 1967); West Midland Metropolitan County Council, since 1973. Served on Department of the Environment Central Housing Advisory Committee.

Mr Thomas Litterick was elected in October, 1974; contested the seat in February, 1974. University lecturer. B May, 1929; ed Dundee School of Economics and Warwick University. Member, Kenilworth UDC, 1970-74. Member, Tribune Group. ASTMS.

Mr Paul Clifford, President of the Selly Oak Colleges. B February, 1913; ed Mill Hill School and Balliol College, Oxford.

BIRMINGHAM, Small Heath

Electorate: 46,602   1974: 51,405

*Howell D. H. (Lab)	17,735
Savage D. J. (C)	6,268
Minnis D. (L)	4,470
Caffery M. (Nat Front)	490
Adamson C. C. (Soc Unity)	349
Lab majority	11,467

No Change

	1974		1979
Total Votes	29,611		29,312
Turnout	57·6%		62·9%
Lab	19,703	66·5%	60·5%
C	5,648	19·1%	21·4%
L	4,260	14·4%	15·2%
Nat Front	—	—	1·7%
Soc Unity	—	—	1·2%
Lab maj	14,055	47·4%	39·1%
Swing		−5·4%	+4·1%

Mr Denis Howell, Minister of State (Sport and Recreation) in the Department of the Environment, 1974-79; Opposition spokesman on housing, local government and sport 1970-74; Minister of State for Housing and Local Government 1969-70; Under Secretary for Education and Science 1964-69. Returned at a by-election March, 1961; represented the All Saints division, 1955-59; contested former Kings Norton division, 1951. B September, 1923; ed elementary O.S.C. School, Birmingham. Football referee. President of Apex since 1971, Sponsored by APEX.

Mr David Savage, solicitor and a General Commissioner of Income Tax. Contested Birmingham, Sparkbrook, in February and October, 1974. Member, Farnborough Urban Council, 1964-73, and Rushmoor Borough Council. B 1939; ed Hurstpierpoint College, Sussex, and the College of Law, London.

Mr Dennis Minnis, political organizer. B September 1938; ed elementary schools. Fought All Saints, Birmingham, 1970; Small Heath, February 1974; Meriden, October 1974. Member, Birmingham City Council, since 1969; Leader of Liberal group since 1972. Member, West Midlands County Council, 1973-77. Proprietor of motor insurance brokers firm.

BIRMINGHAM, Sparkbrook

Electorate: 45,910   1974: 49,683

*Hattersley R. S. G. (Lab)	18,717
Webb N. (C)	10,398
Murray R. (Comm)	715
Lab majority	8,319

No Change

	1974		1979
Total Votes	29,899		29,830
Turnout	60·2%		65·0%
Lab	17,476	58·5%	62·7%
C	8,955	30·0%	34·9%
L	2,920	9·8%	
I Civ Rights	548	1·8%	
Comm	—	—	2·4%
Lab maj	8,521	28·5%	27·8%
Swing		−2·9%	+0·3%

Mr Roy Hattersley, Secretary of State for Prices and Consumer Protection and member of the Cabinet, 1976-79; Minister of State for Foreign and Commonwealth Affairs, 1974-76; Opposition spokesman on education 1972-74, spokesman for Foreign and Commonwealth Affairs, 1970-72, and defence, 1972. Minister of Defence for Administration, 1969-70; Under Secretary, Department of Employment and Productivity, 1968-69; Parliamentary Secretary, Ministry of Labour, 1967-68. Elected in 1964; contested Sutton Coldfield, 1959. Health service executive. B December, 1932; ed Sheffield City Grammar School and Hull University. ASTMS.

Mr Nicholas Webb, barrister (Middle Temple, 1972). B October, 1949; ed Nottingham High School, Downing College, Cambridge; Council of Legal Education. Member, Central Birmingham Community Health Council, chairman, South-West Birmingham CPC.

Mr Roger Murray works at the Rover factory. Shop steward, TGWU.

BIRMINGHAM, Stechford

Electorate 61,115   1974; 62,516

Davis, T. A. G. (Lab)	21,166
*Mackay, A. (C)	19,517
Gopsill G. A. (L)	2,349
Russell F. (Nat Front)	698
Lab Majority	1,649

Labour gain from C

	1974		1979
Total Votes	40,087		43,730
Turnout	64·1%		71·6%
Lab	23,075	57·6%	48·4%
C	11,152	27·8%	44·6%
L	5,860	14·6%	5·4%
Nat Front	—	—	1·6%
Lab maj	11,923	29·8%	3·8%
Swing		−3·5%	+13·0%

1977 by-election: Total vote 36,240 (58·8%)—C 15,731 (43·4%); Lab 13,782 (38·0%); Nat Front 2,955 (8·2%); L 2,901 (8·0%); others 871 (2·4%)—C majority 1,949 (5·4%). C gain from Lab.

Mr Terence Davis, a manager in the motor industry, won Bromsgrove for Labour in the 1971, by-election, having contested seat, 1970. Defeated at new seat of Bromsgrove and Redditch, February and October 1974 and in 1977 by-election. B January, 1938; ed King Edward VI Grammar School, Stourbridge; London University, Michigan University. Member, Expenditure Committee, 1973-74; Yeovil RDC, 1967-68, Sponsored by ASTMS.

Mr Andrew Mackay won the seat for the Conservatives at the by-election in March 1977. Partner in an estate agency practice and consultant to house building firm. B August 1949; ed Solihull School. Member, Central Council of the National Union, 1971-74. Chairman, 'Britain in Europe' campaign in Meriden constituency during 1975 referendum. Member, Conservative Friends of Israel and backbench committees on industry, urban affairs and environment.

Mr Graham Gopsill, insurance agent, contested the seat, in the 1977 by-election and in October and

February, 1974. B December, 1938; ed Mosely School of Art. Birmingham City and District councillor, since 1969.

	1974		1979
Total Votes	51,435		55,799
Turnout	70·9%		74·7%
Lab	27,181	52·8%	48·7%
C	16,086	31·3%	37·9%
L	8,168	15·9%	13·3%
Lab maj	11,095	21·5%	10·8%
Swing		−3·8%	+5·3%

Mr Derek Foster, an assistant director of education in Sunderland. B June, 1937; ed Bede Grammar School, Sunderland and Oxford University. Former chairman, North of England Development Council and of economic development committee, Tyne and Wear County Council. NUT. Member of Salvation Army.

Mr Michael Irvine, barrister (Inner Temple 1964). B 1939; ed Rugby and Oriel College, Oxford. Member, Richmond and Barnes Conservative Association executive committee; vice-chairman, Richmond and Barnes CPC, since 1975.

Mrs Jill Frise, teacher, fought the seat, February, 1974. Aged 41; ed Durham University. District and town councillor.

BIRMINGHAM, Yardley

Electorate 57,574   1974; 59,052

Bevan D. G. (C)	20,193
*Tierney S. (Lab)	19,029
Anderson Miss S. M. (L)	2,491
Challendar H. (Nat Front)	749
C majority	1,164

C gain from Lab

	1974		1979
Total Votes	43,161		42,462
Turnout	73·1%		73·8%
Lab	20,834	48·3%	44·8%
C	16,664	38·6%	47·6%
L	4,518	10·5%	5·9%
Nat Front	1,034	2·4%	1·8%
Pros Brit	111	0·3%	—
Lab maj	4,170	9·7%	—
C maj	—	—	2·8%
Swing		−2·8%	+6·2%

Mr David Bevan, an incorporated auctioneer and estate agent, valuer and surveyor. B April 1928; ed Woodrough School, Moseley, and King Edward's School, Birmingham. Member, Birmingham City Council 1959-74 and West Midlands Metropolitan County Council, since 1974. Fellow and past chairman (Midlands) and Council member for the Incorporated Association of Architects and Surveyors, present chairman and Fellow of the West Midlands branch of the Incorporated Society of Valuers and Auctioneers and a Fellow of the Rating and Valuation Association. Fellow of the Faculty of Building and of the Corporation of Agents; member, Royal Society of Health.

Mr Sydney Tierney was elected in February, 1974. Sponsored by USDAW. Former milkman, Elected to Labour Party national executive committee in October, 1978. B September, 1923; ed Dearne Secondary Modern School and Plater College, Oxford. Vice-chairman PLP West Midlands Group, 1977.

Miss Sue Anderson, a teacher. West Midlands county councillor. Aged 33.

Mr Harold Challendar, tool setter, fought seat in October 1974. B April, 1921; ed Hartfield Crescent School. TGWU (Chief Shop Steward 1964-74).

BISHOP AUCKLAND

Electorate 74,696   1974; 72,581

Foster D. (Lab)	27,200
Irvine M. F. (C)	21,160
Frise Mrs. J. D. (L)	7,439
Lab majority	6,040

No Change

BLABY

Electorate 68,576   1974: 65,073

*Lawson, N. (C)	33,221
Hill, T. K. (Lab)	12,581
Inman, D. (L)	9,277
Gegan, P. (Nat Front)	2,056
C majority	20,640

No Change

	1974		1979
Total Votes	50,939		57,135
Turnout	78·3%		83·3%
C	25,405	49·9%	58·1%
Lab	13,244	26·0%	22·0%
L	12,290	24·1%	16·2%
Nat Front	—	—	3·6%
C maj	12,161	23·9%	36·1%
Swing		0·0%	+6·1%

Mr Nigel Lawson became Financial Secretary to the Treasury, in May, 1979. An Opposition spokesman on Treasury affairs 1977-79, was elected in February, 1974. Contested Eton and Slough, 1970. Company director. B March, 1932; ed Westminster School, Christ Church, Oxford. An Opposition whip 1976-77. Special assistant to Prime Minister (Sir Alec Douglas-Home), 1963-64; special political adviser, Conservative Party, 1973-74; Former member, Public Expenditure Committee; Select Committtee on Wealth Tax, 1975. Editorial staff, *Financial Times*, 1956-60; City Editor, *The Sunday Telegraph*, 1961-63; Editor of *The Spectator*, 1966-70. Fellow, Nuffield College, Oxford, 1972-73.

Mr Trevor Hill, political liaison officer of NUR. B July, 1943; ed City of Leicester Boys' School, Oxford University.

Mr **David Inman,** a solicitor, contested the seat,
October, 1974, and Nuneaton, February, 1974. B
May, 1936; ed King Edwards School, Birmingham,
and University College, London. Member, Leicester-
shire County Council and Hinckley and Bosworth
District Council.

BLACKBURN

Electorate 52,479   1974: 54,213

Straw, J. W. (Lab)	19,683
McGaw, I. D. (C)	14,193
Beetham F. J. (L)	4,371
Adamson, E. (Nat Front)	565
Lab majority	5,490

No Change

	1974		1979
Total Votes	39,535		38,812
Turnout	72.9%		74.0%
Lab	20,344	51.5%	50.7%
C	12,692	32.1%	36.6%
L	4,741	12.0%	11.3%
Nat Front	1,758	4.4%	1.5%
Lab maj	7,652	19.4%	14.1%
Swing		−2.2%	+2.6%

Mr **Jack Straw,** barrister,
was special adviser to Mrs
Barbara Castle (the previous MP for this seat) as
Secretary of State for Social
Services, 1974-76, and then
to Mr Peter Shore, Secretary of State for the Environment, 1976-77. Pres-
ently working for Granada
Television. Contested Tonbridge and Malling, February 1974. B August, 1946;
ed Brentwood School,
Essex; Leeds University and Inns of Court School of
Law. Former president, National Union of Students.
Member, Islington Borough Council, 1971-78; Inner
London Education Authority, 1971-74 (deputy
leader 1973-74). GMWU; ACTT (member, shop
committee).

Mr **Ian McGaw,** insurance broker, contested the seat
in both 1974 elections and St Helens, 1970. B August,
1940; ed Collegiate School, Liverpool. Member,
Young Conservatives National Advisory Committee,
1966-70; NW Area CPC committee. Has worked for
the Liverpool Insurance Institute charities since 1965;
member, Liverpool Junior Chamber of Commerce.

Mr **Frank Beetham,** engineer, contested the seat,
February and October, 1974, and Heywood and
Royton, 1970. B March, 1932; ed St Albans Higher
Grade Roman Catholic School and Blackburn Tech-
nical College. Service on Blackburn District Council
and Blackburn Borough Council, AUEW.

BLACKPOOL, North

Electorate 59,557   1974: 59,743

*Miscampbell, N. A. (C)	23,209
Verdeille, A. W. (Lab)	12,980
Hayworth, C. (L)	6,127
Hanson, A. (Nat Front)	943
C majority	10,229

No Change

	1974		1979
Total Votes	41,607		43,259
Turnout	69.6%		72.6%
C	19,662	47.3%	53.7%
Lab	14,195	34.1%	30.0%
L	7,750	18.6%	14.2%
Nat Front	—	—	2.2%
C maj	5,467	13.2%	23.7%
Swing		−2.8%	+5.2%

Mr **Norman Miscampbell,**
joint secretary and other
office holder of the Conservative Northern Ireland
Committee since 1974, was
returned at a by-election in
March 1962. Contested
Newton in 1955 and 1959.
Barrister (Inner Temple,
1952). B February, 1925;
ed St Edward's School,
Oxford, and Trinity Col-
lege, Oxford. Member
Hoylake Urban District
Council. 1955-61.

Mr **Andrew Verdeille,** senior clerk with Manchester
Corporation. B February, 1948; ed St Joseph's, Redd-
ish; All Hallows, Wythenshawe. Member, Stockport
County Borough Council, 1972-73, and Stockport
Metropolitan Borough Council, since 1973. UCATT.

Mr **Christopher Hayworth,** lecturer. Aged 32; ed
Reading University and Teacher Training College,
Liverpool.

BLACKPOOL, South

Electorate: 58,615   1974: 57,951

*Blaker P. A. R. (C)	21,762
Carrington Mrs P. (Lab)	12,914
Wynne E. E. (L)	7,057
Machin A. (Nat Front)	524
C majority	8,848

No Change

	1974		1979
Total Votes	40,482		42,257
Turnout	69.9%		72.1%
C	18,188	44.9%	51.5%
Lab	12,967	32.0%	30.6%
L	9,327	23.0%	16.7%
Nat Front	—	—	1.2%
C maj	5,221	12.9%	20.9%
Swing		−3.1%	+4.0%

Mr **Peter Blaker,** appointed
Minister of State for
Foreign and Com-
monwealth Affairs in May,
1979, was Under-Secretary
for Foreign and Com-
monwealth Affairs, 1974,
and Under-Secretary for
Defence for the Army,
1972-74. Vice-chairman of
the Conservative
Parliamentary Foreign and
Commonwealth Affairs
Committee. Farmer.
Elected in 1964. B October, 1922; ed Shrewsbury
School, Toronto University and New College, Oxford
(President of the Union and University Law Society).
Barrister (Lincoln's Inn, 1952). In the foreign service,
1953-64. Assistant Opposition whip, 1966-67. On
executive of 1922 Committee, 1967-70. Secretary,
Conservative parliamentary trade committee, 1967-
70. Member of Lloyds.

Mrs Patricia Carrington, teacher. B September, 1933; ed London and Lancaster Universities. NUT.

Mr Edmund Wynne fought the seat, February and October, 1974. Managing director of soft drinks company. B February, 1917; ed Uddingstone Grammar School, Scotland. Member, Lancashire Council and Blackpool District Council. Former Mayor of Blackpool.

BLAYDON

Electorate: 58,463   1974: 59,908

McWilliam J. D. (Lab)	24,687
Middleton T. (C)	16,178
Hutton D. (L)	5,364
Lab majority	8,509

No Change

	1974		1979
Total Votes	41,459		46,229
Turnout	69·2%		79·1%
Lab	23,743	57·3%	53·4%
C	10,277	24·8%	35·0%
L	7,439	17·9%	11·6%
Lab maj	13,466	32·5%	18·4%
Swing		−2·8%	+7·0%

Mr John McWilliam is a Post Office engineer. B May, 1941; ed Leith Academy. Contested Edinburgh, Pentlands, February, 1974. Member, Edinburgh Corporation, 1970-75, convenor of general purposes sub-committee of education committee, 1973-74, Treasurer of City of Edinburgh, 1974-75. Commissioner for local

government accounts. Member Post Office Engineering Union since 1957; branch secretary, 1969-72; branch representative and committee member. Sponsored by POEU.

Mr Terence Middleton, an assistant sub-postmaster, is vice-chairman of Blaydon Conservative Association. B 1944; ed St Cuthbert's Grammar School, Newcastle and Ushaw College, Durham. Member, Gateshead Council, since 1975.

Mr David Hutton, leader of Liberal group on Gateshead Metropolitan Borough Council since 1977; elected to council, 1975. Travel agency manager. B July 1949; ed St Peter's School, York.

BLYTH

Electorate: 79,727   1974: 74,462

*Ryman J. (Lab)	25,047
Milne E. J. (Ind Lab)	17,987
Nicholson Miss E. (C)	14,194
Parkin D. (L)	5,176
Lab majority	7,060

No Change

	1974		1979
Total Votes	55,305		62,404
Turnout	74·3%		78·3%
Lab	20,308	36·7%	40·1%
Ind Lab	20,230	36·6%	28·8%
L	8,177	14·8%	8·3%
C	6,590	11·9%	22·7%
Lab maj	78	0·1%	11·3%
Swing		−5·7%	+3·7%

Mr John Ryman, barrister (Middle Temple 1957), was elected in October, 1974; contested Derbyshire South-East 1970 and Gillingham, 1964. B November 1930; ed Leighton Park School and Pembroke College, Oxford.

Mr Edward Milne, who was returned for Labour in the 1960 by-election, won the seat in February, 1974, as an Independent when the constituency association decided to select a new candidate but he lost it in October, 1974. Contested Rutherglen for Labour, 1959. Trade union official. B October, 1915; ed Robert Gordon's College, Aberdeen. Area organizer, Union of Shop, Distributive and Allied Workers, 1952-60. Vice-Chairman, Parliamentary Labour Party 1967-68; member of Speaker's panel of chairmen, 1965-66.

Miss Emma Nicholson, computer and management consultant, is forward planning and policy coordinating officer for Save the Children Fund headquarters, London. B 1941; ed St Mary's School, Wantage, and the Royal Academy of Music. Her father, Sir Godfrey Nicholson, was MP for Farnham.

Mr David Parkin, social worker. ed Ashton-Under-Lyne Grammar School and Trent Polytechnic.

BODMIN

Electorate: 61,650   1974: 55,485

*Hicks R. A. (C)	27,922
Tyler P. A. (L)	17,893
Knowles N. (Lab)	3,508
Holmes R. (Meb Kernow)	865
Retallack C. (Ecology)	465
Carter M. (Nat Front)	235
C majority	10,029

No Change

	1974		1979
Total Votes	45,661		50,888
Turnout	82·3%		82·5%
C	20,756	45·5%	54·9%
L	20,091	44·0%	35·2%
Lab	4,814	10·5%	6·9%
Meb Kernow	—	—	1·7%
Ecology	—	—	0·9%
Nat Front	—	—	0·5%
C maj	665	1·5%	19·7%
Swing		+1·2%	+6·5%

Mr Robert Hicks, lecturer and consultant, was MP for Bodmin 1970-February, 1974, having won it from the Liberals, and he regained it in October, 1974; contested Aberavon, 1966. Assistant Government whip, 1973-74. B January, 1938; ed Queen Elizabeth Grammar School, Crediton; University College, London, and Exeter University. Vice-chairman. Conservative backbench Agriculture Committee, since 1976; member, Select Committee on European Secondary Legislation, since 1976. Parliamentary

Liason officer, British Hotels, Restaurants, and Caterers Association 1976-77.

Mr Paul Tyler was MP for Bodmin, February to October, 1974. Contested the seat, 1970, and Totnes, 1966. Parliamentary spokesman on housing and transport, 1974. Journalist and broadcaster. Member, Devon County Council 1964-70 and vice-chairman, Dartmoor National Park Committee. Managing director, Cornwall Courier. B October, 1941; ed Mount House School, Tavistock; Sherborne School and Exeter College, Oxford. NUJ, NFU.

Mr Nigel Knowles, an education officer, General Federation of Trade Unions. B December, 1946; ed King Charles Grammar School, Birmingham Polytechnic, University of Essex, Worcester College of Higher Education. ASTMS.

BOLSOVER

Electorate: 52,740   1974: 51,880

*Skinner D. E. (Lab)	27,495
Favell A. (C)	10,116
Frost I. (L)	3,688
Lab majority	17,379

No Change

	1974		1979
Total Votes	38,660		41,299
Turnout	74·5%		78·3%
Lab	27,275	70·6%	66·6%
C	6,209	16·1%	24·5%
L	5,176	13·4%	8·9%
Lab maj	21,066	54·5%	42·1%
Swing		−0·8%	+6·2%

Mr Dennis Skinner, former miner, is chairman of the Miners Group of Labour MPs. Elected in 1970. Member, Labour Party national executive committee, since October, 1978. B February, 1932; ed Tupton Hall Grammar School and Ruskin College. President. Derbyshire Miners (NUM), 1966-70, and NE Derbyshire Constituency Labour Party, 1968-71. Former member, Clay Cross UDC and Derbyshire County Council. Chairman, Tribune Group, 1973-74. Sponsored by NUM.

Mr Anthony Favell, solicitor with practice in Sheffield. B 1939; ed Birkdale Preparatory School, Sheffield; St Bees School, Cumberland, and Sheffield University. Member, High Peak Conservative Association and hon treasurer since 1974. Round Table community service chairman.

Mr Ian Frost, mining mechanical engineer. B February 1938; ed William Rhodes School, Chesterfield and Clowne Chesterfield and Worksop Technical. Parish councillor.

BOLTON, East

Electorate: 58,482   1974: 60,177

*Young D. W. (Lab)	21,920
Baldwin R. (C)	20,068
Lawrence Mrs S. B. (L)	3,603
Hamilton J. (Nat Front)	457
Lab majority	1,852

No Change

	1974		1979
Total Votes	46,120		46,048
Turnout	76·6%		78·7%
Lab	21,569	46·8%	47·6%
C	17,504	38·0%	43·6%
L	5,792	12·6%	7·8%
Nat Front	1,106	2·4%	1·0%
Pros Brit	149	0·3%	—
Lab maj	4,065	8·8%	4·0%
Swing		−2·7%	+2·4%

Mr David Young, a teacher, won the seat in February, 1974; contested Bath, 1970, Banbury, 1966, and South Worcestershire, 1959. B October, 1930; ed Greenock Academy, Glasgow University and St Paul's College, Cheltenham. Former alderman, Nuneaton Borough Council, and councillor, Nuneaton District Council. Chairman, Coventry East Labour Party, 1964-68. Member, Fabian Society. TGWU.

Mr Roger Baldwin, barrister (1969), contested Newton in October, 1974. B March, 1946; ed St Mary's College, Blackburn, and King's College, London University. Former chairman, Burnley Conservative Association.

Mrs Sara Lawrence, housewife, freelance artist and part-time secretary. B December, 1948; ed Worsley Wardley Grammar School, Manchester Art College and Salford College of Technology.

BOLTON, West

Electorate: 50,221   1974: 50,782

*Taylor Mrs. W. A. (Lab)	17,857
Watson B. H. (C)	17,257
Fish J. (L)	4,392
Bernal K. (Nat Front)	348
Lab majority	600

No Change

	1974		1979
Total Votes	39,227		39,854
Turnout	77·2%		79·4%
Lab	16,967	43·3%	44·8%
C	16,061	40·9%	43·3%
L	5,127	13·1%	11·0%
Nat Front	1,072	2·7%	0·9%
Lab maj	906	2·4%	1·5%
Swing		−2·0%	+0·4%

Mrs Ann Taylor, an assistant Government whip, 1977-79; PPS to Secretary of State for Education and Science, 1975-76, and to Secretary of State for Defence, 1976-77. Contested seat February, 1974, won it October, 1974, from Conservatives. Teacher. B July, 1947; ed Bolton School and Bradford and Sheffield Universities. Member, Select Committee on Violence in Marriage, 1975-76; on Wealth Tax, 1975-77, and on Sound Broadcasting, 1976-77. AUT.

Mr Barry Watson contested Greenwich, Woolwich, East, in both 1974 elections. Publicity and public relations manager for engineering division of large engineering group; ex-marine engineer in Merchant Navy. B June, 1935; ed Manchester Grammar School; Allan Glen's School, Glasgow, and the Royal College of Science and Technology, Glasgow. Member, Westminster City Council since 1968 and deputy chief whip, Conservative group 1970-73. Member, Conservative Greater London Area Council.

Mr John Fish, consultant orthodontist. B January 1943; ed Salford Grammar School and Durham University.

BOOTLE

Electorate: 62,578   1974: 64,236

Roberts A. (Lab)	26,900
Watson R. (C)	11,741
Mahon D. (L)	4,531
Fjortoft Mrs. H. (Ind L)	911
Lab majority	15,159

No Change

	1974		1979
Total Votes	43,158		44,083
Turnout	67·2%		70·4%
Lab	27,633	64·0%	61·0%
C	10,743	24·9%	26·6%
L	4,266	9·9%	10·3%
Comm	516	1·2%	—
Ind L	—		2·1%
Lab maj	16,890	39·1%	34·4%
Swing		−3·5%	+2·3%

Mr Allan Roberts is a City of Manchester councillor. B October, 1943; ed Droylesden Littlemoss County Secondary School. Principal officer (child care) of the City of Salford Social Services Department.

Mr Ronald Watson, a travel agent; President, Southport Chamber of Trade and Commerce. Elected to Southport County Borough Council, 1969. B May 1945; ed South Shields Grammar School and Waterloo Grammar School.

Mr David Mahon, journalist, fought Liverpool, Scotland Exchange, February, 1974, and Liverpool, Toxteth, October, 1974, and South Fylde for Labour, 1970. B June, 1939; ed St Mary's College, Crosby, and St Joseph's College, Durham.

Mrs Helen Fjortoft, fought the seat in October 1974 as the official Liberal Candidate. B May 1925.

BOSWORTH

Electorate: 90,290   1974: 83,820

*Butler A. (C)	37,030
Fatchett D. J. (Lab)	28,595
Brown E. (L)	10,032
Dunn D. (Nat Front)	682
C majority	8,435

No Change

	1974		1979
Total Votes	68,760		76,339
Turnout	82·0%		84·5%
C	28,490	41·4%	48·5%
Lab	28,188	41·0%	37·5%
L	12,082	17·6%	13·1%
Nat Front	—	—	0·9%
C maj	302	0·4%	11·0%
Swing		−1·0%	+5·3%

Mr Adam Butler, second son of Lord Butler, became Minister of State for Industry in May, 1979. Won the seat for the Conservatives in 1970. An assistant Government whip, 1974, and an Opposition whip, 1974-75. B October, 1931; ed Eton and Pembroke College, Cambridge. ADC to Governor-General of Canada, 1954-55; Courtaulds Ltd, 1955-73; director, Aristoc Ltd, 1966-73; Kayser Bondor Ltd, 1971-73, Capital and Counties Property Co Ltd since 1973. PPS to Minister of State for Foreign Affairs, 1971-72, Minister of Agriculture, Fisheries and Food, 1972-74. PPS to Mrs Thatcher as Leader of the Opposition 1975-79. Liveryman of Goldsmiths' Co NFU.

Mr Derek Fatchett is a university lecturer. B August, 1945. ASTMS.

Mr Edward Brown, self employed in wool business. B December 1921; ed Hinckley St Peter's RC and Hinckley Technical College. Member, Hinckley and Bosworth Borough Council, since 1965.

BOTHWELL

Electorate: 61,309   1974: 59,357

*Hamilton J. (Lab)	26,492
Scott J. (C)	11,275
Grieve T. A. (L)	5,225
McCool J. F. (Scot Nat)	5,202
Lab majority	15,217

No Change

	1974		1979
Total Votes	45,406		48,194
Turnout	76·5%		78·6%
Lab	22,086	48·6%	55·0%
Scot Nat	11,138	24·5%	10·8%
C	8,125	17·9%	23·4%
L	4,057	8·9%	10·8%
Lab Maj	10,948	24·1%	31·6%
Swing		−5·3%	−0·5%

Mr James Hamilton, Vice-Chamberlain of the Household 1974-79, became a Lord Commissioner of the Treasury (Government whip) in March, 1974. Former chairman, PLP trade union group. Assistant Government whip, 1969-70; Opposition whip, 1970-74. Elected, 1964. B March, 1918; ed senior secondary schools. Member, Lanarkshire County Council, 1955-65. President, Construc-

tional Engineering Union, 1968-70; member of its national executive, 1958-70, Sponsored by AUEW, constructional section.

Mr James Scott, contracts manager with a building firm. B 1930; ed Whitehill School, Glasgow; Glasgow School of Architecture and Strathclyde University.

Mr Terry Grieve, solicitor, fought seat in October, 1974. B June, 1934.

Mr John McCool, teacher, contested the seat, October, 1974. B 1942; ed Motherwell and Strathclyde University. Former member, Cumbernauld Burgh and Dunbartonshire County Councils.

BOURNEMOUTH, East

Electorate: 56,382   1974: 57,010

*Atkinson D. (C)	25,808
Goodwin J. (Lab)	7,553
Matthew D. (L)	6,738
Pratt J. (New Brit)	581
Dempsey Mrs J. (Ecology)	523
C majority	18,255

No Change

	1974		1979
Total Votes	40,169		41,203
Turnout	70·5%		73·1%
C	20,790	51·8%	62·6%
L	10,129	25·2%	16·4%
Lab	8,422	21·0%	18·3%
Nat Front	828	2·1%	—
New Brit	—	—	1·4%
Ecology	—	—	1·3%
C maj	10,661	26·6%	44·3%
Swing		−1·4%	+6·7%

1977 by-election: Total vote 24,025 (42·6%)—C 15,235 (63·4%); Lab 3,684 (15·3%); L 3,212 (13·4%); Nat Front 725 (3·0%); others 1,169 (4·9%)—C majority 11,551 (48·1%).

Mr David Atkinson, managing director of a printing and marketing company which he founded in 1971, was elected at the November, 1977, by-election. Member, Conservative back bench committees on Health and Social Services and small businesses. Contested Newham, North-West, February, 1974, and Basildon in October, 1974. B 1940; ed St George's College, Weybridge, Southend College of Technology, and the College of Automobile and Aeronautical Engineering, Chelsea. National Young Conservative chairman, 1970-71; member, YC Parliamentary Liaison Committee, 1969-73. Elected to Essex County Council, 1973; re-elected, 1977. Member, O.S.C. Kent and Essex Sea Fisheries Committee. Member, Conservative Group for Europe. Worked on Israeli kibbutz.

Mr Joseph Goodwin fought the seat in the 1977 by-election. Lecturer. B June, 1948; ed Bournemouth School and London University. Member, Bournemouth District Council, 1973-76. Branch chairman, NATFHE. National executive member and SW regional organiser, Campaign for Real Ale.

Mr Donald Matthew economist and lecturer, contested the by-election in 1977. Co-opted member, Dorset County Education Committee. NATFHE officer. B November, 1923; ed Rochdale Grammar School; St Luke's College, Exeter; and universities of London and Southampton.

BOURNEMOUTH, West

Electorate: 61,359   1974: 61,211

*Eden Sir J. (C)	25,873
Brushett P. J. (Lab)	9,247
Richards T. D. G. (L)	7,677
Hubbard G. (Nat Front)	438
C majority	16,626

No Change

	1974		1979
Total Votes	42,026		43,235
Turnout	68·7%		70·5%
C	21,294	50·7%	59·8%
Lab	10,566	25·1%	21·4%
L	10,166	24·2%	17·8%
Nat Front	—		1·0%
C maj	10,728	25·6%	38·4%
Swing		−1·7%	+6·4%

Sir John Eden, Minister of Posts and Telecommunications, 1972-74, was Minister for Industry, 1970-72, and Minister of State for Technology, 1970. Returned at a by-election in February, 1954; contested Paddington, North, December, 1953. B September, 1925; ed Eton and in the United States. Chairman, Select Committee on European legislation since 1976. Director, Chesham Amalgamations and Investments, Central and Sheerwood Ltd, Lady Eden's Schools Ltd. President, Independent Schools Association, 1969-71; vice-president, National Chamber of Trade, since 1974.

Mr Peter Brushett contested New Forest, October, 1974. Poultry Distributor. B June, 1931; ed Kemp Welch School and Seale Hayne Agricultural College. TGWU.

Mr Terence Richards, publishing executive, contested the seat February and October, 1974. B September, 1947; ed Oakmead School for Boys, Bournemouth, and Bournemouth College of Technology.

BRADFORD, North

Electorate 68,530   1974: 66,135

*Ford, B. T. (Lab)	25,069
Hamilton, N. (C)	17,548
Bagshawe, A. (L)	5,819
Brons, A. (Nat Front)	614
Smith, Miss. C. E. (WRP)	158
Lab majority	7,521

No Change

	1974		1979
Total Votes	46,568		49,208
Turnout	70·4%		71·8%
Lab	22,841	49·0%	50·9%
C	14,252	30·6%	35·7%
L	9,475	20·3%	11·8%
Nat Front	—		1·2%
WRP	—		0·3%
Lab maj	8,589	18·4%	15·2%
Swing		−2·8%	+1·6%

Mr Benjamin Ford was elected in 1964. Engineer. B April, 1925; ed Rowan Road Central School, Surrey. Alderman, Essex County Council, 1959-67. Member, Clacton UDC, 1960-63. Chairman, joint committee on broadcasting. Member, Services Committee. Vice-chairman, PLP defence committee. Chairman, Inter-Parliamentary Union

(British Branch). Treasurer, PLP Benevolent Fund, Chairman, all-party wool textile group. Director, Welltrade International Ltd. Member, British Shooting Sports Council. Sponsored by AUEW.

Mr Neil Hamilton, barrister and director of a travel company, contested Abertillery, February, 1974. B 1950; ed Amman Valley Grammar School, University College of Wales, Aberystwyth and Corpus Christi College, Cambridge.

BRADFORD, South

Electorate 76,353   1974: 73,272

*Torney, T. W. (Lab)	26,323
Hirst, J. K. (C)	22,005
Taylor, R. (L)	7,127
Wright, G. (Nat Front)	422

Lab majority	4,318

No Change

	1974		1979
Total Votes	52,469		55,877
Turnout	71·6%		73·2%
Lab	25,219	48·1%	47·1%
C	16,944	32·3%	39·4%
L	10,306	19·6%	12·8%
Nat Front	—	—	0·8%
Lab maj	8,275	15·8%	7·7%
Swing		−1·3%	+4·0%

Mr Thomas Torney, elected in 1970, was Derby and district area organizer, USDAW, 1946-70. B July, 1915; ed elementary school. Former chairman, PLP Agriculture and Food Group. Member, Select Committee on Race Relations and Immigration. Secretary, wine and spirit industry liaison committee. Sponsored by USDAW.

Mr John Hirst, director of a retail motor cycle company, has served as chairman of the Housing Committee of Bradford Metropolitan District Council. B May, 1919; ed Great Horton Modern School and Negus Business College.

Mr Roderic Taylor, self-employed designer, craftsman and weaver. Contested Hemsworth, October, 1974, and Bradford West, February, 1974. B March, 1938; ed Bradford schools.

BRADFORD, West

Electorate 65,407   1974: 62,684

*Lyons, E. (Lab)	24,309
Stow, T. (C)	16,554
Flood, N. (L)	3,668
Brown, G. (Nat Front)	633

Lab majority	7,755

No Change

	1974		1979
Total Votes	43,548		45,164
Turnout	69·5%		69·1%
Lab	21,133	48·5%	53·8%
C	16,192	37·2%	36·7%
L	5,884	13·5%	8·1%
Pros Brit	339	0·8%	—
Nat Front	—	—	1·4%
Lab maj	4,941	11·3%	17·1%
Swing		−3·3%	−2·9%

Mr Edward Lyons, QC, was elected in February, 1974; represented Bradford, East, 1966-74. Barrister (Lincoln's Inn, 1952). Crown court recorder since 1972. B May, 1926; ed City of Leeds School, Roundhay High School, and Leeds University. Russian interpreter with Control Commission, Germany, 1946-48. Joint chairman, PLP Home Office Group.

Member, Select Committee on European Secondary Legislation and Joint Select Committee on Consolidation of Statute Law, since 1947.

Mr Thomas Stow, farmer, contested Leeds, South, October 1974. B 1947; ed South Craven Comprehensive School and Askham Bryan Agricultural College. Member, Skipton rural council, 1970-74; North Yorkshire County Council since 1973. Vice-chairman, Skipton Conservative Association, 1970-75. Sidesman at Lothersdale Parish Church since 1967; elected a churchwarden in 1974.

Mr Nicholas Flood, civil engineer. B October 1951; ed City of London School, Solihull School and Leeds University.

BRAINTREE

Electorate 75,103   1974: 65,538

*Newton, A. H. (C)	31,593
Gyford, J. E. B. (Lab)	19,075
Bryan, J. (L)	10,115

C majority	12,518

No Change

	1974		1979
Total Votes	52,032		60,783
Turnout	79·4%		80·9%
C	20,559	39·5%	52·0%
Lab	19,469	37·4%	31·4%
L	12,004	23·1%	16·6%
C maj	1,090	2·1%	20·6%
Swing		−0·8%	+9·2%

Mr Antony Newton, who became an assistant Government Whip in May, 1979, was elected in February, 1974; contested Sheffield, Brightside, 1970. Economist. B August, 1937; ed Friends' School, Saffron Walden, and Trinity College, Oxford. President of Oxford Union, 1959. Joint secretary, Conservative backbench Health and Social Security Committee, since 1976. Assistant director, Conservative Research Department, 1970-74; head of economic section, 1965-70; research secretary, Bow Group, 1964-65.

Mr John Gyford, lecturer in town planning. B April, 1939; ed St Paul's School, Jesus College, Oxford, and Manchester University. Member, Witham Council, 1970-74, and Essex County Council, 1970-77. AUT.

Mr John Bryan, a social worker. B March, 1940; ed St Bonaventures RC Grammar School, London. NALGO.

BRECON AND RADNOR

Electorate 56,975   1974: 54,300

Hooson, T. (C)	22,660
*Roderick, C. E. (Lab)	19,633
Lewis, N. (L)	4,654
Power, Mrs. J. (Pl Cymru)	1,031
C majority	3,027

C gain from Lab

	1974		1979
Total Votes	44,214		47,978
Turnout	81·4%		84·2%
Lab	18,622	42·1%	40·9%
C	15,610	35·3%	47·2%
L	7,682	17·4%	9·7%
Pl Cymru	2,300	5·2%	2·1%
Lab maj	3,012	6·8%	
C maj	—		6·3%
Swing		−0·9%	+6·5%

Mr Tom Hooson, a publishing director, is former chairman of the Bow Group and Crossbow. Fought Caernarvon, 1959. B March 1933, ed Rhyl Grammar School and University College, Oxford. Lived in United States and France during business career. Conservative Party Director of Communications, 1976-78. Cousin of Mr Emlyn Hooson, defeated Liberal candidate for Montgomery.

Mr Caerwyn Roderick, elected in 1970, was a lecturer at Cardiff College of Education. PPS to Mr Michael Foot as Secretary of State for Employment. B July, 1927; ed University College of North Wales. Former member, local executive, NUT; national advisory committee for comprehensive schools and Welsh secondary committee of NUT. Senior master, Hartridge High, Newport, 1960-69. Member, Public Accounts Committee.

Mr Norman Lewis, cost and management accountant, fought Caerphilly, October, 1974. Employed by Wales Gas. Treasurer, Welsh Liberal Party. B December 1925; ed Vaynor and Penderyn and Merthyr Tydfil County Grammar Schools.

Mrs Janet Power, teacher. B March, 1933; ed Bristol University. Community councillor for Llandrindod.

BRENT, East

Electorate 57,034   1974: 63,168

*Freeson, R. (Lab)	20,351
Howes, J. (C)	14,008
Wilding, C. (L)	2,799
Davies, J. (Nat Front)	706
Downing, G. (WRP)	290
Lab majority	6,343

No Change

	1974		1979
Total Votes	37,929		38,154
Turnout	60·0%		66·9%
Lab	20,481	54·0%	53·3%
C	11,554	30·5%	36·7%
L	4,416	11·6%	7·3%
Nat Front	1,096	2·9%	1·9%
I Civ Rights	382	1·0%	—
WRP	—	—	0·8%
Lab maj	8,927	23·5%	16·6%
Swing		−2·9%	+3·4%

Mr Reginald Freeson, Minister for Housing and Construction, Department of the Environment, 1974-79. Parliamentary Secretary, Ministry of Housing and Local Government, 1969-70; Parliamentary Secretary, Ministry of Power, 1967-69. B February, 1926; ed Jewish Orphanage, West Norwood, Returned for Brent East, February,

1974; MP for Willesden, East, 1964-74. An Opposition spokesman on housing and construction, 1970-74. Willesden Borough Council member, 1952-65; Leader, 1958-65. Member, Brent Council, 1964-68; Chairman, 1964-65 Member, Natsopa, 1942-55; NUJ since 1956.

Mr James Howes, deputy regional manager for London and SE of England for the trustee, taxation and investment department of a major bank. B 1929; ed Beehive Preparatory School and Cranbrook College, Ilford. Member, Conservative Friends of Israel; governor, Woodford County High School for Girls.

Mr Christopher Wilding, food shares analyst. Aged 24; ed Trinity College, Cambridge.

Mr Gerald Downing, aged 28, building labourer, UCATT representative on Brent Trades Council.

BRENT, North

Electorate 72,158   1974: 72,122

*Boyson, R. (C)	29,995
Lebor, J. (Lab)	18,612
Ketteringham, A. (L)	5,872
John, G. (Nat Front)	873
C majority	11,383

No Change

	1974		1979
Total Votes	51,849		55,352
Turnout	71·9%		76·7%
C	24,853	47·9%	53·8%
Lab	17,541	33·8%	34·0%
L	8,158	15·7%	10·6%
Nat Front	1,297	2·5%	1·6%
C maj	7,312	14·1%	19·8%
Swing		+0·1%	+2·8%

Mr Rhodes Boyson was appointed Under Secretary of State for Education and Science in May, 1979. An Opposition spokesman on education 1976-79, was elected in February, 1974; contested Eccles, 1970. Former headmaster, Highbury Grove School. B May, 1925; ed Haslingden Grammar School, University College, Cardiff, Manchester University, LSE and Corpus Christi College, Cambridge. Chairman, National Council for Educational Standards. Member, Waltham Forest Borough Council, 1968-74.

Mr John Lebor, a solicitor specialising in trade union and labour law. B January, 1929; ed Mora Elementary School and Kilburn Grammar School. Ten years' service Brent Council, and Leader, London Borough of Brent. APEX and CAWU.

Mr Andrew Ketteringham, corporate planner. B July, 1950; ed Lascelles Secondary Modern School, Harrow County, and Hull University.

BRENT, South

Electorate 59,620   1974: 61,244

*Pavitt, L. A. (Lab and Co-op)	24,178
Heathcoat-Amory, D. (C)	12,562
Hannon, P. (L)	2,859
Downes, Miss A. (Nat Front)	811
O'Neill, R. (WRP)	277

Lab and Co-op majority	11,616

No Change

	1974		1979
Total Votes	37,486		40,687
Turnout	61·2%		68·2%
Lab & Co-op	21,611	57·7%	59·4%
C	10,558	28·2%	30·9%
L	3,929	10·5%	7·0%
Nat Front	1,388	3·7%	2·0%
WRP	—	—	0·7%
Lab/Co-op maj	11,053	29·5%	28·5%
Swing		−2·5%	+0·5%

Mr Laurence Pavitt was an Assistant Government Whip, 1974-76. MP for Willesden, West, 1959-74; returned for Brent, South, in February, 1974. National organizer of the Medical Practitioners' Union, 1956-59. B February, 1914; ed elementary and central schools. Member, Medical Research Council, 1969-72, Hearing Aid Council, 1968-74, and Select Committee on Overseas aid, 1969-71. Chairman, PLP health group, 1964-77, vice-chairman since 1977. Vice-president, British Association for the Hard of Hearing; chairman, British China All Party Group and All Party Group on Action on Smoking and Health. NUPE.

Mr David Heathcoat-Amory, chartered accountant and financial executive with a holding company. B 1949; ed Oxford University (president of Conservative Association). Member, management committee, Shepherd's Bush Housing Association.

Mr Paul Hannon, assistant director, National Association of Deaf Children. Aged 27; ed Royal Veterinary College, London.

Mr Raymond O'Neill, aged 35, telephone engineer. EETPU.

BRENTWOOD AND ONGAR

Electorate 59,759   1974: 58,363

*McCrindle, R. A. (C)	29,113
Peddie, I. J. C. (Lab)	12,182
Jones, C. (L)	6,882

C majority	16,931

No Change

	1974		1979
Total Votes	45,051		48,177
Turnout	77·2%		80·6%
C	21,136	46·9%	60·4%
Lab	13,190	29·3%	25·3%
L	10,725	23·8%	14·3%
C maj	7,946	17·6%	35·1%
Swing		−1·7%	+8·7%

Mr Robert McCrindle, an insurance broker, elected in February, 1974; MP for Billericay, 1970-74; contested Thurrock, 1964, and Dundee, East 1959. B September, 1929; ed Allen Glen's College, Glasgow. Associate of the Chartered Insurance Institute and Fellow of the Corporation of Insurance Brokers. Parliamentary consultant to British Insurance Brokers' Association and Guild of Business Travel Agents, Member, Select Committee on Wealth Tax and of North Atlantic Assembly.

Mr Ian Peddie, barrister, was educated at University College. B December, 1945. Member, Society of Labour Lawyers.

Mr Colin Jones is a teacher of the adult mentally handicapped. B April, 1945; ed Southend.

BRIDGWATER

Electorate 73,040   1974: 69,755

*King, T. J. (C)	31,259
Beasant, J. (Lab)	16,809
Baron, Miss C. (L)	9,793

C majority	14,450

No Change

	1974		1979
Total Votes	53,878		57,861
Turnout	77.2%		79.2%
C	23,850	44.3%	54.0%
Lab	17,663	32.8%	29.1%
L	12,077	22.4%	16.9%
UDP	288	0.5%	
C maj	6,187	11.5%	24.9%
Swing		−1.3%	+6.7%

Mr Tom King, Minister of State for the Environment from May, 1979. Chief Opposition spokesman on energy 1976-79; formerly an Opposition spokesman on industry. Vice-chairman, Conservative industry committee, 1974-75. Won the by-election in March, 1970. Chairman, Sale, Tilney Co Ltd; former general manager, E. S. and A. Robinson Ltd, Bristol. B June, 1933; ed Rugby and Emmanuel College, Cambridge.

Mr John Beasant, publicity officer for New Hebridean Vanuaakun Party, was personal assistant to Sir Edgar Whitehead, Leader of the Opposition in the Rhodesian Parliament 1963-67. B July, 1941; ed Lyford House, St Andrew's and the White Horse School.

Miss Christina Baron, a home help organizer, has served on Wells City Council since 1976. Her husband was Liberal candidate in Wells. B October 1950; ed St Andrews, and City University, London. Member, Nalgo.

BRIDLINGTON

Electorate 68,849   1974: 65,759

Townend, J. (C)	27,988
Doyle, P. J. (Lab)	12,693
Horsley, D. (L)	10,390
C majority	15,295

No Change

	1974		1979
Total Votes	44,629		51,071
Turnout	67.9%		74.2%
C	21,901	49.1%	54.8%
L	11,795	26.4%	20.3%
Lab	9,946	22.3%	24.9%
Nat Front	987	2.2%	
C maj	10,106	22.7%	29.9%
Swing		−2.5%	+1.5%

Mr John Townend, a wine merchant and chartered accountant, contested Kingston upon Hull, North, 1970. B June, 1934; ed Hymers College, Hull. Leader Humberside County Council; member, accounts policy committee. Hull City councillor, 1966. Chairman and managing director, J. Townend and Sons (Hull) Ltd and associate companies. Chairman,

Merchant Vintners Coy Ltd. Divisional chairman, Haltemprice and Beverley Young Conservatives, 1952-54. Governor. Hymers College.

Mr Patrick Doyle is a lecturer. B January 1939; ed Queen Mary's Grammar School, Walsall, and University College, Durham. Member, Hull City Council since 1972 and chairman, Technical Services Committee. Member, NATFHE.

Mr David Horsley is a teacher. Aged 36; ed St David's College, Lampeter, and Westminster College, Oxford.

BRIGG AND SCUNTHORPE

Electorate 94,822   1974: 90,159

Brown, M. (C)	31,130
*Ellis, J. (Lab)	30,644
Beard, M. (L)	7,764
Nottingham, C. (Dem Lab)	2,042
Nottingham, M. (Ind)	123
C majority	486

C gain from Lab

	1974		1979
Total Votes	63,568		71,703
Turnout	70.5%		75.6%
Lab	28,929	45.5%	42.7%
C	22,187	34.9%	43.4%
L	12,452	19.6%	10.8%
Dem Lab	—		2.8%
Ind	—	—	0.2%
Lab maj	6,742	10.6%	
C maj	—	—	0.7%
Swing		−3.1%	+5.6%

Mr Michael Brown is parliamentary research assistant to an MP. B 1951; ed Andrew Cairns County Secondary Modern School, Littlehampton, and York University. Vice-president, York University Students' Union, 1971-72. Vice-chairman, York University Conservative Association, 1971-72.

Mr John Ellis, an assistant Government whip 1974-76, was elected in February, 1974. MP for Bristol, North-West, 1966-70; contested Wokingham, 1964. B October, 1934; ed Doncaster Grammar School, Rastrick Grammar School, Brighouse. Vice-chairman, staff side, Air Ministry Whitley Council, 1961-63. Served on Bristol City Council. Member, Select Committee on Nationalised Industries. Former member, Commons Expenditure Committee. Sponsored by TGWU.

Mr Michael Beard, aged 32, is an executive officer. Trained as a teacher.

BRIGHOUSE AND SPENBOROUGH

Electorate 65,415   1974: 63,645

Waller, G. P. A. (C)	23,448
McGowan, M. (Lab)	21,714
Thomas, R. (L)	7,278
C majority	1,734

C gain from Lab

	1974		1979
Total Votes	50,016		52,440
Turnout	78·6%		80·2%
Lab	21,964	43·9%	41·4%
C	19,787	39·6%	44·7%
L	8,265	16·5%	13·9%
Lab maj	2,177	4·3%	
C maj	—	—	3·3%
Swing		−0·8%	+3·8%

Mr Gary Waller contested Rother Valley February and October, 1974. Contested London borough elections 1971, 1974, and GLC elections 1973. Journalist. B June, 1945; ed Rugby School and Lancaster University. School manager. Former chairman, Newham South Conservative Association. NUJ.

Mr Michael McGowan, education officer, contested Ripon, 1966. B May, 1940; ed Heckmondwike Grammar School and Leicester University. Former BBC television and radio producer. Former member, West Riding County Council, Spenborough Borough Council, 1962-65.

Mr Roger Thomas, barrister, B August, 1954; ed Worksop College, Notts, and Hull University. Interested in sport, music and reading.

BRIGHTON, Kemptown

Electorate 64,170   1974: 65,443

*Bowden, A. (C)	25,512
Barry, Q. (Lab)	17,504
Osborne, S. (L)	4,179
Tyndall, Mrs V. (Nat Front)	404

C majority	8,008

No Change

	1974		1979
Total votes	47,326		47,599
Turnout	72·3%		74·2%
C	21,725	45·9%	53·6%
Lab	19,060	40·3%	36·8%
L	6,214	13·1%	8·8%
Eng Nat	155	0·3%	—
Marx Len	125	0·3%	—
Ind	47	0·1%	—
Nat Front	—	—	0·8%
C maj	2,665	5·6%	16·8%
Swing		−1·2%	+5·6%

Mr Andrew Bowden, a per sonnel consultant and company director, won the seat in 1970; contested the seat in 1966; Kensington North, 1964; Hammersmith, North 1955. Joint chairman, all-party group for pensioners, 1972-74. B April, 1930; ed Ardingly College, Sussex. Member, Select Committee on Expenditure. 1973-74; Select Committee on Abortion (Amendment) Bill, 1975-76. National chairman, Young Conservatives, 1960-61. Member, Wandsworth Borough Council, 1956-62. USDAW.

Mr Quinton Barry, solicitor, contested Lewes in 1970, and Shoreham in February and October, 1974. B

March, 1936; ed Eastbourne College. TGWU, and Society of Labour Lawyers.

Mr Stephen Osborne, a self-employed company director, contested the seat, October, 1974. Ed Lancing College.

BRIGHTON, Pavilion

Electorate 57,003   1974: 53,351

*Amery, H. J. (C)	22,218
Hill, D. S. (Lab)	12,099
Venables, Mrs D. (L)	5,965
Beale, J. (Ecology)	638
Jones, H. (Nat Front)	436

C majority	10,119

No Change

	1974		1979
Total votes	39,313		41,356
Turnout	68·5%		72·6%
C	19,041	48·4%	53·7%
Lab	11,624	29·6%	29·3%
L	8,648	22·0%	14·4%
Ecology	—	—	1·5%
Nat Front	—	—	1·1%
C maj	7,417	18·8%	24·4%
Swing		−2·9%	+2·8%

Mr Julian Amery, Minister of State, Foreign and Commonwealth Office, 1972-74. Minister for Housing and Construction, 1970-72. Minister of Public Building and Works, 1970. Returned at by-election in 1969. Minister of Aviation, 1962-64; Secretary of State for Air from October, 1960; Under-Secretary, Colonial Office from 1958; Under-Secretary, War Office, from 1957. Held Preston, North, 1950-66; contested the two-member Preston seat in 1945. Author, journalist and company director. B March, 1919; ed Eton and Balliol College, Oxford.

Mr David Hill, a college of education lecturer at London and Sussex universities. B October, 1945; ed secondary modern, Westlain Grammar School, Brighton, and Manchester University. Member, Brighton Borough Council, 1975-76. NATFHE.

Mrs Delia Venables, computer specialist in management science. Contested the seat, October, 1974. B May, 1943; ed Perse Girls School, Cambridge, and Illinois University.

Mr John Beale, lecturer in communications studies. Aged 44. Ed Banbury and Cambridge. Member, Conservation Society.

BRISTOL, North-East

Electorate 51,053   1974: 51,970

*Palmer, A. M. F. (Lab Co-op)	19,337
Mulvany, Mrs M. (C)	13,685
Drinan, N. (L)	3,693
Dorey, Mrs G. (Ecology)	469
Brown, K. D. C. (Nat Front)	320

Lab Co-op majority	5,652

No Change

	1974		1979
Total votes	37,006		37,504
Turnout	71·2%		73·5%
Lab & Co-op	19,647	53·1%	51·6%
C	11,056	29·9%	36·5%
L	6,303	17·0%	9·8%
Ecology	—		1·3%
Nation Front	—		0·9%
Lab/Coop m.	8,591	23·2%	15·1%
Swing		−3·9%	+4·0%

Mr Arthur Palmer, chairman of Select Committee on Science and Technology since 1974 and 1966-70. Returned in February, 1974; represented Bristol, Central, 1964-74; Wimbledon, 1945-50; Cleveland, 1952-59. Contested Merton and Morden, 1950 and 1951. Chartered engineer. B August, 1912; ed Ashford Grammar School and Brunel Technical College. Member Select Committee on Nationalized Industries, 1964-66; Select Committee on Members' interests, 1974 and since 1976. Vice-chairman, PLP energy group. Officer and editor, Electrical Power Engineers' Association.

Mrs Mollie Mulvany, author, lecturer and broadcaster. B 1931; ed Wallington Grammar School and London University.

Mr Neil Drinan, a writer and Liberal agent, has fought local government elections. Aged 49.

Mrs Gundula Dorey, probation officer in Bristol Prison. Aged 36; ed Newcastle Central High School and Exter University.

BRISTOL, North-West

Electorate 65,601   1974: 66,381

Colvin, M. K. B. (C)	25,915
*Thomas, R. R. (Lab)	21,238
Davis, P. M. (L)	5,857
Kingston, P. M. (Nat Front)	254
Keen, T. L. (CFMPB)	73
C majority	4,677

C gain

	1974		1979
Total votes	52,593		53,337
Turnout	79·2%		81·3%
Lab	22,156	42·1%	39·8%
C	21,523	40·9%	48·6%
L	8,914	16·9%	11·0%
Nat Front	—		0·5%
CFMPB	—		0·1%
Lab maj	633	1·2%	—
C maj	—		8·8%
Swing		−1·2%	+5·0%

Mr Michael Colvin, farmer, landowner, company director and public house licensee. Part-time member of Conservative Research Department, specializing in avation, 1975-78. Qualified pilot and parachutist. B September, 1932; ed Eton, RMA Sandhurst and Royal Agricultural College, Cirencester. Served with Grenadier Guards 1950-57. Member, Andover RDC 1965-73; Test Valley District Council 1973-75. Vice-chairman, Southern Sports Council, 1968-73.

Church warden. NFU and National Union of Licensed Victuallers.

Mr Ronald Thomas, university lecturer, contested the seat, February, 1974; elected October, 1974. B March, 1929, ed Ruskin College and Balliol College, Oxford. Member, Select Committee on European Legislation, Bristol District Council. Sponsored by ASTMS.

Mr Gordon Davis, company director; chairman, Austin Davis Developments Ltd and subsidiary companies. B July, 1927; ed Bristol Grammar School and Brasenose College, Oxford.

BRISTOL, South

Electorate 60,149   1974: 61,040

*Cocks, M. F. L. (Lab)	25,038
Dicks, T. P. (C)	13,855
Bidwell, C. J. (L)	3,815
Elliot, K. G. (Nat Front)	392
Cheek, Mrs L. J. (WRP)	135
Lab majority	11,183

No Change

	1974		1979
Total votes	42,316		43,235
Turnout	69·3%		71·9%
Lab	25,108	59·3%	57·9%
C	10,124	23·9%	32·0%
L	6,289	14·9%	8·8%
Nat Front	795	1·9%	0·9%
WRP	—		0·3%
Lab maj	14,984	35·4%	25·9%
Swing		−3·1%	+4·7%

Mr Michael Cocks, Parliamentary Secretary to the Treasury (Government Chief Whip) 1976-79; Assistant Government Whip 1974-76. Elected in 1970; contested South Gloucestershire, 1964-66 and Bristol, West, 1959. Lecturer. B August, 1929; ed Bristol University. President, Bristol Borough Labour Party, 1961-63. Sponsored by GMWU.

Mr Terence Dicks, administrative office in local government. B 1937; ed LSE and Oxford. Former member, Oxford University Conservative Club; former vice-chairman, LSE Conservative Association. Nalgo.

Mr Charles Bidwell, barrister. Ed Stonyhurst College of Law.

Mrs Linda Cheek, housewife and former teacher. Aged 26.

BRISTOL, South-East

Electorate 69,937   1974: 69,427

*Wedgwood Benn, A. N. (Lab)	24,878
Godwin J. (C)	22,988
Tatam, N. W. (L)	6,371
Dowler, Mrs K. D. (Nat Front)	523
Keen, T. L. (CFMPB)	66
Lab majority	1,890

No Change

	1974		1979
Total votes	52,881		54,826
Turnout	76·2%		78·4%
Lab	25,978	49·1%	45·4%
C	16,605	31·4%	41·9%
L	8,987	17·0%	11·6%
Nat Front	775	1·5%	1·0%
Mid Class	457	0·9%	—
Comm Pe	79	0·1%	—
CFMPB	—	—	0·1%
Lab maj	9,373	17·7%	3·5%
Swing		−1·9%	+7·1%

Mr Anthony Wedgwood Benn, Secretary of State for Energy, 1975-79; Secretary of State for Industry 1974-75; Minister for Posts and Telecommunications, 1974. Chief Opposition spokesman on trade and Industry 1970-74; Minister of Technology, 1966-70; Postmaster General, 1964-66. Elected in 1950. Debarred from the Commons on the death of his father, Viscount Stansgate, in November, 1960, he contested and won the by-election in May, 1961, but an Election Court declared his Conservative opponent elected. He renounced his title under the Peerage Act and was re-elected in August, 1963. Member, Labour Party Executive, 1959-60 and since 1962; chairman 1971-72. Unsuccessfully contested deputy leadership of PLP in November, 1971 and leadership, 1976. Journalist. B April, 1925; ed Westminster and New College, Oxford. NUJ.

Mr John Godwin, a solicitor, contested the seat, February and October, 1974. B June, 1942; ed King Edward VI Grammar School, Chelmsford and Leeds University. Avon County Councillor.

Mr Nicholas Tatam, a planner with Wessex Water Authority. B May, 1947; ed Essex and Lancaster universities and Bretton Hall College of Education.

BRISTOL, West

Electorate 59,140   1974: 60,447

Waldegrave, W. A. (C)	22,257
Bath, Miss V. (Lab)	9,690
Silver, B. (L)	8,880
Ingham, J. K. (Ecology)	1,154
Jones, M. (Nat Front)	246
Redmore, R. R. (UDP)	93

C majority	12,567

No Change

	1974		1979
Total votes	39,525		42,320
Turnout	65·4%		71·6%
C	18,555	46·9%	52·6%
L	11,598	29·3%	21·0%
Lab	9,372	23·7%	22·9%
Ecology	—	—	2·7%
Nat Front	—	—	0·6%
UDP	—	—	0·2%
C maj	6,957	17·6%	29·7%
Swing		−1·7%	+3·2%

Mr William Waldegrave was a member of the Central Policy Review Staff, Cabinet Office, 1971-73 and on the Political Staff at No 10 Downing Street, 1973-74. He was head of Mr Edward Heath's political office, 1974-75. Since 1975, he has been with GEC Ltd. B August, 1946; ed Eton, Corpus Christi, Oxford (President of the Union) and Harvard (Kennedy Fellow in Politics). Fellow of All Souls College, Oxford, JP, Inner London Juvenile Court. Published book on future of Conservatism, 1978.

Miss Vivien Bath, teacher. Chairman, Bristol Tribune Group. B August, 1944; ed Chatham Girls' School, Central School of Speech and Drama. Member, Bristol Teachers' Association; Bristol District Council, 1973-76.

Mr Bernard Silver, managing director of an advertising agency, contested St Marylebone, February and October, 1974. B October, 1973; ed Kilburn Grammar School and the College for Distributive Trades.

Mr John Ingham is a trainee inspector with an insurance company. Age 26. Member, Conservation Society and Friends of the Earth.

BROMLEY, Beckenham

Electorate 57,939   1974: 59,512

*Goodhart, P. C. (C)	24,607
Mordecai, J. W. (Lab)	10,856
Forrest, Mrs C. (L)	6,450
Vernon, W. (Ecology)	762
Dickson, N. (Nat Front)	606

C majority	13,751

No Change

	1974		1979
Total votes	41,516		43,281
Turnout	69·8%		74·7%
C	19,798	47·7%	56·9%
Lab	11,140	26·8%	25·1%
L	10,578	25·5%	14·9%
Ecology	—	—	1·8%
Nat Front	—	—	1·4%
C maj	8,658	20·9%	31·8%
Swing		−2·4%	+5·4%

Mr Philip Goodhart appointed an Under Secretary of State for Northern Ireland in May 1959. Author. Returned for Beckenham at a by-election in March 1957; contested Consett, 1950. B November, 1925; ed Hotchkiss School, United States, and Trinity College, Cambridge. Joint secretary, 1922 Committee, since 1960. Secretary, Conserva-

tive Parliamentary Defence Committee, 1967-72, chairman 1972-74, vice-chairman 1974-79. Chairman, Conservative parliamentary Northern Ireland Committee since 1976. Advisory Council on Public Records, since 1970; Executive Committee, British Council, since 1974. Member, Council, Consumer's Association 1959-68, and since 1970. United Kingdom representative North Atlantic Assembly since 1964; (Chairman, Arms standardization subcommittee 1972-74).

Mr Jonathan Mordecai, local government officer. B November, 1951; ed Cowbridge Grammar School and City of Birmingham Polytechnic. Member, Brent Borough Council, since 1978. NALGO.

Mrs Christina Forrest, economist, was formerly a research officer, General Federation of Trade Unions. B May, 1950; ed Hutchesons' Girls' Grammar School, Glasgow, and Glasgow University.

BROMLEY, Chislehurst

Electorate 54,024   1974: 53,699

*Sims, R. E. (C)	23,259
Howes, C. (Lab)	13,494
Taylor, B. (L)	5,335
Hoy, R. (Nat Front)	564
C majority	9,765

No Change

	1974		1979
Total votes	40,858		42,652
Turnout	76·1%		79·0%
C	18,926	46·3%	54·5%
Lab	15,032	36·8%	31·6%
L	6,900	16·9%	12·5%
Nat Front	—	—	1·3%
C maj	3,894	9·5%	22·9%
Swing		−1·4%	+6·7%

Mr Roger Sims, an export manager, was elected in February 1974; contested Shoreditch and Finsbury, 1966 and 1970. B January 1930; ed City Boys' Grammar School, Leicester, and St Olave's Grammar School, London. Joint secretary, Conservative parliamentary home affairs committee, since 1976; secretary, all-party paper industry committee.

Member, Select Committee on Race Relations and Immigration; Royal Choral Society.

Mr Brian Taylor, dental surgeon, served on Bromley Borough Council, 1957-60 and 1962-65; then London Borough of Bromley Council, 1966-68. B December 1919; ed City of London School and Guys Hospital Dental School.

BROMLEY, Orpington

Electorate 67,917   1974: 65,686

*Stanbrook, I. R. (C)	32,150
Cook, J. (L)	16,074
Weyman, Miss A. J. (Lab)	6,581
Hitches, F. (Nat Front)	516
MacKillican, I. (Homeland)	146
C majority	16,076

No Change

	1974		1979
Total votes	51,899		55,467
Turnout	79·0%		81·7%
C	24,394	47·0%	58·0%
L	19,384	37·3%	29·0%
Lab	8,121	15·6%	11·9%
Nat Front	—	—	0·9%
Democrat	—	—	0·3%
C maj	5,010	9·7%	29·0%
Swing		−1·9%	+7·3%

Mr Ivor Stanbrook, a barrister, won Orpington for the Conservatives in 1970; contested East Ham, South, 1966. B January 1924; ed Willesden Central School, University College, London and Pembroke College, Oxford. Member, Joint Committee on Consolidation Bills. Colonial district officer in Nigeria, 1950-60. Secretary, Conservative parliamentary home affairs

committee, 1973-75. Former member, Nalgo. Author and film producer.

Mr John Cook, farmer, town planning consultant and management consultant, was educated at Chislehurst and Sidcup Grammar School. B April, 1929.

Miss Anne Weyman, an administrative manager with Amnesty International. Member, Westminster City Council, since 1978. B February 1943; ed Bristol University and LSE ASTMS.

BROMLEY, Ravensbourne

Electorate 47,601   1974: 48,541

*Hunt, J. L. (C)	22,501
Shipley, W. (L)	7,111
Holbrook, J. R. (Lab)	6,848
Greene, S. (Nat Front)	478
C majority	15,390

No Change

	1974		1979
Total votes	35,909		36,938
Turnout	74·0%		77·6%
C	18,318	51·0%	60·9%
L	9,813	27·3%	19·3%
Lab	7,204	20·1%	18·5%
Nat Front	574	1·6%	1·3%
C maj	8,505	23·7%	41·6%
Swing		−1·6%	+5·7%

Mr John Hunt, a public relations consultant, was returned in February 1974; MP for Bromley 1964-74; contested Lewisham, South, 1959. B October 1929; ed Dulwich College. Mayor of Bromley, 1963-64; member, Bromley Borough Council, 1953-65. Vice-chairman, Greater London Conservative MPs, since 1972. Joint Secretary, Parliamentary human rights

group. Former Vice-chairman, now Vice-President of British-Caribbean Association. Vice-chairman, Indo-British Parliamentary group. Member, BBC General Advisory Council.

Mr William Shipley, pharmacist, contested Bromley, 1964, and Newham, South, in February and October, 1974. Also fought a by-election in 1974. Served on Bromley Borough Council, 1963-64. B January, 1923; ed Eggar's Grammar School, Alton, Hants, Chelsea College of Science and Technology and the Open University.

Mr John Holbrook, teacher; director of the League Against Cruel Sports. B January 1945; ed Sir John Talbot's Grammar School and London University. NUT.

BROMSGROVE AND REDDITCH

Electorate: 104,375   1974: 87,849

*Miller, H. D. (C)	44,621
Davis, Mrs A. (Lab)	28,736
Phillips, N. (L)	8,066
Deakin, B. A. (Nat Front)	752
C majority	15,885

No Change

	1974		1979
Total votes	69,917		82,175
Turnout	79·6%		78·7%
C	31,153	44·6%	54·3%
Lab	29,085	41·6%	35·0%
L	9,679	13·8%	9·8%
Nat Front	—	—	0·9%
C maj	2,068	3·0%	19·3%
Swing		−1·0%	+8·1%

Mr Hilary Miller, a company director, gained the seat in February, 1974. Joint secretary, Conservative housing and construction committee, since 1974. Delegate, Council of Europe and WEU since 1974. Contested Bromsgrove in a 1971 by-election and Barrow-in-Furness, 1970. Company director. B March, 1929; ed Eton, Merton College, Oxford, and London University. Joint chairman, all-party motor industry group, 1978. Member, Select Committee on Race Relations and Immigration. With the Colonial Service in Hongkong 1955-68. Fellow of the Economic Development Institute of the World Bank. Treasurer, all-party Anglo-Chinese group.

Mrs Anne Davis, housewife and former teacher. Member, Hereford and Worcester County Council since 1973, and of Redditch Development Corporation Board. B September 1938, ed Newton-le-Willows Grammar School, University College, London and University of London. Member, National Council for One-Parent Families.

Mr Nigel Phillips, sales executive. B April 1956; ed Prince Henry's Grammar School, Evesham, and Leicester University.

BUCKINGHAM

Electorate 103,511   1974: 79,077

*Benyon, W. R. (C)	41,719
Fryer, J. S. (Lab)	27,752
Crooks, S. B. (L)	11,045
Smith, M. (Nat Front)	803
C majority	13,967

No Change

	1974		1979
Total votes	62,983		81,319
Turnout	79·6%		78·6%
C	26,597	42·2%	51·3%
Lab	23,679	37·6%	34·1%
L	12,707	20·2%	13·6%
Nat Front	—		1·0%
C maj	2,918	4·6%	17·2%
Swing		−0·1%	+6·3%

Mr William Benyon, an Opposition Whip since 1974, won the seat for the Conservatives in 1970. Farmer. B January, 1930; ed Royal Naval College, Dartmouth. Member, Select Committee on Expenditure; Berkshire County Council, 1964-74; Bradfield Rural Council, 1960-62; Council of Reading University; Council of Bradfield College. Trustee, Thames Valley Trustee Savings Bank. Governor, Dominion Students Hall Trust.

Mr John Fryer, journalist, fought Harwich, February and October 1974. B February 1945, ed Chigwell School. NUJ branch secretary and regional council member.

Mr Samuel Crooks, university teacher, contested the seat February and October, 1974. B Dec, 1946; ed Campbell College, Belfast and Jesus College, Cambridge. AUT.

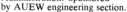

BURNLEY

Electorate 51,050   1974: 52,930

*Jones, D. (Lab)	20,172
Widdecombe, Miss A. (C)	14,062
Steed, M. (L)	5,091
Tyrrall, F. (Democrat)	352
Lab majority	6,110

No Change

	1974		1979
Total votes	39,527		39,677
Turnout	74·7%		77·7%
Lab	21,642	54·8%	50·8%
C	9,766	24·7%	35·4%
L	8,119	20·5%	12·8%
Democrat	—		0·9%
Lab maj	11,876	30·1%	15·4%
Swing		−3·3%	+7·3%

Mr Daniel Jones, an engineer and AUEW official for more than 20 years, has represented the constituency since 1959; contested Barry, 1955. B September, 1908; ed Ynyshir (Rhondda) School and National Council of Labour Colleges, where he became a lecturer. Member, Select Committee on Parliamentary Commissioner for Administration. Sponsored by AUEW engineering section.

Miss Ann Widdecombe, financial administrator at University of London, was educated at Royal Naval School (Singapore), La Sainte Union Convent (Bath), University of Birmingham and Lady Margaret Hall (Oxford). Secretary and Treasurer of Oxford Union. Research assistant to Mr Richard Luce, a Conservative spokesman on foreign affairs. Joint secretary to Conservative Parliamentary Group on disablement income. AUT.

Mr Michael Steed, university teacher, contested Manchester Central, February 1974, Manchester, Exchange, by-election, June 1973; Truro, 1970, and the Brierley Hill, 1967 by-election. B January, 1940; ed Corpus Christi College, Cambridge and Nuffield College, Oxford. AUT. President of the Liberal Party, 1978-79.

BURTON

Electorate 70,130   1974: 67,801

*Lawrence, I. J. (C)		29,821
Jones, G. S. (Lab)		20,020
Stevens, K. (L)		5,383
C majority		9,801

No Change

	1974		1979
Total votes	52,863		55,224
Turnout	78·0%		78·7%
C	23,496	44·4%	54·0%
Lab	21,398	40·5%	36·3%
L	7,969	15·1%	9·7%
C maj	2,098	3·9%	17·7%
Swing		−1·2%	+6·9%

Mr Ivan Lawrence, barrister, was elected in February 1974. B December, 1936; ed Brighton, Hove and Sussex Grammar School; Christ Church, Oxford. Contested Peckham in 1966 and 1970. Member, Expenditure select committee sub-committee on social services and employment. Secretary, Conservative legal committee 1974-77. Member, joint parliamentary committee on consolidation of statutes. President, National Association of Approved Driving Instructors.

Mr Gordon Jones, industrial relations officer, NCB; member, Stoke on Trent City Council, for 10 years, Midlands Electricity Consultative Council and the British Association of Colliery Managers. B June, 1928; ed Ruskin College, Oxford. AUEW (TASS).

Mr Keith Stevens, farmer and journalist, fought Seat in October, 1974. Chairman, British Youth Council, 1970-71, and of National Federation of Young Farmers Clubs, 1971. B December, 1935; ed grammar school and agricultural college.

BURY AND RADCLIFFE

Electorate 78,021   1974: 77,798

*White, F. R. (Lab)		29,194
Le Bosquet, P. J. (C)		29,156
Vickers, S. (L)		5,711
Bridge, J. M. (Nat Front)		414
Lab majority		38

No Change

	1974		1979
Total votes	62,881		64,475
Turnout	80·8%		82·6%
Lab	26,430	42·0%	45·3%
C	25,988	41·3%	45·2%
L	10,463	16·6%	8·9%
Nat Front	—	—	0·6%
Lab maj	442	0·7%	0·1%
Swing		−0·7%	+0·3%

Mr Frank White, industrial relations manager, was assistant Government whip 1976-November, 1978. Won the seat in October, 1974; contested it in February, 1974. B November, 1939, ed Bolton Technical College. Member, industry and trade union groups, PLP. Member, all-party textile and paper industry groups. Vice-chairman, Parliamentary Labour Friends of Israel. Member, Bolton County Borough Council 1963-64; and of Greater Manchester County Council, 1973-75. Sponsored by GMWU. Member, committee of inquiry into Commons refreshment department, 1975.

Mr Peter Le Bosquet unsuccessfully contested Don Valley in both the 1974 elections. A director and chief executive of a large furniture group. B December, 1947; ed High Pavement Grammar School, Nottingham, and Clarendon College, Nottingham. Former Chairman, East Midlands Young Conservatives and YC national vice-chairman, 1971-72. Former member, National Union Executive Committee of National Union General Purposes Committee and of Young Conservatives National Advisory Committee. Vice-chairman, West Nottingham Conservative Association.

Mr Stuart Vickers, an accountant. Chairman, Radcliffe Liberal Association. B October, 1950; ed North Salford Secondary School. NACO.

BURY ST EDMUNDS

Electorate 95,621   1974: 87,321

*Griffiths, E. W. (C)		41,426
Gibson, Mrs A. (Lab)		21,167
Jones, G. (L)		10,386
C majority		20,259

No Change

	1974		1979
Total votes	63,907		72,979
Turnout	73·2%		76·3%
C	32,179	50·4%	56·8%
Lab	21,097	33·0%	29·0%
L	10,631	16·6%	14·2%
C maj	11,082	17·4%	27·8%
Swing		−0·7%	+5·2%

Mr Eldon Griffiths was Opposition spokesman on Europe in 1975-76; a spokesman on trade and industry 1974-75, Under-Secretary for the Environment, with special responsibilities for sport, 1970-74. Returned at a by-election in May, 1964. Parliamentary Secretary, Ministry of Housing and Local Government, 1970. Journalist; Parliamentary adviser to the Police Federation of England and Wales 1966-70 and since 1974. B May 1925; ed Ashton Grammar School; Emmanuel College, Cam-Chairman, British Iranian Parliamentary Group. Served in the Conservative research department. Chief European correspondent of *Washington Post,* 1961-63. Director of several companies.

Mrs Anne Gibson, advertising manager of *The House* magazine; previously Labour Party organiser. B December, 1940; ed Caistor Grammar School and Essex University. TGWU.

Mr Graham Jones, chief auditor. Aged 35.

CAERNARVON

Electorate 43,041   1974: 42,508

*Wigley, D. (Pl Cymru)	17,420
Hughes, T. M. (Lab)	8,696
Paice, J. E. T. (C)	6,968
Edwards, J. T. (L)	1,999

Pl Cymru majority	8,724

No Change

	1974		1979
Total votes	34,369		35,083
Turnout	80·9%		81·5%
Pl Cymru	14,624	42·5%	49·7%
Lab	11,730	34·1%	24·8%
C	4,325	12·6%	19·9%
L	3,690	10·7%	5·7%
Pl Cymru maj	2,894	8·4%	24·9%

Mr Dafydd Wigley won the seat February, 1974, and became party spokesman on finance and taxation. Vice chairman of Plaid Cymru. Financial controller, Hoover Ltd, 1971-74; chief cost accountant and financial planning manager, Mars Ltd, 1967-71; finance staff, Ford Motor Company, 1964-67. Served on Merthyr Borough Council. B April 1943; ed Caernarvon Grammar School, Rydal School, Colwyn Bay, and Manchester University.

Mr Thomas Hughes, barrister. B April, 1949; ed Liverpool University.

Mr James Paice, stock farmer and branding contractor. B 1949; ed Framlingham College, Suffolk; Essex College of Agriculture. Member, Suffolk Coastal District Council, since 1976. Treasurer, Eye Conservative Association.

Mr John Edwards, legal executive. Aged 48.

CAERPHILLY

Electorate 58,008   1974: 56,162

Davies, E. H. (Lab)	27,280
Ranelagh, J. O. (C)	8,783
Williams, P. J. S. (Pl Cymru)	6,931
Jones, N. (L)	3,430

Lab majority	18,497

No Change

	1974		1979
Total votes	42,694		46,424
Turnout	75·6%		78·8%
Lab	24,161	56·6%	58·8%
Pl Cymru	10,452	24·5%	14·9%
C	4,897	11·5%	18·9%
L	3,184	7·5%	7·4%
Lab maj	13,709	32·1%	39·9%
Swing		-0·8%	+2·6%

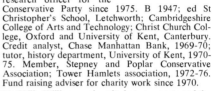

Mr Ednyfed Hudson Davies was MP for Conway 1966-70. Lecturer and barrister. B December, 1929; ed Dunevor Grammar School, Swansea, University College of Wales, Swansea, and Balliol College, Oxford. Member, Select Committee on Agriculture, 1966-70. Former chairman, Wales Tourist Board. TGWU.

Mr John Ranelagh, a research officer for the Conservative Party since 1975. B 1947; ed St Christopher's School, Letchworth; Cambridgeshire College of Arts and Technology; Christ Church College, Oxford and University of Kent, Canterbury. Credit analyst, Chase Manhattan Bank, 1969-70; tutor, history department, University of Kent, 1970-75. Member, Stepney and Poplar Conservative Association; Tower Hamlets association, 1972-76. Fund raising adviser for charity work since 1970.

Mr Philip Williams, university lecturer, contested the seat, 1964, 1968 by-election, 1970, and February and October, 1974. B January, 1939; ed Lewis School, Pengam, and Clare College, Cambridge. ASTMS.

Mr Norman Jones, lecturer in management education, Polytechnic of Wales. B April, 1944; ed Newport High School and Exeter and Bath Universities.

CAITHNESS AND SUTHERLAND

Electorate 29,564   1974: 28,837

*MacLennan, R. A. R. (Lab)	9,613
Wardrop, R. H. (C)	7,074
Shaw, R. (Scot Nat)	6,487

Lab majority	2,539

No Change

	1974		1979
Total votes	22,511		23,174
Turnout	78·1%		78·4%
Lab	7,941	35·3%	41·5%
Scot Nat	5,381	23·9%	28·0%
L	4,949	22·0%	—
C	4,240	18·8%	30·5%
Lab maj	2,560	11·4%	11·0%
Swing		-1·0%	+2·7%

Mr Robert MacLennan, Under Secretary for Prices and Consumer Protection, 1974-79. Opposition spokesman on Scottish Affairs, 1970-72, and defence, 1972 to 1974. Won the seat in March, 1966. Barrister (Gray's Inn, 1962). B June 1936; ed Glasgow Academy, Balliol College, Oxford, Trinity College, Cambridge and Columbia University, New York. Member, Estimates Committee 1967-69; Scottish Labour Committee for Europe; 1963 Club; Fabian Society. GMWU.

Mr Richard Wardrop, business agent. Chairman, Conon Bridge branch of Ross and Cromarty Conservative Association, 1975-78. Member, Scottish Northern Area Conservative Council. B 1923; ed high school and Scottish College of Commerce, Glasgow.

Mr Robert Shaw, novelist. B April, 1937; ed Glasgow University and Western Washington University.

CAMBRIDGE

Electorate 77,666   1974: 75,947

*James, R. V. R. (C)	25,568
Smith, M. H. (Lab)	20,772
Wakelin, J. D. (L)	9,285
Holland, D. W. (Nat Front)	311

C majority	4,796

No Change

	1974		1979
Total votes	52,821		55,936
Turnout	69·5%		72·0%
C	21,790	41·3%	45·7%
Lab	19,017	36·0%	37·1%
L	11,129	21·1%	16·6%
UDP	885	1·7%	—
Nat Front	—		0·6%
C maj	2,773	5·3%	8·6%
Swing		−1·3%	+1·6%

1976 by-election: Total votes 38,451 (49·1%)—C 19,620 (51·0%); Lab 9,995 (26·0%); L 7,051 (18·3%); Nat Front 700 (1·8%); others 1,085 (2·8%). C majority 9,625 (25·0%).

Mr Robert Rhodes James, a historian and business consultant, was elected to the seat for the Conservatives in the December, 1976, by-election. B April, 1933, ed Sedbergh School, Yorkshire and Worcester College, Oxford. Member, Commons Expenditure Committee. Secretary, Conservative constitutional committee; member, foreign and Commonwealth

affairs committee, smaller businesses committee. Senior Clerk, House of Commons, 1961-64. Fellow of All Souls, Oxford. Executive assistant to the Secretary-General the United Nations, 1973-76. Political biographer.

Mr Martin Smith contested the seat in the 1976 by-election. Industrial adviser. B April, 1951; ed King Edward's School, Birmingham, and Cambridge University. ASTMS.

Mr John Wakelin, headmaster and author. B January, 1929; ed Maldon Grammar School and Christ Church, Oxford.

CAMBRIDGESHIRE

Electorate 93,179   1974: 84,434

*Pym, F. L. (C)	41,218
Collins, R. (Lab)	17,929
Jakobi, S. R. (L)	13,780

C majority	23,289

No Change

	1974		1979
Total votes	64,202		72,927
Turnout	76·0%		78·3%
C	30,508	47·5%	56·5%
Lab	17,853	27·8%	24·6%
L	15,841	24·7%	18·9%
C maj	12,655	19·7%	31·9%
Swing		−0·8%	+6·1%

Mr Francis Pym, who became Secretary of State for Defence in May 1979, was chief Opposition spokesman on devolution and House of Commons Affairs until November, 1978, when appointed spokesman on Foreign and Commonwealth Affairs; previously spokesman on agriculture, fisheries and food and Northern Ireland. Secretary of State for

Northern Ireland 1973-74. Returned in the 1961 by-election. Parliamentary Secretary to the Treasury and Government Chief Whip, 1970-73. Contested Rhondda, West, 1959. Company director and farmer. B February, 1922; ed Eton and Magdalene College, Cambridge. Assistant Government whip 1962-64. Opposition whip, 1964-67; Opposition Deputy Chief Whip 1967-70. Chairman, Conservative constitutional backbench committee since 1976. Member, Herefordshire County Council, 1958-61.

Mr Robert Collins, commercial manager of British Transport Docks Board. B September, 1942; ed St James Secondary School, Burnt Oak, Middlesex. Deputy leader of Labour group, Harrow Borough Council. TSSA.

Mr Stephen Jakobi, a solicitor. Aged 44; ed Clare College, Cambridge and Swansea College of Technology. Contested the seat in February and October, 1974, Windsor and Maidenhead, 1966, Cities of London and Westminster, 1965, and Battersea, North, 1964.

CAMDEN, Hampstead

Electorate 64,004   1974: 64,085

*Finsberg, G. (C)	20,410
Livingstone, K. R. (Lab)	16,729
Radford, D. (L)	5,753
White, Mrs J. (Nat Front)	255

C majority	3,681.

No Change

	1974		1979
Total votes	40,414		43,147
Turnout	63·1%		67·4%
C	18,139	44·9%	47·3%
Lab	16,414	40·6%	38·8%
L	5,566	13·8%	13·3%
I Civ Rights	146	0·4%	—
Soc Pty of GB	118	0·3%	—
Ind	31	0·1%	—
Nat Front	—		0·6%
C maj	1,725	4·3%	8·5%
Swing		−0·4%	+2·1%

Mr Geoffrey Finsberg, Opposition spokesman on London, 1974-79, gained Hampstead for the Conservatives in 1970; contested Islington East. 1955. Industrial relations adviser. B June 1926; ed City of London School, Member, Hampstead Borough Council 1949-65; Camden Borough Council, 1964-74 (leader, 1968-70). Vice-chairman, Conservative

parliamentary committee on trade 1972-73. Member, Commons Expenditure Committee (defence and external affairs sub-committee) since 1974; executive 1922 committee. Chief industrial relations adviser and personnel controller, Great Universal Stores Ltd. ASTMS.

Mr **Kenneth Livingstone,** teacher. B June 1945, ed Tulse Hill Comprehensive School and Phillipa Fawcett College of Education. Member, Lambeth Council, 1971-78, and Greater London Council, since 1973. TGWU.

Mr **David Radford,** barrister, B January, 1947; ed Cranleigh School and Selwyn College, Cambridge.

CAMDEN, Holborn and St Pancras, South

Electorate 40,376   1974: 39,171

Dobson, F. G. (Lab)	12,026
Key, R. (C)	9,703
Hibbert, T. (L)	2,190
Theobald, F. (Nat Front)	334
Farrell, P. (WRP)	134
Lab majority	2,323

No Change

	1974		1979
Total votes	21077		24,387
Turnout	53·8%		60·4%
Lab	11,790	55·9%	49·3%
C	6,349	30·1%	39·8%
L	2,938	13·9%	9·0%
Nat Front	—		1·4%
WRP	—		0·5%
Lab maj	5,441	25·8%	9·5%
Swing		−4·6%	+8·1%

Mr **Frank Dobson** is an assistant secretary, local government Ombudsman. Member, Camden Borough Council, 1971-76, and leader of the council, 1973-75. B March, 1940; ed Archbishop Holgate Grammar School, York, and LSE.

Mr **Robert Key,** teacher. B 1945; ed Sherborne School, Dorset, and Clare College, Cambridge. Former vice-chairman, Harrow, Central, Conservative Association. Former member, Harrow education committee. Chairman, governors of special school, Great Ormond Street Hospital for Sick Children.

Mr **Thomas Hibbert,** an educationist, contested the seat, October, 1974, and Camden, Holborn and St Pancras, South, February, 1974. B March, 1925; ed Hawick High School, Cheshire Commercial College, Morley College, London. Employed by ILEA. NUT.

CAMDEN, St Pancras, North

Electorate 42,106   1974: 41,629

*Stallard, A. W. (Lab)	14,556
Kirwan, P. (C)	9,110
Valentine, M. (L)	2,654
Andrews, S. (Nat Front)	360
Jones, G. (WRP)	159
Lab majority	5,446

No Change

	1974		1979
Total votes	24,185		26,839
Turnout	58·1%		63·7%
Lab	14,155	58·5%	54·2%
C	6,602	27·3%	33·9%
L	3,428	14·2%	9·9%
Nat Front	—		1·3%
WRP	—		0·6%
Lab maj	7,553	31·2%	20·3%
Swing		−3·4%	+5·4%

Mr **Albert Stallard,** a Government whip, was elected in 1970. Chairman, all-party committee for homeless and rootless. Member, all-party groups on pensioners and mental health. B November, 1921; ed Low Waters, and Hamilton Academy. Training officer. Member, St Pancras Borough Council, 1953-64, and Camden Council, 1964-79. Sponsored by AUEW (engineering section). Chairman, Camden Town Disablement Committee and Camden Association for Mental Health.

Mr **Peter Kirwan,** stockbroker and associated member of the British Institute of Management. Formerly a regular soldier. B 1930; educated in India, Portora, Northern Ireland and at Sandhurst.

Mr **Malcolm Valentine,** company director, contested Dunfermline, February and October, 1974. B February, 1937; ed Clifton Hall School, Midlothian and Sedbergy School, Yorkshire.

CANNOCK

Electorate 59,511   1974: 56,572

*Roberts, G. E. (Lab)	25,050
Vereker, J. (C)	17,704
Davis, P. J. (L)	4,729
Lab majority	7,346

No Change

	1974		1979
Total votes	43,011		47,483
Turnout	76·0%		79·8%
Lab	23,887	55·5%	52·8%
C	11,665	27·1%	37·3%
L	7,459	17·3%	10·0%
Lab maj	12,222	28·4%	15·5%
Swing		−2·3%	+6·4%

Mr **Gwilym Roberts** was elected in February, 1974. MP for Bedfordshire, South, 1966-70. Contested Conway, 1964, and Ormskirk, 1959. B August, 1928; ed Brynefail Grammar School and University of Wales. Principal lecturer, Hendon College of Technology, 1957-66. Industrial consultant, market and operational research.

Mr **John Vereker** contested the seat in 1964. A personnel manager and member of the Institute of Personnel Management and an Associate of the British Institute of Management. B 1935; ed Kelly College, Tavistock. Member, Warwickshire County Council, 1961-73, and of new county council, since 1973.

Mr **Peter Davis,** social worker, fought Birmingham, Edgbaston, in October, 1974. B September, 1933; ed Queen Mary's School, Walsall, St Luke's College, Exeter, and the Open University. Nalgo.

73

CANTERBURY

Electorate 89,104   1974: 85,718

*Crouch, D. L. (C)	38,805
Spencer, R. P. (Lab)	16,168
Purchese, J, (L)	10,665
White, Miss J. (Nat Front)	941

C majority	22,637

No Change

	1974		1979
Total votes	62,243		66,579
Turnout	72·6%		74·7%
C	31,002	49·8%	58·3%
Lab	16,247	26·1%	24·3%
L	13,898	22·3%	16·0%
Nat Front	1,096	1·8%	1·4%
C maj	14,755	23·7%	34·0%
Swing		−1·8%	+5·1%

Mr David Crouch, company
director, public relations
and marketing consultant.
Elected in 1966; contested
Leeds West, 1959. B June,
1919; ed University College
School, London. Member,
Select Committee on
Nationalised Industries,
1966-74; Select Committee
on Public Accounts, since
1974. Vice-chairman, Con-
servative Industry com-
mittee, 1971-74. Member,

South-East Thames Regional Health Authority.
Member, Council of University of Kent. Director,
Burson Marsteller Ltd, Pfizer Ltd and David Crouch
& Co.

Mr Robin Spencer, transport manager with National
Freight Corporation. B August, 1947; ed Woking
County Grammar School, Bristol University. TSSA.

Mr John Purchese, printer, served on Canterbury City
Council, 1976 and Kent County Council, 1977.
Former sound recordist; now runs a printing business.
B February, 1925; ed Steyning Grammar School and
Ardingly College, both Sussex.

CARDIFF, North

Electorate 47,973   1974: 43,858

*Grist, I. (C)	17,181
Petrou, M. D. (Lab)	13,133
German, M. J. (L)	4,921
Thomas, O. J. (Pl Cymru)	1,081

C majority	4,048

No Change

	1974		1979
Total votes	32,151		36,316
Turnout	73·3%		75·7%
C	13,480	41·9%	47·3%
Lab	11,479	35·7%	36·2%
L	5,728	17·8%	13·6%
Pl Cymru	1,464	4·6%	3·0%
C maj	2,001	6·2%	11·1%
Swing		−2·6%	+2·4%

Mr Ian Grist was an
information officer at the
Welsh Conservative Party
office. Elected in February,
1974; contested Aberavon,
1970. Born December,
1938; ed Repton and Jesus
College, Oxford. Secretary,
Welsh Conservative MPs
since 1974. Member, Select
Committee on Violence in
the Family; chairman, Conservative West African
Affairs Committee.

Mr Owen John Thomas, deputy head teacher. B
October, 1939; ed Howardian High School, Cardiff,
and Glamorgan College of Education. UCAC
(National Union of Teachers in Wales).

Mr Michael German, teacher, contested the seat,
October, 1974. B May, 1945; ed St Mary's College,
Twickenham, the Open University and Bristol
Polytechnic. National official (honorary), NAS.

CARDIFF, North-West

Electorate 43,639   1974: 43,787

*Roberts, M. H. (C)	17,925
Owen, P. H. (Lab Co-op)	11,663
Roberts, J. T. (L)	4,832
Palfrey, C. F. (Pl Cymru)	743

C majority	6,262

No Change

	1974		1979
Total votes	34,571		35,163
Turnout	79·0%		80·6%
C	15,652	45·3%	51·0%
Lab	11,319	32·7%	33·2%
L	6,322	18·3%	13·7%
Pl Cymru	1,278	3·7%	2·1%
C maj	4,333	12·6%	17·8%
Swing		−2·1%	+2·6%

Mr Michael Roberts
became an Under Secretary
of State for Wales in May
1979. An Opposition Whip
since July, 1974, he was
elected in February, 1974;
MP for Cardiff, North, from
1970-74. Contested
Cardiff, South-East, in
1959 and 1955, and
Aberdare in the 1954 by-
election. Former
headmaster. B May, 1927;

ed Neath Grammar School
and University College, Cardiff. Former chairman,
Conservative education committee; past president,
Cardiff Association, National Union of Teachers.
Joint vice-chairman, Conservative education committee, 1974.

Mr Peter Owen, a senior lecturer, contested Weston-
Super-Mare, October, 1974. B May, 1927; ed Penarth
County School, Glamorgan; University College,
Cardiff; Trinity College, Carmarthen and London
University. Member, Cardiff City Council, 1973-76;
deputy chairman, liaison committee and tattoo com-
mittee. NATFHE.

Mr Colin Palfrey, local government officer, contested
the seat, February and October, 1974. B July, 1939;
ed University College, Cardiff, and King's College,
London. Member, Caerphilly UDC, 1970-74, and of
Rhymney Valley District Council, since 1976.

Mr John Roberts, solicitor, Welsh Liberal Party
chairman. Aged 32.

CARDIFF, South-East

Electorate 54,556   1974: 57,299

*Callaghan, L. J. (Lab)	23,871
Jones, I. A. S. (C)	15,170
Roberts, E. R. (Pl Cymru)	628
Aldridge, R. W. (SL)	375
Arrowsmith, Miss P. (Ind Soc)	132
Spencer, R. H. (Comm)	112
Lab majority	8,701

No Change

	1974		1979
Total votes	40,554		40,288
Turnout	70·8%		73·8%
Lab	21,074	52·0%	59·3%
C	10,356	25·5%	37·7%
L	8,066	19·9%	—
Pl Cymru	983	2·4%	1·6%
Marx Len	75	0·2%	—
SL	—	—	0·9%
Ind Soc	—	—	0·3%
Comm	—	—	0·3%
Lab maj	10,718	26·5%	21·6%
Swing		−4·8%	+2·4%

Mr James Callaghan the Leader of the Opposition from May 1979 succeeded Mr (now Sir Harold) Wilson as Prime Minister on April 5, 1976, upon election as leader of the Labour Party. Secretary of State for Foreign and Commonwealth Affairs, 1974-76. Was chief Opposition spokesman on Foreign and Commonwealth Affairs 1972-74; employment

1971-72; Home Office matters, 1970-71. Home Secretary 1967-70, and Chancellor of the Exchequer, 1964-67. Chairman of the Labour Party 1973-74, member, national executive 1957-67, and party treasurer 1967-76. Parliamentary Secretary to the Admiralty, 1950-51, after three years as Parliamentary Secretary to the Ministry of Transport. Labour spokesman on Treasury Affairs, 1961-64. Elected for Cardiff, South, 1945 and for Cardiff, South-East, 1950. B March, 1912; ed at elementary and Portsmouth Northern Secondary Schools.

Mr Alun Jones, contested Pontypridd, February and October, 1974. B December 1937; ed grammar school and University College of Wales, Aberystwyth. Solicitor and company director. Former chairman, Pontypridd Conservative Association.

Mr Eric Roberts, bus driver. Aged 46. Ex regular soldier. Steward, National Stadium, Cardiff.

Miss Pat Arrowsmith, professional gardener. B March 1930; ed Stover, Cheltenham and the universities of Cambridge, Liverpool and Ohio. Leading activist against nuclear armaments; campaigned on withdrawal of troops from Northern Ireland. Contested Fulham, 1966 and 1970.

Mr Richard Spencer, aged 62, senior lecturer in French at University College, Cardiff. President, local branch AUT.

CARDIFF, West

Electorate 51,982   1974: 52,083

*Thomas, G. (The Speaker)	27,035
Ogwen, A. (Pl Cymru)	3,272
Gibbon, C. (Nat Front)	1,287
Speaker majority	23,763

No Change

	1974		1979
Total votes	36,311		31,594
Turnout	69·7%		60·8%
Lab	18,153	50·0%	—
The Speaker	—	—	85·6%
C	11,481	31·6%	—
L	4,669	12·9%	—
Pl Cymru	2,008	5·5%	10·4%
Nat Front	—	—	4·1%
Lab maj	6,672	18·4%	—
The Speaker maj	—	—	75·2%
Swing		−4·8%	—

Mr George Thomas was elected Speaker in February, 1976, on the retirement of the then Mr Selwyn Lloyd. Chairman of Ways and Means and Deputy Speaker, 1974-76. Secretary of State for Wales, 1968-70; Chief Opposition spokesman for Wales, 1970-74. Elected in 1945 for Cardiff, Central, and in 1950 for Cardiff, West. Minister of State,

Commonwealth Office, 1967-68; Minister of State, Welsh Office, 1966-67. Under-Secretary, Home Office, 1964-66. Teacher. B January, 1909; ed at Tonypandy Secondary School and University College, Southampton. Chairman, Welsh Parliamentary Party, 1958-59. Vice-president, Methodist Conference, 1960-61. Elected Fellow, University College, Cardiff, 1973.

Mr Alun Ogwen, head of science departments at a bilingual comprehensive school. Fought West Flint, 1970. B August 1939; ed Grove Park Boys Grammar School, Wrexham, and Liverpool University. Member, Holywell UDC, 1970-74.

CARDIGAN

Electorate 45,555   1974: 43,052

*Howells, G. W. (L)	13,227
Thomas, E. (C)	11,033
Powell, L. J. (Lab)	7,488
Hughes, Dr D. (Pl Cymru)	5,382
L majority	2,194

No Change

	1974		1979
Total votes	34,654		37,130
Turnout	80·5%		81·5%
L	14,612	42·2%	35·6%
Lab	12,202	35·2%	20·2%
Pl Cymru	4,583	13·2%	14·5%
C	3,257	9·4%	29·7%
L maj	2,410	7·0%	5·9%

Mr Geraint Howells, president, and former chairman, of the Welsh Liberal Party. A farmer, he won the seat in February, 1974. Liberal spokesman on agriculture and Wales since July, 1976. Contested Brecon and Radnor, 1970. B April, 1925, ed Ardwyn Grammar School. Member, Cardiganshire County Council since 1952. Served as Welsh Board member, British Wool Marketing Board.

Mr Emlyn Thomas owns a glass fibre company; formerly a farmer. B 1923; ed Llandovery Grammar School and Wolverhampton Technical College.

Former general secretary, Farmers' Union of Wales.
Mr John Powell, barrister and former lecturer. B September, 1950; ed Christ College, Brecon, Amman Valley Grammar School and Cambridge University. Member, Society of Labour Lawyers, NATFHE.

Dr Dafydd Hughes, consultant psychiatrist, University College of Wales Hospital. First Plaid Cymru member of Cardiff City Council. The party's health spokesman. Aged 42.

CARLISLE

Electorate 53,703   1974: 21,079

*Lewis, R. H. (Lab)	21,343
Bloomer, D. (C)	16,777
Potts, T. (L)	4,829
Lab majority	4,566

No Change

	1974		1979
Total votes	41,210		42,949
Turnout	78·8%		80·0%
Lab	21,079	51·2%	49·7%
C	14,825	36·0%	39·1%
L	5,306	12·9%	11·2%
Lab maj	6,254	15·2%	10·6%
Swing		−1·7%	+2·3%

Mr Ronald Lewis, a former British Rail employee, was elected in 1964; contested West Derbyshire, 1951; South Northants 1955; and Darlington, 1959. B July, 1909; ed elementary school and Cliff Methodist College. Member, Select Committee on Expenditure. Sponsored by NUR. Vice-chairman, PLP Trade Union Group. Vice-chairman, PLP Transport

Group. President, Pleasley Cooperative Society Ltd since 1954. Member, executive committee, British section International Union of Local Authorities. Served on Derbyshire County Council and Blackwell RDC. Director, Ansuar Insurance Company.

Mr David Bloomer, a publisher and barrister (Gray's Inn), contested Barrow-in-Furness in February, 1974 and Carlisle in October, 1974. B August, 1941; ed Marlborough College, and Lincoln College, Oxford.

Mr Thomas Potts is a company director, aged 53.

CARLTON

Electorate 76,593   1974: 71,779

*Holland, P. J. (C)	31,762
Palmer, A. (Lab)	18,989
West, J. (L)	9,077
Watts, M. J. (Nat Front)	606
C majority	12,773

No Change

	1974		1979
Total votes	55,789		60,434
Turnout	77·7%		78·9%
C	24,638	44·2%	52·6%
Lab	20,019	35·9%	31·4%
L	9,859	17·7%	15·0%
Nat Front	1,273	2·3%	1·0%
C maj	4,619	8·3%	21·2%
Swing		−1·8%	+6·4%

Mr Philip Holland, an industrial relations consultant, was elected in 1966; MP for Acton, 1959-64; contested Birmingham, Yardley, 1955. B March, 1917; ed Sir John Deane's Grammar School, Northwich. Joint secretary, Conservative parliamentary employment and productivity committee, 1967-70. Vice-chairman, Anglo-Senegalese

parliamentary committee and of Anglo-Laotian parliamentary committee. President, Conservative Trade Union National Advisory Committee, 1971-73. Member, Committee of Selection, since 1974.

Mr Arthur Palmer, miner, leader of the Labour group on Gedling Borough District Council. Urban district councillor for 11 years. Member, NUM, for 43 years. NUM committee member. B April, 1920; ed WEA.

Mr John West, college lecturer. B February, 1929; ed Queens' College, Cambridge. Member, NATFHE. Author and translator of books on Faroe Islands. Mountaineer.

CARMARTHEN

Electorate 61,714   1974: 60,402

Thomas, Dr R. G. (Lab)	18,667
*Evans, G. (Pl Cymru)	16,689
Thomas, N. M. (C)	12,272
Thomas, R. C. C. (L)	4,186
Grice, C. G. (Nat Front)	149
Clarke, E. J. (KBUP)	126
Lab majority	1,978

Lab gain from Pl Cymru

	1974		1979
Total votes	51,707		52,089
Turnout	85·6%		84·4%
Pl Cymru	23,325	45·1%	32·0%
Lab	19,685	38·1%	35·8%
L	5,393	10·4%.	8·0%
C	2,962	5·7%	23·6%
Brit C	342	0·7%	
Nat Front	—		0·3%
KBUD	—		0·2%
Pl Cymru maj	3,640	7·0%	—
Lab maj	—		3·8%
Swing	—		+10·1%

Dr Roger Thomas is a general practitioner. B November, 1925; ed Ammanford Grammar School and London Hospital Medical College. Member, Dyfed County Council, since 1977.

Mr Gwynfor Evans, president of Plaid Cymru since 1945, was MP for Carmarthen, 1966-70. Won this seat again in October

1974; contested the seat in February, 1974, 1966, and 1964; Merioneth, 1945, 1950, 1955 and 1959; and the Aberdare by-election 1954. B September, 1912; ed Barry County School; University College of Wales, Aberystwyth; and St John's College, Oxford. Served on Carmarthenshire County Council, 1949-74. Farmer and market gardener.

Mr Nigel Thomas is a barrister. B 1952; ed Whitland Grammar School, University College, Wales, and Emmanuel College, Cambridge. Chairman, University College Federation of Conservative

Students for three years. Founded student branch of Society of Conservative Lawyers.

Mr Clem Thomas, farmer, company director and journalist, contested Gower in February, 1974. Chief Rugby correspondent of *The Observer*. B January 1929; ed Blondell's School and St John's College, Cambridge. Member, executive committee, Wales Council for the Disabled.

CHEADLE

Electorate 67,362   1974: 65,558

*Normanton, T. (C)	32,407
Austrick, D. (L)	15,268
Done, Mrs F. W. (Lab)	7,415
C majority	17,139

No Change

	1974		1979
Total votes	52,598		55,090
Turnout	80·2%		81·8%
C	25,863	49·2%	58·8%
L	18,687	35·5%	27·7%
Lab	8,048	15·3%	13·5%
C maj	7,176	13·7%	31·1%
Swing		−2·0%	+5·7%

Mr Tom Normanton won the seat for the Conservatives in 1970; contested Rochdale, 1964 and 1959. Industrialist and company director. Council member, CBI. B March, 1917; ed Manchester Grammar School, Manchester University and Manchester College of Technology. Member, European Parliament since 1973. Past President, British Textile Employers' Association; Vice-President International Textile Federation. Member, Textile Industrial Training Board, 1967-70, and, since 1968, of Central Training Council.

Mr David Austick, bookseller, won Ripon at the 1973 by-election and lost the seat to the Conservatives in February, 1974, which they retained the following October. Member, Leeds City Council, 1969-75, and West Yorkshire County Council, 1973-77. B March, 1920; ed Leeds. Member, Liberal Party Council.

Mrs Frances Done is a chartered accountant. B May, 1950, ed Colston's Girls School, Bristol, and Manchester University. Member of Manchester City Council from 1975. ASTMS.

CHELMSFORD

Electorate 84,155   1974: 80,042

*St John-Stevas, N. A. F. (C)	33,808
Mole, S. G. (L)	28,337
Reeves, Mrs S. A. (Lab)	6,041
C majority	5,471

No Change

	1974		1979
Total votes	63,377		68,186
Turnout	79·2%		81·0%
C	26,334	41·6%	49·6%
L	22,332	35·2%	41·6%
Lab	14,711	23·2%	8·9%
C maj	4,002	6·4%	8·0%
Swing		−0·2%	+11·1%

Mr Norman St John-Stevas was appointed Chancellor of the Duchy of Lancaster and Leader of the House with responsibility for the arts, May, 1979. Chief Opposition spokesman on education, science and the arts 1974-78 and a member of the shadow Cabinet since June 1974. In November, 1978, appointed spokesman on constitutional and Commons affairs and arts. Minister of State for Education and Science with responsibility for the arts, 1973-74; Under-Secretary for Education and Science, 1972-73. Elected, 1964. Contested Dagenham, 1951. Barrister (Middle Temple, 1953), author and journalist. B May 1929; ed Ratcliffe College, Fitzwilliam College, Cambridge (president of the Union, 1950). Christ Church, Oxford and Yale University. Member. Select Committee on Race Relation and Immigration, 1968-69; Former member, 1922 Commitee executive; former vice-chairman, Northern Ireland and Home Affairs Committees; former secretary, Education Committee Member of Committee of Privileges.

Mr Stuart Mole, charity director, contested the seat, February and October, 1974. Member, Chelmsford Borough Counbcil, since 1972; B January, 1949; ed St Paul's Cathedral Choir School; St John's, Leatherhead; Nottingham, Oxford and London Universities.

Mrs Susan Reeve, housewife and former child guidance worker. B March 1943; ed Dartford Grammar School.

CHELTENHAM

Electorate 64,726   1974: 62,746

*Irving, C. (C)	25,618
Jones, N. (L)	15,080
Reilley, M. (Lab)	9,185
Jacklin, R. (Nat Front)	342
C majority	10,538

No Change

	1974		1979
Total votes	47,062		50,225
Turnout	75·0%		77·6%
C	21,691	46·1%	51·0%
L	13,237	28·1%	30·0%
Lab	12,134	25·8%	18·3%
Nat Front	—	—	0·7%
C maj	8,454	18·0%	21·0%
Swing		+1·5%	6·2%

Mr Charles Irving, a director of the Dowty group of companies and other companies, won the seat, October, 1974; contested Bilston, 1970, and Kingswood, February, 1974. Member, Cheltenham Borough Council and Gloucestershire County Council, since 1948; Mayor of Cheltenham, 1958-60 and 1971-72. B May, 1926; ed Glengarth School, Cheltenham, and Lucton School, Herefordshire. Member, Services Committee (catering sub-committee) and Conservative backbench committees on health and social services, aviation and home affairs. Founder and Chairman, National Victims Association.

Mr Nigel Jones, computer consultant. B March, 1948; ed Prince Henry's Grammar School, Evesham. Employed by International Computers Ltd.

Mr Michael Reilly, solicitor. B. 1949; ed Emmanuel School, London and London College of Law. ASTMS.

CHERTSEY AND WALTON

Electorate 68,749   1974: 67,527

*Pattie, G. E. (C)	25,810
Sturgis, A. (L)	13,786
O'Byrne, S. P. (Lab)	12,211
Gillibrand, Mrs M. (Nat Front)	819

C majority	12,024

No Change

	1974		1979
Total votes	49,616		52,626
Turnout	73·5%		76·5%
C	25,151	50·7%	49·0%
Lab	14,847	29·9%	23·2%
L	9,194	18·5%	26·2%
Ind	424	0·9%	—
Nat Front	—	—	1·6%
C maj	10,304	20·8%	22·8%
Swing		−0·5%	+2·5%

Mr Geoffrey Pattie, became Under Secretary of Defence for the RAF in May, 1979. Company director. B January, 1936; ed Durham and St Catharine's College, Cambridge, Barrister. Contested Barking, 1966 and 1970. GLC member for Lambeth, 1968-70. Chairman, Inner London Education Authority finance committee, 1968-70. Member, Public Accounts Committee. Vice-chairman, Conservative aviation committee; joint secretary, Conservative defence committee. Director leading British advertising agency.

Mr Andrew Sturgis, solicitor, served on Walton and Weybridge Council and Surrey County Council, both for four years. B October, 1917; ed Oundle and Balliol College, Oxford.

Mr Shaun O'Byrne, computer consultant. B April 1943; ed Merton Boys' Secondary School; Kingston Technical College; King's College, London University. ASTMS.

CHESHAM AND AMERSHAM

Electorate 67,224   1974: 63,385

*Gilmour, Sir I. (C)	32,924
Bradnock, R. (L)	12,328
Barratt, Mrs E. M. (Lab)	7,645
Clinch, Mrs S. (Nat Front)	697

C majority	20,596

No Change

	1974		1979
Total votes	49,494		53,594
Turnout	78·1%		79·7%
C	25,078	50·7%	61·4%
L	14,091	28·5%	23·0%
Lab	10,325	20·9%	14·3%
Nat Front	—	—	1·3%
C maj	10,987	22·2%	38·4%
Swing		−1·4%	+8·6%

Sir Ian Gilmour, appointed Lord Privy Seal and Commons spokesman on Foreign and Commonwealth Affairs in May 1979. Chief Opposition spokesman on defence 1975-79; spokesman on Northern Ireland, 1974-75. Secretary of State for Defence, 1972-74; Minister of State for Defence Procurement, 1971-72; Under Secretary of State for Defence for the Army, 1970-71. Former chairman, Conservative Research Department. Returned in February, 1974; MP for Norfolk, Central, 1962-74; contested Hounslow, West, by-election, 1962. Journalist and barrister. Editor, Spectator 1954-59. B July, 1926; ed Eton and Balliol College, Oxford. Called to the Bar (Inner Temple) 1952.

Mr Robert Bradnock, university lecturer, Branch committee member, AUT. B December, 1943; ed Eltham College; Fitzwilliam College, Cambridge. Member, Bach Choir; elder, Amersham Free Church.

Mrs Elizabeth Barratt, teacher, former member of parish, urban and district councils. JP. NUT; past district president. B August, 1929; ed Wycombe High School; Goldsmith's College.

Mrs Sheila Clinch, aged 35, housewife.

CHESTER, City of

Electorate 72,027   1974: 69,605

*Morrison, P. H. (C)	28,764
Blair, R. D. (Lab)	19,450
Stunnell, A. (L)	7,711

C majority	9,314

No Change

	1974		1979
Total votes	52,479		55,925
Turnout	75·4%		77·6%
C	23,095	44·0%	51·4%
Lab	18,477	35·2%	34·8%
L	10,907	20·8%	13·8%
C maj	4,618	8·8%	16·6%
Swing		−1·7%	+3·9%

Mr Peter Morrison, appointed a Lord Commissioner of the Treasury, (Government whip) in May, 1979. An Opposition whip since 1976, was elected in February, 1974. Secretary, North-West group of Conservative MPs, 1975-76. Director of farming and hotel companies. B 1944; ed Eton College and Keble College, Oxford. Personal assistant to Mr Peter Walker, 1966-67 and investment manager with Slater Walker Securities Ltd, 1968-70. Partner in farming enterprise in Scotland. Joint vice-chairman, Conservative constitutional committee. Younger brother of Mr Charles Morrison, Conservative MP for Devizes.

Mr Richard Blair, a solicitor in local government. B August 1946; ed Chester Cathedral Choir School; Bromsgrove School, Worcs; Liverpool Polytechnic Law School and Durham University. Member, Amnesty International and Howard League. Parish councillor.

Mr Andrew Stunell, architectural assistant, NALGO branch executive officer and member, staff side of new towns Whitley Council. B November, 1942; ed Surbiton Grammar School and Manchester University. Baptist.

CHESTERFIELD

Electorate 73,738   1974: 71,210

*Varley, E. G. (Lab)	31,049
Hill, S. (C)	17,445
Payne, M. (L)	5,617
Lab majority	13,604

No Change

	1974		1979
Total votes	51,695		54,111
Turnout	72·6%		73·4%
Lab	30,953	59·9%	57·4%
C	13,393	25·9%	32·2%
L	7,349	14·2%	10·4%
Lab maj	17,560	34·0%	25·2%
Swing		−3·4%	+4·4%

Mr Eric Varley, Secretary of State for Industry 1975-79, was Secretary of State for Energy, 1974-75. An Opposition spokesman on regional policy, 1970-72; chief spokesman on fuel and power, 1972-74. Chairman, PLP trade union group, 1972-74. Minister of State, Technology and Power, 1969-70; assistant Government whip, 1967-69. Elected in 1964. Craftsman  in mining industry. B August, 1932; ed secondary school, technical college, and Ruskin College, Oxford. Member, Derbyshire area executive of National Union of Mineworkers, 1955-64. Sponsored by NUM.

Mr Stewart Hill, engineer in electronics firm, and part-time lecturer. B 1945; ed Gateways Boys School and Bristol University. Former chairman, Leicestershire Young Conservatives and former member, National Union Executive Committee. Young Conservative national vice-chairman, 1973.

Mr Max Payne, lecturer, contested Carlton, 1964 and 1966. B January, 1930; ed Heanor Grammar School and Manchester University.

CHESTER-LE-STREET

Electorate 83,415   1974: 68,350

*Radice, G. H. (Lab)	38,672
Couchman, J. R. (C)	16,112
McCourt, D. (L)	9,247
Lab majority	22,560

No Change

	1974		1979
Total votes	51,012		64,031
Turnout	74·6%		76·8%
Lab	33,511	65·7%	60·4%
L	9,233	18·1%	14·4%
C	8,268	16·2%	25·2%
Lab maj	24,278	47·6%	35·2%
Swing		−2·5%	+7·1%

Mr Giles Radice was returned at the 1973 by-election. Contested Chippenham, 1964 and 1966. Head of research department, NUGMW, 1966-73. Vice-chairman, PLP industry group. Member, general sub committee of Expenditure. Committee and of Procedure Committee. Chairman, Fabian Society, 1976-77. B October, 1936;

ed Winchester and Magdalen College, Oxford. Sponsored by GMWU.

Mr James Couchman, general manager of family licensed trade companies. Member, Bexley Borough Council. Chairman, Bexleyheath Conservative Association, 1975-78. B 1942; ed Cranleigh School, Surrey; University of Durham.

CHICHESTER

Electorate 73,720   1974: 69,768

*Nelson, R. A. (C)	34,696
Rix, J. (L)	10,920
Cooke, G. N. (Lab)	8,569
Iremonger, E. (UCP)	863
Bagnall, N. (Ecology)	656
C majority	23,776

No Change

	1974		1979
Total votes	51,310		55,704
Turnout	73·5%		75·6%
C	26,942	52·5%	62·3%
L	15,601	30·4%	19·6%
Lab	8,767	17·1%	15·4%
UCP			1·5%
Ecology	—	—	1·2%
C maj	11,341	22·1%	42·7%
Swing		−1·8%	+5·7%

Mr Anthony Nelson, elected in October, 1974. Business consultant and director of an investment company. Contested Leeds, East, in February, 1974. B. June, 1948; ed Harrow and Christ's College, Cambridge. Member, Select Committee on Science and Technology, Secretary, all-party penal affairs group. Member, all-party dental health  group. Secretary, Conservative industry committee, 1974-77.

Mr John Rix, a chartered accountant, contested Gosport, February, 1974. B. March, 1934; ed Sherborne School.

Mr Geoffrey Cooke, researcher and computer programmer in marine engineering; member, London Borough of Barnet Council, since 1978. B January, 1948; ed Sandown Grammar School, Isle of Wight; University College, London and London University Institute of Computer Science. ASTMS.

CHIPPENHAM

Electorate 74,519   1974: 67,852

Needham, R. (C)	29,308
Banks, R. E. J. (L)	24,611
Inchley, Mrs C. L. B. (Lab)	5,146
Pettit, B. (Ecology)	521
C majority	4,697

No Change

	1974		1979
Total votes	53,187		59,586
Turnout	78·4%		80·0%
C	22,721	42·7%	49·2%
L	20,792	39·1%	41·3%
Lab	9,396	17·7%	8·6%
UTD Dem	278	0·5%	—
Ecology	—		0·9%
C maj	1,929	3·6%	7·9%
Swing		−1·2%	+7·8%

Mr Richard Needham fought Pontefract and Castleford in February, 1974, and Gravesend in October, 1974. Company director. Personal and political assistant to Mr James Prior. B 1942; ed Eton, Lincoln's Inn, and Harvard Business School. Member, Somerset County Council, 1967-74. Co-founder, Monday Club, but left in 1964 and joined

PEST. Former member, Young European Managers' Association.

Mr Ronald Banks, investment company director and lecturer in economics. Contested Chippenham, February 1974; Croydon North-West, 1964, 1966 and 1970. B April, 1933; ed John Ruskin Grammar School, Croydon and RAF College, Cranwell.

Mrs Catherine Inchley, teacher, authoress of school textbooks; B December, 1940; ed universities of Cambridge, Essex, Stanford (USA) and del Valle (Guatemala). NUT.

CHORLEY

Electorate 81,016   1974: 76,218

Dover, D (C)	31,125
*Rodgers, G. (Lab)	28,546
Orrell, Mrs N. (L)	6,388
Dean, M. (Nat Front)	379
C majority	2,579

C gain from Lab

	1974		1979
Total votes	61,883		66,438
Turnout	81·2%		82·0%
Lab	27,290	44·1%	43·0%
C	24,577	39·7%	46·8%
L	9,831	15·9%	9·6%
Pros Brit	185	0·3%	
Nat Front	—		0·6%
Lab maj	2,713	4·4%	
C maj	—		3·8%
Swing		−1·9%	+4·1%

Mr Denshore Dover fought Caerphilly in October 1974. A civil engineer and member of the institution of Civil Engineers. B 1938; ed Manchester Grammar School and Manchester University. Member, Barnet Borough Council, 1968-71. Former member of the Greater London Area Education and Local Government Advisory Committees and of the

General Council and of the Housing Study Group. Director, Housing Construction, GLC, since 1977.

Mr George Rodgers won the seat for Labour in February, 1974. Engineer. B November, 1925; ed Longview School, Huyton, Lancs. Chairman, north-west group of Labour MPs and vice-chairman, Labour social services study group. Member, Huyton UDC 1963-74; Liverpool Regional Hospital Board, 1968-74. AEUW.

Mrs Neva Orrell is a teacher. Contested the seat in both 1974 general elections. B July, 1915; ed High School for Girls, Wigan and Brighton Municipal Training College. Member, Leyland Urban Council, 1960-70; South Ribble borough council, 1973-76, and Lancashire County Council, 1973-77. NUT.

CHRISTCHURCH AND LYMINGTON

Electorate 58,182   1974: 55,299

*Adley, R. J. (C)	29,817
Harrison, F. (L)	7,654
Hatts, L. K. (Lab)	6,722
Keeling, J. (Ecology)	975
C majority	22,163

No Change

	1974		1979
Total votes	41,325		45,168
Turnout	74·7%		77·6%
C	23,728	57·4%	66·0%
L	9,838	23·8%	16·9%
Lab	7,759	18·8%	14·9%
Ecology	—	—	2·2%
C maj	13,890	33·6%	49·1%
Swing		−1·4%	+6·2%

Mr Robert Adley, marketing director of international hotel company, was elected for this seat in February, 1974; MP for Bristol, North-East, 1970-74; contested Birkenhead, 1966. B March, 1935; ed Uppingham School. Vice-chairman, all-party tourism committee. First chairman and founder member, Brunel Society, Member,

steering committee, SS Great Britain project. Vice-chairman, British-Chinese parliamentary group. Secretary, Conservative Committee on Transport Industries, since 1975, and of National Council of British Hotels, Restaurants and Caterers Association. European Marketing Director, Holiday Inns of Canada Ltd. Chairman of the British—Jordanian parliamentary group.

Mr Frank Harrison, research scientist. Aged 44. Ed Balliol College, Oxford.

Mr Leigh Hatts, contested the seat, October, 1974. B December, 1946; ed King's College, Taunton. Writer. Secretary, Christian Socialist Movement. TSSA and NUJ.

Mr James Keeling is a plumber and engineer, aged 46. Member, West Hampshire Wildfowlers and of Friends of the Earth.

CIRENCESTER AND TEWKESBURY

Electorate 85,444   ¹1974: 80,408

*Ridley, N. (C)	37,651
Beckerlegge, P. (L)	18,057
Trafford, R. S. (Lab)	11,575
C majority	19,594

No Change

	1974		1979
Total votes	61,673		67,283
Turnout	76·7%		78·7%
C	28,930	46·9%	56·0%
L	18,770	30·4%	26·8%
Lab	13,973	22·7%	17·2%
C maj	10,160	16·5%	29·2%
Swing		−1·1%	+7·3%

Mr Nicholas Ridley, who was appointed Minister of State, Foreign and Commonwealth Office, May, 1979. Under-Secretary for Trade, 1970-72; Parliamentary Secretary, Minister of Technology, 1970. Chairman, Conservative parliamentary finance committee 1972-73 and joint vice-chairman since 1974. Member, Expenditure Committee.

An Opposition spokesman on technology and trade, 1969-70, and on defence, 1955-66. Elected 1959; contested Blyth, 1955. Civil engineer. B February 1929; ed Eton and Balliol College, Oxford.

Mr Philip Beckerlegge, partner in a firm of solicitors. B December, 1942; ed Tapton House Grammar School, Chesterfield. Member, Cotswold District Council, since 1977. Chairman, Western Counties Regional Liberal Party.

Mr Robert Trafford, senior lecturer in education. B August, 1928; ed Hertford College and Leicester University. NATFHE.

CITIES OF LONDON AND WESTMINSTER,
City of London and Westminster, South

Electorate 50,357   1974: 52,170

*Brooke, P. (C)	16,851
Profitt, R. (Lab)	7,067
Ball-Wilson, H. (L)	3,375
Mathews, K. (Nat Front)	478

C majority	9,784

No Change

	1974		1979
Total votes	27,747		27,771
Turnout	53·2%		55·1%
C	14,350	51·7%	60·7%
Lab	8,589	31·0%	25·4%
L	4,122	14·9%	12·2%
Nat Front	686	2·5%	1·7%
C maj	5,761	20·7%	35·3%
Swing		−2·6%	+7·3%

1977 by-election: Total vote 20,251 (39·6%)—C 11,962 (59·1%); Lab 3,997 (19·7%); L 1,981 (9·8%); Nat Front 1,051 (5·2%); others 1,260 (6·2%). C majority 7,965 (39·3%).

Mr Peter Brooke became an assistant Government whip in May, 1979. A management consultant, he was elected at a by-election in February, 1977; con tested Bedwellty in October, 1974. B March, 1934; ed Marlborough, Balliol College, Oxford, and Harvard Business School. Member, all-party committees on widows and one-parent families,

pensioners and the homeless. General Agent for Oxford University Conservative Assoc, 1955; vice-president, National Union of Students, 1955-56; president, Oxford Union, 1957, Member, Camden Borough Council, 1968-69; chairman, Camden Committee for Community Relations, 1968-69. Former Swiss correspondent of *Financial Times.* Chairman of London firm of international management consultants. Liveryman, Drapers Company. Underwriting member of Lloyd's.

Mr Russell Profitt, teacher. B December, 1947, in Georgetown, Guyana, and came to Britain in August, 1961. Ed Barnsbury Secondary School and Goldsmith's College, London. Former President of Students Union and former vice-president, National Union of Students. Member, Lewisham Borough Council, since 1974. NUT.

Mr Harry Ball-Wilson, fought Bermondsey in 1951 and 1955. Partnership counsellor and member, Institute of Management Services and Chartered Institute of Transport. B February, 1916; ed Preston Grammar School.

CITIES OF LONDON AND WESTMINSTER,
City of Westminster, Paddington

Electorate 56,234   1974: 58,499

Wheeler, J. (C)	16,189
*Latham, A. C. (Lab)	16,083
Brett, A. (L)	2,815
Cameron, J. (Nat Front)	402
Banjo, O. T. (WRP)	117

C majority	106

C gain from Lab

	1974		1979
Total votes	36,068		35,606
Turnout	61·7%		63·3%
Lab	17,155	47·6%	45·2%
C	14,844	41·2%	45·5%
L	3,742	10·4%	7·9%
LCCP	192	0·5%	—
I Civ Rights	135	0·4%	—
Nat Front	—	—	1·1%
WRP	—	—	0·3%
Lab maj	2,311	6·4%	—
C maj	—	—	0·3%
Swing		−2·2%	+3·3%

Mr John Wheeler, Director-General of the British Security Industry Association Ltd. Police officer, 1959-62; Assistant Governor at Wandsworth Prison, 1968-72, and Brixton, 1972-73. Former Research Officer at the Home Office. Member of party policy groups on individual rights and freedoms, and home affairs—prisons.

B May, 1940; ed Bury St Edmunds County School and Prison Services Staff College. Director (unpaid), the National Supervisory Council for Intruder Alarms.

Mr Arthur Latham, elected, February, 1974, was MP for Paddington, North, 1969-74; contested Rushcliffe, 1964, and Woodford, 1959. Lecturer in further education. B August, 1930; ed Romford Royal Liberty School, Garnett College of Education. Chairman, Tribune Group, 1975-76. Chairman, Greater London Labour Party. Member, Havering Council and leader, Labour group. CAWU, TGWU, ATTI.

Mr Alastari Brett, solicitor and senior legal assistant, Times Newspapers Ltd. B May, 1950; ed Sedbergh School, Yorkshire, and Exeter College, Oxford.

Mr Ola Banjo, mechanic and TGWU shop steward.

CITIES OF LONDON AND WESTMINSTER,
City of Westminster, St Marylebone

Electorate 40,885   1974: 43,633

*Baker, K. W. (C)	14,899
Hegarty, J. (Lab)	6,586
Mann, E. (L)	2,459
Porritt, J. (Ecology)	691
Elrick, C. (Nat Front)	239
C majority	8,313

No Change

	1974		1979
Total votes	24,884		24,874
Turnout	57·0%		60·8%
C	13,660	54·9%	59·9%
Lab	7,157	28·8%	26·5%
L	4,067	16·3%	9·9%
Ecology	—	—	2·8%
Nat Front	—	—	1·0%
C maj	6,503	26·1%	33·4%
Swing		−2·2%	+3·6%

Mr Kenneth Baker, was Parliamentary Secretary, Civil Service Department, 1972-74. Elected 1970 by-elected; MP for Acton, 1968-70 and contested the seat, 1966; fought Poplar, 1964. Industrial consultant. Member, 1922 Committee executive. B November 1934; ed St Paul's School and Magdalen College, Oxford. Member, Twickenham Borough Council 1961-63. Former member, Public Accounts Committee. Member and Procedure Committee. PPS to Mr Edward Health 1974. Director, Geest Holdings, Celestion Industries.

Mr Joseph Hegarty, local government officer. B January, 1944; ed St Marylebone Grammar School, Battersea College of Technology, and London University. Member, Westminster City Council. Nalgo.

Mr Andrew Mann writers' agent B June, 1935; ed Shaftesbury Grammar School. Member, Writers Guild.

Mr Jonathon Porritt, a teacher, is party national vice-chairman. Aged 28.

CLEVELAND AND WHITBY

Electorate 65,488   1974: 60,674

*Brittan, L. (C)	26,735
Pimlott, B. J. (Lab)	19,818
Pitts, M. (L)	5,870
C majority	6,917

No Change

	1974		1979
Total votes	46,213		52,423
Turnout	76·2%		80·0%
C	19,973	43·2%	51·1%
Lab	18,445	39·9%	37·8%
L	7,795	16·9%	11·2%
C maj	1,528	3·3%	13·2%
Swing		−2·0%	+4·9%

Mr Leon Brittan, was appointed Minister of State, Home Office, in May 1979. Barrister and journalist, was elected in February 1974; contested Kensington, North, 1970 and 1966. An Opposition spokesman on devolution and House of Commons affairs since 1976. In November 1978 also appointed as additional employment spokesman. B September, 1939; ed Haberdashers' Aske's School, Trinity College, Cambridge (President of Union) and Yale University. Vice-chairman, National Association of School Governors and Managers. Member, advisory committee on housing of Community Relations Commissions. Vice-chairman of Conservative Employment Committee 1974-76. Editor of *Crossbow,* 1966-68.

Mr Benjamin Pimlott, university lecturer. B July, 1945; ed Marlborough College, and Worcester College, Oxford. Contested the seat October, 1974, and Arundel, February, 1974. British Acadamy Research Fellow, 1972-73 and Nuffield Foundation Special Science Research Fellow, 1977-78. AUT and TGWU.

Mr Michael Pitts, teacher, contested Scarborough, February 1974, Scarborough and Whitby, 1970; Cleveland, 1966, and Warrington, 1964. B March 1936; ed Scarborough High School and Pembroke College, Oxford. Member, Scarborough District Council, since 1973. NUT. Founder member, North York Moors Railway.

CLITHEROE

Electorate 54,468   1974: 52,086

*Waddington, D. (C)	25,081
Sutton, L. R. (Lab)	13,502
Wilson, F. (L)	5,362
C majority	11,579

No Change

	1974		1979
Total votes	40,921		43,945
Turnout	77·5%		80·7%
C	19,643	48·0%	57·1%
Lab	12,775	31·2%	30·7%
L	8,503	20·8%	12·2%
C maj	6,868	16·8%	26·4%
Swing		−1·5%	+4·8%

1979 by-election: Total votes 34,114 (62·8%)—C 22,185 (65·0%); Lab 9,685 (28·4%); L 2,242 (6·6%). C majority 12,500 (36·6%).

Mr David Waddington, QC, was appointed a Lord Commissioner of the Treasury (Government Whip) in May 1979. Retained the seat for the Conservatives at the by-election in March 1979; MP for Nelson and Colne 1968-October 1974; contested Heywood and Ryton, 1966, Nelson and Colne, 1964, and Farnworth 1955. Barrister (Gray's Inn, 1951), QC 1971. B.August, 1929; ed Sedbergh School and Hertford College, Oxford. Director, Padiham Loom and Power Co Ltd; Progess Mill Ltd; J. and J. Roberts Ltd; and Wolstenholme Rink Ltd.

Mr Lindsay Sutton Journalist, contested the seat in by-election of March, 1979. B November, 1948; ed

Carlton Grammar School, Bradford; Bradford Technical College, Sheffield University. Journalist. NUJ.

Mr Frank Wilson, technical representative. B December, 1924; ed Wallasey Grammar School and Emmanuel College, Cambridge.

COATBRIDGE AND AIRDRIE

Electorate 60,133   1974: 59,903

*Dempsey, J. (Lab)	27,598
Love, J. (C)	12,442
Johnstone, Mrs M. (Scot Nat)	5,260
Lab majority	15,156

No Change

	1974		1979
Total votes	44,629		45,300
Turnout	74·5%		75·3%
Lab	23,034	51·6%	60·9%
Scot Nat	12,466	27·9%	11·6%
C	7,683	17·2%	27·5%
L	1,446	3·2%	—
Lab maj	10,568	23·7%	33·4%
Swing		−4·5%	+0·5%

Mr James Dempsey, elected in 1959, was a clerk with a haulage firm; later a lecturer on political economy and a writer on local government. B February 1917; ed Holy Family School, Mossend; Cooperative College, Loughborough and National Council of Labour Colleges. Member, Lanarkshire Council for many years.

Mr John Love fought the seat, October, 1974. B August, 1941; ed Airdrie Academy. Financial accountant. Member, Burgh of Airdrie Council and Monklands District Council.

Mrs Mary Johnstone, sales manager. B June, 1928. Chairman, Association of Scottish Nationalist Trade Unionists.

COLCHESTER

Electorate 90,589   1974: 81,836

*Buck, A. (C)	36,740
Russell, R. E. (Lab)	22,877
Gage, M. (L)	9,794
C majority	13,863

No Change

	1974		1979
Total votes	62,307		69,411
Turnout	76·1%		76·6%
C	27,693	44·4%	52·9%
Lab	22,193	35·6%	33·0%
L	12,421	19·9%	14·1%
C maj	5,500	8·8%	19·9%
Swing		−0·8%	+5·5%

Mr Anthony Buck, Under Secretary for Defence for the Royal Navy, 1972-74, was returned at a by-election in 1961. Barrister (Inner Temple), 1954) and company director. B December 1928; ed King's School, Ely, and Trinity Hall, Cambridge, Legal adviser, National Association of Parish Councils, 1957-59. Chairman of Select Committee on Parliamentary Commissioner for Administration (Ombudsman) since 1977. Secretary, Conservative Home Affairs Committee, 1964-70.

Mr Robert Russell, press officer for GPO telecommunications. B March, 1946; ed St Helena Secondary School, Colchester, and North East Technical College. Contested Sudbury and Woodbridge, October, 1974. Member, Colchester Borough Council, since 1971. NUJ.

Mr Martin Gage is a senior clerk. Aged 27.

COLNE VALLEY

Electorate 64,139   1974: 60,774

*Wainwright, R. S. (L)	20,151
Hildrew, P. J. (Lab)	17,799
Kaye, S. G. (C)	14,450
Keen, T. L. (CMPB)	101
L majority	2,352

No Change

	1974		1979
Total votes	49,665		52,501
Turnout	81·7%		81·9%
L	21,997	44·3%	38·4%
Lab	20,331	40·9%	33·9%
C	7,337	14·8%	27·5%
CFMPB	—	—	0·2%
L maj	1,666	3·4%	4·5%

Mr Richard Wainwright won the seat for the Liberals in 1966 after contesting it in 1964, the 1963 by-election and in 1959. He lost it in 1970 and regained it in February, 1974. Liberal parliamentary spokesman on economic and industrial affairs 1966-70 and spokesman on trade and industry since 1974. Member, Commons Public Expenditure Committee since April, 1974. Member, committee of inquiry, Commons Refreshment Department, 1975. Chartered accountant. President, Leeds, Bradford and district chartered accountants, 1965-66. B April, 1918; ed Shrewsbury School and Clare College, Cambridge. Director, Charles F. Thackeray, Jowett and Sowry (Office Supplies).

Mr Peter Hildrew is a journalist. Contested Westmorland, February, 1974, and Manchester, Withington, October, 1974. B May, 1943; ed Windermere Grammar School, Christ's Hospital, and Cambridge University. Member, Manchester City Council. NUJ.

Mr Stephen Kaye, chartered accountant and director of several companies. B April 1935; ed Bishops Stortford College, Hertfordshire. Treasurer, Huddersfield and District Army Veterans Association.

CONSETT

Electorate 57,547   1974: 59,014

*Watkins, D. J. (Lab)	26,708
Lycett, M. (C)	10,841
Kennedy, R. (L)	6,048
Lab majority	15,867

No Change

	1974		1979
Total votes	40,495		43,597
Turnout	68·6%		75·8%
Lab	27,123	67·0%	61·3%
C	7,677	19·0%	24·9%
L	5,695	14·1%	13·9%
Lab maj	19,446	48·0%	36·4%
Swing		−3·6%	+5·8%

Mr David Watkins was elected in 1966; contested Bristol, North-West, 1964. Toolmaker. B August, 1925; ed secondary school and Bristol College of Technology. Member, Bristol City Council, 1954-57, and Education Committee, 1958-66. Member, Commons panel of chairmen, Select Committee on Unopposed Bills, and Select Committee on Standing  Orders. Consultant to Gauge and Tool Makers' Association. Secretary, AUEW parliamentary group, 1968-77. Sponsored by AUEW.

Mr Michael Lycett fought the seat, October, 1974. Insurance broker and underwriting member of Lloyds. Former managing director of Rhodesian Insurances Ltd in Salisbury and Bulawayo, of Wright Deen Lycett Ltd., of Lycett Browne-Swinburne, Donglass Ltd. B December, 1915; ed Radley School and Merton College, Oxford. Former member, Council and Churchwarden of Salisbury Cathedral, Rhodesia.

Mr Robert Kennedy, postal executive, and partner in hairdressing firm. Member, Post Office Management Staff Association. B October, 1931; ed Benfieldside Modern Secondary School, Consett and Durham technical colleges. North-East Area education officer for Hairdressers' Federation.

CONWAY

Electorate 51,350   1974: 51,730

*Roberts, J. W. P. (C)	18,142
Davies, G. W. (Lab)	12,069
Roberts, Rev J. R. (L)	6,867
Price, E. (Pl Cymru)	3,497
C majority	6,073

No Change

	1974		1979
Total votes	39,434		40,575
Turnout	76·2%		79·0%
C	15,614	39·6%	44·7%
Lab	12,808	32·5%	29·7%
L	6,344	16·1%	16·9%
Pl Cymru	4,668	11·8%	8·6%
C maj	2,806	7·1%	15·0%
Swing		−1·9%	+3·9%

Mr Wyn Roberts appointed Under Secretary of State for Wales in May, 1979, became an Opposition spokesman on Welsh affairs in 1974. Television executive and journalist. Won the seat for the Conservatives in 1970. B July, 1930; ed Beaumaris County School, Harrow, and University College, Oxford. Formerly Welsh Controller, TWW Ltd, and a former executive of Harlech Television. Joint secretary, Conservative Broadcasting committee, 1974-79. Member Wilson Chair in International Politics Advisory Board, University of Wales.

Mr Gerson Davies, adult education officer, was educated at Holyhead Comprehensive School, Jesus College, Oxford, and Inner Temple. B January, 1945. NAS.

The Rev John Roberts, Methodist minister. B October, 1935; ed John Bright Grammar School, Llandudno; University College, Bangor. Member, Aberconway Borough Council, since 1976; Methodist Relief Fund and Board of Social Responsibility; Liberal Party committee, since 1974.

Mr Emyr Price, senior lecturer, history department, Normal College, Bangor. Ed Pwllheli Grammar School, Ysgol Gyfun Eifionnydd, Porthmadog, and University College, Bangor.

CORNWALL, North

Electorate 55,076   1974: 51,779

Neale, G. A. (C)	24,489
*Pardoe, J. W. (L)	20,742
Tremlett, R. B. (Lab)	1,514
Faull, J. (Ecology)	442
Bridgwater, R. (Nat Front)	224
C majority	3,747

C gain from L

	1974		1979
Total votes	41,691		47,411
Turnout	80·5%		86·1%
L	21,368	51·3%	43·7%
C	17,512	42·0%	51·7%
Lab	2,663	6·4%	3·2%
Anti Party	148	0·4%	—
Ecology	—		0·9%
Nat Front	—		0·5%
L maj	3,856	9·3%	—
C maj	—		8·0%
Swing		—	+6·4%

Mr Gerrard Neale, solicitor and company director, contested the seat, October 1974. B June, 1941; ed Bedford School, Bedford. Member, Conservative Party group on environmental and regional planning. Milton Keynes borough councillor, mayor 1976-77. Founder of Milton Keynes City Forum. Consultant to legal practice and business consultants;  director of chemical company. Chairman, area crime prevention panel.

Mr John Pardoe, Liberal spokesman on economic affairs, was also deputy Liberal whip until 1974. Won seat from Conservatives in 1966; contested Finchley, 1964. Treasurer, Liberal Party 1968-69. Member Select Committee on Wealth Tax. Former member Public Accounts Committee. B July, 1934; ed Sherborne School and Corpus Christi College, Cambridge. Former consultant, National Association of School-masters. Member, Independent Broadcasting Authority's general advisory council, since 1973; London Metal Exchange. Director, International Metal Company.

Mr Roderick Tremlett, GPO postal officer, contested the seat, October, 1974. B May, 1933; ed technical secondary school. UPOW.

Mr Jeremy Faull, aged 49, farmer. County councillor; chairman, South West Energy Committee; member, Ecology Party National Executive Committee.

COVENTRY, North-East

Electorate 64,806   1974: 63,605

*Park, G. M. (Lab)	27,010
Shelburne, The Earl of (C)	16,487
Singh, Raj-Mal (L)	2,291
Robbins, H. (Nat Front)	546
Corrigan, P. (Comm)	390
Perkin, S. (WRP)	378

Lab majority	10,523

No Change

	1974		1979
Total votes	44,516		47,102
Turnout	70·0%		72·7%
Lab	26,489	59·5%	57·3%
C	10,520	23·6%	35·0%
L	6,846	15·4%	4·9%
WRP	352	0·8%	0·8%
Comm	309	0·7%	0·8%
Nat Front	—		1·2%
Lab maj	15,969	35·9%	22·3%
Swing		−1·8%	+6·8%

Mr George Park, elected in February, 1974. Chairman, West Midlands group of Labour MPs since 1977. Member, Coventry City Council 1961-74; Coventry District Council 1973-74 (Leader, Labour Group, 1972-74). Member, West Midlands Metropolitan County Council, 1973-77. B September, 1914; ed Onslow Drive Secondary School, Glasgow, Whitehill Grammar School, Glasgow, and Coventry Technical College. Former convener of shop stewards, Chrysler (UK) Ltd. Member and former branch president. Sponsored by AUEW.

The Earl of Shelburne, estate manager and company director. B 1941; ed Spyway, Eton College and Cirencester Agricultural College. Chairman, North Wiltshire District Council 1973-76; member, Calne and Chippenham RDC, 1963-73 (chairman 1972-73); Wiltshire County Council, since 1970.

Mr Raj Mal Singh, machinist. Aged 55.

Mr Paul Corrigan, aged 30, university lecturer. Member, AUT.

COVENTRY, North-West

Electorate 49,008   1974: 49,247

*Robinson, G. (Lab)	19,460
Miles, D. (C)	15,489
Poole, C. (L)	3,413
Stewart, A. (Nat Front)	359
Keen, T. (CMPB)	98

Lab majority	3,971

No Change

	1974		1979
Total votes	37,033		38,819
Turnout	75·2%		79·2%
Lab	19,205	51·9%	50·1%
C	11,717	31·6%	39·9%
L	5,798	15·7%	8·8%
People	313	0·8%	—
Nat Front	—	—	0·9%
CFMPB	—	—	0·3%
Lab maj	7,488	20·3%	10·2%
Swing		−1·7%	+5·0%

1976 by-election: Total vote 35,871 (72·9%)— Lab 17,118 (47·7%); C 13,424 (37·4%); L 4,062 (11·3%); Nat Front 986 (2·7%); others 281 (0·8%). Lab majority 3,694 (10·3%).

Mr Geoffrey Robinson won by-election, March, 1976. Former financial controller, British Leyland; managing director, Leyland Innocenti, Italy, 1972-73; chief executive, Jaguar Cars, Coventry, 1974-75. Consultant to Meriden Co-operative. Research assistant, Labour Party, 1965-68. B May, 1938; ed Emmanuel School, Cambridge University, and Yale. TGWU.

Mr Derek Miles, chartered civil engineer, fought the 1976 by-election Member, Ramsgate Council, 1965-74; Kent County Council, 1967-77. B July 1937; ed Slough Grammar School and Bristol University. Senior technical advisor to Intermediate Technology Development Group. Consultant to foreign governments, World Bank and other international agencies on construction management and infrastructure development.

Mr Christopher Poole, lecturer in law. B September, 1948; ed Liverpool University. NATFHE.

COVENTRY, South-East

Electorate 50,961   1974: 50,818

*Wilson, W. (Lab)	19,583
Sawdon, T. (C)	12,097
Brazier, M. (L)	2,984
Clarke, R. (Nat Front)	513
Wilkins, A. (WRP)	426

Lab majority	7,486

No Change

	1974		1979
Total votes	34,371		35,603
Turnout	67·6%		69·9%
Lab	20,771	60·4%	55·0%
C	8,648	25·2%	34·0%
L	4,952	14·4%	8·4%
Nat Front	—	—	1·4%
WRP	—	—	1·2%
Lab maj	12,123	35·2%	21·0%
Swing		−3·5%	+7·1%

Mr William Wilson was elected in February, 1974. MP for Coventry, South, 1964-74. Contested Warwick and Leamington, 1951, 1955, 1957 by-election, and 1959. Member, Select Committee on Race Relations and Immigration. B June 1913; ed Wheatley Street School, Cheylesmore School and Junior Technical College, Coventry. Senior partner, Coventry firm of solicitors. Member, Warwickshire County Council, 1958-70, and since 1972.

Mr Timothy Sawdon, ophthalmic optician. B June 1949; ed Pocklington School, Yorkshire, and Bradford University. Member, Coventry City Council since 1974. ASTMS.

Mr Michael Brazier, economics teacher. Ed Prince Henry's Grammar School, Evesham, and Portsmouth Polytechnic. Member, executive committee, Coventry branch of NAS.

Mr Alan Wilkins, aged 43, aero-engine fitter at Rolls Royce. AUEW.

COVENTRY, South-West

Electorate 69,552   1974: 67,841

Butcher, J. P. (C)	27,928
*Wise, Mrs A. (Lab)	22,274
Chapple, N. B. (L)	5,921
Williamson, M. (Nat Front)	482
Keen, T. (CMPB)	79
C majority	5,654

C gain from Lab

	1974		1979
Total votes	53,877		56,684
Turnout	79.4%		81.5%
Lab	23,225	43.1%	39.3%
C	21,107	39.2%	49.3%
L	8,579	15.9%	10.4%
Nat Front	822	1.5%	0.9%
CFMPB	144	0.3%	0.1%
Lab maj	2,118	3.9%	
C maj	—	—	10.0%
Swing		−1.5%	+6.9%

Mr John Butcher contested Birmingham, Northfield, in February, 1974. Computer sales manager. B February, 1946; Ed Huntingdon Grammar School, Birmingham University. At the Institute of Strategic Studies he did research into guerrilla warfare and Nato. Member, Birmingham City and District Councils, 1972-78.

Mrs Audrey Wise, shorthand typist and author, was elected in February, 1974. B January, 1935; ed Rutherford High School. Chairman, PLP social security group; member, Select Committee on Violence in the Family, 1976-78 and of Institute for Workers' Control. Tottenham councillor for four years. USDAW.

Mr Brian Chapple fought the seat in February and October, 1974. Lecturer. B May, 1926; ed Stationers' Company's School and Merton College, Oxford. Former member, Bushey and Solihull Councils. NATFHE.

CREWE

Electorate 59,530   1974: 59,227

*Dunwoody, Mrs G. P. (Lab)	22,288
Butcher, J. V. (C)	18,051
Bithell, C. (L)	5,430
Tonks, W. (Nat Front)	352
Lab majority	4,327

No Change

	1974		1979
Total votes	43,372		46,121
Turnout	73.2%		77.5%
Lab	21,534	49.6%	48.3%
C	14,279	32.9%	39.1%
L	7,559	17.4%	11.8%
Nat Front	—	—	0.8%
Lab maj	7,255	16.7%	9.2%
Swing		−2.8%	+3.7%

Mrs Gwyneth Dunwoody was elected in February, 1974. Member, European Parliament since 1975. Parliamentary Secretary, Board of Trade, 1967-70. MP for Exeter, 1966-70, after contesting the seat in 1964. B December, 1930; ed Fulham County Secondary School and the Convent of Notre Dame. Director, Film Producers' Association of Great Britain, 1970-74. Parliamentary adviser to Association of Independent Cinemas.

Mr John Butcher, chartered accountant. B November 1942; ed Malvern College. Political officer, Bow Group, 1974-75, and treasurer, 1968-70. Member, Royal Borough of Kensington and Chelsea. Council, 1974-78. Financial Controller, U.K. Toys Division, Dunbee-Combex-Marx Ltd. ASTMS.

Mr Colin Bithell, senior production clerk. Member, Flintshire Council, 1970-74; Alyn and Deeside District Council, since 1974. Aged 44.

CROSBY

Electorate 81,208   1974: 78,605

*Page, R. G. (C)	34,768
Mulhearn, A. (Lab)	15,496
Hill, A. (L)	9,302
Hussey, P. (Ecology)	1,489
C majority	19,272

No Change

	1974		1979
Total votes	57,782		61,055
Turnout	73.5%		75.2%
C	29,764	51.5%	56.9%
Lab	17,589	30.4%	25.4%
L	10,429	18.0%	15.2%
Ecology	—	—	2.4%
C maj	12,175	21.1%	31.5%
Swing		−2.0%	+5.2%

Mr Graham Page, Minister for Local Government within the Department of the Environment, 1970-74; Minister of State for Housing and Local Government, 1970; Opposition spokesman on land and housing, 1964-70. Returned at by-election in 1953; contested Islington, North 1950 and 1951. B June 1911; ed Magdalen College School, Oxford, and London University. Solicitor. Director of civil engineering and property companies. Chairman, Select Committee on Statutory Instruments, 1964-70 and since 1974, and of Joint Lords and Commons Select Committee on Statutory Instruments, since 1974. Joint vice-chairman, Conservative planning and local government committee, since 1974. Member, Select Committee on European Secondary Legislation, since 1974.

Mr Anthony Mulhearn, compositor. B January, 1939; ed secondary modern school. NGA.

Mr Anthony Hill contested the seat, October, 1974. Lecturer in law. B April, 1942; ed Merchant Taylor's School, Crosby, and Liverpool Polytechnic. NATFHE.

Mr Peter Hussey works in retailing. Aged 38; ed Tenby and Pembroke Grammar Schools.

CROYDON, Central

Electorate 66,629   1974: 66,746

*Moore, J. E. M. (C)	26,457
White, D. F. (Lab)	18,499
Johnson, J. P. (L)	5,112
Soper, M. J. (Ind C)	238
Gibson, P. (WRP)	116

C majority	7,958

No Change

	1974		1979
Total votes	48,450		50,422
Turnout	72·6%		75·7%
C	20,390	42·1%	52·5%
Lab	20,226	41·7%	36·7%
L	7,834	16·2%	10·1%
Ind C	—		0·5%
WRP	—		0·2%
C maj	164	0·4%	15·8%
Swing		−1·1%	+7·7%

Mr John Moore, investment banker, stockbroker and company director, became a vice-chairman of the Conservative Party with responsibility for youth in March, 1975. B November 1937; ed Licensed Victuallers' School, Slough, London School of Economics (President of the Union 1959-60). Councillor, London borough of Merton, 1971-74. Member, Public Accounts Committee, 1974-75. Lived in United States 1961-65 where he was Precinct Captain (1962) and Ward Chairman (1964), Democratic Party.

Mr David White is a solicitor. B August, 1948; ed Trinity School, Croydon, and Gonville and Caius College, Cambridge. Member, GLC 1973-77 and Croydon Council since 1978. ASTMS.

Mr Paul Johnson contested Dartford, 1970, and Woolwich, West, February and October, 1974. Assistant claims manager with motor insurers. B March, 1943; ed Erith Technical School.

Mr Peter Gibson, aged 47, is the TGWU representative at Thornton Heath bus garage.

CROYDON, North-East

Electorate 57,022   1974: 58,306

*Weatherill, B. B. (C)	21,560
Simpson, D. H. (Lab)	14,784
Streeter, P. T. (L)	5,459
Moss, P. W. (Nat Front)	464

C majority	6,776

No Change

	1974		1979
Total votes	41,404		42,267
Turnout	71·0%		74·1%
C	17,938	43·3%	51·0%
Lab	15,787	38·1%	35·0%
L	7,228	17·5%	12·9%
Ind Brit Nat	451	1·1%	
Nat Front	—	—	1·1%
C maj	2,151	5·2%	16·0%
Swing		−1·6%	+5·4%

Mr Bernard Weatherill was elected Chairman of Ways and Means and Deputy Speaker, in May 1979. Deputy Chief Opposition Whip 1974-79; Government Deputy Chief Whip, 1973-74; Comptroller of the Household (whip) 1972-73; Lord Commissioner of the Treasury (whip) 1970-72; Opposition whip 1967-70. Elected 1964. Master tailor and director, Kilgour Weatherill. Freeman of City of London. B November 1920; ed Malvern College. Member, National Union of Conservative Party, 1963-64.

Mr David Simpson contested the seat, October, 1974. B March, 1934; ed Sandbach School, Nottingham University, and LSE. Lecturer. Member, Fabian Society; GLC, 1973-74. NATFHE.

Mr Patrick Streeter contested the seat in February and October, 1974. B August, 1946; ed Harrow. ASTMS.

CROYDON, North-West

Electorate 55,608   1974: 55,176

*Taylor, R. G. (C)	19,928
Boden, S. J. (Lab)	16,159
Pitt, W. H. (L)	4,239

C majority	3,769

No Change

	1974		1979
Total votes	38,203		40,326
Turnout	69·2%		72·5%
C	16,035	42·0%	49·4%
Lab	14,556	38·1%	40·1%
L	6,563	17·2%	10·5%
Nat Front	1,049	2·7%	—
C maj	1,479	3·9%	9·3%
Swing		−1·7%	+2·7%

Mr **Robert Taylor** was elected in 1970. Architectural ironmonger. Contested Battersea, North, 1964 and 1959. Member, Public Accounts Committee, since 1974. Chairman, Building Materials Export Group. B December 1932; ed Cranleigh School, Director of G. and S. Allgood Ltd and chairman of South African subsidiary. Former Sussex county rugby player. TA parachutist.

Mr **Stanley Boden,** teacher, contested the constituency, February and October, 1974. B September, 1935; ed Coalbrookdale High School, Shropshire, and London and Birmingham Universities. Member, Croydon Borough Council, since 1971. NUT.

Mr **William Pitt** contested the seat, February and October, 1974. Local government officer. B July, 1937; ed Heath Clark School, Croydon, London Nautical School, and Polytechnic of the South Bank. Nalgo.

CROYDON, South

Electorate 62,022   1974: 60,090

*Clark, W. G. (C)		30,874
Billenness, P. (L)		10,006
Bloom, J. M. (Lab)		6,249
Dummer R. (Nat Front)		469

C majority	20,868

No Change

	1974		1979
Total votes	44,420		47,598
Turnout	73·9%		76·7%
C	25,703	57·9%	64·9%
L	11,514	25·9%	21·0%
Lab	7,203	16·2%	13·1%
Nat Front	—		1·0%
C maj	14,189	32·0%	43·9%
Swing		−1·6%	+5·0%

Mr **William Clark,** returned in February 1974, was MP for Surrey, East, 1970-74; contested Northampton, 1955; MP for Nottingham, South, 1959-66. B October, 1917; ed London Secondary School. Chairman, Select Committee on Taxation, 1973. Member, Select Committee on Wealth Tax. Opposition spokesman on Treasury affairs 1964-66. Joint treasurer of Conservative Party 1974-75. Accountant and company director. Member, Institute of Taxation; chairman, Income Tax Payers Society.

Mr **Peter Billenness,** marketing consultant. Contested Hendon, South, 1959 and 1964; Bromley, 1966; Epsom, 1970; and East Grinstead, February, 1974. B May, 1927; ed University College, London.

Mr **John Bloom,** research officer with the National Union of Public Employees. Contested Petersfield, October, 1974. B October, 1934; ed Trinity School, Croydon, and London School of Economics. Former member, Carshalton UDC. NUPE and APEX.

DARLINGTON

Electorate 63,218   1974: 62,955

*Fletcher, E. J. (Lab)		22,565
Kirkhope, T. (C)		21,513
Walker, K. (L)		5,054
Outhwaite, H. (Nat Front)		444

Lab majority	1,052

No Change

	1974		1979
Total votes	46,834		49,576
Turnout	74·4%		78·4%
Lab	21,332	45·5%	45·5%
C	17,620	37·6%	43·4%
L	7,882	16·8%	10·2%
Nat Front	—		0·9%
Lab maj	3,712	7·9%	2·1%
Swing		−1·9%	+2·9%

Mr **Edward Fletcher,** elected in 1964, contested Middlesbrough, West, 1959. Chairman, Tribune Group of Labour MPs. Trade Union official. B February, 1911; ed elementary school and Fircroft College, Birmingham. Member, Expenditure Committee, 1964-70; Newcastle City Council, 1951-64. Northern area organizer, APEX, 1950-53, and northern area secretary, 1953-64. Sponsored by APEX.

Mr **Timothy Kirkhope,** solicitor, fought Durham in February, 1974. B April 1945; ed Royal Grammar School, Newcastle upon Tyne and College of Law, Guildford. Past chairman, Northern Area Conservative Political Centre. Member, Society of Conservative Lawyers. Chairman, Tyneside Hospital Broadcasting Service.

Mr **Kenneth Walker,** senior technical officer with British Rail. B July, 1947; ed Darlington Technical School and Darlington College of Further Education. Member, Norton-on-Derwent Council. TSSA.

DARTFORD

Electorate 57,507   1974: 57,038

Dunn, R. (C)		21,195
*Irving, S. (Lab/Co-op)		19,803
Josephs, I. (L)		4,407
Nobbs, Mrs I. (Nat Front)		476
Beddowes, J. (Fancy Dress Party)		328

C majority	1,392

C gain from Lab and Co-op

	1974		1979
Total votes	43,693		46,209
Turnout	76·6%		80·4%
Lab & Co-op	20,817	47·6%	42·9%
C	15,331	35·1%	45·9%
L	6,606	15·1%	9·5%
Nat Front	939	2·1%	1·0%
FDP	—		0·7%
Lab/Coop m.	5,486	12·5%	
C maj	—		3·0%
Swing		−2·4%	+7·7%

Mr **Robert Dunn** contested Eccles in both the elections of 1974. Senior buyer with a chain of foodstores. B July, 1946; ed Manchester Polytechnic; Brighton Polytechnic; and Salford University. Member, Southwark Borough Council, since 1974; member, Lancashire Education Authority, 1968-71; governor, Inner London Education Authority schools. Member, Society for Individual Freedom and of the Primrose League.

Mr **Sydney Irving** held the seat from 1955 to 1970 and regained it in February, 1974. Deputy Speaker and Chairman of Ways and Means, 1968-70; Treasurer of the Household and Deputy Chief Whip, 1964-66; Deputy Chairman of Ways and Means, 1966-68. Teacher and lecturer. B July, 1918; ed Pendower School, Newcastle upon Tyne, and London School of Economics. Member, Select Committee on Direct Elections, 1976; Select Committee on Members' Interests 1975-79; Committee of Privileges 1974-79. Member, Franks Committee on the feasibility of a register of immigrants, 1976, and of the Liaison Committee, PLP, 1975-79. Chairman Manifesto Group, 1976-77, of Co-operative Parliamentary Group, 1977-78, and PLP Europe Group, 1976-79. NUT and AUT.

Mr **Ian Josephs,** managing director of a school of English hotel. Contested Bexley, Sidcup, October, 1974; Dartford, February, 1974; also Isle of Thanet, 1970, as an independent. B January, 1932; ed Pembroke College, Oxford. Member, Kent County Council, 1960-66.

DARWEN

Electorate 75,008   1974: 70,611

*Fletcher-Cooke, C. (C)	30,789
Ellman, Mrs L. (Lab)	17,763
Cooper, A. (L)	9,928
C majority	13,026

No Change

	1974		1979
Total votes	54,075		58,480
Turnout	76·6%		78·0%
C	23,577	43·6%	52·6%
Lab	17,926	33·2%	30·4%
L	12,572	23·2%	17·0%
C maj	5,651	10·4%	22·2%
Swing		−3·0%	+5·9%

Mr **Charles Fletcher-Cooke,** QC, was elected in 1951. Under Secretary, Home Office, 1961-63. Contested  East Dorset as Labour candidate, 1945. Member, European Parliament, 1977-79. B May, 1914; ed Malvern College and Peterhouse, Cambridge (President of Union, 1936). Barrister (Lincoln's Inn, 1938), QC, 1958. Chairman, Select Committee on Parliamentary Commissioner, 1974-77. Chairman, North-West Conservative MPs, since 1974. Director, Hulton Publications Ltd.

Mrs **Louise Ellman,** housewife and former lecturer. B November, 1945; ed Manchester High School; Hull University; and York University. Leader, Labour group, Lancashire County Council; member, West Lancashire District Council. NATFHE.

Mr **Alan Cooper,** primary school headmaster, contested the seat, 1970, and in February and October, 1974; Bolton, East, 1966; Altrincham and Sale, 1964; and Rossendale, 1959. B March, 1927; ed St Andrew's School, Eccles and Didsbury College of Education. Member, Eccles Borough Council, 1958-74 (Mayor, 1971-72) and Salford City Council since 1975.

DAVENTRY

Electorate 90,892   1974: 83,253

*Prentice, R. (C)	41,422
Rawlings, J. L. (Lab)	19,939
Woodside, R. (L)	11,286
Younger, G. (Nat Front)	522
C majority	21,483

No Change

	1974		1979
Total votes	64,180		73,169
Turnout	77·1%		80·5%
C	29,801	46·4%	56·6%
Lab	20,739	32·3%	27·3%
L	13,640	21·3%	15·4%
Nat Front	—	—	0·7%
C maj	9,062	14·1%	29·3%
Swing		0·0%	+7·6%

Mr **Reginald Prentice,** appointed Minister of State for Social Security with responsibility for disabled, in May, 1979. Member of Labour Governments from 1966 to 1976; resigned from the Labour Party in disagreement over policy in 1977 and joined the Con-  servative Party but continued to sit for Newham, North East. Resigned from the Government in 1976 when Minister of Overseas Development, a post to which he was appointed in 1975. Secretary of State for Education and Science, 1974-75; Labour Opposition spokesman on employment 1971-74; Resigned in October, 1969 after four days as Minister of State for Technology and Power. Minister of Overseas Development, 1967-69; Minister of Public Building and Works, 1966-67; Minister of State, Education and Science 1964-66. Represented Newham, North-East, 1974-78; East Ham, North 1957-74; contested Streatham 1955 and Croydon, North in 1950 and 1951. B July 1923; ed Whitgift School and London School of Economics. Scientific instrument maker; former adviser to TGWU.

Mr **John Rawlings** senior youth and community worker. B March, 1943; ed Northampton secondary modern school. Member, Northampton Borough Council, 1970-76 (Mayor, 1974-75). CTSA/NUT.

Mr **Richard Woodside,** teacher. B May, 1947; ed Sir John Deane's Grammar School, Northwich, and Sir John Cass College, University of London. NUT.

DEARNE VALLEY

Electorate 64,183   1974: 63,265

*Wainwright, E. (Lab)	31,783
Pattman, Miss J. R. (C)	9,048
Hargreaves, P. (L)	5,352
Lab majority	22,735

No Change

	1974		1979
Total votes	44,949		46,183
Turnout	71·0%		72·0%
Lab	33,315	74·1%	68·8%
C	6,046	13·5%	19·6%
L	5,588	12·4%	11·6%
Lab maj	27,269	60·6%	49·2%
Swing		−2·8%	+5·7%

Mr Edwin Wainwright, secretary of the PLP trade union group since 1966. Elected in 1959. Member, Select Committee on Nationalized Industries, since 1974. B August 1908; ed Darfield Council School, Wombwell and Darfield WEA, Barnsley and Mexborough Technical Colleges. Miner, member NUM since 1922; branch official, 1932-1959; member NEC of NUM, 1952-1959. Sponsored by NUM.

Miss Jacqueline Pattman, barrister, and legal manager with multinational company. B March 1951; ed George Abbot School, Guildford, Paris, Switzerland, Vienna, Florence and Queen's University, Belfast, and Exeter University.

Mr Peter Hargreaves, a regional sales manager, contested the seat, October and February, 1974 and 1970, for the Liberals and in 1966 as an Independent. B December, 1935; ed secondary modern school. Member, Wombwell UDC, 1965-69, and 1970-74, and district council since 1973.

DENBIGH

Electorate 65,902   1974: 63,506

*Morgan, W. G. O. (C)	23,683
Williams, Dr D. L. (L)	14,833
Thomas, Rev H. R. (Lab)	9,276
Jones, I. W. (Pl Cymru)	4,915
C majority	8,850

No Change

	1974		1979
Total votes	48,529		52,707
Turnout	76·4%		80·0%
C	18,751	38·6%	44·9%
L	14,200	29·3%	28·1%
Lab	9,824	20·2%	17·6%
Pl Cymru	5,754	11·9%	9·3%
C maj	4,551	9·3%	16·8%
Swing		−1·8%	+4·4%

Mr Geraint Morgan, QC, was elected in 1959; contested Merioneth 1951, Huyton 1955. Barrister (Gray's Inn, 1947); QC, 1971. B November, 1920; ed University College of Wales, Aberystwyth; Trinity Hall, Cambridge; University of London. Vice-chairman, Welsh Conservative MPs, since 1972.

Dr David Williams contested the seat, February and October, 1974. General practioner. B December, 1926; ed Birkenhead School, Liverpool University. Chairman, Welsh General Medical Services Committee; vice-chairman, Welsh Medical Committee, Welsh Council BMA.

The Rev Huw Thomas, minister and former teacher. B September, 1949; ed University of Swansea.

Mr Ieuan Jones, solicitor, contested the seat, October, 1974. B May, 1949; ed Pontardawe Grammar School, Ysgol-y-Berwyn, Bala, and Liverpool Polytechnic.

DERBY, North

Electorate 83,580   1974: 82,697

*Whitehead, P. (Lab)	28,797
Kemm, R. N. (C)	28,583
Whitehouse, R. F. (L)	6,093
Bayliss, C. (Nat Front)	592
Gibson, S. P. (Eng Nat)	116
Lab majority	214

No Change

	1974		1979
Total Votes	60,564		64,181
Turnout	73·2%		76·8%
Lab	26,960	44·5%	44·9%
C	22,767	37·6%	44·5%
L	10,595	17·5%	9·5%
Pros Brit	242	0·4%	
Nat Front	—		0·9%
Eng Nat	—		0·2%
Lab maj	4,193	6·9%	0·4%
Swing		−2·5%	+3·2%

Mr Phillip Whitehead, writer and television producer. Elected 1970; contested West Derbyshire, 1966. B May, 1937; ed Lady Manners School, Bakewell; Exeter College, Oxford. Member, Services Committee and Procedure Committee, chairman of sub-committee computers. Vice-chairman, Fabian Society, 1978. Member, UK delegation to Council of Europe. Member, Annan committee on future of broadcasting. NUR sponsored. NUJ. Chairman, PLP human rights sub-committee, 1977-78. Member, PLP liaison committee, 1978.

Mr Richard Kemm contested Ashfield in both elections in 1974 and in 1970. Lecturer in accountancy; fellow, Chartered Insurance Institute and Associate of the Institute of Chartered Accountants. B November, 1940; ed Blundell's School, Tiverton. Former member, National Young Conservatives Advisory Committee. Former chairman, Somerset and Leicestershire YCs.

Mr Richard Whitehouse, teacher. Was Liberal agent in Bridlington, February, 1974, and in Wolverhampton, South-East, October, 1974. B November, 1951; ed Hull University. NUT.

DERBY, South

Electorate 75,422   1974: 74,342

*Johnson, W. H. (Lab)	26,945
Stern, M. C. (C)	20,853
Somerset Sullivan, J. D. (L)	5,196
Verity, L. A. (Nat Front)	587
Biggs, W. A. (WRP)	146
Short, J. (Eng Nat)	122
Lab majority	6,092

No Change

	1974		1979
Total Votes	51,665		53,849
Turnout	69·5%		71·4%
Lab	26,342	51·0%	50·0%
C	17,010	32·9%	38·7%
L	7,520	14·6%	9·6%
Up & Eng Nat	793	1·5%	—
Nat Front	—	—	1·1%
WRP	—	—	0·3%
Eng Nat	—	—	0·2%
Lab maj	9,332	18·1%	11·3%
Swing		−2·7%	+3·4%

Mr Walter Johnson, President of Transport Salaried Staffs Association, and a member since 1944. Elected in 1970. Contested Acton by-election 1968; South East Bedfordshire, 1959 and Bristol West, 1955. Assistant Government whip, 1974-75. Member, PLP committees on transport, aviation, energy and employment. B November, 1917; ed Devon House School, Margate. Senior executive, personnel, London Transport. Member, Brentford and Chiswick Council six years. Sponsored by TSSA.

Mr Michael Stern, chartered accountant in private practice. B 1942; ed Christ's College Grammar School, Finchley. Political officer, Bow Group, and former treasurer, assistant research secretary, and managing director, Bow Publications Ltd.

Mr Somerset Sullivan, bus conductor, and lecturer on life and works of Bernard Shaw. B August, 1929; ed The Christopher Wren School, London. TGWU.

DERBYSHIRE, North-East

Electorate 70,767   1974: 68,869

Ellis, R. J. (Lab)	27,218
Oliver, E. (C)	21,889
Hall, P. (L)	7,436
Lab majority	5,329

No Change

	1974		1979
Total Votes	50,571		56,543
Turnout	75·6%		79·9%
Lab	25,238	49·9%	48·1%
C	14,997	29·7%	38·7%
L	10,336	20·4%	13·2%
Lab maj	10,241	20·2%	9·4%
Swing		−3·1%	+5·4%

Mr Raymond Ellis is President of the Derbyshire area NUM, and a former branch secretary. B December, 1923; ed elementary schools, Sheffield University and Ruskin College. Derbyshire county councillor. Sponsored by NUM.

Mr Edward Oliver is a chartered accountant. B April 1942; ed Felsted School, Essex. Member, Hertfordshire Council, since 1973. Secretary, King George's pension fund for actors and actresses. Former Samaritan councillor.

Mr Phillip Hall is a teacher. Aged 32; ed Corpus Christi College, Oxford.

DERBYSHIRE, South-East

Electorate 57,516   1974: 53,739

*Rost, P. L. (C)	24,004
Bermingham, G. E. (Lab)	16,617
Lustig, R. (L)	5,518
Neil, Miss C. (Nat Front)	498
C majority	7,387

No Change

	1974		1979
Total Votes	43,111		46,637
Turnout	80·2%		81·1%
C	18,856	43·7%	51·5%
Lab	17,851	41·4%	35·6%
L	6,404	14·9%	11·8%
Nat Front	—	—	1·1%
C maj	1,005	2·3%	15·9%
Swing		−2·2%	+6·8%

Mr Peter Rost, former stockbroker, won the seat for the Conservatives in 1970; contested Sunderland, North, 1966. B September, 1930; ed Aylesbury Grammar School and Birmingham University. Former teacher and financial journalist. Member, Select Committee on Science and Technology. Joint Secretary, Conservative parliamentary committee on trade, 1972-74; joint secretary, energy committee, 1974.

Mr Gerald Bermingham, solicitor. B 1940. APEX.

Mr Richard Lustig, management consultant, B December, 1931; ed Salford Grammar School and LSE.

DERBYSHIRE, West

Electorate 50,655   1974: 66,869

Parris, M. (C)	21,478
Warboys, P. M. (L)	11,261
Moore, W. (Lab)	8,134
C majority	10,217

No Change

	1974		1979
Total Votes	38,546		40,873
Turnout	78·4%		80·7%
C	18,468	47·9%	52·5%
L	10,622	27·6%	27·6%
Lab	9,456	24·5%	19·9%
C maj	7,846	20·3%	24·9%
Swing		−1·0%	+4·6%

Mr Matthew Parris was a member of the private office of Mrs Margaret Thatcher when she was Leader of the Opposition. B 1940; ed in Africa and Cambridge University.

Mr Peter Worboys, solicitor, contested the seat, February and October, 1974. B March, 1947; ed Perse School, Cambridge, and Selwyn College, Cambridge. Nalgo.

Mr William Moore, polytechnic lecturer. Member, Derbyshire County Council. B August, 1933; ed Birmingham College of Commerce and Sheffield University. ATTI.

DEVIZES

Electorate 80,028   1974: 77,793

*Morrison, C. A. (C)	32,439
Finlayson, V. E. (Lab)	16,351
Ainslie, J. (L)	14,059
Burcham, R. (Ecology)	713
Mockler, A. B. (Wessex Reg)	142
C majority	16,088

No Change

	1974		1979
Total Votes	58,514		63,704
Turnout	75·2%		79·6%
C	24,842	42·5%	50·9%
Lab	17,821	30·5%	25·7%
L	15,851	27·1%	22·1%
Ecology	—		1·1%
Wessex Reg	—		0·2%
C maj	7,021	12·0%	25·2%
Swing			−1·9%	+6·6%

Mr Charles Morrison, farmer and company director, was returned at the 1964 by-election. Member of Lloyd's. B June, 1932; ed Eton and Royal Agricultural College, Cirencester. Chairman, trustees of Young Volunteer Force Foundation. Elder brother of Mr Peter Morrison, Conservative MP for City of Chester. Joint vice-chairman agriculture committee and vice-chairman, 1922 Committee, from 1974.

Mr Victor Finlayson contested the seat, October, 1974. Science tutor at Open University and former engineer. B December, 1924; ed elementary, secondary school and London University. AUT.

Mr Jack Ainslie contested the seat, October, 1974. Farmer and director of cooperative marketing groups. B August, 1921; ed Harrow and Trinity College, Oxford. Member, Wiltshire County Council, since 1964, and Liberal leader since 1973; chairman, education committee, 1973-77.

	1974		1979	
Total Votes	58,621		63,514	
Turnout	79·7%		81·7%	
L	28,209	48·1%		36·7%
C	21,488	36·7%		50·1%
Lab	8,356	14·3%		11·2%
ENP	568	1·0%		0·2%
Nat Front	—	—		0·4%
Ecol	—	—		1·1%
DLP	—	—		0·1%
Wessex Reg	—	—		0·1%
DMPSWR	—	—		0·0%
L maj	6,721	11·4%		—
C maj				13·4%
Swing				—

Mr Antony Speller, an executive director, contested the seat in October, 1974. B June, 1929; ed Exeter School, Universities of London and Exeter. Exeter city councillor 1964-74 (Chairman, Education Committee); Chairman, Devon River Authority. Executive director, the Copyshops of South West England.

Mr Jeremy Thorpe was leader of the Liberal Party from 1967 to 1976. Won North Devon from the Conservatives in 1959, having contested it in 1955. Spokesman foreign and commonwealth affairs 1976-78. B April, 1929; ed in United States, Eton, and Trinity College, Oxford. President of Oxford Union 1951. Barrister (Inner Temple) 1954. Resigned directorships of London and County Securities, Capital Securities and other companies in December, 1973. Father and grandfather were MPs. Member Committee of Privileges and Select Committee on direct elections to European Parliament.

Mr Anthony Saltern, teacher. B May, 1943; ed Bude Grammar School and St Paul's College of Education, Cheltenham. NUT.

Mr Anthony Whittaker, holder of honours law degree, works as a smallholder on Exmoor where he is secretary of his local Church Council. Member, Rotary Club of Exmoor. Aged 46.

Mr Frank Hansford-Miller contested the seat in October, 1974, and Lewisham, East, in February, 1974, for the Freedom Party. B November, 1916; ed Colfe's School, Lewisham, and London University. Teacher. Member, Lewisham council, 1959-68.

Mr Auberon Waugh, author, journalist and satirist. B November, 1939; ed Downside and Christ Church, Oxford.

Lieut Commander William Boakes has been contesting general elections and by-elections since 1951. B May 1904; ed elementary school and Royal Navy College. Greenwich.

DEVON, North

Electorate 77,715   1974: 73,598

Speller, A. (C)	31,811
*Thorpe, J. J. (L)	23,338
Saltern, A. J. (Lab)	7,108
Whittaker, A. M. (Ecology)	729
Price, J. P. (Nat Front)	237
Hansford-Miller, F. H. (ENP)	142
Waugh, A. (DLP)	79
Rous, Miss H. (Wessex Reg)	50
Boaks, W. G. (DMPSWR)	20
C majority	8,473

C gain from L

DEVON, West

Electorate 61,408   1974: 57,431

*Mills, P. M. (C)	29,428
Howell, V. (L)	12,256
Maddern, R. D. (Lab)	6,174
Bearsford-Walker, R. (Nat Front)	393
C majority	17,172

No Change

	1974		1979
Total Votes	45,158		48,251
Turnout	78·6%		78·6%
C	22,594	50·0%	61·0%
L	16,665	36·9%	25·4%
Lab	5,899	13·1%	12·8%
Nat Front	—		0·8%
C maj	5,929	13·1%	35·6%
Swing		−1·3%	+5·6%

Mr Peter Mills was Under Secretary, Northern Ireland Office, 1972-74; Parliamentary Secretary, Agriculture, Fisheries and Food, April to November, 1972. Elected February, 1974; represented Torrington, 1964-74. B September, 1921; ed Epsom College and Wye College. Farmer and Company director, Insurance and agricultural consultant. Joint vice-chairman, Conservative agriculture committee, and member, Select Committee on European Secondary Legislation, Since 1974. Member, executive committee, Commonwealth Parliamentary Association.

Mr Victor Howell, a builder, contested Honiton, February and October 1974. B August, 1945; ed Kelly College, Tavistock, Whitelands Teacher Training College, Putney and Exeter Technical College. Exeter councillor, 1970-76.

Mr Ralph Maddern, publisher and former teacher and construction worker. B May, 1927, in Australia, where he was educated. UCATT.

DEWSBURY

Electorate 63,379   1974: 61,508

*Ginsburg, D. (Lab)	22,829
Galley, R. (C)	18,448
Derbyshire, N. (L)	7,580
Lab majority	**4,381**

No Change

	1974		1979
Total Votes	44,846		48,857
Turnout	72·9%		77·1%
Lab	20,378	45·4%	46·7%
C	13,477	30·1%	37·8%
L	10,991	24·5%	15·5%
Lab maj	6,901	15·3%	8·9%
Swing		−2·2%	+3·2%

Mr David Ginsburg, elected in 1959. Market research consultant. D March, 1921, ed University College School, Hampstead, and Balliol College, Oxford. Member, Select Committee on Science and Technology, since 1967; a vice-president and former chairman, Parliamentary and Scientific Committee. TGWU.

Mr Roy Galley, Post Office manager. B December, 1947; ed King Edward VII Grammar School, Sheffield, and Worcester College, Oxford. Former chairman, Leeds Young Conservatives and Yorkshire YCs.

Mr Neil Derbyshire, lecturer. Ed Huddersfield Polytechnic. Aged 27.

DONCASTER

Electorate 60,487   1974: 59,464

*Walker, H. (Lab)	22,184
Beard, P. (C)	19,208
Broadhead, G. (L)	3,646
Day, M. (Nat Front)	300
Lab majority	**2,976**

No Change

	1974		1979
Total Votes	43,260		45,338
Turnout	72·7%		75·0%
Lab	22,177	51·3%	48·9%
C	14,747	34·1%	42·4%
L	6,336	14·6%	8·0%
Nat Front	—		0·7%
Lab maj	7,430	17·2%	6·5%
Swing		−2·9%	+5·3%

Mr Harold Walker, Minister of State, Department of Employment, 1976-79, was Under Secretary for Employment, 1974-76; an Opposition spokesman on employment 1970-74. Under Secretary, Department of Employment and Productivity, 1968-70; Assistant Government Whip, 1967-68. Elected in 1964. Engineer. B July, 1927; ed at council school and Manchester College of Technology. Sponsored by AUEW.

Mr Paul Beard, barrister and crown court recorder, B May, 1930; ed The City Grammar School, Sheffield, and King's College, London. Contested Huddersfield, East, 1959; Oldham, East, 1966; and Wigan, February and October, 1974.

Mr Gerald Broadhead, managing director. Aged 50; ed Doncaster Technical College and Luton Polytechnic.

DON VALLEY

Electorate 95,287   1974: 88,777

*Welsh, M. C. (Lab)	39,603
Freeman, R. (C)	22,243
Simpson, E. (L)	8,238
Connolly, I. (Workers P)	720
McCabe, T. (WRP)	398
Lab majority	**17,360**

No Change

	1974		1979
Total Votes	65,115		71,202
Turnout	73·3%		74·7%
Lab	41,187	63·3%	55·6%
C	13,767	21·1%	31·2%
L	10,161	15·6%	11·6%
Workers P	—		1·0%
WRP	—		0·6%
Lab maj	27,420	42·2%	24·4%
Swing		−1·0%	+8·9%

Mr **Michael Welsh** is a miner and has been a member of the NUM for 36 years and local councillor for 16 years. B November 1926; ed at elementary school. Sponsored by NUM.

Mr **Roger Freeman,** banker and chartered accountant. B May 1942; ed Whitgift School and Balliol College, Oxford. President of Oxford University Conservative Association, 1964. Former treasurer of Bow Group, and managing director, Bow Publications, 1968.

Mr **Edwin Simpson,** project engineer, contested the seat, October, 1974. B November, 1940; ed technical high school, Oakwood, Rotherham.

Mr **Terence McCabe,** aged 32, painter. Member, Yorkshire area committee, UCATT and branch chairman.

DORKING

Electorate 60,630   1974: 58,955

Wickenden, K. (C)	29,003
Hope, Mrs R. (L)	9,240
Weir, J. A. S. (Lab)	8,970
C majority	19,763

No Change

	1974		1979
Total Votes	44,215		47,213
Turnout	75·0%		77·9%
C	22,403	50·7%	61·4%
L	12,098	27·4%	19·6%
Lab	9,714	22·0%	19·0%
C maj	10,305	23·3%	41·8%
Swing		−2·1%	+6·8%

Mr **Keith Wickenden** is executive chairman of European Ferries Ltd and Felixstowe Dock & Railway Co. Director, Brighton and Hove Albion Football Club. Fellow of the Institute of Chartered Accountants. In 1971 was joint liquidator of Rolls-Royce Ltd. B November, 1932; ed East Grinstead Grammar School. Former ward secretary and chairman, Coventry North Constituency Association.

Mrs **Rachel Hope,** teacher. B June, 43; ed Hove Grammar School; La Sainte Union College of Education, and Brighton College of Technology.

Mr **John Weir,** chartered engineer. B September, 1937; ed John Fisher School and Crabfield School of Management. ASTMS.

DORSET, North

Electorate 80,732   1974: 71,325

Baker, N. (C)	40,046
Court, G. (L)	16,750
Rowlands, M. C. (Lab)	7,543
C majority	23,296

No Change

	1974		1979
Total Votes	56,486		64,339
Turnout	79·2%		79·7%
C	28,891	51·1%	62·2%
L	20,350	36·0%	26·0%
Lab	7,245	12·8%	11·7%
C maj	8,541	15·1%	36·2%
Swing		−1·2%	+6·1%

Mr **Nicholas Baker** contested Southwark, Peckham, in both elections in 1974. Partner in firm of solicitors. B November, 1938; ed St Neot's School, Hampshire, and Clifton College and Exeter College, Oxford. Former executive officer, Oxford University Conservative Association and editor of *Oxford Tory*; president, Oxford Carlton Club and member, consultative committee, Union Society. Member, Bow Group; member of political committee since 1974; council member in 1968; secretary 1970-71; and political officer, 1971-72. Former advertising manager and member of editorial board, *Crossbow*.

Mr **Glyn Court,** teacher and writer, contested Westbury in both elections in 1974. B May, 1924; ed Taunton School, University College, Exeter; and Universities of Paris and Grenoble. Member, Ilfracombe UDC, 1965-68; Somerset County Council, 1973-77. IAAM.

Mr **Murray Rowlands,** a principal lecturer at Farnborough College of Technology. B March, 1941; ed Victoria University, Wellington, and Liverpool University. Member, Thamesdown Borough Council, 1976-78. Secretary, Swindon Branch, NATFHE.

DORSET, South

Electorate 74,239   1974: 70,416

Viscount Cranborne (C)	32,372
Chedzoy, A. (Lab)	17,133
Howe, P. St J. (L)	8,649
C majority	15,239

No Change

	1974		1979
Total Votes	53,078		58,154
Turnout	75·4%		78·3%
C	24,351	45·9%	55·7%
Lab	17,652	33·3%	29·5%
L	11,075	20·9%	14·9%
C maj	6,699	12·6%	26·2%
Swing		−1·2%	+6·8%

Viscount Cranborne is a banker. B 1946; ed Eton and Christ Church, Oxford. President, Hatfield and Welwyn Garden City Society for Mentally Handicapped Children; Regional president, Gateway Clubs; president, Hertfordshire Association of Youth Clubs; governor, International Students' House; patron, Anglo-Gambia Diocesan

Association; member, council, Royal Society of St George; vice-president, Chelwood and District Welfare Association (Liverpool).

Mr Alan Chedzoy, lecturer, contested the seat, February and October, 1974. B March, 1935; ed Reading and Southampton Universities. Member, Weymouth and Portland Borough Council. NATFHE.

Mr Peter Howe, solicitor. B October, 1940; ed at Epsom School.

DORSET, West

Electorate 56,658   1974: 53,569

*Spicer, J. W. (C)	26,281
Jones, T. (L)	9,776
Skevington, H. J. (Lab)	7,999
Tillotson, J. (Nat Front)	514
McEwan, Mrs G. (Wessex Reg)	192

C majority	16,505

No Change

	1974		1979
Total Votes	41,699		44,762
Turnout	77·8%		79·0%
C	20,517	49·2%	58·7%
L	11,832	28·4%	21·8%
Lab	9,350	22·4%	17·9%
Nat Front	—		1·1%
Wessex Reg	—		0·4%
C maj	8,685	20·8%	36·9%
Swing		−1·7%	+7·0%

Mr James Spicer, company director and farmer. B 1925; ed Latymer. Elected in February, 1974; contested Southampton, Itchen, by-election in 1971. Member, European Parliament, since 1975. Member, Select Committee on European Secondary Legislation, 1974-75. Director, Conservative Group for Europe; member of national executive since 1966. Vice-chairman, Wessex Area CPC Committee; chairman, National CPC Advisory Committee, 1969-72.

Mr Trevor Jones, a local government officer, contested Preston, North, 1970. B June, 1944; ed London School of Economics. Leader, Liberal group, West Dorset Council, 1973-77. Member, Dorchester Council, 1976-77. Nalgo.

Mr John Skevington, teacher. B March, 1941; ed Bridport Grammar School and Weymouth College of Education. Member, Bridport Town Council. NUT.

DOVER AND DEAL

Electorate 75,883   1974: 74,704

*Rees, P. W. I. (C)	30,606
Chapman, Mrs J. L. (Lab)	22,664
Cohen, J. (L)	6,906
Fox, J. (Silly)	642
Johnson, P. (Nat Front)	378

C majority	7,942

No Change

	1974		1979
Total Votes	58,767		61,196
Turnout	78·7%		80·6%
C	25,647	43·6%	50·0%
Lab	23,353	39·7%	37·0%
L	9,767	16·6%	11·3%
Silly	—		1·0%
Nat Front	—		0·6%
C maj	2,294	3·9%	13·0%
Swing		−1·9%	+4·5%

Mr Peter Rees, QC was appointed Minister of State. Treasury, in May, 1979. Won the seat in 1970; fought Liverpool, West Derby, 1966, and Abertillery in 1965 by-election and 1964. Barrister (Inner Temple) 1953. B December, 1926; ed Stowe and Christ Church, Oxford. Member, Select Committee on Wealth Tax; Select Committee on Company Taxation. An Opposition spokesman on Treasury affairs. Former member, executive of 1922 Committee. Joint secretary, Conservative finance committee, since 1974, and officer of legal committee. Member, Institute of Taxation and Inns of Court Conservative and Unionist Society.

Mrs Jane Chapman, lecturer, contested Dorking, October, 1974. B May, 1950; ed London University and Cambridge. Member, Haringey Council since 1974. NATFHE.

Mr Jack Cohen, dental surgeon. B October, 1935; ed University School, Bexley, and Royal Dental Hospital London. Member, Dover District Council, as an Independent.

DOWN, North

Electorate 99,861   1974: 93,604

*Kilfedder, J. A. (UU)	36,989
Jones, K. (Alliance)	13,364
Smyth, C. (Off UU)	11,728

UU majority	23,625

No Change

	1974		1979
Total Votes	57,006		62,081
Turnout	60·9%		62·2%
UUUC	40,996	71·9%	
UU	—		59·6%
Alliance	9,973	17·5%	21·5%
Off UU	—		18·9%
UPNI	6,037	10·6%	
UUUC maj	31,023	54·4%	
UU maj	—		38·1%

Mr James Kilfedder, Official Unionist MP for North Down 1970-79, resigned from the party to stand as Ulster Unionist in 1979 election. Represented Belfast, West 1964-66. Former Secretary and Chief Whip Official Unionist Parliamentary Party. Secretary of the Northern Ireland Committee of the Conservative Party. Member of the Northern Ireland Assembly and Northern Ireland Convention. B 1928; ed Portora Royal School, Enniskillen and Trinity College, Dublin. Barrister (King's Inn, Dublin, 1952); (Grays Inn, 1958). Joint secretary, Conservative Parliamentary Committee on Northern Ireland since 1972.

Mr Keith Jones, Alliance party spokesman on industry and commerce. Contested seat, October, 1974. Member of North Down Council; at present Deputy Mayor. B 1940.

Mr Clifford Smyth, teacher, was a member of the Northern Ireland Assembly and the Northern Ireland Constitutional Convention. Former chairman of Queen's University Belfast, Conservative and Unionist Association. B 1934; ed. Dunfermline High School and Queen's University, Belfast.

DOWN, South

Electorate 89,562   1974: 91,354

*Powell, J. E. (Off UU)	32,254
McGrady, E. K. (SDLP)	24,033
Forde, P. M. (Alliance)	4,407
Markey, J. E. (IIP)	1,853
O'Hagan, D. (Rep Clubs)	1,682
Rice, S. G. (IDP)	216
Courtney, P. B. (Reform)	31

Off UU majority	8,221

No Change

	1974		1979
Total Votes	66,140		64,476
Turnout	72·4%		72·0%
Off UU	—	—	50·0%
UUUC	33,614	50·8%	—
SDLP	30,047	45·4%	37·3%
Repub	2,327	3·5%	2·6%
Marx Len	152	0·2%	—
Alliance	—	—	6·8%
IIP	—	—	2·9%
IDP	—	—	0·3%
Reform	—	—	0·0%
UUUC maj	3,567	5·4%	—
Off UU maj	—	—	12·7%

Mr Enoch Powell was returned for the seat in October, 1974. In February of that year he had refused to stand as a Conservative in  his former seat of Wolverhampton, South-West, denouncing the general election as "fraudulent". He was dismissed as defence spokesman for the Opposition by Mr Heath in 1968 following a controversial speech referrring to immigration. Unsuccessful candidate for Conservative leadership in 1965. Minister of Health 1960-63; Financial Secretary to Treasury, 1957-58 when he resigned in protest at Government spending. Parliamentary Secretary, Ministry of Housing and Local Government, 1955-57. Member, Select Committee on Procedure. Represented Wolverhampton, South-West, 1950-74. B July 1912; ed King Edward's School, Birmingham, and Trinity College, Cambridge. Professor of Greek, Sydney University, 1937-39.

Mr Edward McGrady, chartered accountant. Minister for Co-ordination in Northern Ireland Executive, 1974. Founder member and first chairman, SDLP 1970-72. Party treasurer, 1976-78. B 1943; ed St Patrick's High School, Downpatrick.

Mr Patrick Forde, farmer. B 1921. Member of South Down District Council.

Mr Eugene Markey, journalist. B 1944; ed Christian Brothers' School, Newry. Member, Newry District Council.

Desmond O'Hagan, journalist. Formerly senior lecturer in sociology and philosophy in Stranmillis College, Belfast before becoming full-time worker for Republican Clubs. B 1935; ed London School of Economics and Queen's University, Belfast.

Mr F. G. Rice, garage proprietor. B 1938. Ed Technical College, Ballynahick and studied in London.

Peter Courtney, a district councillor since 1961. B 1923; ed Public Elementary School and technical college. Candidate, 1974 for Northern Ireland Convention.

DUDLEY, East

Electorate 59,661   1974: 60,381

*Gilbert, J. W. (Lab)	22,521
Williams, W. D. (C)	14,834
Lewis, G. P. T. (L)	3,639
Baker, A. J. (Nat Front)	844

Lab Majority	7,687

No Change

	1974		1979
Total Votes	41,225		41,838
Turnout	68·3%		70·1%
Lab	23,621	57·3%	53·8%
C	11,430	27·7%	35·5%
L	5,003	12·1%	8·7%
Nat Front	1,171	2·8%	2·0%
Lab maj	12,191	29·6%	18·3%
Swing		−1·4%	+5·6%

Mr John Gilbert, Minister of State for Defence, since September 1976-79; Financial Secretary to Treasury, 1974-75; Minister for Transport, Department of Environment, 1975-76. Elected, February 1974; MP for Dudley, 1970-74, contested by-election, Dudley, 1968 and Ludlow, 1966. Opposition spokesman on Treasury matters, 1972-74. B April, 1927; ed, Merchant Taylors School, Northwood; St John's College, Oxford and New York University. NUGMW.

Mr Donald Williams, chartered accountant and director of a West Midlands food company and of an electronic engineering company. MP for Dudley from the by-election in 1968 to general election, 1970. Fought the seat, 1966. B October 1919; ed Royal Grammar School, Worcester. Member, Hereford and Worcester County Council, since 1973.

Mr Gerald Lewis, student counsellor, B March, 1926; ed Aberdeen University; Queen's University, Belfast; Aston University, Birmingham. NATFHE.

DUDLEY, West

Electorate 77,525   1974: 74,746

Blackburn, J. G. (C)	30,158
Hartley-Brewer, M. J. (Lab)	29,019

C majority	1,139

C gain from Lab

	1974		1979
Total Votes	56,214		59,177
Turnout	75·2%		76·3%
Lab	28,740	51·1%	49·0%
C	20,215	36·0%	51·0%
L	7,259	12·9%	—
Lab maj	8,525	15·1%	—
C maj	—	—	2·0%
Swing		−3·7%	+8·5%

Mr John Blackburn is a sales manager. Former member of the Royal Military Police and detective constable in Liverpool for nine years. B September 1933; ed Liverpool Collegiate School and Liverpool University. Member, Institute of Sales Engineers and of Institute of Commercial and Technical Representatives. Elected Wolverhampton Borough Council in  1971 and to Wolverhampton District Council in 1973. Member, Post Office Users' National Council, since 1973.

Mr Michael Hartley-Brewer, political adviser to Mr David Ennals as Secretary of State for Social Services, contested Birmingham, Selly Oak, 1970. B September, 1943; ed Salesian College and Birmingham University. COHSE and NUJ.

DUMFRIES

Electorate 64,311   1974: 61,856

*Monro, H. S. P. (C)	22,704
Wood, A. (Lab)	13,700
Wallace, J. (L)	7,169
Gibson, E. (Scot Nat)	6,647

C majority	9,004

No Change

	1974		1979
Total Votes	47,447		50,220
Turnout	76·7%		78·1%
C	18,386	38·8%	45·2%
Lab	12,558	26·5%	27·3%
Scot Nat	12,542	26·4%	13·2%
L	3,961	8·3%	14·3%
C maj	5,828	12·3%	17·9%
Swing		−3·0%	+2·8%

Mr Hector Monro appointed an Under Secretary of State for Environment with special responsibilities for Sport in May 1979, was Opposition spokesman on sport since 1974, on Scotland, 1974-75; Under Secretary for Health and Education, Scottish Office, 1971-74; Lord Commissioner of the Treasury (whip), 1970-71; Opposition whip, 1967-70.  Elected in 1964. B October, 1922; ed Canford School and King's College, Cambridge. Member, Dumfries County Council, 1952-67. Chairman, Anchor Extrusions Ltd. Manager, Scottish rugby XV during tour of Australia. Member, backbench committees on Scotland, agriculture and aviation.

Mr Alec Wood, teacher. B 1950. Has held various posts in Edinburgh, North CLP. EIS.

Mr James Wallace has been a member of the Scottish Liberal Party executive since 1976. Barrister's clerk. B August, 1954; ed Annan Academy; Downing College, Cambridge; Edinburgh University (Chairman, university Liberal Club, 1976-77).

Mr Ernest Gibson, teacher. B November, 1928; ed Portobello Secondary School and Jordanhill College. District councillor.

DUNBARTONSHIRE, Central

Electorate 49,381   1974: 49,357

*McCartney, H. (Lab)	20,515
Soames, N. (C)	8,512
Lindsay, W. (Scot Nat)	6,055
McCreadie, Mrs L. (L)	3,099
McCafferty, D. (Comm)	1,017
Darroch, R. (CD)	312

Lab majority	12,003

No Change

	1974		1979
Total Votes	39,393		39,510
Turnout	79·8%		80·0%
Lab	15,837	40·2%	51·9%
Scot Nat	11,452	29·1%	15·3%
C	6,792	17·2%	21·5%
Comm	3,417	8·7%	2·6%
L	1,895	4·8%	7·8%
CD	—		0·8%
Lab maj	4,385	11·1%	30·4%
Swing		−3·3%	−4·1%

Mr Hugh McCartney, sales representative, was returned for the seat in February 1974; MP for Dunbartonshire, East 1970-74. B January 1920; ed John Street Secondary School, Glasgow, and Royal Technical College, Glasgow. Secretary, Scottish Labour Group of MPs. Member, Dunbarton County Council; burgh councillor since 1955. Sponsored by  TGWU.

Mr Nicholas Soames, insurance broker, was educated at Eton. B February, 1948.

Mr William Lindsay, sales manager and buyer. Contested Glasgow, Shettleston, February, 1974, 1970, and 1966. B May, 1936; ed Woodside Secondary School and Allan Glen's. Former SNP leader on Glasgow Corporation.

Mr Danny McCafferty, 29, primary school teacher. EIS.

DUNBARTONSHIRE, East

Electorate 73,261   1974: 61,788

Hogg, N. (Lab)	23,268
Hirst, M. W. (C)	20,944
*Bain, Mrs M. A. (Scot Nat)	12,654
Waddell, R. (L)	4,600

Lab majority	2,324

Lab gain from Scot Nat

	1974		1979
Total Votes	49,838		61,466
Turnout	80·7%		83·9%
Scot Nat	15,551	31·2%	20·6%
C	15,529	31·2%	34·1%
Lab	15,122	30·3%	37·9%
L	3,636	7·3%	7·5%
Scot Nat maj	22	0·0%	
Lab maj	—		3·8%
Swing		—	−2·4%

Mr **Norman Hogg,** a trade union officer, has worked full-time with Nalgo since 1967. B March, 1938, ed Ruthrieston Secondary School, Aberdeen.

Mr **Michael Hirst,** chartered accountant, contested Dunbartonshire, Central, February and October, 1974. B January, 1946; ed Glasgow Academy, Glasgow University and University of Iceland, Reykjavik, where he was exchange scholar. Chairman, Conservative Parliamentary Candidates Association; Vicechairman, Scottish Young Conservatives; past president Glasgow University Conservative Club.

Mrs **Margaret Bain,** teacher, won the seat in October, 1974. Appoint SNP spokesman on education and social services, October, 1974. Member, SNP national executive. Fought seat in February, 1974. B September, 1945; ed Biggar High School, Glasgow University and Jordanhill College.

Mr **Ronald Waddell,** works in transport planning. B May, 1954; ed Bearsden Academy; Strathclyde and Salford universities; Cranfield Institute of Technology.

DUNBARTONSHIRE, West

Electorate 54,507   1974: 51,943

*Campbell, I. (Lab)		21,166
Munro, J. C. (C)		14,709
Stratton, S. (Scot Nat)		7,835
Lab majority		6,457

No Change

	1974		1979
Total Votes	40,658		43,710
Turnout	78·3%		80·2%
Lab	15,511	38·1%	48·4%
Scot Nat	13,697	33·7%	17·9%
C	9,421	23·2%	33·7%
L	2,029	5·0%	—
Lab maj	1,814	4·4%	14·7%
Swing		−4·3%	+0·1%

Mr **Ian Campbell,** chairman of the all-party Scotch whisky industry group, was elected in June, 1970; secretary, Scottish Labour Group, 1975-76. Electrical power engineer with South of Scotland Electricity Board, 1953-70. B April, 1962; ed Dunbarton Academy, Royal Technical College (now Strathclyde University) Member Dunbarton Town and County

councils, 1958-70; Provost of Dunbarton, 1962-70. NUGM.

Mr **James Munro,** primary school teacher. B, 1953; ed, Paisley Grammar School, Langside College and Jordanhill College of Education. Member, Central Council, Scottish Conservative Association, and of executive of Scottish Federation of Conservative Students.

Mr **Stanley Stratton,** head of planning department, BBC Scotland. B July 1932; ed George Heriot School.

DUNDEE, East

Electorate 64,330   1974: 63,152

*Wilson, R. G. (Scot Nat)		20,497
Reid, J. (Lab)		17,978
Townsend, B. J. T. (C)		9,072
Brodie, C. (L)		2,317
Battersby, R. (WRP)		95
Scot Nat majority		2,519

No Change

	1974		1979
Total Votes	46,343		49,959
Turnout	73·4%		77·7%
Scot Nat	22,120	47·7%	41·0%
Lab	15,137	32·7%	36·0%
C	7,784	16·8%	18·2%
L	1,302	2·8%	4·6%
WRP	—	—	0·2%
Scot Nat maj	6,983	15·0%	5·0%

Mr **Gordon Wilson** won the seat in February, 1974; contested it in the March, 1973, by-election. Partner in a law practice. B April, 1938; ed Douglas High School and Edinburgh University. Senior vice-chairman SNP; appointed Deputy Leader, SNP Parliamentary Party and spokesman on energy and oil, March, 1974. Member, Law Society of Scotland.

Mr **James Reid,** engineer. Convenor shop stewards AUEW national committee; district committee. B 1932. Chairman, Scottish Council, Mobility for the Disabled.

Mr **Brian Townsend,** chief press officer, Ford Motor company. B 1941; ed International School of Geneva, Ecole D'Humanite, Switzerland; Aberdeen University. Formerly features writer and motoring correspondent, *Aberdeen Press and Journal.* NUJ.

DUNDEE, West

Electorate 63,883   1974: 63,916

Ross, E. (Lab)		23,654
Fairlie, J. (Scot Nat)		13,197
Stevenson, I. (C)		12,892
Mennie, R. (Comm)		316
Lab majority		10,457

No Change

	1974		1979
Total Votes	47,503		50,059
Turnout	74·3%		78·4%
Lab	19,480	41·0%	47·3%
Scot Nat	16,678	35·1%	26·4%
C	8,769	18·5%	25·8%
L	2,195	4·6%	—
Comm	381	0·8%	0·6%
Lab maj	2,802	5·9%	20·9%
Swing		−5·0%	+0·5%

Mr **Ernest Ross,** quality control engineer. B July, 1942; ed local schools. Sponsored by AUEW (TASS).

Mr James Fairlie, a teacher, contested the seat in both 1974 elections. B May, 1940; Ed St John's Perth, Perth Academy, Dundee University and Dundee College of Education.

Mr Ian Stevenson, registered chiropodist. 1945; ed Ellesmere Port GS and Edinburgh School of Chiropody. Member, Tayside Regional Council, since 1974; chairman, Scottish Young Conservatives, since 1973.

DUNFERMLINE

Electorate 64,868   1974: 60,679

Douglas, R. G. (Lab)	22,803
Lester, A. (C)	15,490
Cameron, Miss A. (Scot Nat)	7,351
Whitelaw, G. (L)	5,803
Lab and Co-op majority	7,313

No Change

	1974		1979
Total Votes	46,060		51,447
Turnout	75·9%		79·3%
Lab	18,470	40·1%	44·3%
Scot Nat	13,179	28·6%	14·3%
C	10,611	23·0%	30·1%
L	3,800	8·3%	11·3%
Lab maj	5,291	11·5%	14·2%
Swing		−4·1%	+1·4%

Mr Richard Douglas was MP for Stirlingshire, East, and Clackmannan, 1970 to February, 1974; unsuccessfully contested that seat in October, 1974; contested Glasgow, Pollock, in 1967 by-election; Edinburgh, West, in 1966 and South Angus in 1964. B January 1932; ed senior secondary school, Cooperative College, Stanford Hall, Loughborough, and University of Strathclyde.

Mr Anthony Lester, district manager, assurance company. 1928; ed Morgan Academy, Dundee. Member, Lothian Regional Council, since 1974. Contested Clackmannan and East Stirlingshire, February, 1974; West Lothian, October 1974.

Miss **Athole Cameron,** primary school headmistress, contested Inverness, 1970, and Dunfermline, October, 1974. B January, 1926; ed Perth Academy, Dundee College of Education.

Mr Gordon Whitelaw, sales representative. B August, 1950, ed Onslow Drive Secondary School, Glasgow.

DURHAM

Electorate 77,463   1974: 74,711

*Hughes, W. M. (Lab)	30,903
Lavis, M. (C)	19,666
Wood, C. (L)	8,572
Lab majority	11,237

No Change

	1974		1979
Total Votes	53,505		59,141
Turnout	71·6%		76·3%
Lab	31,305	58·5%	52·3%
C	13,189	24·7%	33·3%
L	9,011	16·8%	14·5%
Lab maj	18,116	33·8%	19·0%
Swing		−4·2%	+7·4%

Mr Mark Hughes, elected in 1970; member, European Parliament, 1975-79. Lecturer in economic history at Durham University, 1964-70. B December, 1932; ed Stowcliffe School, Durham School and Balliol College, Oxford. Served on Durham Rural Council. Former member, Select Committee on Parliamentary Commissioner for Administration and of Public Expenditure Committee.

Mr Matthew Lavis, assistant registrar, University of Durham. B December, 1944; ed Cheltenham Grammar School and St John's College, University of Durham. Past chairman, Durham Conservative Association.

DURHAM, North-West

Electorate 63,387   1974: 61,283

*Armstrong, E. (Lab)	29,525
Fenwick, T. (C)	14,245
Hannibell, Mrs J. (L)	4,394
Lab majority	15,280

No Change

	1974		1979
Total Votes	43,568		48,164
Turnout	71·1%		76·0%
Lab	27,953	64·2%	61·3%
C	9,197	21·1%	29·6%
L	6,418	14·7%	9·1%
Lab maj	18,756	43·1%	31·7%
Swing		−3·4%	+5·7%

Mr Ernest Armstrong, Under Secretary for Environment, 1975-79, was Under Secretary for Education and Science, 1974-75; Opposition spokesman on education and science, 1973-74; Opposition whip, 1970-73; Lord Commissioner of the Treasury 1969-70; Assistant Government whip, 1967-69. Elected in 1964; contested Sunderland, South, 1955 and 1959. Schoolmaster. B January, 1915; ed Wolsingham Grammar School and Leeds City Teacher Training College, NUT and NUGM.

Mr Thomas Fenwick, managing director, forestry products company and executive director, family farming company. B 1926, ed Charterhouse and Jesus Coll, Cambridge. Manager, approved school at Stanhope Castle, since 1958. Chairman, North-West Durham Conservative Association.

Mrs Julienne Hannibell, housewife. Aged 37. District and town councillor.

EALING, Acton

Electorate 56,875   1974: 56,689

*Young, Sir G. (C)	21,056
Barnham, G. A. (Lab)	15,258
Rowley, S. (L)	3,549
Wakley, C. (Nat Front)	501
O'Leary, J. (INP)	243
C majority	5,798

No Change

	1974		1979
Total Votes	39,099		40,607
Turnout	69·0%		71·4%
C	17,669	45·2%	51·9%
Lab	16,861	43·1%	37·6%
L	4,569	11·7%	8·7%
Nat Front	—		1·2%
INP	—		0·6%
C maj	808	2·1%	14·3%
Swing		−0·7%	+6·1%

Sir George Young, became an Under Secretary of State for Health and Social Secretary in May 1979. Opposition whip, 1976-79. Economist, elected in February, 1974. B July, 1941; ed Eton and Christ Church, Oxford. Member, Select Committee on Violence in Marriage, since 1975; Conservative watchdog group for the self-employed since 1975; GLC, 1970-73; Lambeth Borough Council, 1968-71. Economic adviser, Post Office Corporation, 1969-79. ASTMS.

Mr Glen Barnham, official of Equity, contested Esher, February, 1974, and Ealing Acton, October, 1974. B April 1945; ed at local schools. Member, Ealing Council, since 1971, and chairman of the Social Services committee since 1973. Chairman of governors of comprehensive school.

Mr Simon Rowley, manager with microfilm service firm. B March, 1949; ed Wellington and University of York.

EALING, North

Electorate 76,805   1974: 73,898

Greenway, H. (C)	27,524
*Molloy, W. J. (Lab)	26,044
Taylor, J. (L)	5,162
Shaw, J. (Nat Front)	1,047
C majority	1,480

C gain from Lab

	1974		1979
Total Votes	54,577		59,777
Turnout	73·9%		77·8%
Lab	24,574	45·0%	43·6%
C	21,652	39·7%	46·0%
L	8,351	15·3%	8·6%
Nat Front	—		1·8%
Lab maj	2,922	5·3%	
C maj	—		2·4%
Swing		−0·6%	+3·8%

Mr Harry Greenway, deputy headmaster at a London school. Contested Stepney, 1970; Stepney and Poplar, February and October, 1974. B 1934; ed Warwick School, College of St Mark and St John, London and Caen University. Member, Bow Group and Conservative National Advisory Committee on Education; British delegate to Assembly of Atlantic Treaty Association, 1971-74, and senior vice-chairman, Atlantic Education committee; Council of British Horse Society and founder and chairman of the London Schools' Horse Society. President, London Schoolboys' Hockey Association. AMA.

Mr William Molloy was elected in 1964. B October, 1918; ed St Thomas Council School, Swansea, and University of Wales. Member of European Parliament, 1976-77 and of Council of "Get Britain Out" (of EEC) campaign. Founder and vice-chairman, PLP Common Market and European Group; chairman, PLP social services group, since 1974. Former chairman, Staff-Side Whitley Council, Germany and Austria Sections, FO. Member, Council of Europe and Western European Union, 1969-73, Inter-Parliamentary Union and Council of Royal Geographical Society.

Mr Jack Taylor, deputy general secretary, Workers' Educational Association, and honorary secretary, International Federation of Workers' Educational Associations. B June, 1925; ed Harrow County School, University of New Zealand, and Sydney University. Vice-chairman, Association of Liberal Trade Unionists. TGWU.

EALING, Southall

Electorate 73,146   1974: 70,832

*Bidwell, S. J. (Lab)	28,498
Patten, R. C. (C)	17,220
Hains, R. (L)	3,920
Fairhurst, J. (Nat Front)	1,545
Gupta, S. (Ind)	637
Ali, T. (Soc Unity)	477
Paul, S. S. (Ind Businessman)	115
Lab majority	11,278

No Change

Ealing Southall 211

	1974		1979
Total Votes	45,010		52,412
Turnout	63·5%		71·7%
Lab	24,218	53·8%	54·4%
C	14,235	31·6%	32·9%
L	6,557	14·6%	7·5%
Nat Front	—		2·9%
Ind	—		1·2%
Soc Unity	—		0·9%
Ind Businessmen	—		0·2%
Lab maj	9,983	22·2%	21·5%
Swing		−2·6%	+0·3%

Mr Sydney Bidwell was elected in 1966. B January, 1917; ed elementary school and evening classes. Contested Hertfordshire, South West, 1964; Hertfordshire, East, 1959. Member, Select Committee on Race Relations and Immigration. Lecturer; former tutor and organizer for National Council of Labour Colleges. Previously railway worker. Former NUR and now

TGWU. Chairman, Tribune Group, 1975. Vice-chairman, PLP transport group, 1977. Sponsored by TGWU.

Mr Robert Patten, solicitor and JP. B 1937; ed The Stationers' Company's School, London. Contested constituency, October, 1974.

Mr Richard Hains contested Birmingham, Northfield, October, 1974, and Walsall, South, February, 1974. B January, 1945. Adviser to children and people's homes.

EASINGTON

Electorate 65,242   1974: 63,815

*Dormand, J. D. (Lab)	29,537
Smailes, J. S. (C)	11,981
Morley, Mrs V. (L)	6,979
Lab majority	17,556

No Change

	1974		1979
Total Votes	44,036		48,497
Turnout	69·0%		74·3%
Lab	28,984	65·8%	60·9%
C	8,047	18·3%	24·7%
L	7,005	15·9%	14·4%
Lab maj	20,937	47·5%	36·2%
Swing		−1·8%	+5·6%

Mr John Dormand, Lord Commissioner of the Treasury (Government Whip) 1974-79; assistant Government Whip, 1974. Elected in 1970. B August, 1919; ed Wellfield Grammar School, Bede College, Durham, Loughborough College and Oxford and Harvard Universities. Former member, Select Committee on Nationalised Industries.

Secretary, Northern Group of Labour MPs. Member, Easington RDC, 1949-52; education officer for Easington RDC, 1963-70. APEX. Formerly NALGO and NUT.

Mr Stephen Smailes, maintenance engineer. B 1940; ed Newham Grange School; Stockton and Billingham Technical College. Member, Stockton Borough Council; Northern Area Conservative Council. Contested Easington February and October, 1974.

Mrs Vivienne Morley, senior medical social worker. B February, 1947; ed Cambridge High School, Cambridge, College of Arts and Technology, and Oxford University. NALGO.

EASTBOURNE

Electorate 76,880   1974: 74,697

*Gow, I. R. E. (C)	37,168
Bellotti, D. (L)	11,084
Caine, L. J. (Lab)	10,166
Mitchell, C. (Nat Front)	533
C majority	26,084

No Change

	1974		1979
Total Votes	55,689		58,951
Turnout	74·6%		76·7%
C	30,442	54·7%	63·0%
L	14,417	25·9%	18·8%
Lab	10,830	19·4%	17·2%
Nat Front	—	—	0·9%
C maj	16,025	28·8%	44·2%
Swing		−3·2%	+5·2%

Mr Ian Gow is a solicitor. Elected in February, 1974; contested Coventry, East, 1964, and Clapham, 1966. B February, 1937; ed Winchester. Member, Select Committee on Wealth Tax and Select Committee on Parliamentary Commissioner for Administration Secretary, Conservative Party backbench committees on Northern Ireland since

1976 and Constitutional Committee since 1977. Appointed PPS to Mrs Thatcher as Prime Minister in May, 1979.

Mr Davis Bellotti, South-East regional secretary of the YMCA. B August, 1943; ed Exeter School and YMCA National College, Member, Lewes Town Council.

Mr Leonard Caine, clerical assistant, contested the seat, October 1974. B June 1926; ed Bedewell Church of England School, Eastbourne. Member, Eastbourne Borough Council, since 1962; secretary, Eastbourne and District Trades Council. TGWU.

EAST GRINSTEAD

Electorate 59,124   1974: 55,602

*Johnson Smith, G. (C)	28,279
Nieboer J. (L)	11,102
Taylor, R. J. (Lab)	6,196
C majority	17,177

No Change

	1974		1979
Total Votes	41,438		45,577
Turnout	74·5%		77·1%
C	22,035	53·2%	62·0%
L	12,755	30·8%	24·4%
Lab	6,648	16·0%	13·6%
C maj	9,280	22·4%	37·6%
Swing		−1·8%	+5·6%

Mr Geoffrey Johnson Smith, Parliamentary Secretary, Civil Service Department, 1972-74; Under Secretary of Defence for the Army, 1971-73. Elected at a by-election, 1965. Opposition Whip, 1965-66. Represented Holborn and St Pancras, South, 1959-1964. Member, Select Committee on MPs' interests, 1976. Vice chairman, Con-

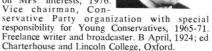

servative Party organization with special responsibility for Young Conservatives, 1965-71. Freelance writer and broadcaster. B April, 1924; ed Charterhouse and Lincoln College, Oxford.

Mr Jeremy Nieboer, solicitor. B October, 1940; ed Harrow School and Oriel College, Oxford.

Mr Richard Taylor, school teacher and former civil servant. B September, 1945; ed King Edward VI Grammar School, Morpeth, and Newcastle University. NUT.

EAST KILBRIDE

Electorate 73,094   1974: 65,799

*Miller, Dr M. S. (Lab)	31,401
Hodgson, W. G. (C)	17,128
Murray, G. (Scot Nat)	9,090
McDowell, D. (Comm)	658
Lab majority	14,273

No Change

	1974		1979
Total Votes	52,073		58,277
Turnout	79·1%		79·7%
Lab	21,810	41·9%	53·9%
Scot Nat	19,106	36·7%	15·6%
C	8,513	16·3%	29·4%
L	2,644	5·1%	—
Comm	—	—	1·1%
Lab maj	2,704	5·2%	24·5%
Swing		−5·3%	+0·5%

Dr Maurice Miller won the seat in February 1974; MP for Glasgow, Kelvingrove, 1964-74. Government whip, 1968-69. Medical practitioner and company director. B August, 1920; ed Shawlands Academy, Glasgow and Glasgow University. Member, Glasgow Corporation, 1950-64; Bailie 1954-57. Chairman, Glasgow and West of Scotland Socialist Medical Association. Member, Commons Expenditure Committee, Select Committee on Abortion (Admendment) Bill, 1975-76. Chairman, PLP health group. Sponsored by ASTMS.

Mr William Hodgson, estate manager. B, 1937; ed Edinburgh Academy and at agriculture college. Farmed in Australia for eight years. Delegate, Naracoote District, Liberal and Country League of South Australia, 1966-71 and president, 1971.

Mr Gordon Murray, a civil engineer, contested the seat, February and October, 1974. B July, 1927; ed Aberdeen Grammar School and Robert Gordon's College of Technology. Member, Strathclyde Regional Council. Member, SNP national executive committee and former executive vice-chairman.

Mr David McDowall is a lecturer in English. Ed Glasgow University and Jordanhill College of Education.

EASTLEIGH

Electorate 85,400   1974: 75,826

*Price, D. E. C. (C)	38,516
Roberts, Mrs. C. E. (Lab)	18,222
Johnson, G. D. (L)	12,143
C majority	20,294

No Change

	1974		1979
Total Votes	59,755		68,881
Turnout	78·8%		80·7%
C	26,869	45·0%	55·9%
Lab	19,054	31·9%	26·5%
L	13,832	23·1%	17·6%
C maj	7,815	13·1%	29·4%
Swing		−1·4%	+8·1%

Mr David Price was Under Secretary for Aerospace, Department of Trade and Industry, 1971-72; Parliamentary Secretary, Ministry of Aviation Supply, 1970-71; Parliamentary Secretary, Ministry of Technology, June to October, 1970. Opposition spokesman on technology and science, 1964-70. Parliamentary Secretary, Board of Trade, 1962-64. Elected 1955. B November, 1924; ed Eton, Trinity College, Cambridge, and Yale University (Research Fellow); President Cambridge Union, 1948. Economist and industrial executive. General consultant, Institute of Works Managers.

Mrs Cynthia Roberts, housewife and former secretary. B December, 1936; ed South Borough Secondary Girls' School, Maidstone, and Gilmore House, London.

Mr David Johnson contested the seat, February and October, 1974. Headmaster. B July, 1937; ed Shaftesbury Grammar School and King Alfred College, Winchester. Member, Romsey Borough Council, 1967-73; Test Valley Council, since 1973.

EBBW VALE

Electorate 36,207   1974: 37,640

*Foot, M. M. (Lab)	20,028
Inkin, G. (C)	3,937
Pope, A. T. (L)	3,082
Robert, G. ap. (Pl Cymru)	1,884
Lab majority	16,091

No Change

	1974		1979
Total Votes	28,647		28,931
Turnout	76·1%		79·9%
Lab	21,226	74·1%	69·2%
L	3,167	11·1%	10·7%
C	2,153	7·5%	13·6%
Pl Cymru	2,101	7·3%	6·5%
Lab maj	18,059	63·0%	55·6%
Swing		−2·4%	+5·5%

Mr Michael Foot was Lord President of the Council and Leader of the Commons 1976-79. Runner-up to Mr Callaghan in election for Labour Party leadership. Secretary of State for Employment, 1974-76. Opposition spokesman on the power and steel industries, 1970-71; shadow Leader of the House principally concerned with Common Market legislation, 1971-72; from 1972-74 concerned with EEC only. Unsuccessfully contested deputy leadership of PLP in July, 1970, and November, 1971. Returned for Ebbw Vale at a by-election in 1960; MP for Plymouth, Devonport, 1945-55, he contested the seat in 1959, and

Monmouth, 1935. Journalist and author, former managing director of *Tribune*. B July, 1913; ed Swanage, Leighton Park School, Reading and Wadham College, Forres School, Oxford; president of Union, 1933. Member, Committee of Privileges; Labour Party National Executive, 1947-50, and since 1972. Became Deputy Leader of the Opposition in May, 1979.

Mr Geoffrey Inkin, farmer. B 1934; ed Dean Close School, Cheltenham; RMA Sandhurst, RMCS Shrivenham, Staff College, Camberley, Royal Agricultural College, Cirencester. Gwent county councillor.

Mr Ambrose Pope, mechanical engineer. B October, 1923; ed local school, technical college and RAF. Former councillor, Ebbw Vale UDC. Former councillor, Ebbw Vale UDC. Former shop steward. Engineering staff representative for AEUW at BSC Ebbw Vale.

Mr Gwilym ap Robert fought the seat at the last general election. B May, 1976; ed Cardiff High School; Wales and Oxford universities, and Harvard Seminary Foundation, USA. Lecturer, Wales University. AUT.

ECCLES

Electorate 58,496   1974: 57,549

*Carter-Jones, L. (Lab)	24,280
Reid, J. (C)	16,221
Knight, G. (L)	4,448
Keenan, T. (Comm)	368
Lab majority	8,059

No Change

	1974		1979
Total Votes	41,908		45,317
Turnout	72·8%		77·5%
Lab	22,328	53·3%	53·6%
C	13,062	31·2%	35·8%
L	6,170	14·7%	9·8%
Comm	348	0·8%	0·8%
Lab maj	9,266	22·1%	17·8%
Swing		−2·5%	+2·1%

Mr Lewis Carter-Jones, elected in 1964, contested City of Chester, 1956 by-election and 1959. Teacher, lecturer and industrial training adviser. B November, 1920; ed Bridgend Grammar School and University College of Wales, Aberystwyth. Chairman, Committee for Research for Apparatus for Disabled and of PLP Disablement Group. Vice-chairman, all-party group for chemical industry; PLP aviation group; disabled income group. Secretary, all party BLESMA group. Parliamentary adviser to RNIB. Sponsored by TGWU.

Mr John Reid, section head of industrial group sales office for paint company. B 1941; ed St Bede's College, Manchester. Vice chairman, Ashton-under-Lyne Conservative Association; school manager and governor. Past member, Court of Lancaster University.

Mr Gordon Knight, commercial manager in a shipping company. B November, 1911; ed Stand Grammar School, Whitefield, Manchester, and Bolton Technical College.

Mr Terry Keenan, primary school deputy headmaster. Aged 36. Member, Salford Trades Council. NUT.

EDINBURGH, Central

Electorate 37,740   1974: 40,956

*Cook, R. F. (Lab)	12,191
McLetchie, D. W. (C)	7,530
Donaldson, S. (L)	3,096
Kennedy, G. (Scot Nat)	2,486
Boyd, C. D. (Scot Lab)	176
Lab majority	4,661

No Change

	1974		1979
Total Votes	27,634		25,479
Turnout	67·5%		67·5%
Lab	11,129	40·3%	47·8%
C	7,176	26·0%	29·6%
Scot Nat	6,866	24·8%	9·8%
L	2,463	8·9%	12·2%
Scot Lab	—	—	0·7%
Lab maj	3,953	14·3%	18·2%
Swing		−5·6%	−2·0%

Mr Robin Cook was elected in February, 1974; contested Edinburgh, North, 1970. Tutor and organizer in adult education. B February, 1946; ed Aberdeen Grammar School, Royal High School, Edinburgh and Edinburgh University. Vice-chairman, PLP Defence Group; chairman, housing sub-committee, Scottish Labour Group, and all-party group on penal reform in Scotland. Member, Advisory Panel on Arms Control and Disarmament. Sponsored by NUR.

Mr David McLetchie, solicitor. B 1952; ed George Heriot's School, Edinburgh and Edinburgh University. Vice chairman, Federation of Conservative Students, 1974-75.

Mr Stewart Donaldson, chairman of the Scottish Young Liberals since 1978. Investment analyst. B December, 1953; ed Morrison's Academy, Crieff, Perthshire, and Edinburgh University.

Mr Gavin Kennedy, lecturer in economics and author, contested Chelmsford for Labour in 1970. B February, 1940; ed Strathclyde and Brunel Universities. AUT and Writers' Guild.

EDINBURGH, East

Electorate 57,473   1974: 57,460

*Strang, G. S. (Lab)	23,477
Campbell, G. (C)	14,660
MacDougall, G. C. (Scot Nat)	5,296
Downes, Miss C. (Comm)	173
Brotherstone, T. (WRP)	124
Lab majority	8,817

No Change

	1974		1979
Total Votes	43,784		43,730
Turnout	76·2%		76·1%
Lab	19,669	44·9%	53·7%
Scot Nat	11,213	25·6%	12·1%
C	10,111	23·1%	33·5%
L	2,578	5·9%	—
Comm	213	0·5%	0·4%
WRP	—	—	0·3%
Lab maj	8,456	19·3%	20·2%
Swing		−4·9%	+0·8%

Mr Gavin Strang, Parliamentary Secretary, Ministry of Agriculture, Fisheries and Food, 1974-79; Under Secretary for Oil, Department of Energy, 1974. Elected in 1970. Member, Select Committee on Science and Technology, 1970-74. An Opposition spokesman on trade and industry, 1973-74. Agricultural scientist. B July, 1943; ed Morrison's Academy, Edinburgh University, and Churchill College, Cambridge. Sponsored by ASTMS.

Mr Geoffrey Campbell, chartered mechanical engineer and engineering superintendent. B 1926; ed Liff Road School, Lochee, Dundee, and Dundee Technical College. Town and county councillor in Midlothian. Chairman Scottish Conservative Trade Union Advisory Committee, 1968-75 and since 1977. Contested Stirling, Falkirk and Grangemouth, February and October, 1974.

Mr George MacDougall contested the seat, February and October, 1974. Journalist. B March, 1928; ed Edinburgh Corporation schools.

Miss Carol Downes, aged 29, teacher. EIS.

EDINBURGH Leith

Electorate 37,204   1974: 39,407

Brown, R. (Lab)	12,961
McLernan, A. J. (C)	8,944
Aitken, K. (L)	3,382
Platt, W. R. (Scot Nat)	2,706
Lab majority	4,017

No Change

	1974		1979
Total Votes	29,495		27,993
Turnout	74·8%		75·2%
Lab	11,708	39·7%	46·3%
C	8,263	28·0%	32·0%
Scot Nat	7,688	26·1%	9·7%
L	1,836	6·2%	12·1%
Lab maj	3,445	11·7%	14·3%
Swing		−4·7%	−1·3%

Mr Ronald Brown, full-time union official and former fitter. B June, 1940; ed Ainslie Park High School, Edinburgh. Member, Royston/Granton Regional Council. AUEW.

Mr Aidan McLernan, financial consultant. B 1944; ed St Joseph's College, Dumfries. Member, Edinburgh District Council, since 1974; Edinburgh Festival Council; Junior Chamber of Commerce.

Mr Richard Platt, surveyor. B March, 1927; ed Hyndland Secondary School, Glasgow.

EDINBURGH, North

Electorate 45,303   1974: 47,215

*Fletcher, A. M. (C)	14,170
Lindsay, N. (Lab)	9,773
Guild, R. (L)	5,045
MacCormick, N. (Scot Nat)	3,521
C majority	4,397

No Change

	1974		1979
Total Votes	32,679		32,509
Turnout	69·2%		71·8%
C	12,856	39·3%	43·6%
Lab	8,465	25·9%	30·1%
Scot Nat	7,681	23·5%	10·8%
L	3,677	11·3%	15·5%
C maj	4,391	13·4%	13·5%
Swing		−3·1%	0·0%

Mr Alexander Fletcher was appointed Under Secretary of State for Scotland in May, 1979, after being an Opposition spokesman on Scottish affairs. Chartered accountant and company director. Won the by-election in 1973. B August 1929; ed Greenock High School and Institute of Chartered Accountants. Contested West Renfrewshire, 1970. Member, East Kilbride Development Corporation, 1971-73. Elder of Church of Scotland. Member, Select Committee on Science and Technology, 1974-76. Member, European Parliament, 1976-77.

Mr Neil Lindsay, electrician. B May, 1939; ed Ainslie Park High School. Member, Lothian Council.

Mr Neil MacCormick, Regius Professor of Public Law, Edinburgh University. B May, 1941; ed High School, Glasgow; Glasgow University, and Balliol College, Oxford. Member, Houghton Committee on financial aid to political parties, 1975-76, and signed minority report. AUT.

EDINBURGH, Pentlands

Electorate 58,652   1974: 54,955

*Rifkind, M. L. (C)	17,684
Johnstone, A. J. (Lab)	16,486
Luckhurst, C. (L)	5,919
Maxwell, S. (Scot Nat)	4,934
C majority	1,198

No Change

	1974		1979
Total Votes	41,509		45,023
Turnout	75·5%		76·8%
C	14,083	33·9%	39·3%
Lab & Coop	12,826	30·9%	36·6%
Scot Nat	10,189	24·5%	11·0%
L	4,411	10·6%	13·1%
C maj	1,257	3·0%	2·7%
Swing		−3·8%	−0·2%

Mr Malcolm Rifkind, an
advocate, was appointed
Under Secretary of State for
Scotland in May, 1979. He
was an Opposition spokes-
man on Scotland from 1975
until he resigned over
devolution in 1977. B June,
1946; ed George Watson's
College, Edinburgh and
Edinburgh University.
Elected in February, 1974;
contested Edinburgh, Cen-
tral, 1970. Member, Select

Committee on Overseas Development; Edinburgh
Council, 1970-74. Joint Secretary Conservative Par-
liamentary Foreign and Commonwealth Affairs
Committee. Lecturer in politics, University College of
Rhodesia, 1967-69.

Mr Arthur Johnstone, lecturer. B 1949.

Mr Stephen Maxwell, journalist and university lecturer. B October, 1942; ed Pocklington School, York,
and Cambridge University.

EDINBURGH, South

Electorate 58,556   1974: 56,154

Ancram, M. A. (C)	17,986
Brown, J. G. (Lab)	15,526
Lovell, J. P. B. (L)	7,400
Shirley, R. (Scot Nat)	3,800
Biggar, S. M. (Ecology)	552
C majority	2,460

No Change

	1974		1979
Total Votes	41,653		45,264
Turnout	74·2%		77·3%
C	14,962	35·9%	39·7%
Lab	11,736	28·2%	34·3%
Scot Nat	9,034	21·7%	8·4%
L	5,921	14·2%	16·3%
Ecology	—		1·2%
C maj	3,226	7·7%	5·4%
Swing		−3·3%	−1·2%

Mr Michael Ancram, advo-
cate, was MP for Berwick
and East Lothian from February to October, 1974;
contested West Lothian in
1970. B 1945; ed Amp-
leforth and Oxford and
Edinburgh Universities.
First chairman, Thistle
Group. Eldest son of Mar-
quess of Lothian. Vice-
chairman, Scottish Conservative Party.

Mr Gordon Brown, college
lecturer. B February, 1951; ed Kirkcaldy High School
and Edinburgh University (Rector of University,
1972-75). ASTMS.

Mr Bryan Lovell, lecturer in Geology, Edinburgh
University. B February 1942; ed Oxford and Harvard.

Mr Robert Shirley, economic lecturer at an education
college in Edinburgh, fought seat in both 1974 elections. Convenor, SNP taxation policy committee. B
March 1928; ed Beardsden Academy and Glasgow
University.

Mr Stewart Biggar, educated at Edinburgh Univ
sity. Aged 28. Member of Torness Alliance.

EDINBURGH, West

Electorate 54,727   1974: 52,569

*Douglas-Hamilton, Lord James (C)	19,360
McGregor, M. C. B. (L)	12,009
Callender, Mrs R. (L)	7,330
Bell, C. (Scot Nat)	3,904
C majority	7,351

No Change

	1974		1979
Total Votes	40,247		42,603
Turnout	76·6%		77·8%
C	15,354	38·1%	45·4%
Lab	10,152	25·2%	28·2%
Scot Nat	8,135	20·2%	9·2%
L	6,606	16·4%	17·2%
C maj	5,202	12·9%	17·2%
Swing		−3·5%	+2·1%

Lord James Douglas-
Hamilton, advocate,
brother of the Duke of
Hamilton, became a Lord
Commissioner of the
Treasury (Government
Whip) in May, 1979. Was
an Opposition whip.
Elected in October, 1974;
contested Hamilton, Feb-
ruary, 1974. B July, 1942;
ed Strathavon, Eton, Balliol
College, Oxford and Edin-
burgh University. Presi-

dent, Scottish Amateur Boxing Association. Mur-
rayfield District Councillor, 1974. Secretary, Conservative backbench constitutional committee, since
1976. Boxing blue and former president, Oxford
Union.

Mr Michael McGregor, organization and methods
analyst. B June, 1940; ed Daniel Stewart's College,
Edinburgh. Member, Edinburgh City Council, 1972-
75. ASTMS.

Mr Colin Bell, journalist. B April, 1938; ed St Paul's
School and King's College, Cambridge. Father, NUJ
Chapel, The Scotsman.

ENFIELD, Edmonton

Electorate 58,860   1974: 61,476

*Graham, T. E. (Lab and Co-op)	20,713
Attwood, J. (C)	18,733
Wintle, W. (L)	3,276
Bruce, D. J. (Nat Front)	1,213
Lab and Co-op majority	1,980

No Change

	1974		1979
Total Votes	41,224		43,935
Turnout	67·1%		74·6%
Lab & Co-op	20,229	49·1%	47·1%
C	13,401	32·5%	42·6%
L	5,699	13·8%	7·5%
Nat Front	1,895	4·6%	2·8%
Lab/Co-op maj	6,828	16·6%	4·5%
Swing		−2·1%	+6·0%

Mr Edward Graham, Lord Commissioner of the Treasury (Government Whip) 1976-79. Elected in February, 1974. National Secretary of the Co-operative Party until April, 1974. Contested Enfield, West, 1966. Former Labour group leader, Enfield Council; chairman, Housing and Redevelopment Committee, 1961-68.

Member National Association of Co-operative Officials; Expenditure Committee, 1974-75.

Mr John Attwood contested the seat, October, 1974. Aministrative officer at Middlesex Polytechnic. B 1949; ed Enfield Grammar School and Exeter and Sheffield Universities.

Mr George Wintle, pharmacist and managing director of a dispensing chemists. B January, 1933; ed County Grammar School, Bassaleg, Gwent, and Bristol College of Technology.

ENFIELD, North

Electorate 66,427   1974: 67,818

Eggar, T. (C)		24,927
*Davies, B. (Lab)		21,444
Crawford, K. (L)		4,681
Wotherspoon, J. (Nat Front)		816
C majority		3,483

C gain from Lab

	1974		1979
Total votes	47,823		51,868
Turnout	70·5%		78·1%
Lab	20,880	43·7%	41·3%
C	16,087	33·6%	48·1%
L	9,526	19·9%	9·0%
Nat Front	1,330	2·8%	1·6%
Lab maj	4,793	10·1%	—
C maj	—		6·8%
Swing		−1·9%	+8·4%

Mr Timothy Eggar, merchant banker. B 1951; ed, Winchester College, Magdalene College, Cambridge, and College of Law, London. Chairman, Cambridge Univ Cons Assoc, 1972. Vice-chairman, Federation of Conservative Students, 1973-74. Personal assistant to Mr William Whitelaw in October, 1974, General Election.

Mr Bryan Davies, Lord Commissioner to the Treasury, 1979. Elected in February, 1974; contested Norfolk, Central, 1966. Member, Select Committee on Overseas Development and of Expenditure Committee 1974-79. B November, 1939; ed Redditch High School, University College, London, Institute of Education, London, and London School of Economics. Vice-chairman, PLP education and science group, 1977. Member, Medical Research Council. Former teacher and lecturer.

Mr Keith Crawford, postgraduate student and part-time lecturer. Aged 29; ed South Bank Polytechnic.

ENFIELD, Southgate

Electorate 67,355   1974: 70,935

*Berry, A. G. (C)	31,663
Wilson, I. S. (Lab)	11,584
Baker, A. (L)	7,223
Pert, R. (Nat Front)	895
C majority	20,079

No Change

	1974		1979
Total votes	48,031		51,365
Turnout	67·7%		76·3%
C	25,888	53·9%	61·6%
Lab	10,966	22·8%	22·6%
L	9,922	20·7%	14·1%
Nat Front	1,255	2·6%	1·7%
C maj	14,922	31·1%	39·0%
Swing		−0·4%	+3·9%

Mr Anthony Berry was appointed Vice-Chamberlain of HM Household, in May 1979. An Opposition whip 1975-79. Elected in 1964. Deputy chairman, Leopold Joseph and Sons Ltd; formerly assistant editor of *The Sunday Times* and director of Kemsley Newspapers Ltd, 1954-59. B February, 1925; ed Eton and Christ Church, Oxford. PPS to Mr

Peter Walker, 1970-74, as Secretary of State for Environment and then for Trade and Industry. Joint vice-chairman, Conservative transport industries committee, since 1974 and secretary, 1967-70. Joint vice-chairman since 1974 and joint secretary, Conservative London members' committee, 1966-70. Member, Anglo-Israel Council.

Mr Ian Wilson, teacher. B March 1951; ed Colchester Royal Grammar School, Churchill College, Cambridge, and Chelsea Centre for Science Education. NUT.

Mr Anthony Baker, chartered surveyor. Aged 33.

Mr Royston Pert, aged 30, incorporated administrative accountant.

EPPING FOREST

Electorate 66,723   1974: 64,055

*Biggs-Davison, J. A. (C)	29,447
Shepherd, W. D. (Lab)	13,994
Kitching, D. (L)	6,528
Wilkins, B. (Nat Front)	1,110
C majority	15,453

No Change

	1974		1979
Total votes	46,962		51,079
Turnout	73·3%		76·6%
C	22,392	47·7%	57·6%
Lab	15,618	33·3%	27·4%
L	8,952	19·1%	12·8%
Nat Front	—		2·2%
C maj	6,774	14·4%	30·2%
Swing		1·3%	+7·9%

Mr **John Biggs-Davison,** an Opposition spokesman on Northern Ireland 1974-78, was elected for the seat in February, 1974; MP for Chigwell, 1955-74; contested Coventry, South, 1951. Author and freelance journalist and broadcaster. B June 1918; ed Clifton College and Magdalen College, Oxford. Elected chairman, Monday Club, 1974; chairman (previously vice-chairman) Conservative parliamentary Northern Ireland Committee, since 1974. Member, Select Committee on Abortion (Amendment) Bill, 1975-76; chairman, UK Falkland Islands parliamentary group, 1977. Joint vice-chairman (1972) and former secretary, Conservative Foreign and Commonwealth Affairs committee.

Mr **David Shepherd** is a section manager, Post Office data processing service. B November, 1942; ed Queen Mary College, London University. Member, Waltham Forest Council since 1974. Member, Society of Post Office Executives.

Mr **David Kitching,** charity administrator and former diplomat and senior civil servant. B December, 1926; ed University College School, Hampstead, and New College, Oxford.

EPSOM AND EWELL

Electorate 82,126   1974: 80,597

*Hamilton, A. (C)	39,104
Anderson, M. (L)	12,746
Smith, C. R. (Lab)	11,315
C majority	26,358

No Change

	1974		1979
Total votes	59,399		63,165
Turnout	73·7%		76·9%
C	32,109	54·1%	61·9%
L	15,819	26·6%	20·2%
Lab	11,471	19·3%	17·9%
C maj	16,290	27·5%	41·7%
Swing		−1·7%	+4·6%

1978 by-election: Total votes: 44,402.—C 28,242 (63.6%), Lab 7,314 (16.5%), L 5,673 (12.8%), Royalist 2,350 (5.3%), Nat Front 823 (1.9%).—C majority 20,928 (47.1%).

Mr **Archibald Hamilton** became MP at the by-election in April, 1978; contested Dagenham, February and October, 1974. Managing director, British Quadruplex, engineers. B December, 1941; ed Eton. Member, Council of Royal Borough of Kensington and Chelsea. 1968-71.

Mr **Michael Anderson,** personnel manager, contested the seat at 1978 by-election. B September, 1930; ed Perse School, Cambridge, and Emmanuel College, Cambridge. Fellow of Institute of Personnel Management.

Mr **Christopher Smith,** housing association worker. B July 1951; ed George Watson's College, Edinburgh, Pembroke College, Cambridge, and Harvard University. Member, London Borough of Islington Council, since 1978.

ESHER

Electorate 47,860   1974: 47,572

*Mather, D. C. M. (C)	24,152
Welchman, C. (L)	7,311
Pickles, J. T. (Lab)	5,634
C majority	16,841

No Change

	1974		1979
Total votes	35,351		37,097
Turnout	74·3%		77·5%
C	19,741	55·8%	65·1%
L	8,881	25·1%	19·7%
Lab	6,729	19·0%	15·2%
C maj	10,860	30·7%	45·4%
Swing		−2·0%	+6·5%

Mr **Carol Mather** was appointed a Lord Commissioner of the Treasury in May, 1979. Elected in 1970. An Opposition whip 1975-79. Member, Conservative Research Department, 1962-70. Contested Leicester North-West, 1966. B January, 1919; ed Harrow and Trinity College, Cambridge. Member of Lloyd's. Joint secretary, Conservative home affairs

committee, 1974-76 and of Foreign and Commonwealth Affairs committee, 1972-74. Joint vice-chairman, Northern Ireland Committee, 1974-76, joint secretary, 1972-74. Served with Welsh Guards, 1940-1962, and was a liaison officer to General Montgomery in the Western Desert campaign, the Normandy landings and the advance into Europe.

Mr **Charles Welchman,** barrister, contested the seat, October, 1974. B April, 1943; ed West Buckland School, Exeter Technical College, and University College, London.

Mr **John Pickles,** British Petroleum manager. B January 1944; ed Lancaster Royal Grammar School and Manchester University. APEX.

ESSEX, South East

Electorate 82,350   1974: 76,013

*Braine, Sir Bernard (C)	40,497
Smith, N. J. M. (Lab)	15,965
Alexander, Mrs F. (L)	6,858
C majority	24,532

No Change

	1974		1979
Total votes	56,035		63,320
Turnout	73·7%		76·9%
C	27,348	48·8%	64·0%
Lab	18,638	33·3%	25·2%
L	10,049	17·9%	10·8%
C maj	8,710	15·5%	38·8%
Swing		0·2%	+11·6%

Sir Bernard Braine, a member of the executive of the 1922 committee and former chairman of the Select Committees on Overseas Aid (1967-70) and Overseas Development (1973-74), was a Conservative spokesman on foreign and Commonwealth affairs and overseas development, 1967-70. Parliamentary Secretary, Ministry of Health, 1962-64; Under Secretary, Commonwealth Relations Office, 1961-62; Parliamentary Secretary, Ministry of Pensions and National Insurance, 1960-61. Elected for the seat in 1955; represented Billericay, 1950-55; contested Leyton, East, 1945. B June 1914; ed Hendon County School. Parliamentary adviser to Police Superintendents' Association of England and Wales. Member, Select Committee on Abortion (amendment) Bill. A Governor, Commonwealth Institute, since 1968. Chairman, National Council on Alcholism.

Mr Nigel Smith, teacher, contested Chichester in February and October, 1974. B October, 1947; ed Manchester Polytechnic and Kent State University, USA. Member, Basildon Council, since 1975, NUT.

Mrs Frances Alexander, teacher of nursing studies, contested the seat, February, 1974, and Tower Hamlets, Stepney and Poplar, October, 1974. B November, 1935; ed Brentwood County High School, the London Hospital and Weymouth College of Education and Southampton University.

ETON AND SLOUGH

Electorate 64,916   1974: 63,813

*Lestor, Miss J. (Lab)	20,710
Ward, C. (C)	19,370
Goldenberg, P. (L)	5,254
Brooker, G. (Ind C)	2,359
Jones, D. (Nat Front)	943
Lab majority	1,340

No Change

	1974		1979
Total votes	46,387		48,636
Turnout	72·7%		74·9%
Lab	22,238	47·9%	42·6%
C	14,575	31·4%	39·8%
L	8,213	17·7%	10·8%
Nat Front	1,241	2·7%	1·9%
Anti Extremist	120	0·3%	
Ind C	—	—	4·9%
Lab maj	7,663	16·5%	2·8%
Swing		−1·5%	+6·8%

Miss Joan Lestor was chairman of the Labour Party, 1977-78; vice-chairman, 1976-77. Under Secretary for Education and Science, October, 1969-70 and 1975-76. Resigned in protest at public spending cuts. Under Secretary, Foreign and Commonwealth Office, 1974-75. Won the seat for Labour in 1966; contested Lewisham, West, 1964. Teacher. B

November, 1931; ed Blaenavon Secondary School, Monmouth, William Morris High School, Walthamstow, and London University. Member, National Executive of the Labour Party since 1967. Former Member, Select Committee on Race Relations and Immigration. Chairman, PLP, Southern Africa sub-committee, 1977-78. GMWU.

Mr Christopher Ward, a solicitor, was MP for Swindon from 1969, when he won the by-election, until 1970. B December, 1942; ed Magdalen College, Oxford. Member, Berkshire County Council, 1965-70 and from 1974; deputy leader, Conservative group and chairman, finance sub-committee. Member, standing conference on London and South East Regional Planning Council.

Mr Philip Goldenberg, solicitor, contested the seat, February and October, 1974. B April, 1946; ed St Paul's School and Pembroke College, Oxford.

EXETER

Electorate 68,825   1974: 67,184

*Hannam, J. G. (C)	27,173
Hobbs, G. W. (Lab)	19,146
Marsh, H. (L)	8,756
Frings, P. (Ecology)	1,053
C majority	8,027

No Change

	1974		1979
Total votes	53,934		56,128
Turnout	80·3%		81·6%
C	21,970	40·7%	48·4%
Lab	19,622	36·4%	34·1%
L	12,342	22·9%	15·6%
Ecology	—		1·9%
C maj	2,348	4·3%	14·3%
Swing		−2·4%	+5·0%

Mr John Hannam, secretary of the all-party disablement group, won the seat in 1970. B August, 1929; ed Yeovil Grammar School. Director, Inghams Travel Ltd; President of British Motels Federation. Vice-chairman, Conservative energy committee, arts and heritage committee and sports and recreation committee. Somerset county councillor, 1967-69. Captain of the

Lords and Commons tennis club and ski club. Member, Glyndebourne Festival Opera Society.

Mr Gary Hobbs, teacher, contested Poole, February and October 1974. B December 1945; ed Plymouth College and Exeter University. Member, Poole Council, 1971-74. Methodist lay preacher; qualified football referee. NUT.

Mr Howard Marsh, teacher. B January, 1944; ed Queen Elizabeth's Grammar School, Barnet, and London Bible College. Member, Exeter City Council, since 1974. NAS/UWT.

Mr Peter Frings, self-employed printer and writer. Aged 22; ed Exeter University.

EYE

Electorate 69,843   1974: 65,710

Gummer, J. S. (C)	28,707
Koppel, P. E. (Lab)	13,686
Kemsley, P. (L)	12,259
Flint, J. J. (Ind)	324
Rogers, N. H. (ACMC)	268
C majority	15,021

No Change

	1974		1979
Total votes	50,865		55,244
Turnout	77.4%		79.1%
C	22,387	44.0%	52.0%
L	14,530	28.6%	22.2%
Lab	13,948	27.4%	24.8%
Ind	—		0.6%
ACMC	—		0.5%
C maj	7,857	15.4%	27.2%
Swing		−0.6%	+5.3%

Mr Selwyn Gummer, a pub-
lisher, was MP for
Lewisham, West, 1970 to
February, 1974. Contested
Greenwich, 1964 and 1966.
A vice-chairman of the
Conservative Party, 1972-
74. B November, 1939; Ed
King's School, Rochester
and Selwyn College, Cam-
bridge (president of the
Union, 1962). Chairman,
Federation of Conservative
Students, 1961. Co-opted

member, ILEA 1967-70. PPS to Mr James Prior, as
Minister of Agriculture, Fisheries and Food, 1971.

Mr Paul Koppel, insurance accountant. B March,
1931 in Vienna; ed Letchworth Grammar School.
Member, Ipswich Borough Council and Suffolk
County Council. ASTMS.

Mr Peter Kemsley, farmer and director of farming
companies. B April; 1932; ed Marlborough and Royal
Agricultural College, Cirencester.

FALMOUTH AND CAMBORNE

Electorate 69,705   1974: 66,921

*Mudd, W. D. (C)	30,523
Tebbutt, P. M. (Lab)	13,923
Hall-Say, J. (L)	7,489
Truran, L. (Meb Kernow)	1,637
Swingler, M. (Nat Front)	280
C majority	16,600

No Change

	1974		1979
Total votes	50,718		53,852
Turnout	75.8%		77.3%
C	23,950	47.2%	56.7%
Lab	18,094	35.7%	25.9%
L	6,428	12.7%	13.9%
Nat Front	—		0.5%
Meb Kernow	—		3.0%
Ind L	2,246	4.4%	—
C maj	5,856	11.5%	30.8%
Swing		+1.7%	+9.6%

Mr David Mudd, journalist,
broadcaster and author,
won the seat in 1970. B
June, 1933; Ed Truro
Cathedral School. Member,
Tavistock Urban Council,
1959-61. Secretary, West
Country group of Conserva-
tive MPs, 1973-76. NUJ;
Father (chairman) of
Westward Television
Chapel, 1968-70. Consul-
tant to National Federation
of Site Operators.

Mr Peter Tebbutt, consulting engineer, contested
Sutton Coldfield, 1970, and Gosport, October 1974.
B February 1931; ed Sidcot School, Somerset and
Bembridge, Isle of Wight. Member, Birmingham City
Council, 1971-74. AUEW.

Mr John Hall-Say, company director. B August, 1932;
ed privately. Member, English clay pigeon shooting
team.

FAREHAM

Electorate 61,612   1974: 57,330

Lloyd, R. (C)	28,730
Boulden, P. (L)	11,685
Townsend, B. R. (Lab)	8,041
Vine, D. C. (Nat Front)	252
C majority	17,045

No Change

	1974		1979
Total votes	44,155		48,708
Turnout	77.0%		79.1%
C	19,053	43.2%	59.0%
L	14,605	33.1%	24.0%
Lab	8,153	18.5%	16.5%
Ind C	1,727	3.9%	—
Nat Front	617	1.4%	0.5%
C maj	4,448	10.1%	35.0%
Swing		−2.7%	+8.9%

Mr Peter Lloyd, marketing
and development manager
for a biscuit manufacturer,
contested Nottingham,
West, February and
October, 1974. B
November 1937; ed Ton-
bridge School and Pem-
broke College, Cambridge;
Chairman, Cambridge Uni-
versity Conservative
Association, 1959.
Research officer, London
Municipal society, 1960-62.

Chairman, Bow Group, 1972-73, research secretary,
1970-72, and editor of *Crossbow* until 1976. Member,
European Movement.

Mr William Boulden, managing director of an advertising firm; contested the seat as an Independent
Conservative in February and October, 1974. B April,
1943; ed Penzance Grammar School and Cornwall
Technical College.

Mr Brian Townsend, a designer, contested the seat,
October 1974. B February 1942; ed Porchester Secondary Modern School. TGWU (ACTS).

FARNHAM

Electorate 64,607   1974: 62,738

*Macmillan, M. (C)	30,127
Raynes, P. (L)	13,658
Davis, P. W. (Lab)	7,497
Bradford, S. L. (CPV)	204
Peel, R. (UCP)	170
C majority	16,469

No Change

	1974		1979
Total votes	47,816		51,656
Turnout	76.2%		77.6%
C	23,885	50.0%	58.3%
L	15,626	32.7%	26.4%
Lab	8,305	17.4%	14.5%
CPV	—		0.4%
UCP	—		0.3%
C maj	8,259	17.3%	31.9%
Swing		−2.5%	+5.6%

Mr Maurice Macmillan was Paymaster General attached to the Treasury, 1973-74; Secretary of State for Employment, 1972-73; Chief Secretary to the Treasury, 1970-72. Elected in 1966; MP for Halifax, 1955-64; contested Seaham, 1945, Lincoln, 1951 and Wakefield (by-election), 1954. Economic Secretary to the Treasury, 1963-64. B January, 1921;

ed Eton and Balliol College, Oxford, Chairman, Macmillan and Company Ltd, 1966-70, and since 1974, Son of Mr Harold Macmillan. Formerly director, Yorkshire Television and Monotype Corporation. Executive chairman, Wider Share Ownership Council, 1964-70. Member, Shadow Cabinet and a spokesman on Treasury and economic affairs 1974-75. Member, Select Committee on Wealth Tax, 1975-76.

Mr Peter Raynes, managing director of an executive recruitment company. B January, 1932; ed Kingswood School, Bath. Member, Surrey County Council, 1975-77.

Mr Peter Davis, research officer, APEX. B May, 1951; ed RGS Newcastle, Oxford and Manchester universities. Former bus conductor.

FARNWORTH

Electorate 71,844   1974: 70,565

*Roper, J. F. H. (Lab and Co-op)	27,965
Windle, S. (C)	19,858
Rothwell, Mrs M. P. (L)	8,043
Lab and Co-op majority	8,107

No Change

	1974		1979
Total votes	52,732		55,866
Turnout	74·7%		77·8%
Lab & Co-op	28,184	53·4%	50·1%
C	13,489	25·6%	35·5%
L	11,059	21·0%	14·4%
Lab/Co-op m.	14,695	27·8%	14·6%
Swing		−2·1%	+6·6%

Mr John Roper is an economist. Member, Select Committee on European Secondary Legislation since 1974 and Expenditure Committee; chairman Labour Committee for Europe since 1976. Elected in 1970; contested High Peak, 1964. B September, 1935; ed William Hulme's Grammar School, Manchester, Reading School, Magdalen College, Oxford,

and University of Chicago. Director, Co-operative Wholesale Society, 1969-74; Co-operative Insurance Society, 1973-74. Chairman, General Council of the United Nations Associations, since 1973. Delegate, Consultative Assembly, Council of Europe, and WEU, since 1974. Member, Select Committee on the Wealth Tax, 1974-75; General Advisory Council, IBA, since 1974; Council of Institute of Fiscal Studies, since 1975. Secretary, Anglo-Benelux Parliamentary Group.

Mr Stanley Windle, engineering works manager and chairman of the North-West Area Conservative Clubs. B 1925; ed Stockport and engineering training college, London.

Mrs Margaret Rothwell, teacher, fought the seat, February and October, 1974. B June, 1931; ed Farnworth Grammar School and Elizabeth Gaskell College of Education. Member, Kearsley Council, 1965-74 (chairman, 1971-72). NUT.

FAVERSHAM

Electorate 78,509   1974: 76,000

*Moate, R. D. (C)	33,513
Sherwen, T. (Lab)	21,351
Aldous, A. (L)	6,349
Webb, A. (Nat Front)	439
C majority	12,162

No Change

	1974		1979
Total votes	58,276		61,652
Turnout	76·7%		78·5%
C	25,087	43·0%	54·4%
Lab	22,210	38·1%	34·6%
L	10,979	18·8%	10·3%
Nat Front	—	—	·0·7%
C maj	2,877	4·9%	19·8%
Swing		−1·9%	+7·4%

Mr Roger Moate, insurance broker, won the seat in 1970; contested it in 1966. Member, Statutory Instruments Committee, since 1975; Vice-chairman, Conservative transport committee, 1978. Director of Alexander Howden Insurance Brokers Ltd. B May, 1938; ed Latymer Upper School, Hammersmith. Vice-chairman, Greater London

area Young Conservatives, 1964-66.

Mr Tim Sherwen, educational publisher and freelance editor. B November, 1937; ed Tonbridge School and Cambridge University. NUJ.

Mr Anthony Aldous, senior systems analyst. B October, 1945; ed Bournemouth Grammar School and Bournemouth College of Advanced Technology.

FERMANAGH AND SOUTH TYRONE

Electorate 71,481   1974: 71,343

*Maguire, M. F. (Ind)	22,398
Ferguson, R. (Off UU)	17,411
Currie, A. (SDLP)	10,785
Baird, E. (UUUP)	10,607
Acheson, P. (Alliance)	1,070
Ind majority	4,987

No Change

	1974		1979
Total votes	63,265		62,271
Turnout	88·7%		87·1%
Ind	32,795	51·8%	36·0%
Off UU	—	—	28·0%
SDLP	—	—	17·3%
UUUP	—	—	17·0%
Alliance	—	—	1·7%
UUUC	30,285	47·9%	—
Marx Len	185	0·3%	—
Ind maj	2,510	3·9%	8·0%

Mr Frank Maguire, publican, won the seat in October, 1974. B September, 1929; ed St Mary's Marist Brothers School, Athlone. Joined his uncle in business in Lisnaskea and later formed his own company.

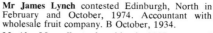

Mr Raymond Ferguson, solicitor. Member, Fermanagh District Council and of Orange Order. B 1941; ed Portora Royal School, Enniskillen and Queen's University, Belfast.

Mr Austin Currie was elected Nationalist member for East Tyrone in Stormont, 1964 and 1969. Principal organiser, first Civil Rights March 1968, in protest against housing allocations. Foundation member of SDLP, becoming chief whip of the party. Minister of Housing in power-sharing executive; subsequently represented Fermanagh-South Tyrone in Convention. B 1939; ed St Patrick's Academy, Dungannon and Queen's University, Belfast.

Mr Ernest Baird, chemist, represented the constituency in Assembly and Convention. Deputy leader and Chief Whip, United Ulster Unionist Coalition. First chairman of Vanguard Unionist Party, subsequently taking over leadership of United Ulster Unionist Movement. Member of Orange Order and Apprentice Boys of Derry. B 1931.

Mr Peter Acheson, solicitor and former company director. B 1939.

FIFE, Central

Electorate 61,476   1974: 58,402

*Hamilton, W. W. (Lab)	27,619
McCrone, I. A. (C)	9,597
Lynch, J. (Scot Nat)	9,208
Maxwell, A. (Comm)	1,172

Lab majority	18,022

No Change

	1974		1979
Total votes	43,162		47,596
Turnout	73·9%		77·4%
Lab	22,400	51·9%	58·0%
Scot Nat	14,414	33·4%	19·3%
C	5,308	12·3%	20·2%
Comm	1,040	2·4%	2·5%
Lab maj	7,986	18·5%	37·8%
Swing		−3·1%	+0·9%

Mr William Hamilton was elected in February, 1974. Was MP for West Fife, 1950-74 and contested that seat in 1945. Member, European Parliament, 1975-79. Member, Estimates Committee, 1953-72; chairman, 1964-70. Member, Select Committee on Violence in Marriage. Teacher. B June, 1917; ed Washington Grammar School, County Durham, and Sheffield University. Former member, Public Expenditure Committee. Vice-chairman, Parliamentary Labour Party, 1964-70. NUT. Sponsored by COHSE.

Mr Iain McCrone, farmer; director, fish farming company and of frozen food distributors. B 1934; ed Trinity College, Glenalmond and West of Scotland College of Agriculture. Past president, Fife and Kinross Area Executive of NFU.

Mr James Lynch contested Edinburgh, North in February and October, 1974. Accountant with wholesale fruit company. B October, 1934.

Mr Alex Maxwell, employed by the NCB, contested the seat in both 1974 elections. B November 1931; ed Airdrie Academy and Coatbridge Technical College.

FIFE, East

Electorate 59,297   1974: 56,453

Henderson, B. (C)	20,117
Campbell, W. M. (L)	10,762
McLeish, H. B. (Lab)	9,339
Marshall, J. (Scot Nat)	6,612

C majority	9,355

No Change

	1974		1979
Total votes	41,605		46,830
Turnout	73·7%		79·0%
C	16,116	38·7%	43·0%
Scot Nat	13,202	31·7%	14·1%
Lab	7,040	16·9%	19·9%
L	5,247	12·6%	23·0%
C maj	2,914	7·0%	20·0%
Swing		−5·6%	+0·6%

Mr Barry Henderson, management consultant and director of Gilmerston Management Services Ltd, was MP for East Dunbartonshire, February to October, 1974; contested that seat in 1970 and Edinburgh, East, 1966. B April, 1936; ed Lothallan School and Stowe. Member, British Computer Society. Chairman, Scottish Conservative Candidates' Association, since 1975; information officer, Scottish Central Office, 1966-70.

Mr Menzies Campbell, advocate, fought Greenock and Port Glasgow in both 1974 elections. Ex-international sprinter; captain UK athletics team. B May 1941; ed Hillhead High School, Glasgow; Glasgow University and Staniford University, California. Former Chairman, Scottish Liberal Party.

Mr Henry McLeish, local government officer, part-time university lecturer, and a former professional footballer. B June, 1948; ed Buckhaven High School and Heriot Watt University. Member, Royal Town Planning Institute. NUPE.

Mr Jack Marshall, self-employed. B April, 1936; ed Bathgate Academy and Falkirk College of Technology.

FLINT, East

Electorate 74,262   1974: 69,273

*Jones, S. B. (Lab)	29,339
Warburton-Jones, P. (C)	23,116
Carlile, A. (L)	6,736
Rogers, J. (Pl Cymru)	1,198
Davies, G. (Comm)	307

Lab majority	6,223

No Change

	1974		1979
Total votes	55,183		60,696
Turnout	79·7%		81·7%
Lab	27,002	48·9%	48·3%
C	17,416	31·6%	38·1%
L	8,986	16·3%	11·1%
Pl Cymru	1,779	3·2%	2·0%
Comm	—	—	0·5%
Lab maj	9,586	17·3%	10·2%
Swing		−1·1%	+3·5%

Mr Barry Jones was Under Secretary of State for Wales, 1974-79. Elected in 1970; contested Northwich, 1966. Teacher and former regional organizer, NUT. B June, 1938; ed Hawarden Grammar School and Bangor College of Education. Former UK delegate to Council of Europe and WEU.

Mr Peter Warburton-Jones, barrister and part-time legal adviser to a newspaper group. B 1946; ed Trinity College, Glenalmond; Madrid University and Corpus Christi College, Cambridge. Committee member, Lambeth Central Conservative Association.

Mr Alexander Carlile, barrister, contested the seat, February, 1974. B February, 1948; ed Epsom College, London University.

Mr John Rogers, teacher, contested Ebbw Vale, February, 1974. B February, 1943; ed Rhyl Grammar School; St Mary's College, Crosby; Leeds University. UCAC (National Association of Teachers of Wales).

Mr Glyn Davies, building worker. Aged 40. Delegate to Deeside Trades Council. UCATT.

FLINT, West

Electorate 68,418   1974: 64,302

*Meyer, Sir Anthony (C)	26,364
Hughes, R. M. (Lab)	16,678
Parry, J. H. (L)	9,009
Edwards, B. M. (Pl Cymru)	1,720
C majority	9,686

No Change

	1974		1979
Total votes	48,475		53,771
Turnout	75·4%		78·6%
C	20,054	41·4%	49·0%
Lab	15,234	31·4%	31·0%
L	10,881	22·4%	16·8%
Pl Cymru	2,306	4·8%	3·2%
C maj	4,820	10·0%	18·0%
Swing		−1·9%	+4·0%

Sir Anthony Meyer, former diplomat, was elected in 1970; represented Eton and Slough, 1964-66. Underwriter at Lloyds. B October, 1920; ed Eton and New College, Oxford. Member, Select Committee on Expenditure, serving on Education, Arts and Home Office Sub-committee and of Joint Select Committee on Consolidated Bills. A trustee of the Shakespeare Memorial National Theatre; founder and editor of political journal *Solon.* PPS to Chief Secretary to the Treasury, 1970-72 and Secretary of State for Employment, 1972-74.

Mr Merion Hughes, social worker, B February, 1948; ed Bangor Normal College and Liverpool Polytechnic. Nalgo.

Mr John Parry, solicitor. B March, 1934; ed Clifton College, Bristol University.

Mr Brian Edwards, computer consultant, contested Cardiff, North, 1970. B July, 1934; ed LSE.

FOLKESTONE AND HYTHE

Electorate 66,297   1974: 64,714

*Costain, A. P. (C)	26,837
Budd, B. (L)	10,817
Priestman, G. J. (Lab)	10,015
Lavine, M. (Nat Front)	478
C majority	16,020

No Change

	1974		1979
Total votes	45,322		48,147
Turnout	70·0%		72·6%
C	20,930	46·2%	55·7%
L	12,488	27·6%	22·5%
Lab	11,639	25·7%	20·8%
Ind	265	0·6%	—
Nat Front	—	—	1·0%
C maj	8,442	18·6%	32·3%
Swing		−1·8%	+7·2%

Mr Albert Costain, a member of the Speaker's panel of chairmen since 1975, Public Accounts Committee, 1961-64 and since 1974. Elected in 1959. Chairman of Richard Costain Ltd, 1966-69. FIOB. B July, 1910; ed Merchant Taylor's Crosby, Liverpool; King James's Grammar School, Knaresborough, and College of Estate Management, London. Chairman, horticulture sub-committee of Conservative agriculture committee; treasurer, Anglo-Hongkong Parliamentary Group.

Mr Bernard Budd, QC, B December 1912; ed Cardiff High School, West Leeds High School and Pembroke College, Cambridge. Contested Dover, 1964 and 1966, and Folkestone and Hythe, February and October 1974.

Mr Gordon Priestman, electrical engineer. B June, 1930; ed Richmond Road Boys' School, Gillingham and Medway College of Technology. Former leader of Rochester Council, Labour leader on Medway Council. EPEA.

GAINSBOROUGH

Electorate 65,654   1974: 61,749

*Kimball, M. R. (C)	24,040
Blackmore, R. B. (L)	16,885
Bach, W. S. G. (Lab)	10,335
August, R. E. (Ind C)	570
C majority	7,155

No Change

	1974		1979
Total votes	46,155		51,830
Turnout	74·7%		78·9%
C	19,163	41·5%	46·4%
L	15,195	32·9%	32·6%
Lab	11,797	25·6%	19·9%
Ind C	—	—	1·1%
C maj	3,968	8·6%	13·8%
Swing		−2·2%	+5·3%

Mr Marcus Kimball, company director and farmer, has been chairman of the British Field Sports Society since 1964. Returned at a by-election in 1956; contested Derby, South, 1955. B October, 1928; ed Eton and Trinity College, Cambridge. Member, Rutland County Council, 1955-62. Joint Secretary, Conservative agriculture committee, 1959-63, and forestry committee, 1960-62. Joint master and huntsman, Cottesmore Hounds, 1963-68, and Fitzwilliam, 1951-52. Privy Council representative on Royal College of Veterinary Surgeons, since 1969.

Mr Roger Blackmore contested the seat, February and October, 1974, and 1970. College lecturer. B December, 1941; ed Abingdon School, Berkshire, Shebbear College, North Devon, and Leicester University. NATFHE.

Mr William Bach is a barrister. B December, 1946; ed Oxford University. Member, Leicester City Council since 1976.

GALLOWAY

Electorate 41,110   1974: 39,407

Lang, I (C)	15,306
*Thompson, G. H. (Scot Nat)	12,384
Hannay, Dr D. R. (L)	2,852
Johnston, D. D. (Lab)	2,841
C majority	2,922

C gain from Scot Nat

	1974		1979
Total votes	30,377		33,383
Turnout	77·1%		81·2%
Scot Nat	12,242	40·3%	37·1%
C	12,212	40·2%	45·8%
L	3,181	10·5%	8·5%
Lab	2,742	9·0%	8·5%
Scot Nat maj	30	0·1%	—
C maj	—	—	8·7%
Swing	—	—	+3·0%

Mr Ian Lang is an insurance broker and Lloyd's underwriting agent. B June, 1940; ed Rugby and Sidney Sussex College, Cambridge. Contested Central Ayrshire, 1970, and Glasgow, Pollok, February, 1974. Trustee, West of Scotland Trustee Savings Bank; director, Glasgow Chamber of Commerce.

Mr George Thompson gained the seat for the SNP in October, 1974; contested it, February, 1974. A former SNP assistant secretary. Taught modern languages at Kirkcudbright High School. SNP spokesman on health since 1974. B September, 1928; ed Dalry School, Kirkcudbright Academy and University of Edinburgh.

Dr David Hannay, medical practitioner. B January, 1939; ed Winchester College; Trinity College, Cambridge; St George's Hospital, London. Contested seat, February and October, 1974.

Mr Derek Johnston, solicitor. B April, 1940; ed Dalbeattie High School, Kirkcudbright Academy, and Edinburgh University. GMWU.

GATESHEAD, East

Electorate 62,475   1974: 63,496

*Conlan, B. (Lab)	28,776
Rogers, F. (C)	14,078
Batey, C. (L)	4,201
Lab majority	14,698

No Change

	1974		1979
Total votes	44,589		47,055
Turnout	70·2%		75·3%
Lab	27,620	61·9%	61·2%
C	10,021	22·5%	29·9%
L	6,948	15·6%	8·9%
Lab maj	17,599	39·4%	31·3%
Swing		−4·2%	+4·0%

Mr Bernard Conlan, a member of the Defence and External Affairs sub-committee of the Select Committee on Expenditure, was elected in 1964; contested High Peak, 1959. Engineer. B October, 1923; ed Manchester primary and secondary schools. Member, Manchester City Council, 1954-66. Officer of Amalgamated Engineering Union, 1944-66; sponsored by AUEW engineering section. Joint vice-chairman, PLP trade union group, 1977.

Mr Francis Rogers, schoolmaster. B April, 1928; ed Gateshead Grammar School, Oriel College, Oxford and Durham University. Member, Gateshead Borough Council, 1952-65, and North Tyneside Metropolitan Borough Council, since 1975.

Mr Cliff Batey, aged 35, systems analyst. ed Sunderland Technical College.

GATESHEAD, West

Electorate 29,037   1974: 30,768

*Horam, J. R. (Lab)	13,533
Kelly, D. R. (C)	5,221
Patterson, F. E. (L)	1,185
Beadle, H. (Nat Front)	186
Lab majority	8,312

No Change

	1974		1979
Total votes	20,200		20,125
Turnout	65·7%		69·3%
Lab	13,859	68·6%	67·2%
C	1,132	21·9%	25·9%
L	1,909	9·5%	5·9%
Nat Front	—	—	0·9%
Lab maj	9,427	46·7%	41·3%
Swing		−4·7%	+2·7%

Mr John Horam Under Secretary of State for Transport, 1976-79. Elected in 1970; contested Folkestone and Hythe, 1966. An economist. B March, 1939; ed Silcoates School, Wakefield, and St Catharine's College, Cambridge. Founder, Commodities Research Unit Ltd, managing director, 1968-70. Sponsored by TGWU. Feature and leader writer, *Financial Times*, 1962-65, *The Economist*, 1965-68, *Tribune* contributor, 1966-68. Chairman, Manifesto Group, 1976. Member, Select Committee on Wealth Tax.

Mr David Kelly, managing director of a packing company. B, 1936; ed Sedbergh and St John's College, Cambridge.

Mr Frank Patterson, lecturer, and leader, Liberal group, Easington Council. Aged 34.

GILLINGHAM

Electorate 63,951   1974: 62,099

*Burden, F. F. A. (C)	26,791
Love, S. (Lab)	16,292
Sidebottom, D. (L)	6,219
Campbell, S. (Nat Front)	528
Fry, S. (Ecology)	501
Beckwith, T. (WRP)	92

C majority	10,499

No Change

	1974		1979
Total votes	47,141		50,423
Turnout	75·9%		78·8%
C	19,042	40·4%	53·1%
Lab	15,046	31·9%	32·3%
L	12,131	25·7%	12·3%
Nat Front	922	2·0%	1·0%
Ecology	—	—	1·0%
WRP	—	—	0·2%
C maj	3,996	8·5%	20·8%
Swing		−1·8%	+6·1%

Mr Frederick Burden was elected in 1950; contested South Shields, 1935, Finsbury 1945, Rotherhithe 1947 by-election. Chairman, parliamentary animal welfare group. Former vice-chairman, Conservative civil aviation committee. Director of a group of companies connected with the construction industry. B December, 1905; ed Sloane Grammar School, Chelsea.

Mr Stephen Love, comprehensive school headmaster. B August, 1934; ed Forest Grammar School, Berks and University College, Oxford. Member, West Sussex Education Authority, teacher representative. NUT representative, TUC South East Region.

Mr David Sidebottom, teacher. B April 1949; ed Stockport School and Imperial College, London. Member, Malvern Hills District Council, 1975-78. NUT

GLASGOW, Cathcart

Electorate 48,574   1974: 49,826

Maxton, J. A. (Lab)	17,550
*Taylor, E. M. (C)	15,950
Ewing, A. (Scot Nat)	2,653
Wills, H. (L)	2,042

Lab majority	1,600

Lab gain from C

	1974		1979
Total votes	38,195		38,195
Turnout	76·7%		78·6%
C	16,301	42·7%	41·8%
Lab	14,544	38·1%	45·9%
Scot Nat	6,292	16·5%	6·9%
L	1,058	2·8%	5·3%
C maj	1,757	4·6%	
Lab maj	—	—	4·1%
Swing		−0·3%	−4·4%

Mr John Maxton, lecturer in social studies at Hamilton College of Education. National chairman, Association of Lecturers in Colleges of Education, Scotland. Has contested local elections. B May 1936; ed Lord Williams' Grammar School, Thame, Oxfordshire, Oxford University.

Mr Edward Taylor, chief Opposition spokesman on Scotland, 1977-79, was Under-Secretary (Development), Scottish Office, 1974; Under-Secretary, Scottish Office, 1970-71, when he resigned in disagreement with Government policy on EEC. Elected in 1964; contested Glasgow, Springburn, 1959. Industrial relations officer and journalist. B April, 1937; ed Glasgow High School and Glasgow University. Member, Glasgow City Council, 1960-64.

Mr Alex Ewing, who works in newspaper publicity, and promotion, contested the seat in 1974. B February 1942; ed Holyrood School and Glasgow School of Art. Former secretary, Cathcart branch of SNP and chairman, Gorbals constituency. SLADE.

GLASGOW, Central

Electorate ,19,826   1974: 25,516

*McMillan, T. M. (Lab)	8,542
Saleem, F. (C)	1,937
Bird, S. (Scot Nat)	1,308

Lab majority	6,605

No Change

	1974		1979
Total votes	14,506		11,787
Turnout	56·9%		59·5%
Lab	9,231	63·6%	72·5%
Scot Nat	2,790	19·2%	11·1%
C	1,880	13·0%	16·4%
L	605	4·2%	
Lab maj	6,441	44·4%	56·1%
Swing		−6·7%	−2·8%

Mr Thomas McMillan, formerly a woodcutting machinist at Cowlairs railway workshops. Elected in 1966. B February, 1919; secondary education and National Council of Labour Colleges. Member, Glasgow City Council since 1962. Secretary, Glasgow Central CLP. Sponsored by NUR.

Mr Farouq Saleem, restaurateur and printing company owner. B 1943; ed Karachi and Strathclyde Universities. Founder secretary, Arab Scottish Friendship Association, Glasgow.

Mr Stephen Bird, printer in local newspaper. B July 1951.

GLASGOW, Craigton

Electorate 44,326   1974: 44,333

*Millan, B. (Lab)	19,952
Mair, J. (C)	9,480
Silver, R. (Scot Nat)	3,881
Lab majority	10,472

No Change

	1974		1979
Total votes	33,585		33,313
Turnout	75·8%		75·2%
Lab	16,952	50·5%	59·9%
Scot Nat	8,171	24·3%	11·7%
C	6,734	20·1%	28·5%
L	1,728	5·1%	—
Lab maj	8,781	26·2%	31·4%
Swing		−4·9%	−0·5%

Mr Bruce Millan was appointed Secretary of State for Scotland in April, 1976; Minister of State for Scotland, responsible for Scottish Economic Planning Department and aid for development, 1974-76. An Opposition spokesman on Scottish affairs, 1973-74, and on industry, 1970-73. Under Secretary for Scotland, 1966-70; Under Secretary of Defence for the RAF, 1964-66. Elected in 1959; contested the seat, 1955, and West Renfrewshire, 1951. Chartered accountant. B October, 1927; ed Harris Academy, Dundee. Sponsored by APEX.

Mr John Mair, solicitor. B 1929; ed Glasgow Academy; Trinity College, Glenalmond; Oxford University. Contested Glasgow, Govan, November 1973 by-election, and February, 1974, General Election. Member, Glasgow Corporation 1971-75; Strathclyde Regional Council since 1974.

Mr Robert Silver, Professor of Mechanical Engineering, Glasgow University, since 1967. Member, SNP National Council. B March 1913; ed Montrose Academy and Glasgow University.

GLASGOW, Garscadden

Electorate 52,440   1974: 54,700

*Dewar, D. (Lab)	23,591
Lawson, I. M. (C)	8,393
Bain, J. (Scot Nat)	6,012
Barr, S. (Comm)	374
Lab majority	15,198

No Change

	1974		1979
Total votes	38,756		38,370
Turnout	70·9%		73·2%
Lab	19,737	50·9%	61·5%
Scot Nat	12,100	31·2%	15·7%
C	5,004	12·9%	21·9%
L	1,915	4·9%	—
Comm	—	—	1·0%
Lab maj	7,637	19·7%	39·6%
Swing		−5·0%	−0·8%

1978 by-election: Total vote 36,364 (69%)—Lab 16,507 (45.4%); Scot Nat 11,955 (32.9%) C 6,746 (18.6%) Scot Lab 583 (1.6%); Comm 407 (1.1%); Soc. Workers 166 (0.4%). Lab majority 4,552 (12.5%).

Mr Donald Dewar was returned at the April 1978 by-election. MP for Aberdeen, South, 1966-70; contested the seat, 1964 and 1970. Solicitor. B August 1937; ed Glasgow Academy and Glasgow University (president of the Union 1961-62). Member, Expenditure Committee, since 1978; Select Committee for Scottish Affairs, 1969-70; Public Accounts Committee, 1966-68.

Mr Iain Lawson, sales administration executive. B 1952; ed Clydebank School. Chairman, West of Scotland Young Conservatives. Contested 1978 by-election.

Mr James Bain, sales representative. B December 1937; ed Stevenston Junior Secondary School and David Dale College. Group leader, Glasgow District Council.

Mr Samuel Barr, aged 47, welder. ABS. Shop stewards' convenor, Scotstoun Marine division, Govan Shipbuilders. Vice-chairman, Glasgow Trades Council.

GLASGOW, Govan

Electorate 24,894   1974: 32,094

McMahon, A. (Lab)	11,676
Walker, J. (C)	3,188
Wilson, T. (Scot Nat)	2,340
Lab majority	8,488

No Change

	1974		1979
Total votes	23,012		17,204
Turnout	71·7%		69·1%
Lab	11,392	49·5%	67·9%
Scot Nat	9,440	41·0%	13·6%
C	1,623	7·1%	18·5%
L	444	1·9%	—
Nat Front	86	0·4%	—
Ind	27	0·1%	—
Lab maj	1,952	8·5%	49·4%
Swing		−6·0%	−3·5%

Mr Andrew McMahon, a shipyard worker. B March 1920; ed St Saviour's School, Govan. Member, Glasgow District Council. Convenor of stewards' district committee. Boilermakers' Union. Member Boilermakers' Union since 1936.

Mr Jack Walker, aged 30, teacher at Crookston Castle Secondary School. Elected representative, Glasgow School Council No. 16. Ed Hillhead High School, Glasgow and Glasgow University. Chairman, Govan Conservative Association.

Mr Thomas Wilson, travel firm marketing executive; convener, tourism and recreation policy committee of SNP. B September, 1945; ed Glasgow University.

115

GLASGOW, Hillhead

Electorate 39,793   1974: 41,726

*Galbraith, T. G. D. (C)	12,368
Mowbray, R. A. (Lab)	10,366
Harris, M. (L)	4,349
Borthwick, G. (Scot Nat)	3,050

C majority	2,002

No Change

	1974		1979
Total votes	30,203		30,133
Turnout		72·4%	75·7%
C	11,203	37·1%	41·0%
Lab	8,507	28·2%	34·4%
Scot Nat	6,897	22·8%	10·1%
L	3,596	11·9%	14·4%
C maj	2,696	8·9%	6·6%
Swing		−5·3%	−1·2%

Mr Thomas Galbraith was Parliamentary Secretary, Ministry of Transport, 1963-64; Under Secretary, Scottish Office, from 1959, resigned in November, 1962. Civil Lord of the Admiralty from 1957; Treasurer of the Household, 1955; Comptroller of the Household, 1954. Returned at 1948 by-election; contested Paisley, 1945, and East Edinburgh by-election the same year. Chairman, Scottish Conservative MPs, committee, 1970-72. B March, 1917; son and heir of Lord Strathclyde; ed Aytoun House, Glasgow, Wellington College, Christ Church, Oxford and Glasgow University.

Mr Richard Mowbray, a lecturer in economics at Paisley College. Born September, 1946; ed Chesterfield Grammar School, London School of Economics and Glasgow University. APEX. Member of Association of Lecturers in Scottish Central Institutions.

Mr Marshall Harris, Scottish national officer, United Nations Association. B March, 1928; ed Heriot Watt's Edinburgh.

Mr Gordon Borthwick, journalist and photographer, contested the seat, October, 1974. B April, 1931; ed Wallacehall Academy, Dumfries and Hyndland School, Glasgow. Vice-president, New Glasgow Society. Proprietor of photography, publishing and display business.

GLASGOW, Kelvingrove

Electorate 33,701   1974: 42,654

*Carmichael, N. G. (Lab)	11,133
MacDougall, A. C. S. (C)	6,374
Bennett, E. (L)	2,412
Bayne, I. O. (Scot Nat)	2,199

Lab majority	4,759

No Change

	1974		1979
Total votes	27,024		22,118
Turnout		63·4%	65·6%
Lab	11,567	42·8%	50·3%
C	7,448	27·6%	28·8%
Scot Nat	6,274	23·2%	9·9%
L	1,735	6·4%	10·9%
Lab maj	4,119	15·2%	21·5%
Swing		−3·5%	−3·2%

Mr Neil Carmichael, Under Secretary, Department of Environment, 1974-76; an Opposition spokesman on Scottish affairs, 1970-74. Parliamentary Secretary, Ministry of Technology, 1969-70, and to Ministry of Transport, 1967-69. Returned in February, 1974; MP for Glasgow, Woodside, 1962-74. Engineer. B October, 1921; ed Estbank Academy and Royal College of Science and Technology, Glasgow. Sponsored by GMWU.

Mr Alan MacDougall, managing director, North Ayrshire Properties Ltd. B 1934; ed George Watson's College, Edinburgh. Contested Lanark, 1970, and February, 1974. Member, Ayrshire County Council, 1971-74 and Stewarton Town Council.

Mr Eric Bennett, estimator, fought Glasgow, Central, October 1974. B September 1951; ed Eastbank Academy, Glasgow. TGWU.

Mr Ian Bayne, teacher, contested Rutherglen, October, 1974. B March, 1940; ed St Aloysius College, Glasgow, Edinburgh University and Moray House College of Education.

GLASGOW, Maryhill

Electorate 50,434   1974: 51,545

*Craigen, J. M. (Lab and Co-op)	22,602
White, M. (C)	5,106
McGlashan, D. (Scot Nat)	3,812
Attwooll, Miss E. (L)	2,332
Smith, P. (Comm)	287

Lab and Co-op majority	17,496

No Change

	1974		1979
Total votes	33,983		34,139
Turnout		65·9%	67·7%
Lab & Co-op	19,589	57·6%	66·2%
Scot Nat	10,171	29·9%	11·2%
C	3,160	9·3%	15·0%
L	1,063	3·1%	6·8%
Comm	—	—	0·8%
Lab/Co-op m.	9,418	27·7%	51·2%
Swing		−5·1%	−1·5%

Mr James Craigen, industrial liason officer, was elected in February, 1974; contested Ayr, 1970. B August, 1938; ed Shawlands Academy, Glasgow; University of Strathclyde and Heriot-Watt University, PPS to Secretary of State for Scotland, 1974-76. Chairman, Scottish PLP Group. Substitute member, UK delegation to Council of Europe and WEU. Member, Select Committee on European Secondary Legislation; Glasgow Corporation, 1965-68; Scottish Police Advisory Board. Governor of the Scottish Police College since 1970. NUGMW.

Mr Matthew White, aged 60, office manager. Ed Kelvinside Academy, Glasgow. Chairman, Maryhill Conservative Association, 1969-73; vice-chairman from 1973.

Mr David MacGlashen, organiser for a national voluntary organization. B January 1951; ed Westwood School.

Mr Peter Smith, aged 37; lecturer in economics and industrial relations at Glasgow College of Technology.

GLASGOW, Pollok

Electorate 59,032   1974: 59,451

*White, J. (Lab)	21,420
Roser, D. A. (C)	12,928
McIntosh, A. (Scot Nat)	4,187
McKell, G. (L)	3,946
Armstrong, Ms N. G. (Ind Lab)	869
Skinner, Mrs I. (Nat Front)	104
Hilton, R. B. (Ind Dem)	41
Lab majority	8,492

No Change

	1974		1979
Total votes	43,014		43,495
Turnout	72·4%		73·7%
Lab	18,695	43·5%	49·2%
C	11,604	27·0%	29·7%
Scot Nat	10,441	24·3%	9·6%
L	2,274	5·3%	9·1%
Ind Lab	—	—	2·0%
Nat Front	—	—	0·2%
Ind Dem	—	—	0·1%
Lab maj	7,091	16·5%	19·5%
Swing		−4·6%	−1·5%

Mr James White won the seat for Labour in 1970. Member, Select Committee on Abortion (Amendment) Bill, 1975, which he sponsored. B April, 1922; ed Knightswood Senior Secondary School. Managing director, Glasgow Car Collection Ltd. TGWU. Member, Commonwealth Parliamentary Association Delegation, Bangladesh, 1973.

Mr David Roser is a partner in a clothing wholesalers and managing director of an import company. B 1940; ed Glasgow Academy and Strathclyde University. Contested Bothwell, October 1974. Member, Scottish Conservative Trade Union Advisory Committee. ASTMS.

Mr Angus McIntosh contested Glasgow, Maryhill, February and October, 1974. B 1928; ed Camphill Senior Secondary School. Glasgow councillor, 1968-71.

Mr George McKell, greengrocer. B May, 1939; ed The Abbey, Birmingham, and St. Joseph's, Salop.

GLASGOW, Provan

Electorate 52,482   1974: 54,975

*Brown, H. D. (Lab)	24,083
Langdon, S. M. (C)	5,239
Cunning, R. (Scot Nat)	4,767
Jackson, J. (Comm)	377
Campbell, M. (WRP)	193
Lab majority	18,844

No Change

	1974		1979
Total votes	35,181		34,659
Turnout	64·0%		66·0%
Lab	20,602	58·6%	69·5%
Scot Nat	10,628	30·2%	13·8%
C	3,448	9·8%	15·1%
Comm	503	1·4%	1·1%
WRP	—	—	0·6%
Lab maj	9,974	28·4%	54·4%
Swing		−2·0%	−2·8%

Mr Hugh Brown was Under-Secretary, Scottish Office, with responsibilities for housing and agriculture and fisheries, 1974-79. Elected 1964. Former civil servant, Ministry of Pensions and National Insurance. B May, 1919; ed Allan Glen's School and Whitehall Secondary School, Glasgow. Member, Glasgow Corporation, 1954-64. Chairman, social services group, PLP, 1966-68, and Scottish Labour group, 1973-74. TGWU.

Mr Michael Langdon, electrical engineer. B July, 1944; ed Royal High School, Edinburgh; Edinburgh and Oxford universities. ASTMS.

Mr Robert Cunning, newspaper photo-compositor. B December, 1931. Deputy Provost, Strathkelvin District Council.

Mr John Jackson, paperworker, contested the seat twice in 1974, 1970 and 1966. B September, 1924; ed Kent Road School, Glasgow, and Finnieston Street School, Glasgow. Member, Sogat district committee.

Mr Mark Campbell, aged 23, postman. Scottish representative of the Young Socialists National Committee. UOPW.

GLASGOW, Queens Park

Electorate 34,332   1974: 38,776

*McElhone, F. P. (Lab)	15,120
Collins, J. (C)	5,642
Greene, P. (Scot Nat)	2,276
Kay, J. R. (Comm)	263
Kerrigan, Miss J. (WRP)	99
MacLellan, W. (Soc. Unity)	92
Lab majority	9,478

No Change

	1974		1979
Total votes	25,975		23,492
Turnout	67·0%		68·4%
Lab	14,574	56·1%	64·4%
Scot Nat	5,660	21·8%	9·7%
C	4,421	17·0%	24·0%
L	966	3·7%	—
Comm	354	1·4%	1·1%
WRP	—	—	0·4%
Soc Unity	—	—	0·4%
Lab maj	8,914	34·3%	40·4%
Swing		−4·8%	−0·7%

Mr Frank McElhone, Under-Secretary of State for Scotland, 1975-79, was returned in February, 1974, MP for Glasgow, Gorbals, 1969-74. Member, Glasgow City Council, 1963-74; Glasgow magistrate, 1966-68; B April, 1929; ed St Bonaventure's Secondary School. Former member, Commons Expenditure Committee; PPS to Mr Benn as Secretary of State for Industry, 1974-75. Sponsored by USDAW.

Mr Julius Collins, fashion agent. B 1922; ed Queen's Park Secondary School, Glasgow. Former president, Glasgow Speakers Club.

Mr Philip Greene, social worker. B December 1944; ed Jordanhill College.

117

Mr **John Kay,** draughtsman. ASTMS. Former Scottish secretary, Association of Scientific Workers. Industrial organizer of Communist Party in Scotland.

Miss **Jean Kerrigan,** aged 35, is a member of USDAW. Formerly NUT.

GLASGOW, Shettleston

Electorate 31,910   1974: 38,324

Marshall, D. (Lab)	13,955
McClure, Miss M. (C)	4,794
MacDonald, M. (Scot Nat)	3,022
Lab majority	9,161

No Change

	1974		1979
Total votes	24,666		21,771
Turnout		64·4%	68·2%
Lab	13,391	54·3%	64·1%
Scot Nat	7,042	28·5%	13·9%
C	3,543	14·4%	22·0%
L	690	2·8%	
Lab maj	6,349	25·8%	42·1%
Swing		−5·4%	−1·1%

Mr **David Marshall,** Scottish Area Secretary for Manor Hospital. B May, 1941; ed Larbert High School, Denny High School, Falkirk High School and Woodside Senior Secondary School, Glasgow. Councillor for six years. Chairman, Strathclyde Regional Council Manpower Committee; Member of Police Council for United Kingdom,

National Joint Council for Fire Brigades. Former shop steward. Sponsored by TGWU. District committee delegate; Scottish Trades Union Congress delegate.

Miss **Myra McClure,** biochemist engaged in medical research for Cancer Research Campaign. B 1948; ed Glasgow High School for Girls and University of Glasgow. Former research assistant, Glasgow Royal Infirmary, on Vitamin D deficiency.

Mr **Murdo MacDonald,** airline pilot. B 1949; ed Hillhead High School and Air Services Training College, Perth.

GLASGOW, Springburn

Electorate 42,116   1974: 48,066

Martin, M. J. (Lab)	18,871
McKay, G. R. (C)	6,100
Morton, W. J. (Scot Nat)	3,587
Lab majority	12,771

No Change

	1974		1979
Total votes	31,955		28,558
Turnout		66·5%	67·8%
Lab	17,444	54·6%	66·1%
Scot Nat	9,049	28·3%	12·6%
C	4,245	13·3%	21·4%
L	865	2·7%	
Comm	352	1·1%	—
Lab maj	8,395	26·3%	44·7%
Swing		−4·9%	−1·7%

Mr **Michael Martin,** trade union officer, has served on Glasgow Corporation, 1973-74, and Glasgow District Council since 1974. B July, 1945; ed St Patrick's School, Glasgow. National Union of Sheet Metal Workers (1962), AUEW (1970) and NUPE (1976).

Mr **George McKay** contested Glasgow, Provan, October 1974, (agent in February 1974 election) and Glasgow, Woodside, in 1970 as an independent candidate. B 1948; ed Hillhead High School, Glasgow and Glasgow University.

Mr **William Morton,** maintenance engineer, contested the seat, February and October, 1974. B April 1933; ed Allan Glen's School Glasgow. Former Glasgow councillor.

GLOUCESTER

Electorate 64,958   1974: 62,503

*Oppenheim, Mrs S. (C)	25,163
Golder, M. D. (Lab)	18,747
Halford, D. G. (L)	7,213
Morgan, R. (Nat Front)	527
C majority	6,416

No Change

	1974		1979
Total votes	49,157		51,650
Turnout		78·6%	79·5%
C	22,664	46·1%	48·7%
Lab	19,136	38·9%	36·3%
L	7,357	15·0%	14·0%
Nat Front	—		1·0%
C maj	3,528	7·2%	12·4%
Swing		−1·1%	+2·6%

Mrs **Sally Oppenheim** was appointed Minister for Consumer Affairs in May 1979. Joined the shadow Cabinet in February, 1975, as chief Opposition spokesman on consumer affairs for which she had been a spokesman since 1974. Won the seat in 1970.

B July 1928; ed Sheffield High School, Lowther College, North Wales and the Royal Academy of Dramatic Art. Member, BBC Advisory Council since 1971. National vice-president, Royal Society for Prevention of Accidents, the Association of Townswomen's Guilds and the National Mobile Homes Residents' Association. Vice-President, Association of District Councils.

Mr **Michael Golder,** economist and managing director of catering company, contested Windsor and Maidenhead, February and October, 1974. B January, 1945; ed Witney Grammar School. Director of Galleon World Travel Association Ltd. ASTMS.

Mr **David Halford,** who is in nylon production, fought the seat in both 1974 elections. Member, Gloucester City Council, since 1976. B May 1944; ed Crypt Grammar School and Gloucester Technical College.

GLOUCESTERSHIRE, South

Electorate 84,867   1974: 79,439

*Cope, J. (C)	35,627
Mullins, M. K. (Lab)	20,465
Conrad, G. (L)	12,850
Kerridge, D. (Ecology)	695
C majority	15,162

No Change

	1974		1979
Total votes	63,228		69,637
Turnout	79·6%		82·1%
C	26,581	42·0%	51·2%
Lab	22,235	35·2%	29·4%
L	14,412	22·8%	18·5%
Ecology	—		1·0%
C maj	4,346	6·8%	21·8%
Swing		−1·5%	+7·5%

Mr John Cope became an assistant Government Whip in May, 1979. A chartered accountant, he was elected in February, 1974; contested Woolwich East, 1970. B May, 1937; ed Oakham School, Rutland. Conservative research department, 1965-67. Secretary, Conservative parliamentary smaller businesses committee, since 1974. Member, Commons Expenditure Committee since 1974, and of Select Committee on Parliamentary Commissioner for Administration since 1975. Joint secretary, Conservative finance committee since 1976.

Mr Michael Mullins, comprehensive school headmaster. B February, 1932; ed grammar school, University College, Swansea, King's College, London. NUT.

Mr George Conrad, general medical practitioner, B April, 1949; ed Latymer Upper School and Bristol University.

Mr David Kerridge, lecturer in economics. aged 35; ed Wycliffe School, Stroud.

GLOUCESTERSHIRE, West

Electorate 70,104   1974: 67,255

Marland, P. (C)	28,183
*Watkinson, J. T. (Lab)	24,009
Joachim, Mrs M. (L)	6,370
Storkey, G. (Nat Front)	270
C majority	4,174

C gain from Lab

	1974		1979
Total votes	53,906		58,832
Turnout	80·2%		83·9%
Lab	22,481	41·7%	40·8%
C	22,072	40·9%	47·9%
L	9,353	17·4%	10·8%
Nat Front	—		0·5%
Lab maj	409	0·8%	—
C maj	—		7·1%
Swing		1·0%	+3·9%

Mr Paul Marland, a farmer and company director, contested the seat, February and October, 1974, and Bedwellty, 1970. B March, 1940; ed Gordonstoun School and Trinity College. Dublin. Former member, North Cotswold RDC, Member, Lloyd's, NFU.

Mr John Watkinson was elected in October, 1974; contested Warwick and Leamington, 1970. Barrister and former teacher. B January, 1941; ed Bristol Grammar School and Oxford University. Member, Public Accounts Committee and Expenditure Committee. Honorary Secretary, Anglo-Irish group and Anglo-Swiss group. Member, Council of Europe and WEU; rapporteur, defence and armaments, legal affairs and agriculture committees. TGWU, previously NUT.

Mrs Margaret Joachim, geologist, university research associate and lecturer. B June, 1949; ed Brighton and Hove High School, St Hugh's College, Oxford, West Midlands College of Education and Birmingham University. Member, committee of National Traction Engine Club and Ironbridge Gorge Museum Trust.

GOOLE

Electorate 66,042   1974: 64,631

*Marshall, E. I. (Lab)	27,690
Higgins, Dr F. (C)	16,439
Davidson, A. (L)	3,976
Lab majority	11,251

No Change

	1974		1979
Total votes	44,796		48,105
Turnout	69·4%		72·8%
Lab	26,804	59·8%	57·6%
C	12,707	28·4%	34·2%
L	5,285	11·8%	8·3%
Lab maj	14,097	31·4%	23·4%
Swing		−2·3%	+4·0%

Mr Edmund Marshall, a mathematician, was elected in 1971; contested Louth as a Liberal in 1964 and 1966; joined Labour Party, 1967. B May, 1940; ed Humberstone Foundation School, Clee; Magdalen College, Oxford; Liverpool University. Chairman, trade and industry sub-committee of Expenditure Committee, since 1976. Vice-chairman, PLP environment group, 1977. Methodist local preacher; member, British Council of Churches; treasurer, Christian Socialist Movement. Member, Wallasey County Borough Council, 1963-65. TGWU.

Mr Frank Higgins, local government officer. B 1940; ed Hull University and University College of North Wales, Bangor. Member, Tory Reform Group. Anglican lay reader since 1962.

Mr Andrew Davidson, export shipping officer.

GOSPORT

Electorate 51,318   1974: 48,871

*Viggers, P. J. (C)	24,553
Slater, J. A. (Lab)	10,460
Lewis, C. (L)	4,741
C majority	14,093

No Change

	1974		1979
Total votes	36,809		39,754
Turnout	75·3%		77·5%
C	17,487	47·5%	61·8%
Lab	10,621	28·9%	26·3%
L	8,701	23·6%	11·9%
C maj	6,866	18·6%	35·5%
Swing		0·1%	+8·4%

Mr Peter Viggers, solicitor, company director and underwriting member of Lloyd's, was elected in February, 1974. B March 1938; ed Portsmouth Grammar School and Trinity Hall, Cambridge. Joint secretary, 1975-76, and a vice-chairman, Conservative energy committee. Secretary, Wessex group of Conservative MPs.

Mr John Slater, solicitor. B December, 1950; ed Portsmouth Grammar School. APEX.

Mr Craig Lewis, science and engineering research worker. Aged 45, ed Liverpool University.

GOWER

Electorate 58,023   1974: 56,867

*Davies, I. (Lab)	24,963
Llewellyn, T. (C)	14,322
Blakeborough-Pownal, R. (L)	4,245
Thomas, E. (Pl Cymru)	3,357
Lab majority	10,641

No Change

	1974		1979
Total votes	43,752		46,887
Turnout	76·9%		80·8%
Lab	25,067	57·3%	53·2%
C	8,863	20·3%	30·5%
L	5,453	12·5%	9·1%
Pl Cymru	4,369	10·0%	7·2%
Lab maj	16,204	37·0%	22·7%
Swing		−1·8%	+7·1%

Mr Ifor Davies was Under Secretary, Welsh Office, 1966-69, and Lord Commissioner of the Treasury, 1964-66. Elected in 1959. Industrial personnel officer. B June 1910; ed Gowerton School, Swansea Technical College and Ruskin College, Oxford. Chairman, Welsh Parliamentary Labour Party, 1970-71; Welsh Labour group of MPs, since 1973. Chairman, Welsh Grand Committee. Member, Court of University of Wales and board of Civic Trust for Wales. Vice-president, National Association of Local Councils. Sponsored by APEX.

Mr Trefor Llewellyn, chartered accountant and financial manager of BOC Ltd. B July 1947; ed Eton and University of Wales. Contested Cardiganshire, February 1974.

Mr Roger Blakeborough-Pownal, solicitor. B September, 1944; ed Rhyl Grammar School, and Queen's College, Cambridge.

Mr Eifion Thomas, designer. Aged 32, ed secondary schools, technical college, University College, Swansea.

GRANTHAM

Electorate 84,479   1974: 78,404

Hogg, D. (C)	36,697
Bell, Mrs V. (Lab)	18,547
Bailey, W. T. (L)	10,852
Lab majority	18,150

No Change

	1974		1979
Total votes	58,198		66,096
Turnout	74·2%		78·2%
C	27,738	47·7%	55·5%
Lab	19,708	33·9%	28·1%
L	10,752	18·5%	16·4%
C maj	8,030	13·8%	27·4%
Swing		−2·1%	+6·8%

Mr Douglas Hogg barrister, is duty lawyer for a national newspaper. Was a journalist with the *Sunday Express.* B 1943; ed Eton, Christ Church, Oxford and Lincoln's Inn. A past President of Oxford Union. Member, legal research committee, Association of Conservative Lawyers, and part author of several publications. Son of Lord Hailsham, the Lord Chancellor.

Mrs Vivienne Bell contested Rushcliffe, October, 1974. Housewife and freelance economist. Member, Long Eaton UDC, 1971-74. B July, 1943; ed Verdin Grammar School, Winsford, Horsham High School and University College, London. ASTMS.

Mr Winston Bailey, farmer, tought the seat as independent Liberal in February, 1974, and as Liberal in October, 1974. B March, 1941; ed Lincoln City Grammar School.

GRAVESEND

Electorate 88,895   1974: 87,269

Brinton, T. D. (C)	37,592
*Ovenden, J. F. (Lab)	28,246
Goodwin, I. J. A. (L)	5,917
Willden, G. D. (Nat Front)	603
Con majority	9,346

C gain from Lab

	1974		1979
Total votes	68,620		72,358
Turnout	78·6%		81·4%
Lab	29,569	43·1%	39·0%
C	27,264	39·7%	52·0%
L	10,244	14·9%	8·2%
Nat Front	1,304	1·9%	0·8%
Pros Brit	239	0·3%	—
Lab maj	2,305	3·4%	—
C maj	—	—	13·0%
Swing		−0·6%	+8·2%

Mr Timothy Brinton, broadcasting consultant, freelance commentator and interviewer. B 1929; ed Summer Fields, Oxford; Eton, Geneva University and Central School of Speech and Drama, London. Staff announcer and newsreader, BBC radio, 1951-57; head of English programmes, Radio Hong Kong, 1957-59, and newscaster and reporter ITN, 1959-62. Member, Kent County Council, since 1974. Schools governor and member, Kent Education Committee.

Mr John Ovenden, telecommunications engineer, won the seat in February, 1974; contested Sevenoaks, 1970. Member, Public Accounts Committee. Secretary, all-party committee for widows, one-parent families. B August, 1942; ed Chatham House Grammar School, Ramsgate. Member, Gillingham Borough Council, 1966-69 and 1972-74. Former secretary, Kent Federation of Labour Party. Society of Post Office Executives.

Mr Ian Goodwin, freelance sports writer. B October, 1942; ed Sir Joseph Williamson's Mathematical School, Rochester, and the School of Oriental and African Studies, London University.

GREENOCK AND PORT GLASGOW

Electorate 61,610   1974: 62,126

*Mabon, Dr J. D. (Lab and Co-op)	24,071
Boyd, J. (L)	12,789
Glasgow, R (C)	4,926
Wright, J. K. (Scot Nat)	3,435
Mathieson, Mrs I. (WRP)	176

Lab and Co-op majority	11,282

No Change

	1974		1979
Total votes	44,152		45,397
Turnout	71·1%		73·7%
Lab & Co-op	21,279	48·2%	53·0%
Scot Nat	9,324	21·1%	7·6%
L	8,580	19·4%	28·2%
C	4,969	11·3%	10·9%
WRP	—	—	0·4%
Lab/Co-op maj	11,955	27·1%	24·8%
Swing		−3·6%	−2·6%

Dr Dickson Mabon was Minister of State for Energy, 1976-79; Under Secretary of State for Scotland, 1964-67; Minister of State, Scottish Office, 1967-70; deputy Opposition spokesman on Scotland 1970-72 (resigned in protest at party's Common Market policy). Chairman, Labour Committee for Europe 1974-76; chairman, Scottish Parliamentary Labour Party, 1972-73 and, 1975-76. Member, Council of Europe, 1970-72 and 1974-76; Assembly, WEU 1970-72 and 1974-76; president, European Movement, 1975-76; founder and chairman of Manifesto Group 1974. Physician and medical historian. B November, 1925; ed state schools and Glasgow University. Returned, February, 1974. MP for Greenock 1955-74; contested Bute and North Ayrshire, 1951 and West Renfrewshire, 1955. MPU, NUGMW and BMA.

Mr James Boyd, a supervisor at Tate and Lyle refinery at Greenock. Aged 59; ed Greenock High School. Former Provost of Greenock. Councillor in Greenock for 18 years.

Mr Ronald Glasgow, public relations officer with Crewe and Nantwich Borough Council. B 1949; ed Liberton Secondary School, Edinburgh and St Andrews University. Member, Court of University of St Andrews.

Mr Kenneth Wright, civil engineer, contested seat in both 1974 elections. B February, 1945; ed Greenock High School and Glasgow University.

Mrs Isobella Mathieson, aged 47, a sister in charge at Ravenscraig Psychiatric Hospital. COHSE, branch delegate to Greenock Trades Council.

GREENWICH, Greenwich

Electorate 51,519   1974: 52,847

*Barnett, N. G. (Lab)	18,975
Saroop, N. (C)	12,133
Knight, G. (L)	3,870
Steven, Mrs H. (Nat Front)	951
Mallone, R. (FP)	460

Lab majority	6,842

No Change

	1974		1979
Total votes	34,496		36,389
Turnout	65·3%		70·6%
Lab	19,155	55·5%	52·1%
C	9,249	26·8%	33·3%
L	5,838	16·9%	10·6%
Ind	254	0·7%	—
Nat Front	—		2·6%
FP	—		1·3%
Lab maj	9,906	28·7%	18·8%
Swing		−3·1%	+4·9%

Mr Guy Barnett, Under Secretary for the Environment since 1976, retained the seat for Labour in the July, 1971 by-election. MP for Dorset, South, 1962-64; contested Scarborough and Whitby, 1959. Member, European Parliament, 1975-76, and of Council of Get Britain Out (of EEC) Campaign. Teacher; former chief education officer of Commonwealth Institute. B August, 1928; ed Highgate School and St Edmund Hall, Oxford. Secretary, Oxford Union, 1953. Member, Select Committee on Race Relations, 1972-74. Former Parliamentary consultant to Society of Civil Servants. Sponsored by SCS and NUT.

Mr Narindar Saroop, business executive with a firm of Lloyd's brokers. B 1929; ed privately in England and at Aitchison Chief's College, Lahore and Indian Military Academy, Dehra Dun. Regular officer in the Indian Army, 1946-54; Councillor, Kensington and Chelsea, since 1974.

Mr Graham Knight has contested local elections. Aged 38.

GREENWICH, Woolwich East

Electorate 52,523   1974: 50,998

*Cartwright, J. C. (Lab)	21,700
Rock, P. (C)	11,240
Woodhead, D. J. (L)	2,998
Steven, I. (Nat Front)	884
Lab majority	10,460

No Change

	1974		1979
Total votes	32,837		36,822
Turnout	64·4%		70·1%
Lab	19,812	60·3%	58·9%
C	7,387	22·5%	30·5%
L	4,638	14·1%	8·1%
Nat Front	1,000	3·0%	2·4%
Lab maj	12,425	37·8%	28·4%
Swing		−3·0%	+4·7%

Mr John Cartwright, former director, Royal Arsenal Cooperative Society, was elected in October, 1974; contested Bexleyheath, February, 1974, and Bexley, 1970. B November, 1933; ed Woking County Grammar School. Chairman, Manifesto Group of PLP. Executive civil servant, 1942-55; Labour Party organizer, 1955-67; political secretary, RACS, 1967-72. Chairman, National Union of Labour Organizers, 1969-70. Leader of Greenwich Borough Council, 1971-74 and chief whip, London Boroughs Association, 1971-75. Member, Labour Party NEC, 1971-75 and 1976-78. Member, select committees on wealth tax, European elections and EEC secondary legislation. Trustee National Maritime Museum. Member, North Atlantic Assembly. Sponsored by USDAW.

Mr Patrick Rock, on staff of Conservative Research Department, specializing in housing, land and construction. B 1951; ed Beaumond College, Stonyhurst College and Worcester College, Oxford. Board member, Hanover Housing Association, since 1976. School governor.

Mr David Woodhead, polytechnic lecturer, contested the seat in February and October, 1974. B March, 1944; ed Huddersfield New College and Manchester University. NATFHE.

GREENWICH, Woolwich West

Electorate 56,327   1974: 56,368

*Bottomley, P. J. (C)	21,222
Page, Mrs D. (Lab)	18,613
Churchill, J. (L)	4,363
Skeggs, M. (Nat Front)	630
C majority	2,609

No Change

	1974		1979
Total votes	41,649		44,828
Turnout	73·9%		79·6%
Lab	19,614	47·1%	41·5%
C	16,073	38·6%	47·3%
L	5,962	14·3%	9·7%
Nat Front			1·4%
Lab maj	3,541	8·5%	
C maj			5·8%
Swing		−1·6%	+7·1%

1975 by-election: Total vote 35,421. C 17,280 (48.8%); Lab 14,898 (42.1%); L 1,884 (5.3%); Nat Front 856 (2.4%); others 503 (1.4%). C majority 2,382 (6.7%). C gain from Lab.

Mr Peter Bottomley, an industrial economist, has held the seat since the by-election in June, 1975. B July, 1944; ed Westminster School and Trinity College, Cambridge. Secretary, Conservative health and social services committee, 1976; member, Select Committee on Violence in the Family, 1976 and Select Committee on Overseas Develpment, since 1978. Chairman, British Union of Family Organizations, TGWU.

Mrs Diana Page, teacher. B October, 1935; ed Camden School for Girls, City of London Secretarial College and Bishop Otter College, Chichester. Member, Race Relations Action Group, Child Poverty Action Group. President, Socialist Environmental and Resources Association. NUT.

Mr John Churchill, company director. B August, 1941; ed Blundell's School, Tiverton and Imperial College, London.

Mr Malcolm Skeggs, a chartered librarian, contested Woolwich, East, October, 1974; Ilford, South, 1970 and St Marylebone by-election, 1970. B August, 1940; ed Brockley County School and University College of Wales. Chairman, Greenwich branch of National Front since 1971.

GRIMSBY

Electorate 66,644   1974: 66,302

*Mitchell, A. V. (Lab)	26,282
Blair, R. (C)	20,041
Rigby, D. M. (L)	3,837
Lennard, J. (Mod Lab)	214
Hayes, J. (Nat Front)	137
Lab majority	6,241

No Change

	1974		1979
Total votes	45,979		50,511
Turnout	69·3%		75·8%
Lab	21,657	47·1%	52·0%
C	14,675	31·9%	39·7%
L	9,481	20·6%	7·6%
Ind Dem Lab	166	0·4%	
Mod Lab			0·4%
Nat Front			0·3%
Lab maj	6,982	15·2%	12·3%
Swing		−2·0%	+1·4%

By-election April 1977: Total vote: 46,697. Lab 21,890 (46.9%), C 21,370 (45.8%), L 3,128 (6.7%); Others 309 (0.7%).—Lab maj 520 (1.1%).

Mr Austin Mitchell, journalist, retained the seat for Labour in the April, by-election. Jounalist, Yorkshire Television, 1969-71 and 1973-77; presenter BBC current affairs group, 1972-73. B September, 1934: ed Woodbottom Council School, Bingley Grammar School and Manchester and Oxford universities. Lecturer in history, University of Otago, Dunedin, New Zealand, 1959-63. Senior lecturer in politics, University of Canterbury, Christchurch, New Zealand, 1963-67. Official Fellow, Nuffield College, Oxford, 1967-69. NUJ.

Mr Robert Blair, United Kingdom fish supplies coordinator for a frozen food company. B 1925; ed King Street Public School, Aberdeen and Robert Gordon's College, Aberdeen. Contested by-election, April, 1977.

Mr Derek Rigby proprietor of tool and equipment hire company, contested the seat, February and October, 1974 and Isle of Ely, 1966. B May, 1934; ed Deytheur Grammar School, Montgomeryshire, and Wigan Technical College. Lancashire councillor.

GUILDFORD

Electorate 73,251   1974: 72,302

*Howell, D. A. (C)	31,595
Blagbrough, P. H. (Lab)	11,689
Donnelly, H. (L)	11,673
Scott, P. (RF)	232
C majority	19,906

No Change

	1974		1979
Total votes	51,951		55,189
Turnout	71·9%		75·3%
C	25,564	49·2%	57·2%
L	14,660	28·2%	21·2%
Lab	11,727	22·6%	21·2%
RF	—		0·4%
C maj	10,904	21·0%	36·0%
Swing		−1·5%	+4·7%

Mr David Howell, became Secretary of State for Energy in May 1979. Opposition spokesman on Home Office affairs and previously on Treasury and economic affairs and energy; Minister of State for Energy, 1974; Minister of State for Northern Ireland, November, 1972-74; and Under Secretary for Northern Ireland, 1972; Lord Commissioner of the Treasury, 1970-71; Parliamentary Secretary, Civil Service Department, 1970-72; and Under-Secretary for Employment, 1971-72. Elected in 1966; contested Dudley 1964. B January, 1936; ed Eton and King's College, Cambridge. Director of Conservative Political Centre, 1964-66. Editor of **Crossbow,** 1962-64; chairman Bow Group, 1961.

Mr Paul Blagbrough, company secretary for City financial institution, formerly economist, Bank of England. B July 1946; ed William Ellis Grammar School and Sussex University. Member, Labour Committee for Britain in Europe, Fabian Society, APEX. Woking councillor, 1973-76.

Mr Henry Donnelly, industrial relations consultant. B July, 1913 in Tientsin, China; ed in India, Plymouth, Devon, and School of Military Engineering, Chatham. Member, Liberal Party Council. Nalgo.

HACKNEY, Central

Electorate 46,464   1974: 48,524

*Davis, S. C. (Lab)	16,506
Bennett, N. (C)	7,718
Georghiades, E. (L)	1,835
May, R. (Nat Front)	1,418
Johnson, M. (WRP)	340
Lab majority	8,788

No Change

	1974		1979
Total votes	25,621		27,953
Turnout	52·8%		60·2%
Lab	17,650	68·9%	59·0%
C	4,797	18·7%	27·6%
L	3,174	12·4%	6·6%
Nat Front	—	—	5·1%
Comm	—	—	1·2%
WRP	—	—	0·5%
Lab maj	12,853	50·2%	31·4%
Swing		−4·6%	+9·4%

Mr Clinton Davis, Under Secretary for Trade (companies, aviation and shipping) 1974-79. Elected in 1970; contested Yarmouth, 1964 and 1959, and Portsmouth, Langstone, 1955. Solicitor. B December, 1928; ed Mercers' School and King's College, London University (Chairman, Labour Society). APEX.

Mr Nicholas Bennett teacher. B 1949; ed Sedgehill School, Southwark College and Walbrook College, North London Polytechnic. Lewisham Borough councillor. Founder and first chairman, Polytechnic of North London Conservative Association. NAS.

Mr Elikkos Georghiades, barrister. Aged 27.

Mr Michael Johnson, aged 23, plasterer's mate. Member editorial board, Young Socialist weekly newspaper.

HACKNEY, North and Stoke
Newington

Electorate 46,776   1974: 52,870

Roberts, E. A. C. (Lab)	14,688
Miller, T. (C)	9,467
Gates, T. (L)	3,033
May, Mrs. S. (Nat Front)	860
Goldman, M. (Comm)	440
Lab majority	5,221

No Change

	1974		1979
Total votes	27,914		28,488
Turnout	52·8%		60·9%
Lab	16,525	59·2%	51·6%
C	5,972	21·4%	33·2%
L	3,796	13·6%	10·6%
Nat Front	1,044	3·7%	3·0%
Comm	418	1·5%	1·5%
WRP	159	0·6%	—
Lab maj	10,553	37·8%	18·4%
Swing		−4·6%	+9·1%

Mr Ernest Roberts was Assistant General Secretary of the AUEW for 20 years; member of the union for 45 years. Chairman, Labour Parliamentary Association, 1979. Fought Stockport, 1955. B April 1912; ed St Chad's Boys' Elementary School, Shrewsbury. Member, Coventry City Council, 1949-57. Author of books and pamphlets. Founder member of Institute of Workers' Control, Anti-Nazi League and CND. Member of Government EDCs and other organizations. Sponsored by AUEW.

Mr Timothy Miller, marketing consultant. B 1940; ed Douay School and Magdalen College, Oxford.

Mr Tudor Gates,writer and film producer and director, contested Tower Hamlets, Bethnal Green and Bow in February and October, 1974, Isle of Thanet, 1970; and Bethnal Green 1966 and 1964. B January, 1930; ed Raine's Foundation Grammar School, Stepney and London University. Chairman, writers section, Association of Cinema and Television Technicians.

Mr Monty Goldman, accountant, contested the seat in October 1974, 1970 and 1966. B October 1931; ed Parmiter's Grammar School. Member, Hackney Community Relations Executive Committee. APEX.

HACKNEY, South and Shoreditch

Electorate 43,090   1974: 49,540

*Brown, R. W. (Lab)	14,016
Evennett, D. (C)	7,312
Roberts, J. (L)	2,387
Tyndall, J. (Nat Front)	1,958
Curtis, P. (WRP)	215
Lab majority	6,704

No Change

	1974		1979
Total votes	27,088		25,888
Turnout	54·7%		60·1%
Lab	17,333	64·0%	54·1%
C	4,038	14·9%	28·2%
L	3,173	11·7%	9·2%
Nat Front	2,544	9·4%	7·6%
WRP	—		0·8%
Lab maj	13,295	49·1%	25·9%
Swing		−5·3%	+11·6%

Mr Ronald Brown, returned in February, 1974, was MP for Shoreditch and Finsbury 1964-74. An assistant Government whip, 1966-67. B September 1921; ed elementary school, south London and Borough Polytechnic. Brother of Lord George-Brown. Senior lecturer in electrical engineering; principal of industrial training school; parliamentary adviser to and sponsored by Furniture, Timber and Allied Trades Union; parliamentray consultant, NALGO. Member, European Parliament, 1977-79. Chairman, PLP Greater London area group. Member, Select Committee on Science and Technology.

Mr David Evennett, insurance broker and underwriting member of Lloyds. Former schoolmaster. B 1949; ed Buckhurst County High School and LSE. Elected to Redbridge Borough Council, 1974.

Mr Jeffery Roberts, oil investment analyst. B June, 1943; ed Waterloo Grammar School, Liverpool; New College, Oxford; University of Wales. Representative of the Liberal Candidates' Association on Liberal Party Council.

Mr John Tyndall, is chairman, national directorate of the National Front.

Mr Peter Curtis, hospital porter. Former secondary school teacher. Aged 30. NUPE.

HALESOWEN AND STOURBRIDGE

Electorate 84,534   1974: 82,198

*Stokes, J. H. R. (C)	33,247
Etheridge, R. A. (Lab)	24,282
Harvey, C. (L)	8,597
Goodwin, S. (Nat Front)	921
C majority	8,965

No Change

	1974		1979
Total votes	62,596		67,047
Turnout	76·2%		79·3%
C	24,387	39·0%	49·6%
Lab	23,537	37·6%	36·2%
L	14,672	23·4%	12·8%
Nat Front	—	—	1·4%
C maj	850	1·4%	13·4%
Swing		−2·4%	+6·0%

Mr John Stokes, management consultant, was elected for the constituency February, 1974; represented Oldbury and Halesowen, 1970-74; contested Gloucester, 1964, and Hitchin, 1966. B July, 1917; ed Haileybury and Queens College, Oxford. Member, Conservative Parliamentary Defence Committee. Chairman, General Purposes Committee, Primrose League; vice-chairman, Royal Society of St George.

Mr Richard Etheridge, chartered engineer and university teacher. B December, 1933; ed Halesowen Secondary Modern School, Birmingham College of Technology, University of Aston. AEU, ATTI, AUT. Member, Black Country Society.

Mr Christopher Harvey, Chamber of Commerce executive. B January, 1949; ed Kidderminster College of Further Education and Bristol Polytechnic. Member, Wyre Forest District Council, since 1977.

HALIFAX

Electorate 63,768   1974: 63,562

*Summerskill, Dr Shirley (Lab)	21,416
Ford, J. (C)	20,182
Clegg A. (L)	6,853
Wadsworth, B. (Nat Front)	455
Lab majority	1,234

No Change

	1974		1979
Total votes	47,386		48,906
Turnout	74·6%		76·7%
Lab	20,976	44·3%	43·8%
C	16,798	35·4%	41·3%
L	8,693	18·3%	14·0%
Powellite	919	1·9%	—
Nat Front	—		0·9%
Lab maj	4,178	8·9%	2·5%
Swing		−1·6%	+3·2%

Dr Shirley Summerskill, Under-Secretary, Home Office, 1974-79. An Opposition spokesman on health, 1970-74. Elected in 1964; contested Blackpool, North, 1962 by-election, Medical practioner. B September, 1931; ed St Paul's School; Somerville College, Oxford; St Thomas' Hospital. Vice-president, Socialist Medical Association; chairman, PLP health group, 1968-70, vice-chairman 1964-68. United Kingdon delegate to the UN Status of Women Commission, 1968 and 1969. Daughter of Lady Summerskill. MPU. ASTMS.

Mr John Ford, company director. B December, 1944 and ed Malsis Hall, Keighley and Stowe School. Member, Halifax Borough Council, 1968-71, and Calderdale Council, since 1975. Director of family group of companies.

Mr Allen Clegg, textile technologist, contested the seat, February and October, 1974, and Bradford, South, 1964. B May, 1938; ed Heath Grammar School, Halifax and Bradford University. Member, Halifax Borough Council, 1963-74, and Calderdale Metropolitan District Council, 1973-76. APEX.

HALTEMPRICE

Electorate 80,058   1974: 76,257

*Wall, P. H. S. (C)	34,525
Walker R. (L)	14,637
Elcock, H. J. (Lab)	12,743
C majority	19,888

No Change

	1974		1979
Total votes	57,155		61,905
Turnout	75·0%		77·3%
C	28,206	49·4%	55·8%
L	16,566	29·0%	23·6%
Lab	12,383	21·7%	20·6%
C maj	11,640	20·4%	32·2%
Swing		−2·7%	+3·7%

Mr Patrick Wall, was returned at a by-election in February, 1954; contested Cleveland, 1951 and 1952 by-election. B October, 1916; ed Downside. Joint vice-chairman, Conservative parliamentary committee on defence, 1965-77; chairman, Conservative sub-committee on fisheries and of Southern African group since 1970. Member, Westminster City

Council, 1953-62. Chairman, North Atlantic Assembly military committee since 1977; chairman, Conservative/Christian Democrat group, North Atlantic Assembly, since 1977. Treasurer, British group IPU, since 1976. Substitute delegate, Council of Europe and WEU since 1974. Royal Marines, 1935-50. IoJ.

Mr Robert Walker, contested the seat, February and October, 1974. Was in the diplomatic service for 25 years; in 1972 became Deputy Registrar of Hull University. B May, 1924; ed Sowerby Bridge Secondary School and Peterhouse College, Cambridge. Former chairman, staff side, Diplomatic Service Whitley Council. AUT.

Mr Howard Elcock, lecturer. Aged 36.

HAMILTON

Electorate 51,802   1974: 50,346

*Robertson, G. (Lab)	24,593
Davison, P. S. (C)	9,794
Stoddart, C. (Scot Nat)	6,842
Lab majority	14,799

No Change

	1974		1979
Total votes	38,883		41,229
Turnout	77·2%		79·6%
Lab	18,487	47·5%	59·6%
Scot Nat	15,155	39·0%	16·6%
C	3,682	9·5%	23·8%
L	1,559	4·0%	—
Lab maj	3,332	8·5%	35·8%
Swing		−5·1%	+1·1%

1978 by-election: Total vote 37,035 (72·0%)—Lab 18,880 (51·0%); Scot-Nat 12,388 (33·4%); C 4,818 (13·0%); L 949 (2·6%). Lab majority 6,492 (17·5%).

Mr George Robertson, won the by-election in May, 1978. Scottish organizer for the GMWU, 1970-78. B April, 1946; ed Dunoon Grammar School and Dundee University. Chairman, Scottish Council, Labour Party, 1977-78. Board member, Scottish Development Agency, 1975-78, and of Scottish Tourist Board, 1974-76. Sponsored by GMWU.

Mr Peter Davison, scientist and farmer. Director of Research, Scientific Documentation Centre; editor of *Euro Abstracts* which published notifications of all research carried out by the EEC. B January 1930; ed George Watson's Boys College, Edinburgh University. Fife regional councillor.

Mr Charles Stoddart, university law lecturer. B April, 1948; ed Edinburgh University and McGill University.

HAMMERSMITH, Fulham

Electorate 57,018   1974: 58,303

Stevens, M. (C)	20,249
Stead, B. J. (Lab)	18,750
Rendel, D. D. (L)	3,882
Roberts, D. K. (Nat Front)	499
C majority	1,499

C gain from Lab

	1974		1979
Total votes	41,343		43,380
Turnout	70·9%		76·1%
Lab	20,616	49·9%	43·2%
C	15,295	37·0%	46·7%
L	4,577	11·1%	8·9%
Nat Front	855	2·1%	1·2%
Lab maj	5,321	12·9%	—
C maj	—	—	3·5%
Swing		−2·6%	+8·2%

Mr Martin Stevens, partner in a marketing consultancy group, contested the seat in both 1974 elections and Dulwich, 1966 and 1964. B July 1929; ed Bradfield and Trinity College, Oxford. Member L.C.C. (Dulwich) 1955-58; Camberwell Borough Council, 1959-65. Chairman, national appeal, Cancer Research Campaign. APEX.

Mr Barrington Stead, solicitor, contested Kensington, South, 1964. B December, 1935; ed Chislehurst and Sidcup County Grammar School, and St John's College, Oxford. Leader, Hammersmith Borough Council, since 1973; member since 1971. Member, Kensington and Chelsea council, 1964-68. TGWU.

Mr David Rendel, oil company employee. B April, 1949; ed Eton College, Magdalen College and St Cross College, Oxford. Member, Hammersmith Borough Council.

HAMMERSMITH, North

Electorate 50,821   1974: 52,371

Soley, C. S. (Lab)		17,241
Cripps J. (C)		13,735
Knott, S. H. J. A. (L)		4,147
Pearse, R. (Nat Front)		462
Stewart, C. (WRP)		193

Lab majority		3,506

No Change

	1974		1979
Total votes	33,833		35,778
Turnout	64·6%		70·4%
Lab	18,061	53·4%	48·2%
C	9,939	29·4%	38·4%
L	5,200	15·4%	11·6%
Ind	633	1·9%	—
Nat Front	—	—	1·3·
WRP	—	—	0·5%
Lab maj	8,122	24·0%	9·8%
Swing		−2·9%	+7·1%

Mr Clive Soley, is a probation officer. B May, 1939; ed Downshall, Ilford, secondary modern school. Hammersmith councillor, 1974-78. GMWU.

Mr Jeremy Cripps, European controller of a company manufacturing fluid power system components. B 1943; ed Eton and Case Western Reserve University, Ohio. Chartered accountant in Britain and USA. Co-founder, in 1975, of Society of Conservative Accountants, becoming joint hon secretary. Hon treasurer, London Branch, English Speaking Union.

Mr Simon Knott, a member of the Stock Exchange and company director, contested the seat, February and October, 1947, and Barons Court, 1959, 1964, 1966 and 1970. B June, 1931; ed Malvern College and Trinity College, Cambridge.

Mr Calvin Stewart, engineer. Aged 49. Former freelance photographer. TGWU.

HARBOROUGH

Electorate 68,989   1974: 65,855

*Farr, J. A. (C)	33,328
Soulsby, P. A. (Lab)	11,350
Weatherall, P. (L)	9,529
Ashby, A. (Nat Front)	1,002

C majority	21,978

No Change

	1974		1979
Total votes	50,277		55,209
Turnout	76·3%		80·0%
C	25,776	51·3%	60·4%
L	12,567	25·0%	17·3%
Lab	11,934	23·7%	20·6%
Nat Front	—	—	1·8%
C maj	13,209	26·3%	39·8%
Swing		−1·1%	+6·1%

Mr John Farr, elected in 1959; contested Ilkeston 1955. B September, 1922; ed Harrow. Member of Lloyd's, company director and landowner. Vice-chairman, Conservative Northern Ireland Committee 1974-78. Secretary, party's committee on agriculture, 1970-74. Member, Commons Standing Orders Committee; former Select Committees on agriculture. Secretary, all-party conservation committee, and Anglo-Irish Parliamentary group. Substitute delegate, Council of Europe and WEU.

Mr Peter Soulsby, teacher. B December, 1948, ed Minchenden School, Southgate, London, Leicester College of Education & Leicester University. Member, Leicester City Council, since 1974. NUT.

Mr Paul Weatherall, librarian. B June, 1950; ed Henry Smith School, Hartlepool and Leeds Polytechnic. NALGO.

HARINGEY, Hornsey

Electorate 58,409   1974: 58,279

*Rossi, H. A. L. (C)	20,225
Knight, E. R. (Lab)	16,188
O'Brien, P. W. (L)	4,058
Pell, P. (Nat Front)	337
Berry, D. W. (Ind C)	156

C majority	4,037

No Change

	1974		1979
Total votes	39,926		40,964
Turnout	68·5%		70·1%
C	17,226	43·1%	49·4%
Lab	16,444	41·2%	39·5%
L	5,283	13·2%	9·9%
Nat Front	973	2·4%	0·8%
Ind C	—	—	0·4%
C maj	782	1·9%	9·9%
Swing		−1·6%	+4·0%

Mr Hugh Rossi, was appointed Minister of State for Northern Ireland in May, 1979. An Opposition spokesman on housing and construction since 1976 and on housing and land from 1974. Under-Secretary for the Environment, 1974; Lord Commissioner of the Treasury, 1972-74; Assistant Government Whip 1970-72. Elected in June, 1966. B June, 1927; ed Finchley Catholic Grammar School and King's College, London University. Member, Haringey Borough Council, 1964-68; Hornsey Borough Council, 1956-65 (deputy mayor, 1964-65); Middlesex County Council, 1961-65. Secretary, Conservative housing committee, 1967-70; vice-chairman, legal committee, 1970. Deputy leader, Government delegation to Council of Europe and Western European Union, 1970-73.

Mr Edward Knight, member of Lambeth Council since 1974 and leader since 1978. B June, 1933; ed Strand Grammar School, London. ASTMS and USDAW.

Mr Patrick O'Brien, barrister, contested the seat, February, 1974, and Brent, East, October, 1974. B June, 1945; ed St Joseph's Academy, Blackheath, and Queen's College, Cambridge.

HARINGEY, Tottenham

Electorate 46,821   1974: 47,530

*Atkinson, N. (Lab)	16,299
Carrington, M. H. M. (C)	9,166
Alexander, Miss K. (L)	2,177
Mates, C. S. (Nat Front)	833
Gutteridge, E. D. J. (WRP)	94
Rolph, G. A. (Fellowship Party)	71

Lab majority	7,133

No Change

	1974		1979
Total votes	26,699		28,640
Turnout	56·2%		61·2%
Lab	15,708	58·8%	56·9%
C	6,492	24·3%	32·0%
L	2,288	8·6%	7·6%
Nat Front	2,211	8·3%	2·9%
WRP	—	—	0·3%
FP	—	—	0·2%
Lab maj	9,216	34·5%	24·9%
Swing		−2·6%	+4·8%

Mr Norman Atkinson, treasurer of the Labour Party since 1976. Elected in 1964; contested Wythenshawe, 1955; Altrincham and Sale 1959. Mechanical engineer and chief design engineer, Manchester University, 1957-64. B March, 1923; ed elementary and technical schools. Member, Tribune Group. Former chairman, Select Committee on Science and Technology; former member, Select Committee on Immigration and Race Relations. Member, Manchester City Council, 1945-49. Governor, Imperial College of Science and Technology. Sponsored by AUEW.

Mr Matthew Carrington, banker with the First National Bank of Chicago. B 1947; ed Lycee Francais de Londres; Imperial College of Science and Technol-

ogy, London University, and London Graduate School of Business Studies.

Miss Katherine Alexander, family property manager, contested the seat, February and October, 1974. B December, 1941; ed London University and Birbeck College.

Mr Eric Gutteridge, secretary of the AUEW Tottenham No 7 branch and a delegate to Haringey Trades Council. Aged 34.

HARINGEY, Wood Green

Electorate 52,039   1974: 52,019

Race, R. (Lab)	16,465
Riley, Miss J. (C)	13,950
Davies, G. (L)	3,665
Frost, R. (Nat Front)	998

Lab majority	2,515

No Change

	1974		1979
Total votes	32,384		35,078
Turnout	62·3%		67·4%
Lab & Co-op	16,605	51·3%	46·9%
C	8,394	25·9%	39·8%
L	4,782	14·8%	10·4%
Nat Front	2,603	8·0%	2·8%
Lab/Co-op m	8,211	25·4%	7·1%
Swing		−2·3%	+9·1%

Mr Reginald Race, research officer with NUPE, sponsored by that union. Contested Ruislip-Northwood, February and October 1974. B June, 1947; ed Sale Grammar School, universities of Kent and Essex. NUPE and APEX.

Miss Jenny Riley, export planning manager with a cigarette manufacturer. B April 1946; ed St Mary's Hall, Brighton and Girton College, Cambridge. GLC member for Wood Green, since 1977. ASTMS.

Mr Geoffrey Davies, solicitor. Aged 39; ed Law Society School.

Mr Robert Frost, a self-employed businessman, is 41. Formerly served in the Life Guards.

HARLOW

Electorate 67,494   1974: 62,964

*Newens, A. S. (Lab & Co-op)	22,698
Powley, J. (C)	21,306
Browne, R. (L)	8,289
Childs, J. (Nat Front)	840

Lab majority	1,392

No Change

	1974		1979
Total votes	47,340		53,133
Turnout	75·2%		78·7%
Lab & Co-op	24,961	52·7%	42·7%
C	11,510	24·3%	40·1%
L	10,869	23·0%	15·6%
Nat Front	—	—	1·6%
Lab/Co-op m	13,451	28·4%	2·6%
Swing		−2·0%	+12·9%

Mr Stanley Newens, former teacher and miner, returned in February, 1974. MP for Epping, 1964-70. B March, 1930; ed Buckhurst High School, University College, London, and Westminster Teacher Training College. President, London Cooperative Society. Chairman, PLP Eastern Area group, since 1974; vice-chairman, PLP Foreign and Commonwealth affairs group. Member, NUM 1952-56, NUT since 1956.

Mr John Powley, director of the electrical goods business he started in 1960. B August 1936; ed Cambridge Grammar School for Boys and Cambridge College of Arts and Technology. Trained as radio and television service engineer. Member on former Cambridge and Isle of Ely County Councils; Cambridgeshire County and Cambridge District Councils, 1973. Elected Leader, Conservative Group, Cambridge City Council, 1973.

Mr Robert Brown, reinsurance broker. B May, 1943; ed Birkbeck College, London University, Universities of Barcelona and Poitiers, and St Ignatius College, Stamford Hill.

HARROGATE

Electorate 69,182   1974: 64,759

*Banks, R. G. (C)	30,551
Kent, R. (L)	12,021
Fleming, A. (Lab)	8,221
Waite, Mrs D. (Nat Front)	585

C majority	18,530

No Change

		1974		1979
Total votes		45,648		51,378
Turnout		70·5%		74·3%
C	24,583	53·9%		59·5%
L	11,269	24·7%		23·4%
Lab	8,047	17·6%		16·0%
Nat Front	1,030	2·3%		1·1%
Whig	719	1·6%		—
C maj	13,314	29·2%		36·1%
Swing		−2·7%		+3·6%

Mr Robert Banks, horticultural nurseryman and farmer, was elected in February, 1974. Paddington councillor, 1959-65. B January 1937; ed Haileybury. Naval reserve officer, former executive in publishing, now partner in an investment company. Joint secretary, Conservative parliamentary defence committee; vice-chairman, party's horticultural sub-committee; secretary, all-party tourism group and Anglo-Sudan all-party group. Substitute member, Council of Europe and WEU.

Mr Rodney Kent, antique dealer, contested Thirsk and Malton, October, 1974. B October, 1932; ed Ashville College, Newcastle-on-Tyne. Mayor of Harrogate, 1973-74; alderman and leader of Liberal group, Harrogate Council, 1960-74.

Mr Aidan Fleming, industrial marketing engineer. B September, 1934; ed Michigan State University. AUEW/TASS.

HARROW, Central

Electorate 44,747   1974; 45,260

*Grant, J. A. (C)	16,627
Quicke, A. C. (Lab)	12,124
Bancroft, R. (L)	4,785
Marshall, H. (Nat Front)	427

C majority	4503

No Change

		1974		1979
Total votes		33,023		33,963
Turnout		73·0%		75·9%
C	14,356	43·5%		49·0%
Lab	12,288	37·2%		35·7%
L	5,566	16·9%		14·1%
Nat Front	813	2·5%		1·3%
C maj	2,068	6·3%		13·3%
Swing		−0·9%		+3·5%

Mr Anthony Grant was vice-chairman of the Conservative Party, with responsibilities for candidates, 1974-76. Under Secretary for Trade and Industry, 1972-74; Parliamentary Secretary, Board of Trade, 1970-72. Elected in 1964; contested Hayes and Harlington, 1959. Solicitor and company director. B May, 1925; ed St Paul's School and Brasenose College, Oxford. Master, Guild of Freemen of City of London. Vice-chairman, backbench trade committee, 1974. Opposition whip 1966-70. Substitute member, Council of Europe and W.E.V. since 1977.

Mr Andrew Quicke, TV film producer, contested Kingston upon Thames, October 1974 election. B October, 1936; ed New College, Oxford.

Mr Ralph Bancroft, aged 27, senior parlimentary assistant. Ed Sussex University.

HARROW, East

Electorate 49,354   1974: 49,315

*Dykes, H. J. (C)	20,871
Miles, D. (Lab)	12,993
Savitt, M. (L)	3,984
le Croissette, L. (Nat. Front)	572

C majority	7,878

No Change

		1974		1979
Total votes		36,936		38,420
Turnout		74·9%		77·8%
C	17,073	46·2%		54·3%
Lab	13,595	36·8%		33·8%
L	6,268	17·0%		10·4%
Nat Front	—			1·5%
C maj	3,478	9·4%		20·5%
Swing		−0·9%		+5·5%

Mr Hugh Dykes, stockbroker, won the seat for the Conservatives in 1970; contested Tottenham, 1966. B May, 1939; ed Weston-super-Mare Grammar School and Pembroke College, Cambridge (chairman, University Conservative Association, 1962). Member, European Parliament, 1974-1976. Secretary, Conservative European Affairs Committee.

Member, Wider Share Ownership Council. Sponsored Heavy Commercial Vehicles (Controls and Regulation) Bill which became law in July 1973 and is known as the Dykes Act.

Mr David Miles, senior lecturer in business studies at Kingston Polytechnic. B October, 1945; ed King Edward VI Grammar School, Morpeth, Northumberland; Enfield College of Technology, Middlesex. Deputy Leader of Opposition, Westminster City Council. Co-opted member ILEA, 1976-77. NATFHE.

HARROW, West

Electorate 56,907   1974: 56,641

*Page, J. A. (C)	26,007
Catterson, Miss M. T. (Lab)	10,794
Dick, R. (L)	7,350
Bennett, T. (Nat. Front)	646
C majority	15,213

No Change

	1974		1979
Total votes	42,169		44,797
Turnout	74·4%		78·7%
C	21,924	52·0%	58·1%
Lab	10,342	24·5%	24·1%
L	9,903	23·5%	16·4%
Nat Front	—	—	1·4%
C maj	11,582	27·5%	34·0%
Swing		−0·8%	+3·2%

Mr John Page was returned in a by-election in March, 1960; contested Eton and Slough, 1959. B September, 1919; ed Harrow and Magdalene College, Cambridge. Chairman, Conservative parliamentary labour affairs committee, 1970-74; secretary, Conservative broadcasting committee, 1974-76; president, Conservative Trade Unionists National Advisory Council, 1967-

69; member, Select Committee on Race Relations and Immigration, 1970-71; delegate to Council of Europe and WEU since 1972 and chairman, Budget Committee, 1973-74, and Social and Health Committee since 1975. President, Independent Schools Association since 1971; chairman, Council for Independent Education, since 1974.

Miss Marie Catterson, barrister and former research assistant in labour law, LSE. B October, 1948; ed Wyggeston Girls Grammar School, Leicester and University College, London. TGWU (ACTS).

Mr Ronald Dick, management consultant. B February, 1936; ed in London and Scotland.

HARTLEPOOL

Electorate 65,732   1974: 65,345

*Leadbitter, E. L. (Lab)	27,039
Miller, K. (C)	18,877
Abbott, C. (L)	3,193
Lab majority	8,162

No Change

	1974		1979
Total votes	47,300		49,109
Turnover	72·4%		74·7%
Lab	24,440	51·7%	55·1%
C	16,546	35·0%	38·4%
L	6,314	13·3%	6·5%
Lab maj	7,894	16·7%	16·7%
Swing		−4·1%	0·0%

Mr Edward Leadbitter was elected in 1964. A teacher. B June, 1919; ed state schools and Cheltenham Teacher Training College. Member, Select Committee on Science and Technology. Former member, West Hartlepool Borough Council; president, Hartlepool Labour Party, 1958-62. Chairman PLP transport group ports sub-committee. Sponsored by NUPE.

Mr Keith Miller is a barrister. B January, 1948; ed Southampton University and Middle Temple. Former vice-chairman, Hackney Conservative Association. Twice contested seat on Hackney Borough Council.
Mr Christopher Abbott, self-employed electrical engineer. Aged 28.

HARWICH

Electorate 92,908   1974: 88,710

*Ridsdale, J. E. (C)	37,685
Brooks, C. W. (Lab)	16,998
Goodenough, R. (L)	14,094
Pearson, A. (Nat Front)	597
C majority	20,687

No Change

	1974		1979
Total votes	64,146		69,374
Turnout	72·3%		74·7%
C	29,963	46·7%	54·3%
Lab	19,135	29·8%	24·5%
L	15,048	23·5%	20·3%
Nat Front	—		0·9%
C maj	10,828	16·9%	29·8%
Swing		−1·2%	+6·4%

Mr Julian Ridsdale, company director, was returned at a by-election in February, 1954. Under Secretary, Air Ministry, 1962-64; Under Secretary for Defence for the RAF, 1964. Chairman, British Japanese parliamentary group, since 1964; vice-chairman, United Nations Parliamentary Association, since 1966. Chairman, Japanese Society, London, since 1976.

Member, Public Accounts Committee, 1970-74. B June, 1915; ed Tonbridge, the Royal Military College, Sandhurst, and London Unversity School of Oriental Languages. Contested Paddington, North, 1951.

Mr Christopher Brooks, economist. B October, 1960; ed Mellow Lane Comprehensive School, Hayes and Nottingham University. Member, Lambeth Borough Council. APEX.

Mr Robert Goodenough, teacher, aged 30. Ed Open University.

HASTINGS

Electorate 57,699   1974: 57,023

*Warren, K. R. (C)	21,311
Foster, M. J. (Lab)	12,392
Leggett, A. E. (L)	6,474
McNally, G. L. (Ind)	839
Anderson, Mrs H. J. (Nat Front)	344

C majority	8,919

No Change

	1974		1979
Total votes	40,815		41,360
Turnout	71·6%		71·7%
C	18,337	44·9%	51·5%
Lab	13,685	33·5%	30·0%
L	8,793	21·5%	15·7%
Ind	—		2·0%
Nat Front	—		0·8%
C maj	4,652	11·4%	21·5%
Swing		−2·2%	+5·0%

Mr Kenneth Warren was elected in 1970; contested St Pancras North, 1964. Aeronautical engineer and management consultant. substitute delegate, Council of Europe and WEU since 1974 and chairman WEU's science, Technology and aerospace committee since 1975. Member, Select Committee on Science and technology. Chairman, Conservative parliamentary aviation committee, 1975-77; secretary, Anglo-Soviet parliamentary committee. Paddington Borough Councillor, 1953-65. B August, 1926; ed Midsomer Norton Grammar School, Aldenham School, De Havilland Aeronautical Technical School, King's College, London and London School of Economics.

Mr Michael Foster, solicitor's legal clerk, contested the seat, February, 1974 and October, 1974. B February, 1946; ed Hastings Grammar School. Leader, Labour Group, Hastings Borough Council, 1973-76 and of Hastings County Borough Council, 1973-74. East Sussex County Council, 1973-77; Labour Chief Whip. GMWU.

Mr Albert Leggett contested the seat, October, 1974. Representative in Post Office telecommunications. B January, 1935; ed Bec Grammar School, Tooting.

HAVANT AND WATERLOO

Electorate 82,116   1974: 75,472

*Lloyd, I. S. (C)	35,580
Hoodless, D. B. (Lab)	15,240
Amies, D. (L)	11,274

C majority	20,340

No Change

	1974		1979
Total votes	55,643		62,094
Turnout	73·7%		75·6%
C	24,880	44·7%	57·3%
L	16,148	29·0%	18·2%
Lab	14,615	26·3%	24·5%
C maj	8,732	15·7%	32·8%
Swing		−2·6%	+7·2%

Mr Ian Lloyd, returned in February, 1974, represented Portsmouth, Langstone, 1964-74. Economist and chairman of International Shipping Information Services. B May, 1921; ed Michaelhouse, Natal, Witwatersrand University, King's College, Cambridge (former president of Union), and Administrative Staff College, Henley. Member, Select Committee on Science and Technology. Fellow of Royal Statistical Society. Economic adviser to Central Mining and Investment Corporation, 1949-53; member, South African Board of Trade and Industries, 1953-56.

Mr Donald Hoodless, director of a housing trust. B October 1942; ed Isleworth Grammar School and Durham University. Member, London Borough of Islington Council, since 1968; N E Thames Regional Health Authority. ACTS.

Mr David Amies, account and housing manager to the Barbican estate. B February 1942; ed Bexhill Grammar School and Leeds University. Member, Rother District Council; branch chairman of Nalgo.

HAVERING, Hornchurch

Electorate 60,865 1874: 60,423

Squire, R. C. (C)	21,340
*Williams, A. L. (Lab)	20,571
Lewcock, C. (L)	4,657
Harris, A. (Nat Front)	994

C majority	769

C gain from Lab

	1974		1979
Total votes	43,952		47,562
Turnout	72·7%		78·1%
Lab	21,336	48·5%	43·3%
C	14,535	33·1%	44·9%
L	7,284	16·6%	9·8%
PAA	797	1·8%	—
Nat Front	—		2·1%
Lab maj	6,801	15·4%	—
C	—		1·6%
Swing		−1·3%	+8·5%

Mr Robin Squire, deputy chief account of a banking group, fought the seat, October 1974. B July, 1944; ed Tiffin School. Member, London Borough of Sutton Council, since 1968; leader of majority party since 1976. Vice-chairman, National Young Conservatives, 1974.

Mr Alan Lee Williams, a lecturer and writer, was elected in February, 1974; MP for Hornchurch, 1966-70; contested Epsom, 1964. Former Thames waterman and lighterman. B November, 1930; ed Roan School, Greenwich, and Ruskin College, Oxford. Chairman, PLP defence and services committee; all-party waterways group. Joint chairman, all-party motor industry group, 1978.

Director, British Atlantic Committee, 1972-74. Member, PLP defence group, 1966-70. Head of United Nations Association, Youth Department, 1962-66. Member, Greenwich Borough Council, 1953-55.

Mr Christopher Lewcock, town planner with Swale Borough Council. B June 1953; ed Woodroffe School, Lyme Regis; Churcher's College, Petersfield and St George's School, Hongkong. Nalgo branch secretary.

HAVERING, Romford

Electorate 55,154   1974: 55,337

*Neubert, M. J. (C)	22,714
Bartlett, Mrs S. M. (Lab)	13,902
Bates, J. (L)	4,818
Caine, Mrs M. (Nat Front)	820

C majority	8,812

No Change

	1974		1979
Total votes	39,540		42,254
Turnout	71·5%		76·6%
C	17,164	43·4%	53·8%
Lab	14,513	36·7%	32·9%
L	7,663	19·4%	11·4%
PAA	200	0·5%	—
Nat Front	—	—	1·9%
C maj	2,651	6·7%	20·9%
Swing		−0·2%	+7·1%

Mr Michael Neubert, secretary of the Conservative parliamentary committee for prices and consumer affairs since 1976 and of the committee for trade, was elected in February 1974; contested Romford 1970, Hammersmith North, 1966. Travel consultant. B September, 1933; ed Queen Elizabeth's School, Barnet, Bromley Grammar School and Downing College, Cambridge. Member, Bromley Borough Council, 1960-63; London Borough of Bromley Council, 1964-68, alderman 1968-74, Leader of Council 1967-70, Mayor 1972-73.

Mrs Suzanne Bartlett, a student counsellor, contested Worthing, 1970, and Thanet East, October 1974. B May 1933; ed Willesden County Grammar School and LSE. Member, Hampshire County Council, since 1970. ASTMS.

Mr John Bates, barrister. B May, 1951; ed Harrow. Vice-chairman, Liberal Ecology Group.

HAVERING, Upminster

Electorate 65,966   1974: 64,429

*Loveridge, J. W. (C)	27,960
Stephenson, J. K. (Lab)	18,895
Harvey, D. (L)	5,216
Neary, W. (Nat Front)	965

C majority	9,065

No Change

	1974		1979
Total votes	49,082		53,036
Turnover	76·2%		80·4%
C	20,966	42·7%	52·7%
Lab	20,272	41·3%	35·6%
L	7,844	16·0%	9·8%
Nat Front	—	—	1·8%
C maj	694	1·4%	17·1%
Swing		−0·3%	+7·8%

Mr John Loveridge, Principal of St Godric's College, London, since 1954, and farmer. Elected in February, 1974; MP for Hornchurch, 1970-74; fought Aberavon in 1951. B September, 1925; ed St John's College, Cambridge. Member, Hampstead Borough Council, 1953-59. Vice-chairman, Conservative Smaller Businesses Committee, since 1974. Member, Select Committee on Expenditure. Former member, Select Committee on Procedure.

Mr John Stephenson, a lecturer at N E London Polytechnic, contested Bury St Edmunds, February and October 1974. B May, 1939; ed Barrow in Furness County Grammar School, LSE, and London University. AMA/NATFHE.

Mr David Harvey, research scientist. B July, 1939; ed North Manchester Grammar School and various polytechnics. ASTMS.

HAZEL GROVE

Electorate 70,005   1974: 67,648

*Arnold, T. R. (C)	32,420
Bingham, V. (L)	17,148
Lowe, J. G. (Lab)	8,846

C majority	15,272

No Change

	1974		1979
Total votes	55,720		58,414
Turnout	82·4%		83·4%
C	25,012	44·9%	55·5%
L	22,181	39·8%	29·4%
Lab	8,527	15·3%	15·1%
C maj	2,831	5·1%	26·1%
Swing		−1·3%	+5·4%

Mr Tom Arnold, theatre producer and company director, won the seat in October, 1974; contested it February, 1974, and Manchester, Cheetham, June, 1970. B January, 1947; ed Bedales, Le Rosey (Geneva) and Pembroke College, Oxford. Member, Select Committee on European Legislation since November, 1976. Secretary, Conservative North-West MPs group. Treasurer, House of Commons Flying Club. Executive member, Society of West End Theatre. Joint Secretary. All Party Group on the Theatre. Member, Theatrical Manangement Association. ASTMS. 10J.

Mr Vivian Bingham, management consultant, fought Heywood and Royton in both 1974 elections. B April, 1932; ed Duke's Grammar School, Alnwick; King Edward's, Birmingham, and New College, Oxford. Founder of own company, Workplace Consultants Ltd.

Mr John Lowe, quantity surveyor. Member, Cheadle Labour Party.

131

HEMEL HEMPSTEAD

Electorate 91,843   1974: 83,795

Lyell, N. (C)	37,953
*Corbett, R. (Lab)	32,964
Penwarden, D. (L)	6,314
Walters, T. (Nat Front)	649

C majority	4,989

C gain from Lab

	1974		1979
Total votes	68,458		77,880
Turnout	81·7%		84·8%
Lab	29,223	42·7%	42·3%
C	28,738	42·0%	48·7%
L	10,497	15·3%	8·1%
Nat Front	—	—	0·8%
Lab maj	485	0·7%	6·4%
Swing		−0·5%	+3·5%

Mr Nicholas Lyell, barrister, contested Lambeth, Central, in October, 1974. B December, 1938; ed Stowe School and Christ Church, Oxford.

Mr Robin Corbett, journalist, was elected in October, 1974; contested the seat, February, 1974, and 1966; fought West Derbyshire by-election, 1967. B December 1933; ed Holly Lodge Grammar School, Smethwick. Member, Expenditure Committee, since 1976, employment and social services sub-committee. Chairman, PLP agriculture and food group, 1979. Secretary, PLP civil liberties group. Vice-president, all-party animal welfare group. NUJ (national executive council, 1965-69).

Mr David Penwarden, assistant director of the Industrial Relations Training Resource Centre, Ashridge Management College, contest Bedfordshire, South, in both 1974 elections, the Deptford by-election, 1963, and West Ham, North, 1955. B September 1932; ed Taunton School and Keble College, Oxford. Member, West Ham Council, 1960-63, and Reading Council, 1965-66.

HEMSWORTH

Electorate 71,581   1974: 69,810

*Woodall, A. (Lab)	36,509
Whitfield, J. (C)	10,466
Fussey, T. (L)	5,474

Lab majority	26,043

No Change

	1974		1979
Total votes	48,969		52,449
Turnout	70·1%		73·3%
Lab	37,467	76·5%	69·6%
C	5,895	12·0%	20·0%
L	5,607	11·5%	10·4%
Lab maj	31,572	64·5%	49·6%
Swing		0·5%	+7·4%

Mr Alec Woodall, a colliery surface foreman, has held the seat since February, 1974. B September, 1918; ed Southmoor Road County School, Hemsworth. Member, Hemsworth Urban District Council, 1966-74. Member, joint committee on consolidation Bills. Life member of the NUM which he joined in 1933. Sponsored by NUM.

Mr John Whitfield, solicitor. B October, 1941; ed Sedbergh School and Leeds University. Specialist in taxation and company law. Secretary, Badsworth and Thorpe Audlin branch of Hemsworth Conservative Association.

Mr Antony Fussey fought Wakefield in both 1974 elections. Town planner. B July 1950; ed Hymers College, Hull; LSE and Leeds Polytechnic. Nalgo shop steward. Baptist deacon and lay reader.

HENLEY

Electorate 65,933   1974: 62,475

*Heseltine, M. R. D. (C)	29,982
Atack, S. (L)	11,693
Whiting, D. J. (Lab)	9,435

C majority	18,289

No Change

	1974		1979
Total votes	45,983		51,110
Turnout	73·6%		77·5%
C	22,554	49·0%	58·7%
L	12,288	26·7%	22·9%
Lab	11,141	24·2%	18·5%
C maj	10,266	22·3%	35·8%
Swing		−1·4%	+7·7%

Mr Michael Heseltine was appointed Secretary of State for Environment in May, 1959. Joined the Shadow Cabinet as chief Opposition spokesman on industry, 1974-76, and has since been chief spokesman on trade, March to June 1974. Minister for Aerospace and Shipping, 1972-74; Under Secretary for the Environment, 1970-72; Parliamentary Secretary, Ministry of Transport, June-October 1970. Elected in February 1974; represented Tavistock, 1966-74; contested Coventry, North, 1964, and Gower, 1959. B March 1933; ed Shrewsbury and Pembroke College, Oxford (President of Union, 1954). Publisher; chairman 1966-70 and since 1974, of Haymarket publishing group.

Mr Stephen Atack, aged 26, sales director; ed Eastbourne College of Education. Previously candidate in local government elections.

Mr David Whiting, periodical publisher. B June, 1944; ed Henry Thornton Secondary School, Clapham, School of Oriental and African Studies and Harvard Graduate School of Arts and Science. Member, London Borough of Southwark Council. Natsopa.

HEREFORD

Electorate 61,447   1974: 57,830

*Shepherd, C. R. (C)	23,012
Green, C. F. (L)	18,042
Adshead, I. R. (Lab)	7,150
C majority	4,970

No Change

	1974		1979
Total votes	43,828		48,204
Turnout	75·8%		78·4%
C	17,060	38·9%	47·7%
L	15,948	36·4%	37·4%
Lab	10,820	24·7%	14·8%
C maj	1,112	2·5%	10·3%
Swing		−1·1%	+9·3%

Mr Colin Shepherd, marketing director. B January, 1938; ed Oundle, Caius College, Cambridge, McGill University, Montreal. Joined Haigh Engineering Company, 1963, with responsibility for marketing and development of new products. Served in Royal Canadian Navy, 1959-63. Joint secretary, Conservative agriculture committee since December, 1976.

Mr Christopher Green, partner in industrial relations company, fought Cheadle in both 1974 elections and Surbiton, 1970. B May 1943; ed Wrekin College and King's College, London. NUJ.

Mr Ian Adshead, contracts officer and a part-time further education lecturer. B November, 1949; ed Stretford Grammar School and Liverpool Polytechnic. Member, Stretford Borough Council, Manchester, 1971-74. APEX.

HERTFORD AND STEVENAGE

Electorate 87,623   1974: 82,218

Wells, P. (C)	31,739
*Williams, Mrs. S. (Lab)	30,443
Rigby, B. (L)	7,660
Pell, J. (Nat Front)	581
C majority	1,296

C gain from Lab

	1974		1979
Total votes	62,701		70,423
Turnout	76·3%		80·4%
Lab	29,548	47·1%	43·2%
C	20,502	32·7%	45·1%
L	11,419	18·2%	10·9%
Nat Front	1,232	2·0%	0·8%
Lab maj	9,046	14·4%	
C maj			1·9%
Swing		−1·2%	+8·1%

Mr Bowen Wells was senior executive of the Commonwealth Development Corporation, 1961-73. Owner and managing director of Substation Group Services Ltd. B August, 1935; ed St. Paul's School, London and Exeter University. Former member, Bow Group research team on overseas aid and development, and former chairman, "Westminster for Europe" campaign.

Mrs Shirley Williams was Secretary of State for Education and Science, 1976-79; Secretary of State for Prices and Consumer Protection, 1974-76 and additionally Paymaster General from April, 1976. Returned for seat in February, 1974; MP for Hitchin, 1964-74. Chief Opposition spokesman on social services, 1970-71, when elected to the Shadow Cabinet. Spokesman on Home Office affairs, 1971-73, and on prices, 1973-74. Minister of State, Home Office, 1969-70; Minister Education and Science, 1967-69; Parliamentary Secretary, Ministry of Labour, 1966-67. Contsted Harwich in 1955 and 1954 by-election and Southampton, Test, in 1959. B July, 1930; ed Summit School, Minnesota, St Paul's School, Hammersmith, Somerville College, Oxford, and Columbia University, New York. Member, Labour Party NEC, since 1970. Chairman, Labour Committee for Europe, 1965. Sponsored by APEX.

Mr Brian Rigby, teacher. B July, 1944; ed Friars Grammar School, Bangor; Hull University and the Open University. School representative (shop steward) NAS/UWT. Former National General Secretary, Association of Liberal trade Unionists.

HERTFORDSHIRE, East

Electorate 96,327   1974: 88,848

*Walker-Smith, Sir D. (C)	41,599
Evans, I. J. (Lab and Co-op)	20,139
Abdela, Mrs L. (L)	11,393
Smith, J. (Nat Front)	1,819
C majority	21,460

No Change

	1974		1979
Total votes	65,779		74,950
Turnout	74·0%		77·8%
C	29,334	44·6%	55·5%
Lab	20,999	31·9%	26·9%
L	15,446	23·5%	15·2%
Nat Front	—	—	2·4%
C maj	8,335	12·7%	28·6%
Swing		−1·6%	+7·9%

Sir Derek Walker-Smith, QC, was Minister of Health, 1957-59; Parliamentary Secretary, Board of Trade, 1955-56; Economic Secretary to the Treasury, 1956-57; and Minister of State, Board of Trade, 1957. Represented Hertford, 1945-55 and East Hertfordshire since 1955. Barrister (Middle Temple, 1934), QC 1955. B April, 1910; ed Rosall and Christ Church, Oxford. Member, Committee of Privileges. Chairman, 1922 Committee, 1951-55. Chairman, Society of Conservative Lawyers, 1969-75. Member, European Parliament, 1973-79. Associate of Royal Institution of Chartered Surveyors.

Mr Julian Evans, education secretary with a retail Co-operative Society. B July 1950; ed grammar school and college of further education.

Mrs Lesley Abdela, agricultural adviser. B November, 1945; ed Queen Anne's School, Caversham and Châtelard, Switzerland. Member, Commonwealth Forestry Association. Divisional director of the Gingerbread group for one-parent families.

HERTFORDSHIRE, South

Electorate 65,198   1974: 64,666

*Parkinson, C. E. (C)	27,857
Male, N. G. (Lab)	16,059
Sattin, G. (L)	7,001
Fenn, S. (Nat Front)	605
C majority	11,798

No Change

	1974		1979
Total votes	49,201		51,522
Turnout	76·1%		79·0%
C	21,018	42·7%	54·1%
Lab	18,790	38·2%	31·2%
L	9,393	19·1%	13·6%
Nat Front	—	—	1·2%
C maj	2,228	4·5%	22·9%
Swing		−0·7%	+9·2%

Mr Cecil Parkinson was appointed Minister of State for Trade in May, 1979. An Opposition spokesman on trade 1976-79; Opposition whip 1974-76; assistant Government whip, 1974. Returned in February, 1974; MP for Enfield West, 1970-74; contested Northampton, 1970. Chartered accountant; founder and chairman, Parkinson Hart Securities Ltd, chairman of other companies. B September, 1931; ed Royal Grammar School, Lancaster and Emmanuel College, Cambridge.

Mr Nicholas Male, clerical officer. B March, 1953; ed Boreham Wood Grammar School, University of Warwick. Member, Elstree Town Council. Nalgo.

Mr Gerald Sattin, antique dealer and company director, was parliamentary agent at Islington, Central, in both 1974 elections. B July, 1927; ed St Edwards School, Oxford, and Christ College, Cambridge. Fellow, Royal Philatelic Society.

HERTFORDSHIRE, South-West

Electorate 75,930   1974: 75,992

*Dodsworth, G. H. (C)	33,112
Colman, A. J. (Lab)	16,784
Cass, G. (L)	9,808
Graves, P. (Nat Front)	839
C majority	16,328

No Change

	1974		1979
Total votes	58,507		60,543
Turnout	77·0%		79·7%
C	24,939	42·6%	54·7%
Lab	19,098	32·6%	27·7%
L	14,470	24·7%	16·2%
Nat Front	—		1·4%
C maj	5,841	10·0%	27·0%
Swing		−1·4%	+8·5%

Mr Geoffrey Dodsworth was elected in February, 1974. Chartered accountant; director, Grindlays Bank Ltd. Contested Hartlepools, 1964, and Don Valley, 1959. B June, 1928; ed St Peter's School, York. Member, Select Committee on Statutory Instruments. Former member, Select Committee on Wealth Tax. Member, Union of Conservative and Unionist Associ-

ations; Primrose League, Bow Group, Member, York City Council, 1959-65.

Mr Anthony Colman, retail executive. B July, 1943; ed Paston Grammar School, North Walsham, and Magdalene College, Cambridge. Member, Price Commission.

Mr Gerald Cass, chartered secretary, fought Hastings in February 1974, and Hendon, North, 1966 and 1970. Former chairman, London Liberal Party. B August, 1929; ed Priory School, Acton. Manager, accounts department of West End company.

HEXHAM

Electorate 66,798   1974: 65,088

*Rippon, G. (C)	25,483
Bell, S. (Lab)	16,935
Shipley, J. (L)	10,697
C majority	8,548

No Change

	1974		1979
Total votes	49,054		53,115
Turnout	75·4%		79·5%
C	21,352	43·5%	48·0%
Lab	16,711	34·1%	31·9%
L	10,991	22·4%	20·1%
C maj	4,641	9·4%	16·1%
Swing		−2·8%	+3·3%

Mr Geoffrey Rippon, QC, leader of the Conservative Group in the European Parliament 1977-79; member 1976-79. Appointed to the Shadow Cabinet in March, 1974 as a spokesman on foreign and Commonwealth affairs and Europe and from November, 1974 to 1977 was chief spokesman. Secretary of State for the Environment, 1972-74; Chancellor of the Duchy of Lancaster with responsibility for EEC negotiations 1970-72; Minister of Technology, June-July, 1970. Opposition spokesman on defence, 1968-70. Minister of Public Buildings and Works, 1962-64, joining Cabinet in 1963; Parliamentary Secretary Ministry of Housing and Local Government, 1961-62, and Ministry of Aviation, 1959-61. Returned for seat on 1966; represented Norwich, South, 1955-64. B May, 1924; ed King's College, Taunton, and Brasenose College, Oxford. Barrister (Middle Temple, 1948) and QC 1964. Chairman, Brittanica Arrow Holdings.

Mr Stuart Bell, barrister and member of Lloyds. B May, 1938; ed Hookergate Grammar School, Co. Durham. Member, Labour NEC sub-committee on rural areas; society of Labour Lawyers.

Mr John Shipley, North regional secretary of the Open University, contested Blyth in both elections in 1974. B July, 1946; ed Whitby Grammar School and University College, London (President of the Union, 1968-69). Member, Newcastle City Council, since 1975. AUT.

HEYWOOD AND ROYTON

Electorate 82,199   1974: 77,705

*Barnett, J. (Lab)	28,489
Morgan, P. (C)	26,202
Hewitt, M. (L)	7,644
Marsh, R. (Nat Front)	641
Lab majority	2,287

No Change

	1974		1979
Total votes	59,482		62,976
Turnout	76·5%		76·6%
Lab	27,206	45·7%	45·2%
C	19,307	32·5%	41·6%
L	12,969	21·8%	12·1%
Nat Front	—		1·0%
Lab maj	7,899	13·2%	3·6%
Swing		−1·0%	+4·8%

Mr Joel Barnett was Chief Secretary to the Treasury in 1974-79, and in the Cabinet 1977-79. Elected in 1964; contested Runcorn, 1959. An Opposition spokesman on Treasury matters, 1970-74. Accountant. B October, 1923; ed Jewish School, Derby Street, Manchester, and Manchester Central High School. Member, Prestwich Borough Council 1956-59.

Chairman (1967-70) and vice-chairman (1966-67) PLP economic and finance group. TGWU.

Mr Peter Morgan, chartered surveyor, contested the seat, October 1974. B May, 1946; ed Malvern College. FRICS. Former secretary, Crew Chamber of Trade and Commerce; past president, South Cheshire junior chamber and former vice-president, London junior chamber. ASTMS.

Mr Michael Hewitt, aged 44, lecturer.

HIGH PEAK

Electorate 59,323   1974: 57,095

*Le Marchant, S. (C)	22,532
Bookbinder, D. (Lab)	17,777
Brown, D. (L)	8,200

C majority	4,755

No Change

	1974		1979
Total votes	45,959		48,509
Turnout	80·5%		81·8%
C	19043	41·4%	46·4%
Lab	17,041	37·1%	36·6%
L	9,875	21·5%	16·9%
C maj	2,002	4·3%	9·8%
Swing		−0·2%	+2·7%

Mr Spencer Le Marchant was appointed Comptroller of H M Household in May 1979. An Opposition whip 1974-79. Elected in 1970; contested Vauxhall, 1966. Member of the Stock Exchange; partner, L. Messel & Co. B January, 1931; ed Eton. Member, Westminster City Council, 1956-71. Joint secretary, Conservative energy committee.

Mr David Bookbinder, a wholesale confectioner, contested the seat, October 1974. B March, 1941; ed secondary modern school and technical college. Member, Derbyshire County Council, (leader of Labour Opposition). TGWU.

Mr David Brown, television producer. B September, 1945; ed Bradford Grammar School and New College, Oxford. Member, High Peak District Council.

HILLINGDON, Hayes and Harlington

Electorate 56,165   1974: 55,960

*Sandelson, N. D. (Lab)	20,350
Tyrell, A. (C)	17,048
Smallbone, Mrs H. (L)	3,900
Callow, G. T. (Nat Front)	582
Mansfield, J. (Comm)	249

Lab majority	3,302

No Change

	1974		1979
Total votes	38,885		42,129
Turnout	69·5%		75·0%
Lab	20,291	52·2%	48·3%
C	10,871	28·0%	40·5%
L	6,336	16·3%	9·3%
Nat Front	1,189	3·1%	1·4%
WRP	198	0·5%	—
Comm	—	—	0·6%
Lab maj	9,420	24·2%	7·8%
Swing		−0·2%	+8·2%

Mr Neville Sandelson retained the seat for Labour in the 1971 by-election. Barrister (Inner Temple, 1946). B November, 1923; ed Westminster and Trinity College, Cambridge. Contested Chichester, 1970; Leicester, South-West by-election, 1967; Heston and Isleworth, 1966; Rushcliffe, 1959; Beckenham by-election, 1957, and Ashford, 1950, 1951 and 1955.

Member, Expenditure Committee and defence and external affairs subcommittee. Vice-chairman PLP foreign and home affairs groups. Joint chairman All Party Group on the Theatre. Member, LCC, 1952-58, Society of Labour Lawyers, Fabian Society; GMWU. Member, Speaker's Conference on Electoral Law and Select Committee on Wealth Tax.

Mr Albert Tyrrel, former garage proprietor. B 1915; ed Priory School, Acton. Chairman, Hayes and Harlington Conservative Association. Leader Conservative group, Hayes and Harlington Urban District Council, 1958-61; member, Hillingdon Borough Council, 1968-71; deputy mayor, 1970-71.

Mrs Hester Smallbone contested Sutton, Carshalton, in both 1974 elections and Battersea, North, 1970. B May, 1924; ed Ecclesfield Grammar School, Sheffield, and Somerville College, Oxford. Member, Richmond Borough Council, 1961-65. Former psychiatric social worker.

Mr John Mansfield, aged 58, toolmaker. Chairman, Hillindon Borough Council Federation. AUEW.

HILLINGDON, Ruislip-Northwood

Electorate 55,505   1974: 54,119

Wilkinson, J. (C)	26,748
Lloyd, M. E. (Lab)	9,541
Stephenson, R. (L)	6,867
Martin, A. (Nat Front)	477

C majority	17,207

No Change

	1974		1979
Total votes	40,348		43,633
Turnout	74·6%		78·6%
C	20,779	51·5%	61·3%
Lab	10,490	26·0%	21·9%
L	8,621	21·4%	15·7%
UDP	458	1·1%	—
Nat Front	—		1·1%
C maj	10,289	25·5%	39·4%
Swing		−0·2%	+6·9%

Mr John Wilkinson was MP for Bradford, West,, 1970-February, 1974, and contested that seat in October, 1974. Sales manager of an aviation company. B September, 1940; ed Eton, RAF College, Cranwell, and Churchill College, Cambridge. Former flying instructor at Cranwell. ADC to Commander 2nd Allied Tactical Air Force, Germany, 1967.
Member, Select Committee on Science and Technology, 1972-74, and for Race Relations and Immigration 1972-74. Secretary Conservative parliamentary aviation committee 1972-74, defence committee 1972-74 and chairman South East Asia group of foreign affairs committee 1973-74. Head of Universities Department, Conservative Central Office, 1967-68; Aviation Specialist, Conservative Research Department, 1969. Vice-chairman, Royal United Services Institute of Defence Studies.

Mr Michael Lloyd, information officer. B 1937; NUJ and TGWU.

Mr Raymond Stephenson, solicitor. Contested Holland with Boston, February and October, 1974. Aged 54; ed London University.

HILLINGDON, Uxbridge

Electorate 60,313   1974: 59,746

*Shersby, J. M. (C)	24,967
Pringle, G. E. (Lab)	16,972
Hunt, J. (L)	5,031
Budgen, Mrs P. (Nat Front)	595
C majority	7,995

No Change

	1974		1979
Total votes	44,866		47,565
Turnout	75·1%		78·9%
C	19,969	44·5%	52·5%
Lab	17,816	39·7%	35·7%
L	7,081	15·8%	10·6%
Nat Front	—		1·3%
C maj	2,153	4·8%	16·8%
Swing		−0·1%	+6·0%

Mr Michael Shersby held the seat for the Conservatives in the 1972 by-election. Director General, British Sugar Bureau; secretary, British Sugar Refiners Association. B February, 1933; ed John Lyon School, Harrow-on-the Hill. Chairman, Conservative Party trade committee 1974-76, vice-chairman 1977. Secretary, Parliamentary and Scientific Commit-
tee. Joint secretary, Conservative Party industry committee, 1972-74. Member, Paddington Borough Council, 1959-64, and Westminster City Council, 1964-71. (Deputy Lord Mayor, 1967-68.)

Mr George Pringle, headteacher, contested seat October 1974. B July, 1924; ed Wallington County Grammar School; Leavesden Training College and Open University. Member (co-opted), Hillingdon Education Committee. NUT and National Association of Head Teachers. Chairman, Teachers Council, Hillingdon.

Mr Jonathan Hunt, journalist on *The Observer.* B July, 1943; ed Colebrook School, Bognor Regis and Worthing College of Further Education. NUJ.

HITCHIN

Electorate 76,807   1974: 72,815

*Stewart, B. H. I. H. (C)	33,169
O'Flynn, D. R. (Lab)	19,940
Dix, E. (L)	8,224
Goodale, B. (Ecology)	911
Logan, V. (Nat Front)	881
C majority	13,229

No Change

	1974		1979
Total votes	57,952		63,125
Turnout	79·6%		82·2%
C	25,842	44·6%	52·5%
Lab	22,656	39·1%	31·6%
L	9,454	16·3%	13·0%
Ecology	—		1·4%
Nat Front	—		1·4%
C maj	3,186	5·5%	20·9%
Swing		−0·5%	+7·7%

Mr Ian Stewart won the seat in February, 1974. Banker, director of Brown Shipley and Co Ltd. Fought Hammersmith, North, 1970. B August, 1935; ed Hailonbury and Jesus College, Cambridge. Member, Expenditure Committee, since December 1977. Director, British Numismatic Society, 1965-67. Treasurer, Westminster Committee for the Protection of
Children, 1960-70. Secretary, Conservative Finance Committee, 1975-76 and 1978.

Mr Denis O'Flynn contested Havering, Romford, February and October 1974. A machine moulder in the car industry. B January, 1934; ed St Patrick's School, Cork. Member, Havering Borough Council for seven years; AUEW (Foundry Section).

Mr Eric Dix, personnel manager, fought the seat, October, 1974. B November, 1923; ed Westminster City School and Trinity College, Cambridge.

Mr Brian Goodale, editor of *Electronic Engineering Journal.* Member, British Antarctic Survey, for three years and of Conservation Corps. Aged 27; ed Reading and Open Universities.

HOLLAND WITH BOSTON

Electorate 85,578   1974: 80,454

*Body, R. B. F. S. (C)	35,440
Fox, M. (Lab)	17,908
Wright, J. (L)	10,480
C majority	17,532

No Change

	1974		1979
Total votes	58,082		63,828
Turnout	72·2%		74·6%
C	28,145	48·5%	55·5%
Lab	19,461	33·5%	28·1%
L	10,476	18·0%	16·4%
C maj	8,684	15·0%	27·4%
Swing		−2·2%	+6·2%

Mr Richard Body, elected in 1966. Member, Joint Committee on Consolidation, &c. Bills, since 1976. Represented Billericay from 1955-59; contested Leek, 1951, Rotherham, 1950, and Abertillery by-election, 1950. Barrister (Middle Temple, 1949) and farmer. B May, 1927; ed Reading School. Former officer of Conservative backbench sub-committee on horticulture. Chairman, Open Seas Forum since 1970. Joint chairman of the council on "Get Britain Out" (of EEC) Referendum Campaign, 1975. A vice-president of The Selsdon Group.

Mr Malcolm Fox, lecturer, fuel consultant and former chemist, contested Blaby, October, 1974. B May, 1939; ed Hatfield Polytechnic and London University. District councillor. HATFHE.

Mr John Wright, lecturer in mechanical services, has been a member of Boston Borough Council since 1970. B July, 1934; ed People's College Junior Technical, Nottingham District Technical College and Bolton College of Education.

HONITON

Electorate 78,303   1974: 73,070

*Emery, P. F. H. (C)	37,832
Ruffle, R. (L)	12,601
Luesby, T. (Lab)	8,756
Bacon, Mrs M. H. (Ecol)	1,423
C majority	25,231

No Change

	1974		1979
Total votes	55,268		60,612
Turnout	75·6%		77·4%
C	29,720	53·8%	62·4%
L	16,500	29·9%	20·8%
Lab	9,048	16·4%	14·4%
Ecology	—	—	2·3%
C maj	13,220	23·9%	41·6%
Swing		−1·2%	+·3%

Mr Peter Emery was Under-Secretary for Energy, 1974; Under-Secretary for Trade and Industry, 1972-74, with responsibility for industry. Returned as by-election in 1967. MP for Reading 1959-66; contested Poplar, 1951, and Lincoln, 1955. An Opposition spokesman on Treasury, economic affairs and trade, 1964-65. Joint founder of the Bow

Group in 1951. Manufacturer. B February, 1926; ed Scotch Plains, New Jersey, and Oriel College, Oxford. Member, Hornsey Borough Council, 1951-58 (deputy mayor, 1957-58). Chairman, Shenley Trust Services Ltd and Axion Ltd. Director, Phillips Petroleum (UK) Ltd, 1961-72. Director General, European Federation of Purchasing, 1963-72. Chairman, Consultative Council of Professional Management Organisations, 1964-72.

Mr Rodney Ruffle, aged 38, joined Liberal Party 1957. Trained as teacher at St Luke's College, Exeter. Area officer, NUT.

Mr Trevor Luesby, university lecturer. B September, 1935; ed Lincoln College, Oxford. NATFHE.

Mrs Margaret Bacon, proof reader for Penguin Books; trained as a teacher. Aged 43; ed Howells School, Denbigh and Oxford University.

HORNCASTLE

Electorate 51,531   1974: 49,627

*Tapsell, P. H. B. (C)	21,362
Starky, M. J. C. (L)	10,833
Collins, D. P. (Lab)	6,240
Hook, M. (Nat Front)	319
C majority	10,529

No Change

	1974		1979
Total votes	35,105		38,754
Turnout	70·7%		75·2%
C	16,750	47·7%	55·1%
L	11,506	32·8%	28·0%
Lab	6,849	19·5%	16·1%
Nat Front	—		0·8%
C maj	5,244	14·9%	27·1%
Swing		−2·0%	+5·4%

Mr Peter Tapsell was an Opposition spokesman on Treasury and economic affairs, 1977; a spokesman on Foreign and Commonwealth affairs, 1976-77. Elected in 1966; MP for Nottingham, West, 1959-64; contested Wednesbury, 1957 by-election. Stockbroker, a senior member and shareholder of James Capel and Co. B February, 1930; ed Tonbridge School and Merton College, Oxford.

Mr Michael Starky, lecturer, fought the seat, October 1974. B August, 1936; ed St John's School, Leatherhead. Member, East Lindsey District Council, since 1973. AMA.

Mr David Collins, a Leicestershire Cooperative dairy salesman. B August, 1941; ed New Park Secondary School, Leicester; WEA. Member, Leicester City Council, 1972-76. USDAW.

HORSHAM AND CRAWLEY

Electorate 100,059   1974: 90,944

*Hordern, P. M. (C)	42,529
Newman, P. W. (Lab)	27,508
Foley, M. H. (L)	10,920
Murch, A. (Nat Front)	493
C majority	15,021

No Change

	1974		1979
Total votes	70,984		81,450
Turnout	78·1%		81·4%
C	29,867	42·1%	52·2%
Lab	26,168	36·9%	33·8%
L	13,848	19·5%	13·4%
Nat Front	1,101	1·6%	0·6%
C maj	3,699	5·2%	18·4%
Swing		−1·9%	+6·6%

Mr Peter Hordern, MP for Horsham, 1964-74, was returned in 1974. Chairman, Conservative finance committee, 1970-72, and joint vice-chairman since 1974. Member, Public Accounts Committee, since 1969. B April, 1929; ed Geelong Grammar School, Australia, and Christ Church, Oxford. Member, executive, 1922 Committee. Member of London

Stock Exchange. Director, Petrofina (UK) Ltd and Atlas Electric and General Trust Ltd.

Mr Patrick Newman, senior analyst, Productivity Services, London Borough of Lambeth. B January, 1947; ed West Tarring County Secondary School, Worthing, and Lanchester Polytechnic, Coventry. Member, West Sussex County Council, 1974-77. Nalgo and TASS-AUEW.

Mr Michael Foley, linguist and teacher, contested the seat, February and October 1974. B January, 1936; ed Bishop Otter College, Chichester and Surrey University. NAS.

HOUGHTON-LE-SPRING

Electorate 60,491   1974: 59,905

*Urwin, T. W. (Lab)	30,181
Straw, P. (C)	9,105
Ellis, J. (L)	4,479
Temple, D. (WRP)	326
Lab majority	21,076

No Change

	1974		1979
Total votes	43,396		44,091
Turnout	72·4%		72·9%
Lab	29,699	68·4%	68·5%
L	9,298	21·4%	10·2%
C	4,399	10·1%	20·7%
WRP	—	—	0·7%
Lab maj	20,401	47·0%	47·8%
Swing		−2·3%	0·7%

Mr Thomas Urwin has been leader of the British parliamentary delegation to the Council of Europe and WEU since 1976 and chairman of the Council of Europe Socialist Group, also since 1976. Minister of State, Local Government and Regional Planning, 1969-70; Minister of State, Department of Economic Affairs, 1968-69. Elected in 1964. B June, 1912;

elementary education. Chairman, PLP industry group; member, PLP liaison committee. Member, Houghton-le-Spring Urban Council, 1949-65, chairman, 1954-55. Full-time organizer, Amalgamated Union of Building Trade Workers, 1954-64; branch officer, 1933-54. Sponsored by UCATT.

Mr Philip Straw barrister (Inner Temple 1971) practising on the North East circuit. B November, 1945; ed Royal Grammar School, Newcastle-upon-Tyne and Inns of Court School of Law. Member, Northumberland and North Durham Legal Aid Certifying Committee. Hon Secretary, Chester-le-Street Conservative Association.

Mr John Ellis, mine geologist. Aged 32; ed University College, London.

Mr David Temple, aged 35, was a founder-member of the party. Coal face electrician and NUM lodge delegate.

HOUNSLOW, Brentford and Isleworth

Electorate 71,337   1974: 71,199

*Hayhoe, B. J. (C)	27,527
Walker, P. J. (Lab)	22,533
Parry, J. (L)	4,208
Attridge, P. (Nat Front)	738
Coates, Miss I. (Ecology)	454
Simmerson, R. (C ACM)	257
C majority	4,994

No Change

	1974		1979
Total votes	52,203		55,717
Turnout	73·3%		78·1%
C	22,527	43·2%	49·4%
Lab	22,295	42·7%	40·4%
L	6,019	11·5%	7·6%
Nat Front	1,362	2·6%	1·3%
Ecology	—	—	0·8%
CACM	—	—	0·5%
C maj	232	0·5%	9·0%
Swing		−0·4%	+4·2%

Mr Barney Hayhoe became Under Secretary of Defence for the Army in May 1979. An Opposition spokesman on employment 1974-79. Returned in February, 1974; MP for Heston and Isleworth, 1970-74; contested Lewisham, South, 1974. Mechanical engineer, member of Lloyds, broadcaster, lecturer and writer. B August, 1925; ed elementary school and Stanley

Technical School, South Norwood. Vice-chairman, Conservative Group for Europe, and member, executive committee and general purposes committee, European Movement. Vice-chairman, Conservative Party International. IPCS.

Mr Peter Walker, campaign worker for Amnesty International, contested the seat, October 1974 and Sutton Carshalton, February 1974. B August, 1945; ed Secondary Modern, London Polytechnic and London University. Member, Croydon Borough Council, since 1971. Political aide to the Labour Leader of the GLC, 1973-77. TGWU.

Mr John Parry, a BBC producer, fought Worcester, 1964. B February, 1927; ed Queen's College, Cambridge.

Miss Irene Coates, aged 54, full-time worker with the Conservation Society, playwright; ed King Alfred School, Hampstead.

HOUNSLOW, Feltham and Heston

Electorate 79,873   1974: 78,983

*Kerr, R. W. (Lab)	28,675
Ground, R. P. (C)	24,570
Norcott, B. (L)	5,051
Reid, Mrs J. M. (Nat Front)	898
Lugg, R. (WRP)	168
Lab majority	4,105

No Change

	1974		1979
Total votes	53,613		59,362
Turnout	67·9%		74·3%
Lab	26,611	49·3%	48·3%
C	17,464	32·6%	41·4%
L	7,554	14·1%	8·5%
Nat Front	1,984	3·7%	1·5%
WRP	—	—	0·3%
Lab maj	9,147	17·0%	6·9%
Swing		−1·9%	+5·0%

Mr Russell Kerr, an air charter executive, was returned for the seat in February, 1974; MP for Feltham, 1966-74. Chairman, Select Committee on Nationalized Industries since November, 1974; vice-chairman, 1970-74; member since 1967. Chairman, Tribune Group, 1969-70. Member, national executive, and sponsored by ASTMS. B February, 1921; ed Shore School, Sydney, and Sydney University. Director (unpaid) Tribune Publications Ltd. Chairman, PLP aviation group.

Mr Reginald Group, a barrister, contested the seat, February and October, 1974. B August, 1932; ed Selwyn College, Cambridge, and Magdalen College, Oxford. President, Oxford University Conservative Association, 1958. Member, Hammersmith Borough Council, 1968-1971.

Mr Barry Norcott, househusband and voluntary social worker. B April, 1941; ed Haymill Secondary Modern School and Merchant Seaman's College. Contested Wolverhampton, South East, October, 1974.

Mr Richard Lugg, aged 27, works at Heathrow Airport; assistant branch secretary, TGWU.

HOVE

Electorate 70,318   1974: 73,034

*Sainsbury, T. A. D. (C)	30,256
Fitch, B. R. (Lab)	10,807
Walsh, Dr J. M. M. (L)	8,771
Sheridan, F. (Nat Front)	508
C majority	**19,449**

No Change

	1974		1979
Total votes	50,993		50,342
Turnout	69·8%		71·6%
C	27,345	53·6%	60·1%
L	12,469	24·5%	17·4%
Lab	11,179	21·9%	21·5%
Nat Front	—	—	1·0%
C maj	14,876	29·1%	38·6%
Swing		−5·6%	+3·4%

Mr Tim Sainsbury, director of J. Sainsbury Ltd and other companies, was elected at the 1963 by-election. B June, 1932; ed Eton and Worcester College, Oxford. Member, Public Expenditure Committee, Select Committee on Wealth Tax. Vice-Chairman, Conservative Environment Committee. Chairman, All Party Parliamentary Committee for the Release of Soviet Jewry. Joint treasurer, Conservative Friends of Israel.

Mr Brian Fitch, self-employed painter and decorator. Member, Brighton Borough and East Sussex County Councils. B February, 1941; ed in Brighton. AUEW.

Dr James Walsh, medical practitioner, fought the seat, October 1974. B January, 1943; ed Wimbledon College and London University. Member, Arun District Council and Littlehampton Town Council, since 1976. B.M.A. Surgeon Commander R.N.R. being principal medical officer, Sussex Division, R.N.R.

HOWDEN

Electorate 63,708   1974: 57,512

*Bryan, Sir P. (C)	26,550
Shields, Mrs E. (L)	12,006
Davenport, A. B. (Lab)	8,827
C majority	**14,544**

No Change

	1974		1979
Total votes	41,757		47,383
Turnout	72·6%		74·4%
C	19,583	46·9%	56·0%
L	14,803	35·5%	25·3%
Lab	7,371	17·7%	18·6%
C maj	4,780	11·4%	30·7%
Swing		−1·7%	+4·1%

Sir Paul Bryan, Minister of State for Employment, 1970-72, was chairman, Conservative employment committee 1973-74; vice-chairman, 1974. Member, Select Committee on Sound Broadcasting. Elected in 1955. B August, 1913; ed St John's School, Leatherhead, and Gonville and Caius College, Cambridge. Assistant whip, 1956; a Lord Commissioner of the Treasury, 1958-61. Contested Sowerby, 1951, 1950 and 1949 (by-election). Director, Granada Television Ltd since 1972, Granada Theatres Ltd since 1973 and Greater Manchester Independent Radio since 1972.

Mrs Elizabeth Shields, teacher, ed London University. Married to Mr David Shields who contested East Stirlingshire and Clackmannan in October, 1974.

Mr Bromley Davenport, social worker. B April, 1933; ed Radcliffe Technical College, Lancashire, and Queen's University, Belfast. Member, Skipton UDC, 1970-73. Apex (York branch).

HUDDERSFIELD, East

Electorate 53,983   1974: 53,515

Sheerman, B. J. (Lab and Co-op)	19,040
Bendelow, M. (C)	15,945
MacPherson, G. (L)	4,890
Hirst, H. (Ind)	243
Lab majority	**3,095**

No Change

	1974		1979
Total votes	38,720		40,118
Turnout	72·4%		74·3%
Lab	19,522	50·4%	47·5%
C	11,108	28·7%	39·7%
L	7,326	18·9%	12·2%
Nat Front	764	2·0%	
Ind	—		0·6%
Lab maj	8,414	21·7%	7·8%
Swing		−2·3%	+6·9%

Mr Barry Sheerman, university lecturer and broadcaster. B August, 1940; ed Hampton Grammar School, Kingston Technical College and LSE. Contested Taunton, October, 1974. Member, Loughor UDC 1972-74 and Lliw Valley Borough Council, 1973-78. AUT and ASTMS.

Mr Martin Bendelow, a Fellow at the Centre for Policy Studies. B July, 1945; ed Ashville College, Harrogate.

Mr Gavin Macpherson, chartered engineer, is a traffic and transport engineering consultant. B May, 1946; ed Espom College, Hatfield College of Technology and Leeds University. Chairman, Liberal Party transport panel. NATFHE.

HUDDERSFIELD, West

Electorate 55,066 1974: 53,510

Dickens, G. (C)	18,504
Faulkner, R. O. (Lab)	16,996
Hasler, Mrs K. J. L. (L)	6,225
Keen, T. (CFMPB)	101
C majority	1,508

C gain from Lab

	1974		1979
Total votes	40,799		41,826
Turnout	76·2%		76·0%
Lab	16,882	41·4%	40·6%
C	15,518	38·0%	44·2%
L	7,503	18·4%	14·9%
Nat Front	760	1·9%	—
CFMPB	136	0·3%	0·2%
Lab maj	1,364	3·4%	
C maj	—	—	3·6%
Swing		−1·0%	+3·5%

Mr Geoffrey Dickens contested Ealing, North, October 1974 and Teesside, Middlesborough, February 1974. Company director. B August, 1931; ed Harrow and Acton Technical College. Member, Hertfordshire County Council. 1970-74; St Albans district council, 1967-73 (chairman, 1970-71).
Mr Richard Faulkner, communications adviser, contested Monmouth in October, 1974, and Devizes in 1970 and February, 1974. B March, 1946; ed Merchant Taylors' School and Worcester College, Oxford. Member, London Borough of Merton Council, 1971-78. Corporate affairs adviser to a number of leading companies and associations. In 1976 was co-founder of *The House Magazine,* Parliament's weekly journal. Member, Management Committee, Wimbledon F.C. Sponsored by NUR; member, NUJ.
Mrs Kathleen Hasler, teacher, contested the seat February and October 1974. B March, 1939; ed Twickenham County School and Exeter University.

HUNTINGDONSHIRE

Electorate 93,862 1974: 79,724

Major, J. (C)	40,193
Fulbrook, J. (Lab)	18,630
Rowe, D. G. (L)	12,812
Robinson, K. (Nat Front)	983
C majority	21,563

No Change

	1974		1979
Total votes	59,886		72,618
Turnout	75·1%		77·4%
C	26,989	45·1%	55·3%
Lab	17,745	29·6%	25·7%
L	15,152	25·3%	17·6%
Nat Front	—		1·4%
C maj	9,244	15·5%	29·6%
Swing		−1·5%	+7·0%

Mr John Major contested Camden, St Pancras, North, in February and October, 1974. Senior business development executive of British overseas merchant bank, and Associate of the Institute of Bankers. B March, 1943; ed Rutlish Grammar School. Member, London Borough of Lambeth Council, 1968-71. Founded Lambeth Borough Young Conservatives in 1965. Chairman, Brixton Conservative Association, 1970-71. Chairman, Beckenham Conservative Association. Member, management board of Warden Housing Association. National Union of Bank Employees.

Mr Julian Fulbrook, lecturer in law at LSE; barrister. B May, 1948; ed Exeter, Cambridge and Harvard universities. Member, Camden Borough Council, since 1978. TGWU.

Mr Dennis Rowe, teacher, fought the seat in both 1974 elections. B October 1923; ed Drayton Manor Grammar School, Hanwell, and Larkfield Teachers Training College, N Ireland. AMA.

HUYTON

Electorate 73,006 1974: 73,485

*Wilson, Sir H. (Lab)	27,449
Harrison, G. (C)	19,939
Cottier, P. (L)	5,476
Lab majority	7,510

No Change

	1974		1979
Total votes	52,223		52,864
Turnout	71·1%		72·4%
Lab	31,750	60·8%	51·9%
C	15,517	29·7%	37·7%
L	4,956	9·5%	10·4%
Lab maj	16,233	31·1%	14·2%
Swing		−1·9%	+8·4%

Sir Harold Wilson was Prime Minister and First Lord of the Treasury from March, 4, 1974 until he resigned on April 5, 1976. Leader of the Opposition, 1970-1974; Prime Minister, 1964-70; Leader of the Opposition, 1963-64. Opposition spokesman on foreign affairs, 1961-63, and previously on Treasury matters. Former member and chairman (1961-62) Labour Party NEC. MP for Huyton since 1950 and for Ormskirk, 1945-50. B March, 1916; ed Milnsbridge Council School, Royds Hall School, Huddersfield, Wirral Grammar School, and Jesus College, Oxford. Parliamentary Secretary, Ministry of Works, 1945-46; Secretary for Overseas Trade, 1946-47; President, Board of Trade, 1947-51 (resigned). Chairman, Public Accounts Committee, 1959-63. Chancellor, Bradford University. Fellow of the Royal Society since 1969. Chairman, committee to review functioning of financial institutions since 1976.

Mr Garnet Harrison, stockbroker and member of the Stock Exchange. B 1951; ed Stand Grammar School for Boys, Whitefield, Lancashire. Young Conservative branch chairman and divisional chairman. Former chairman, Whitefield Conservative Association; member, North West Area speakers' panel.

Mr David Cottier, teacher. B April, 1946; ed high school and Padgate College of Education, Warrington. NAS.

ILKESTON

Electorate 75,305 1974: 74,980

*Fletcher, L. R. (Lab)	29,760
Clark, M. (C)	21,160
Blackburn, D. (L)	7,879

Lab majority	8,600

No Change

	1974		1979
Total votes	56,119		58,799
Turnout	74·8%		78·1%
Lab	31,153	55·5%	50·6%
C	15,295	27·3%	36·0%
L	9,671	17·2%	13·4%
Lab maj	15,858	28·2%	14·6%
Swing		−2·4%	+6·8%

Mr Raymond Fletcher was elected in 1964; contested Wycombe in 1955. Journalist and author and contributor to *The Times* and other publications. B December, 1921; secondary education and university extra-mural classes. Sponsored by TGWU since 1964; member since 1954. Chairman, parliamentary airships group, and parliamentary branch, Labour

Friends of Israel. United Kingdom representative, North Atlantic Assembly.

Mr Michael Clark, marketing manager. B August, 1935; ed King Edward VI Grammar School, Retford; King's College, London; St John's College, Cambridge; and University of Minnesota. Treasurer, Cambridge Conservative Association, 1975-78. ASTMS.

Mr Desmond Blackburn, wine merchant, contested Altrincham and Sale, February and October, 1974. B June, 1920; ed Shrewsbury School.

INCE

Electorate 83,019 1974: 77,113

*McGuire, M. T. (Lab)	34,599
Brown, P. (C)	20,263
Gibb, J. K. (L)	6,294
Simons, J. (WRP)	442

Lab majority	14,336

No Change

	1974		1979
Total votes	55,812		61,598
Turnout	72·4%		74·2%
Lab	35,453	63·5%	56·2%
C	11,923	21·4%	32·9%
L	8,436	15·1%	10·2%
WRP	—	—	0·7%
Lab maj	23,530	42·1%	23·3%
Swing		−1·1%	+9·4%

Mr Michael McGuire is a former coal miner and full-time official of the NUM. Elected in 1964, B May, 1926; elementary education. Sponsored by NUM. Member, Select Committee on Nationalized Industries, 1967-70. Former member, PLP trade union group executive. Member, Council of Europe, since 1977, and of executive committee, Inter-Parliamentary Union, since 1977.

Mr Peter Brown, accountant, contested Gateshead, West, October 1974. B 1948; ed St Michael's College, Leeds and Liverpool University (President, students' union, 1970).

Mr John Gibb, company director, contested the seat, October, 1974. B September, 1926; ed St Egberts College, Chingford; King George V Grammar School, Southport; and Dolcoath Technical College, Camborne.

Mr John Simons, aged 35, has been unemployed for three years. Former GMWU shop steward.

INVERNESS

Electorate 62,571 1974: 57,527

*Johnston, R. (L)	15,716
Hunter-Gordon, R. (C)	11,559
Barr, D. (Scot Nat)	9,603
Wilson, B. D. H. (Lab)	9,586
Bell, U. (FG)	112

L majority	4,157

No Change

	1974		1979
Total votes	40,531		46,576
Turnout	70·5%		74·4%
L	13,128	32·4%	33·7%
Scot Nat	11,994	29·6%	20·6%
C	8,922	22·0%	24·8%
Lab	6,332	15·6%	20·6%
Fine Ghaidheil	155	0·4%	0·2%
L maj	1,134	2·8%	8·9%

Mr Russell Johnston was elected in 1974. First United Kingdom Liberal member of European Parliament (1973-75, 76-79). Former Liberal spokesman on foreign affairs and defence. Former member Select Committee on EEC secondary legislation. B July, 1932; ed Portree High School, Isle of Skye, and Edinburgh University. Former teacher and party

research assistant. Chairman, Scottish Liberal Party, 1970-74; vice-chairman, 1965-70. Member, Royal Commission on Local Government in Scotland, 1966-69.

Mr Richard Hunter-Gordon, aged 23, accountant. Ed Beaul, Edinburgh and Yorkshire, and Reading University.

Mr Donald Barr contested the seat, October, 1974; Caithness and Sutherland, 1970. Music teacher and lecturer. B February, 1941; ed Glasgow High School and Royal Scottish Academy of Music. Member, SNP national executive; Wick Town Council, 1969-72.

Mr Brian Wilson, journalist, contested Ross and Cromarty, October, 1974. B December, 1948; ed Dunoon School, Dundee University and University College, Cardiff. NUJ.

IPSWICH

Electorate 88,470 1974: 87,675

*Weetch, K. T. (Lab)	34,444
Erith, R. (C)	30,703
Keeling, P. (L)	5,772
Robinson, P. (Nat Front)	449
Hodge, R. (WRP)	115
Lab majority	3,741

No Change

	1974		1979
Total votes	69,694		71,483
Turnout	79.5%		80.8%
Lab	31,566	45.3%	48.2%
C	29,833	42.8%	43.0%
L	8,295	11.9%	8.1%
Nat Front	—	—	0.6%
WRP	—	—	0.2%
Lab maj	1,733	2.5%	5.2%
Swing		−1.5%	−1.4%

Mr Kenneth Weetch, a college lecturer, was elected in October, 1974; contested the seat in February, 1974, and Saffron Walden in 1970. B September, 1933; ed Newbridge Grammar School and LSE. Member, Select Committee on Science and Technology. Former national executive member, National Association of Schoolmasters; member, ATCDE. President of house owner's cooperative.

Mr Robert Erith is a partner in a firm of stockbrokers. B August, 1938; ed Ipswich School and Essex Institute of Agriculture. Major in the TAVR. Member, Colchester Young Conservatives, 1955-65, and of local branch of Saffron Walden Conservative Association since 1969 (chairman 1971-76). Member, Society of Investment Analysts, Dedham Vale Society, Colne-Stour Countryside Association and MCC. Partner, E. B. Savory, Miller Co; director, Erith & Co Ltd (builders' merchants).

Mr Preston Keeling, voluntary services organiser. B May, 1945; ed Aldersbrook Secondary Modern and Cambridge University. Vice-chairman, Eastern Regional Liberal Party, since 1974. Former member NEC, and former leader of local government department, Liberal Party Headquarters.

Mr Rudolph Hodge, aged 28, has been unemployed for three years. Born in Dutch West Indies. AUEW.

ISLE OF ELY

Electorate 69,954 1974: 68,491

*Freud, C. R. (L)	26,397
Stuttaford, Dr I. T. (C)	23,067
Saunders, C. H. (Lab)	7,067
L majority	3,330

No Change

	1974		1979
Total votes	52,815		56,531
Turnout	77.1%		80.8%
L	22,040	41.7%	46.7%
C	19,355	36.6%	40.8%
Lab	11,420	21.6%	12.5%
L maj	2,685	5.1%	5.9%

Mr Clement Freud won the seat for the Liberals in the 1973 by-election. Writer and broadcaster and trustee of Playboy International. Rector of Dundee University. B April, 1924; ed Dartington Hall and St Paul's School. Party spokesman on education, 1973-1976; spokesman on prices and consumer protection, Northern Ireland, broadcasting and the arts.

Member, Select Committee on Broadcasting. NUJ. Equity. Sponsored Freedom of Information Bill in 1978-79 session.

Dr Thomas Stuttaford contested the seat in October, 1974. MP for Norwich, South, 1970-4. Visiting physician at BUPA medical centre and holder of clinical assistantship at Queen Mary's hospital for the East End. Member, Select Committee on Science and Technology, 1970-74; former secretary, Conservative parliamentary committee for health and social services. Honorary member, British Cancer Council; member, management committeees of Birth Control Campaign and Doctor and Over-population Group. B May, 1931; ed Greshams School, Brasenose College, Oxford, and West London Hospital. Former member, Blofield and Flegg RDC and Norwich City Council.

Mr Colin Saunders, prison hospital officer. B July, 1940; ed Old Buckenham Area School. Former member, Bedford Borough Council and Bedfordshire County Council. Member, Prison Officers' Association.

ISLE OF WIGHT

Electorate 90,961 1974: 85,897

*Ross, S. S. (L)	35,889
Fishburn, J. D. (C)	35,537
Wilson, Mrs C. (Lab)	3,014
L majority	352

No Change

	1974		1979
Total votes	65,916		74,440
Turnout	76.7%		81.8%
L	29,697	45.1%	48.2%
C	27,657	42.0%	47.7%
Lab	8,562	13.0%	4.0%
L maj	2,040	3.1%	0.5%

Mr Stephen Ross won the seat for the Liberals in February, 1974, having contested it in 1966 and 1970. Party spokesman on local government and planning, 1974-76; environment, 1966-77; and housing and local government since 1977. Chartered surveyor and farmer. B July, 1926; ed Bedford School. Member, Isle of Wight County Council, 1967-74. NFU.

Mr Dudley Fishburn is assistant editor of *The Economist.* Contested seat October, 1974. B June, 1946; ed Harvard College. NUJ.

Mrs Catherine Wilson, housewife. Formerly a secretary and hotelier. Member, Co-operative Party. B June, 1943.

ISLINGTON, Central

Electorate 40,884 1974: 45,347

*Grant, J. D. (Lab)	13,415
Goodson-Wickes, Dr C. (C)	9,276
Dunn, Mrs M. (L)	2,242
Chaney, S. (Nat Front)	797
Williams, A. (Ecology)	310
Lab majority	4,139

No Change

	1974		1979
Total votes	25,106		26,040
Turnout	55·4%		63·7%
Lab	14,689	58·5%	51·5%
C	5,296	21·1%	35·6%
L	3,786	15·1%	8·6%
Nat Front	1,335	5·3%	3·1%
Ecology	—		1·2%
Lab maj	9,393	37·4%	15·9%
Swing		−3·8%	+10·7%

Mr John Grant, Under-Secretary for Employment since 1976; Under-Secretary, Overseas Development, 1974-76; Parliamentary Secretary, Civil Service Department, March to October, 1974. MP for Islington, East, 1970-74; returned for Islington, Central, February, 1974. Formerly an Opposition spokesman on broadcasting and other media. Contested Beckenham, 1966. Journalist. B October, 1932; ed Stationers Company's School, Hornsey. Former member, Select Committee on Expenditure. NUJ and TGWU. Sponsored by EETPTU.

Dr Charles Goodson-Wickes, specialist physician at St Bartholomew's Hospital, a consulting physician to BUPA, and a barrister (Inner Temple). B November, 1945; ed Charterhouse, St Bartholomew's Hospital. Member, BMA and Medico-Legal Society.

Mrs M Dunn, a copywriter. Ed Hendon College of Technology.

Mr Adrian Williams, Post Office worker. Aged 33; ed Sheffield University.

ISLINGTON, North

Electorate 38,253 1974: 41,390

*O'Halloran, M. J. (Lab)	12,317
Kerr, N. (C)	7,861
Clarke, K. (L)	2,079
Hook, S. (Nat Front)	501
Simpson, M. (Soc Unity)	438
McCullough, R. (WRP)	217
Lab majority	4,456

No Change

	1974		1979
Total votes	22,422		23,413
Turnout	54·2%		61·2%
Lab	12,973	57·9%	52·6%
C	6,155	27·5%	33·6%
L	2,736	12·2%	8·9%
Lab & Dem	558	2·5%	—
Nat Front	—	—	2·1%
Soc Unity	—	—	1·9%
WRP	—	—	0·9%
Lab maj	6,818	30·4%	19·0%
Swing		−2·5%	+5·7%

Mr Michael O'Halloran was returned at a by-election in October 1969. Builder, railwayman and office manager. B August, 1928; ed Clohanes National School, Eire. Member, Islington Borough Council, 1967-71. Member of and sponsored by NUR.

Mr Neil Kerr, financial analyst and journalist. Former primary school teacher. B December 1943; ed Merchant Taylors' School, Crosby and Lincoln College Oxford. Master of Business Administration at Cranfield Business School. Chairman, Highbury Ward, Islington Central Conservative Association, since 1975; Leader of opposition on Islington Borough Council since 1978.

Mr Kenneth Clarke, building surveyor. Aged 29; ed Magdalen College, Oxford.

Mr Roy McCullough, aged 31, building worker. UCATT.

ISLINGTON, South and Finsbury

Electorate 38,427 1974: 45,251

*Cunningham, G. (Lab)	12,581
Waterson, N. (C)	8,237
Dean, A. (L)	1,991
Kavanagh, P. (Nat Front)	824
Betteridge, Mrs M. (Comm)	330
Delderfield, D. (New Brit)	136
Critchfield, R. (SPGB)	78
Lab majority	4,344

No Change

	1974		1979
Total votes	23,668		24,177
Turnout	56·0%		62·9%
Lab	14,544	61·5%	52·0%
C	4,951	20·9%	34·1%
L	3,661	15·5%	8·2%
Comm	512	2·2%	1·4%
Nat Front	—	—	3·4%
New Brit	—	—	0·6%
SPGB	—	—	0·3%
Lab maj	9,593	40·6%	17·9%
Swing		−4·8%	+11·3%

Mr George Cunningham a member of the British delegation to the European Parliament, 1978-79. Returned in February 1974; MP for Islington, South-West, 1970-74; contested Henley, 1966. B June 1931; ed Dunfermline High School, Blackpool Grammar School and Manchester and London Universities. Member, Select Committee on Proceedure; Select Committee on Overseas Development, 1973-74, and Expenditure Committee, 1971-74; Public Accounts Committee. since 1974. Chairman, PLP Parliamentary affairs and social services groups. On staff of Commonwealth Relations Office, 1956-63; Second Secretary, British High Commission at Ottawa, 1958-60; Ministry of Overseas Development, 1966-69. TGWU.

Mr Nigel Waterson, marine lawyer. Member, London Borough of Hammersmith Council, 1974-78. Treasurer and president Oxford University Conservative Association, 1970, and of Oxford Union standing committee, 1970-71. Vice-president, Edmund Burke Society, 1971. B October 1950; ed Leeds Grammar School and Queen's College, Oxford. Called to the Bar, 1973. Attached to parliamentary committee on consumer protection 1972-73 when research assistant to Mrs Sally Oppenheim, the Conservative front bench spokesman on consumer protection.

Mr Antony Dean, advertising representative and qualified teacher. B April, 1956; ed Rutherford Comprehensive School, Marylebone, and Culham College, Abingdon.

Mrs Marie Betteridge, chairman of local tenants association member of community health council. Member, executive committee, Communist Party. Contested the seat, 1966, 1970 and February and October, 1974.

JARROW

Electorate 55,619 1974: 54,735

Dixon, D. (Lab)	24,057
Auld, D. (C)	12,529
McDonnell, Mrs A. (L)	3,907
Downey, H. (Ind Lab)	2,247
Brown, N. (WRP)	374
Lab majority	11,528

No Change

	1974		1979
Total votes	39,083		43,114
Turnout	74·1%		77·5%
Lab	24,558	62·8%	55·8%
C	8,707	22·3%	29·1%
L	5,818	14·9%	9·1%
Ind Lab	—		5·2%
WRP	—		0·9%
Lab maj	15,851	40·5%	26·7%
Swing		−3·6%	+6·9%

Mr Donald Dixon is a trade union official. B March 1929; ed Ellison Street Church of England School, Jarrow. Member, Jarrow Borough Council, 1963-74; leader, 1969-74. Member, South Tyneside District Council since 1974; chairman, labour group and housing committee. Vice-president, Jarrow and Heb- 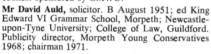 burn Trades Council. Member, GMWU regional council. Sponsored by GMWU.

Mr David Auld, solicitor. B August 1951; ed King Edward VI Grammar School, Morpeth; Newcastle-upon-Tyne University; College of Law, Guildford. Publicity director, Morpeth Young Conservatives 1968; chairman 1971.

Mrs Alex McDonnell, field worker for Age Concern. B October, 1940; ed Whitehill School and Langside College, Glasgow. Member, Durham County Council, 1973-77.

Mr Nicholas Brown, aged 43, engineering worker and shop steward.

KEIGHLEY

Electorate 54,428 1974: 51,741

*Cryer, G. R. (Lab)	19,698
Dawson, J. (C)	19,620
Holmstedt, Miss M. (L)	4,062
Fairey, R. L. (Nat Front)	234
Wade, Mrs J. (Ecology)	208
Lab majority	78

No Change

	1974		1979
Total votes	42,934		43,822
Turnout	83·0%		80·5%
Lab	19,569	45·6%	45·0%
C	16,488	38·4%	44·8%
L	5,839	13·6%	9·3%
Nat Front	859	2·0%	0·5%
Pros Brit	179	0·4%	—
Ecology	—		0·5%
Lab maj	3,081	7·2%	0·2%
Swing		−2·6%	+3·5%

Mr Robert Cryer resigned in November 1978 as Under-Secretary for Industry, to which he was appointed in 1976, in protest at a decision to cut off public funds to a Merseyside workers' cooperative. Former technical college teacher. Member, Keighley Borough Council, 1971-73.  B December, 1934; ed Salt High School, Shipley and Hull University. Chairman, PLP employment group, 1975-76. TGWU and ATTI.

Mr John Dawson contested Leeds, East, in October 1974. Solicitor and principal lecturer at Leeds Polytechnic Law School. B September 1947; ed Leeds Grammar School, Leeds University and Liverpool College of Commerce. Vice-chairman, Leeds University Union Conservative Association, 1967-69; secretary, Far Headingly Young Conservatives, 1970-71; vice-chairman, North West Leeds Young Conservatives, 1971-72; chairman 1972-73.

Miss Margareta Homstedt, a university lecturer, contested the seat, October 1974, and Bradford South, February 1974. B July, 1941; ed Stockholm University. International liaison officer of the Liberal Party, 1974-77. Member, Todmorden Town Council, from 1976. Wife of Liberal Party President, Mr Michael Steed, candidate at Burnley.

Mrs Joyce Wade, lecturer.

KENSINGTON AND CHELSEA
Chelsea

Electorate 57,515 1974: 64,554

*Scott, N. P. (C)	21,782
Pandy, R. (Lab)	6,092
Driver, P. (L)	4,544
Reeve, A. (Nat Front)	342
Fellowes, Mrs B. (CSD)	146
Fielding, Miss A. (Ind)	49
C majority	15,690

No Change

	1974		1979
Total votes	32,260		32,955
Turnout	50·0%		57·3%
C	19,674	61·0%	66·1%
Lab	6,507	20·2%	18·5%
L	5,758	17·8%	13·8%
SLAG	321	1·0%	—
Nat Front	—	—	1·0%
CSD	—	—	0·4%
Ind	—	—	0·1%
C maj	13,167	40·8%	47·6%
Swing		−1·0%	+3·4%

Mr Nicholas Scott was a member of the Shadow Cabinet and chief Opposition spokesman on housing, 1974–75. Elected in October, 1974; represented Paddington, South, 1966–74; contested Cities of London and Westminster, Paddington, February 1974. Under Secretary for Employment, January–February, 1974. Contested Islington, South-West, 1964 and 1959. B August 1933; ed Clapham College. Director of printing and publishing and other companies. National chairman, Young Conservatives, 1963, and president, Greater London YCs. Member, Holborn Borough Council, 1956-59 and 1962-65. ASTMS.

Mr Robert Pandy, member of Kensington and Chelsea council. Refuse collector.

Mr Peter Driver, oil company executive. B December, 1934; ed Epsom College.

KENSINGTON AND CHELSEA
Kensington

Electorate 52,396 1974: 61,105

*Rhys Williams, Sir B. (C)	17,361
Holmes, Mrs P. (Lab)	11,898
Vincent-Emery, Miss B. (L)	3,537
Albery, N. (Ecology)	698
Hopewell, C. (Nat Front)	356
C majority	5,463

No Change

	1974		1979
Total votes	34,443		33,850
Turnout	56·4%		64·6%
C	15,562	45·2%	51·3%
Lab	13,645	39·6%	35·1%
L	5,236	15·2%	10·4%
Ecology	—	—	2·1%
Nat Front	—	—	1·1%
C maj	1,917	5·6%	16·2%
Swing		−3·7%	+5·3%

Sir Brandon Rhys Williams, an industrial consultant, elected in February, 1974, represented Kensington, South, 1968-74. Member, European Parliament since 1974. Contested Pontypridd, 1959 and Ebbw Vale in 1960 by-election and 1964. B November, 1927; ed Eton, Chairman National Birthday Trust. Assistant director (appeals) Spastics Society, 1962-63.

Formerly with ICI Ltd. Former vice-chairman, parliamentary health and social security, parliamentary finance committee.

Mrs Patricia Holmes, lecturer-researcher. B 1946.

Miss Bobbie Vincent-Emery, press officer with Equal Opportunities Commission. Aged 35; ed Sheffield Polytechnic.

Mr Nicholas Albery, aged 30, architect's research assistant.

KETTERING

Electorate 88,396 1974: 85,802

Homewood, W. D. (Lab)	31,579
Allason, R. (C)	30,101
Raven, G. (L)	8,424
Lab majority	1,478

No Change

	1974		1979
Total votes	62,808		70,104
Turnout	73·2%		79·3%
Lab	30,970	49·3%	45·0%
C	19,800	31·5%	42·9%
L	12,038	19·2%	12·0%
Lab maj	11,170	17·8%	2·1%
Swing		−1·8%	+7·8%

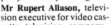

Mr William Homewood, a full-time organizer of the Iron and Steel Trades Confederation; previously branch secretary and district committee secretary. B March, 1920; ed elementary school and Ruskin College, Oxford. Rural district councillor for seven years. A former constituency party secretary and agent.

Mr Rupert Allason, television executive for video cassette television company. B November 1951; ed Downside School, Grenoble University and London University. Member, British Industrial and Scientific Film Association's cassette group. His father, Mr James Allason, was Conservative MP for Hemel Hempstead, 1959-74. NUJ.

Mr Gerard Raven, political and EEC correspondent of *Farmers' Weekly*, B June, 1948; ed Wellingborough School. Member, Electoral Reform Society, Mensa and NUJ.

KIDDERMINSTER

Electorate 80,131 1974: 78,965

*Bulmer, J. E. (C)	33,523
Wright, A. W. (Lab)	17,871
Adams, G. (L)	9,939
Luckman, A. (Nat Front)	1,052
C majority	15,652

No Change

	1974		1979
Total votes	59,168		62,385
Turnout	74·9%		77·6%
C	25,602	43·3%	53·7%
Lab	18,833	31·8%	28·6%
L	14,733	24·9%	15·9%
Nat Front	—	—	1·7%
C maj	6,769	11·5%	25·1%
Swing		−1·1%	+6·8%

Mr Esmond Bulmer was elected in February, 1974. Director of H. P. Bulmer Ltd of Hereford, cider makers. B May, 1935; ed Rugby and King's College, Cambridge. Secretary, Conservative employment committee, since 1974. NFU.

Mr Anthony Wright, university lecturer. B March, 1948; ed Kettering Grammar School, LSE; Balliol College, Oxford; Harvard University. AUT.

Mr Garratt Adams, haulier. Chairman and administrator of trust for elderly. Contested local government elections. Aged 57; ed Birmingham University.

KILMARNOCK

Electorate 60,351 1974: 60,380

McKelvey, W. (Lab)		25,718
Corbett, J. (C)		14,251
MacInnes, A. (Scot Nat)		8,963
Lab majority		11,467

No Change

	1974		1979
Total votes	48,550		48,932
Turnout	80·4%		81·1%
Lab	22,184	45·7%	52·6%
Scot Nat	14,655	30·2%	18·3%
C	9,203	19·0%	29·1%
L	2,508	5·2%	—
Lab maj	7,529	15·5%	23·5%
Swing		−3·6%	+1·6%

Mr William McKelvey is a former full-time Labour Party and union official. B July, 1934; ed Dundee Academy and Dundee College of Technology. Sponsored by AUEW engineering section.

Mr John Corbett contested Glasgow, Garscadden, October, 1974. Farmer and estate agent. B March 1947; ed Eton and Royal Agricultural College, Cirencester. Chairman, Kilmaurs and Fenwick Conservative Association, and member of executive and advisory committees of Kilmarnock Conservative Association.

Mr Alistair MacInnes, engineering surveyor, contested the seat, February and October, 1974, and 1970. B July, 1927; ed Glenwood High School, Durban and Robert Gordon's Institute of Technology, Aberdeen. Member, Kilmarnock Town Council, 1966-69.

KINGSTON-UPON-HULL, Central

Electorate 60,801 1974: 63,278

*McNamara, J. K. (Lab)	22,318
Tillett J. (C)	14,725
Bryant, J. (L)	5,069
Braithwaite, A. (Nat Front)	422
Stanton, Ms P. M. (Soc Unity)	274
Lab majority	7,593

No Change

	1974		1979
Total votes	42,823		42,808
Turnout	67·7%		70·4%
Lab	22,417	52·3%	52·1%
C	12,596	29·4%	34·4%
L	7,810	18·2%	11·8%
Nat Front	—	—	1·0%
Soc Unity	—		0·6%
Lab maj	9,821	22·9%	17·7%
Swing		−3·2%	+2·6%

Mr Kevin McNamara was returned for the seat in February, 1974, having been MP for Kingston upon Hull, North, 1966-74; contested Bridlington, 1964. B September, 1934; ed St Mary's College, Crosby, and Hull University. Lecturer in law. Chairman, Select Committee on Overseas Development, since 1978. Chairman, PLP Northern Ireland Group. Sponsored by TGWU. Member, UK delegation to the Council of Europe.

Mr Jeffery Tillett, lecturer, author and music publisher, contested Salford, West, February and October 1974; Nottingham, North, 1966; Ilkeston, 1964. B December 1927; ed Derby School and Nottingham University. Deputy leader Derby borough council, member since 1957, (Mayor 1977-78); chairman of Derby education committee, 1968-72. NUT.

Mr John Bryant, sales officer. B April, 1955; ed King Henry VIII Grammar School, Coventry and Hull University.

KINGSTON-UPON-HULL, East

Electorate 89,023 1974: 81,624

*Prescott, J. L. (Lab)	39,411
Bean, M. M. B. (C)	15,719
Horne, M. J. (L)	7,543
Matson, D. J. (Nat Front)	374
Lab majority	23,692

No Change

	1974		1979
Total votes	54,783		63,074
Turnout	67·1%		70·8%
Lab	34,190	62·4%	62·5%
C	10,397	19·0%	24·9%
L	10,196	18·6%	12·0%
Nat Front	—		0·6%
Lab maj	23,793	43·4%	37·6%
Swing		−1·7%	+2·9%

Mr John Prescott, member of European Parliament 1975-79 and leader of the Labour delegation there 1976-79. Former official of the National Union of Seamen. Elected in 1970; contested Southport, 1966. B May, 1938; ed Grange Secondary Modern School, Ellesmere Port, Ruskin College and Hull University. Sponsored by NUS. Former member, Select Committee on Nationalised Industries. PPS to Mr Peter Shore as Secretary of State for Trade, 1974-76.

Mr **Michael Bean,** market gardener and director. B 1943; ed Ampleforth College. Member Hull City Council 1969-72.

Mr **Michael Horne,** university technician. Aged 23; ed Hull University.

KINGSTON-UPON-HULL, West

Electorate 52,489 1974: 57,592

*Johnson, J. (Lab)	19,750
Smith, R. E. (C)	11,592
Foston, S. J. (L)	3,656
Fox, M. D. (Nat Front)	411

Lab majority	8,158

No Change

	1974		1979
Total votes	37,173		35,409
Turnout	64·5%		67·5%
Lab	20,393	54·9%	55·8%
C	10,272	27·6%	32·7%
L	6,508	17·5%	10·3%
Nat Front	—		1·2%
Lab maj	10,121	27·3%	23·1%
Swing		−4·2%	+2·1%

Mr **James Johnson,** chairman of PLP and All-party fisheries committees; chairman PLP Yorkshire & Humberside group since 1977. Member, Select Committee on Overseas Development, since 1974. Returned in 1964; represented Rugby, 1950-59. Teacher and lecturer. B September, 1908; ed Duke's School, Alnwick and Leeds and London universities. Chairman, PLP Commonwealth committee since 1968. Member executive, Commonwealth Parliamentary Association, chairman of UK groups. Served on Coventry City Council and Fabian Society executive. Sponsored by GMWU.

Mr **Rodney Smith,** business consultant. B 1935; ed Westminster and Highfield Colleges and Wupertaal School, Rhine Valley. Member Southend County Borough Council, 1964-68. Chairman Southend West Young Conservatives, 1958-60. Chairman Eastern Area Conservative Political Centre 1971-74; member Eastern Area executive committee.

KINGSTON UPON THAMES

Electorate 57,572 1974: 59,251

*Lamont, N. H. S. (C)	24,944
Torode, J. A. (Lab)	11,400
Terry, D. (L)	6,771

C majority	13,544

No Change

	1974		1979
Total votes	42,526		43,115
Turnout	71·8%		74·9%
C	20,680	48·6%	57·9%
Lab	12,226	28·8%	26·4%
L	9,580	22·5%	15·7%
C maj	8,414	19·8%	31·5%
Swing		−2·4%	+5·8%

Mr **Norman Lamont,** appointed as Under-Secretary of State for Energy in May 1979. An Opposition spokesman on industry, 1976-79, and on consumer affairs and prices 1975-76. Merchant banker. Returned at a by-election in 1972; contested Kingston-upon-Hull, East, 1970. Secretary, Conservative Parliamentary Health and Social Security Committee,

1972-74. B May, 1942; ed Loretto School and Fitzwilliam College, Cambridge. (President of Union, 1964.) Chairman, Bow Group, 1971-72. Joint secretary, Conservative finance committee, 1976. Member, Select Committee in Procedure.

Mr **John Torode,** leader writer for *The Guardian.* B January, 1939; ed Wanstead County High School, Lincoln College, Oxford, and Cornell universities. Former member, Younger Committee on Privacy. NUJ.

Mr **Declan Terry,** aged 37 consultant electrical engineer. Member, Kingston Council 1974-78.

KINGSTON UPON THAMES, Surbiton

Electorate 46,922 1974: 46,073

*Fisher, Sir N. (C)	20,063
Moore, C. P. (Lab)	9,261
Tilley, Mrs C. J. (L)	6,093

C majority	10,802

No Change

	1974		1979
Total votes	33,570		35,417
Turnout	72·9%		75·5%
C	15,330	45·7%	56·6%
Lab	9,309	27·7%	26·1%
L	8,931	26·6%	17·2%
C maj	6,021	18·0%	30·5%
Swing		−0·8%	+6·2%

Sir Nigel Fisher, director or a group of pharmaceutical companies. Member, executive, 1922 Committee. Spokesman on Commonwealth Affairs, 1964-66; Under Secretary for Commonwealth Relations and the Colonies, 1963-64; Under Secretary for the Colonies, 1962-63. Contested Chislehurst, 1945; represented Hitchin, 1950-55; elected for Surbi-

ton, 1955. B July, 1913; ed Eton and Trinity College, Cambridge. Biographer of Ian Macleod.

Mr **Colin Moore,** an administrative assistant, North London Polytechnic. Former Labour Party research assistant. B May 1950; ed King George V Grammar School, Southport, Oxford University. Nalgo.

Mrs **Christine Tilley,** member, Kingston upon Thames Council, 1974-78. B June, 1942; ed St Paul's Girls' School, Hammersmith.

KINGSWOOD

Electorate 60,229   1974: 55,436

Aspinwall, J. H. (C)	23,553
*Walker, T. W. (Lab)	23,250
Wilson, A. (L)	4,852
Bale, R. (Nat Front)	258
C majority	303

C gain from Lab

	1974		1979
Total votes	47,056		51,913
Turnout	84·1%		86·2%
Lab	20,703	44·0%	44·8%
C	18,137	38·5%	45·4%
L	8,216	17·5%	9·3%
Nat Front	—	—	0·5%
Lab maj	2,566	5·5%	—
C maj	—	—	0·6%
Swing	—	−1·1%	+3·0%

Mr Jack Aspinwall, company director, contested the seat in February and October, 1974, as a Liberal. B February, 1933; ed Prescott Grammar School, Bootle, and Marconi College, Chelmsford. Member, Avon County Council and Kingswood District Council. Chairman of governers of several local schools.

Mr Terence Walker was elected in February, 1974. Accountant. B October, 1935; ed Clarks Grammar School, Bristol and Bristol College of Further Education. Second Church Estates Commisioner, 1974-79. Sponsored by TGWU.

Mr Anthony Wilson, solicitor. B July, 1951; ed Shirley House, Watford; Bushey Grammar School.

KINROSS AND WEST PERTHSHIRE

Electorate 38,591   1974: 35,237

*Fairbairn, N. H. (C)	15,523
Smith, I. (Scot Nat)	9,045
Chapman, Mrs J. (L)	3,572
Macleod, D. R. (Lab)	2,593
C majority	6,478

No Change

	1974		1979
Total votes	26,470		30,733
Turnout	75·1%		79·6%
C	11,034	41·7%	50·5%
Scot Nat	10,981	41·5%	29·4%
L	2,427	9·2%	11·6%
Lab	2,028	7·7%	8·4%
C maj	53	0·2%	21·1%
Swing	—	−4·5%	+4·0%

Mr Nicholas Fairbairn, QC, became Solicitor-General for Scotland in May, 1979. Elected October, 1974. Contested Edinburgh, Central, 1964 and 1966. Farmer, company director, advocate, author, painter and poet. Served on Edinburgh Festival Committee. Former member, Joint Select Committee on Statutory Instruments. Member, Council of World Population Crisis, 1968-70. Chairman, Traverse Theatre, 1964-72. B December, 1933; ed Loretto and Edinburgh University.

Mr Ian Smith, photographer. B January, 1937; ed Nicolson Institute. Chairman, SNP health policy committee.

Mr Donald Macleod, advocate. B September, 1948; ed High School, Stirling, and Glasgow University.

KIRKCALDY

Electorate 61,057   1974: 60,824

*Gourlay, H. P. H. (Lab)	25,449
Stewart, Mrs J. (C)	12,386
Currie, A. (Scot Nat)	9,416
Lab majority	13,063

No Change

	1974		1979
Total votes	45,602		47,251
Turnout	75·0%		77·4%
Lab	20,688	45·4%	53·9%
Scot Nat	14,587	32·0%	19·9%
C	7,539	16·5%	26·2%
L	2,788	6·1%	—
Lab maj	6,101	13·4%	27·7%
Swing	—	−4·7%	+0·6%

Mr Harry Gourlay, elected in 1959, contested South Angus, 1955. Chairman, PLP Scottish group, 1977; member, Select Committee on Procedure. Deputy Chairman of Ways and Means, 1968-70; a Lord Commissioner of the Treasury, 1966-68; assistant Government whip, 1964-66. Vehicle examiner. B July, 1916; ed Sinclairtown Public School and Kirkcaldy High School. Member, Estimates Committee, 1959-64. Member, Kirkcaldy Town Council 1946-60; Fife County Council, 1947-60; National Union of Vehicle Builders, 1934-71. Sponsored by TGWU.

Mrs Jean Stewart, barrister and former teacher. B 1926; ed Brondesbury, Albury, Hertfordshire; St Andrew's University. Member, East Fife Conservative Association; executive committee, West Aberdeenshire Conservative Association, 1963-70. Hon secretary, Canada group of Conservative Commonwealth and Overseas Council; Conservative Foreign Affairs Forum. Member, Council of the China Society (a non-political society).

Mr Andrew Currie, training officer with Citizens Advice Bureau. Secretary to SNP industry committee and convenor, consumer protection committee. B November, 1936; ed Glasgow University and Strathclyde and Open universities.

KNUTSFORD

Electorate 57,671   1974: 55,238

*Bruce-Gardyne, J. (C)	26,795
Barton, A. G. (Lab)	8,992
Ingham, R. (L)	8,499
Brown, J. (Ind C)	690

C majority	17,803

No Change

	1974		1979
Total votes	42,411		44,976
Turnout	76·8%		78·0%
C	21,636	51·0%	59·6%
L	11,210	26·4%	18·9%
Lab	9,565	22·6%	20·0%
Ind C	—	—	1·5%
C maj	10,426	24·6%	39·6%
Swing		−2·3%	+5·6%

1979 by-election: Total vote 32,902 (57·4%)—C 22,086 (67·1%); L 5,206 (15·8%); Lab 5,124 (15·6%); others 486 (1·5%). C majority 16,880 (51·3%).

Mr John Bruce-Gardyne, a journalist, was elected at the March 1979 by-election. Held South Angus for the Conservatives from 1964 to October, 1974. Secretary of Scottish Conservative MPs' group, 1967-72; vice-chairman, Conservative parliamentary finance committee, 1972-74; member, Commons Expenditure Committee, 1972-74. Economic leader writer for *The Daily Telegraph.* B April, 1930; ed Winchester College and Magdalen College, Oxford.

Mr Alan Barton, teacher. B November, 1942; ed Holt School, Liverpool, and St. Peter's College, Oxford. NUT.

Mr Robert Ingham, nuclear power engineer, branch chairman, IPCS nuclear power branch. B November, 1931; ed Llangollen Grammar School; Bangor University.

LAMBETH, Central

Electorate 43,678   1974: 48,722

*Tilley, J. (Lab and Co-op)	15,101
Hanley, J. (C)	9,125
Blunt, D. (L)	2,339
Lillington, Mrs V. (Nat Front)	830
Redgrave, C. (WRP)	152
Whereat, A. (Ind)	50

Lab and Co-op majority	5,976

No Change

	1974		1979
Total votes	25,617		27,597
Turnout	52·6%		63·2%
Lab	15,381	60·0%	54·7%
C	6,704	26·2%	33·1%
L	3,211	12·5%	8·5%
WRP	233	0·9%	0·6%
Marx Len	88	0·3%	—
Nat Front	—	—	3·0%
Ind	—	—	0·2%
Lab maj	8,677	33·8%	21·6%
Swing		−4·7%	+6·1%

1978 by-election: Total votes 20,846 (44·5%)—Lab 10,311 (49·5%); C 7,170 (34·4%); Nat Front 1,291 (6·2%); L 1,104 (5·3%); others 970 (4·6%). Lab majority 3,141 (15·1%).

Mr John Tilley, journalist, industrial correspondent, retained the seat for Labour in the 1978 by-election. Contested Kensington in both 1974 elections. B June, 1941. Leader, Wandsworth Council, and member since 1971. NUJ, Co-operative Party and Fabian Society. Joint Secretary, all-party group on the theatre.

Mr Jeremy Hanley, senior lecturer and company director. B 1945; ed Rugby. Member, Ruislip and Northwood Conservative Association; Conservative Group for Europe and European Movement. Member of Mensa; semi-finalist in Brain of Mensa, 1976.

Mr David Blunt, barrister, contested the seat at the 1978 by-election. B October, 1944; ed Farnham Grammar School; Cambridge University.

Mr Corin Redgrave, aged 39, is an actor and brother of Miss Venessa Redgrave, the WRP candidate at Manchester, Moss Side. Member of party's central committee and secretary, London district committee; ed Cambridge University. Equity.

LAMBETH, Norwood

Electorate 48,857   1974: 52,893

*Fraser, J. D. (Lab)	16,282
Pritchard, J. (C)	14,342
Charlesworth, D. (L)	3,051
Williams, Mrs C. (Nat Front)	707

Lab majority	1,940

No Change

	1974		1979
Total votes	32,727		34,382
Turnout	61·9%		70·4%
Lab	16,449	50·3%	47·4%
C	11,678	35·7%	41·7%
L	4,377	13·4%	8·9%
Gay Lib	223	0·7%	—
Nat Front	—	—	2·1%
Lab maj	4,771	14·6%	5·7%
Swing		−1·9%	+4·4%

Mr John Fraser became Minister of State, Department of Prices and Consumer Protection, in April, 1976; Under Secretary for Employment, 1974-76. An Opposition spokesman on the Home Office, 1971-74. Won the seat in 1966 and contested it, 1964. Solicitor. B June, 1934; ed Sloane Grammar School and Law Society College. GMWU. Former chairman, PLP

Greek Democratic Committee; former member, Select Committees on Education and Science and on Broadcasting Proceedings of House of Commons. Former deputy chairman, PLP Environment Group. Member, Lambeth Borough Council, 1962-68. Founder member, Co-ownership Development Society.

Mr John Pritchard, employed in housing management, contested Wrexham in February and October, 1974. B July, 1946; ed Haberdashers' Aske's School and St David's University College, Lampeter. Member, Bromley Borough Council, since 1974. Former chairman, West Lewisham Young Conservatives and vice-chairman, Cities of London and West-minster Young Conservatives. Vice-chairman, London regional branch National Association of Conservative Graduates.

Mr David Charlesworth, aged 26, economist. Ed Lancaster University.

LAMBETH, Streatham

Electorate 53,347   1974: 56,453

*Shelton, W. J. M. (C)	19,630
Daniel, T. P. C. (Lab)	14,130
Pincham, J. S. (L)	3,779
Bryant, G. W. (Nat Front)	523
Hollander, A. J. (PTC)	102
C majority	5,500

No Change

	1974		1979
Total votes	36,177		38,164
Turnout	64·1%		71·5%
C	16,515	45·7%	51·4%
Lab	13,648	37·7%	37·0%
L	4,987	13·8%	9·9%
Nat Front	817	2·3%	1·4%
Ind	210	0·6%	—
PTC	—	—	0·3%
C maj	2,867	8·0%	14·4%
Swing		−1·5%	+3·2%

Mr William Shelton, PPS to Mrs Thatcher as Leader of the Opposition, 1975-79. Elected for Streatham in February, 1974. MP for Clapham 1970-74. Chairman of advertising agency. B October, 1929; ed Radley College, Worcester College, Oxford, Tabor Academy, Mass, and Texas University. Member, GLC, 1967-70. Vice chairman, Conservative Education

Committee and Greater London Conservative MPs' Committee; secretary, Conservative Foreign Affairs and Trade Committee Member. Select Committee on Procedure.

Mr Timothy Daniel, solicitor. B May, 1944; ed Bristol University. Contested Harrow, West, 1970. Leader of Labour group, Westminster City Concil, since 1977. Chairman, Deptford Housing Aid Centre. TGWU.

Mr John Pinchan, insurance broker, fought Hillingdon, Uxbridge, February and October, 1974. Member, Liberal Tax Panel; joint author, Liberal Report on Land Use and Site Value Rating Commission. Chairman, J. S. Pinchan (Holdings) Ltd and associated companies. Member, Lloyds. Fellow, Chartered Insurance Institute of the Corporation of Insurance Brokers; Institute of Directors; Scottish Woodland Owners' Association. B May, 1932; ed Kingston Grammar School.

LAMBETH, Vauxhall

Electorate 39,870   1974: 46,502

Holland, S. (Lab)	13,058
Heslop, P. (C)	8,358
Harrison, F. (L)	1,842
Atkinson, V. (Nat Front)	879
Elliot, D. (Lab AP)	565
Hannigan, Miss S. (WRP)	153
Boaks, W. (DMPSWR)	44
Lab majority	4,700

No Change

	1974		1979
Total votes	24,520		24,899
Turnout	57·7%		62·5%
Lab	15,493	63·2%	52·4%
C	5,727	23·4%	33·6%
L	3,300	13·5%	7·4%
Nat Front	—	—	3·5%
Lab AP	—	—	2·3%
WRP	—	—	0·6%
DMPSWR	—	—	0·2%
Lab maj	9,766	39·8%	18·8%
Swing		−4·9%	+10·5%

Mr Stuart Holland, political economist and lecturer, was chairman of the Public Enterprise Group, 1973-75; economist assistant, Cabinet Office, 1966-67, and personal assistant to the Prime Minister, 1967-68. B

March, 1940; ed Christ's Hospital, University of Missouri, Balliol College, Oxford, and St Antony's College, Oxford. Special adviser, Commons Expenditure Committee, 1971-72; consultant, economic and social affairs committee, Council of Europe, 1973; Open University 1973. Associate editor, *European Economic Review,* since 1970.

Mr Philip Heslop, barrister, was president of the Cambridge Union, 1971. B 1948; ed Haileybury, University of Perugia, Christ's College, Cambridge, Loncoln's Inn. Chairman, Cambridge University Conservative Association, 1969.

Mr Frederick Harrison, journalist contested Brent, North 1974 elections. B March, 1944; ed London and Oxford universities. NUJ.

LANARK

Electorate 51,320   1974: 48,408

*Hart, Mrs J. (Lab)	18,118
Bell, A. (C)	12,979
McAlpine, T. (Scot Nat)	7,902
McDermid, F. (L)	2,967
Lab majority	5,139

No Change

	1974		1979
Total votes	39,794		41,966
Turnout	82·2%		81·8%
Lab	14,948	37·6%	43·2%
Scot Nat	14,250	35·8%	18·8%
C	9,222	23·2%	30·9%
L	1,374	3·5%	7·1%
Lab maj	698	1·8%	12·3%
Swing		−4·6%	+1·0%

Mrs Judith Hart was Minister for Overseas Development, 1977-79. She had been appointed in March, 1974, but resigned in June, 1975. Opposition spokesman on overseas development, 1970-74. Minister of Overseas Development, 1969-70, Paymaster General, 1968-69, with seat in Cabinet; Minister of Social Security, 1967-68; Minister of State, Commonwealth

Office, 1966-67; Under Secretary, Scottish Office, 1964-66. Won seat for Labour, 1959; contested Bournemouth, West, 1951; Aberdeen, South, 1955.

B September, 1924; ed Royal Grammar School, Clitheroe; London School of Economics and London University. Member, Labour Party National Executive since 1969.

Mr Arthur Bell, managing director and marketing consultant, contested the seat, October, 1974 and Kirkcaldy, February, 1974. B October, 1946; ed Royal High School, Edinburgh and Edinburgh University. Chairman Central and Southern region, Young Conservatives, 1968-69; vice-chairman, Scottish Young Conservatives, 1969-71, vice-chairman, Federation of Conservative Students, 1969-70.

Mr Thomas McAlpine, chartered engineer and managing director, contested the seat in February, and October, 1974, and Bothwell, 1970. SNP vice-president. B September, 1929; ed Dalziel High School, Motherwell and Glasgow University. Member, Hamilton Council, 1960-63. ASTMS.

LANARKSHIRE, North

Electorate 56,565 1974: 54,147

*Smith, J. (Lab)	25,015
Robertson, G. J. (C)	14,195
Ralston, J. (Scot Nat)	5,887

Lab majority	10,820

No Change

	1974		1979
Total votes	43,027		45,097
Turnout	79·5%		79·7%
Lab	19,902	46·3%	55·5%
Scot Nat	11,561	26·9%	13·1%
C	9,665	22·5%	31·5%
L	1,899	4·4%	—
Lab maj	8,341	19·4%	24·0%
Swing		−4·3%	0·1%

Mr John Smith Secretary of State for Trade, 1978-79; Minister of State, Privy Council Office, 1976-78; Minister of State, Department of Energy, 1975-76; Under Secretary, Department of Energy, 1974-75. Elected in 1970; contested East Fife by-election, 1961, and in 1964. Advocate. B September, 1938; ed Dunoon Grammar School and Glasgow University. Sponsored by Amalgamated Society of Boilermakers.

Mr Grant Robertson, solicitor. B 1949; ed Clydebank High School and Glasgow University. Member Central Council of the Scottish Conservative and Unionist Association, and the Scottish Young Conservatives. Leader, Conservative group, Glasgow parliamentary debating association.

Mr John Ralston is a teacher. B February, 1933; ed Trinity College, Cambridge.

LANCASTER

Electorate 51,252 1974: 46,643

*Kellett-Bowman, Mrs M. E. (C)	19,400
Henig, Mrs R. B. (Lab)	15,174
Mumford, M. J. (L)	5,949
White, D. F. (Nat Front)	196

C majority	4,226

No Change

	1974		1979
Total votes	38,820		40,719
Turnout	78·2%		79·4%
C	16,540	42·6%	47·6%
Lab	15,119	38·9%	37·3%
L	7,161	18·4%	14·6%
Nat Front	—	—	0·5%
C maj	1,421	3·7%	10·3%
Swing		−1·2%	+3·3%

Mrs Elaine Kellett-Bowman won the seat in 1970. Barrister (Middle Temple, 1964), farmer and social worker. Contested Buckingham, 1966 and 1964, South West Norfolk 1959, and the 1959 by-election, and Nelson and Colne, 1955. Member, European Parliament, since 1975. B July, 1924; ed Queen Mary's School, Lytham; The Mount, York, and St Anne's College, Oxford. Alderman of Borough of Camden, 1968-71. Member of Press Council, 1964-68.

Mrs Ruth Henig, university lecturer. B November, 1943; ed Wyggeston Girls' Grammar School, Leicester, and Bedford College, London. Secretary, women's section, Lancaster Fabians. TGWU.

Mr Michael Mumford, university teacher, contested the seat, October, 1974. B April, 1939; ed Royal Grammar School, Guildford, Liverpool University, and McMaster University, Canada. Member, Cardiganshire County Council, 1968-70. Senior lecturer, University of Nairobi, 1971-72. AUT.

LEEDS, East

Electorate 67,048 1974: 67,091

*Healey, D. W. (Lab)	26,346
Carter, A. (C)	15,810
Ellis, M. L. (L)	4,622
Rigby, S. J. (Nat Front)	445
Hill, Mrs A. C. (Ecology)	206
Slaughter, Mrs B. (WRP)	103

Lab majority	10,536

No Change

	1974		1979
Total votes	44,476		47,532
Turnout	65·7%		70·9%
Lab	24,745	55·6%	55·4%
C	12,434	28·0%	33·3%
L	6,970	15·7%	9·7%
People	327	0·7%	—
Nat Front	—	—	0·9%
Ecology	—	—	0·4%
WRP	—	—	0·2%
Lab maj	12,311	27·6%	22·1%
Swing		−3·4%	+2·7%

Mr Denis Healey, was Chancellor of the Exchequer March, 1974-79; unsuccessfully contested the party leadership election in 1976. Chief Opposition spokesman on Treasury matters, 1972-74; chief Opposition spokesman on foreign and Commonwealth affars, 1970-72; Secretary of State for Defence, 1964-70. Elected for Leeds, South-East, at a by-election in 1952, and for Leeds, East, in 1955; contested Pudsey and Otley, 1945. B August, 1917; ed Bradford Grammar School and Balliol College, Oxford. Member, Labour Party national executive committee, 1970-75.

Mr Andrew Carter, contracts manager with tile manufacturers. B 1949; ed Fulneck School, Pudsey; Ingledew College, Leeds and Leeds College of Building. Member, Leeds Metropolitan District Council, since 1973; Pudsey Borough Council, since 1974. School manager and governor.

Mr Michael Ellis, teacher. Aged 28; ed Universities of Wales and Sheffield.

Mrs Barbara Slaughter, aged 51, teacher and former social worker. NUT.

LEEDS, North-East

Electorate 59,113   1974: 58,968

*Joseph, Sir Keith (C)	20,297
Sedler, R. H. (Lab)	14,913
Hollingworth, R. (L)	5,329
Parkin, Mrs S. (Ecology)	813
Tibbitts, E. L. (Anti-Corr)	103

C majority	5,384

No Change

	1974		1979
Total votes	38,607		41,455
Turnout	65·5%		70·1%
C	18,749	48·6%	49·0%
Lab	13,121	34·0%	36·0%
L	6,737	17·5%	12·9%
Ecology	—	—	2·0%
Anti-Corr	—	—	0·2%
C maj	5,628	14·6%	13·0%
Swing		−1·0%	−0·8%

Sir Keith Joseph, was appointed Secretary of State for Industry in May, 1979. Chief Opposition spokesman on industry, with overall responsibility for Conservative Party policy and research 1974-79. Chief Opposition spokesman on home affairs, 1974-75. Secretary of State for Social Services, 1970-74; Minister of Housing and Local Government and Minister for Welsh Affairs, 1962-64; Parliamentary Secretary, Ministry of Housing and Local Government, 1959-61, and Minister of State, Board of Trade, 1961-62. Returned at a by-election in February, 1956; contested Barons Court, 1955. B January, 1918; ed Harrow and Magdalen College, Oxford. Barrister (Middle Temple, 1946). Fellow of All Souls, 1946-60, and since 1972. Company director. Founder and chairman of management committee of Centre for Policy Studies since 1974.

Mr Ronald Sedler, solicitor, city councillor, 1957-60 and 1972-74. B April, 1926; ed Parmiter's School, London, and Leeds University. APEX.

Mr Roy Hollingworth, medical laboratory technician. Member, Health Service National Advisory Council, of which he was branch secretary and chairman and now branch vice-chairman. B December, 1941; ed Osmondthorpe County Secondary School. ASTMS.

Mrs Sara Parkin, aged 32, housewife and part-time nurse. Member, Leeds West Community Health Council.

LEEDS, North-West

Electorate 68,702   1974: 65,062

*Kaberry, Sir Donald (C)	23,837
O'Grady, P. A. (Lab)	17,623
Keates, C. (L)	7,899
Rushworth, K. (Ecology)	847

C majority	6,214

No Change

	1974		1979
Total votes	43,122		50,206
Turnout	66·3%		73·1%
C	19,243	44·6%	47·5%
Lab	15,216	35·3%	35·1%
L	8,663	20·1%	15·7%
Ecology	—	—	1·7%
C maj	4,027	9·3%	12·4%
Swing		−2·1%	+1·5%

Sir Donald Kaberry, member, Select Committee on Nationalised Industries since November, 1974; member, Speaker's panel of chairmen. Elected, 1950. Vice-chairman, Conservative Party Organisation, 1955-61; solicitor and company director. Member, Law Society. B August, 1907; ed Leeds Grammar School. Parliamentary Secretary, Board of Trade, April-October, 1955; assistant Government whip, 1952-55. Chairman, Association of Conservative Clubs, since 1961.

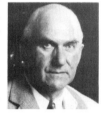

Mr Peter O'Grady, a service manager in the furnishing industry, contested Ripon, 1964. B September, 1926; ed elementary school, Leeds College of Technology, Leeds College of Music. UCATT.

Mr Laurence Keats, aged 50, is a lecturer. Ed Birmingham University. Contested local government elections.

LEEDS, South

Electorate 50,119   1974: 52,700

*Rees, M. (Lab)	22,388
Ratcliffe, R. (C)	8,058
Hurst, F. (L)	3,568
Spink, B. (Nat Front)	416

Lab majority	14,330

No Change

	1974		1979
Total votes	33,604		34,430
Turnout	63·8%		68·7%
Lab	21,653	64·4%	65·0%
C	6,388	19·0%	23·4%
L	5,563	16·6%	10·4%
Nat Front	—	—	1·2%
Lab maj	15,265	45·4%	41·6%
Swing		−5·2%	+1·9%

Mr **Merlyn Rees** was Home Secretary, 1976-79 and Secretary of State for Northern Ireland, 1974-76. Chief Opposition spokesman on Northern Ireland, 1972-74; an Opposition spokesman on the Home Office, 1970-72; Under-Secretary, Home Office, 1968-70; Under-Secretary for Defence for the RAF, 1966-68; Under-Secretary for Defence for the Army,

1965-66. Returned at a by-election in June, 1963; contested Harrow, East, 1955 and 1959. Economics lecturer. B December, 1920; ed Harrow Weald Grammar School, Goldsmith's College and London School of Economics. NUT and GMWU.

Mr **Richard Ratcliffe,** managing director. B 1937; ed Harrow County Grammar School for Boys, Queen Mary College, University of London. Member Woodstock Conservative Association since 1968; vice-chairman, North Oxfordshire Conservative Association, since 1976.

LEEDS, South-East

Electorate 43,472   1974: 49,787

*Cohen, S. (Lab)	15,921
Sexton, Mrs M. (C)	6,549
Clay, Miss M. G. (L)	5,430
Rodgers, J. M. (Comm)	190
Flint, P. (Nat Front)	168

Lab majority	9,372

No Change

	1974		1979
Total votes	28,050		27,258
Turnout	56·3%		65·0%
Lab	17,160	61·2%	56·3%
C	6,144	21·9%	23·2%
L	4,429	15·8%	19·2%
Comm	317	1·1%	0·7%
Nat Front	—		0·6%
Lab maj	11,016	39·3%	33·1%
Swing		−5·6%	+3·1

Mr **Stanley Cohen,** elected in 1970, has been a delegate, Consultative Assembly, Council of Europe and WEU, since 1974. British Railways clerical officer, 1951-70. Elected in 1970; contested Barkston Ash, 1966. B July, 1927; ed St Patrick and St Charles Roman Catholic Schools, Leeds. Member, Leeds City

Council, since 1952. Member, Duke of Edinburgh's Commonwealth study conference to Australia, 1968. Sponsored by TSSA.

Mrs **May Sexton** contested the seat, October and February, 1974. Director of the YWCA, Leeds. Member, Leeds City Council, since 1960. B 1924; ed Belle Vue Road School.

Miss **Margaret Clay,** careers advisor, contested the seat, February and October 1974. B April, 1947; ed Sheffield and Leeds Universities. Member, Leeds District Council, since 1978. NATFHE.

Mr **James Rodgers,** an English teacher in a technical college. Aged 29; ed Leeds University. Co-founder and secretary, City and Woodhouse Ward Campaign for Racial Harmony. Member, Yorkshire District Committee, Communist Party. NATFHE.

LEEDS, West

Electorate 58,798   1974: 60,402

*Dean, J. (Lab)	21,290
Simmonds, H. (C)	11,626
Greenfield, C. (L)	9,734
Duckenfield, J. (Nat Front)	466

Lab majority	9,664

No Change

	1974		1979
Total votes	41,638		43,116
Turnout	68·9%		73·3%
Lab	20,669	49·6%	49·4%
L	13,062	31·4%	22·6%
C	7,907	19·0%	27·0%
Nat Front	—		1·1%
Lab maj	7,607	18·2%	22·4%
Swing		−6·5%	+4·1%

Mr **Joseph Dean,** an engineer, was elected in February, 1974. B June, 1922; ed St Anne's Roman Catholic School, Manchester. Member, Services Committee. Member, Manchester City Council, 1960-74. Vice-chairman, PLP housing and construction group, 1977. Spon-

sored by AUEW.

Mr **Hugh Simmonds,** solicitor, farm director and former computer systems analyst. B April, 1948; ed Merchant Taylors' School and the College of Law. Mayor, Beaconsfield, 1976. Member, Beaconsfield Urban District Council, 1971-74, Beaconsfield Town Council, since 1973; Beaconsfield District Council, since 1976. Treasurer, Selsdon Group, since 1974.

Mr **Christopher Greenfield,** teacher, contested Leeds, North-East, February and October, 1974. Member, Leeds City Council, 1973-76 and of West Yorkshire County Council since 1976. Vice-president, Leeds University Union, 1970-71. Member, NUT. B December, 1948; ed Kingswood Grammar School, Gloucester, and Leeds University.

LEEK

Electorate 87,502   1974: 83,930

*Knox, D. L. (C)	36,508
Fisher, M. (Lab)	25,937
Conway, Mrs M. (L)	6,474
Bailey, C. I. (Ratepayer)	1,451

C majority	10,571

No Change

	1974		1979
Total votes	65,883		70,370
Turnout	78·5%		80·4%
C	30,796	46·7%	51·9%
Lab	26,472	40·2%	36·9%
L	8,615	13·1%	9·2%
Ratepayer	—		2·1%
C maj	4,324	6·5%	15·0%
Swing		−0·9%	+4·2%

Mr David Knox, economist and management consultant, won the seat for the Conservatives in 1970. A vice-chairman of the Conservative Party, 1974-75. Contested Birmingham Stechford, 1964 and 1966; Nuneaton by-election, 1967. B May, 1933; ed Lockerbie Academy, Dumfries Academy and London University. Joint Secretary, Conservative Finance Committee, 1972-73; secretary, Conservative trade committee, 1974; joint secretary, Conservative employment committee, since 1976. Member, Select Committee on European legislation, since 1976.

Mr Mark Fisher, principal of an education centre. B October, 1944; ed Eton and Trinity College, Cambridge. NUT.

Mrs Megan Conway, playgroup supervisor and part-time barmaid. Councillor since 1976. Aged 32.

LEICESTER, East

Electorate 67,269   1974: 63,899

*Bradley, T. G. (Lab)	23,844
Waterhouse, M. (C)	20,988
Andrews, B. (L)	4,623
Calver, B. J. (Nat Front)	1,385
Lab majority	2,856

No Change

	1974		1979
Total votes	46,200		50,840
Turnout	72·3%		75·6%
Lab	20,688	44·8%	46·9%
C	16,877	36·5%	41·3%
L	5,668	12·3%	9·1%
Nat Front	2,967	6·4%	2·7%
Lab maj	3,811	8·3%	5·6%
Swing		−2·7%	+1·3%

Mr Tom Bradley, a railway clerk, was an Opposition spokesman on transport, 1970-74. Elected, July, 1962, in by-election; contested Rutland and Stamford, 1950, 1951 and 1955, and Preston, South in 1959. B April, 1926; ed Kettering Central School. President, Transport Salaried Staffs' Association, 1964-77; treasurer, 1961-64; acting general secretary January-May, 1977 when defeated in election for post of general secretary. Member, Labour Party national executive, since 1966. Chairman, Labour Party, 1975-76. Chairman, Kettering Town Football Club. Sponsored by TSSA.

Mr Michael Waterhouse, commercial banker, is Assistant Vice-President with the Morgan Guaranty Trust Company with special responsibilities for the building products, chemical and pharmaceutical industries. B May, 1949; ed Eton and Trinity College, Cambridge.

Mr Basil Andrews, journalist, and member, Leicestershire County Council, 1967-77. B July, 1919; ed Coopers' Company's School, Bow. NUJ.

LEICESTER, South

Electorate 70,714   1974: 72,558

*Marshall, J. (Lab)	24,548
Godsall, R. (C)	22,550
Pick, J. (L)	4,856
Cartwright, A. R. (Nat Front)	940
Lab majority	1,998

No Change

	1974		1979
Total votes	49,960		52,894
Turnout	68·9%		74·8%
Lab	21,588	43·2%	46·4%
C	20,455	40·9%	42·6%
L	5,709	11·4%	9·2%
Nat Front	2,072	4·1%	1·8%
Comm Pe	136	0·3%	—
Lab maj	1,133	2·3%	3·8%
Swing		−2·8%	+0·8%

Mr James Marshall, lecturer, was elected in October 1974; contested the seat in February, 1974, and Harborough, 1970. Government whip. B March, 1941; ed Sheffield City Grammar School and Leeds University. Member, Leicester City Council, 1971-76 (leader, 1974); Leeds City Council, 1965-68. Chairman PLP East Midlands Group. NUAAW.

Mr Raymond Godsall is a senior executive in an industrial company. B October, 1937; ed Wycliffe. Gloucester Technical Grammar School, Cranfield and University of Birmingham and Aston. Former chairman, Birdingbury and Marton branch of Rugby Conservative Association. Vice-chairman, Birdingbury Parish Council.

Mr John Pick, company director and author, contested Melton, 1970, February and October, 1974. B December, 1921; ed Sidcot School, Somerset and Emmanuel College, Cambridge. Former chairman, East Midlands Region Liberal Party.

LEICESTER, West

Electorate 67,209   1974: 64,650

*Janner, G. E. (Lab)	26,032
Goobey, A. R. (C)	17,194
Lycett, A. (L)	4,032
Ash, P. (Nat Front)	1,308
Lab majority	8,838

No Change

	1974		1979
Total votes	44,240		48,566
Turnout	68·4%		72·3%
Lab	23,406	52·9%	53·6%
C	13,446	30·4%	35·4%
L	5,135	11·6%	8·3%
Nat Front	2,253	5·1%	2·7%
Lab maj	9,960	22·5%	18·2%
Swing		−2·3%	+2·1%

Mr Greville Janner, QC, writer and lecturer, was elected in 1970; contested Wimbledon, 1955. B July, 1928; ed Bishop's College School, Quebec; St Paul's School, London; Trinity Hall, Cambridge, and Harvard Law School. President of the Cambridge Union and Chairman of the University Labour Club. Member, Joint Committee on Consolidation Bills since 1974. Public Accounts Committee, 1970-74. Chairman, all-party industrial safety group. Vice-chairman, all-party retirement group; all-party committee for the Release of Soviet Jewry. Vice-president, Board of Deputies of British Jews. NUJ.

Mr Alastair Goobey, investment manager with investment trust. B December, 1945; ed Marlborough College and Trinity College, Cambridge. Member, Bow Group, since 1971. Co-Author of Bow Group pamphlets.

Mr Alan Lycett, computer operator. B December, 1948; ed King Edward VII Grammar School, Coalville, Leicestershire.

LEIGH

Electorate 66,603   1974: 64,493

Cunliffe, L. (Lab)	27,736
Shaw, D. (C)	18,713
Godwin, M. (L)	4,796
Lab majority	9,023

No Change

	1974		1979	
Total votes	48,077		51,245	
Turnout	73.9%		76.9%	
Lab	27,036	56.2%	54.1%	
C	12,401	25.8%	36.5%	
L	8,640	18.0%	9.4%	
Lab maj	14,635	30.4%	17.6%	
Swing		−2.0%	+6.4%	

Mr Lawrence Cunliffe, an engineer with the National Coal Board. B 1929. Sponsored by NUM.

Mr David Shaw, a chartered accountant. B 1950; ed Broomfield House, King's College School, and the City of London Polytechnic. Member, Royal Borough of Kingston upon Thames Council. Former treasurer, Twickenham Constituency Young Conservatives.

Mr Michael Godwin, lift engineer. Aged 49.

LEOMINSTER

Electorate 48,211   1974: 44,055

*Temple-Morris, P. (C)	21,126
Pincham, R. J. (L)	16,261
Dobbs, P. J. (Lab)	2,099
C majority	4,865

No Change

	1974		1979	
Total votes	34,527		39,486	
Turnout	78.4%		81.9%	
C	15,741	45.6%	53.5%	
L	15,162	43.9%	41.2%	
Lab	3,624	10.5%	5.3%	
C maj	579	1.7%	12.3%	
Swing		0.3%	+6.5%	

Mr Peter Temple-Morris, elected February, 1974. Barrister. B February, 1938; ed Malvern and St Catherine's College, Cambridge. Contested Norwood, Lambeth, 1970, and Newport, 1964 and 1966. Secretary, Conservative Party transport and legal committees; British-Iranian and British-Lebanese parliamentary groups. Executive member, British branch, Inter-Parliamentary Union. Chairman, Bow Group home affairs standing committee. Member, Royal Institute of International Affairs. Former chairman, Cambridge University Conservative Association.

Mr Patrick Dobbs, farmer. B December, 1935; ed London University (Wye College). NUAAW.

Mr Roger Pincham, contested the seat, February and October, 1974 and 1970. B October, 1935; ed Wimbledon Park School and Kingston Grammar School. Partner, Phillips and Drew, stockbrokers.

LEWES

Electorate 76,290   1974: 72,060

*Rathbone, J. R. (C)	33,992
Hook, G. (L)	12,279
Forrester, T. (Lab)	11,152
Webb, Mrs B. (Nat Front)	764
C majority	21,713

No Change

	1974		1979
Total votes	53,186		58,187
Turnout	73.8%		76.3%
C	27,588	51.9%	58.4%
L	13,741	25.8%	21.1%
Lab & Coop	11,857	22.3%	19.2%
Nat Front	—	—	1.3%
C maj	13,847	26.1%	37.3%
Swing		−2.2%	+4.8%

Mr Timothy Rathbone was elected February, 1974. B March, 1933; ed Eton and Christ Church, Oxford, and Harvard Business School. Advertising director, Charles Barker ABH International Ltd; deputy chairman, Ayer Barker Hegemann Ltd. Secretary, Conservative media committee. Member, National Committee for Electoral Reform. Chief Publicity and Public Relations Officer, Conservative Central Office, 1966-68.

Mr Gordon Hook, teacher, contested Lewes, October, 1974. Deacon, Eastgate Baptist Church, Lewes. Former county rugby player. Lt RNR/CCF. B October, 1945; ed Sir Thomas Rich's Grammar School, Gloucester.

Mr Tom Forrester, an industrial journalist. B 1949. NUJ.

LEWISHAM, Deptford

Electorate 56,096   1974: 61,210

*Silkin, J. E. (Lab)	19,391
Grant, D. (C)	11,638
Rowden, N. (L)	2,774
Mitchell, Dr R. (Nat Front)	1,490
Maguire, Mrs J. (Soc Unity)	274
Dacres, G. (WRP)	198
Lab majority	7,753

No Change

	1974		1979
Total votes	35,818		35,765
Turnout	58·5%		63·8%
Lab	21,045	58·8%	54·2%
C	8,111	22·6%	32·5%
L	4,931	13·8%	7·8%
Nat Front	1,731	4·8%	4·2%
Soc Unity	—	—	0·8%
WRP	—	—	0·6%
Lab maj	12,934	36·2%	21·7%

Mr John Silkin was Minister of Agriculture, Fisheries and Food, 1976-79. Minister for Planning and Local Government, Department of Environment, from March 1974 to 1976, with a seat in the Cabinet from October 1974. Opposition spokesman on social services, 1972-74, and on local government and development, 1970-72. Returned at a by-election in 1963. Minister of Public Building and Works, 1969-70; Parliamentary Secretary to the Treasury, Deputy Leader of the House and Government Chief Whip, 1966-69; Treasury of the Household and deputy Chief Whip, April-July, 1966; Lord Commissioner of the Treasury (Whip), 1966; Government whip, 1964-66. Contested St Marylebone, 1950; Woolwich, West, 1951, and Nottingham, South, 1959. Solicitor. B March, 1923; ed Dulwich College; University of Wales, and Trinity Hall, Cambridge. Sponsored by TGWU.

Mr David Grant, economist with Messrs Fielding, Newson-Smith & Co. (stockbrokers). B November, 1947; ed Cardiff High School and Queen's College, Cambridge. Former chairman, Cardiff Central Young Conservatives; former secretary, Paris Bow Group. Member, Hornsey Conservative Association, City Conservative Forum. Chairman, London Conservative Parliamentary Candidates' Association.

Mr Gilbert Dacres, aged 28, freelance typographic designer. Ed Camberwell School of Arts and Crafts after coming to England from Jamaica.

LEWISHAM, East

Electorate 67,066   1974: 69,540

*Moyle, R. D. (Lab)	22,916
Malins, H. (C)	21,323
Forrest, J. (L)	4,265
Ellis, M. (Nat Front)	1,168
Harewood, H. (WRP)	190
Lab majority	1,593

No Change

	1974		1979
Total votes	47,817		59,862
Turnout	68·8%		74·3%
Lab	24,350	50·9%	46·0%
C	15,398	32·2%	42·8%
L	8,069	16·9%	8·6%
Nat Front	—	—	2·3%
WRP	—	—	0·4%
Lab maj	8,952	18·7%	3·2%
Swing		−3·5%	+7·7%

Mr Roland Moyle, Minister of State for Health in the DHSS 1976-79; Minister of State for Northern Ireland, 1974-76, and Parliamentary Secretary, Ministry of Agriculture, Fisheries and Food, 1974, was elected for Lewisham, East in February, 1974; MP for Lewisham, North, 1966-74. Opposition spokesman on higher education, 1971-74. Barrister and former industrial relations executive with gas and electricity industries. B March, 1928; ed elementary schools in Bexleyhealth, Kent; county school Llanidloes, Montgomeryshire; University College of Wales, Aberystwyth, Trinity Hall, Cambridge, and Gray's Inn. Member, Select Committee on Race Relations and Immigration, 1968-72. Vice-chairman, PLP defence committee, 1968-72. Sponsored by NUPE.

Mr Humfrey Malins, solicitor, contested Liverpool, Toxteth, in February and October, 1974. B July, 1945; ed St John's School, Leatherhead, Brasenose College, Oxford. Member, Mole Valley District Council, since 1973. Former chairman, Dorking Young Conservatives; Member, South East Area Provincial Conservative Council. Played for Southern Counties Rugby team against the New Zealand All Blacks, 1972; also played for Oxford University and Richmond.

Mr James Forrest, journalist. B February, 1947; ed Allan Glen's School, Glasgow; Glasgow University. NUJ.

Mr Herbert Harewood, aged 40, Post Office worker. Born in Barbados. UPOW.

LEWISHAM West

Electorate 59,292   1974: 62,435

*Price, C. (Lab)	20,932
Kemp, N. P. (C)	19,882
Payne, G. A. (L)	3,350
Williams, P. (Nat Front)	901
Lab majority	1,050

No Change

	1974		1979
Total votes	43,741		45,065
Turnout	70·1%		76·0%
Lab	21,102	48·2%	46·4%
C	15,573	35·6%	44·1%
L	5,592	13·6%	7·4%
Nat Front	1,114	2·5%	2·0%
Lab maj	5,529	12·6%	2·3%
Swing		−3·8%	+5·1%

Mr Christopher Price, freelance journalist and broadcaster, was elected in February, 1974; represented Birmingham, Perry Barr, 1966-70; contested Shipley, 1964. Member, European Parliament, 1977-78. B January, 1932; ed Leeds Grammar School and Queen's College, Oxford (secretary, Labour Club, 1953). Member, Sheffield City Council, 1962-66. Editor, *New Education* 1967-68; education correspondent, *New Statesman* 1968-74. NUJ.

Mr Noel Kemp contested Goole in February and October, 1974 and Northamptonshire, South, by-election in 1962. B December, 1937; ed Westminster School and Christ Church, Oxford. Broadcaster, writer and organizer, union of independent companies; City editor of *The Spectator,* 1971-72. Member, Trust House Forte management, 1973-75. Member, Equity, West of England organizer for Help the Aged. Former treasurer, Oxford Union Society. Member, executive committee, Cities of London and Westminster Conservative Association, 1964-69.

Mr Godfrey Payne, sales supervisor, contested Gillingham, 1964 and 1966. B March 1933; ed Welling County Modern School and Open University.

LICHFIELD AND TAMWORTH

Electorate 101,343   1974: 89,752

Heddle, J. (C)	41,454
*Grocott, B. J. (Lab)	33,006
Rule, P. (L)	7,408
Wallace, Mrs P. (Nat Front)	475
C majority	8,448

C gain from Lab

	1974		1979
Total votes	70,127		82,343
Turnout	78·1%		81·3%
Lab	29,872	42·6%	40·1%
C	29,541	42·1%	50·3%
L	10,714	15·3%	9·0%
Nat Front	—	—	0·6%
Lab maj	331	0·5%	
C maj	—	—	10·2%
Swing	—	−1·5%	+5·3%

Mr John Heddle, consultant surveyor and Lloyds underwriter, contested Bolton, East, October, 1974, and Gateshead, West, February, 1974. B September, 1941; ed Bishop's Stortford College and College of Estate Management (London University). Member, Kent County Council, since 1973. Freeman of the City of London. Member, Bow Group and 1900 Club. Fellow, Incorporated Society of Valuers and Auctioneers (National chairman associate members, 1968-69), Fellow Rating and Valuation Association; Fellow Institute of Directors; Fellow Royal Society of Arts.

Mr Bruce Grocott, a polytechnic lecturer, was elected in October 1974; contested the seat, February 1974, and South-West Hertfordshire, 1970. Joint secretary, all-party penal reform group. Member Select Committee on Overseas Developments. B November, 1940; ed Hemel Hempstead Grammar School and Leicester and Manchester Universities. Bromsgrove urban district councillor, 1971-74. Sponsored by ASTMS.

Mr Philip Rule, company chairman, contested the seat, October, 1974. B June, 1936; ed Stowmarket Grammar School, Suffolk, and Hull University.

LINCOLN

Electorate 55,194   1974: 53,022

Carlisle, K. (C)	17,777
*Jackson, Miss M. M. (Lab)	17,175
Melton, K. (L)	5,638
Stockdale, F. (Dem Lab)	1,743
Noble, J. (Nat Front)	107
Kyle, T. (Rev Ref)	77
C majority	602

C gain from Lab

	1974		1979
Total votes	39,635		42,577
Turnout	74·8%		77·0%
Lab	14,698	37·1%	40·4%
Social Dem	13,714	34·6%	—
C	11,223	28·3%	41·8%
L	—	—	13·3%
Dem Lab	—	—	4·1%
Nat Front	—	—	0·3%
Rev Ref	—	—	0·2%
Lab maj	984	2·5%	1·4%
C maj	—	—	1·4%
Swing	—	−4·2%	+5·1%

Mr Kenneth Carlisle, farmer and barrister. B March, 1941; ed Harrow, Magdalen College, Oxford and London Business School. Employed by Brooke Bond Liebig, 1966-74, working in Argentina and Paraguay. Chairman Stanton branch, Bury St Edmunds Conservative Association. Member Bow Group; NFU. Set up research with Cambridge University on the long-term effect of forestry on the flora of old deciduous woodlands in Suffolk.

Miss Margaret Jackson was Under-Secretary for Education and Science 1976-79; assistant Government whip, 1975-76. Elected, October 1974; contested the seat, February, 1974. Metallurgist. B January, 1943; ed St Mary's RC Primary School, Ashton-under-Lyme, Notre Dame High School, Norwich, and Manchester College of Science and Technology. Research assistant, Labour Party, 1970-74. Experimental officer, Department of Metallurgy, Manchester University, 1967-70. Member, House of Commons Services Committee, 1974-75. Political adviser, Ministry of Overseas Development, February to October 1974. Sponsored by TGWU.

Mr Keith Melton, senior lecturer in marketing. Member, Staythorpe Parish Council. B June, 1947; ed North Kesteven Grammar School and Manchester University. NATFHE.

LIVERPOOL, Edge Hill

Electorate 35,350   1974: 40,970

*Alton, D. (L)	12,701
Wareing, R. (Lab)	8,453
Ward, N. (C)	3,098
Hawksley, H. (Nat Front)	152

Lab majority	4,248

No Change

	1974		1979
Total votes	25,083		24,404
Turnout	61·2%		69·0%
Lab	13,023	51·9%	34·6%
L	6,852	27·3%	52·0%
C	5,208	20·8%	12·7%
Nat Front	—	—	0·6%
Lab maj	6,171	24·6%	—
L maj	—	—	17·4%
Swing		−4·3%	—

March, 1979, by-election: Total vote 20,199 (56.6%).—L. 12,945 (64.1%), Lab 4,812 (23.8%), C 1,906 (9.4%), Law and Order 337 (1.8%), Soc Unity 127 (0.6%), Gay L 40 (0.2%).—L maj 8,133 (40.3%).

Mr David Alton, teacher, won the seat for the Liberals at the by-election on March 29, 1979, and took his place in the Commons on April 1, two days before it adjourned for the general election. Contested the seat, February and October, 1974. City councillor, 1972-78. B March, 1951; ed Campion School, Hornchurch and Christ's College of Education, Liverpool. NUT.

Mr Robert Wareing, lecturer, fought the March, 1979, by-election; contested Berwick-upon-Tweed, 1970. B August, 1930; ed Alsop High School, Liverpool and Bolton College of Education. Principal lecturer, Central Liverpool College of Further Education. President, Liverpool District Labour Party since 1972. Chairman, Merseyside County Labour Party, 1976-78. NATFHE.

Mr Nicholas Ward, chartered accountant and chief executive of a Liverpool based group of companies. Fought March 1979 by-election. B 1941; ed Charterhouse and European Institute of Business Administration, Fontainbleu. Treasurer, City of Chester Conservative Association.

LIVERPOOL, Garston

Electorate 79,248   1974: 81,030

Thornton, G. M. (C)	28,105
*Loyden, E. (Lab)	25,318
Davison, W. J. (L)	4,890
Kelly, T. (WRP)	142

C majority	2,787

C gain from Lab

	1974		1979
Total votes	58,279		58,455
Turnout	71·9%		73·8%
Lab	27,857	47·8%	43·3%
C	24,557	42·1%	48·1%
L	5,865	10·1%	8·4%
WRP	—	—	0·2%
Lab maj	3,300	5·7%	—
C maj	—	—	4·8%
Swing		−2·3%	+5·2%

Mr George Thornton, a River Mersey pilot. B April, 1939; ed Wallasey Grammar School. Member Wallasey County Borough Council, 1965-67; Wirral Metropolitan Council, since 1973; leader of council until 1977. Conservative leader on AMA education committee; member of Burnham Committee and North-West Economic Planning Council.

Mr Edward Loyden was elected in February, 1974. Member, Liverpool City and District Councils, 1960-74, and Merseyside Metropolitan Council, 1973-74. Port worker; member, national committee, docks section, TGWU. B May, 1923; ed Friary RC elementary school. President, Liverpool Trade Council, 1967, and Merseyside Trades Council, 1974. Sponsored by TGWU. Vice-chairman, TGWU Parliamentary Committee.

Mr Wilfrid Davison, lecturer, contested Doncaster, February and October, 1974. B June, 1938; ed St Mary's College, Liverpool, and Liverpool University.

Mr Terence Kelly, aged 35, is in the fire service. Secretary, Crewe Fire Brigades' Union.

LIVERPOOL, Kirkdale

Electorate 43,304   1974: 45,344

*Dunn, J. A. (Lab)	17,043
Fitzsimmons, Mrs M. (C)	9,334
Mahon, P. (L)	3,819
Williams, W. (Nat Front)	198

Lab majority	7,709

No Change

	1974		1979
Total Votes	28,799		30,394
Turnout	63·5%		70·2%
Lab	17,686	61·4%	56·1%
C	8,205	28·5%	30·7%
L	2,908	10·1%	12·6%
Nat Front	—	—	0·7%
Lab maj	9,481	32·9%	25·4%
Swing		−6·1%	+3·7%

Mr James Dunn was Under Secretary of State for Northern Ireland 1976-79. Lord Commissioner of the Treasury (Government whip) 1974-76; Opposition whip 1971-74. Engineer. Elected in 1964. B January, 1926; ed St Teresa's School, Liverpool, and LSE. Member, Liverpool City Council, 1958-65; Commons Estimates Committee, 1964-70; Procedure Committee, 1964-67, North Atlantic Assembly, 1968-74. Sponsored by TGWU.

Mr Myra Fitzsimmons, part-time business administrator. B May, 1920; ed Liverpool Church of England Voluntary School and Queen Mary High School. Former part-time non-teaching assistant, Liverpool Education Authority. Member, Liverpool County Borough Council, 1969-74; Liverpool District Council, since 1975. Vice-president, National Education Association.

Mr Paul Mahon, partner in family business. Aged 28.

LIVERPOOL, Scotland Exchange

Electorate 32,303   1974: 35,146

*Parry, R. (Lab)	13,920
Bligh, J. M. (C)	2,264
Davies, C. (L)	1,939
O'Hara, R. (Comm)	421

Lab majority	11,656

No Change

	1974		1979
Total votes	18,888		18,544
Turnout	53·7%		57·4%
Lab	15,154	80·2%	75·1%
C	2,234	11·8%	12·2%
L	944	5·0%	10·5%
Comm	556	2·9%	2·3%
Lab maj	12,920	68·4%	62·9%
Swing		−3·9%	+2·7%

Mr Robert Parry, returned in February, 1974; represented Liverpool, Exchange, 1970-74. Trade union official. B January, 1933; ed Bishop Goss Roman Catholic School, Liverpool. Chairman, Merseyside group of Labour MPs, since 1975. Member, Liverpool City Council, 1963-74. Full-time officer for NUPE, 1960-68, and now sponsored by TGWU.

Mr John Bligh, assistant teacher and former headmaster. B July, 1927; ed Downside School, Bath, and Neville's Cross Teacher Training College, Durham. Chairman and founder, Merseyside branch, Monday Club. Member, North West Area Conservative advisory committee on education.

Mr Christopher Davies, teacher. B July, 1954; ed Cheadle Hulme School, Stockport, and Cambridge University.

Mr Roger O'Hara, aged 46, area secretary of the Communist Party. Governor of St Finbar's and St Nicholas' Roman Catholic Schools. AUEW.

LIVERPOOL, Toxteth

Electorate 41,859   1974: 45,883

*Crawshaw, R. (Lab)	14,833
Shone, A. W. (C)	8,690
Addison, Miss R. (L)	3,206
Adams, P. (Soc Unity)	238
Elliott, Ms D. (WRP)	148

Lab majority	6,143

No Change

	1974		1979
Total votes	26,915		27,115
Turnout	58·7%		64·8%
Lab	15,312	56·9%	54·7%
C	8,062	30·0%	32·0%
L	3,176	11·8%	11·8%
WRP	365	1·4%	0·5%
Soc Unity	—		0·9%
Lab maj	7,250	26·9%	22·7%
Swing		−4·2%	+2·1%

Mr Richard Crawshaw, was elected Second Deputy Chairman of Ways and Means and a Deputy Speaker in May, 1979, after being a member of the Speaker's panel of chairmen. Elected in 1964. Barrister (Inner Temple, 1948). B September, 1917; ed Pendleton Grammar School, Tatterford School, Pembroke College, Cambridge and London University. Member, Liverpool City Council, 1957-65. In 1972 established record for non-stop walking of 255.8 miles.

Mr Anthony Shone, Chairman of a Liverpool flour-milling company. Aged 40. Former member, Merseyside Chamber of Commerce Council; former president, Liverpool and District Millers' Association; member, Executive committee of Liverpool Council of Social Service.

Miss Ruth Addison, lecturer and administrator, B January, 1947; ed Manchester High School for Girls; York University and Bolton College of Education. NATFHE.

LIVERPOOL, Walton

Electorate 50,303   1974: 51,967

*Heffer, E. S. (Lab)	20,231
Gould, R. (C)	12,673
Cardwell, N. (L)	3,479
Haire, W. F. (Nat Front)	254

Lab majority	7,558

No Change

	1974		1979
Total votes	35,495		36,637
Turnout	68·3%		72·8%
Lab	20,568	57·9%	55·2%
C	10,706	30·2%	34·6%
L	4,221	11·9%	9·5%
Nat Front	—		0·7%
Lab maj	9,862	27·7%	20·6%
Swing		−2·9%	+3·5%

Mr Eric Heffer was appointed Minister of State for Industry, March, 1974 and resigned in 1975. In Opposition Front Bench team on Industrial Relations Bill, 1970-71. Opposition spokesman on employment, 1971-73. Member, Shadow Cabinet, 1972. Elected for Walton in 1964. Carpenter-joiner and journalist. B January, 1922; elementary education. Member, Labour Party national executive committee, since 1975. Member and sponsored by, UCATT, formerly ASW. Vice-chairman, League Against Cruel Sports.

Mr Ronald Gould, retail chemist. B December 1934; ed Liverpool Institute and the School of Pharmacy, Liverpool. Member, Liverpool City Council; Walton Conservative Association, Inland Waterways Association.

Mr Neil Cardwell, journalist. Aged 24.

LIVERPOOL, Wavertree

Electorate 59,040   1974: 59,720

*Steen, A. D. (C)	21,770
Morris, R. (Lab & Co-op)	14,828
Roberts, C. W. (L)	6,705
C majority	6,942

No Change

	1974		1979
Total votes	41,380		43,303
Turnout	69·3%		73·3%
C	18,971	45·8%	50·3%
Lab & Co-op	16,216	39·2%	34·2%
L	6,193	15·0%	15·5%
C maj	2,755	6·6%	16·1%
Swing		−2·7%	+4·7%

Mr Anthony Steen, community worker and youth leader, barrister (Gray's Inn, 1962) and Lloyd's underwriter, was elected in February, 1974. B July 1940 ed Westminster School. Member Select Committee on Race Relations and Immigration. Chairman, Conservative Party policy group on young people. Secretary, Conservative urban affairs group. Founder and first director of Task Force 1964-68, and of Young Volunteer Force Foundation 1968-74.

Mr Roy Morris, public relations officer, fought the seat, October 1974; contested Weston-Super-Mare, February, 1974. B March, 1932; ed Exeter School and Exeter Technical College. Member, Bristol City Council, since 1963; Avon County Council, 1972-76; National Union of Co-op Officials.

Mr Charles Roberts, senior assistant registrar, contested Clitheroe in both 1974 general elections. B July 1943; ed the Royal Masonic School and St David's College, Lampeter.

LIVERPOOL, West Derby

Electorate 57,973   1974: 58,890

*Ogden, E. (Lab)	22,576
Hudson, D. P. M. (C)	14,356
Humphreys, Ms A. (L)	3,765
Lab majority	8,220

No Change

	1974		1979
Total votes	39,624		40,697
Turnout	67·3%		70·2%
Lab	23,964	60·5%	55·5%
C	11,445	28·9%	35·3%
L	4,215	10·6%	9·3%
Lab maj	12,519	31·6%	20·2%
Swing		−3·8%	+5·7%

Mr Eric Ogden, a former miner, was elected in 1964. B August, 1923; ed Queen Elizabeth's Grammar School, Middleton, Leigh Technical College and Wigan Mining College. Sponsored by NUM. Member, Middleton Borough Council, 1958-64. Parliamentary Adviser to the Council of the Pharmaceutical Society of Great Britain. Secretary, all-party Channel Tunnel Group.

Mr David Hudson, director of housebuilding companies. B March 1939; ed Wellington College; Université de Paris à la Sorbonne; Trinity Hall, Cambridge; European Institute of Business Administration, Fontainbleau.

LLANELLI

Electorate 64,429   1974: 64,495

*Davies, D. J. D. (Lab)	30,416
Richards, G. D. J. (C)	10,471
Rees, K. D. (L)	5,856
Roberts, H. (Pl Cymru)	3,793
Hitchon, R. E. (Comm)	617
Lab majority	19,945

No Change

	1974		1979
Total votes	49,585		51,153
Turnout	76·9%		79·4%
Lab	29,474	59·4%	59·5%
L	7,173	14·5%	11·4%
Pl Cymru	6,797	13·7%	7·4%
C	6,141	12·4%	20·5%
Comm	—		1·2%
Lab maj	22,301	44·9%	39·0%
Swing		2·1%	+4·0%

Mr Denzil Davies, was Minister of State, Treasury, 1975-79. Barrister. Elected in 1970. B October, 1938; ed Carmarthen Grammar School and Pembroke College, Oxford. Lectured at Chicago and Leeds universities. Member, European Secondary Legislation Committee, 1974-75; Select Committee on Wealth Tax, 1974-75. Also served on Public Accounts Committee, Select Commitee on Corporation Tax and Joint Select Committee on Delegated Legislation.

Mr Gwilym Richards, solicitor, contested the seat, February and October, 1974. B March, 1930; ed Llandyssol Grammar School and St Catherine's College, Oxford. Chairman, Carmarthen Conservative Association.

Mr Kenneth Rees, planning engineer and draughtsman. B May, 1944.

Mr Henry Roberts, area manager for a computer company. B July, 1953; ed Caernarvon Grammar School and University College of Swansea.

LONDONDERRY

Electorate 94,770   1974: 93,141

*Ross, W. (Off UU.)	31,592
Logue, H. (SDLP)	19,185
Barr, A. (Alliance)	5,830
McAteer, F. (IIP)	5,489
Melough, E. (Rep Clubs)	888
Webster, B. (Derry Lab)	639

Off UU. majority	12,407

No Change

	1974		1979
Total votes	64,632		63,623
Turnout	69·4%		67·1%
UUUC	35,138	54·4%	—
Off UU	—	—	49·7%
SDLP	26,118	40·4%	30·2%
Repub	2,530	3·9%	1·4%
Lab & TU	846	1·3%	—
UUUC maj	9,020	14·0%	—
Off UU maj	—	—	19·5%
Alliance	—	—	8·6%
IIP	—	—	1·4%
Derry Lab	—	—	1·0%

Mr William Ross, farmer, was elected in February, 1974. Party's spokesman on agriculture and fisheries, and local government Member, Apprentice Boys of Derry, the Orange and Black Institutions; former sec, Mid-Londonderry Constituency Unionist Party B February, 1936; ed Dungiven Primary School.

Mr Hugh Logue, company director and projects manager of the joint EEC—Irish Government combat poverty programme. Economic spokesman for SDLP. Active in civil rights movement; Member NI. Assembly and NI. Convention. Post graduate student in European economics at Dublin University B 1937.

Mr Arthur Barr, a Dupont employee. Returned as Alliance councillor for Londonderry.

Mr Fergus McAteer, accountant. Irish Independence candidate. Member, Derry City Council, since 1973; Western Education and Library Board, since 1973. B 1946. Ed St. Columb's College, Londonderry and University College, Dublin.

Mr Eamonn Melough, played prominent part in organizing civil rights movement in Londonderry. B 1934.

Mr Bill Webster, a full-time trade union official. Secretary, Derry Labour and Trade Union Party.

LOUGHBOROUGH

Electorate 76,455   1974: 70,244

Dorrell, S. (C)	29,788
*Cronin, J. D. (Lab)	24,589
Palmer, R. (L)	6,650
Whitebread, D. (Ecology)	595
Peacock, J. (Nat Front)	484

C majority	5,199

C gain from Lab

	1974		1979
Total votes	55,139		62,106
Turnout	78·5%		81·2%
Lab	22,896	41·5%	39·6%
C	20,521	37·2%	48·0%
L	10,409	18·9%	10·7%
Nat Front	1,215	2·2%	0·8%
Pros Brit	125	0·2%	—
Ecology	—	—	1·0%
Lab maj	2,348	4·3%	8·4%
Swing		−1·6%	+6·3%

Mr Stephen Dorrell, export director and protective clothing manufacturer, contested Kingston-upon-Hull, East, October, 1974. B March, 1952; ed Uppingham and Brasenose College, Oxford. Officer cadet RAF volunteer reserve, 1971-73. Personal assistant to Mr Peter Walker in February, 1974, general election.

Mr John Cronin was elected in 1955. Consultant surgeon and company director. B March, 1916; ed London University. Member, BMA and Parliamentary Committee, COHSE. Former surgeon, Royal Free and Prince of Wales Hospitals. Member, London County Council, 1950-53. Opposition whip, 1959-62. Front bench spokesman for air, 1961-62; spokesman on aviation, 1962-64. Chairman, Anglo-French Parliamentary Relations Committee, secretary 1964-70. Sponsored by COHSE.

Mr David Whitebread, aged 30, teacher. Ed Keele University. Worked for two years in British school in Tehran.

LOUTH

Electorate 73,264   1974: 70,498

*Brotherton, M. L. (C)	25,701
Sellick, J. C. L. (L)	19,026
Betts, C. J. C. (Lab)	12,316
Stokes, C. D. B. (Nat Front)	261

C majority	6,675

No Change

	1974		1979
Total votes	51,505		57,304
Turnout	73·1%		78·2%
C	19,819	38·5%	44·9%
L	16,939	32·9%	33·2%
Lab	14,747	28·6%	21·5%
Nat Front	—	—	0·5%
C maj	2,880	5·6%	11·7%
Swing		−4·0%	+6·7%

Mr Michael Brotherton, an advertising executive with *The Times,* 1967-74. Retired Lieutenant-Commander. Elected October, 1974; contested Deptford, 1970. B May, 1931; ed Prior Park and Royal Naval Colleges Dartmouth and Greenwich. Appointed to Select Committee on Violence in Marriage, February 1975. Served in Royal Navy, 1949-64.

Mr John Sellick, company director with farming interests, contested the seat, February and October, 1974. B October, 1943; ed Knossington Grange, and Oakham School, Rutland.

Mr Clive Betts, local government economist, contested Sheffield, Hallam, October, 1974. Member, Sheffield City Council, since 1976. B January, 1950; ed King Edward VII School, Sheffield, and Pembroke College. TGWU, Nalgo.

LOWESTOFT

Electorate 82,733   1974: 76,936

*Prior, J. M. L. (C)	33,376
Lark, A. (Lab)	25,555
Skelcher, B. (L)	6,783
Pye, T. (Ecology)	435
C majority	7,821

No Change

	1974		1979
Total votes	60,123		66,149
Turnout	78·1%		80·0%
C	25,510	42·4%	50·5%
Lab	23,448	39·0%	38·6%
L	11,165	18·6%	10·3%
Ecology	—	—	0·7%
C maj	2,062	3·4%	11·9%
Swing		−1·2%	+4·2%

Mr James Prior was appointed Secretary of State for Employment, in May 1979. Chief Opposition spokesman on employment, 1974-79 after a short period as spokesman on home affairs. Appointed to Shadow Cabinet in March, 1975; unsuccessfully contested leadership of Conservative Party in February, 1975. Lord President of the Council and Leader  of the House of Commons 1972-74; Minister of Agriculture, Fisheries and Food, 1970-72. Deputy chairman, Conservative Party Organisation, 1972-74. Elected in 1959. Vice-chairman of the Conservative Party, April to August, 1965, when he resigned to become PPS to Mr Edward Heath until 1970. Farmer and land agent. B October, 1927; ed Charterhouse and Pembroke College, Cambridge, Member Select Committee on MPs' Interests 1974. Consultant to Trust Houses Forte since 1974.

Mr Jack Lark, vehicle builder. Leader Labour group, Waveney District and Suffolk County councils; Mayor of Lowestoft, 1972-73. B October, 1936; ed Roman Hill School and Lowestoft College. NUVB and TGWU.

Mr Barrie Skelcher, health physicist and company director. B June, 1932; ed Leicester University College and Birmingham University.

LUDLOW

Electorate 50,413   1974: 48,625

Cockeram, E. (C)	20,906
Robinson, E. (L)	12,524
Wymer, I. K. (Lab)	5,717
Adshead, R. J. (Nat Front)	354
Turner, F. (Ind)	106
C majority	8,382

No Change

	1974		1979
Total votes	36,365		39,607
Turnout	74·8%		78·6%
C	17,124	47·1%	52·8%
L	10,888	29·9%	31·6%
Lab	8,353	23·0%	14·4%
Nat Front	—	—	0·9%
Ind	—	—	0·3%
C maj	6,236	17·2%	21·2%
Swing		−0·5%	+7·1%

Mr Eric Cockeram was MP for Bebington, 1970-74; contested Bedington and Ellesmere Port, February and October, 1974. Chairman of family menswear business. B July, 1924; ed The Leys School, Cambridge. Member, Commons Select Committee on Corporation Tax, 1971. Chairman, Liverpool NHS executive, 1969-70. Former member, board of  governors United Liverpool Hospitals. President, Menswear Association of Britain, 1964-65. Director, Liverpool Trustee Savings Bank.

Mr Eric Robinson, Polytechnic lecturer, contested the seat, February and October, 1974, and Wolverhampton, South-West, 1970. B July, 1930; ed Hanley Grammar School and Edinburgh University. Member, Salop County Council, since 1973. Initiator of national parks campaign, 1973.

Mr Ivor Wymer, principal of a sixth form college, contested South-West Staffordshire, February and October, 1974. B May, 1938; ed Leeds University. NAS/UWT (national executive, 1967-74).

LUTON, East

Electorate 52,427   1974: 53,549

Bright, G. F. J. (C)	17,809
*Clemitson, I. M. (Lab)	16,962
Franks, D. (L)	5,285
Kerry, M. G. (Nat Front)	461
Mitchell, C. T. (Comm)	107
Bardwaj, J. N. (CPPS)	61
Lynn, A. (WRP)	45
C majority	847

C gain from Lab

	1974		1979
Total votes	39,323		40,730
Turnout	73·4%		77·7%
Lab	17,877	45·5%	41·6%
C	14,200	36·1%	43·7%
L	6,947	17·7%	13·0%
Prop Dev	299	0·8%	—
Nat Front	—	—	1·1%
Comm	—	—	0·3%
CPPS	—	—	0·1%
WRP	—	—	0·1%
Lab maj	3,677	9·4%	—
C maj	—	—	2·1%
Swing		−3·1%	+5·7%

Mr Graham Bright, managing director of a food company. Contested Dartford, October, 1974, and Thurrock, February, 1974, and 1970. B 1942; ed Hassenbrook County School and Thurrock Technical College. Served on Thurrock UDC and Essex County Council. Former treasurer, deputy chairman and CPC chairman, Thurrock Conservative Association.

Mr Ivor Clemitson Represented the seat February, 1974-79. Secretary, all-party Industrial Common Ownership Group; member, Select Committee on Parliamentary Commissioner for Administration. B December, 1931; ed Harlington (Beds) County Primary School, Luton Grammar School, London School of Economics and Bishop's Theological College. Research officer, National Graphical Association, 1971-74; Director, Singapore Ind Mission, 1969-70; industrial chaplain, Diocese of St Albans, 1964-69; curate, Christ Church, Bramall Lane, Sheffield. APEX.

Mr David Franks, Merchandising administrator. B October, 1944. ASTMS.

Mr Arthur Lynn, aged 36, employed by Vauxhall Motors, Luton. Member, branch committee and delegate to Luton Trades Council.

Mr Tom Mitchell, secretary of the South East Midlands District of the Communist Party for 22 years. Worked for 28 years in iron and steel jobbing.

LUTON, West

Electorate 61,186   1974: 58,272

Carlisle, J. (C)	21,230
*Sedgemore, B. C. J. (Lab)	20,984
Dolling, M. J. (L)	5,233
How, D. (Nat Front)	701
C majority	246

C gain from Lab

	1974		1979
Total votes	43,654		48,148
Turnout	74·9%		78·7%
Lab	20,402	46·7%	43·6%
C	13,963	32·0%	44·1%
L	9,289	21·3%	10·9%
Nat Front	—		1·5%
Lab maj	6,439	14·7%	—
C maj	—		0·5%
Swing		−2·1%	+7·6%

Mr John Carlisle, commodity trader and member of the London Corn Exchange. B August, 1942; ed Bedford School, St Lawrence College and London University. Chairman, Mid-Bedfordshire Conservative Association, 1974-76. President, Mid-Bedfordshire Young Conservatives. Chairman, Bedfordshire Education Advisory Committee.

Mr Brian Sedgemore, Represented the seat February, 1974-79. Barrister (Middle Temple, 1966). B March, 1937; ed Heles School, Exeter, and Oxford

University. Member, Expenditure Committee; Society of Labour Lawyers; Wandsworth Council, 1971-74. Chairman, Wandsworth Council for Community Relations, 1971-74.

Mr Michael Dolling, taxi proprietor, contested the seat, February and October, 1974. B July, 1938; ed Northfields School, Dunstable. TGWU.

MACCLESFIELD

Electorate 87,864   1974: 80,150

*Winterton, N. R. (C)	40,116
Foster, R. A. (Lab)	16,779
Berry, A. J. (L)	11,726
C majority	23,337

No Change

	1974		1979
Total votes	63,041		68,621
Turnout	78·7%		78·1%
C	31,685	50·3%	58·5%
Lab	18,592	29·5%	24·5%
L	12,764	20·2%	17·1%
C maj	13,093	20·8%	34·0%
Swing		−0·3%	+6·6%

Mr Nicholas Winterton, elected in 1971 by-election, was sales and general manager of a plant hire firm from 1960-71. Contested Newcastle-under-Lyme in October 1969 and in 1970. B March, 1938; ed Bilton Grange Preparatory School and Rugby School. Member, Select Committee on Expenditure, since 1974 and its social services and employment sub committee; was a member of Select Committee on Abortion. Secretary, Conservative education and agriculture, fisheries and food committees. Vice-chairman, all-party textile industry group and of British-Danish parliamentary group.

Mr Ronald Foster, work study officer, North-West Gas; member, Tameside MBC since 1975. B November, 1932; ed St Stephen's, Droylsden, Manchester. Member, Fabian Society, Nalgo.

Mr Anthony Berry, university lecturer, contested the seat, February and October, 1974. B August, 1939; ed St Brendan's College, Bristol and Bath, London, Seattle and Manchester universities.

MAIDSTONE

Electorate 90,125   1974: 88,338

*Wells, J. J. (C)	37,727
Burnett, J. (L)	16,676
Evans, R. (Lab)	16,632
Whiting, D. (Nat Front)	703
C majority	21,051

No Change

	1974		1979
Total votes	65,261		71,738
Turnout	74·1%		77·0%
C	28,852	44·2%	52·6%
L	18,581	28·5%	23·2%
Lab	17,828	27·3%	23·2%
Nat Front	—		1·0%
C maj	10,271	15·7%	29·4%
Swing		−2·4%	+6·2%

Mr **John Wells** was elected in 1959; contested Smethwick, 1955. Former joint vice-chairman of the Conservative backbench agriculture committee; chairman of the horticultural committee, 1965-70. Member, Speaker's panel of chairmen since 1974. Marine engineer; horticulturalist and family company directorships. B

March, 1925; ed Heath Mount School, Hertford, Eton and Corpus Christi College, Oxford.

Mr **John Burnett,** chartered accountant, contested the seat, October, 1974. B October, 1931; ed Liverpool Collegiate School, Colfe's Grammar School, Lewisham. Member, Maidstone Borough Council, since 1973.

Mr **Richard Evans,** Teacher. B May, 1951; ed Sutton Valence School, Kent; John Mason School, Abingdon; Bishop Otter College, Chichester and University of Sussex. NUT.

Mr **Dennis Whiting,** aged 45, is a librarian at the University of Kent. Ed Maidstone Grammar School and Oxford University.

MALDON

Electorate 65,659   1974: 61,725

*Wakeman, J. (C)	29,585
Oliver, R. (Lab)	12,848
Wright, M. (L)	8,730
C majority	16,737

No Change

	1974		1979
Total votes	47,056		51,163
Turnout	76·2%		77·9%
C	20,485	43·5%	57·8%
Lab	14,098	30·0%	25·1%
L	12,473	26·5%	17·1%
C maj	6,387	13·5%	32·7%
Swing		−1·9%	+9·6%

Mr **John Wakeham,** was appointed an assistant Government whip in May 1979. Chartered accountant and chairman of family company. Elected February, 1974; contested Putney, Wandsworth, 1970, and Coventry, East, 1966. B June, 1932; ed Charterhouse. Member, Select Committee on Expenditure and its trade and industry subcommittee.

Secretary, Conservative small business committee.

Mr **Robert Oliver,** work study engineer. B December, 1925; ed Duns Public School and Berwickshire High School. Essex County Councillor, 1973-77. TSSA.

Mr **Michael Wright,** a charity director. Contested Stratford-on-Avon, February and October, 1974. B April, 1926; ed universities of Manchester and Birmingham. Member, Warwickshire County Council, 1973-77.

MANCHESTER, Ardwick

Electorate 44,497   1974: 47,937

*Kaufman, G. B. (Lab)	17,235
Swan, W. R. (C)	9,963
Thomson, P. (L)	2,934
West, J. S. (Soc Unity)	287
Lab majority	7,272

No Change

	1974		1979
Total votes	28,156		30,419
Turnout	58·7%		68·4%
Lab	15,632	55·5%	56·7%
C	8,849	31·4%	32·8%
L	3,675	13·1%	9·6%
Soc Unity	—	—	0·9%
Lab maj	6,783	24·1%	23·9%
Swing		−4·4%	+0·1%

Mr **Gerald Kaufman,** Minister of State, Department of Industry, since 1975-79; formerly Under-Secretary in same department; Under-Secretary, Department of Environment, 1974-75. Former parliamentary press liaison officer for the Labour Party. Elected in 1970; contested Gillingham, 1959, and Bromley, 1955. B June, 1930; Ed Leeds Grammar

School and Queen's College, Oxford. Assistant secretary, Fabian Society, 1954-55; former political correspondent, *New Statesman.*

Mr **William Swan,** chairman and managing director of a chain of piano and organ shops. ed Princess Road School, Manchester. Former member, Manchester City Council and former chairman of constituency association.

MANCHESTER, Blackley

Electorate 52,878   1974: 54,860

Easton, K. (Lab)	20,346
Green, A. (C)	15,842
Ashley, J. (L)	3,868
Wallace, N. (Nat Front)	326
Lab majority	4,504

No Change

	1974		1979
Total votes	38,752		40,382
Turnout	70·6%		76·4%
Lab	19,720	50·9%	50·4%
C	12,601	32·5%	39·2%
L	5,517	14·2%	9·6%
Nat Front	914	2·4%	0·8%
Lab maj	7,119	18·4%	11·2%
Swing		−2·6%	+3·6%

Mr **Kenneth Easton,** planning engineer with GEC, Trafford Park. Aged 51. Member, Manchester City Council, since 1962; deputy leader of council and chairman of education committee. Sponsored by AUEW.

Mr **Arthur Green,** sales manager. B September, 1930; ed Secondary and adult education classes. Member, Greater Manchester County Council, since

1974; Manchester City Council, since 1973.

Mr James Ashley, regional director of a building centre. Contested Manchester, Gorton, 1970. B 1940; ed Manchester Polytechnic.

MANCHESTER, Central

Electorate 31,312   1974: 39,857

*Lever, N. H. (Lab)	14,117
Cummins, H. P. (C)	4,413
Wilmott, G. M. R. (L)	1,052
Bentall, D. S. (Nat Front)	365
Lab majority	9,704

No Change

	1974		1979
Total votes	21,277		19,947
Turnout	53.4%		63.7%
Lab	14,753	69.3%	70.8%
C	4,142	19.5%	22.1%
L	2,382	11.2%	5.3%
Nat Front	—	—	1.8%
Lab maj	10,611	49.8%	48.7%
Swing		−4.4%	+0.5%

Mr Harold Lever Chancellor of the Duchy of Lancaster, and special adviser to Mr Harold Wilson and Mr James Callaghan on financial and economic affairs, 1974-79. Given responsibility for small businesses, 1978. Opposition spokesman on European affairs, 1970-72; chairman, Public Accounts Committee, 1970-74. Elected to shadow Cabinet, 1970 and resigned in April 1972 in protest at party's EEC policy; reelected to shadow cabinet in December 1972, and until 1974 had responsibility for company law, mergers and competition, civil aviation and shipping. Paymaster General 1969-70 with a seat in Cabinet, serving in the Ministry of Technology with special responsibility for power matters. Financial Secretary to the Treasury 1967-69; Under Secretary, Department of Economic Affairs, January-August 1967. Member, Speaker's panel of chairmen 1964-66. Won Manchester Exchange 1945, Cheetham 1950, and Central, February 1974. B January, 1914; ed Manchester Grammar School and Manchester University.

Mr Paul Cummins, manager of forwarding agents. B April, 1951; ed Ravensbury Secondary School, Manchester, Openshawe College, Manchester. Member, Manchester City Council, since 1975.

Mr Gordon Willmott, lecturer, contested Manchester, Ardwick, October, 1974. B June, 1930; ed Bassaleg Grammar School and Oriel College, Oxford.

MANCHESTER, Gorton

Electorate 53,943   1974: 55,955

*Marks, K. (Lab)	22,293
Lord, M. N. (C)	16,009
Shaw, G. (L)	2,867
Chadfield, R. (Nat Front)	469
Lab majority	6,284

No Change

	1974		1979
Total votes	39,694		41,638
Turnout	70.9%		77.2%
Lab	21,287	53.6%	53.5%
C	12,423	31.3%	38.4%
L	5,984	15.1%	6.9%
Nat Front	—		1.1%
Lab maj	8,864	22.3%	15.1%
Swing		−0.9%	+3.6%

Mr Kenneth Marks, Under-Secretary for the Environment, 1975-79. Returned at a by-election in November, 1967; contested Moss Side, 1955. Headmaster. B June, 1920; ed Central High School, Manchester, and Didsbury College of Education, Manchester. Former chairman, PLP social security group. Opposition whip, 1970-71. Member, Select Committee on Education and Science, 1968-70; Public Expenditure Committee, 1974-75. NUT.

Mr Michael Lord, managing director and arboricultural consultant. B October, 1938; ed William Hulme's Grammar School, Manchester, and Christ's College, Cambridge. Member, North Bedfordshire Borough Council, 1974-77. Associate member, British Institute of Management. Fellow, Arboricultural Association. Rugby blue and England trialist.

MANCHESTER, Moss Side

Electorate 47,811   1974: 51,444

*Morton, G. M. (Lab)	17,765
Murphy, T. E. (C)	13,234
Commons, G. P. B. (L)	2,981
Redgrave, Miss V. (WRP)	225
Lab majority	4,531

No Change

	1974		1979
Total votes	32,333		34,205
Turnout	62.9%		71.5%
Lab	15,212	47.0%	51.9%
C	11,101	34.3%	38.7%
L	5,686	17.6%	8.7%
I Civil Rights	238	0.7%	—
Pros Brit	96	0.3%	—
WRP	—	—	0.7%
Lab maj	4,111	12.7%	13.2%
Swing		−3.0%	−0.3%

1978 by-election: Total votes 27,073 (51.6%)—Lab 12,556 (46.4%); C 10,998 (40.6%), L 2,502 (9.2%), Nat Front 623 (2.3%); WRP 394 (1.5%). Lab majority 1,558 (5.6%).

Mr George Morton, an architect, returned at a by-election July, 1978. B February, 1940; ed Fettes College, Edinburgh, Edinburgh College of Art and Glasgow University. Member, Manchester City Council, 1971-74, and Greater Manchester Council, 1973-77. Nalgo.

Mr Thomas Murphy, director, advertising and tobacco group. B 1941; ed Salford College of Technology. Member, Manchester City Council, since 1967.

Mr John Commons, aged 23, student. ed Manchester Polytechnic.

Miss Vanessa Redgrave, actress, is sister of the WRP candidate at Jarrow. Contested Newham, North-East, February and October, 1974 and this seat, 1978 by-election. B January, 1937; ed Queensgate School and Central School of Speech and Drama.

MANCHESTER, Openshaw

Electorate 37,816   1974: 42,554

*Morris, C. R. (Lab)	17,099
Hilton, P. (C)	9,955
Coles, A. (Nat Front)	296
Widdall, P. (Comm)	174
Lab majority	7,144

No Change

	1974		1979
Total votes	27,985		27,524
Turnout	65·8%		72·8%
Lab	16,109	57·6%	62·1%
C	7,596	27·1%	36·2%
L	3,980	14·2%	—
Comm	300	1·1%	0·6%
Nat Front	—		1·1%
Lab maj	8,513	30·5%	25·9%
Swing		−3·2%	+2·3%

Mr Charles Morris was Minister of State, Civil Service Department, October, 1974-79. Elected in 1962 at by-election; contested Cheadle, 1959. PPS to Mr Harold Wilson, 1970-74. Appointed Government whip, January, 1966; Vice-Chamberlain to Royal Household, 1967-69; Treasurer of the Household (Deputy Chief Whip), 1969-70. Formerly a postal  and telegraph officer, and member of executive council of the Union of Post Office Workers, 1959-63. B December, 1926; ed Brookdale Park School, Manchester. Sponsored by UPOW.

Mr Peter Hilton, self-employed. B May, 1946; ed Burnage Grammar School, Manchester, and Sheffield University. Licensed lay reader, Church of England 1972-75. Member, Diocesan Standing Committee. Honorary Treasurer, Diocse of Northern Zambia, 1971-75.

Mr Philip Widdall, social worker, contested the seat, February and October, 1974. Aged 34; ed Ashton-under-Lyne Grammar School. Nalgo department secretary in social services department and a member of Manchester branch executive council.

MANCHESTER, Withington

Electorate 53,408   1974: 58,200

*Silvester, F. J. (C)	18,862
Hodgson, G. M. (Lab)	15,510
Mitchell, J. T. (L)	5,387
Gibson, M. G. (Feudal)	157
C majority	3,352

No Change

	1974		1979
Total votes	39,428		39,916
Turnout	67·7%		74·7%
C	16,937	43·0%	47·3%
Lab	14,936	37·9%	38·9%
L	7,555	19·2%	13·5%
Feal	—		0·4%
C maj	2,001	5·1%	8·4%
Swing		−2·7%	+1·6%

Mr Frederick Silvester was an Opposition whip, 1974-76. Elected February, 1974; held Walthamstow, West, for the Conservatives, 1967-70, contesting the seat 1966. Advertising executive and barrister (Gray's Inn, 1957). B September, 1933; ed Sir George Monoux Grammar School, Walthamstow, and Sidney Sussex College, Cambridge.  Member, Select Committee on Expenditure, since 1976; Select Committee on Procedure. Vice-chairman, Conservative prices and consumer protection committee, 1974; vice-chairman, Conservative employment committee, since 1976. Senior associate partner in a leading advertising agency.

Mr Geoffrey Hodgson, economics lecturer. B July, 1946; ed Cheshunt Grammar School and Manchester University. Member, NATFHE and Institute for Workers' Control.

Mr John Mitchell, textile consultant. B January, 1932; ed Paisley College of Technology.

MANCHESTER, Wythenshawe

Electorate 60,602   1974: 65,123

*Morris, A. (Lab and Co-op)	26,860
Sumberg, D. (C)	14,747
Griffiths, L. (L)	3,853
Lab and Co-op majority	12,113

No Change

	1974		1979
Total votes	44,788		45,460
Turnout	68·8%		75·0%
Lab & Co-op	26,448	59·1%	59·1%
C	12,269	27·4%	32·4%
L	6,071	13·6%	8·5%
Lab/Co-op m	14,179	31·7%	26·7%
Swing		−3·0%	+2·5%

Mr Alfred Morris was Under Secretary for Health and Social Security with special responsibility for the disabled, 1974-79. Elected in 1964; contested seat 1959, and Liverpool, Garston 1951. Chairman, parliamentary cooperative group, 1970-71; Opposition spokesman on social services, 1970-74.  Promoted Chronically Sick and Disabled Persons Act, 1970. B March 1928; ed Manchester elementary schools, Ruskin College and St Catherine's College, Oxford; post-graduate studies at Manchester University. Former chairman, food and agriculture group, Parliamentary Labour Party and Labour MP's disablement group. Sponsored by Cooperative movement.

Mr **David Sumberg,** solicitor. B June, 1941; ed Tettenhall College, Staffordshire. Executive member, Manchester youth and community service.

MANSFIELD

Electorate 71,851   1974: 69,555

*Concannon, J. D. (Lab)	29,051
Daly, K. (C)	17,720
Chambers, D. J. (L)	8,536
Donovan, P. (Nat Front)	259

Lab majority	11,331

No Change

	1974		1979
Total votes	50,455		55,566
Turnout	72·5%		77·3%
Lab	28,946	57·4%	52·3%
C	11,685	23·2%	31·9%
L	9,358	18·5%	15·4%
Comm	448	0·9%	—
Nat Front	—	—	0·5%
Lab maj	17,279	34·2%	20·4%
Swing		−2·0%	+6·9%

Mr **Dennis Concannon** was Minister of State, Northern Ireland Office, 1976-79; Under Secretary, Northern Ireland Office, June 1974-76. Vice-Chamberlain of the Household, March to June 1974; Opposition whip, 1970-74; assistant Government whip, 1968-70. Returned in 1966. Miner and NUM official. B May, 1930; ed Rossington Secondary School,

Doncaster Technical School, WEA and Nottingham University. Member, Mansfield Council 1962-68. Sponsored by NUM.

Mr **Kenneth Daly,** director, insurance broking company and company manufacturing fire retardant materials. B August, 1938; ed Belvedere College, Dublin, and the Associate Chartered Insurance Institute. Member, Tandridge District Council, 1976-78. Chairman, Burstow Branch, East Surrey Conservative Association. Member, East Surrey Trades Union Advisory Committee. ASTMS.

Mr **David Chambers,** chiropodist, contested the seat, October, 1974. B February, 1947; ed Great Yarmouth Grammar School, City of Norwich School, Chelsea School of Chiropody. Member, Notts County Council, since 1977; Society of Chiropodists.

MELTON

Electorate 87,319   1974: 82,139

*Latham, M. A. (C)	40,242
Read, Miss I. M. (Lab)	15,882
Farrer, D. (L)	12,596

C majority	24,360

No Change

	1974		1979
Total votes	63,257		68,720
Turnout	77·0%		78·7%
C	30,943	48·9%	58·6%
Lab	16,747	26·5%	23·1%
L	15,567	24·6%	18·3%
C maj	14,196	22·4%	35·5%
Swing		−0·6%	+6·5%

Mr **Michael Latham,** elected February, 1974 contested Liverpool, West Derby, 1970. Non-executive director, Lovell Homes Ltd, a building firm, since 1975. B November, 1942; ed Marlborough College, King's College, Cambridge. Director and chief executive of House Builders' Federation, 1971-73; Parliamentary Liaison Office, National

Federation of Building Trades Employees, 1967-73. Conservation Research Department, 1965-67. Member, Expenditure Committee since 1974; Westminster City Council, 1968-71; board of Shelter.

Miss **Imelda Read,** research assistant. B January, 1939. ASTMS.

Mr **David Farrer,** barrister. B March, 1943; ed Queen Elizabeth's Grammar School, Barnet; Downing College, Cambridge.

MERIDEN

Electorate 98,914   1974: 97,364

Mills, I. (C)	37,151
*Tomlinson, J. E. (Lab)	33,024
Spurling, D. (L)	4,976
Parkes, A. (Nat Front)	1,032

C majority	4,127

C gain from Lab

	1974		1979
Total votes	73,098		76,183
Turnout	75·1%		77·0%
Lab	34,641	47·4%	43·3%
C	25,675	35·1%	48·8%
L	12,782	17·5%	6·5%
Nat Front	—	—	1·4%
Lab maj	8,966	12·3%	—
C maj	—	—	5·5%
Swing		−3·3%	+8·9%

Mr **Iain Mills,** marketing planning manager with Dunlop, responsible for marketing new tyre projects; was responsible for all racing tyre development, 1966-70. B April, 1940; ed Prince Edward School, Bulawayo, Rhodesia, and Cape Town University. Member, Tichfield District

Council, 1973-74. Burgess of the City of Glasgow.

Mr **John Tomlinson,** was Under Secretary, Ministry of Overseas Development, 1977-79; Under Secretary, Foreign and Commonwealth Office, 1976-79. Lecturer in industrial relations. Elected February 1974; contested Walthamstow, East, 1970, and Bridlington, 1966. B August, 1939; ed Westminster City School and Co-operative College. Formerly political organiser and head of research department, AUEW. Member, Sheffield City Council, 1964-67, and Dartford Borough Council. TGWU and ATTI.

Mr **David Spurling,** senior lecturer in transport economics. B July, 1940; ed Owen's School, London, Royal Grammar School, Guildford, and Bristol University. Southend Borough councillor, 1973-74. NATFHE.

MERIONETH

Electorate 27,250   1974: 26,728

*Thomas, D. E. (Pl Cymru)	9,275
Harvey, R. (C)	5,365
Jones, R. H. (Lab)	5,332
Parsons, J. H. (L)	2,752
Pl Cymru majority	3,910

No Change

	1974		1979
Total votes	22,457		22,724
Turnout	84·0%		83·4%
Pl Cymru	9,543	42·5%	40·8%
Lab	6,951	31·0%	23·5%
L	3,454	15·4%	12·1%
C	2,509	11·2%	23·6%
Pl Cymru maj	2,592	11·5%	17·2%

Mr Dafydd Thomas, adult education tutor, broadcaster and writer, won the seat in February 1974; contested Conway, 1970. B October, 1946; ed University College of North Wales. Became Playid Cymru parliamentary spokesman on social, educational and cultural policy in 1975; party spokesman on agricultural and rural development, 1974. Honorary secretary, all-party mental health group. Member, Child Poverty Action Group, Mind, Institute for Workers Control and Shelter. TGWU.

Mr Robert Harvey contested Caernarvon, October 1974. Journalist and broadcaster. B August 1953; ed Eton and Christ Church, Oxford. Chairman, Oxford Bow Group, 1973-74; member, Bow Group; executive member, Kensington Conservative Association; member, Montgomeryshire Conservative Association; Royal Institute for International Affairs.

Mr Rhion Jones, personnel manager. B May, 1948; ed Llanelli Grammar School, University College of Wales, Aberystwth and Balliol College, Oxford. Member, NALGO.

Mr John Parsons, solicitor and former agent for Mr Emlyn Hooson, former Liberal MP for Montgomery. Aged 49.

MERTHYR TYDFIL

Electorate 39,680   1974: 39,714

*Rowlands, E. (Lab)	22,386
de Wilde, A. R. (C)	4,426
ap Gwilym, E. (Pl Cymru)	2,962
Oliver, R. D. (L)	1,275
Dennett, C. C. (Comm)	223
Gould, R. T. (WRP)	114
Lab majority	17,960

No Change

	1974		1979
Total votes	30,111		31,386
Turnout	75·8%		79·1%
Lab	21,260	70·6%	71·3%
Pl Cymru	4,455	14·8%	9·4%
C	2,587	8·6%	14·1%
L	1,300	4·3%	4·1%
Comm	509	1·7%	0·7%
WRP	—	—	0·4%
Lab maj	16,805	55·8%	57·2%
Swing		−3·1%	+2·4%

Mr Edward Rowlands was Minister of State, Foreign and Commonwealth Office, 1976-79; Under Secretary, 1975-76. Under Secretary, Welsh Office, 1974-75. Won the seat in 1972 by-election; MP for Cardiff, North, 1966-70. Under Secretary, Welsh Office, 1969-70. Former lecturer, Welsh College of Advanced Technology. B January, 1940; ed Rhondda Grammar School, Wirral Grammar School, and King's College, London. ASTMS.

Mr Robin de Wilde, barrister, qualified London Tourist Board guide and part-time journalist. B 1945; ed Dean Close School, Cheltenham, RAF College, Cranwell, and the Inns of Court School of Law. Member, Chelsea Conservative Association; chairman, Law Students Conservative Association, 1970-71.

Mr Eurfyl ap Gwilym, industrialist, is National Chairman of Plaid Cymru. B November, 1944; ed Ardwyn Grammar School and London University. Senior manager, John Williams group of companies.

Mr Travis Gould, aged 29, machine tool fitter.

MERTON, Mitcham and Morden

Electorate 62,365   1974: 65,398

*Douglas-Mann, B. L. H. (Lab)	21,668
Samuel, D. (C)	21,050
Locke, R. (L)	4,258
Perryman, J. (Nat Front)	966
Lab majority	618

No Change

	1974		1979
Total votes	46,461		47,942
Turnout	73·1%		76·9%
Lab	22,384	48·2%	45·2%
C	16,193	34·9%	43·9%
L	7,429	16·0%	8·9%
Comm	281	0·6%	—
Ind	106	0·2%	—
ARPSWR	68	0·1%	—
Nat Front	—	—	2·0%
Lab maj	6,191	13·3%	1·3%
Swing		−3·7%	+6·0%

Mr Bruce Douglas-Mann, a solicitor, was elected February, 1974; MP for Kensington, North, 1970-74; contested Maldon, 1966, and St Albans, 1964. B June 1927; ed in Canada and Jesus College, Oxford. Chairman, PLP housing and construction group, since 1974. Chairman, Society of Labour Lawyers; president, Socialist Environment Research Association. Member, board of Shelter. Member, Kensington Borough Council, 1962-65; Kensington and Chelsea Council, 1966-68.

Mr David Samuel, property consultant and company director, contested the seat in October, 1974; Nuneaton, 1974. B 1939; ed Randwick High School, Sydney. Member, Kensington and Chelsea Council, since 1968, and of the Association of Municipal Corporation's housing committee, 1969-72. Chairman, Federation of Private Residents Association, 1974.

Mr **Ronald Locke,** chartered engineer, contested Wandsworth, Central, 1959, and 1964. B October, 1912; ed Wandsworth Junior Technical College and London University.

MERTON, Wimbledon

Electorate 65,471   1974: 70,726

*Havers, Sir Michael (C)	27,567
Tansey, R. B. (Lab)	14,252
Twigg, D. (L)	7,604
Bailey, A. (Nat Front)	612

C majority	13,315

No Change

	1974		1979
Total votes	48,657		50,035
Turnout	68·8%		76·4%
C	23,615	48·5%	55·1%
Lab	14,909	30·6%	28·5%
L	10·133	20·8%	15·2%
Nat Front	—		1·2%
C maj	8,706	17·9%	26·6%
Swing		−2·3%	+4·3%

Sir Michael Havers, QC, became Attorney General in May, 1971. Opposition spokesman on law, from 1974, he was appointed to advise party leader's consultative committee on legal matters. Solicitor-General, 1972-74. Chairman, Conservative Legal Committee. Member, Committee of Privileges and Select Committee on MPs' interests 1974 and since 1976.

Elected in 1970. B March, 1923; ed Westminster School and Corpus Christi College, Cambridge. Called to the Bar (Inner Temple). 1948. Recorder of Dover, 1962-68; Recorder of Norwich, 1968.

Mr **Rock Tansey,** barrister. B July, 1939; ed grammar school. Member, Haldane Society of Socialist Lawyers; NCCL; Merton Borough Council, since 1978. TGWU(ACTS).

Mr **David Twigg,** consulting civil engineer. B March, 1934; ed Queen Elizabeth I Grammar School, Alford.

MIDDLETON AND PRESTWICH

Electorate 77,291   1974: 76,737

*Callaghan, J. (Lab)	27,918
Park, J. (C)	26,820
Whatmough, D. (L)	5,888
Andrew, S. (Nat Front)	350

Lab majority	1,098

No Change

	1974		1979
Total votes	58,138		60,976
Turnout	75·8%		78·9%
Lab	26,639	45·8%	45·8%
C	22,925	39·4%	44·0%
L	8,340	14·3%	9·7%
Pros Brit	234	0·4%	—
Nat Front	—	—	0·6%
Lab maj	3,714	6·4%	1·8%
Swing		−2·8%	+2·3%

Mr **James Callaghan** was elected in February, 1974. Former lecturer at St John's College, Manchester. B January, 1927; ed Manchester University and London University. Member, Commons Standing Orders Committee; Middleton Borough Council, 1971-74. Football coach and referee.

Mr **James Park,** solicitor, contested Crewe in February and October, 1974, B 1941; ed Wadham House School, Malvern College and Manchester University. Former chairman, Knutsford Young Conservatives, 1968, and North-West area Young Conservatives, 1971-73. Member, Young Conservatives national advisory council, 1971-73. Vice chairman, Knutsford Constituency Association, 1977.

Mr **David Whatmough,** management accountant. B April, 1944; ed Manchester Central Grammar School. Treasurer, Hyndburn and Rossendale Community Relations Council. Local authority appointee to board of managers of four primary schools. ASTMS.

MIDLOTHIAN

Electorate 101,482   1974: 89,191

*Eadie, A. (Lab)	37,733
Mann, H. W. (C)	20,797
Spiers, G. A. F. (Scot Nat)	13,260
Brodie, A. P. (L)	7,129

Lab majority	16,936

No Change

	1974		1979
Total votes	69,059		78,919
Turnout	77·4%		77·8%
Lab	28,652	41·5%	47·8%
Scot Nat	24,568	35·6%	16·8%
C	11,046	16·0%	26·4%
L	4,793	6·9%	—
Rad L	—		9·0%
Lab maj	4,084	5·9%	21·4%
Swing		−4·7%	+2·0%

Mr **Alexander Eadie** was Under Secretary for Energy, 1974-79. Former Opposition spokesman on energy and former chairman of PLP miners' group and of parliamentary power and steel group. Elected in 1966, contested Ayr, 1964 and 1959. Former miners' agent. B June, 1920; ed Buckhaven senior secondary school, Fife, and technical college. Sponsored by NUM.

Mr **Hugh Mann,** farmer. B February, 1927; ed Melville College, Edinburgh; Dalkeith High School, Strathallan School, Perthshire, and Oxford University. Member, Bonnyrigg Town Council, 1962-64, and Midlothian Conservative Association. Committee member and former secretary, Dalkeith Agricultural Society; director Royal Highland Show.

Mr **Glen Spiers** English teacher. Member, SNP's national council. B January, 1936; ed St Patrick's School, Leicester, and Aberdeen University.

MONMOUTH

Electorate 80,085   1974: 74,838

*Thomas, J. S. (C)	33,547
Steel, T. M. (Lab)	23,785
Hando, D. (L)	8,494
Williams, G. (Pl Cymru)	641
C majority	**9,762**

No Change

	1974		1979
Total votes	59,493		66,467
Turnout	79·5%		83·0%
C	25,460	42·8%	50·5%
Lab	23,118	38·9%	35·8%
L	10,076	16·9%	12·8%
Pl Cymru	839	1·4%	1·0%
C maj	2342	3·9%	14·7%
Swing		−1·7%	+5·4%

Mr John Stradling Thomas
was appointed Treasurer of
HM Household and Gov-
ernment Deputy Chief
Whip in May, 1979. An
Opposition whip, 1974-79.
Won the seat for the Con-
servatives in 1970. Assistant Government whip,
1971-72; Lord Commis-
sioner of the Treasury
(whip) 1973-74. Contested
Cardiganshire, 1966;
Aberavon, 1964. Farmer. B

June, 1925; ed Rugby and London University.
Member, Carmarthen Borough Council, 1961-64.
Chairman, Carmarthenshire NFU, 1964, NFU council, 1963-70; Select Committee on Civic List, 1970-
71.

Mr Timothy Steel, marketing manager with Leyland
Cars. B April, 1944; ed Royal Grammar School,
Guildford. TGWU(ACTS).

Mr David Hando, deputy headmaster, contested the
seat, 1970, and February and October, 1974. B April,
1938; ed St Julian's High School, Newport; LSE;
University of Wales, Cardiff. NUT.

Mr Gwyn Williams, aged 42, teacher. Ed Brynmawr
Grammar School and University College, Aberystwyth.

MONTGOMERY

Electorate 35,786   1974: 33,583

Williams, D. J. D. (C)	11,751
*Hooson, H. E. (L)	10,158
Price, J. (Lab)	4,751
Clowes, C. (Pl Cymru)	2,474
C majority	**1,593**

C gain from L

	1974		1979
Total votes	26,172		29,134
Turnout	77·9%		81·4%
L	11,280	43·1%	34·9%
C	7,421	28·4%	40·3%
Lab	5,031	19·2%	16·3%
Pl Cymru	2,440	9·3%	8·5%
L maj	3,859	14·7%	
C maj			5·4%
Swing			+7·4%

Mr Delwyn Williams, a sol-
icitor. B November 1938;
ed Welshpool Grammar
School and University Col-
lege of Wales, Aberystwyth.
Member, Powys County
Council, and former
member, Montgomeryshire
County Council. Fought
Cardigan, October 1974,
and Montgomery, 1970.
Junior vice-president,
Welshpool Rotary Club.

Mr Emlyn Hooson, QC,
leader of the Welsh Liberal Party, was elected at a
by-election in April, 1962. Member of Liberal Party
Executive since 1964. Liberal spokesman on
agriculture and prices, 1974-76, when he became
spokesman on home affairs and defence. Barrister
(Gray's Inn 1949), QC 1960. Hill farmer. B March
1925; ed Denbigh Grammar School and University
College of Wales. Contested Conway, 1950 and 1951.

Mr John Price, Post Office engineer, is chairman of
Chester and North Wales Council of Post Office
unions and secretary, North Wales and Chester
POEU co-ordinating committee, and of Chester and
District Trades Council. Member, Cheshire County
Council. Vice-chairman, Chester Labour Party, and
press officer,Cheshire County Labour Party. Aged 37.

Dr Carl Clowes, specialist in community medicine. B
December, 1943; ed Manchester University.

MORAY AND NAIRN

Electorate 45,802   1974: 41,174

Pollack, A. (C)	14,220
*Ewing, Mrs W. (Scot Nat)	13,800
Rodan, S. (L)	4,361
Scobie, G. E. W. (Lab)	3,104
C majority	**420**

C gain from Scot Nat

	1974		1979
Total votes	30,766		55,485
Turnout	74·7%		77·5%
Scot Nat	12,667	41·2%	38·9%
C	12,300	40·0%	40·1%
Lab	2985	9·7%	8·7%
L	2,814	9·1%	12·3%
Scot Nat maj	367	1·2%	—
C maj	—	—	1·2%
Swing	—	—	+0·5%

Mr Alexander Pollack, an
advocate, Scottish Bar
(called in 1973), contested
the seat, October, 1974,
and West Lothian,
February, 1974. B July,
1974; ed Glasgow
Academy, Brasenose Col-
lege, Oxford, and
Edinburgh University.
Former Counsellor for
Edinburgh Marriage
Guidance Council; former
treasurer, Order of

Christian Unity. Founder member, Thistle Group.

Mrs Winifred Ewing, vice-president of the SNP, won
the seat February, 1974; MP for Hamilton 1967-70.
Became SNP spokesman on external affairs and the
EEC in 1974, and has also been spokesman on home
affairs. Member, European Parliament, since 1975.
Appointed to Select Committee on Violence in
Marriage, 1975. B July, 1929; ed Queen's Park Senior
Secondary School, Glasgow, and Glasgow University.

Mr Stephen Rodan, pharmacist. B April, 1954; ed
Glasgow High School and Heriot Watt University.
Chairman, Scottish Young Liberals, 1974-77.

Mr Geoffrey Scobie, university lecturer. B July, 1937; ed Sutton High School, Plymouth and Universities of Bristol, Birmingham and Glasgow. Bishopbriggs Burgh councillor. AUT.

MORECAMBE AND LONSDALE

Electorate 68,625   1974: 68,473

Lennox-Boyd, M. A. (C)	29,068
Collier, G. (Lab)	13,253
Tinker, H. R. (L)	10,150
C majority	15,815

No Change

	1974		1979
Total votes	49,914		52,471
Turnout	72·9%		76·5%
C	24,877	49·8%	55·4%
Lab	12,633	25·3%	25·3%
L	12,404	24·9%	19·3%
C maj	12,244	24·5%	30·1%
Swing		−1·7%	+2·8%

Mr Mark Lennox-Boyd barrister, business interests in farming, contested Brent, South, October, 1974. B May, 1943; ed Eton and Christ Church, Oxford. Worked for Save the Children Fund in Jordan, 1965.

Mr Gerard Collier, product quality engineer. B January, 1947; ed George Heriot's School, Edinburgh, NE Essex Technical College and School of Art; Portsmouth Polytechnic; Slough Technical College. AUEW (TASS).

Mr Hugh Tinker, professor of international politics. Aged 57; ed Sidney Sussex College, Cambridge.

MORPETH

Electorate 49,881   1974: 48,518

*Grant, G. (Lab)	21,744
Edwards, S. (C)	9,913
Thompson, A. (L)	6,972
Lab majority	11,831

No Change

	1974		1979
Total votes	35,571		38,629
Turnout	73·3%		77·4%
Lab	22,696	63·8%	56·3%
C	8,009	22·5%	25·7%
L	4,866	13·7%	18·0%
Lab maj	14,687	41·3%	30·6%
Swing		1·0%	3·3%

Mr George Grant, elected 1970, was a miner for eight years and conciliation officer in the NUM northern area. B October, 1924; ed elementary school, WEA and evening classes. Chairman, PLP Northern area group, 1977. Member, Bedlingtonshire Urban Council, 1959-70 (chairman 1964-66); chairman, Ashington branch, NUM 1959-66 and compensation secretary, 1959-66.

Mr Stephen Edwards, designer, and former art teacher. B 1938; ed St Bees School, Cumberland,

Durham University, Kings' College, Newcastle upon Tyne, and Oxford University. Member, Northumberland and Newcastle Society committee; founder chairman, Tyne Valley Action Group. Lecturer for the National Trust.

Mr Alan Thompson, chartered engineer and company director, contested Dunbartonshire, East, October, 1974. B May, 1936; ed Dicksons College.

MOTHERWELL AND WISHAW

Electorate 50,317   1974: 51,506

*Bray, J. W. (Lab)	22,263
Thomson, J. (C)	11,326
Mackay, J. (Scot Nat)	4,817
Sneddon, J. (Comm)	740
Lab majority	10,937

No Change

	1974		1979
Total votes	38,817		39,146
Turnout	75·4%		77·8%
Lab	17,319	44·6%	56·9%
Scot Nat	12,357	31·8%	12·3%
C	7,069	18·2%	28·9%
L	1,126	2·9%	—
Comm	946	2·4%	1·9%
Lab maj	4,962	12·8%	28·0%
Swing		−5·2%	−0·8%

Mr Jeremy Bray, returned for the seat in October, 1974, was MP for Middlesbrough West, 1962 (by-election) to 1970; contested Thirsk and Malton, 1959. Parliamentary Secretary, Ministry of Technology, 1967-69; Parliamentary Secretary, Ministry of Power, April, 1966 to January, 1967. Member, Select, Committee on Wealth Tax, 1974; Expenditure Committee since 1978. B June, 1930; ed Aberystwyth Grammar School; Kingswood School, Bath; Jesus College, Cambridge. Choate Fellow, Harvard. Economist. Consultant, Booksellers' Association. TGWU.

Mr John Thomson, teacher, contested Rutherglen, February and October, 1974. B December, 1934; ed Jordanhill College of Education, Coatbridge Technical College. Fellow in Education, Winston Churchill Management Trust, 1970. Member, Motherwell and Wishaw town council, 1965-70; district council since 1977.

Mr James Mackay, engineering firm's area manager. B October, 1928; ed East Plean School and Riverside Technical College, Stirling. Contested the seat, October, 1974.

Mr James Sneddon, steelworks maintenance engineer. Aged 60. Motherwell council. AUEW convenor. President, Dalziel Co-operative Society. Member, Scottish and national executive committees, Communist Party.

NANTWICH

Electorate 64,211   1974: 61,196

Bonsor, Sir Nicholas. (C)	25,624
Shaw, D. (Lab)	17,919
Walsh, C. (L)	6,571
Green, J. (Nat Front)	814
C majority	7,705

No Change

	1974		1979
Total votes	46,625		50,928
Turnout	76·2%		79·3%
C	20,395	43·7%	50·3%
Lab	17,021	36·5%	35·2%
L	9,209	19·8%	12·9%
Nat Front	—	—	1·6%
C maj	3,374	7·2%	15·1%
Swing		−1·6%	+3·9%

Sir Nicholas Bonsor, barrister, farmer and company director, contested Newcastle under Lyme, February and October, 1974. B December, 1942; ed Eton and Keble College, Oxford. Chairman, Wing Branch, Buckingham Conservative Association, 1974-76. Fellow, Royal Society of Arts. NFU. Secretary-general, Committee for Industrial Cooperation.

Mr Deric Shaw, company secretary. B July 1933; ed Old Moat Lane Secondary Modern, and Withington, Manchester. Financial and economic business interests. ASTMS.

Mr Christopher Walsh, probation officer. Aged 24; ed Newcastle upon Tyne Polytechnic.

NEATH

Electorate 51,659   1974: 52,257

*Coleman, D. R. (Lab)	27,071
Sandy, C. (C)	8,455
Gwyn, Rev A. (Pl Cymru)	6,430
Lab majority	**18,616**

No Change

	1974		1979
Total votes	40,733		41,956
Turnout	77·9%		81·2%
Lab	25,028	61·4%	64·5%
Pl Cymru	7,305	17·9%	15·3%
C	4,641	11·4%	20·2%
L	3,759	9·2%	—
Lab maj	17,723	43·5%	44·3%
Swing		−2·0%	+2·8%

Mr Donald Coleman, elected in 1964, a Lord Commissioner of the Treasury (Government whip) 1974-79; Opposition whip 1970-74. Member, Select Committee on Overseas Aid, 1969-74, and delegate, Council of Europe and Western European Union 1968-74. Metallurgist; sponsored by Iron and Steel Trades Confederation. B September, 1925; ed Cadoxton School, Barry, and Cardiff Technical College. Tenor soloist and former member, Welsh National Opera Company.

Mr Christopher Sandy contested Dorset, South, as a Liberal in October, 1974. Joined Conservative Party, 1975. Chartered accountant. B April 1949; ed Bishop Wordsworth's Grammar School, Salisbury; Canford School, Wimborne; Exeter University. Member, Richmond Conservative Association Political Committee. Former editor, Conservative *Small Business News.*

Rev Aled Gwyn, minister of religion, is a member of West Glamorgan County Council. B August, 1940; ed University of Wales, Aberystwyth, and Memorial College, Swansea.

NELSON AND COLNE

Electorate 47,739   1974: 48,356

Lee, J. (C)	17,522
*Hoyle, E. D. H. (Lab)	17,086
Hewitt, D. (L)	4,322
C majority	**436**

C gain from Lab

	1974		1979
Total votes	39,191		38,930
Turnout	81·0%		81·5%
Lab	17,505	44·7%	43·9%
C	16,836	43·0%	45·0%
L	4,850	12·4%	11·1%
Lab maj	669	1·7%	—
C maj	—		1·1%
Swing		−1·1%	+1·4%

Mr John Lee, chartered accountant, and company director, contested Moss Side, Manchester, in October, 1974. B 1942; ed William Hulme's Grammar School, Manchester. Former divisional treasurer, Stretford Young Conservatives; former group chairman, North West Bow Group, 1968-69. Member, executive council, Manchester Youth and Community Service, and trustee; vice-chairman, North West Conciliation Committee, Race Relations Board; member, North West Committee, British Digestive Foundation; political secretary to Lord Carr in 1974.

Mr Douglas Hoyle, sales engineer, won the seat for Labour in October, 1974; contested it in February, 1974, and 1970; Clitheroe, 1964. Elected to Labour Party National Executive Committee, October, 1978. B February, 1924; ed Adlington School, Horwich Technical College and Bolton Technical College. Member, Council of "Get Britain Out" (of EEC) Campaign Member, Manchester Regional Hospital Board, 1968-74; ASTMS since 1958 (member, national executive since 1968, and president, 1978). Sponsored by ASTMS.

Mr David Hewitt, conference organiser, director of two companies. B November, 1948; ed Nelson Secondary Technical School, Manchester Polytechnic.

NEWARK

Electorate 75,612   1974: 71,346

Alexander, R. (C)	27,711
*Bishop, E. S. (Lab)	25,960
Baker, J. (L)	6,773
C majority	**1,751**

C gain from Lab

	1974		1979
Total votes	55,541		60,444
Turnout	77·8%		79·9%
Lab	26,598	47·9%	42·9%
C	20,827	37·5%	45·8%
L	8,116	14·6%	11·2%
Lab maj	5,771	10·4%	—
C maj	—		2·9%
Swing		−1·4%	+6·6%

Mr Richard Alexander, solicitor, contested Lincoln, 1966 and 1970. B June, 1934; ed Eastbourne Grammar School, Dewsbury Grammar School, University College London, and Institute of Advanced Legal Studies, University of London. Member, Bassetlaw District Council since 1975; Retford Borough Council, 1965-74, Nottinghamshire County Council, 1967-74, Former member, East Midlands Regional Economic Planning Council, and East Midlands Transport User's Consultative Committee.

Mr Edward Bishop was Minister of State for Agriculture, Fisheries and Food, 1974-79; Parliamentary Secretary, Ministry of Agriculture, Fisheries and Food, June-October, 1974. Former spokesman on trade, industry and aerospace. Elected in 1964; contested Gloucestershire South, 1955, Exeter 1951, and Bristol, West, 1950. Assistant Government whip, 1966-67. Aeronautical design draughtsman. B October, 1920; ed Merchant Venturers' Technical College, Bristol and Bristol University, Member Bristol City Council for 17 years. Sponsored by AUEW (TASS).

Mr John Baker, a senior lecturer. B May, 1928; ed High Storrs Grammar School, Sheffield, and Leeds University.

NEWBURY

Electorate 80,355   1974: 72,587

*McNair-Wilson, M (C)	33,677
Richards, A. (L)	23,388
Ruddock, Mrs J. (Lab)	6,676

C majority	10,289

No Change

	1974		1979
Total votes	55,366		63,741
Turnout	76·3%		79·3%
C	23,499	42·4%	52·8%
L	22,477	40·6%	36·7%
Lab	9,390	17·0%	10·5%
C maj	1,022	1·8%	16·1%
Swing		+0·1%	+8·4%

Mr Michael McNair-Wilson was returned for Newbury in February, 1974. Member, Select Committee on Nationalised Industries since November, 1974. Won Walthamstow, East in 1969 by-election and held it in 1970; contested Lincoln, 1964. B October, 1930; ed Eton. Public relations executive; director, Sidney-Barton Ltd. Brother of MP for New Forest. Chairman, Conservative Aviation Committee, 1972-74; Joint Secretary, United Nations Parliamentary Group, 1970-72, and to Greater London Conservative MPs' Committee, 1969-70. NUJ, 1962-68.

Mr Anthony Richards, economic and public affairs adviser, B May, 1947; ed Friars School, Bangor; Sheffield and Essex Universities. Former director of research, Liberal Party.

Mrs Joan Ruddock, careers officer, youth opportunities programme. Ex-director Oxford housing aid centre. B December, 1943; ed Pontypool Grammar School, Imperial College, London. Nalgo.

NEWCASTLE UNDER LYME

Electorate 72,442   1974: 72,781

*Golding, J. (Lab)	28,649
Ashley, Mrs E. (C)	24,421
Evans, G. (L)	5,878
Rowe, S. (BSEP)	156

Lab majority	4,228

No Change

	1974		1979
Total votes	56,798		59,104
Turnout	78·0%		81·6%
Lab	28,154	49·6%	48·5%
C	20,784	36·6%	41·3%
L	7,604	13·4%	9·9%
UK Front	256	0·5%	—
BSEP	—	—	0·3%
Lab maj	7,370	13·0%	7·2%
Swing		−1·8%	+2·9%

Mr John Golding, Under Secretary of State, Employment, 1976-79; member of the Labour Party National Executive Committee since October, 1978. Lord Commissioner of the Treasury (Government Whip) February-October, 1974; Opposition whip 1970-74, Elected at the 1969 by-election. B March, 1931; ed City Grammar School, Chester, University College of North Staffordshire and London School of Economics. Member, Select Committee on Statutory Instruments, 1969-70. Sponsored by POEU.

Mrs Elsie Ashley, director of a firm of timber merchants, contested Stoke-on-Trent, Central, February 1974 and 1970. B 1919; ed Newcastle-under-Lyme secondary modern schools and privately. Member, Newcastle-under-Lyme Borough Council, since 1963; deputy Mayor 1977; member Staffordshire County Council, since 1966. President, North Staffordshire Spastic Society; county vice-president, British Red Cross Society; chairman, North Staffordshire RSPCA; member, West Midlands Gas Consumer Council.

Mr Gwyn Evans, electricity supply planner. Aged 55; ed Cardiff University College.

NEWCASTLE UPON TYNE, Central

Electorate 23,678   1974: 25,156

*Cowans, H. L. (Lab)	10,395
Merchant, P. (C)	2,982
Ellis, A (L)	2,073

Lab majority	7,413

No Change

	1974		1979
Total votes	14,694		15,450
Turnout	58·4%		65·3%
Lab	10,546	71·8%	67·3%
C	2,432	16·6%	19·3%
L	1,716	11·7%	13·4%
Lab maj	8,114	55·2%	48·0%
Swing		−3·2%	+3·6%

1976 by-election: Total votes 9,856 (41·0%)—Lab 4,692 (47·6%); L 2,854 (29·0%); C 1,945 (19·7%); others 184 (1·86%); Nat Front 181 (1·8%). Lab majority 1,838 (18·6%).

Mr Harry Cowans, former British Railways technical officer, retained the seat for Labour in November, 1976, by-election. B December, 1932, ed Atkinson Road Technical School, Newcastle upon Tyne, Member, Gateshead Borough Council, 1970-78, and Tyne and Wear County Council, 1972-76. Chairman, PLP Northern Group. Sponsored by NUR.

Mr Piers Merchant, journalist. B 1951; ed Durham University. Editor of local Conservative magazine.

Mr Andrew Ellis, printer, contested the seat October, 1974, and at a by-election 1976. B May, 1952; ed Trinity College, Cambridge, and Newcastle University.

NEWCASTLE UPON TYNE, East

Electorate 44,484   1974: 45,651

*Thomas, M. S. (Lab and Co-op)		18,257
Conway, D. (C)		12,087
Nelson, J. (L)		2,818
Lab and Co-op majority		6,170

No Change

	1974		1979
Total votes	32,766		33,162
Turnout	71·8%		74·5%
Lab & Co-op	17,312	52·8%	55·1%
C	11,063	33·8%	36·4%
L	4,391	13·4%	8·5%
Lab/Co-op m	6,249	19·0%	18·7%
Swing		−0·8%	+0·1%

Mr Mike Thomas was elected in October, 1974; contested Hertfordshire, East, 1970. Director of the National Volunteer Centre, 1973-74. B May, 1944; ed Latymer Upper School, Hammersmith. King's School, Macclesfield, and Liverpool University. Member, Select Committee on Nationalised Industries, since 1975. Head of Co-operative Party Research Department, 1966-68; Senior Research Officer, Political and Economic Planning, 1968-73. USDAW.

Mr Derek Conway contested Durham, October, 1974. Regional organiser for Action Research for the Crippled Child. B 1953; ed Beacon Hill Boy's School and London Academy of Music and Dramatic Art. Member, Tyne and Wear Metropolitan Council. Vice-Chairman, Northern Area Conservative Council. Former member, Gateshead Metropolitan Borough Council.

Mr John Nelson, sales manager. B February, 1923; ed South Shields Grammar School.

NEWCASTLE UPON TYNE, North

Electorate 39,307   1974: 40,238

*Elliott, Sir William (C)		12,721
Ward, Mrs S. (Lab)		11,010
Marlowe, C. (L)		2,983
C majority		1,711

No Change

	1974		1979
Total votes	26,154		26,714
Turnout	65·0%		68·0%
C	11,217	42·9%	47·6%
Lab	10,748	41·1%	41·2%
L	4,189	16·0%	11·2%
C maj	469	1·8%	6·4%
Swing		−4·2%	+2·3%

Sir William Elliott, vice-chairman of the Conservative Party Organisation from 1970 until April 1974. Comptroller of the Household (Whip), 1970-74; an Opposition Whip, 1964-70. Assistant Government whip, 1963-64. Elected at 1957 by-election; contested Morpeth, 1955, and 1954 by-election. Farmer. B December, 1920; ed King Edward VI Grammar School, Morpeth. Member, Select Committee on Race Relations and Immigration since 1976; Select Committee on Violence in Marriage, February, 1975. President, Northern Area Young Conservative Council, 1953. Director of water company.

Mrs Susan Ward is a research assistant on pensions for the GMWU. B September, 1949; ed St James' School, West Malvern, and St Hugh's College, Oxford. Fought Kensington and Chelsea, February, 1974, and Southend, East, October, 1974. Member, Wandsworth Borough Council, 1972-78. Former conciliation officer with Race Relations Board.

Mr Christopher Marlowe, salesman. Ed universities of St Andrews and Edinburgh. Agent, Edinburgh, South, October 1974.

NEWCASTLE UPON TYNE, West

Electorate 83,156   1974: 76,966

*Brown, R. C. (Lab)		32,827
Gilbert, D. (C)		21,591
Dickinson, Miss J. (L)		5,801
Lab majority		11,236

No Change

	1974		1979
Total votes	52,985		60,219
Turnout	68·8%		72·4%
Lab	30,057	56·7%	54·5%
C	14,983	28·3%	35·9%
L	7,945	15·0%	9·6%
Lab maj	15,074	28·4%	18·6%
Swing		−4·1%	+4·9%

Mr Robert Brown, Under Secretary for Defence for the Army, 1974-79; Under Secretary for Social Security Department of Health and Social Security, 1974; an Opposition Spokesman on environment until 1974. Former vice-chairman, Parliamentary Labour Party trade union group. Parliamentary Secretary, Ministry of Transport, 1968-70. Elected in 1966.

B May, 1921; ed Rutherford Technical College. Secretary of constituency Labour Party and election agent, 1950-66. Councillor and alderman, Newcastle City Council for 10 years. Sponsored by GMWU.

Mr Donald Gilbert, managing director of carpet and textile business. B 1927; ed Royal Grammar School, Newcastle and Christ's College, Cambridge. Member,

Tyne and Wear Metropolitan Council; Newcastle City Council for 10 years (former deputy leader of the council).

Miss Jane Dickinson, designer and printer. Aged 32.

NEW FOREST

Electorate 85,137   1974: 79,109

*McNair-Wilson, P. M. E. D.	(C)		39,124
Kyrle, M. (L)			13,674
Whitehead, A. P. V.	(Lab)		12,950

C majority	25,450

No Change

	1974		1979
Total votes	57,958		65,748
Turnout	74·2%		77·2%
C	28,778	49·7%	59·5%
L	15,355	26·5%	20·8%
Lab	13,825	23·9%	19·7%
C maj	13,423	23·2%	38·7%
Swing		−1·4%	+7·0%

Mr Patrick McNair-Wilson, was an Opposition spokesman on energy, 1974-76, and previously on the private steel sector. Vice-chairman, Conservative fuel and power committee, 1968-70. Elected at 1968 by-election; represented Lewisham, West, 1964-66. Director of the London Municipal Society, 1960-63. Company director. B  May, 1929; ed Hall School, Hampstead, and Eton. Member, Select Committee on Nationalised Industries, 1974, and Select Committee on Science and Technology, 1968-70. Brother of MP for Newbury, PPS to Minister for Transport Industries, 1970-74.

Mr Martin Kyrle, teacher, contested Christchurch and Lymington, February, 1974. B March, 1933; ed Southampton University, Sussex University. Member, Eastleigh Trades Council, NAS/UWT.

Mr Alan Whitehead, deputy director Outset, a charity assisting disabled. B September, 1950; ed Isleworth Grammar School, Southampton University. ACTS.

NEWHAM, North East

Electorate 66,371   1974: 65,975

Leighton, R. (Lab)	22,818
Wood, Mrs K. (C)	12,778
Corney, D. J. (L)	4,027
Northcott, W. H. H. (Nat Front)	1,769
Regan, J. (Ind)	208
Van Der Poorten, M. A (WRP)	154
Boaks, W. (DMPSWR)	118

Lab majority	10,040

Lab gain from C

	1974		1979
Total votes	39,036		41,872
Turnout	59·2%		63·1%
Lab	22,205	56·9%	54·5%
C	8,664	22·2%	30·5%
L	4,880	12·5%	9·6%
Nat Front	2,715	7·0%	4·2%
WRP	572	1·5%	0·4%
Ind	—	—	0·5%
DMPSWR	—	—	0·3%
Lab maj	13,541	34·7%	24·0%
Swing		−2·4%	+5·3%

Mr Ronald Leighton, a printer, is chairman of the Labour Common Market Safeguards Committee. B January, 1930; ed elementary and Ruskin College, Oxford. Contested Horsham and Crawley, February, 1974, and Middleton and Prestwich, 1964. Sponsored by Natsopa.

Mrs Kay Wood, speech therapist. B 1943; ed Queen School, Chester, Oldrey Fleming College of Speech Therapy, and Guys Hospital Medical School, University of London. Honorary treasurer and councillor, College of Speech Therapists, 1973-76; administrative secretary, Conservative Medical Society.

Mr David Corney fought West Bromwich, West, in October, 1974. Lecturer. B March, 1946; ed Wednesbury High School, Essex University and Birbeck College, London University.

NEWHAM, North-West

Electorate 54,030   1974: 53,489

*Lewis, A. W. J. (Lab)	18,392
Amess, D. (C)	7,937
McCarthy, B. (L)	2,377
Maloney, M. (Nat Front)	1,217

Lab majority	10,455

No Change

	1974		1979
Total votes	27,596		29,923
Turnout	51·6%		55·4%
Lab	18,388	66·6%	61·5%
C	5,007	18·1%	26·5%
L	4,201	15·2%	7·9%
Nat Front	—	—	4·1%
Lab maj	13,381	48·5%	35·0%
Swing		−4·3%	+6·7%

Mr Arthur Lewis was elected for this seat in February, 1974, after representing West Ham, North, 1950-74. Returned at Upton, 1945. Member, Council of Europe since January, 1976, and WEU. Industrial consultant. Former trade union official (GMWU) and chairman of the Eastern Regional group of Labour MPs. B February,  1917; ed elementary school and Borough Polytechnic, National Council of Labour Colleges and WEA. Former member of the London Labour Party Executive committee, member, Commons Expenditure Committee since April, 1974. Chairman, All-Party Committee for Freedom of information. GMWU, APEX and ASTMS.

Mr David Amess, employment consultant. B 1952; ed St. Bonaventure's Grammar School and Bournemouth College of Technology.

Mr Brian McCarthy, computer systems manager, contested Havering, Hornchurch, February and October 1974, and West Ham, North, 1970. B June, 1939; ed Whitechapel Grammar School and West Ham College of Technology. Member, Newham Borough Council, 1964-71.

NEWHAM, South

Electorate 53,431   1974: 57,695

*Spearing, N. J. (Lab)	19,636
Elphicke, Mrs M. J. (C)	6,863
Ozimek, J. (L)	2,085
Anderson, T. (Nat Front)	1,899
Lab majority	12,773

No Change

	1974		1979
Total votes	30,835		30,483
Turnout	53·4%		57·1%
Lab	21,372	69·3%	64·4%
L	3,611	11·7%	6·8%
C	3,440	11·2%	22·5%
Nat Front	2,412	7·8%	6·2%
Lab maj	17,761	57·6%	41·9%
Swing		−2·1%	+8·1%

Mr Nigel Spearing, teacher, elected by-election, May, 1974. B October, 1930; ed Latymer Upper School, Hammersmith, and St Catharine's College, Cambridge. Regained Acton for Labour in 1970, lost it in February 1974; contested Warwick and Leamington, 1964. Member, Select Committees on Sound Broadcasting, since 1978, Overseas Development, since 1977; and on procedure; vice-chairman, European group of PLP since November, 1974. Member, Council of "Get Britain out" (of EEC) Campaign. Chairman, Safeguard Britain Campaign, since October, 1977. NUT.

Mrs Mary-Jo Elphicke, leader of Conservative controlling group on Huntingdon District Council, since 1976. B 1937. Chairman, Cambridge standing conference. Ed boarding school.

Mr John Ozimek, student. B November, 1957, ed Wadham College, Oxford.

NEWPORT

Electorate 75,121   1974: 75,061

*Hughes, R. J. (Lab)	30,919
Davies, G. G. (C)	21,742
Lambert, A. (L)	6,270
Vickery, A. R. (Pl Cymru)	473
Woodward, Mrs G. R. (Nat Front)	454
Lab majority	9,177

No Change

	1974		1979
Total votes	56,745		59,858
Turnout	75·6%		79·7%
Lab	30,069	53·0%	51·7%
C	16,253	28·6%	36·3%
L	9,207	16·2%	10·5%
Pl Cymru	1,216	2·1%	0·8%
Nat Front	—	—	0·8%
Lab maj	13,816	24·4%	15·4%
Swing		−2·8%	+4·5%

Mr Roy Hughes was elected in 1966. Former administrative officer in a Coventry car firm, and officer in Transport and General Workers Union, 1959-66. B June, 1925; ed Pontlilanfraith County Grammar School and Ruskin College, Oxford, Member, Coventry City Council, and secretary, Coventry Labour Party, 1962-66. Chairman, PLP steel group and all-party sports group. Vice-chairman, Labour Middle East Council. Sponsored by TGWU.

Mr Gerald Davies, chairman of menswear retailing company. B 1941; ed Rougemont School, Newport, and Wyncliffe College, Stonehouse. Member, Newport Borough Council; Magor and St Mellons Rural District Council, 1967-70; Monmouth Conservative Association.

Mr Anthony Lambert, Post Office senior auditor for Wales and the Marches, contested Gloucestershire, South 1970, and South West Staffordshire, October 1974. Former member, national executive, Post Office Management Staff Association. Member, Thornbury (Gloucestershire) Council, 1970. B September 1943; ed Hitchin Boys Grammar School and St Edmund Hall, Oxford University.

Mr Robert Vickery, company director. Contested seat, 1970. Played for Newport and Newport Saracens Rugby Clubs. B May, 1935; ed Newport High School and Newport Technical College.

NEWTON

Electorate 102,885   1974: 95,268

*Evans, J. (Lab)	41,466
Huntley, T. (C)	30,125
Smith, R. (L)	8,471
Fishwick, Mrs A. (Nat Front)	641
Lab majority	11,341

No Change

	1974		1979
Total votes	73,178		80,703
Turnout	76·8%		78·4%
Lab	38,956	53·2%	51·4%
C	22,484	30·7%	37·3%
L	11,738	16·0%	10·5%
Nat Front	—		0·8%
Lab maj	16,472	22·5%	14·1%
Swing		−1·8%	+4·2%

Mr John Evans, an assistant Government whip 1979. Elected in February, 1974. Member, European Parliament, 1975-79, and chairman of its regional policy and transport committee, 1976-79. Former member, Commons Public Accounts Committee. Fitter. B October, 1930; ed Jarrow Central School, Member, Hebburn Urban District Council, 1962-74 (chairman 1972-73, leader 1969-1974, and of South Tyneside Metropolitan District Council, 1973-74. Sponsored by AUEW.

Mr Thomas Huntley, senior staff engineer for a motor insurance company. B 1930; ed Stopsley Secondary School, Luton, Luton Technical College. Member, Rossendale District Council; Deputy Traffic Commissioner, North-West; President, North-West Federation of Pigeon Clubs.

Mr **Rodney Smith** contested Antrim, South, 1970; and Warley, East, October, 1974. Lecturer. B April, 1945; ed Campbell College, Belfast; St John's College, Cambridge; Queen's University, Belfast; Bolton College of Education. NATFHE.

NORFOLK, North

Electorate 98,135   1974: 90,526

*Howell, R. F. (C)	43,952	
Dimmick, R. S. (Lab)	22,126	
Collings, G. R. (L)	10,643	
Sizeland, A. C. R. (Nat Front)	548	

C majority	21,826

No Change

	1974		1979
Total votes	69,279		77,269
Turnout	76·5%		78·7%
C	33,312	48·1%	56·9%
Lab	22,191	32·0%	28·6%
L	13,776	19·9%	13·8%
C maj	11,121	16·1%	28·3%
Swing		−1·5%	+6·1%
Nat Front	—	—	0·7%

Mr **Ralph Howell,** member, European Parliament, 1974-79. Farmer and member of Lloyd's. Was joint vice-chairman, back bench committee on agriculture and employment. Won seat for the Conservatives in 1970; contested it, 1966. B May, 1923; ed Diss Grammar School. Former local NFU chairman. Member, Mitford and Launditch Rural Council, 1961-74.

Mr **Robert Dimmick,** computer technical specialist. B November, 1947; ed London primary schools, St Paul's School, Hammersmith, Gonville and Caius College, Cambridge. Sprowston parish councillor, Norfolk, 1974-76. Past chairman, Norwich Fabian Society. ASTMS.

Mr **Gustave Collings,** book publisher, contested Portsmouth, Langstone, 1964. B June, 1925; ed John Lyon's School. Director, Malvern Typesetting Ltd and other companies.

NORFOLK, North-West

Electorate 83,702   1974: 79,743

*Brocklebank-Fowler, C. (C)	33,796	
Williams, R. L. (Lab)	25,868	
Mynott, M. (L)	6,588	

C majority	7,928

No Change

	1974		1979
Total votes	62,545		66,252
Turnout	78·4%		79·2%
C	27,513	44·0%	51·0%
Lab	26,170	41·8%	39·0%
L	8,862	14·2%	9·9%
C maj	1,343	2·2%	12·0%
Swing		0·5%	+4·9%

Mr **Christopher Brocklebank-Fowler,** elected in February, 1974; MP for King's Lynn, 1970-74; contested West Ham, North, 1964. Marketing and advertising consultant. B January, 1934; ed Perse School, Cambridge. Former chairman and secretary, Bow Group. Member, Junior Carlton Club. Joint Secretary, United Nations Parliamentary Group, since 1971; former chairman, Conservative horticultural committee; joint secretary, Conservative Foreign and Commonwealth Affairs Committee, 1974. Member, Select Committee on Overseas Development, since 1973.

Mr **Richard Williams,** solicitor, contested the seat, October, 1974. B October 1940; ed Tywyn primary and secondary schools, Gwynadd. State advocate in Zambia, 1968-71 Member, Socialist Agricultural Society.

Mr **Michael Mynott,** managing director of a retail menswear and ladies fashion business. Aged 49.

NORFOLK, South

Electorate 100,243   1974: 90,810

*MacGregor, J. R. R. (C)	42,792	
Davies, P. J. (Lab)	23,755	
Bristol, J. (L)	11,990	

C majority	19,037

No Change

	1974		1979
Total votes	69,195		78,537
Turnout	76·2%		78·3%
C	31,478	45·5%	54·5%
Lab	22,713	32·8%	30·2%
L	14,687	21·2%	15·3%
UDP	317	0·5%	—
C maj	8,765	12·7%	24·3%
Swing		−1·0%	+5·8%

Mr **John MacGregor,** became a Lord Commissioner of the Treasury (Government whip) in May, 1979. Director, Hill Samuel and Co Ltd, and Hill Samuel Registers Ltd, Elected in February, 1974. An Opposition whip 1977-79. Member, Public Accounts Committee, 1974-75; Expenditure Committee, 1975-77. Chairman, Bow Group, 1963-64. Secretary, Conservative Finance Committee, 1976-77. B February, 1937; ed Merchiston Castle School, Edinburgh, St Andrews University and King's College, London. Former journalist with *New Society;* special assistant to Sir Alec Douglas-Home when Prime Minister and head of Mr Heath's private office, 1965-68.

Mr **Paul Davies,** teacher. B May, 1949; ed University of Leeds, Keswick Hall College of Education, New University of Ulster. NUT.

Mr **Jonathan Bristol,** company director. B April, 1940; ed Salt Grammar School, Fulneck Boys' School, Royal Agricultural College, Cirencester.

NORFOLK, South-West

Electorate 57,901   1974: 53,719

*Hawkins, P. L. (C)	24,767
Rosenberg, A. (Lab)	14,063
Baxter, B. (L)	6,363
C majority	10,704

No Change

	1974		1979
Total votes	41,286		45,793
Turnout	76·9%		78·1%
C	19,778	47·9%	54·8%
Lab	14,850	36·0%	31·1%
L	6,658	16·1%	14·1%
C maj	4,928	11·9%	23·7%
Swing		−0·9%	+5·9%

Mr Paul Hawkins was Vice-Chamberlain of the Household (whip) 1973-74; a Lord Commissioner of the Treasury (whip) 1971-73 and an assistant Government whip, 1970-71. Opposition whip, March to October, 1974. Elected 1964. Chartered surveyor in agricultural practice. B August, 1912; ed Cheltenham College. Member, Norfolk County Council, 1949-70; alderman 1968-70. Member, Select Committee on Wealth Tax, 1974; Select Committee on Agriculture, 1968-69. Member, United Kingdom delegation to Council of Europe, since 1976.

Mr Alan Rosenberg, teacher. B June, 1938, ed Archbishop Tenison's Grammar School, Kennington; Regent Street Polytechnic. NUT.

Mr Brian Baxter, farmer, contested the seat, October 1974. B November, 1932; ed Dunoon Grammar School, Scottish Hotel School and King's Lynn Technical College.

NORMANTON

Electorate 61,390   1974: 58,936

*Roberts, A. (Lab)	26,591
Cavendish, M. H. (C)	14,398
Paton, A. R. C. (L)	6,134
Lab majority	12,193

No Change

	1974		1979
Total votes	41,495		47,123
Turnout	70·4%		76·8%
Lab	24,372	58·7%	56·4%
C	9,739	23·5%	30·6%
L	7,384	17·8%	13·0%
Lab maj	14,633	35·2%	25·8%
Swing		−0·4%	+4·7%

Mr Albert Roberts was elected in 1951. Mining engineer and mines inspector. NUM branch secretary, 1935-41. B May, 1908; ed Woodlesford County School and Whitwood Technical College. Member, Rothwell Urban Council, 1937-52, chairman 1948-49. Executive member, Inter-Parliamentary Union (British group) since 1953,

chairman 1968-71. Deputy Lieutenant, West Riding, 1967. Sponsored by NUM.

Mr Michael Cavendish, deputy head teacher. Member West Yorkshire County Council and Yorkshire Area Advisory Committee on Education. B April, 1936; ed King Edward VII School, Lytham, Jesus College Oxford, and Jesus College, Cambridge.

Mr Andrew Paton, controller on British Rail, fought Lancaster in 1970. B 1946; ed Shrewsbury School and Durham University.

NORTHAMPTON, North

Electorate 50,739   1974: 49,030

Marlow, A. (C)	18,597
*Colquhoun, Mrs M. M. (Lab)	13,934
Rounthwaite, A. (L)	5,659
Rickord, R. G. W. (Nat Front)	373
C majority	4,663

C gain from Lab

	1974		1979
Total votes	37,250		38,563
Turnout	76·0%		76·0%
Lab	16,314	43·8%	36·1%
C	14,776	39·7%	48·2%
L	6,160	16·5%	14·7%
Nat Front	—		1·0%
Lab maj	1,538	4·1%	
C maj	—		12·1%
Swing		−0·8%	+8·1%

Mr Anthony Marlow, development manager with a grain shippers company, contested Normanton, February 1974, and Rugby, October, 1974. B June 1940; ed Wellington School, Royal Military Academy, Sandhurst, and St Catharine's College, Cambridge. Former chairman, Daventry Conservative Political Centre committee and East Midlands Area CPC working party.

Mrs Maureen Colquhoun, economist, was elected in February, 1974; contested Tonbridge, 1970. B August, 1928; ed convent, Eastbourne, commercial college, Brighton, and London School of Economics. Member, Shoreham Council, 1965-74, county councillor, West Sussex, County Council 1973-75. Member, Commons Expenditure Committee, since 1975. GMWU.

Mr Anthony Rounthwaite, administrative officer, B February, 1951; ed King's School, Tynemouth; Newcastle upon Tyne Polytechnic. NUPE.

NORTHAMPTON, South

Electorate 51,151   1974: 44,343

*Morris, M. W. L. (C)	19,125
Mason, G. (Lab)	15,491
Amey, D. (L)	3,478
James, Mrs M. (Nat Front)	407
C majority	3,634

No Change

	1974		1979
Total votes	33,487		38,501
Turnout	75·5%		75·3%
C	14,393	43·0%	49·7%
Lab	14,252	42·6%	40·2%
L	4,842	14·5%	9·0%
Nat Front	—	—	1·1%
C maj	141	0·4%	9·5%
Swing		−0·1%	+4·5%

Mr Michael Morris, marketing director of advertising agency. B November, 1936; ed Bedford School and St Catharine's College, Cambridge. Elected, February, 1974; contested Islington, North, 1966. Alderman, London Borough of Islington 1971-74; member, Islington Council 1968-70. Hon Secretary, All-Party Anglo-Sri Lanka Committee, since 1974; Conservative environment committee, since 1977; Conservative trade committee, 1974-76; Conservative Local government committee, 1975-76 and Conservative housing committee, 1974.

Mr Graham Mason, boot and shoe operative. B March, 1935; ed Kingsthorpe Grove and Bective Secondary Modern. Member, Northampton Borough Council, since 1973. NUFLAT (footwear trade section).

Mr Michel Amey, bus driver. B December, 1959; ed Aldercar Secondary School. TGWU.

NORTH FYLDE

Electorate 78,130   1974: 74,799

*Clegg, W. (C)	35,366
Fox, R. (Lab)	14,376
Herbert, P. (L)	8,630
Warbarton, K. (Nat Front)	481
C majority	20,990

No Change

	1974		1979
Total votes	53,437		58,853
Turnout	71·4%		75·3%
C	29,661	55·5%	60·1%
Lab	12,522	23·4%	24·4%
L	11,254	21·1%	14·7%
Nat Front	—	—	0·8%
C maj	17,139	32·1%	35·7%
Swing		−2·4%	+1·8%

Mr Walter Clegg, Lord Commisioner of the Treasury (whip) 1970-72; Vice-Chamberlain of the Household (whip) 1972-73; Comptroller of the Household (whip) 1973-74. Partner in firm of solicitors. Elected in 1966; contested Ince, 1959. B April, 1920; ed Arnold School, Blackpool, Bury Grammar School, and Manchester University. Member, Lancashire County Council, 1955-61. Opposition whip, March to October, 1974. Member, executive, 1922 committee. Member, Select Committee on Procedure, since 1974.

Mr Malcolm Fox, barrister. B November, 1951; ed Baines Grammar School, Poulton le Fylde; Cambridge University. Member, Fabian Society, Anti-Apartheid Movement. TGWU.

Mr Peter Herbert, senior laboratory technician. Member, Garstang and Wyre Councils, since 1976. Aged 32; ed Lancashire College of Agriculture.

NORTHWICH

Electorate 54,362   1974: 52,626

*Goodlad, A. R. (C)	23,201
Silverman, B. H. (Lab)	14,455
Little, G. (L)	6,311
C majority	8,746

No Change

	1974		1979
Total votes	41,361		43,967
Turnout	78·6%		80·9%
C	18,663	45·1%	52·8%
Lab	14,053	34·0%	32·9%
L	8,645	20·9%	14·4%
C maj	4,610	11·1%	19·9%
Swing		−1·7%	+4·4%

Mr Alistair Goodlad, elected February, 1974; contested Crewe, 1970. B July, 1943; ed St Faith's School, Cambridge, Marlborough College and King's College, Cambridge. Director, Bowater Overseas Holdings Ltd. Was personal assistant to Mr Peter Walker when Opposition spokesman on transport.

Mr Barry Silverman, general manager with the Co-operative Wholesale Society, contested Macclesfield, February, 1974 and Hillingdon, Ruislip-Northwood, 1970. B October, 1931; ed Pinner County Grammar School. Councillor, Borough of Ealing, 1958-61. Member, Harrow Education Committee, 1970-72; ASTMS.

Mr Geoffrey Little, barrister. B May, 1950; ed Stockport School and Emmanuel College, Cambridge.

NORWICH, North

Electorate 46, 687   1974: 45,079

*Ennals, D. H. (Lab)	17,927
Rippon, P. H. (C)	12,336
Moore, P. (L)	4,253
Hannah, G. (Ecology)	334
Goold, L. (Nat Front)	250
Panes, A. (Comm)	106
Colling, S. (WRP)	92
Lab majority	5,591

No Change

	1974		1979
Total votes	32,090		35,298
Turnout	71·2%		75·6%
Lab	17,958	56·0%	50·8%
C	8,754	27·3%	34·9%
L	5,378	16·8%	12·0%
Ecology	—		0·9%
Nat Front	—		0·7%
Comm	—		0·3%
WRP	—		0·3%
Lab maj	9,204	28·7%	15·9%
Swing		−4·0%	+6·4%

Mr David Ennals was Secretary of State for Social Services, 1976-79; Minister for State for Foreign and Commonwealth Affairs, 1974-76. Elected in February, 1974; represented Dover, 1964-70. Minister of State for Health and Social Security, 1968-70; Under-Secretary, Home Office, 1967-68, and Under-Secretary for Defence (Army), 1966-67. Contested Richmond as a Liberal in 1950 and 1951. B August, 1922; ed Queen Mary's Grammar School, Walsall, and at Windsor, Connecticut. Campaign director, National Association for Mental Health until 1974. Secretary, United Nations Association, 1952-57. Overseas secretary, Labour Party, 1958-64.

Mr Paul Rippon, solicitor. B 1937; ed Highgate School, London. Norfolk county councillor. Chairman, North West Norfolk Conservative Association Political Committee, 1973-74.

Mr Philip Moore, local Government officer. B September, 1948; ed Boston Grammar School, Peterborough Technical College. Nalgo.

Mr George Hannah, aged 37, employed in computer bureau.

Mr Andy Panes, bus conductor, aged 35. Vice-chairman, East Anglia District, Communist Party. Literature and publicity officer, Norwich and District Trades Council.

Mr Steven Colling, aged 24, factory worker and shop steward. GMWU.

NORWICH, South

Electorate 45,073   1974: 44,862

*Garrett, J. L. (Lab)	16,240
Coutts, I. (C)	15,042
Mackintosh, P. (L)	4,618
Fountaine, A. (Nat Front)	264

Lab majority	1,198

No Change

	1974		1979
Total votes	35,204		36,164
Turnout	78·5%		80·2%
Lab	16,590	47·1%	44·9%
C	13,185	37·5%	41·6%
L	5,429	15·4%	12·8%
Nat Front			0·7%
Lab maj	3,405	9·6%	3·3%
Swing		−4·0%	+3·1%

Mr John Garrett was elected in February, 1974. Management consultant. B September, 1931; ed Sir George Monoux School, London; Oxford University; and University of California. Member, Greenwich Borough Council. Vice-chairman PLP, trade and industry groups. Member, procedure and expenditure committees. TGWU.

Mr Ian Coutts, chartered accountant. B 1927; ed Ipswich School and Culford School, Suffolk. Member and former vice-chairman, Forehoe and Henstead RDC, 1963-72. Member, Norfolk County Council since 1970; leader 1977. Member, Association of County Councils and University of East Anglia Council; governor, Theatre Royal, Norwich; president and secretary, Norfolk Caledonian Society.

Mr Peter Mackintosh, teacher, contested local government elections. Aged 44; ed Gonville and Caius Colleges, Cambridge.

NOTTINGHAM, East

Electorate 47,838   1974: 53,786

*Dunnett, J. J. (Lab)	15,433
Brandon-Bravo, M. (C)	12,199
Hiley, J. D. (L)	2,270
Coles, M. (Nat Front)	426
Juniper, I. B. (Soc Unity)	252

Lab majority	3,234

No Change

	1974		1979
Total votes	32,282		30,580
Turnout	60·0%		63·9%
Lab	16,530	51·2%	50·5%
C	10,574	32·8%	39·9%
L	4,442	13·8%	7·4%
Ind Lab	736	2·3%	
Nat Front	—		1·4%
Soc Unity	—		0·8%
Lab maj	5,956	18·4%	10·6%
Swing		−3·8%	+3·9%

Mr Jack Dunnett, a solicitor, was elected February, 1974; represented Nottingham, Central, 1964-74. B June, 1922; ed Whitgift Middle School, Croydon, and Downing College, Cambridge. Member, Greater London Council, 1964-67; Middlesex County Council, 1958-61; and Enfield Borough Council, 1958-63. Member, NUGMW since 1961. Chairman, Notts County Football Club; member, Football League Managment Committee, and Football Association Council. Director of property company.

Mr Martin Brandon-Bravo, company director and Nottingham City councillor. B March 1932; ed Latymer.

Mr John Hiley, work study officer. B August, 1954; ed Central London Poytechnic. Member, Sleaford District Trades Council. GMWU.

NOTTINGHAM, North

Electorate 78,996   1974: 76,490

*Whitlock, W. C. (Lab)	25,028
Waine, P. (C)	21,956
Stockley, J. (L)	4,900
Peck, J. H. (Comm)	1,071
Pratt, R. (Nat Front)	454
Lab majority	3,072

No Change

	1974		1979
Total votes	51,334		53,409
Turnout		67·1%	67·6%
Lab	24,694	48·1%	46·9%
C	17,853	34·8%	41·1%
L	7,470	14·6%	9·2%
Nat Front	792	1·5%	0·9%
Comm	525	1·0%	2·0%
Lab maj	6,841	13·3%	5·8%
Swing		−2·7%	+3·7%

Mr William Whitlock,
Under-Secretary for
Foreign and Com-
monwealth Affairs, 1967-
69; Deputy Chief Whip and
Lord Commissioner of the
Treasury, March-July,
1967; Comptroller of the
Household, 1966-67; Lord
Commissioner of the
Treasury, March-July,
1966; Vice-Chamberlain of
the Household, 1964-66.
Elected 1959. Opposition

whip, 1962-64. Area organizer, Union of Shop,
Distributive and Allied Workers, 1947-59. B June,
1918, ed Itchen Grammar School, Southampton, and
Southampton University. Member, All-Party Roads
Study Group.

Mr Peter Waine, personnel manager with an industrial
group. B June 1949; ed Bilton Grange and Worksop
College, Bradford University. Member, Rugby
Borough Council, 1973-77; chairman, Birmingham
Bow Group, 1975, and national vice-chairman, Bow
Group 1976.

Mr John Stockley, lecturer in technology. B
December, 1934; ed Swanage Grammar School,
Royal Navy Technical Schools, Basingstoke Technical
College Open University. NATHFE.

Mr John Peck contested the seat, February and
October, 1974, 1970, 1966, 1964, 1959 and 1955.
Nottingham Co-operative Society employee. B
August, 1922; ed Scunthorpe Grammar School
USDAW.

NOTTINGHAM, West

Electorate 77,155   1974: 77,711

*English, M. (Lab)	26,301
Stoneman, Mrs M. (C)	23,801
Willis, M. (L)	5,497
Wilkinson, T. J. (Nat Front)	718
James, A. (WRP)	192
Lab majority	2,500

No Change

	1974		1979
Total votes	55,079		56,509
Turnout		70·9%	73·2%
Lab	27,373	49·7%	46·5%
C	18,108	32·9%	42·1%
L	9,598	17·4%	9·7%
Nat Front	—	—	1·3%
WRP	—	—	0·3%
Lab maj	9,265	16·8%	4·4%
Swing		−3·6%	+6·2%

Mr Michael English has
held the seat since 1964;
contested Shipley, 1959. B
December, 1930; ed King
George V Grammar
School, Southport, and
Liverpool University.
Member, Rochdale
Borough Council, 1953-65.
Sponsored by NUGMW.
Chairman, General Sub-
committee of the
Expenditure Committee.
Member, Speaker's Panel
of Chairmen and Proceedure Committees. Chairman,
PLP Parliamentary Affairs Group, 1970-77, and
vice-chairman since 1977. Chairman, PLP East
Midlands Group, 1977. Member of Council of Get
Britain Out (of EEC) Campaign.

Mrs Margaret Stoneman, lecturer and student
councillor. B 1925; ed Barr's Hill Grammar School,
Birmingham University, Coventry College of
Education and Tavistock Institute for Human
Relations, London. Member, Coventry City Council,
1955-62 and 1967-70; former vice-president,
Coventry Conservative Association; member, West
Midlands Speakers Panel; executive member, East
Midlands Area Women's Advisory Committee, since
1976.

Mr Michael Willis, radio presenter. B October, 1945;
ed Tal Handaq Royal Naval School and Royal Air
Force, Hereford. ABS; ACTT.

Mr Arthur James, lorry driver and former mine
worker.

NUNEATON

Electorate 80,225   1974: 77,892

*Huckfield, L. J. (Lab)	31,403
Stevens, L. (C)	23,715
Williams, C. E. G. (L)	6,184
Matthews, R. P. (Nat Front)	1,028
Davis, G. E. (Ind Lab)	629
Lab majority	7,688

No Change

	1974		1979
Total votes	57,584		62,959
Turnout		73·9%	78·5%
Lab	32,308	56·1%	49·9%
C	14,547	25·3%	37·7%
L	10,729	18·6%	9·8%
Nat Front	—	—	1·6%
Ind Lab	—	—	1·0%
Lab maj	17,761	30·8%	12·2%
Swing		−1·7%	+9·3%

Mr Leslie Huckfield was Under-Secretary, Department of Industry, 1976-79. Elected at by-election in 1967; contested Warwick and Leamington, 1966. Elected to National Executive Committee of Labour Party, 1978. B April, 1942; ed Prince Henry's Grammar School, Evesham; Keble College, Oxford; and University of Birmingham. Former lecturer in economics and former Parliamentary adviser, British Safety Council. Former member, Select Committee on Expenditure. Former chairman, PLP transport group and West Midlands group of Labour MPs. Served on Birmingham Regional Hospital Board. Sponsored by TGWU.

Mr Lewis Stevens, production manager. B 1936; ed Oldbury Grammar School, Liverpool University, and Lancaster College of Technology. Member, Nuneaton Borough Council, 1966-72.

Mr Cecil Williams, building surveyor, contested Birmingham, Sparkbrook, 1974. B August, 1948; ed Birmingham Polytechnic. President, Birmingham Communuty Association.

OGMORE

Electorate 70,156   1974: 67,927

Powell, R. (Lab)		29,867
Walters, L. (C)		13,780
Gibbs, Mrs J. T. (L)		9,812
Jones, D. I. (Pl Cymru)		2,450
Lab majority		16,087

No Change

	1974		1979
Total votes	51,195		55,909
Turnout	75·4%		79·7%
Lab	30,453	59·5%	53·4%
C	8,249	16·1%	24·6%
L	8,203	16·0%	17·5%
Pl Cymru	4,290	8·4%	4·4%
Lab maj	22,204	43·4%	28·8%
Swing		4·1%	+7·3%

Mr Raymond Powell, a senior administrative officer with the Welsh Water Authority. B 1928. Chairman, Labour Party of Wales, 1977; member Ogwr Borough Council. Former lecturer, National Council of Labour Colleges. Sponsored by USDAW.

Mr Leslie Walters, production foreman and formerly an industrial chemist with the British Steel Corporation, contested Merthyr Tydfil, October 1974, and Neath, February 1974. B 1937; ed Cowbridge Grammar School, Bridgend, and Margam Technical College. Mayor of Bridgend Town Council and deputy Conservative leader of Ogwr District Council, 1977.

Mrs Jennie Gibbs, housewife and former teacher of retarded children, contested the seat twice in 1974 and in 1966. B October, 1920; ed Maestag Grammar School; University College of Wales, Aberystwyth. Member, Ogwr District Council and Mid-Glamorgan County Council, since 1973; Maestag UDC, 1963-74, and Glamorgan CC, 1967-74.

Mr Dafydd Jones, teacher. B December, 1943; ed Aberaeron Grammar School and Aberystwyth University. Contested the seat, 1974. UCAC.

OLDHAM, East

Electorate 52,420   1974: 50,737

*Lamond, J. A. (Lab)		18,248
Walker, R. (C)		13,616
Hilyer, C. G. (L)		4,149
Lab majority		4,632

No Change

	1974		1979
Total votes	36,113		36,013
Turnout	71·2%		68·7%
Lab	19,054	52·8%	50·7%
C	10,917	30·2%	37·8%
L	6,142	17·0%	11·5%
Lab maj	8,137	22·6%	12·9%
Swing		−3·1%	+4·8%

Mr James Lamond, a design engineer, was elected in 1970. B November 1928; ed Burrelton School, Coupar Angus junior secondary school. Member, Aberdeen Town Council 1958-70; leader, Labour group 1967-70; Lord Provost, 1970-71; Lord Lieutenant of Aberdeen, 1970-71. Member, Public Accounts Committee. Sponsored by AUEW-TASS, and a member since 1944. Vice-chairman, PLP employment group, 1957. Vice-president, World Peace Council.

Mr Roy Walker, lecturer and tutor, contested Sheffield Brightside, October 1974. B 1943; ed Firth Park Grammar School, Sheffield, Exeter University Institute of Education, and Manchester University. Member, Stockport Metropolitan Borough Council and Stockport Area Health Authority. Secretary, Bredbury Conservative Association; member, Hazel Grove Divisional Executive Council.

Mr Christopher Hilyer, architect, contested the seat, February and October, 1974. B March, 1940; ed Prescot Grammar School and Manchester University.

OLDHAM, West

Electorate 46,763   1974: 48,062

*Meacher, M. H. (Lab)		17,802
Smith, J. (C)		12,025
Stocks, K. (L)		3,604
Halliwell, G. (Nat Front)		515
Lab majority		5,777

No Change

	1974		1979
Total votes	34,689		33,946
Turnout	72·2%		72·6%
Lab	18,444	53·2%	52·4%
C	10,407	30·0%	35·4%
L	5,838	16·8%	10·6%
Nat Front	—	—	1·5%
Lab maj	8,037	23·2%	17·0%
Swing		−3·1%	+3·1%

Mr Michael Meacher was Under-Secretary for Trade, 1976-79; Under-Secretary for Health and Social Security, 1975-76; Under-Secretary for Industry, 1974-5. Regained seat for Labour in 1970; contested Colchester, 1966. B November, 1939; ed Berkhamstead School; New College, Oxford; and LSE. Lecturer in social administration. Member, Fabian Society. Sponsored by COHSE.

Mr John Smith contested Sheffield, Brightside, February, 1974. B December, 1943; ed Cheltenham Grammar School, York and London Universities. Industrial consultant. Member, Brighton Borough Council.

Mr Kenneth Stocks, teacher, contested the seat, October, 1974. B May, 1937; ed Knaresborough Grammar School, Manchester University. Six years as teacher-missionary in Peshawar and Lahore. Speaks Urdu.

ORKNEY AND SHETLAND

Electorate 28,884   1974: 26,289

*Grimond, J. (L)	10,950
Donaldson, C. (C)	4,140
Goodlad, Miss R. (Lab)	3,385
Spens, M. (Scot Nat)	935

L majority	6,810

No Change

	1974		1979
Total votes	17,572		19,410
Turnout	66·8%		67·2%
L	9,877	56·2%	56·4%
Scot Nat	3,025	17·2%	4·8%
C	2,495	14·2%	21·3%
Lab	2,175	12·4%	17·4%
L maj	6,852	39·0%	35·1%

Mr Jo Grimond was Leader of the Liberal Party from 1956 to 1967. He won the seat 1950 after contesting it in 1945. Liberal spokesman on Scottish affairs, energy and the arts. Barrister (Middle Temple, 1937); director, The Manchester Guardian and Evening News Ltd from 1967. B July, 1913; ed Eton and Balliol College, Oxford. Secretary, Scottish National Trust, 1947-49; Rector, Edinburgh University, 1960-63; Chancellor, University of Kent since 1970. President, Scottish Liberal Party, 1970.

Mr Charles Donaldson, partner in a firm of chartered architects. B 1933; ed Buckie High School, Banffshire; Scott Sutherland School of Architecture; Robert Gordon's Institute of Technology, Aberdeen. Member, Edinburgh Central and North Conservative Associations; a director, Whitburn College for Adult Handicapped.

Miss Robina Goodlad, adult educator with 'The Planning Exchange'. B August, 1950; ed Scalloway Junior School, Shetland, Anderson High School, Lerwick, Aberdeen and Glasgow Universities. ASTMS.

Mr Michael Spens, architect/planner. Secretary, SNP International Committee. B October, 1939; ed Eton and Cambridge University.

ORMSKIRK

Electorate 97,764   1974: 96,593

*Kilroy-Silk, R. (Lab)	37,222
Keefe, B. (C)	36,364
Pirani, S. (WRP)	820

Lab majority	858

No Change

	1974		1979
Total votes	70,320		74,406
Turnout	72·8%		76·1%
Lab	35,392	50·3%	50·0%
C	26,541	37·7%	48·9%
L	8,387	11·9%	—
WRP	—	—	1·1%
Lab maj	8,851	12·6%	1·1%
Swing		−1·0%	+5·7%

Mr Robert Kilroy-Silk, a university lecturer and author, was elected February, 1974; contested the seat, 1970. B May, 1942; ed Saltley Grammar School, Birmingham; LSE and London University. Vice-chairman, PLP Home Affairs Group. Member, Public Accounts Committee, 1975-77; Select Committee on wealth tax, 1974-75; select committee on Race Relations and Immigration, 1975. Member, PLP employment, industry and health service groups.

Mr Brian Keefe, Liverpool University examiner and visiting lecturer, contested Liverpool, Scotland, in the by-election and general election February 1974, Liverpool Toxteth in 1966 and 1970, and Ormskirk, October 1974. B 1934; ed St Margaret's C of E School, Liverpool; Chester and Sheffield Colleges of Education; Rutgers and Michigan Universities. Fellow, Royal Geographical Society; vice-president, Liverpool Conservative Association. Qualified Rugby Union referee.

Mr Simon Pirani, aged 22, journalist on *Young Socialist*. Member, Young Socialists national committee.

OSWESTRY

Electorate 58,334   1974: 56,429

*Biffen, W. J. (C)	23,551
Sandland-Nielsen, P. E. (Lab)	10,150
Evans, D. J. (L)	9,405

C majority	13,401

No Change

	1974		1979
Total votes	40,539		43,106
Turnout	71·8%		73·9%
C	19,165	47·3%	54·6%
Lab	10,751	26·5%	23·5%
L	10,623	26·2%	21·8%
C maj	8,414	20·8%	31·1%
Swing		−1·9%	+5·1%

Mr John Biffen was appointed Chief Secretary to the Treasury, May, 1979, with a seat in the Cabinet. Chief Opposition spokesman on energy and industry, 1976-77. In November 1978, appointed spokesman on small businesses and self employed. Returned at by-election in 1961; contested Coventry, East, 1959. Economist. B

November, 1930; ed Dr Morgan's Grammar School, Bridgwater; Jesus College, Cambridge. Member, executive of 1922 Committee; ex-chairman, Conservative industry committee; librarian, Bow Group, 1961-62. Former member, Select Committee on Procedure, Public Accounts Committee, 1964-67; Select Committee on Nationalised Industries.

Mr Peter Sandland-Nielsen computer systems analyst. B December, 1941; ed Handsworth Technical School, Birmingham. Member, Hereford-Worcester County Council, since 1977. TGWU/ACTS.

Mr David Evans, lecturer, contested the seat, February and October, 1974, and Wallasey, 1970. B February 1947; ed Teignmouth Grammar School and Liverpool University.

OXFORD

Electorate 81,708   1974: 77,270

Patten, J. (C)	27,459
*Luard, D. E. T. (Lab)	25,962
Roaf, D. (L)	6,234
Cheeke, A. (Ox Ecol)	887
Smith, Mrs B. (Ind)	72

C majority	1,497

C gain from Lab

	1974		1979
Total votes	54,692		60,614
Turnout	70·8%		74·2%
Lab	23,359	42·7%	42·8%
C	22,323	40·8%	45·3%
L	8,374	15·3%	10·3%
Nat Front	572	1·0%	—
Ind	64	0·1%	0·1%
Ecology	—	—	0·1%
Lab maj	1,036	1·9%	—
C maj	—	—	2·5%
Swing		−1·7%	+2·2%

Mr John Pattern, university lecturer and director of an industrial relations company. B July. 1945; ed Wimbledon College and Sidney Sussex College, Cambridge. Member, Oxford City Council, 1973-76. Part-time member, Conservative Research Department; member, Oxford Conservative Association. AUT.

Mr Evan Luard was Under-Secretary for Foreign and Commonwealth Affairs, 1976-79, a post he held in 1969-70. MP for the constituency, 1966-70; returned in October, 1974. Contested the seat, 1964 and February, 1974. B October, 1926; ed Felsted and King's College, Cambridge. Fellow, St Anthony's College, Oxford. Member, Oxford City Council, 1958-61. University lecturer.

Mr Dermot Roaf, mathematics fellow of Exeter College, Oxford. B March, 1937; ed Winchester College, Christ Church, Oxford, Trinity College, Cambridge. Chairman, Oxford AUT, 1970-72.

Mr Anthony Cheeke, librarian of the Edward Grey Institute, stood for the Oxford Ecology Movement.

OXON, Mid

Electorate 63,212   1974: 59,607

*Hurd, D. R. (C)	28,465
Hedge, J. (Lab)	13,004
Burton, Miss M. (L)	8,367
Madden, P. (Ind)	174

C majority	15,461

No Change

	1974		1979
Total votes	45,591		50,010
Turnout	76·4%		79·1%
C	20,944	45·9%	56·9%
Lab	13,641	29·9%	26·0%
L	11,006	24·1%	16·7%
Ind	—	—	0·3%
C maj	7,303	16·0%	30·9%
Swing		−0·2%	+7·4%

Mr Douglas Hurd was appointed Minister of State for Foreign and Commonwealth Affairs in May 1979. Opposition spokesman on Europe since 1976-79; Head of Mr Edward Heath's political office, 1968-74. Elected February, 1974. B March, 1930; ed Eton and Trinity College, Cambridge. Worked in the Foreign Service 1952-66 in China,

the United States and Europe, becoming a chief secretary. Conservative Research Department, 1966-68. Author of five political thrillers. Member, Advisory Panel on Arms Control and Disarmament. Director, British section, European League for Economic Co-operation, since 1977.

Mr John Hedge, senior probation officer and member of the National Association of Probation Officers. B October, 1947; ed Royal Masonic School and Manchester University. Agent in Mid-Oxon for both elections in 1974.

Miss Muriel Burton, lecturer, contested the seat, October 1974, and Oldham, East, 1964. B June, 1934; ed Counthill Grammar School, Oldham, Manchester, Oxford and Reading Universities. Former member, Oldham Council; South Oxon District Council.

PAISLEY

Electorate 63,765   1974: 66,059

Adams, A. (Lab)	25,894
Willis, G. (C)	12,139
Rollo, D. R. (Scot Nat)	7,305
Monaghan, B. (Scot Lab)	811
Tait, Mrs J. (Comm)	145
White, T. (WRP)	122

Lab majority	13,755

Lab gain from Scot Lab

	1974		1979
Total votes	47,702		46,416
Turnout	72·2%		72·8%
Lab	21,368	44·8%	55·8%
Scot Nat	15,778	33·1%	15·7%
C	7,440	15·6%	26·2%
L	3,116	6·5%	—
Scot Lab	—	—	1·7%
Comm	—	—	0·3%
WRP	—	—	0·3%
Lab maj	5,590	11·7%	29·6%
Swing		−5·6%	−0·2%

Mr Allen Adams is a computer analyst. B February, 1946; ed Camphill High School, Paisley, and Reid-Kerr Technical College, Paisley. Vice-chairman, Strathclyde Social Services Council, for 10 years. APEX.

Mr George Willis, partner in car hire business. B 1943; ed Bellahouston Academy, Glasgow.

Mr David Rollo, chartered electrical engineer, contested the seat, February and October, 1974; Glasgow, Woodside, 1970; Hamilton, 1959. B July, 1919; ed Lenzie Academy and Glasgow University.

Mrs June Tait, cartographic draughtsman. Aged 30. AUEW/TASS.

Mr Thomas White, aged 43, shop steward at Chrysler's Linwood plant.

PEMBROKE

Electorate 76,268   1974: 72,053

*Edwards, R. N. (C)	30,483
Evans, A. (Lab)	23,015
Livesey, R. (L)	6,249
Dawe, R. (Pl Cymru)	1,573
Kingzett, B. (Ecology)	694
C majority	7,468

No Change

	1974		1979
Total votes	57,304		62,014
Turnout	79·5%		81·3%
C	23,190	40·5%	49·2%
Lab	22,418	39·1%	37·1%
L	9,116	15·9%	10·1%
Pl Cymru	2,580	4·5%	2·5%
Ecology	—	—	1·1%
C maj	772	1·4%	12·1%
Swing		−0·6%	+5·3%

Mr Nicholas Edwards was appointed Secretary of State for Wales in May, 1979. Became a member of the Shadow Cabinet as chief Opposition spokesman on Wales in 1975 having become a spokesman on Welsh affairs 1974-79. Won the seat in 1970. Insurance broker. B February, 1934; ed Westminster School and Trinity College,

Cambridge. Member, Select Committee on Members' Interests 1976-79. Secretary, Welsh group of Conservative MPs, 1972-74. Member of Lloyd's. Company director.

Mr Alan Evans, official of the National Union of Teachers. B February, 1939; ed Llanelli Grammar School and LSE. Member, ILEA, 1971-75; London Borough of Camden, 1974-78. NUT and NUGMW.

Mr Richard Livesey, senior lecturer in farm management, Welsh Agricultural College, Aberystwyth. B May 1935; ed Talgaeth CP School; Bedales School, Seale-Hayne Agricultural College, Reading University. Fought Perth and East Perthshire, 1970. NAFTHE.

Mr Ronald Dawe, partner in a firm of heating and plumbing engineers, is a former NUM lodge officer. B November, 1936; ed Nant-y-Moel County Secondary School. Served on Ogmore and Garw UDC.

PENISTONE

Electorate 72,370   1974: 67,060

*McKay, A. (Lab)	28,010
Dobkin, I. (C)	18,309
Chadwick, D. (L)	10,772
Lab majority	9,701

No Change

	1974		1979
Total votes	50,057		57,091
Turnout	74·6%		78·9%
Lab	27,146	54·2%	49·1%
C	12,011	24·0%	32·1%
L	10,900	21·8%	18·9%
Lab maj	15,135	30·2%	17·0%
Swing		−2·9%	+6·6%

1978 by-election: Total votes 42,718 (59·8%). Lab 19,424 (45·5%); C 14,053 (32·8%); L 9,241 (21·6%). Lab maj 5,371 (14·3%).

Mr Allen McKay won the seat in the by-election in 1978. Industrial relations officer with the National Coal Board. B February, 1927; ed Hoyland Kirk Balk School; Extra-Mural Department of University of Sheffield. Served on Hoyland Nether UDC, 1965-74; chairman, 1973-74. Member, Barnsley Metropolitan Borough Council, 1974-78. Com-

mittee member and branch president, NUM.

Mr Ian Dobkin, barrister, fought the 1978 by-election. B 1948; ed Leeds Grammar School and Queen's College, Oxford. Called to the Bar, 1971. Executive member, Leeds Council of Christians and Jews; member, Leeds Community Relations Council, since 1973. Treasurer North West Leeds Young Conservatives, 1972-73; former chairman, Leeds Federation of Young Conservatives; vice-chairman, Yorkshire Area Young Conservatives, 1973-76

Mr David Chadwick, lecturer, contested the seat in the 1978 by-election and twice in 1974; Blackpool, South, 1970; Nelson and Colne by-election, 1968. B September, 1939; ed Blackpool College of Technology. Member, Blackpool County Borough Council, 1968-72; Sheffield City Council, since 1976. NATFHE.

PENRITH AND THE BORDER

Electorate 57,210   1974: 55,602

*Whitelaw, W. S. I. (C)	26,940
West, L. R. (Lab)	9,844
Wates, B. (L)	7,257
C majority	17,096

No Change

	1974		1979
Total votes	40,553		44,041
Turnout	72·9%		77·0%
C	23,547	58·1%	61·2%
Lab	9,791	24·1%	22·4%
L	7,215	17·8%	16·5%
C maj	13,756	34·0%	38·8%
Swing		−2·7%	+2·4%

Mr William Whitelaw was appointed Home Secretary in May 1979. Deputy Leader of the Opposition 1975-79 after unsuccessfully contesting the leadership of the Conservative Party. Chief Opposition spokesman on devolution, 1974-76, and on home affairs and broadcasting, 1976-79. Chairman of the Conservative Party, 1974-75;

Opposition spokesman on employment 1974; Secretary of State for Employment, 1973-74; Secretary of State for Northern Ireland, 1972-73, and Lord President of the Council and Leader of the House of Commons, 1970-72. President, National Union of Conservative and Unionists Associations, 1971. Opposition chief whip, 1964-70; Parliamentary Secretary, Ministry of Labour, 1962-64. Elected 1955; contested East Dunbartonshire, 1950 and 1951. Member, Committee of Privileges. B June, 1918; ed Winchester and Trinity College, Cambridge. Farmer and landowner. Partner, Mount Pleasant Farms, Penrith.

Mr Linden West, tutor and organiser in adult education. B November 1946; ed Hanley High School, Stoke-on-Trent, and Keele University. Member, Carlisle City Council.

Mr Bernard Wates, now retired, contested Workington in 1976 by-election; Morecambe and Lonsdale, Feb 1974 and Westmorland, October 1974. B October, 1920; ed Mill Hill and Trinity Hall, Cambridge. Former teacher and deputy director of education for Westmorland.

PERTH AND EAST PERTHSHIRE

Electorate 62,142   1974: 57,646

Walker, W. C. (C)	20,153
*Crawford, G. D. (Scot Nat)	17,050
McKenzie, W. F. (Lab)	6,432
Goudie, B. (L)	4,410
C majority	3,103

C gain from Scot Nat

	1974		1979
Total votes	42,537		48,045
Turnout	73·8%		77·3%
Scot Nat	17,337	40·8%	35·5%
C	16,544	38·9%	41·9%
Lab	5,805	13·6%	13·4%
L	2,851	6·7%	9·2%
Scot Nat maj	793	1·9%	—
C maj	—	—	6·4%
Swing			+1·6%

Mr William Walker, managing director of his own management, marketing and design consultancy company, contested Dundee East, October 1974. B 1929; ed Logie and Blackness Schools Dundee; Trades College Dundee; College of Arts, Dundee; and College

of Distributive Trades, London. Senior Gliding Instructor Air Cadet Gliding Schools since 1968; former political officer and vice-chairman, Brandwood Branch, Birmingham Hall Green Conservative Association; member, British Institute of Management; fellow, Institute of Personnel Management and Royal Society of Arts.

Mr Douglas Crawford, managing director of a group of economic and development consultants and former journalist. Member and former director of communications, NUJ. SNP spokesman on finance and industry 1974-79. Elected in October 1974; contested seat, February, 1974. B 1941; ed Glasgow Academy and St Catherine's College, Cambridge. A vice-chairman of the SNP.

Mr William McKenzie, architect. B 1937. GMWU.

Mr Britton Goudie, registered indexer (legal). B November, 1914; ed King Edward's School, Birmingham, London University. Member, Society of Civil and Public Servants. Methodist lay preacher.

PETERBOROUGH

Electorate 72,912   1974: 63,044

Mawhinney, Dr B. (C)	27,734
*Ward, M. J. (Lab)	22,632
Green D. (L)	5,685
Wilhelmy, J. (Nat Front)	672
Bishop, M. (WRP)	106
C majority	5,102

C gain from Lab

	1974		1979
Total votes	49,094		56,829
Turnout	77·9%		77·9%
Lab	21,820	44·4%	39·8%
C	19,972	40·7%	48·8%
L	7,302	14·9%	10·0%
Nat Front	—		1·2%
WRP	—		0·2%
Lab maj	1,848	3·7%	—
C maj	—		9·0%
Swing		−1·9%	+6·3%

Dr Brian Mawhinney, university lecturer, Royal Free Hospital School of Medicine, London, contested Teesside, Stockton, in October, 1974. B July, 1940; ed Royal Belfast Academical Institution; Queens University, Belfast; University of Michigan; University of London. Member, Hendon North Conservative Association. AUT.

Mr Michael Ward was elected in October 1974 after contesting the seat, February 1974, 1970 and 1966. Former press officer with Inner London Education Authority. Member, Expenditure Committee, 1976-79 and of its Education, Arts and Home Office sub-committee. B April 1931; ed Royal Liberty Grammar School, Romford, and Manchester University. Member, Romford Borough Council and its successor London Borough of Havering, 1958-78; alderman, 1971-78; Leader of Council, 1971-74. President, London Government PR Association, 1977-79. NUJ and GMWU (MATSA).

Mr David Green, aged 29, bank employee.

Mr Michael Bishop, aged 28, employed in brick works. TGWU.

PETERSFIELD

Electorate 81,887   1974: 74,230

*Mates, M. J. (C)	39,200
Madeley J. (L)	16,825
Clough, B. W. (Lab)	8,082
C majority	22,375

No Change

	1974		1979
Total votes	56,809		64,107
Turnout	76.5%		78.3%
C	28,689	50.5%	61.1%
L	19,702	34.7%	26.2%
Lab	8,301	14.6%	12.6%
UDP	117	0.2%	
C maj	8,987	15.8%	34.9%
Swing		−1.4%	+6.3%

Mr Michael Mates was a regular soldier until he resigned his commission on adoption as prospective Conservative candidate for Petersfield in 1974. Elected October, 1974. B June, 1934; ed Blundell's and King's College, Cambridge. Served on staff of Vice-Chief of Defence Staff. Secretary, Conservative Northern Ireland Committee, since 1974.

Mr John Madeley, economic journalist, contested Christchurch and Lymington, October, 1974. B July, 1934; ed Bury Grammar School and Manchester University. Director, Madeley's Printers (Wilmslow) Ltd. Church of England lay reader. NUJ.

Mr Bertram Clough, Labour Party reseach assistant, and former senior assistant, education department, NATFHE. B July, 1947; ed Waterloo Grammar School, Kirkby College of Further Education, Manchester Polytechnic. TGWU (ACTS).

PLYMOUTH, Devonport

Electorate 48,236   1974: 50,105

*Owen, Dr D. A. L. (Lab)		16,545
Hughes, K. (C)		15,544
James, M. (L)		2,360
Bearsford-Walker, L. (Nat Front)		243
Stoner, R. (Ind)		203

Lab majority	1,001

No Change

	1974		1979
Total votes	36,802		34,895
Turnout	73.4%		72.3%
Lab	17,398	47.3%	47.4%
C	15,139	41.1%	44.5%
L	3,953	10.7%	6.8%
Ind L	312	0.8%	—
Nat Front	—	—	0.7%
Ind	—	—	0.6%
Lab maj	2,259	6.2%	2.9%
Swing		−2.5%	+1.6%

Dr David Owen was Secretary of State for Foreign and Commonwealth Affairs 1977-79; Minister of State, Foreign Office, 1976-77; Minister of State for Health, 1974-76; Under-Secretary for Health 1974. Elected in February, 1974; represented Plymouth, Sutton, 1966-74. Contested Torrington, 1964. Opposition spokesman on defence, 1970-72 but resigned after disagreement on EEC policy. Under-Secretary for Defence for the Royal Navy, 1968-70. B July, 1938; ed Bradfield College, Berkshire; Sidney Sussex College, Cambridge; and St Thomas's Hospital, London. ASTMS (MPU section).

Mr Kenneth Hughes, a company director. B March, 1922; ed The Acland School and Hammersmith

Building College. Fellow, Institute of Builders and Royal Society of Health. Member, Barnet Borough Council until 1974; mayor, 1971-72; former member, Hendon South Conservative Association executive committee; former assistant divisional treasurer, South-East Cornwall Conservative Association.

Mr Michael James, contested Cardiff, West, twice in 1974. Financial consultant and legal assistant. B March, 1934; ed Llandaff Technical College and Cardiff University.

PLYMOUTH, Drake

Electorate 55,711   1974: 55,556

*Fookes, Miss J. E. (C)	21,759
Fletcher, B. W. (Lab)	17,515
Puttick, A. (L)	3,452
Bradbury, C. (Nat Front)	279

C majority	4,244

No Change

	1974		1979
Total votes	41,894		43,005
Turnout	75.4%		77.2%
C	17,287	41.3%	50.6%
Lab	17,253	41.2%	40.7%
L	7,354	17.6%	8.0%
Nat Front	—	—	0.6%
C maj	34	0.1%	9.9%
Swing		−3.0%	+4.9%

Miss Janet Fookes, elected for the seat in 1974; represented Merton and Morden, 1970-74. Teacher. B February, 1936; ed Hastings and St Leonards Ladies' College, Hastings High School and Royal Holloway College, University of London. Member, Speakers' Panel of Chairmen; Expenditure Committee, chairman, Education, Arts and Home

Office subcommittee; Public Petitions Committee. Secretary, Conservative Parliamentary education committee, all-party deserted families group, and parliamentary animal welfare committee.

Mr Brian Fletcher, a faculty director at a secondary school, contested the seat, October, 1974, and Plymouth, Sutton, February, 1974. B March 1942; ed Birmingham University and King's College, London. Chairman, South-West Regional Council of the Labour Party. NAS and UWT.

Mr Anthony Puttick, barrister. Aged 44; ed Royal Naval College, Dartmouth and Brasenose College, Oxford.

PLYMOUTH, Sutton

Electorate 68,516   1974: 61,007

*Clark, A. K. M. (C)	28,892
Priestley, J. G. (Lab)	17,605
Scannell, J. (L)	6,226

C majority	11,287

No Change

	1974		1979
Total votes	45,857		52,723
Turnout	75.2%		76.9%
C	20,457	44.6%	54.8%
Lab	15,269	33.3%	33.4%
L	10,131	22.1%	11.8%
C maj	5,188	11.3%	21.4%
Swing		−2.8%	+5.0%

Mr Alan Clark, elected in February, 1974, is an historian; son of Lord Clark. B April, 1928; ed Eton and Christ Church, Oxford. Barrister, Inner Temple, 1955. Member, Institute for Strategic Studies. Governor, St Thomas's Hospital. Secretary, Conservative home affairs committee.

Mr Julian Priestley, a European civil servant, fought the seat, October, 1974. B May, 1950; ed St Boniface's College, Plymouth, and Balliol College, Oxford. APEX.

Mr John Scannell, laboratory technician. B August, 1915; ed Baltimore School, Irish Republic. Member, Saltash Borough Council and Caradon District Council. Nalgo.

PONTEFRACT AND CASTLEFORD

Electorate 60,697 1974: 60,288

*Lofthouse, G. (Lab)	30,566
Page, H. (C)	10,665
Marsh, L. (L)	3,616
Lab majority	19,901

No Change

By-election, 1978: Total vote 41,070. Lab 19,508 (65.8%); C 8,080 (27.2%); L 2,054 (7.0%). Lab majority 11,428 (38.6%).

	1974		1979
Total votes	42,890		44,847
Turnout	71·1%		73·9%
Lab	30,208	70·4%	68·2%
C	6,966	16·2%	23·8%
L	5,259	12·3%	8·1%
WRP	457	1·1%	—
Lab maj	23,242	54·2%	44·4%
Swing		−1·2%	+4·9%

Mr Geoffrey Lofthouse, a personnel manager, was elected at the by-election in October, 1978. B December, 1925; ed primary, secondary and Leeds University. Spent 20 years in local government service and was for 23 years a member of the NUM, BACM, APEX.

Mr Hugo Page, research officer for the Conservative Action for Electoral Reform, fought the 1978 by-election. B 1951; ed Harrow and Magdalene College, Cambridge. Former member, Cambridge University Conservative Association; member, Inner Temple and the Society of Conservative Lawyers.

Mr Leslie Marsh, aged 53, guest house owner. Contested 1978 by-election.

PONTYPOOL

Electorate 57,187 1974: 55,112

*Abse, L. (Lab)	27,751
Sackville, T. (C)	10,383
Mathias, E. A. R. (L)	5,508
Hyde, W. (Pl Cymru)	1,169
Lab majority	17,368

No Change

	1974		1979
Total votes	40,034		44,811
Turnout	72·6%		78·4%
Lab	25,381	63·4%	61·9%
C	6,686	16·7%	23·2%
L	5,744	14·3%	12·3%
Pl Cymru	2,223	5·6%	2·6%
Lab maj	18,695	46·7%	38·7%
Swing		−2·4%	+4·0%

Mr Leo Abse, a solicitor, was elected at by-election, November, 1958; contested Cardiff North, 1955. B April, 1917; ed Howard Gardens High School, Cardiff, and London School of Economics. Chairman, Cardiff Labour Party, 1951-53; member, Cardiff City Council, 1953-58. Member, Home Office Advisory Council for Penal Reform; Council of Institute for Study and Treatment for Delinquency; National Council for the Unmarried Mother and her Child; departmental committee on adoption; Select Committee on Abortion.

Mr Thomas Sackville, director of family-owned ranching business in Rhodesia and a partner in an exporting business. B 1950; ed St Aubyns School, Sussex, and Oxford University.

Mr Ernest Mathias, civil engineer, contested the seat, 1951, and twice in 1974. Served 10 years on Cwmbran Developmental Corporation. B April, 1916; ed Abersychan and Imperial College. Nalgo.

Mr William Hyde, coal miner. B July, 1946; ed Ruskin College, Oxford. NUM.

PONTYPRIDD

Electorate 75,050 1974: 70,200

*John, B. T. (Lab)	32,801
Clay, M. J. (C)	17,114
Penri-Williams, H. (L)	6,228
Roberts, E. A. (Pl Cymru)	2,200
Davies, R. G. (Nat Front)	263
Lab majority	15,687

No Change

	1974		1979
Total votes	51,797		58,606
Turnout	73·8%		78·1%
Lab	29,302	56·6%	56·0%
C	10,528	20·3%	29·2%
L	8,050	15·5%	10·6%
Pl Cymru	3,917	7·6%	3·8%
Nat Front	—	—	0·4%
Lab maj	18,774	36·3%	26·8%
Swing		−2·7%	+4·7%

Mr **Brynmor John,** was Minister of State, Home Office, 1976-79; Under-Secretary for Defence for the RAF, 1974-76. Elected in 1970. Solicitor, B April 1934; ed Pontypridd Grammar School and University College, London. Specialized in industrial accident law. Governor of Pontypridd secondary schools. Former member, local trades council.

Mr Michael Clay, chartered accountant. B July 1929; ed Winchester College, chairman, Cowbridge Branch, Pontypridd Conservative Association; vice-chairman, constituency Association.

Mr Hugh Penri-Williams, international insurance executive. B September, 1946; ed St Marylebone Secondary School, University College of Wales.

Mr Alun Roberts, aged 32, solicitor, with the South Wales Electricity Board. Ed Porth Grammar School, and University College of Wales.

POOLE

Electorate 87,208   1974: 83,403

Ward, J. (C)	38,846
Bell, D. A. (Lab)	15,291
Sutton, B. (L)	14,001
C majority	23,555

No Change

	1974		1979
Total votes	62,801		68,138
Turnout	75·3%		78·1%
C	28,982	46·1%	57·0%
L	17,557	28·0%	20·5%
Lab	16,262	25·9%	22·4%
C maj	11,425	18·1%	34·6%
Swing		−1·5%	+7·2%

Mr **John Ward,** a chartered civil engineer and managing director of a subsidiary of a major building company, contested Portsmouth, North, in October, 1974. B March, 1925; ed Romford County Technical School, and St Andrew's University. Chairman, Wessex area, 1966-69, and area treasurer since 1969. Member, Executive Committee, National Union of

Conservative and Unionist Associations; Conservative Political Centre National Advisory Committee; European Movement; Conservative Group for Europe. Founder member, Conservative Commonwealth Council; secretary, Mediterranean Group, 1955-60.

Mr David Bell, teacher and social worker, was parliamentary research assistant to Mrs Maureen Colquhoun, former MP for Northampton North. B March, 1947; ed Alleynes School, Stevenage, and Durham University. NUT.

Mr Bryan Sutton, deputy principal of Bournemouth and Poole College of Further Education. Ed LSE.

PORTSMOUTH, North

Electorate 68,870   1974: 69,089

Griffiths, P. (C)	26,356
*Judd, F. A. (Lab)	24,045
Brewin, S. (L)	3,354
Hadlow, R. (Nat Front)	298
Ferrett, W. (WRP)	122
C majority	2,311

C gain from Lab

	1974		1979
Total votes	53,094		54,175
Turnout	76·8%		78·7%
Lab	24,352	45·9%	44·4%
C	23,007	43·3%	48·6%
L	5,208	9·8%	6·2%
Pros Brit	527	1·0%	—
Nat Front	—	—	0·6%
WRP	—	—	0·2%
Lab maj	1,345	2·6%	—
C maj	—	—	4·2%
Swing		−1·0%	+3·4%

Mr **Peter Griffiths** represented Smethwick 1964-66 and contested Portsmouth, North, February, 1974. Senior lecturer. B May, 1928; ed West Bromwich Grammar School, City of Leeds Training College, London University and Birmingham University. Member, Smethwick Borough Council, 1955-64 and alderman, 1964-66; former president, Young Conservatives.

Mr Frank Judd was Minister of State at the Foreign and Commonwealth Office, 1977-79; Under-Secretary, Ministry of Overseas Development, 1976-77; Under-Secretary for Defence for the Royal Navy, 1974-76. Elected February, 1974; represented Portsmouth, West, 1966-74. An Opposition spokesman, 1972-74. B March, 1935; ed City of London School and LSE. PPS to Mr Harold Wilson, 1970-72. Sponsored by ASTMS.

Mr Sydney Brewin, self-employed. Contested Havant and Waterloo, February, 1974. B April, 1931; ed Burton-on-Trent Grammar School. Member, East Sussex Council, 1960-63; East Grinstead District Council, 1959-63.

PORTSMOUTH, South

Electorate 67,346   1974: 70,773

*Pink, R. B. (C)	26,835
Thomas, Mrs S. (Lab)	15,306
Wallis, J. (L)	6,487
Donkin, W. (Nat Front)	457
C majority	11,529

No Change

	1974		1979
Total votes	49,106		49,085
Turnout	69·4%		72·9%
C	23,379	47·6%	54·7%
Lab	15,308	31·2%	31·2%
L	9,807	20·0%	13·2%
Marx Len	612	1·2%	—
Nat Front	—	—	0·9%
C maj	8,071	16·4%	23·5%
Swing		−2·1%	+3·5%

189

Mr Bonner Pink, member of the Speaker's panel of chairmen, was elected in 1966. Company director. B September, 1912; ed Oundle. Member, Estimates Committee, 1967-70; former member, Public Expenditure Committee. Member, Portsmouth City Council from 1948 (Alderman, 1961); Lord Mayor of Portsmouth, 1961-62.

Mrs Sally Thomas, Teacher. B 1946.

Mr Jack Wallis, insurance broker, contested Southampton, Test, twice in 1974, 1970, and Buckingham, 1964. B February, 1923; ed Wilson's Grammar School, London, Goldsmiths Teacher Training College, London, and Sidney Sussex College, Cambridge. Member, Harpenden Urban District Council 1962-65.

PRESTON, North

Electorate 51,756   1974: 50,885

Atkins, R. J. (C)		18,632
*Atkins, R. H. (Lab)		18,603
Braham, M. P. (L)		2,715
Hetherington, J. F. (Nat Front)		329

C majority	29

C gain from Lab

	1974		1979
Total votes	39,390		40,279
Turnout	76·7%		77·8%
Lab	18,044	45·8%	46·2%
C	16,260	41·3%	46·3%
L	4,948	12·6%	6·7%
Pros Brit	138	0·4%	
Nat Front	—		0·8%
Lab maj	1,784	4·5%	
C maj	—		0·1%
Swing		−2·0%	+2·3%

Mr Robert Atkins, a sales executive, contested Luton West in February and October 1974. B February, 1946; ed Highgate School. Member, Haringey Borough Council 1968-76. Member, European Movement and General Council of the Conservative Group for Europe; chairman, Haringey for Europe Campaign, 1975; member, Hornsey Conservative Association since 1964; chairman, Hornsey Young Conservatives, 1967-69; vice-chairman, Greater London Young Conservatives, 1971-72.

Mr Ronald Atkins, elected February, 1974, represented the constituency, 1966-70; contested Lowestoft, 1964. B June, 1916; ed Barry County School and London University. Lecturer in further education college. Member, Preston District Council, 1974; Braintree Rural District Council, 1952-61. Member, Select Committees on Violence in Marriage and Violence in the Family. Chairman, PLP transport group and of all-party retirement group; treasurer, all-party group on health and safety. ASLEF.

Mr Michael Braham contested Huyton, October, 1974. Legal executive. B May, 1949.

PRESTON, South

Electorate 51,820   1974: 51,522

*Thorne, S. G. (Lab)		17,810
Tetlow, B. (C)		17,189
Marshall, R. P. (L)		4,625
Gibson, M. (Nat Front)		258
Stephens, V. A. (WRP)		116

Lab majority	621

No Change

	1974		1979
Total votes	39,355		39,998
Turnout	76·4%		77·2%
Lab	18,449	46·9%	44·5%
C	14,700	37·4%	43·0%
L	5,456	13·9%	11·6%
Nat Front	663	1·7%	0·6%
Pros Brit	87	0·2%	
WRP	—		0·3%
Lab maj	3,749	9·5%	1·5%
Swing		−2·5%	+4·0%

Mr Stanley Thorne, lecturer in industrial sociology, elected February 1974; contested Liverpool, Wavertree, 1964. B July, 1918; ed Ruskin College, Oxford and Liverpool University. Vice-chairman, PLP Northern Ireland group; member PLP health, housing and aviation groups. Liverpool councillor, 1963-66 and 1971-74, former deputy

chairman, Liverpool education committee. Sponsored by ASTMS.

Mr Brian Tetlow, estate agent and insurance broker, fought Westhoughton, February and October 1974. B August 1929; ed Xaverian College, Manchester. Chairman, Bolton East Conservative Association, 1971-74. Member, Greater Manchester County Council, since 1973; previously a member, Bolton Town Council.

Mr Ronald Marshall, vice-principal of college of further education, contested the seat, twice in 1974. B March, 1927; ed Woodhouse Grove School, Yorkshire; Handsworth College, Birmingham, and Manchester University. Member, Preston Borough Council. NATFHE.

PUDSEY

Electorate 67,853   1974: 65,354

*Shaw, J. G. D. (C)		24,591
Cooksey, S. J. (L)		15,852
McBride, P. D. (Lab)		13,727
Lewenz, P. (Ecology)		340

C majority	8,739

No Change

	1974		1979
Total votes	51,072		54,510
Turnout	78·1%		80·3%
C	20,180	39·5%	45·1%
L	15,599	30·5%	29·1%
Lab	15,293	29·9%	25·2%
Ecology	—		0·6%
C maj	4,581	9·0%	16·0%
Swing		−1·1%	+5·1%

Mr **Giles Shaw,** appointed an Under Secretary of State for Northern Ireland, in May, 1979, was elected in February 1974; contested Kingston upon Hull, West, 1966. B November, 1931; ed Sedbergh School and St John's College, Cambridge (President of the Union, 1954). Vice-chairman, Conservatives prices and consumer affairs com-  mittee, and all-party wool textile group. Member, select committee on nationalised industries 1976-79; served on Flaxton RDC from 1956-62. Joint secretary, Yorkshire Conservative MPs since 1974. Consultant, Rowntree Mackintosh Ltd, and Ogilvy, Benson and Mather Ltd. Director, North Riding Motors Ltd.

Mr **Stephen Cooksey,** an academic administrator. Contested the seat in both 1974 elections and Leeds, South, 1970. B January, 1944; ed Middlesbrough High School and Leeds University. Former member, Horsforth District Council and West Yorkshire County Council.

Mr **Peter McBride,** polytechnic lecturer. B May, 1939; ed St Mary's College, Middlesbrough, and Sheffield, Durham and Newcastle universities. NATFHE.

READING, North

Electorate 65,369   1974: 64,484

*Durant, R. A. B. (C)	25,085
Mason, Rev D. M. (Lab)	17,662
Minton, P. (L)	6,170
Baker, P. (Nat Front)	554
Edwards, L. W. (Ind)	126
C majority	7,423

No Change

	1974		1979
Total votes	46,658		49,597
Turnout	72·4%		75·9%
C	18,734	40·2%	50·6%
Lab	18,266	39·1%	35·6%
L	9,064	19·4%	12·4%
Nat Front	594	1·3%	1·1%
Ind	—	—	0·3%
C maj	468	1·1%	15·0%
Swing		−1·8%	+6·9%

Mr **Anthony Durant,** director and company secretary of an audio visual aids company, was elected, February 1974; contested Rother Valley, 1970. B January, 1928; ed Dane  Court Preparatory School and Bryanston School, Dorset. Member, Select Committee Parliamentary Commissioner for Administration since April 1974. Chairman, all-party committee for widows and single-parent families. Secretary, all-party committee on inland waterways and Conservative industry committee; Treasurer, Parliamentary group for world government. Member, Woking Urban Council, 1968-74; Chairman, Woking education committee, 1969-74; member, Surrey education committee, 1969-74. Consultant to Delta Metal Electrical (Holdings) Ltd, and to British Film Production, Assoc.

The **Rev David Mason,** community worker, contested Norfolk, North, February and October, 1974. B May,

1926; ed London and Boston universities. Member, GLC and Kensington and Chelsea Borough Council. TGWU and COHSE.

Mr **Peter Minton,** investment analyst. B November, 1935; ed Bromley County Grammar School. Served on Orpington UDC and Bromley Borough Council. NUJ.

READING, South

Electorate 73,001   1974: 69,124

*Vaughan, Dr G. F. (C)	30,067
Gale, B. (Lab)	14,422
Watts, K. (L)	10,642
Dunn, P. (Ecology)	700
C majority	15,645

No Change

	1974		1979
Total votes	51,627		55,831
Turnout	74·7%		76·5%
C	21,959	42·5%	53·9%
L	15,293	29·6%	19·1%
Lab	14,375	27·8%	25·8%
Ecology	—	—	1·3%
C maj	6,666	12·9%	28·1%
Swing		−2·0%	+6·7%

Dr **Gerard Vaughan** became Minister of State for Health at the DHSS in May, 1979. Was an Opposition spokesman on the social services 1975-79; Opposition whip, 1974-75. Elected February, 1974; held Reading for the Con-  servatives, 1970-74; contested Poplar, 1955. Specialist at Guy's Hospital and has acted as adviser to voluntary organizations, including National Society for Autistic Children, and National Institute for the Deaf. B June, 1923; ed London University and Guy's Hospital. Alderman, GLC, 1967-72, and LCC, 1955-64. President, Conservative Medical Society.

Mr **Bernard Gale,** employed by Post Office as lecturer in sociology. B June, 1921; ed Grecian Street Central School, Salford and Middlesex Polytechnic. Member, Gloucester CBC, 1958-65. Society of Post Office Executives.

Mr **Keith Watts,** computer systems manager, contested Reading North, October, 1974. B October, 1942; ed Hertford Grammar School and Slough College of Technology. Member, Wokingham Rural District Council, 1972-74; Wokingham District Council, 1973-76. Woodley Town Council, 1973-76. Nalgo.

REDBRIDGE, Ilford, North

Electorate 65,052   1974: 65,195

*Bendall, V. W. H. (C)	26,381
Jowell, Mrs T (Lab)	19,186
Freeman, J. (L)	4,568
Hughes, J. R. (Nat Front)	804
Iremonger, T. L. (Ind C)	452
C majority	7,195

No Change

	1974		1979
Total votes	48,544		51,391
Turnout	74·5%		79·0%
Lab	20,621	42·5%	37·3%
C	19,843	40·9%	51·3%
L	8,080	16·6%	8·9%
Nat Front	—	—	1·6%
Ind C	—	—	0·9%
Lab maj	778	1·6%	—
C maj	—	—	14·0%
Swing		−1·1%	+7·8%

1978 by election: Total votes 44,819 (68.9%) C 22,548 (50.4%), Lab 17,051 (38.0%), L 2,248 (5.0%), Nat Front 2,126 (4.7%) others 846 (1.9%). C majority 5,479 (12.0%). C gain from Lab.

Mr Vivian Bendall, surveyor and valuer, won the seat for the Conservatives in the March, 1978 by-election; contested Hertford and Stevenage, February and October, 1974. B December, 1938; ed Coombe Hill House, Croydon, and Broad Green College, Croydon. Member, Croydon Borough Council, 1964-78, and GLC, 1970-73. Chairman, Greater London Young Conservatives, 1967-68. Partner in firm of surveyors and valuers.

Mrs Tessa Jowell, assistant director of MIND, contested the 1978 by-election. B September, 1947; ed St Margaret's School, Aberdeen, Aberdeen and Edinburgh universities; Goldsmiths College, London. Member, Camden Borough Council, since 1971; chairman, social services committee, 1974-76; now chairman, staff committee. ACTS (branch of TGWU).

Mr John Freeman, headmaster, contested the 1978 by-election. B April, 1931; ed Ilford County High School, Westminster College, London, and Institute of Education, London University. NUT.

Mr Thomas Iremonger was Conservative MP for this seat from a by-election in February, 1954, until he was defeated in October, 1974. Contested seat as independent in 1978 by-election; also fought Birmingham, Northfield, 1950. B March, 1916; ed Oriel College, Oxford. Author of books on penalogy and economics. Member, Royal Commission on Penal System, 1963-66.

REDBRIDGE, Ilford South

Electorate 54,295   1974: 56,257

Thorne, N. G. (C)	19,290
*Shaw, A. J. (Lab)	17,602
Scott, R. J. R. (L)	3,664
Fitzgerald, T. C. (Nat Front)	636

C majority	1,688

C gain from Lab

	1974		1979
Total votes	39,230		41,192
Turnout	69·7%		75·9%
Lab	17,538	44·7%	42·7%
C	15,789	40·2%	46·8%
L	5,734	14·6%	8·9%
Pros Brit	169	0·4%	—
Nat Front	—	—	1·5%
Lab maj	1,749	4·5%	—
C maj	—	—	4·1%
Swing		−0·9%	+4·3%

Mr Neil Thorne, chartered surveyor, contested the seat in October, 1974. B August, 1932; ed City of London School and London University. Lloyd's Underwriter. Member, County of London Territorial Association; vice-president, British Legion, Member, Redbridge Borough Council, 1966-68, and alderman 1976-78, GLC, 1967-73; member; Statutory Committee for Dockland Development; freeman and liveryman, City of London; governor, Mayfield School for Girls; chairman, Beech Co-ownership Housing Society.

Mr Arnold Shaw elected in February, 1974, was MP for Ilford, South, 1966-70. Contested the seat 1964. Teacher. B July, 1909; ed Cooper's Company School, London, and University College. Southampton. Member, Redbridge Council, 1971-74 and from 1965-68; Ilford Borough Council, 1952-65, and Stepney Borough Council, 1934-48. NUT.

Mr Ralph Scott contested Waltham Forest, Leyton, October, 1974. B January, 1939; ed South-East Essex County Technical School, Barking, and North East London, Polytechnic. Contracts officer.

REDBRIDGE, Wanstead and Woodford

Electorate 57,218   1974: 58,378

*Jenkin, C. P. F. (C)	26,214
Macnulty, M G. (Lab)	8,464
Cornish, A. (L)	6,535
Bond, C. (Nat Front)	957

C majority	17,750

No Change

	1974		1979
Total votes	39,850		42,170
Turnout	68·3%		73·7%
C	21,209	53·2%	62·2%
Lab	10,369	26·0%	20·1%
L	8,272	20·8%	15·5%
Nat Front	—	—	2·3%
C maj	10,840	27·2%	42·1%
Swing		−0·7%	+7·4%

Mr Patrick Jenkin, was appointed Secretary of State for Social Services in May, 1979, having been chief Opposition spokesman on the social services since, 1976. Was appointed to the Shadow Cabinet in 1974 as chief spokesman on energy. Minister of Energy, 1972-74; Chief Secretary, Treasury, 1972-74; Financial Secretary to the Treasury, 1970-72. Opposition spokesman on finance, economic and trade affairs, 1965-70. Elected in 1964. B September, 1926; ed Clifton College and Jesus College, Cambridge. Barrister, industrial adviser and director of companies.

Mr Michael Macnulty, data handling manager. Member, Waltham Forest Borough Council, since 1971. B August, 1946; ed Leyton County High School for Boys. NUBE.

Mr Alan Cornish, transport executive, has contested local government elections. B January, 1940; ed London University and North-Western University, US.

REIGATE

Electorate 72,248   1974: 72,745

*Gardiner, G. A. (C)	33,767
Grant, N. (Lab)	12,454
Speyer, J. (L)	10,257
C majority	21,313

No Change

	1974		1979
Total votes	54,774		56,478
Turnout	75·3%		78·2%
C	27,769	50·7%	59·8%
Lab	14,185	25·9%	22·1%
L	12,554	22·9%	18·2%
Pple Power	266	0·5%	—
C maj	13,584	24·8%	37·7%
Swing		−1·4%	+6·4%

Mr George Gardiner, journalist. Editor, *Conservative Monthly News* and author of a biography on Mrs Thatcher. Elected February 1974; contested Coventry South, 1970. B March, 1935; ed Harvey Grammar School, Folkestone, and Balliol College, Oxford. Secretary, Conservative European affairs committee.  Organising secretary, Conservative "Union Flag" (anti-devolution) group. Former member, education sub-committee of Expenditure Committee. Former senior political correspondent for Thomson Newspapers. NUJ.

Mr Nicholas Grant, head of research for the Confederation of Health Service Employees. B March, 1948; ed Bristol Polytechnic and University of Warwick. Member labour NEC social policy and human rights sub-committees; Lambeth Borough Council. COHSE and NUJ.

Mr Jack Speyer, chartered loss adjuster. B April, 1943; ed Strand Grammar School.

RENFREWSHIRE, East

Electorate 64,456   1974: 61,911

Stewart, J. A. (C)	25,910
Sullivan, Mrs E. (Lab)	12,672
Craig, W. G. A. (L)	9,366
Pow, J. (Scot Nat)	3,989
C majority	13,238

No Change

	1974		1979
Total votes	47,996		51,937
Turnout	77·6%		80·6%
C	19,847	41·4%	49·9%
Scot Nat	11,137	23·2%	7·7%
Lab	9,997	20·8%	24·4%
L	7,015	14·6%	18·0%
C maj	8,710	18·2%	25·5%
Swing		−5·0%	+2·4%

Mr Alan Stewart, university lecturer; contested Dundee, East, in 1970. B 1942; ed Bell Baxter High School, Cupar, St Andrew's University and Harvard. Member, London Borough of Bromley, 1974-76. Treasurer, Beckenham Conservative Association, 1974-76.

Mrs Ellen Sullivan, teacher. B September, 1945; ed St Augustine's Secondary School, Glasgow, Glasgow School of Art. Member, Cumbernauld Council, 1974-76. ETS.

Mr William Craig, an export manager, contested the seat twice in 1974. B March, 1925; ed Glasgow High School and Glasgow University. Former president, University Liberal Club.

RENFREWSHIRE, West

Electorate 78,218   1974: 67,078

*Buchan, N. F. (Lab)	28,236
Boyle, W. (C)	19,664
Cameron, C. D. (Scot Nat)	8,333
Finnie, J. R. (L)	7,256
Lab majority	8,572

No Change

	1974		1979
Total votes	53,718		63,489
Turnout	80·1%		81·2%
Lab	20,674	38·5%	44·5%
Scot Nat	15,374	28·6%	13·1%
C	14,399	26·8%	31·0%
L	3,271	6·1%	11·4%
Lab maj	5,300	9·9%	13·5%
Swing		−3·5%	−0·9%

Mr Norman Buchan was Minister of State for Agriculture, Fisheries and Food, 1974; Opposition spokesman on agriculture, 1973-74, and on Scottish affairs, 1970-73; Under-Secretary, Scottish Office, 1967-70. Elected in 1964. Teacher. B October, 1922; ed Kirkwall Grammar School and Glasgow University. Member, Public Accounts Committee, 1975. Chairman, PLP Scottish group. Member, Council of Poetry Societies, since 1977. Sponsored by TGWU.

Mr Walter Boyle, whisky broker. B 1935; ed Hillhead High School, Glasgow. Member, Strathclyde Regional Council, since 1974; Dunbartonshire County Council, 1974-75; Bearsden Burgh Council, 1973-75. Vice-chairman, East Dunbartonshire Conservative Association.

Mr Charles Cameron, chartered accountant, contested the seat, February and October, 1974. B August, 1942; ed Hutcheson Boys' School, Glasgow, Former member, Largs Town Council.

RHONDDA

Electorate 63,412   1974: 65,787

*Jones, T. A. (Lab)	38,007
Leyshon, P. (C)	6,526
James, G. (Pl Cymru)	4,226
True, A. (Comm)	1,819

Lab majority	31,481

No Change

	1974		1979
Total votes	50,112		50,578
Turnout	76·2%		79·8%
Lab	38,654	77·1%	75·1%
PL Cymru	4,173	8·3%	8·4%
C	3,739	7·5%	12·9%
L	2,142	4·3%	—
Comm	1,404	2·8%	3·6%
Lab maj	34,481	68·8%	62·2%
Swing		−3·4%	+3·7%

Mr Alec Jones was Under Secretary for Wales, 1975-79; Under Secretary for Social Security, 1974-75. Elected February, 1974; represented Rhondda, West 1967-74. Former Secretary, Welsh Labour Group. Teacher, B August, 1924; ed Porth Grammar School and training college, Bangor, Chairman, PLP education group, 1969-70; former Wood Green borough councillor. NUT. Sponsored by COHSE.

Mr Peter Leyshon, arts and crafts teacher, contested Rhondda, twice in 1974. B October, 1933; ed Tonypandy Grammar School and Cardiff College of Art. Founder chairman, Rhondda Constituency Conservative Association, 1973; member, British Mountaineering Council Committee of Management; member, executive committee, South Wales Mountain Rescue Association.

Mr Glyn James, engineer with the National Coal Board. County and borough councillor. NUM.

Mr Arthur True, electrician; former shop steward and convenor for ETU. Member, National executive, Communist Party, since 1965.

RICHMOND UPON THAMES, Richmond

Electorate 50,811   1974: 53,821

*Royle, Sir A. (C)	19,294
Watson, A. J. (L)	16,764
Filochowski, J. (Lab)	4,692
King, K. J. (Ind)	315
Murphy, Mrs P. (Nat Front)	244
Wedgwood, D. D. (ENP)	34

C majority	2,530

No Change

	1974		1979
Total votes	40,399		41,343
Turnout	75·1%		81·4%
C	17,450	43·2%	46·7%
L	13,235	32·8%	40·5%
Lab	8,714	21·6%	11·3%
Nat Front	1,000	2·5%	0·6%
Ind	—	—	0·8%
ENP	—	—	0·1%
C maj	4,215	10·4%	6·2%
Swing		−2·0%	+6·9%

Sir Anthony Royle, chairman, party's overseas committee and international office; vice-chairman, Conservative committee on European Affairs, served as Under Secretary of State for Foreign and Commonwealth Affairs, 1970-74. Elected in 1959; contested St Pancras, North, 1955, and Torrington by-election, 1958. B March, 1927; ed Harrow and Sandhurst. Director of several major public companies; member of Lloyd's. Opposition whip, 1967-70. Member Select Committee on Broadcasting. Appointed a vice-chairman of Conservative Party with responsibility for candidates, May 1979.

Mr Alan Watson, head of the television, radio, audio-visual division of the EEC Commission, Brussels. Contested the seat, October, 1974. B February, 1941; ed Kingswood School and Jesus College, Cambridge.

Mr Julian Filochowski, education secretary, Catholic Institute for International Relations. B December, 1947; ed St Michael's College, Leeds, and Churchill College, Cambridge. TGWU (ACTS).

RICHMOND UPON THAMES,

Twickenham

Electorate 71,535   1974: 72,210

*Jessel, T. F. H. (C)	30,017
Waller, J. (L)	17,169
Wetzel, D. (Lab)	9,591
Braithwaite, M. (Nat Front)	686

C majority	12,848

No Change

	1974		1979
Total votes	53,719		57,463
Turnout	74·4%		80·3%
C	24,959	46·5%	52·2%
Lab	15,452	28·8%	16·7%
L	13,021	24·2%	29·9%
Anti EEC	287	0·5%	—
Nat Front	—	—	1·2%
C maj	9,507	17·7%	22·3%
Swing		−1·0%	+8·9%

Mr Toby Jessel was elected in 1970; contested Kingston-upon-Hull, North, at the by-election in 1966 and at the general election two months later; fought Peckham, 1964. B July, 1934; ed Royal Naval College, Dartmouth, and Balliol College, Oxford. Member, GLC, for Richmond upon Thames, 1956-73, and of Southwark Borough Council, 1964-66. Joint secretary, Greater London group of Conservative MPs.

Mr John Waller, managing partner of computer systems manufacturer. B April, 1940; ed Sir Rodger Marwood's School, Sandwich, and Caius College, Cambridge. Member, Richmond upon Thames Borough Council, since 1973.

Mr David Wetzel, political organizer. B October, 1942; ed Spring Grove Grammar School and Ealing College of Higher Education. Councillor, London Borough of Hounslow, 1964-68. TGWU.

RICHMOND, (Yorks)

Electorate 65,319   1974: 62,002

*Kitson, Sir T. (C)	28,958
Hodgson, G. (L)	9,964
Bratton, K. R. (Lab)	8,173
C majority	18,994

No Change

	1974		1979
Total votes	40,709		47,095
Turnout	65·7%		72·1%
C	23,156	56·9%	61·5%
L	9,528	23·4%	21·2%
Lab	8,025	19·7%	17·4%
C maj	13,628	33·5%	40·3%
Swing		−2·3%	+3·4%

Sir Timothy Kitson, Parliamentary Private Secretary to Mr Heath as Prime Minister, 1970-74 and as Leader of the Opposition, 1974-75. Opposition whip, 1967-70. Elected in 1959. Farmer and company director. B January, 1931; ed Charterhouse and the Royal Agricultural College, Cirencester. Secretary, Conservative Agriculture Committee, Member, Public Accounts Committee since 1975, Estimates Committee, 1964-66; North Riding County Council, 1955-60 and Thirsk RDC, 1954-57.

Mr Gerald Hodgson, surveyor. B May, 1939; ed Sherborne, Dorset.

Mr Kenneth Bratton, a lecturer, contested Horncastle, October, 1974. B July, 1946; ed Hull University. NATFHE.

RIPON

Electorate 53,180   1974: 50,172

*Hampson, K. (C)	25,292
Tennant, R. (L)	9,089
Davies, W. N. (Lab)	6,749
Laurence, A. (Ecology)	781
C majority	16,203

No Change

	1974		1979
Total votes	39,598		41,911
Turnout	78·9%		78·8%
C	20,636	52·1%	60·3%
L	13,632	34·4%	21·7%
Lab	5,330	13·5%	16·1%
Ecology	—	—	1·9%
C maj	7,004	17·7%	38·6%
Swing		−0·1%	+2·8%

Mr Keith Hampson regained the seat for the Conservatives in February, 1974. Contested it at by-election in July, 1973. Vice-chairman, Conservative education committee. Personal assistant to Mr Heath in the 1966 general election and also assisted him in the Bexley contest in 1970. B August, 1943; ed King James I Grammar School, Bishop Auckland, and at Bristol and Harvard universities. Former chairman, Bristol University Conservative Associaton. Lecturer in American history, Edinburgh University, 1968-74.

Mr Robert Tennant, chartered librarian, contested Teesside, Thornaby, twice in 1974. B August, 1936; ed Ripon Grammar School and Leeds School of Librarianship. Member, Northallerton Town Council, since 1976. Nalgo.

Mr William Davies, a principal child care adviser. B 1931. Nalgo, NUPE.

Mr Alastair Laurence, aged 31, proprietor of a piano-making business and freelance teacher of local history and environmental studies.

ROCHDALE

Electorate 66,841   1974: 67,029

*Smith, C (L)	22,172
Connell J. (Lab)	16,878
Picton, I. (C)	9,494
Merrick, J. (Nat Front)	690
L majority	5,294

No Change

	1974		1979
Total votes	47,098		49,234
Turnout	70·3%		73·7%
L	20,092	42·7%	45·0%
Lab	17,339	36·8%	34·3%
C	7,740	16·4%	19·3%
Nat Front	1,927	4·1%	1·4%
L maj	2,753	5·9%	10·7%

Mr Cyril Smith gained the seat for the Liberals in the by-election in October, 1972. Fought the seat in 1970. Party spokesman on employment and social services. B June, 1928; ed Rochdale Grammar School Managing director, Smith Springs (Rochdale) Ltd. Mayor of Rochdale, 1966-67. Member, borough council 1952-75. On Parliamentary panel, TGWU, 1955-58. Member, Commons Services Committee, former member, Select Committee on Procedure, Select Committee on Nationalised Industries. Deputy pro-chancellor, Lancaster University.

Mr John Connell, a works convenor of shop stewards, contested the seat in October, 1974. Mayor of Heywood, 1959. Member, Rochdale Metropolitan Borough Council, since 1973; county councillor, 1973-77; mayor, Rochdale, 1977-78, B November, 1928; ed St Joseph's Roman Catholic School, Heywood and Bolton School of Art.

Mr Iain Picton, youth and community officer at Conservative Central Office. B 1951; ed The Grange School, Welwyn; Alleyne's Grammar School, Hertfordshire; and University of Liverpool. Became national vice-chairman, Federation of Conservative Students. Member, North West Area Young Conservatives executive; Committee member, Young European Democrats.

ROCHESTER AND CHATHAM

Electorate 79,872   1974: 79,799

Fenner, Mrs P. E (C)	27,574
*Bean, R. E. (Lab)	24,886
Black, Mrs M. (L)	5,219
King, J. (Nat Front)	417

C majority	2,688

C gain from Lab

	1974		1979
Total votes	58,701		58,096
Turnout	73·6%		72·7%
Lab	25,467	43·4%	42·8%
C	23,049	39·3%	47·5%
L	9,035	15·4%	9·0%
Nat Front	1,150	2·0%	0·7%
Lab maj	2,418	4·1%	—
C maj	—	—	4·7%
Swing		−2·8%	+4·4%

Mrs Peggy Fenner represented the seat 1970-October 74. She served on the Select Committee for the Civil List and the Select Committee on Public Expenditure; Parliamentary Secretary to the Ministry of Agriculture, Fisheries and Food, 1972-73. B November, 1922; ed LCC Elementary School, Brockley and Ide Hill School, Kent. Housewife, Chairman, Sevenoaks UDC 1962-63 on which she served for 15 years. Member, executive of Kent Borough and Urban District Councils Association, 1967-71. Member, West Kent Divisional Executive Education Committee 1962-72 Member, European Parliament, 1974.

Mr Robert Bean, who won the seat in October, 1974, contested Thanet, East, in February, 1974 and Gillingham, 1970. B September, 1935; ed Rochester Mathematical School and Medway College of Technology. Member, Select Committee on Nationalised Industries. Polytechnic Lecturer. Member, Chatham Borough Council, 1958-74, and Medway Borough Council 1974-76. Sponsored by UCATT.

Mrs Mary Black, teacher, contested the seat, October, 1974. B November, 1930; ed Lelvinside Senior Secondary School and Sittingbourne College of Education.

ROSS AND CROMARTY

Electorate 32,892   1974: 29,411

*Gray, J. H. N. (C)	10,650
McRae, W. (Scot Nat)	5,915
Bloomer, K. (Lab)	5,055
Morrison, H. (L)	3,496

C majority	4,735

No Change

	1974		1979
Total votes	20,432		25,116
Turnout	69·5%		76·4%
C	7,954	38·9%	42·4%
Scot Nat	7,291	35·7%	23·6%
Lab	3,440	16·8%	20·1%
L	1,747	8·6%	13·9%
C maj	663	3·2%	18·8%
Swing		2·9%	+0·1%

Mr Hamish Gray, became Minister of State for Energy in May, 1979. An Opposition spokesman on energy 1975-79. Won the seat in 1970. Lord Commissioner of the Treasury (whip), 1973-74; assistant Government whip, 1973-74. B June, 1927; ed Inverness Royal Academy. Former director of a roofing and contracting firm. Member, Inverness Town Council and County Council, 1965-70. Former member, council, Highland Chamber of Commerce and of Highlands and Islands Youth Employment Committee. Member, Select Committee on Scottish Affairs. 1971.

Mr William McRae, a partner in a firm of solicitors, contested the seat twice in 1974. B May, 1923; ed Falkirk High School and Glasgow University. SNP executive vice-chairman and convener of party's land policy committee.

Mr Keir Bloomer, teacher. B July, 1947; ed Greenock Academy and Magdalene College, Cambridge.

Mr Hamish Morrison, policy director of the Scottish Council for Development and Industry. B May, 1944; ed Kilmarnock Academy and RNC, Dartmouth.

ROSSENDALE

Electorate 50,623   1974: 50,463

Trippier, D. A. (C)	20,370
*Noble, M. A. (Lab)	18,497
Arnold, P. (L)	3,534

C majority	1,873

C gain from Lab

	1974		1979
Total votes	40,802		42,401
Turnout	80·9%		83·8%
Lab	16,156	39·6%	43·6%
C	15,953	39·1%	48·0%
L	8,693	21·3%	8·3%
Lab maj	203	0·5%	—
C maj	—	—	4·4%
Swing		−1·2%	+2·4%

Mr David Tripper, a stockbroker, contested Rochdale in October, 1972, by-election and Oldham, West, in February and October, 1974. B May, 1946; ed Bury Grammar School, former lecturer in Stock Exchange economics. Member, Rochdale Metropolitan Borough Council, leader of Conservative Group (member of council since 1969); chairman, Rochdale Young Conservatives, 1965; chairman, South-East Lancashire Young Conservatives, 1966. Member, Stock Exchange. Director of financial planning company. Officer in Royal Marines Reserve.

Mr Michael Noble was elected October, 1974; contested the seat February, 1974, and Manchester, Withington, 1970. B March, 1935; ed Hull Grammar School and Sheffield and Hull universities. Lecturer. Chairman, PLP textile group. Secretary, North-West Labour MPs. Member, Burnley County Borough Council, 1971-74; chairman of education committee.

ASTMS. Parliamentary spokesman for Amalgamated Textile Workers Union. Qualified FA and MCC coach.

Mr Peter Arnold, teacher, contested Stockport, North, twice in 1974. B August, 1944; ed London and Manchester universities.

ROTHERHAM

Electorate 60,871 1974: 61,209

*Crowther, J. S. (Lab)	26,580
Hinckley, D. (C)	13,145
House, Mrs I. (L)	3,686
Davies, K. (Nat Front)	490
Lab majority	13,435

No Change

1976 by-election:- Total vote 28,313 (46.3%); Lab 14,351 (50.8%); C 9,824 (34.7%); L 2,214 (7.8%); Nat Front 1,696 (6.0%); others 228 (0.7%); Lab majority 4,527 (16.1%).

	1974		1979
Total votes	40,064		43,901
Turnout	65·5%		72·1%
Lab	25,874	64·6%	60·5%
C	8,840	22·1%	29·9%
L	5,350	13·4%	8·4%
Nat Front	—		1·1%
Lab maj	17,034	42·5%	30·6%
Swing		−2·7%	+5·9%

Mr Stanley Crowther was elected at a by-election in June, 1976. B May, 1925; ed Rotherham Grammar School and Rotherham College of Technology. Journalist. Member, Rotherham Borough Council, 1958-59 and 1961-76. Mayor of Rotherham, 1971-72, and 1975-76; chairman, planning committee, 1964-76; chairman,  Yorkshire and Humberside Development Association, 1972-76. Member, executive, Town and Country Planning Association. NUJ and Sponsored by TGWU.

Mr Douglas Hinckley, director of a group of family companies, fought the 1976 by-election. B 1933; ed Leys School, Cambridge. Chairman, Wiseton Parish Council. Member, central committee, Sheffield Conservative Associations. Sheffield representative on Yorkshire Area Conservative Advisory Committee on Education.

Mrs Ingrid House, teacher. Past president, Rotherham Teachers' Association and Rotherham Divisional Council, NUT. Membership secretary, Rotherham NUT. B August, 1948; ed Seyne Grammar School, Rayleigh, Essex, and Sheffield City College of Education.

ROTHER VALLEY

Electorate 99,029 1974: 91,963

*Hardy, P. (Lab)	45,986
Barber, R. (C)	19,984
Sykes, C. (L)	7,937
Lab majority	26,002

No Change

	1974		1979
Total votes	66,391		73,907
Turnout	72·2%		74·6%
Lab	44,670	67·3%	62·2%
C	11,893	17·9%	27·0%
L	9,828	14·8%	10·7%
Lab maj	32,777	49·4%	35·2%
Swing		−1·3%	+7·1%

Mr Peter Hardy, elected in 1970, was a teacher. Member, UK delegation to the Consultative Assembly of the Council of Europe, October, 1975. B July, 1931; ed Wath upon Dearne Grammar School; Westminster College, London; Sheffield University. Contested Scarborough and Whitby, 1964; Sheffield, Hallam, 1966. Chairman PLP  energy group; vice-chairman PLP Northern Ireland group. Member, Expenditure Committee. Sponsored by NUPE.

Mr Richard Barber, solicitor, is secretary of the Bow Group and of group's standing committee on defence. B 1946; ed Dean Close School, Cheltenham; Reading University. Chairman, Sutton and Cheam Young Conservatives, 1974-75; President, Greater London YC Debating Union, 1976-77. Author of several Bow Group pamphlets.'

Mr Colin Sykes, bank official, B July, 1941; ed Bentley School, Calne, Wiltshire, and Bishopshalt School, Hillingdon. ASTMS.

ROXBURGH, SELKIRK AND PEEBLES

Electorate 59,691 1974: 57,824

*Steel, D. M. S. (L)	25,993
Malone, G. P. (C)	15,303
Heald, D. (Lab)	4,150
Stewart, A. (Scot Nat)	3,502
L majority	10,690

No Change

	1974		1979
Total votes	45,791		48,948
Turnout	80·6%		82·0%
L	20,006	43·7%	53·1%
C	12,331	27·4%	31·3%
Scot Nat	9,178	20·0%	7·2%
Lab	4,076	8·9%	8·5%
L maj	7,475	16·3%	21·8%

Mr David Steel, was elected Leader of the Liberal Party in July 1976, when he also took charge of the party's role on devolution. Former Liberal Whip. Won the seat from the Conservatives at the 1965 by-election; contested the seat, 1964. Liberal spokesman on foreign affairs from 1975. Sponsored the Abortion Act, 1967 and member, Select Committee on

Abortion (Amendment) Bill, 1975-76. President of the Anti-Apartheid Movement in Great Britain, 1966-69. Director of advertising company. B March, 1938; ed Prince of Wales School, Nairobi; George Watson's College, Edinburgh and Edinburgh University. Member, British Council of Churches. President, National League of Young Liberals.

Mr Gerald Malone contested Glasgow, Pollok, October, 1974, and Glasgow Provan, February 1974. B July, 1950; ed St Aloysius' College, Glasgow, and Glasgow University. Solicitor.

Mr David Heald economics lecturer. B 1947.

Mr Angus Stewart, Secretary, organization committee of Scottish National Party. B December, 1946; ed Edinburgh Academy; Oxford and Edinburgh universities.

ROYAL TUNBRIDGE WELLS

Electorate 71,825   1974: 69,138

*Mayhew, P. B. B. (C)	31,928
Bartlett, A. A. J. (Lab)	11,392
Baker, R. (L)	9,797
Standen, W. (Nat Front)	509
C majority	20,536

No Change

	1974		1979
Total votes	50,130		53,626
Turnout	72·5%		74·7%
C	24,829	49·5%	59·5%
L	12,802	25·5%	18·3%
Lab	12,499	24·9%	21·2%
Nat Front	—		0·9%
C maj	12,027	24·0%	38·3%
Swing		−1·7%	+6·8%

Mr Patrick Mayhew, QC, who became an Under Secretary of State for Employment in May 1979, has held the seat since February 1974; fought Dulwich, Camberwell in 1970. B September, 1929; ed Tonbridge School and Balliol College, Oxford. Member, Executive of 1922 Committee, since 1976 and Joint Vice-chairman, Conservative Home Affairs Committee since 1976. Member, Select Committee on Violence in Marriage, 1975, and Conduct of Members, 1977. Legal assessor for disciplinary committee, GMC and Dental Council.

Mr Alan Bartlett, senior portfolio manager with major nationalised pension fund. B September, 1948. Member, British Association of Colliery Management.

RUGBY

Electorate 61,506   1974: 59,590

Pawsey, J. (C)	24,417
*Price, W. G. (Lab)	21,688
Lomax, B. (L)	4,945
Gresham, A. (Nat Front)	551
C majority	2,729

C gain from Lab

	1974		1979
Total votes	47,560		51,601
Turnout	79·8%		83·9%
Lab	22,926	48·2%	42·0%
C	17,722	37·3%	47·3%
L	6,775	14·2%	9·6%
Soc Credit	137	0·3%	—
Nat Front	—		1·1%
Lab maj	5,204	10·9%	—
C maj	—		5·3%
Swing		0·6%	+8·1%

Mr James Pawsey, chairman and chief executive of a vending machine group and director of six subsidiaries. B 1933; ed Coventry Technical School and Coventry Technical College. Former chairman, Warwickshire Association of Parish Councils. Member, Rugby Rural District Council, 1964-74; Warwickshire County Council, since 1975; Rugby Borough Council.

Mr William Price, was Parliamentary Secretary to Privy Council Office, 1974-79; Parliamentary Secretary, Overseas Development, 1974. Won seat in 1966. Journalist. Parliamentary Private Secretary to Deputy Leader of the Opposition, 1972-74. B June, 1934; ed Forest of Dean Technical College. Former Central Midlands secretary of NUJ.

Mr Brian Lomax, probation officer, contested Knutsford twice in 1974 and Oldham, West, 1970. B March, 1948; ed De La Salle College, Salford, and Pembroke College, Cambridge.

RUNCORN

Electorate 82,126   1974: 69,929

*Carlisle, M. (C)	32,907
Maudsley, G. J. (Lab)	22,226
Kemp, R. (L)	8,783
C majority	10,681

No Change

	1974		1979
Total votes	54,278		63,916
Turnout	77·6%		77·8%
C	25,047	46·1%	51·5%
Lab	19,579	36·1%	34·8%
L	9,188	16·9%	13·7%
Ind L Dem	464	0·9%	
C maj	5,468	10·0%	16·7%
Swing		−1·4%	+3·3%

Mr Mark Carlisle, QC, appointed Secretary of State for Education and Science in May, 1979. Was chief Opposition spokesman for Education and Science 1978-79; Minister of State, Home Office, 1972-74, Under-Secretary, Home Office, 1970-72. Elected in 1964; contested St Helens, 1958 by-election and 1959. B July, 1929; ed Radley College and Manchester University. Barrister (Gray's Inn, 1954). Vice-chairman, Society of Conservative Lawyers, since July, 1975. Former chairman, Federation of University Conservative and Unionist Associations; vice-chairman, North-West Con-

servative MPs 1974. Former member, Home Office Advisory Council on the Penal System. Member, Executive 1922 Committee until November 1978.

Mr George Maudsley, a British Rail engine driver; member, Liverpool City Council. B April, 1929; ed Liverpool primary and secondary schools, former member, Merseyside County Council. ASLEF.

Mr Richard Kemp, estate agent and Liverpool councillor. Aged 26.

RUSHCLIFFE

Electorate 67,286   1974: 63,976

*Clarke, K. H. (C)	34,196
Atkins, C. I. E. (Lab)	11,712
Hamilton, J. E. (L)	9,060
C majority	22,481

No Change

	1974		1979
Total votes	49,505		54,968
Turnout	77·4%		81·7%
C	27,074	54·7%	62·2%
Lab	12,131	24·5%	21·3%
L	10,300	20·8%	16·5%
C maj	14,943	30·2%	40·9%
Swing		−1·4%	+5·3%

Mr Kenneth Clarke, appointed Parliamentary Secretary, Ministry of Transport, in May, 1979, was an Opposition spokesman on industry 1976-79. Won the seat in 1970. An Opposition spokesman for health and social security, 1974-76; Lord Commissioner of the Treasury (Government whip) 1974; assistant whip, 1972-74. Contested  Mansfield, 1964 and 1966. Barrister, B July, 1940; ed Nottingham High School, Gonville and Caius College, Cambridge. Research secretary, Birmingham Bow Group, 1966-67. President Cambridge Union. 1963.

Mr Clive Atkins, miner. B May, 1937; ed secondary school. NUM.

Mr Julian Hamilton contested the seat twice in 1974. Chartered accountant. B August, 1939; ed Nottingham High School, Rugby School and Cranfield Business School.

RUTHERGLEN

Electorate 49,379   1974: 48,824

*Mackenzie, J. G. (Lab)	18,546
Burns, P. (C)	10,523
Brown, R. (L)	7,315
Grieve, M. (Scot Nat)	3,325
Lab majority	8,023

No Change

	1974		1979
Total votes	38,492		39,709
Turnout	78·8%		80·4%
Lab	17,088	44·4%	46·7%
Scot Nat	9,732	25·3%	8·4%
C	9,248	24·0%	26·5%
L	2,424	6·3%	18·4%
Lab maj	7,356	19·1%	20·2%
Swing		−5·0%	+0·1%

Mr Gregor Mackenzie, was Minister of State, Scottish Office, 1976-79; Minister of State for Industry, 1975-76; Under Secretary for Industry, 1974-75. Previously Opposition spokesman on broadcasting and communications. Won the seat in the 1964 by-elections; contested Kinross and West Perth, 1959, and East Aberdeenshire, 1950. Sales manager. B  November, 1927, ed Queens Park School and School of Social Studies. Glasgow University, Sponsored by TGWU.

Mr Paul Burns, solicitor. B 1947; ed St Aloysius College, Glasgow and Glasgow University. Executive member, Glasgow Hillhead and Central Conservative Associations. Lieutenant R.C.T. (Volunteer). Lecturer for the National Trust.

Mr Michael Grieve, television script writer and editor. B July, 1932; ed Whalsay, Shetland Isles, and Kilquhanity House, Kirkcubrightshire. Member, National Council, SNP. NUJ.

RUTLAND AND STAMFORD

Electorate 59,404   1974: 54,656

*Lewis, K. (C)	26,198
Withers, M. R. C. (Lab)	11,383
Blaine, P. (L)	8,801
C majority	14,815

No Change

	1974		1979
Total votes	41,325		46,382
Turnout	75·6%		78·1%
C	19,101	46·2%	56·5%
Lab	12,111	29·3%	24·5%
L	10,113	24·5%	19·0%
C maj	6,990	16·9%	32·0%
Swing		−1·5%	+7·5%

Mr Kenneth Lewis was elected in 1959; contested Ashton-under-Lyne, 1951, and Newton, 1945 and 1950. Member, Estimates Committee, 1962-64; Committee of Selection, 1964-70, and since 1974. B July, 1916; ed Jarrow Central School and Edinburgh University. Former chairman, Conservative Parliamentary Employment Committee.  Member, Middlesex County Council, 1947-1950 Director, Business and Holiday Travel Ltd. Member, Institute of Travel and Tourism, and Institute of Marketing.

Mr Malcolm Withers, financial journalist, contested the seat, October 1974. B March, 1936; ed St Clement Danes Grammar School, Shepherd's Bush and Leicester University. Member, Rutland District Council, since 1973. NUJ.

Mr Peter Blaine, sales engineer. B July, 1944; ed Leeds Grammar School; Pembroke College, Oxford; Southampton University and Imperial College, London.

RYE

Electorate 73,416   1974: 72,261

*Irvine, B. G. (C)	35,516
Moore, D. R. S. (L)	12,438
Smyth, D. (Lab)	6,852
Rix, Miss A. (Ecology)	1,267
Duesbury, T. (Nat Front)	552

C majority	23,078

No Change

	1974		1979
Total votes	53,642		56,625
Turnout	74·2%		77·1%
C	30,511	56·9%	62·7%
L	14,828	27·6%	22·0%
Lab	8,303	15·5%	12·1%
Ecology	—		2·2%
Nat Front	—		1·0%
C maj	15,683	29·3%	40·7%
Swing		−2·3%	+4·6%

Mr Godman Irvine was elected First Deputy Chairman of Ways and Means and a Deputy Speaker in May 1979. He was Second Deputy Chairman of Ways and Means, and a Deputy Speaker, in 1976-79, having been a member of the Speaker's panel of chairmen since 1965 and of the Committee of Selection since 1974. Elected in 1955; contested Wood Green, 1951. Barrister (Inner Temple, 1932) and farmer. B in Canada, 1909; ed St Paul's School, London, and Magdalen College, Oxford. Vice-chairman of Conservative Parliamentary Agricultural Committee, 1964-70, and member Select Committee on Agriculture, 1966-69. Joint vice-chairman, Conservative Parliamentary Foreign and Commonwealth Affairs Committee, 1974-76.

Mr Richard Moore, British staff member, Liberal and Democratic Group of European Parliament, contested Norfolk North, February and October 1974, Antrim, North, 1966 and 1970, Cambridgeshire, 1961 and 1964 and Tavistock, 1955 and 1959. B February, 1931; ed Trinity College, Cambridge. (President of the Union. 1955). Formerly political secretary to Mr Jeremy Thorpe when Leader of the Liberal Party.

Mr Derek Smyth, business economist. B April, 1936; ed Ashford Grammar School. Councillor, Worsley UDC, 1971-72. Director, Ashford Co-operative Society, 1974-75; Farnworth and Walkden Co-operative Society, 1969-72. ASTMS.

Miss Anne Rix, biology teacher. Aged 36; ed Lewes Grammar School, Eastbourne College of Education, Surrey University.

SAFFRON WALDEN

Electorate 65,034   1974: 62,392

*Haselhurst, A. (C)	28,563
Phillips, A. (L)	13,200
Stoneham, B. R. M. (Lab)	10,547
Smedley, O. (Ind)	425
Bailey, R. (Nat Front)	342

C majority	15,363

No Change

	1974		1979
Total votes	48,713		53,077
Turnout	78·1%		81·6%
C	21,291	43·7%	53·8%
L	14,770	30·3%	24·9%
Lab	12,652	26·0%	19·9%
Ind	—		0·8%
Nat Front	—		0·6%
C maj	6,521	13·4%	28·9%
Swing		−0·8%	+8·1%

1977 by-election: Total votes 22,692 (55.7%); C 22,692 (55.7%); L 10,255 (25.2%); Lab 5,948 (14.6%); Ant-EEC 1,818 (4.5%); C majority 12,437 (30.5%).

Mr Alan Haselhurst, elected at the by-election in 1977. Captured Middleton and Prestwich for Conservatives in 1970 but lost seat to Labour in February, 1974. Government affairs consultant to Albright & Wilson Ltd. B June, 1937; ed King Edward VI School, Birmingham, Cheltenham College and Oriel College, Oxford (President, University Conservative Association, and secretary, treasurer and librarian of the Union). Chairman, Young Conservatives National Advisory Committee 1966-68.

Mr Andrew Phillips contested the seat in the 1977 by-election, and Harwich, 1970. Solicitor. Aged 40; ed Uppingham and Trinity Hall, Cambridge.

Mr Benjamin Stoneham fought the 1977 by-election. B August, 1948; ed Cambridge and Warwick universities. Personal aide to National Coal Board chairman. Member, Fabian Society. APEX.

ST ALBANS

Electorate 73,339   1974: 69,693

*Goodhew, V. H. (C)	31,301
Picton, D. (L)	14,057
Greaves, R. J. (Lab and Co-op)	13,638

C majority	17,244

No Change

	1974		1979
Total votes	54,377		58,996
Turnout	78·0%		80·4%
C	24,436	44·9%	53·1%
Lab	15,301	28·1%	23·1%
L	14,640	26·9%	23·8%
C maj	9,135	16·8%	29·3%
Swing		−2·1%	+6·6%

Mr Victor Goodhew, member of the Speaker's panel of chairmen, and the Commons services committee, was a Lord Commissioner of the Treasury (Whip), 1970-73; Assistant Government Whip, 1970. Elected in 1959. Joint vice-chairman of the Conservative committee on defence, 1964-1970, and since 1974. Contested Paddington, North, 1955. Company director and parliamentary adviser to the Brick Development Association. B November, 1919; ed King's College School. Member, Westminster City Council, 1953-59; LCC, 1958-61. United Kingdom representative North Atlantic Assembly.

Mr David Picton, solicitor. Aged 33.

Mr John Greaves, barrister. B August 1948; ed Douay Martyrs School, Ickenham; Uxbridge Technical College and Central London Polytechnic. TGWU.

ST HELENS

Electorate 74,830   1974: 76,067

*Spriggs, L. (Lab)	32,489
Brown, J. (C)	16,934
Smith, I. (L)	4,587
Boylan, J. (WRP)	471
Lab majority	15,555

No Change

	1974		1979
Total votes	50,863		54,481
Turnout	66·9%		72·8%
Lab	32,620	64·1%	59·6%
C	10,554	20·7%	31·1%
L	7,689	15·1%	8·4%
WRP	—		0·9%
Lab maj	22,066	43·4%	28·5%
Swing		−1·9%	+7·4%

Mr Leslie Spriggs was returned at a by-election in 1958; contested North Fylde, 1955. Railwayman. B April, 1910; ed council school and through National Council of Labour Colleges. Sponsored by NUR of which he was president, political council of North-West England district council. Member PLP groups and Cheshire region of Labour Party. Former lecturer for National Council of Labour Colleges.

Mr John Brown, builder and managing director of his own company. B 1933; ed Rainford Secondary Modern School and St Helens Technical College. Chairman, Rainford Sports Council. Member, St Helens District Council and St Helens Sports Council. Former chairman, Rainford Conservative Association.

Mr Ian Smith, teacher. B July, 1951; ed Huyton Hey Secondary School. Chairman, St Helens District and Divisional Liberal Party. NAS.

ST IVES

Electorate 53,715   1974: 51,440

*Nott, J. W. F. (C)	22,352
Evans, R. D. (Lab)	8,636
Cotton, J. (L)	8,299
Murley, D. (Meb Kernow)	1,662
Hoptrough, H. (Ecology)	427
C majority	13,716

No Change

	1974		1979
Total votes	37,916		41,376
Turnout	73·7%		77·0%
C	17,198	45·4%	54·0%
L	11,330	29·9%	20·1%
Lab	9,388	24·8%	20·9%
Meb Kernow	—	—	4·0%
Ecology	—	—	1·0%
C maj	5,868	15·5%	33·1%
Swing		−0·9%	+6·2%

Mr John Nott, became Secretary of State for Trade in May, 1979; chief Opposition spokesman on trade 1977-79; an Opposition spokesman on Treasury and economic affairs, 1975-77, and Minister of State, Treasury, 1972-74. Elected in 1966. B February, 1932; ed Bradfield College and Trinity College, Cambridge (President of the Union 1959). Barrister (Inner Temple, 1960) and Company chairman and director. Member, Select Committee on Wealth Tax, 1974-75; Public Expenditure Committee, 1970-72; secretary, Conservative parliamentary finance committee, 1967-70.

Mr Rik Evans catering contractor. Educated in Canada and Britain. B August, 1945.

Mr John Cotton, teacher. Aged 34; ed Newcastle and Hull Universities.

Mr Howard Hoptrough, lecturer and librarian. Aged 55. Member, Friends of the Earth; former editor, Ecology Party newsletter.

SALFORD, East

Electorate 32,718   1974: 40,144

*Allaun, F. J. (Lab)	13,453
Latimer, S. (C)	7,597
Lab majority	5,856

No Change

	1974		1979
Total votes	23,876		21,050
Turnout	59·5%		64·3%
Lab	14,276	59·8%	63·9%
C	6,440	27·0%	36·1%
L	3,160	13·2%	—
Lab maj	7,836	32·8%	27·8%
Swing		−3·3%	+2·5%

Mr Frank Allaun the present chairman of the Labour Party; vice-chairman 1977-78 was elected in 1955. Chairman, Labour Party NEC housing committee and of Labour Action for Peace. Member, National Executive of Labour Party since 1967. Former deputy chairman, foreign affairs group of the PLP. B February, 1913; ed Manchester Grammar School. Has been an engineer, shop assistant, foreign tours leader, WEA lecturer, chartered accountant, journalist. NUJ and AEU.

Mr Stephen Latimer, partner in a firm of solicitors, contested the seat, October, 1974. B 1950; ed Salford Grammar School and Manchester University. Former chairman, Salford East Young Conservatives; divisional vice-chairman, Salford East Conservative Association.

SALFORD, West

Electorate 43,587   1974: 45,833

*Orme, S. (Lab)	18,411
Markwick, J. (C)	11,157
Carter, S. (WRP)	383
Lab majority	7,254

No Change

	1974		1979
Total votes	29,889		29,951
Turnout	65·2%		68·7%
Lab	17,112	57·3%	61·5%
C	8,540	28·6%	37·3%
L	4,237	14·2%	
WRP	—	—	1·3%
Lab maj	8,572	28·7%	24·2%
Swing		−4·5%	+2·2%

Mr Stanley Orme was Minister for Social Security, with a seat in the Cabinet, 1976-79; Minister of State, Department of Health and Social Security, 1976; Minister of State for Northern Ireland, 1974-76. Elected in 1964. An Opposition spokesman on Northern Ireland, 1972-74. Contested Stockport, South, 1959. Engineer. B April, 1923; ed elementary and technical schools, National Council of Labour Colleges and Workers' Educational Association classes. Member, Sale Borough Council, 1958-64. Sponsored by AUEW, engineering section; shop steward, branch president for 21 years. Former chairman of AUEW parliamentary group of MPs, and of Northern Ireland PLP group.

Mr James Markwick, deputy managing director of Guardian and director, Guardian and Manchester Evening News Ltd. Newspaper Ltd; chairman of Gemini News Service; executive member, Newspaper Publishers Association; council member, National Association for the Training of Journalists. Ed Wrekin College, St Edmund Hall, Oxford, and Harvard.

SALISBURY

Electorate 64,615   1974: 62,817

*Hamilton, M. A. (C)	24,962
Lakeman, J. F. (L)	18,718
Boney, C. R. (Lab)	6,321
C majority	6,244

No Change

	1974		1979
Total votes	46,916		50,001
Turnout	74·7%		77·4%
C	20,478	43·6%	49·9%
L	16,298	34·7%	37·4%
Lab	10,140	21·6%	12·6%
C maj	4,180	8·9%	12·5%
Swing		−1·4%	+7·6%

Mr Michael Hamilton was returned at a by-election in February, 1965; represented Wellingborough, 1959-64. Lord Commissioner of the Treasury (whip), 1962-64; assistant whip, 1961-62. B July, 1918; ed Radley and University College, Oxford. UK representative, UN General Assembly, 1970 and US bicentennial celebrations, 1976. Vice-chairman, Army and Navy Stores Ltd; member, Hops Marketing Board.

Mr John Lakeman, contested the seat, February and October 1974. Self employed. B December, 1947; ed Bishop Wordsworth School, Salisbury, and Exeter University.

Mr Charles Boney, teacher. B March, 1950; ed Felsted School, Essex, University of Bristol, Redland College of Education. NUT.

SCARBOROUGH

Electorate 60,896   1974: 58,553

*Shaw, M. N. (C)	23,669
Lahteela, E. J. (Lab)	11,344
Galloway, S. (L)	9,025
Yelin, T. (Ind)	487
C majority	12,325

No Change

	1974		1979
Total votes	39,877		44,525
Turnout	68·1%		73·1%
C	19,831	49·7%	53·2%
L	10,123	25·4%	20·3%
Lab	9,923	24·9%	25·5%
Ind	—	—	1·1%
C maj	9,708	24·3%	27·7%
Swing		−3·8%	+1·4%

Mr Michael Shaw, a chartered accountant, was elected in February, 1974. Member, European Parliament since 1974. Represented Scarborough and Whitby, 1966-74, and Brighouse and Spenborough, 1960-64. Contested latter division in 1959 and Dewsbury, 1955. B October, 1920; ed Sedbergh. Chairman, Yorkshire Area Conservatives, 1965-66. Vice-chairman, Conservative Trade and Industry Committee, 1967-74, and Yorkshire Conservative MPs since 1972.

Mr Erkki Lahteela, hotelier. B 1920 in Finland. Member, North Yorkshire County Council, since 1973.

Mr Steve Galloway, telecommunications superintendent, contested Pontefract and Castleford, October 1974, York, February 1974. B July 1948; ed St Mary's Grammar School, Darlington, and Harrogate College of Further Education.

SEVENOAKS

Electorate 80,960   1974: 74,969

Wolfson, M. (C)	36,697
Redden, R. H. (Lab)	14,583
Phillips, G. (L)	11,839
Easter, M. (Nat Front)	821
C majority	22,114

No Change

	1974		1979
Total votes	56,759		63,940
Turnout	75·7%		79·0%
C	26,670	47·0%	57·4%
Lab	15,065	26·5%	22·8%
L	15,024	26·5%	18·5%
Nat Front	—	—	1·3%
C maj	11,605	20·5%	34·6%
Swing		−1·9%	+7·0%

Mr Mark Wolfson, personal director with a merchant bank, contested Islington, North, February, 1974 and City of Westminster, Paddington, October 1974. B April, 1934; ed Eton and Pembroke College, Cambridge. Worked for Canadian Pacific Railway for two years and as a teacher in an Indian Reservation in British Columbia. Three years as head of Brathay Hall Centre in the Lake District. London Borough of Wandsworth councillor for three years.

Mr Richard Redden, financial journalist. B December 1942; ed Bromley Grammar School and St Catherine's College, Oxford. Contested London Borough of Bromley elections 1971, 1974 and 1978. NUJ.

Mr Graham Phillips, systems analyst and district councillor since 1975. Aged 32.

SHEFFIELD, Attercliffe

Electorate 62,984   1974: 63,917

*Duffy, A. E. P. (Lab)	29,702
French, D. (C)	11,599
Boothroyd, D. (L)	4,017
Mason, J. (Nat Front)	457
Lab majority	18,103

No Change

	1974		1979
Total votes	42,926		45,775
Turnout	67·2%		72·7%
Lab	29,601	69·0%	64·9%
C	8,043	18·7%	25·3%
L	5,282	12·3%	8·8%
Nat Front	—	—	1·0%
Lab maj	21,558	50·3%	39·6%
Swing		−2·9%	+5·3%

Mr Patrick Duffy, Under Secretary, Defence (Royal Navy) 1976-79. Elected 1970; MP for Colne Valley, 1963-66; contested Tiverton, 1955, 1951 and 1950. Economist and consultant. B June, 1920; ed London and Columbia Universities. GMWU. Chairman, PLP economic affairs and finance group, 1965-66 and in 1974. Member, Select Committee on Public Expenditure, 1970-74 and Vice-Chairman, PLP Northern Ireland Group, 1974. Former chairman, trade and industry sub-committee inquiry into fishing industry. Sponsored by GMWU.

Mr Douglas French, barrister and director of an import-export company. B 1944; ed Glyn Grammar School, Epsom, St Catherines College, Cambridge and the Inns of Court School of Law. While at Cambridge he was a committee member of Cambridge University Conservative Association (1965-66), editor of CUCA 'Guide to Cambridge' (1965) and a member of the Cambridge Union. Member, City of Westminster Social Services House Committee. Committee member. Golborne Branch of Kensington Conservative Association (1972-73).

Mr Dennis Boothroyd, accounts clerk. Aged 58.

SHEFFIELD, Brightside

Electorate 54,459   1974: 54,095

*Maynard, Miss V. J. (Lab)	25,672
Knightly, Mrs B. (C)	7,979
Johnson, M. S. (L)	3,482
Brack, K. T. (Nat Front)	354
Lab majority	17,693

No Change

	1974		1979
Total votes	36,466		37,487
Turnout	67·4%		68·8%
Lab	18,108	49·7%	68·5%
Ind Lab	10,182	27·9%	—
C	4,905	13·5%	21·3%
L	3,271	9·0%	9·3%
Nat Front	—	—	0·9%
Lab maj	7,926	21·8%	47·2%

Miss Joan Maynard, member, Labour Party National Executive Committee, since 1970, was elected in October, 1974. Yorkshire area secretary, National Union of Agricultural and Allied Workers for 22 years; former president; union's only sponsored MP. B 1921. Ed University College of North Wales. Member, PLP agriculture and education groups. Parish councillor, county councillor. Magistrate.

Mrs Betty Knightly, barrister with farming interests in Hampshire, contested Salford, East, February 1974, B 1919; ed Godolphin School, Salisbury, Germany and France and Grays Inn. Initiated the Matrimonial Property Bill 1969 leading to Matrimonial Proceedings and Property Act, 1970. Holborn borough councillor, 1956-59. Former chairman, Walthamstow West Conservative Association. NFU.

Mr Malcolm Johnson, works manager, contested Sheffield Hallam twice in 1974. B January, 1928; ed Aireborough Grammar School and Leeds College of Technology.

SHEFFIELD, HALLAM

Electorate 78,901   1974: 77,400

*Osborn, J. H. (C)	31,436
Bower, M. J. (Lab)	16,502
Salt, K. A. (L)	8,982
Smith, G. F. (Nat Front)	300

C majority	14,934

No Change

	1974		1979
Total votes	53,226		57,220
Turnout	68·8%		72·5%
C	26,083	49·0%	54·9%
Lab	15,419	29·0%	28·8%
L	11,724	22·0%	15·7%
Nat Front	—	—	0·5%
C maj	10,664	20·0%	26·1%
Swing		−0·9%	+3·0%

Mr John Osborn, a steel works director, was elected in 1959. Member, European Parliament 1975-79. Joint secretary, 1922 Committee since 1968; chairman, Conservative parliamentary transport industries committee since 1972 and Anglo-Soviet Parliamentary Group; joint chairman, All-Party Roads Study Group. Member, executive of Inter-Parliamentary Union and Select Committee on Science and Technology, 1970-72. Director, Samuel Osborn and Co Ltd and subsidiaries. B December, 1922; ed Rugby and Trinity Hall, Cambridge. Member, council of CBI and council of Industrial Society.

Mr Michael Bower, former journalist and official of the NUJ. Member, Press Council, 1976-77. B August, 1942; ed Colwyn Bay Grammar School and Salford College of Technology. Member, Sheffield City Council since 1976.

Mr Kenneth Salt, quantity surveyor. Aged 37; ed Open University.

SHEFFIELD, Heeley

Electorate 63,996   1974: 65,244

*Hooley, F. O. (Lab)	24,618
George, D. (C)	19,845
Webb, R. (L)	4,708
Thorpe, P. K. (Nat Front)	274

Lab majority	4,773

No Change

	1974		1979
Total votes	47,924		49,445
Turnout	73·5%		77·3%
Lab	24,728	51·6%	49·8%
C	15,322	32·0%	40·1%
L	7,151	14·9%	9·5%
Nat Front	723	1·5%	0·6%
Lab maj	9,406	19·6%	9·7%
Swing		−3·6%	+4·9%

Mr Frank Hooley, elected February, 1974, and MP for the constituency from 1966-70. Contested it in 1964 and Skipton, 1959. Member, Select Committees on Science and Technology and on Overseas Development. Chairman, PLP overseas aid group, 1977-78. Member, Council on International Development, 1977. Sponsored by Apex. B November 1923; ed King Edward's School, Birmingham and Birmingham University. Assistant registrar, Sheffield University, 1952-65 and senior assistant registrar, 1965-66.

Mr Daniel George, retired pensions consultant. B 1916. Member, Sheffield Metroplitan District Council, South Yorkshire County Council.

Mr Rodney Webb. Aged 32; ed Millbank College of Commerce.

SHEFFIELD, Hillsborough

Electorate 51,088   1974: 52,032

*Flannery, M. H. (Lab)	20,556
Patnick, C. I. (C)	12,206
Neale, Mrs P. A. (L)	3,088
Williams, Mrs S. (Nat Front)	326

Lab majority	8,350

No Change

	1974		1979
Total votes	34,656		36,176
Turnout	66·6%		70·8%
Lab	21,026	60·7%	56·8%
C	8,718	25·2%	33·7%
L	4,912	14·2%	8·5%
Nat Front	—		0·9%
Lab maj	12,308	35·5%	23·1%
Swing		−3·5%	+6·2%

Mr Martin Flannery, elected February, 1974. Head teacher. B March, 1918; ed De La Salle Grammar School and Sheffield Teacher Training College. Member ASTMS and NUT Parliamentary consultant. Chairman PLP education and science group. Secretary, PLP Chile group.

Mr Irvine Patnick, production controller at textile factory. B 1929; ed Sheffield College of Technology. Leader, Conservative group, South Yorkshire County Council. Member, Sheffield Metropolitan District Council.

SHEFFIELD, Park

Electorate 62,174   1974: 67,425

*Mulley, F. W. (Lab)	27,483
Cole, C. (C)	7,159
Butler, F. R. (L)	4,737
Pierson, I. (Nat Front)	302
Ashberry, G. (Comm)	279
Littlehales, P. (WRP)	111

Lab majority	20,324

No Change

	1974		1979
Total votes	42,092		40,071
Turnout	62·4%		64·4%
Lab	30,057	71·4%	68·6%
L	6,093	14·5%	11·8%
C	5,539	13·2%	17·9%
Comm	403	1·0%	0·7%
Nat Front	—	—	0·8%
WRP	—	—	0·3%
Lab maj	23,964	56·9%	50·7%
Swing		−4·7%	+3·7%

Mr Frederick Mulley, Sec-retary of State for Defence, 1976-79, won the seat in 1950. Deputy Defence Sec-retary and Minister for the Army, 1964-65; Minister of Aviation, 1965-67; Minister of State, Foreign and Commonwealth Office, and also Minister for Dis-armament, 1967-69; Minister of Transport, 1969-70; Minister for Transport, Department of

the Environment, 1974-75; Secretary of State for Education and Science, 1975-76. B July, 1918; ed Warwick School and Christ Church, Oxford. Fellow of St Catharine's College, Cambridge, 1948-50. Barrister (Inner Temple, 1954) and economist. Con-tested Sutton Coldfield, 1945. Member, Labour Party National Executive, 1957-58, 1960-64 and since 1965. Vice-chairman, Labour Party, 1973-74; chairman, 1974-75. Sponsored by APEX.

Mr Charles Cole, personnel services manager with an electrical component firm. B 1948; ed Spalding Grammar School and Bristol University. Treasurer, Sutton Coldfield Conservative Political Centre. Member, Holland with Boston Conservative Association; constituency representative on West Midlands Area CPC General Purposes Committee.

Mr Francis Butler, merchandising manager, contested the seat twice in 1974. B May, 1941; ed Owler Lane School, Sheffield, and Sheffield College of Art.

Mr Gordon Ashberry, Sheffield area secretary of the Communist Party, contested the seat, October, 1974. Factory shop steward for 13 years, deputy convenor for five years and factory negotiator for three years. Served on district committee, AUEW.

Mr Paul Littlehales, mechanical engineer. Provisional delegate to AUEW district committee. Aged 37.

SHIPLEY

Electorate 33,318   1974: 32,008

*Fox, J. M. (C)	22,641
Ward, P. R. (Lab)	14,281
Roberts, G. G. (L)	5,673
Pedley, D. (Ecology)	486

C majority	8,360

No Change

	1974		1979
Total votes	42,094		43,081
Turnout	80·9%		80·5%
C	18,518	44·0%	52·6%
Lab	15,482	36·8%	33·1%
L	8,094	19·2%	13·2%
Ecology	—	—	1·1%
C maj	3,036	7·2%	19·5%
Swing		−1·0%	+6·1%

Mr Marcus Fox, appointed Under Secretary of State for Environment in May 1979; Opposition spokesman on transport, 1975-76; on the environment, 1974, and on housing, 1974-75. Elected 1970; contested Dewsbury, 1959, and Huddersfield, West, 1966. Assistant whip, 1972-73; Lord Com-missioner of the Treasury (whip) 1973-74. Member, Select Committee on Race

Relations and Immigration, 1970. Secretary, party transport industries committee, 1970-73. Became a party vice-chairman with responsibility for candidates in January, 1976. Company director.

Mr Peter Ward, an engineer with British Aerospace, contested Southport, February, 1974. B April, 1934; ed Wigan College of Further Education. Former member, Preston RDC. AUEW (TASS).

Mr Glyn Roberts, lecturer, contested the seat in both 1974 elections. B May, 1925; ed Monmouth School and LSE. ATTI.

Mr David Pedley, aged 35, solicitor. Recently acted for motorway objectors. Former legal adviser to Friends of the Earth.

SHOREHAM

Electorate 72,288   1974: 68,498

*Luce, R. N. (C)	34,339
Robinson, C. (L)	12,754
Shamash, G. D. (Lab)	8,867
Benjafield, J. (Nat Front)	406

C majority	21,585

No Change

	1974		1979
Total votes	51,167		56,366
Turnout	74·7%		78·0%
C	26,170	51·1%	60·9%
L	14,797	28·9%	22·6%
Lab	10,200	19·9%	15·7%
Nat Front	—	—	0·7%
C maj	11,373	22·2%	38·3%
Swing		−2·5%	+7·0%

Mr Richard Luce, appointed Under Secretary of State for Foreign and Commonwealth Affairs, in May, 1979; an Opposition spokesman on Foreign and Commonwealth Affairs, 1977-79, and Opposition whip 1974-75. Elected for Arundel and Shoreham at by-election in 1971 and after redistribution for Shoreham in February, 1974. Contested Hitchin,

1970. B October 1936; ed Wellington College, Christ's College, Cambridge and Wadham College, Oxford, Chairman, Courtenay, Stewart International and Selanex Ltd and member European Advisory Board, Corning Glass International. Member, Select Committee on Proceedure.

Mr Clifford Robinson, shipping consultant. B March, 1923; ed Oldham Municipal High School. Member, Lancing Parish Council, since 1971; Adur District Council, since 1973.

Mr Gerald Shamash, solicitor. B May, 1947; ed North Cestrian Grammar School, Cheshire, University of Surrey. Governer, Rutherford Comprehensive School, London; member, Central London Valuation Tribunal. ASTMS, TGWU.

SHREWSBURY

Electorate 63,236   1974: 60,228

*Langford-Holt, Sir J. (C)	23,548
Laurie, A. (L)	13,364
Bishton, J. (Lab)	11,558
C majority	10,184

No Change

	1974		1979
Total votes	44,211		48,470
Turnout	73·4%		76·6%
C	19,064	43·1%	48·6%
L	13,643	30·9%	27·6%
Lab	11,504	26·0%	23·8%
C maj	5,421	12·2%	21·0%
Swing		−1·5%	+3·8%

Sir John Langford-Holt was returned in 1945. Secretary of the Conservative parliamentary labour committee for five years. Member, Commons Expenditure Committee, since December, 1975, Public Accounts Committee and several Conservative backbench committees. B June, 1916; ed Shrewsbury School. Director, Siebe Gorman Holdings Ltd. Freeman and Liveryman of City of London.

Mr Alan Laurie, warden of adult education centre. Councillor since 1962. Aged 57; ed Selwyn College, Cambridge.

Mr John Bishton, senior social worker, Wolverhampton Corporation, contested Oswestry, February and October 1974. B April 1946; ed Wolverhampton Municipal Grammar School, University College, Swansea, Birmingham University. NUPE.

SKIPTON

Electorate 53,881   1974: 52,562

Watson, J. (C)	23,177
Brooks, Mrs K. C. (L)	17,484
Selby, B. M. (Lab)	4,632
C majority	5,693

No Change

	1974		1979
Total votes	43,163		45,293
Turnout	82·1%		84·1%
C	17,822	41·3%	51·2%
L	17,232	39·9%	38·6%
Lab	8,109	18·8%	10·2%
C maj	590	1·4%	12·6%
Swing		−1·4%	+9·2%

Mr John Watson, marketing director of games manufacturer, also qualified as a solicitor. Contested York in February and October 1974. B 1943; ed Bootham School, York and the College of Law, Guildford. Personal assistant to Mr Edward Heath during 1970 election campaign. Joined Young Conservatives in 1961 and has held office at all levels; national chairman in 1971. Member, Law Society and Institute of Arbitrators.

Mrs Claire Brooks, solicitor, contested the seat, February, 1974, and 1959. B June, 1931; ed Settle C of E School, Settle Girls' High School, Skipton Girls' High School and University College, London.

Mr Brian Selby, solicitor. B April, 1948; ed Roundhay School, Leeds, Leeds University, Leeds Polytechnic. Chairman, Leeds North East Labour Party, 1975. Member, Leeds City Council, 1972-74; West Yorkshire County Council, since 1977. TGWU and APEX.

SOLIHULL

Electorate 84,272   1974: 79,992

*Grieve, W. P. (C)	43,027
Hallam, D. J. A. (Lab)	10,820
Gillett, I. (L)	10,214
Stevenson, D. (Nat Front)	978
C majority	32,207

No Change

	1974		1979
Total votes	60,195		65,039
Turnout	75·3%		77·2%
C	31,707	52·7%	66·2%
L	15,848	26·3%	15·7%
Lab	12,640	21·0%	16·6%
Nat Front	—		1·5%
C maj	15,859	26·4%	49·6%
Swing		−2·4%	+8·9%

Mr Percy Grieve, QC, was elected in 1964; contested Lincoln by-election, March, 1962. B March, 1915; ed privately and at Trinity Hall, Cambridge. Barrister (Middle Temple, 1938), QC 1962. Recorder of Northampton since 1965. Chairman, Franco-British Parliamentary Relations Committee, 1970-75; vice-chairman, Anglo-Benelux Group; Delegate, Council of Europe and WEU, since 1969. Master of Bench, Middle Temple, since 1969. Member of Lloyds.

Mr David Hallam, public relations officer. B June, 1948; ed Upton House Secondary School, Hackney, and Sussex University. Member, NALGO, NUJ, and Christian Socialist Movement.

Mr Ian Gillett, senior metallurgist. Aged 34; ed Lanchester Polytechnic.

SOMERSET, North

Electorate 96,606   1974: 89,056

*Dean, A. P. (C)	43,173
Smith, A. J. (Lab)	22,122
Sanders, Rev D. (L)	12,898
Carder, R. (Ecology)	1,254
C majority	21,051

No Change

	1974		1979
Total votes	71,632		79,447
Turnout	80·4%		82·2%
C	32,146	44·9%	54·3%
Lab	22,671	31·6%	27·8%
L	16,428	22·9%	16·2%
Utd Dem	387	0·5%	
Ecology	—	—	1·6%
C maj	9,475	13·3%	26·5%
Swing		−1·5%	+6·6%

Mr Paul Dean, Under Secretary Health and Social Security, 1970-74, was elected in 1964; contested Pontefract by-election, March, 1962. B September, 1924; ed Ellesmere College, Shropshire, and Exeter College, Oxford. Former farmer. Resident tutor, Swinton College, 1956-57; joined Conservative research department 1958 and assistant director, 1962. Chairman, Watchdog group for the self-employed since June, 1975. Member, Select Committee on Overseas Development since 1978. Director, Charterhouse Pensions. Consultant on pension schemes.

Mr Anthony Smith, a BBC producer and former housemaster at an approved school. Contested Westbury twice in 1974. B March, 1938; ed Farmor's Endowed School, Fairford, and Southampton University. ABS.

Mr Richard Carder, music teacher. Aged 36; ed Ardingly College, Sussex. Member, Friends of the Earth, Kennet and Avon Canal Trust.

SOUTHAMPTON, Itchen

Electorate 81,151   1974: 82,009

*Mitchell, R. C. (Lab)	28,036
Hunter, A. (C)	26,434
Pinder, J. (L)	6,132
Lab majority	1,602

No Change

	1974		1979
Total votes	57,612		60,602
Turnout	70·3%		74·7%
Lab	28,168	48·9%	46·3%
C	20,373	35·4%	43·6%
L	9,071	15·7%	10·1%
Lab maj	7,795	13·5%	2·7%
Swing		−2·3%	+5·4%

Mr Richard Mitchell, who has held the seat since the 1971 by-election, was MP for Southampton, Test, 1966-70, having unsuccessfully contested it in 1964, and New Forest, 1959. Member, European Parliament, 1975-79, serving on the bureau of the Socialist Group. Former chairman, PLP education committee. Member, Select Committee on Education and Science, 1968-70. Former deputy headmaster. B August, 1927; ed Godalming Grammar School and Southampton University. Member, Southampton City Council, 1955-67. NUGMW and parliamentary consultant for NUT.

Mr Andrew Hunter, assistant master at a public school. B 1943; ed Durham University and Jesus College, Cambridge. Member, Durham University Liberal Party, 1962-65, Cambridge University Conservative Association, 1966-68. Lay reader in Church of England. Holds commission in TAVR.

Mr John Pinder, teacher. B April, 1955; ed Forest School, Winnersh, Berkshire, Manchester University and Crewe and Alsager College.

SOUTHAMPTON, Test

Electorate 76,890   1974: 73,895

Hill, S. J. A. (C)	27,198
*Gould, B. C. (Lab)	25,075
Hughes, D. (L)	6,393
C majority	2,123

C gain from Lab

	1974		1979
Total votes	54,024		58,666
Turnout	73·1%		76·3%
Lab	22,780	42·2%	42·7%
C	22,250	41·2%	46·4%
L	8,994	16·6%	10·9%
Lab maj	530	1·0%	
C maj	—	—	3·7%
Swing		−1·7%	+2·3%

Mr James Hill, company director, held seat, 1970-October 1974. B 1926; ed Regents Park School, Southampton, North Wales Naval Training College and Southampton University. Member, Select Committee on Expenditure, 1972-73, Secretary, Conservative back-bench committee on housing and construction, 1971-73. Member, European Parliament, 1973-75; transport committee of European Parliament. Chairman, Committee for regional policy and transport (Europe) March 1973-March 1975.

Mr Bryan Gould, fellow and tutor in law, Worcester College, Oxford, 1968-74, who won the seat in October, 1974, contested it in February, 1974. B February, 1939; ed Victoria University and Auckland University, New Zealand, and Balliol College, Oxford. Member, Select Committee on European Legislation; chairman, Safeguard Britain Campaign until October, 1977. ASTMS.

Mr David Hughes, European elections agent. Ed Southampton University.

SOUTHEND, East

Electorate 57,037   1974: 57,295

*McAdden, Sir S. (C)	22,413
Wright, T. N. (Lab)	11,639
Hugill, J. (L)	5,244
Twomey, P. (Nat Front)	676

C majority	10,774

No Change

	1974		1979
Total votes	39,419		39,972
Turnout	68·8%		70·1%
C	18,083	45·9%	56·1%
Lab	13,480	34·2%	29·1%
L	7,856	19·9%	13·1%
Nat Front	—	—	1·7%
C maj	4,603	11·7%	27·0%
Swing		+0·2%	+7·6%

Sir Stephen McAdden, a company director, was elected in 1950. B November, 1907; ed Salesian College, Battersea. Vice-chairman, Anglo-Israeli parliamentary group and Anglo-Austrian group. Member, Speaker's panel of chairmen, Hackney Borough Council, 1935-45; Wanstead and Woodford Borough Council, 1945-48; Essex County Council,  1947-48. Business interests in property development and public relations.

Mr Antony Wright medical liaison officer, contested Southend, West, twice in 1974. B June, 1939; ed Christchurch Secondary Modern School, Southport. Member, Castle Point District Council, 1973-76. ASTMS.

Mr James Hugill, industrial consultant. District councillor, 1973-78. B April 1918; ed Nunthorpe Grammar School, York.

SOUTHEND, West

Electorate 66,958   1974: 67,438

*Channon, H. P. G. (C)	29,449
Evans, D. (L)	12,585
Nisbet, Mrs J. (Lab)	8,341
McKeon, L. J. (Nat Front)	680

C majority	16,864

No Change

	1974		1979
Total votes	49,340		51,055
Turnout	73·2%		76·2%
C	23,480	47·6%	57·7%
L	16,409	33·3%	24·6%
Lab	9,451	19·2%	16·3%
Nat Front	—	—	1·3%
C maj	7,071	14·3%	33·1%
Swing		−1·1%	+6·5%

Mr Paul Channon, became Minister of State, Civil Service Department, in May, 1979. Chief Opposition spokesman on the environment, 1974-75; spokesman on consumer affairs, 1974; member of the Shadow Cabinet, 1974.  Minister for Housing and Construction, 1972-74; Minister of State for Northern Ireland, March-November, 1972; Under Secretary for the Environment, 1970-72; Parliamentary Secretary, Ministry of Housing and Local Government, June to October, 1970. Elected at by-election in January, 1959, succeeding his father. B October, 1935; ed Lockers Park, Hemel Hempstead, Eton and Christ Church, Oxford. Director, CSE Aviation, Arthur Guinness and Son.

Mrs Joy Nisbet, adoption adviser and fostering officer. B January, 1930; ed North London Collegiate School and LSE. NUPE.

SOUTH FYLDE

Electorate 94,335   1974: 90,861

*Gardner, E. L. (C)	45,883
Chadwick, G. (Lab)	13,636
Stevens, J. (L)	11,938
Roberts, M. (Nat Front)	941

C majority	32,247

No Change

	1974		1979
Total votes	65,444		72,398
Turnout	72·0%		76·7%
C	37,193	56·8%	63·4%
L	14,527	22·2%	16·5%
Lab	13,724	21·0%	18·8%
Nat Front	—	—	1·3%
C maj	22,666	34·6%	44·6%
Swing		−1·8%	+4·4%

Mr Edward Gardner, QC, elected in 1970, was MP for Billericay, from 1959 to 1966; contested Erith and Crayford in 1955. Called to the Bar (Gray's Inn) in 1947, admitted to the Nigerian and British Guianan Bars, 1962, and  became a Master of the Bench of Gray's Inn in 1968. B May, 1912; ed Hutton Grammar School. Chairman (1973-74), and vice-chairman (1974) Conservative Parliamentary Home Affairs Committee; chairman, Society of Conservative Lawyers since July, 1975. Crown court recorder.

Mr Graham Chadwick, adult education officer. B November 1941; ed Leicester and Manchester Universities. Member, Greater Manchester Council, 1973-77. NATFHE.

Mr John Stevens, computer project manager, contested Bristol, South, February 1974, and Bristol North-West, 1970. B May, 1943; ed Trowbridge Boys' High School.

SOUTHPORT

Electorate 68,385   1974: 66,109

*Percival, Sir W. I. (C)	25,953
Fearn, R. C. (L)	19,426
James, I. G. (Lab)	5,725
C majority	**6,527**

No Change

	1974		1979
Total votes	48,724		51,104
Turnout	73·7%		74·7%
C	23,014	47·2%	50·8%
L	17,387	35·7%	38·0%
Lab	8,323	17·1%	11·2%
C maj	5,627	11·5%	12·8%
Swing		−2·0%	+4·7%

Sir Ian Percival, QC, who became Solicitor General in May, 1979, had been an Opposition spokesman on law since 1976. Elected in 1959; contested Battersea, North, 1951 and 1955. Barrister (Inner Temple, 1948); QC, 1963. B May, 1921; ed Latymer School and St Catherine's College, Cambridge. Chairman, Conservative legal committee, 1970-74; vice-chairman, 1974-79. Member, Select Committee on EEC secondary legislation, 1974-79. A Recorder.

Mr Ronald Fearn, assistant bank manager, contested the seat twice in 1974 and in 1970. B February, 1931; ed Southport, Norwood Road County School and King George V Grammar School. Former member, Southport Town Council, Sefton Metropolitan District council and Merseyside Metropolitan Distict Council. NUBE.

Mr Ifan James, teacher, contested the seat, October, 1974. B May, 1936; ed Eifionydd, Porthmadog. NUT.

SOUTH SHIELDS

Electorate 70,566   1974: 72,584

Clark, D. (Lab)	28,675
Booth, R. (C)	15,551
Monger, L. (L)	6,003
Lab majority	**13,124**

No Change

	1974		1979
Total votes	46,976		50,229
Turnout	64·7%		71·2%
Lab	26,492	56·4%	57·1%
C	11,667	24·8%	31·0%
L	8,106	17·3%	12·0%
Nat Front	711	1·5%	
Lab maj	14,825	31·6%	26·1%
Swing		−4·2%	+2·7%

Mr David Clark was MP for Colne Valley, 1972-February 1974, and front bench spokesman on agriculture 1972-74. B October, 1939; ed Windermere Grammar School and Manchester and Sheffield Universities. University lecturer. Contested Manchester, Withington, 1966, in Colne Valley, 1970 and February and October 1974. Chairman of Manchester University Labour Club and President of the Union, 1963-64. Vice-chairman of PLP environment group and secretary of all-party wool textile group 1972-74. NUPE sponsored.

Mr Roger Booth, barrister. B 1942; ed King Edward VI School, Stourbridge and Sheffield University. Member, Tyne and Wear County Council, since 1973; TAVR.

Mr Llewellyn Monger, sales manager. B August, 1944; ed South Shields High School and Newcastle Polytechnic. SOGAT.

SOUTHWARK, Bermondsey

Electorate 51,246   1974: 55,254

*Mellish, R. J. (Lab)	19,338
Duma, A. (C)	7,582
Taylor, J. (L)	2,072
Sneath, J. (Nat Front)	1,175
Moore, A. (WRP)	239
Lab majority	**11,756**

No Change

	1974		1979
Total votes	31,177		30,406
Turnout	56·4%		59·3%
Lab	22,875	73·4%	63·6%
C	4,294	13·8%	24·9%
L	2,520	8·1%	6·8%
Nat Front	1,488	4·8%	3·9%
WRP	—		0·8%
Lab maj	18,581	59·6%	38·7%
Swing		−4·0%	+10·4%

Mr Robert Mellish, Parliamentary Secretary, Treasury, and Government Chief Whip, 1974-76, joined the Cabinet in June, 1974. Chairman, Select Committee on Sound Broadcasting. Member, Mortgage Review Board since February 1978. Opposition Chief Whip, 1970-74; became Minister of Housing and Local Government three weeks before 1970 election. Parliamentary Secretary, Treasury, and Government Chief Whip, 1969-70; Minister of Public Building and Works, 1967-69; Parliamentary Secretary, Ministry of Housing and Local Government, 1964-67, with special responsibility for London housing. Elected for Rotherhithe, 1946; returned for Bermondsey, 1950. B March, 1913; ed St Joseph's, Deptford. Knighted by Pope John (Knight Commander of St George) for services to Roman Catholic Church, 1959. Chairman, London Labour Party, 1961-77. Sponsored by TGWU, of which he was an official.

Mr Alexander Duma, director of a merchant bank, barrister and accountant. B 1946; ed privately and at University College, London (Chairman, College Conservative Association, 1967). Vice-president, Bermondsey Conservative Associaton, since 1975.

Mr Joseph Taylor, administration manager, contested the seat, October, 1974. B May, 1923; ed Wilson's Grammar School and Open University.

Mr Anthony Moore is a TGWU shop steward. Active trade unionist in dock industry for 23 years. Aged 39.

SOUTHWARK, Dulwich

Electorate 61,259   1974: 67,542

*Silkin, S. C. (Lab)	18,557
Morley, E. (C)	18,435
Pearson, W. H. (L)	4,759
Thompson, D. (Nat Front)	920
Smart, D. (Ecology)	468

Lab majority	122

No Change

	1974		1979
Total votes	43,987		43,139
Turnout	65·1%		70·4%
Lab	21,790	49·5%	43·0%
C	14,331	32·6%	42·7%
L	7,866	17·9%	11·0%
Nat Front	—	—	2·1%
Ecology	—	—	1·1%
Lab maj	7,459	16·9%	0·3%
Swing		−3·1%	+8·3%

Mr Samuel Silkin, QC, was Attorney-General 1974-79. Member Privileges Committee. An Opposition spokesman on legal matters, 1970-74. Elected, 1964. B March, 1918; ed Dulwich College and Trinity Hall, Cambridge. Barrister (Middle-Temple, 1941). Chairman, Select Committee on Parliamentary Privilege, 1966-67; vice-chairman, PLP Legal and Judicial Group, 1970-74. President, Alcohol Education Centre; Governor, Maudsley Hospital. Member Royal Commission on the Penal System for England and Wales, 1965-66.

Mr Eric Morley who has held directorships with Mecca Ltd and Grand Metropolitan Hotels Ltd, contested seat in October 1974. B 1918; ed St Martin-in-the-Fields; Whitstable Grammar School; Training Ship, 'Exmouth' and Army School. President, Variety Clubs International. Managing director, Outward Bound Trust.

Mr William Pearson, managing director of advertising agency, contested the seat, February and October, 1974. B May, 1927; ed Willington College and Worcester College, Oxford.

Mr David Smart teaches geography at Dulwich College. Aged 51; ed Sherborne and London University.

SOUTHWARK, Peckham

Electorate 59,015   1974: 63,349

*Lamborn, H. G. (Lab)	20,364
Dalton, A. (C)	9,553
Minahan, T. (L)	2,607
Roberts, Mrs M. (Nat Front)	1,503

Lab majority	10,811

No Change

	1974		1979
Total votes	34,317		34,027
Turnout	54·2%		57·7%
Lab	24,586	71·6%	59·8%
C	5,760	16·8%	28·1%
L	3,971	11·6%	7·7%
Nat Front	—	—	4·4%
Lab maj	18,826	54·8%	31·7%
Swing		−5·2%	+11·5%

Mr Harry Lamborn, elected February, 1974, PPS to Mr Denis Healey as Chancellor of the Exchequer, 1974-79. MP for Southwark, May, 1972-74. B May, 1915; ed elementary school. Former director, Royal Arsenal Co-operative Society. Member, Camberwell Borough Council, 1953-65, mayor 1963-64; London County Council, 1958-65. GLC 1964-73, deputy chairman, 1971-72. Sponsored by USDAW and member since 1933.

Mr Andrew Dalton, international fund manager for a merchant bank and director of marine reinsurance brokerage company. B 1949; ed Oundle School, Peterborough, and Magdalen College, Oxford. Research secretary and council member, Bow Group. Member, Conservative parliamentary public sector policy group.

Mr Terence Minahan, Lloyds insurance broker. Aged 42.

SOWERBY

Electorate 49,275   1974: 48,747

Thompson, D. (C)	16,797
*Madden, M. F. (Lab)	15,617
Shutt, D. T. (L)	7,369

C majority	1,180

C gain from Lab

	1974		1979
Total votes	38,589		39,783
Turnout	79·2%		80·7%
Lab	14,971	38·8%	39·3%
C	14,325	37·1%	42·2%
L	9,136	23·7%	18·5%
Pros Brit	157	0·4%	—
Lab maj	646	1·7%	
C maj	—	—	2·9%
Swing		−0·7%	+2·3%

Mr Donald Thompson, company director, contested the seat in both 1974 elections and Batley and Morley in 1970. Former farmer and owner of contract butchering firm. B November 1931; ed Hipperholme Grammar School. Member, West Riding County Council, 1967-74; West Yorkshire County Council, 1973-77; Calderdale District Council, since 1974.

Mr Max Madden, elected February, 1974; contested Sudbury and Woodbridge, 1966. Former member, Trade and Industry subcommittee, Public Expenditure Committee; Select Committee on European Secondary Legislation and Select Committee on Conduct of Members. Chairman, PLP employment group and vice-chairman, textile group. Member, Council of 'Get Britain Out' (of EEC) Campaign. Sponsored by TGWU.

Mr David Shutt, chartered accountant, fought the constituency in 1970 and twice in 1974. B March, 1942; ed Pudsey Grammar School. Member, Calderdale Metropolitan District Council, since 1973; Society of Friends (Quakers). Director, Joseph Rowntree Social Service Trust Ltd.

SPELTHORNE

Electorate 70,898   1974: 69,411

*Atkins, H. E. (C)	31,290
Dodwell, C. H. (Lab)	15,137
Winner, P. E. (L)	7,565
Sawyer, J. (Nat Front)	518

C majority	16,153

No Change

	1974		1979
Total votes	51,694		54,510
Turnout	74·5%		76·9%
C	23,125	44·7%	57·4%
Lab	17,177	33·2%	27·8%
L	10,212	19·8%	13·9%
Nat Front	1,180	2·3%	1·0%
C maj	5,948	11·5%	29·6%
Swing		−1·4%	+9·0%

Mr Humphrey Atkins was appointed Secretary of State for Northern Ireland in May, 1979. Was Opposition Chief Whip 1974-79. Treasurer of the Household (whip) 1970-73. Parliamentary Secretary to the Treasury and Government chief whip, 1974. Opposition whip, 1967-70. Returned for this seat, 1970; represented Morden, 1955-70; contested West

Lothian, 1951. Member of Lloyd's. Former director of financial advertising agency. B August, 1922; ed Wellington College. Secretary, Conservative parliamentary defence committee, 1965-67.

Mr Christopher Dodwell, research chemist. B 1943.
Mr Paul Winner fought the seat twice in 1974. B July, 1934; ed St Lawrence College, Ramsgate; Westminster City Schools; La Sorbonne, Paris; St John's College, Oxford and the LSE Department of Business Administration.

STAFFORD AND STONE

Electorate 83,300   1974: 78,817

*Fraser, H. C. P. J. (C)	34,387
Poulter, M. J. D. (Lab)	21,210
Burman, R. (L)	10,049

C majority	13,177

No Change

	1974		1979
Total votes	59,860		65,646
Turnout	75·9%		78·8%
C	27,173	45·4%	52·4%
Lab	20,845	34·8%	32·3%
L	11,491	19·2%	15·3%
GTBP	351	0·6%	—
C maj	6,328	10·6%	20·1%
Swing		−1·7%	+4·7%

Mr Hugh Fraser, company director and merchant banker, unsuccessfully contested the leadership of the Conservative Party in February, 1975. Appointed Secretary of State for Air, July, 1962; Minister of Defence for RAF, 1964.

Under-Secretary, Colonial Office, 1960-62; War Office, 1958-60. President, Association of Conservative Clubs, 1975-76. Member for Stone, 1945-50, when he was returned for Stafford and Stone. B January 1918; ed Ampleforth, Balliol College, Oxford (President of the Union), and the Sorbonne. Member, Committee of Privileges. Director, Sun Alliance Insurance, Ionian Bank and several other companies.

Mr Michael Poulter, probation officer. B November, 1942; ed St Ignatius' College, Stamford Hill, London, and English College and Gregorian University, Rome. Member, Fabian Society and Institute for Workers Control. ASTMS.

Mr Richard Burman, management services manager, fought Leek in February, 1974, and 1970. B August, 1930; ed Oundle, Leeds College of Technology and Regent Street Polytechnic.

STAFFORDSHIRE, South West

Electorate 67,383   1974: 61,042

*Cormack, P. T. (C)	32,153
Lane, G. J. (Lab)	14,720
Fox, R. (L)	5,460
Thomas, J. (Nat Front)	912

C majority	17,433

No Change

	1974		1979
Total votes	46,024		53,245
Turnout	75·4%		79·0%
C	22,604	49·1%	60·4%
Lab	15,065	32·7%	27·6%
L	8,355	18·2%	10·3%
Nat Front	—		1·7%
C maj	7,539	16·4%	32·8%
Swing		−1·8%	+8·2%

Mr Patrick Cormack, former teacher, elected February, 1974; represented Cannock 1970-74. Contested Grimsby, 1966; Bolsover, 1964. B May, 1939; ed St James Choir and Havelock Schools, Grimsby; Hull University.

Chairman, all party parliamentary committee for Soviet Jews, 1971-75; member, Select Committee on Anti-Discrimination, Chairman, all-party committee for widows and single parent families, 1974-77. IOJ.

Mr Graham Lane, teacher. B November 1943; ed Manchester and Cambridge Universities. NUT, ASTMS.

Mr R Fox, aged 42, archivist, has fought local government elections.

STALYBRIDGE AND HYDE

Electorate 67,772   1974: 66,389

*Pendry, T. (Lab)	27,082
Kershaw, J. (C)	20,502
Pickup, J. (L)	4,642

Lab majority	6,580

No Change

	1974		1979
Total votes	48,608		52,226
Turnout	73·2%		77·1%
Lab	25,161	51·8%	51·9%
C	15,404	31·7%	39·3%
L	7,725	15·9%	8·9%
Ind	318	0·7%	—
Lab maj	9,757	20·1%	12·6%
Swing		−2·4%	+3·7%

Mr Tom Pendry was Under Secretary, Northern Ireland Office, 1978-79; Lord Commissioner of the Treasury (Government whip), 1974-77. Opposition whip, 1971-74. Former member, Public Expenditure Committee. Member, Speaker's Conference on Electoral Reform, 1973-74. Full-time official, NUPE, 1960-70. Elected, 1970. B 1934; ed St Augustine's, Ramsgate and Plater Hall, Oxford. Member, Paddington Borough Council, 1962-65. Member, Consultative Assembly, Council of Europe, 1973-76. Sponsored by NUPE.

Mr John Kershaw, lecturer. B 1950; ed Audenshaw Grammar School; Manchester Polytechnic and Padgate College of Education. Member, Greater Manchester Metropolitan Council. Chairman, Greater Manchester YC's, 1974-77; City of Manchester YC's 1972-75; and Withington Conservative Club, 1975-77.

STIRLING, FALKIRK and GRANGEMOUTH

Electorate 66,164   1974: 64,362

*Ewing, H. (Lab)	29,499
Boyles, W. (C)	13,881
Donachy, J. (Scot Nat)	8,856

Lab majority	15,618

No Change

	1974		1979
Total votes	51,077		52,236
Turnout	79·4%		78·9%
Lab	22,090	43·2%	56·5%
Scot Nat	20,324	39·8%	1·7%
C	7,186	14·1%	26·6%
L	1,477	2·9%	—
Lab maj	1,766	3·4%	29·9%
Swing		−5·4%	−0·4%

Mr Harry Ewing was Under Secretary, Scottish Office, with responsibility for devolution and home affairs, 1974-79. Elected, February, 1974; MP for Stirling and Falkirk, 1971-74. Post Office worker. Former chairman, PLP posts and telecommunications group. B January, 1931; ed Beath High School, Cowdenbeath. Fought Fife, East, 1970. Sponsored by UPOW.

Mr William Boyles, publican. B 1936; ed Dundas School, High School, Grangemouth and Skerry's College, Edinburgh. Grangemouth district councillor.

Mr John Donachy, business consultant and company chairman. B March, 1926; ed George Heriot's School, Edinburgh; Glasgow High School and Glasgow University.

STIRLINGSHIRE, EAST and CLACKMANNAN

Electorate 66,535   1974: 62,693

O'Neil, M. J. (Lab)	22,780
*Reid, G. N. (Scot Nat)	21,796
Begg, T. N. A. (C)	9,778

Lab majority	984

Lab gain from Scot Nat

	1974		1979
Total votes	51,292		54,354
Turnout	81·8%		81·7%
Scot Nat	25,998	50·7%	40·1%
Lab & Co-op	18,657	36·4%	41·9%
C	5,369	10·5%	18·0%
L	1,268	2·5%	—
Scot Nat maj	7,341	14·3%	—
Lab maj	—	—	1·8%
Swing	—	—	+1·0%

Mr Martin O'Neil is a teacher. B 1945. GMWU/MATSA.

Mr George Reid, SNP spokesman on constitutional affairs (United Kingdom and EEC), won the seat in February, 1974, and became party spokesman on housing, health and social services. B June, 1939; ed Tullibody School, Dollar Academy, St Andrew's University and various American universities. Broadcaster and journalist. Member, Council of Europe and WEU. Vice-chairman, 'Yes for Scotland' in 1979 devolution referendum. NUJ.

Mr Thomas Begg, lecturer in economics and industrial relations, contested the seat, October, 1974. B 1942; ed Balfron High School, Clydebank Technical College and Strathclyde University. Served in RAF, 1959-68. Elder, Church of Scotland.

STIRLINGSHIRE, WEST

Electorate 57,602   1974: 52,989

*Canavan, D. A. (Lab)	22,516
McCurley, Mrs A. (C)	12,160
Jones, Mrs J. T. (Scot Nat)	8,627
Cant, D. (L)	3,905
Lab majority	10,356

No Change

	1974		1979
Total votes	42,769		47,208
Turnout	80·7%		82·0%
Lab	16,698	39·0%	47·7%
Scot Nat	16,331	38·2%	18·3%
C	7,875	18·4%	25·8%
L	1,865	4·4%	8·3%
Lab maj	367	0·8%	21·9%
Swing		−4·7%	−0·7%

Mr Dennis Canavan, elected October, 1974. Treasurer, Scottish Parliamentary Labour group, convenor of group's education subcommittee and parliamentary spokesman for Scottish committee on mobility for the disabled. Assistant headmaster. Leader of Labour Group, Stirling District Council, 1974. B August, 1942; ed St Columba's High School, Cowdenbeath and Edinburgh University.

Mrs Anna McCurley, schoolteacher. B 1943; ed Glasgow High School for Girls; Glasgow and Strathclyde Universities. Branch chairman, Glasgow, Hillhead, Conservative Association, 1975. Member, Strathclyde Regional Council.

Mrs Janette Jones contested the seat, February and October, 1974. B August, 1931; ed Kilsyth Academy. Former Member, Kilsyth Town council and Strathclyde Regional Council.

Mr David Cant, trout farmer. B April, 1940; ed Trinity College, Dublin, and Royal Naval College, Dartmouth.

STOCKPORT, North

Electorate 53,533   1974: 52,842

*Bennett, A. F. (Lab)	18,789
Last, J. W. (C)	18,456
Hartley, J. (L)	5,096
Walker, K. (Nat Front)	244
Lab majority	333

No Change

	1974		1979
Total votes	41,219		42,585
Turnout	78·0%		79·5%
Lab	17,979	43·6%	44·1%
C	16,155	39·2%	43·3%
L	7,085	17·2%	12·0%
Nat Front	—	—	0·6%
Lab maj	1,824	4·4%	0·8%
Swing		−2·0%	+1·8%

Mr Andrew Bennett, elected February, 1974; contested Knutsford, 1970. Member, Select Committee on Members' Interests, since 1976; Joint Select Committee on Statutory Instruments; Select Committee on Violence in the Family. Oldham borough councillor, 1964-74. B March, 1939; ed Birmingham University. NUT.

Mr John Last, senior executive with mail order company, contested Liverpool, West Derby, in February and October, 1974. B 1940; ed Sutton Grammar School and Trinity College, Oxford. Member, Merseyside County Council; secretary of Conservative group.

Mr John Hartley, senior administrative assistant. Aged 28.

STOCKPORT, South

Electorate 48,513   1974: 47,795

McNally, T. (Lab)	16,910
Skidmore, D. (C)	15,785
Quayle, M. (L)	4,458
Murphy, R. (Nat Front)	374
Lab majority	1,125

No Change

	1974		1979
Total votes	35,502		37,527
Turnout	74·3%		77·4%
Lab	16,281	45·9%	45·1%
C	12,061	34·0%	42·1%
L	7,160	20·2%	11·9%
Nat Front	—	—	1·0%
Lab maj	4,220	11·9%	3·0%
Swing		−1·8%	+4·4%

Mr Thomas McNally was political adviser to Mr James Callaghan, as Prime Minister. B February, 1943; ed College of St Joseph, Blackpool and University College London. Vice-president NUS, 1965-66. GMWU.

Mr Frederic Skidmore, surgeon and lecturer. B 1939; ed Gonville and Caius, Cambridge, and Birmingham Medical School. Member, executive committee, Conservative Medical Society.

STOKE-ON-TRENT, Central

Electorate 59,493   1974: 61,217

*Cant, R. B. (Lab)	24,707
Williams, W. (C)	12,104
Thomas, A. (L)	4,260
Lab majority	12,603

No Change

	1974		1979
Total votes	39,952		41,071
Turnout	65·3%		69·0%
Lab	24,146	60·4%	60·2%
C	9,493	23·8%	29·5%
L	6,313	15·8%	10·4%
Lab maj	14,653	36·6%	30·7%
Swing		−4·5%	+2·9%

Mr Robert Cant was elected in 1966; contested Shrewsbury, 1950 and 1951. Lecturer. B July, 1915; ed Middlesborough High School and London School of Economics. Chairman, PLP finance and economics group. Former member, Public Accounts Committee; Member, Select Committee on MPs' interests; Stoke-on-Trent City Council, 1953-74, and of Staffordshire County Council, since 1973. AUT.

Mr Wallace Williams, sales engineer and lecturer in management, contested seat October 1974. B 1930; ed Stafford Grammar School. Member, Leek RDC, 1971-73; Staffordshire Moorlands District Council, since 1973; Staffordshire County Council social services advisory committee; West Midlands Provincial Council Employers' Association.

Mr Alan Thomas, training officer for computer programmers, contested the seat, October, 1974. B December, 1939; ed Wallasey Grammar School, Hull University. Branch treasurer, ASTMS.

STOKE-ON-TRENT, North

Electorate 59,402   1974: 59,899

*Forrester, J. S. (Lab)	25,652
Ibbs, R. (C)	13,228
Smedley, C. V. (L)	3,994
Baugh, C. (Nat Front)	341
Lab majority	12,424

No Change

	1974		1979
Total votes	41,695		43,215
Turnout	69·6%		72·8%
Lab	25,264	60·6%	59·4%
C	10,192	24·4%	30·6%
L	6,239	15·0%	9·2%
Nat Front	—	—	0·8%
Lab maj	15,072	36·2%	28·8%
Swing		−3·9%	+3·7%

Mr John Forrester, teacher, was elected in 1966. B June, 1924; ed Eastwood Council School, City School of Commerce, Stoke-on-Trent, and Alsager Teacher Training College. Member, Stoke-on-Trent city and district councils, since 1970. Secretary, constituency Labour Party, 1961; member, executive committee, Stoke-on-Trent City Labour Party, 1958, NUT.

Mr Roger Ibbs, self-employed state registered chiropodist. B January, 1948; ed Alleyne's Grammar School, Stone, Staffordshire, and Northern College of Chiropody, Salford. Chairman, Stoke North Conservative Party. Member, Stoke-on-Trent District Council and secretary to council's Conservative group.

Mr Clive Smedley, an employee relations manager with a computer firm. B August, 1945.

STOKE-ON-TRENT, South

Electorate 74,193   1974: 72,629

*Ashley, J. (Lab)	31,610
Rayner, R. (C)	17,364
Chantrey, Dr D. (L)	4,829
Lab majority	14,246

No Change

	1974		1979
Total votes	50,181		53,803
Turnout	69·1%		72·5%
Lab	30,699	61·2%	58·8%
C	14,204	28·3%	32·3%
L	5,278	10·5%	9·0%
Lab maj	16,495	32·9%	26·5%
Swing		−2·4%	+3·2%

Mr Jack Ashley, journalist and broadcaster, is chairman of the all-party Lords and Commons disablement group and a member of the Labour Party national executive committee since 1976. Elected in 1966; contested Finchley, 1951. B December, 1922; ed elementary school, Ruskin College, Oxford, and Gonville and Caius College, Cambridge (President of the union). Member, PLP liaison committee 1977-78. Member, national executive, Chemical Workers Union. 1946-47; General Advisory Council BBC, 1967-69; Widnes Borough Council, 1946-47, Sponsored by GMWU.

Mr Raymond Rayner, company chairman. B September, 1933; ed Taunton Grammar School. Member, Southampton City Council.

STRATFORD-ON-AVON

Electorate 76,588   1974: 71,895

*Maude, A. E. U. (C)	35,470
Taylor, J. (L)	12,916
Purnell, C. A. (Lab)	10,334
C majority	22,554

No Change

	1974		1979
Total votes	53,229		58,720
Turnout	74·0%		76·7%
C	27,123	51·0%	60·4%
L	14,555	27·3%	22·0%
Lab	11,551	21·7%	17·6%
C maj	12,568	23·7%	38·4%
Swing		−1·7%	+6·7%

Mr Angus Maude was appointed to the Cabinet as Paymaster General in May, 1979. Became a deputy chairman of the Conservative Party and chairman of the Conservative Research Department in February, 1975. Elected at by-election in 1963; represented Ealing, South, 1950-58, when he resigned; contested South Dorset by-election in November, 1962. Author and journalist, B September, 1912; ed Rugby and Oriel College, Oxford. Director, Conservative Political Centre, 1951-55. Editor, *Sydney Morning Herald*, 1958-61. Conservative spokesman on aviation, 1964-65, and on colonies, 1965-66. Member, Select Committee on MPs' interests, 1974 and 1976-79. Former member, executive of 1922 Committee, Select Committee on Procedure, and Select Committee on European Secondary Legislation.

Mr James Taylor, farmer. B 1934; ed Bootham, York, and Royal Agricultural College, Cirencester. Past Chairman, South Worcestershire Liberal Association. NFU Council delegate.

Mr Christopher Purnell, law student. B January, 1949; ed Tonbridge School, Magdalen College, Oxford, and Central Polytechnic School of Law. Member, London Borough of Wandsworth since 1974. TGWU.

STRETFORD

Electorate 69,258   1974: 68,766

*Churchill, W. S. (C)	25,972
Scott, P. N. (Lab)	21,466
Wrigley, D. I. (L)	6,369
C majority	4,506

No Change

	1974		1979
Total votes	52,620		53,807
Turnout		76·5%	77·7%
C	22,114	42·0%	48·3%
Lab	20,877	39·7%	39·9%
L	9,629	18·3%	11·8%
C maj	1,237	2·3%	8·4%
Swing		-2·4%	+3·0%

Mr Winston Churchill was an Opposition spokesman on defence from 1976-78. Author and journalist. Won the seat for the Conservatives in 1970; contested Manchester, Gorton, by-election, 1967. B October, 1940; ed Eton and Christ Church, Oxford. Secretary, Conservative backbench foreign affairs committee, 1973-76. Trustee, National  Benevolent Fund for the Aged, 1973; Governor, English Speaking Union, 1975. Institute of Journalists.

Mr Peter Scott, a full-time official of Apex; NW area secretary. Contested the seat, October, 1974. B December, 1931; ed Ryhope Grammar School, Sunderland. Member, Darlington Town Council, 1963-64.

Mr Dennis Wrigley owns a firm of management and marketing consultants. Contested the seat, February and October 1974, High Peak, 1970, 1966, 1964 and 1961 by-election, and Oldham, East 1959. B January, 1930; ed Manchester Grammar School and Manchester Regional School of Architecture.

STROUD

Electorate 76,137   1974: 69,398

*Kershaw, J. A. (C)	32,534
Marshall, B. J. (Lab)	17,037
Heppell, J. (L)	12,314
C majority	15,497

No Change

	1974		1979
Total votes	55,755		61,885
Turnout		80·3%	81·3%
C	24,406	43·8%	52·6%
Lab & Co-op	17,352	31·1%	27·5%
L	13,756	24·7%	19·9%
UDP	241	0·4%	—
C maj	7,054	12·7%	25·1%
Swing		-0·9%	+6·2%

Mr Anthony Kershaw, a company director, was Under Secretary, Defence (RAF), 1973-74; Under Secretary, Foreign and Commonwealth Office, 1970-73; Parliamentary Secretary, Ministry of Public Building and Works, 1970. Elected in 1955; contested Gloucester, 1950 and 1951. Barrister (Inner Temple, 1939). B  December, 1915; ed Eton and Balliol College, Oxford. Member, Defence and External Affairs Sub-committee of Public Expenditure Committee; joint secretary, Conservative defence committee, 1964-67. PPS to Mr Heath until 1970. Member, Westminster City Council, 1946-50.

Mr Beverly Marshall, teacher. B March, 1951; ed Holmfirth High School, Colne Valley High School, and Worcester College of Higher Education. Member, Worcester CBC, 1972-74; Worcester City DC, since 1973; and Association of District Councils, 1975-77. NUT.

Mr James Heppell, senior planning officer, contested Gloucester, 1970; Shipley, 1966 and 1964. B July, 1938; ed Carres Grammar School, Sleaford; Leeds University, University of Wales. Member, Stroud District Council, since 1973; Gloucestershire County Council, 1973-77. Nalgo. Methodist lay preacher.

SUDBURY AND WOODBRIDGE

Electorate 91,441   1974: 84,286

*Stainton, K. M. (C)	39,544
Hills, Miss J. B. (Lab)	18,972
Beale, R. (L)	13,435
C majority	20,572

No Change

	1974		1979
Total votes	63,241		71,951
Turnout		75·0%	78·7%
C	30,049	47·5%	55·0%
Lab	17,986	28·4%	26·4%
L	15,206	24·0%	18·7%
C maj	12,063	19·1%	28·6%
Swing		-1·5%	+4·7%

Mr Keith Stainton, company director, Lloyd's underwriter and a Fellow of the Institute of Management Consultants, was returned at a by-election, December, 1963. B November, 1921; ed Kendal Grammar School and Manchester University.  Conservative spokesman on aviation 1966-67. Former member, Estimates Committee, Select Committee on Science and Technology, and Public Expenditure Committee. *Financial Times* leader writer, 1949-53. Founder member, Bow Group.

Miss Jill Hills, part-time teacher, served on Colchester Borough Council, 1972-74. B August, 1942; ed Harrow County Grammar School, Wycombe Abbey School and Manchester and Essex universities. NATFHE.

Mr Roderick Beale, lecturer, contested Maldon, February and October 1974 and 1970 and Cambridgeshire, 1966. B October 1932; ed London School of Economics.

SUNDERLAND, North

Electorate 72,994   1974: 75,577

*Willey, F. T. (Lab)	29,213
Keith, L. (C)	16,311
Lennox, J. A. (L)	5,238
Lab majority	12,902

No Change

	1974		1979
Total votes	50,642		50,762
Turnout	67·0%		69·5%
Lab	29,618	58·5%	57·5%
C	13,947	27·5%	32·1%
L	7,077	14·0%	10·3%
Lab maj	15,671	31·0%	25·4%
Swing		−5·3%	+2·8%

Mr Frederick T. Willey, vice-chairman of the Parliamentary Labour Party, was Minister of State, Ministry of Housing and Local Government, 1967; Minister of Land and Natural Resources, 1964-67. Barrister (Middle Temple, 1936). B November, 1910; ed Johnston School, Durham, and St John's College, Cambridge. Elected as  Sunderland MP in 1945 and returned for the North division in 1950. Chairman, Select Committee on Race Relations and Immigration, since 1975; Select Committee on MPs' interests since 1976, and of Committee of Selection. Member, Committee of Privileges since 1974. Former chairman, Select Committee on Education and Science and Select Committee on Abortion (Amendment) Bill. ASTMS (sponsored by that union) and APEX.

Mr Lindsay Keith, solicitor and public notary in partnership. B 1945; ed Fettes College, Edinburgh, College of Law, Guildford, and Liverpool Polytechnic. Member, executive committee, Blyth Conservative Association.

Mr John Lennox, economist, contested the seat, February and October 1974. B June, 1947; ed St Aidan's Grammar School, Sunderland, De La Salle College of Education, Manchester, Durham University.

SUNDERLAND, South

Electorate 79,130   1974: 76,479

*Bagier, G. A. T. (Lab)	29,403
Harris, J. (C)	21,002
Barker, P. (L)	4,984
Lab majority	8,401

No Change

	1974		1979
Total votes	52,044		55,389
Turnout	68·1%		70·0%
Lab	28,623	55·0%	53·1%
C	15,593	30·0%	37·9%
L	7,828	15·0%	9·0%
Lab maj	13,030	25·0%	15·2%
Swing		−5·0%	+4·9%

Mr Gordon Bagier, who won the seat in 1964, was a British Railways signals inspector. B July, 1924; ed Pendower Secondary Technical School, Newcastle upon Tyne. President, Yorkshire District Council, NUR, 1962-64. Member, Keighley Borough Council, 1956-60, and Sowerby Bridge Urban Council, 1962-65. Member, Estimates Committee,  1964-66. Substitute member, Council of Europe (Consultative Assembly) and WEU. Sponsored by NUR.

Mr James Harris, assistant general manager of division of major airline company. B 1928; ed Bristol Grammar School. Former chairman, Surrey Young Conservatives; and vice-chairman, South Eastern Area Young Conservatives.

Mr Paul Barker, probation officer, contested Blaydon, October, 1974. B January, 1933; ed Ellis School and Didsbury College.

SURREY, East

Electorate 57,364   1974: 55,673

*Howe, Sir G. (C)	28,266
Liddell, Mrs S. (L)	8,866
Harries, W. G. (Lab)	7,398
Smith, D. (Nat Front)	452
C majority	19,400

No Change

	1974		1979
Total votes	42,406		44,982
Turnout	76·2%		78·4%
C	22,227	52·4%	62·8%
L	12,382	29·2%	19·7%
Lab	7,797	18·4%	16·4%
Nat Front	—		1·0%
C maj	9,845	23·2%	43·1%
Swing		−1·1%	+6·2%

Sir Geoffrey Howe, QC, was appointed Chancellor of the Exchequer in May, 1979. He became chief Opposition spokesman on Treasury and economic affairs in February, 1975, after having unsuccessfully contested the leadership of the Conservative Party. Opposition spokesman on social services 1974-75; Minister for Trade and Consumer Affairs within  the Department of Trade and Industry, 1972-74; Solicitor General, 1970-72. Elected in February, 1974; represented Reigate, 1970-74 and Bebington, 1964-66; contested Aberavon 1955 and 1959. B December, 1926; ed Winchester and Trinity Hall, Cambridge. Barrister, (Middle Temple, 1952). Director of insurance and market research companies. Member, General Council of Bar, 1957-61; elected Bencher of Middle Temple, 1969.

Mrs Susan Liddell, teacher. B June, 1923; ed Beltane School, Wimbledon; Newham College, Cambridge.

Mr William Harries, economist, employed in telecommunications. B July, 1954; ed Haverfordwest Grammar School and Leeds University.

SURREY, North-West

Electorate 75,197   1974: 68,928

*Grylls, W. M. J. (C)	36,219
Sharpe, R. (Lab)	10,763
Simpson, D. (L)	9,037
Heath, R. (Nat Front)	796

C majority	25,456

No Change

	1974		1979
Total votes	48,823		56,815
Turnout	70·8%		75·6%
C	25,524	52·3%	63·7%
Lab	11,943	24·5%	18·9%
L	11,356	23·3%	15·9%
Nat Front	—		1·4%
C maj	13,581	27·8%	44·8%
Swing		−1·8%	+8·5%

Mr Michael Grylls, vice-chairman of the Conservative backbench industry committee since 1975, was elected in February, 1974; MP for Chertsey, 1970-74; contested Fulham, 1964 and 1966. Consultant to a pharmaceutical and chemical company. B February, 1934; ed Royal Naval College, Dartmouth, and universities in Paris and Madrid. Member, Select Committee on Overseas Development, 1972-77; GLC (Cities of London and Westminster) 1967-68; deputy leader of ILEA, 1969-70; St Pancras Borough Council, 1959-62.

Mr Raymond Sharpe, company secretary. B 1923.

Mr David Simpson, salesman. Aged 26.

SUSSEX, Mid

Electorate 68,232   1974: 61,074

*Renton, R. T. (C)	32,548
Campbell, J. (L)	11,705
Turner, D. S. (Lab)	8,260
Haslett, S. H. M. (Ind C)	697

C majority	20,843

No Change

	1974		1979
Total votes	46,659		53,210
Turnout	76·4%		78·0%
C	25,126	53·9%	61·2%
L	13,129	28·1%	22·0%
Lab	8,404	18·0%	15·5%
Ind C	—		1·3%
C maj	11,997	25·8%	39·2%
Swing		−1·2%	+4·9%

Mr Timothy Renton, company director, was elected in February, 1974; contested Sheffield, Park, 1970. B May, 1932; ed Eton and Magdalen College, Oxford. Vice-chairman, Conservative Parliamentary Trade Committee, since 1974; member, Select Committee on Nationalized Industries, since 1974; Fellowship, Industry and Parliament Trust, 1977-78. Grower of ornamental amenity trees in partnership with wife. ASTMS.

Mr John Campbell, accountant and managing director of Sussex engineering company. Company won 1978 export award to smaller manufacturers. B August, 1930; ed Allan Glen's School, Glasgow.

Mr Desmond Turner, biochemist. B July, 1939; ed Luton Grammar School and London University. AUT.

SUTTON, Carshalton

Electorate 67,255   1974: 66,856

*Forman, N. (C)	26,492
Ormerod, M. G. (Lab)	16,121
Hatherley, J. (L)	8,112
Denville-Faulkner, T. (Nat Front)	919

C majority	10,371

No Change

1976 by-election: Total vote, 40,152 (60.5%). C, 20,753 (51.7%); Lab, 11,021 (27.5%); L, 6,028 (15.0%); Nat Front, 1,851 (4.6%); Others, 499 (1.2%). C majority 9,732 (24.2%).

	1974		1979
Total votes	49,650		51,644
Turnout	74·3%		76·8%
C	22,538	45·4%	51·3%
Lab	18,840	37·9%	31·2%
L	8,272	16·7%	15·7%
Nat Front	—		1·8%
C maj	3,698	7·5%	20·1%
Swing		−1·4%	+6·3%

Mr Nigel Forman, retained the seat for the Conservatives in the by-election in March, 1976. Former assistant director of Conservative Research Department. Contested Coventry, North-East, February, 1974. B March, 1943; ed Shrewsbury School; New College, Oxford; College of Europe, Bruges, Harvard and Sussex Universities. Member, Select Committee on Science and Technology, since 1976; secretary, Conservative backbench committees on education and energy.

Mr Michael Ormerod, contested Reigate, February and October, 1974. B September, 1938; ed Bradfield College, Berkshire. Research scientist at Institute of Cancer Research. ASTMS.

Mr John Hatherley, teacher. Contested the seat at the by-election, March, 1976. Member, National Council, Liberal Party. B October, 1926; ed Witwatersrand University, Cape Town University.

SUTTON, Sutton and Cheam

Electorate 63,038   1974: 60,559

*Macfarlane, D. N. (C)	28,842
Caswill, C. (L)	13,136
Irwin, Mrs N. (Lab)	7,126
Hunt, J. (Nat Front)	465
Smoker, J. (Ind)	128
C majority	15,706

No Change

	1974		1979
Total votes	46,567		49,697
Turnout	76·9%		78·8%
C	22,156	47·6%	58·0%
L	16,995	36·5%	26·4%
Lab	7,118	15·3%	14·3%
Wmn's Rights	298	0·6%	—
Nat Front	—	—	0·9%
Ind	—	—	0·3%
C maj	5,161	11·1%	31·6%
Swing		−0·3%	+5·7%

Mr Neil Macfarlane, was appointed Under Secretary of State for Education and Science in May, 1979. Company director and former executive with an oil company. Regained the seat for the Conservatives, February, 1974; contested East Ham, North, 1970; Sutton and Cheam by-election, 1972. B May 1936; ed St Arbyns, Woodford Green, and

Bancrofts School, Woodford Wells. Member, Select Committee on Science and Technology, 1974-79; secretary, Conservative backbench committees on energy, Greater London and on sport and recreation. Secretary, Anglo-Thai Parliamentary Committee.

Mr Christopher Caswill, public servant, scientific staff. Member, Liberal Party national panels on employment and industrial relations and industrial development. B January, 1944; ed Cranbrook School, Kent, and Queens College, Cambridge. ASTMS.

Mrs Nancy Irwin, teacher. B November, 1932; ed United States and Battersea College of Education. Member, Co-operative Society Political Committee. NUT.

SUTTON COLDFIELD

Electorate 64,093   1974: 60,491

*Fowler, P. N. (C)	34,096
Hooper, C. E. A. (L)	7,989
Partridge, J. F. (Lab)	6,511
Wallace, R. (Nat Front)	466
Hammond, G. C. (Ind C)	459
C majority	26,107

No Change

	1974		1979
Total votes	45,057		49,521
Turnout	74·5%		77·3%
C	25,729	57·1%	68·9%
L	12,373	27·5%	13·1%
Lab	6,955	15·4%	16·1%
Nat Front	—	—	0·9%
Ind C	—	—	0·9%
C maj	13,356	29·6%	52·8%
Swing		−1·8%	+5·5%

Mr Norman Fowler was appointed Minister of Transport May, 1979. He became chief Opposition spokesman on transport in 1976 having been chief spokesman on the social services since February, 1975, when he joined the Shadow Cabinet. A spokesman on home affairs,

1974-75. Jounalist on *The Times*, 1961-70, being its Home Affairs Correspondent 1966-70. Elected for this seat, February, 1974; MP for Nottingham, South, 1970-74. B February, 1938; ed King Edward VI School, Chelmsford, and Trinity Hall, Cambridge. Member, Select Committee on Race Relations and Immigration, 1970-74. Adviser, Group Four Security. NUJ.

Mr Edward Hooper, leather manufacturer and merchant. B August, 1940; ed Bryanston, RNC Dartmouth, St Catherine's College, Oxford.

Mr John Partridge, progress chaser, has served on Solihull Metropolitan Borough Council since 1975. B April, 1948; ed St Philips Grammar School, Birmingham. TGWU.

SWANSEA, East

Electorate 60,350   1974: 54,780

*Anderson, D. (Lab)	31,909
Edwards, Mrs S. (C)	10,689
Ball, J. G. (Pl Cymru)	2,732
Jones, W. (Comm)	308
Lab majority	21,220

No Change

	1974		1979
Total votes	41,900		45,638
Turnout	71·3%		75·6%
Lab	26,735	63·8%	69·9%
C	6,014	14·4%	23·4%
L	5,173	12·3%	—
Pl Cymru	3,978	9·5%	6·0%
Comm	—	—	0·7%
Lab maj	20,721	49·4%	46·5%
Swing		−1·9%	+1·4%

Mr Donald Anderson, barrister, (Inner Temple, 1969), formerly a diplomat and university lecturer, was elected in October, 1974; MP for Monmouth, 1966-70. Chairman, Welsh Labour Group, since 1977. B June 1939; ed Swansea Grammar School and University College, Swansea. Member, Kensington and Chelsea Council,

1971-75. Chairman, PLP Environment Committee, 1974-76, 1977-78; jt hon secretary, Anglo-German Parliamentary group. Methodist local preacher. President, Gower Society, 1976-78. TGWU.

Mrs Sandra Edwards, is a housewife. B 1941; ed Bennington High School and Mount Holyoake College, Massachusetts. Member, Ealing Borough Council since 1978; Westminster City Council, 1974-78. National chairman, pre-school playgroups association, 1974-78; national chairman, fair play for children campaign, 1973-78.

Mr John Ball, stores controller, contested the seat in February and October, 1974. B December, 1947; ed Dynevor Grammar School. Former national youth secretary of Plaid Cymru. ACTSS.

Mr **William Jones**, contested seat in February, 1974, and in 1970 and 1966. Insurance agent. B November, 1918; ed elementary school. Chairman, Penderry Tenants' Action Committee. USDAW.

SWANSEA, West

Electorate 65,872   1974: 65,225

*Williams, A. J. (Lab)	24,175
Mercer, D. (C)	23,774
Ball, M. J. (L)	3,484
Gwent, G. ap (Pl Cymru)	1,012

Lab majority	401

No Change

	1974		1979
Total votes	48,914		52,445
Turnout	75·0%		79·6%
Lab	22,565	46·1%	46·1%
C	17,729	36·2%	45·3%
L	6,842	14·0%	6·6%
Pl Cymru	1,778	3·6%	1·9%
Lab maj	4,836	9·9%	0·8%
Swing		−1·7%	+4·5%

Mr **Alan Williams**, Minister of State, Department of Industry, 1976-79; Minister of State, Prices and Consumer Protection, 1974-76. Won the seat in 1964; contested Poole, 1959. B October, 1930; ed Cardiff High School, Cardiff College of Technology and University College, Oxford. Radio and television broadcaster and freelance journalist. Opposition spokesman on education and science, 1970-73; consumer affairs 1973-74. Parliamentary Secretary, Ministry of Technology and Power 1969-70; Under Secretary, Department for Economic Affairs, 1967-69.

Mr **David Mercer**, solicitor and company secretary, contested Swansea, East, February and October, 1974. B April, 1950; ed Dynevor County Secondary School, Swansea and Nottingham University. Member, Lawn Tennis Umpires' Association of Great Britain; Swansea Junior Chamber of Commerce.

Mr **Martin Ball**, is a lecturer. B February, 1951; ed Exeter School, University College, Bangor, and Essex University.

Mr **Gruffydd ap Gwent**, a solicitor, contested the seat in October, 1974, and 1970. B May, 1942; ed Llandovery College and University of Wales.

SWINDON

Electorate 65,761   1974: 62,900

*Stoddart, D. L. (Lab)	25,218
Hammond, N. (C)	19,319
Collis, Miss G. (L)	5,709

Lab majority	5,899

No Change

	1974		1979
Total votes	46,533		50,246
Turnout	74·0%		76·4%
Lab	24,124	51·8%	50·2%
C	13,854	29·8%	38·4%
L	8,349	17·9%	11·4%
WRP	206	0·4%	—
Lab maj	10,270	22·0%	11·8%
Swing		−2·4%	+5·1%

Mr **David Stoddart**, was a Lord Commissioner of the Treasury, 1976-78, and an Assistant Government Whip, 1975-76. Won the seat in 1970 after contesting it in the 1969 by-election; fought Newbury, 1964 and 1959. Power station administrative assistant. B May, 1926; ed St Clement Danes and Henley Grammar Schools, Bromley Technical College.

Member, Select Committtee on Nationalized Industries. Former chairman PLP environment group and former vice-chairman PLP energy group. Sponsored by EETPU.

Mr **Nigel Hammond**, teacher and author, contested Aberavon, October 1974. B February, 1938; ed Abingdon School, London School of Economics and Bristol University. Member, Oxfordshire Rural Community Council; AMA; Wiltshire CTU—teachers' committee; Bow Group; Conservative National Advisory Committee on Education, 1965-70.

Miss **Gudrun Collis**, solicitor, contested Chigwell, 1964. B 1937; ed Newham College, Cambridge.

TAUNTON

Electorate 66,349   1974: 63,654

*Du Cann, E. D. (C)	28,483
Horne, Mrs S. (Lab)	15,759
Lee, M. (L)	7,928
Garbett, G. (Ecol)	1,403

C majority	12,724

No Change

	1974		1979
Total votes	50,530		53,573
Turnout	79·4%		80·7%
C	22,542	44·6%	53·2%
Lab	15,721	31·1%	29·4%
L	11,984	23·7%	14·8%
UDP	283	0·6%	
Ecology	—	—	2·6%
C maj	6,821	13·5%	23·8%
Swing		−1·3%	+5·1%

Mr **Edward Du Cann**, has been chairman of the 1922 Committee since 1972, and of the Select Committee on Public Accounts, since 1974. Formers chairman (1971), Select Committee on Public Expenditure. Elected at February, 1956 by-election: contested Barrow in Furness, 1955, and West Walthamstow, 1951. B May, 1924: ed Colet Court, Woodbridge

School and St John's College, Oxford. Member, Committee of Privileges, since 1974. Admiral, House of Commons Yacht Club, since 1973; founder of the Unicorn Group of Unit Trusts; chairman, Canon Assurance Ltd; patron, Association of Marine Brokers. Chairman of Conservative Party Organization, 1965-67; Minister of State, Board of Trade. 1963-64; Economic Secretary to the Treasury, 1962-63.

Mrs **Sandra Horne**, trade union official with Nalgo, school manager, and member, Manpower Services Commission. B March, 1947; ed Glasgow University.

Mr **Marcus Lee**, aged 39, conference director, *Financial Times*. Ed Exeter College, Oxford.

TEE

Mr Geoffrey Garbett, aged 26, is a teacher. Treasurer, Taunton Classical Guitar Society.

TEESSIDE, Middlesbrough

Electorate 65,175   1974: 60,259

*Bottomley, A. G. (Lab)	24,872
Fenwick, C. (C)	13,463
Freitag, P. (L)	4,023
Simpson, M. (WRP)	1,018
Wilcox, J. (Ind Lab)	861

| Lab majority | 11,409 |

No Change

	1974		1979
Total votes	36,855		44,237
Turnout		61·2%	67·9%
Lab	22,791	61·8%	56·2%
C	8,984	24·4%	30·4%
L	5,080	13·8%	9·1%
WRP	—		2·3%
Ind Lab	—		1·9%
Lab maj	13,807	37·4%	25·8%
Swing		−2·5%	+5·8%

Mr Arthur Bottomley, member of the Committee of Privileges since 1974, was Minister of Overseas Development, 1966-67; Secretary of State for Commonwealth Relations, 1964-66. Returned in February, 1974; represented Middlesbrough, East, 1962-74; Rochester and Chatham, 1950-59, and Chatham, 1945-50. Sec-

retary for Overseas Trade, 1947-51; Under Secretary for the Dominions, 1946-47. B February 1907; ed council school and Toynbee Hall. Chairman, Select Committee on Race Relations and Immigration, 1968-70; former chairman, House of Commons Services Committee. Sponsored by NUPE.

Mr Christopher Fenwick, director of Fenwick Ltd, a department store group. B August 1937; ed Rugby School and Pembroke College, Cambridge. Member, Camden Borough Council, 1971-74.

Mr Peter Freitag, business consultant, contested Darlington, February and October, 1974. B April, 1929; ed Haberdasher's Aske's School. Member, Darlington District Council and Durham County Council (leader of opposition 1972-74) 1970-77; governing council of Council of European Municipalities, 1978.

TEESSIDE, Redcar

Electorate 62,511   1974: 62,365

*Tinn, J. (Lab)	25,470
Cottrell, Mrs E. (C)	17,417
Elliott, A. (L)	4,225
Lloyd, E. (Ind)	333

| Lab majority | 8,053 |

No Change

	1974		1979
Total votes	43,079		47,445
Turnout		69·1%	75·9%
Lab	23,204	53·9%	53·7%
C	12,774	29·7%	36·7%
L	7,101	16·5%	8·9%
Ind	—		0·7%
Lab maj	10,430	24·2%	17·0%
Swing		−2·3%	+3·6%

Mr James Tinn, returned in February, 1974; MP for Cleveland, 1964-74. Teacher and former steel-worker. B August, 1922; ed Consett Council School and Ruskin College and Jesus College, Oxford. Former

chairman, trade union and steel groups of Labour MPs; former member, Select Committee on Overseas Development. Member Parliamentary Group for World Government, and Labour Middle East Committee. National Union of Blastfurnacemen (former branch secretary) and NUT. Sponsored by NUB.

Mrs Elizabeth Cottrell, consultant archivist and part-time teacher. B March, 1941; ed Grove Park Girls' Grammar School, Wrexham; New Hall, Cambridge, and Nottingham University.

Mr Alan Elliott, aged 44, is a post office telephone sales engineer. Former member, Gisborough Town Council.

TEESSIDE, Stockton

Electorate 89,206   1974: 85,206

*Rodgers, W. T. (Lab)	34,917
Jones, R. B. (C)	23,790
Dunleavy, Mrs S. E. (L)	6,074
Bruce, A. (Nat Front)	384
Fletcher, Mrs V. (Ind)	343
Smith, J. (Comm)	243

| Lab majority | 11,127 |

No Change

	1974		1979
Total votes	59,106		65,751
Turnout		69·1%	73·7%
Lab	32,962	55·8%	53·1%
C	18,488	31·3%	36·2%
L	6,906	11·7%	9·2%
Ind	750	1·3%	0·5%
Nat Front	—		0·6%
Comm	—		0·4%
Lab maj	14,474	24·5%	16·9%
Swing		−2·6%	+3·8%

Mr William Rodgers, was Secretary of State for Transport and member of the Cabinet 1976-79; Minister of State for Defence, 1974-76. B October, 1928; ed Sudley Road Council School, Quarry Bank High School, Liverpool, and Magdalen College, Oxford. General Secretary, Fabian Society, 1953-60. Contested Bristol, West, by-election, March,

1957; represented Stockton-on-Tees, 1962-74. Returned for this seat in February, 1974. Economic consultant. Opposition spokesman on aviation supply, 1970-72; Minister of State, Treasury, 1969-70; Minister of State, Board of Trade, 1968-69; Under-Secretary, Foreign Office, 1967-68; Under-Secretary, Economic Affairs, 1964-67. Sponsored by GMWU.

Mr Robert Jones, is local government adviser to the Federation of Civil Engineering Contractors. B 1950; ed Merchant Taylors and University of St Andrews. Freeman, City of London and of Merchant Taylors Company. Member, Royal Burgh, St Andrews 1972-75; Fife County Council, 1973-75.

Mrs Sandra Dunleavy, a partner in family transport business. B December, 1943; ed Easington Secondary School, Peterlee Technical College.

220

Mr James Smith, process operator at ICI Billingham; chairman and convenor of trade union branch.

TEESSIDE, Thornaby

Electorate 61,783   1974: 62,330

*Wrigglesworth, I. W. (Lab & Co-op)	23,597
Jeffreys, J. (C)	18,073
Patmore, N. (L)	4,255
Evans, M. (Nat Front)	251
Lab and Co-op majority	5,524

No Change

	1974		1979
Total votes	45,054		46,176
Turnout	72·3%		74·7%
Lab/Co-op	22,130	49·1%	51·1%
C	17,482	38·8%	39·1%
L	5,442	12·1%	9·2%
Nat Front	—	—	0·5%
Lab/Co-op m	4,648	10·3%	12·0%
Swing		−3·4%	−0·9%

Mr Ian Wrigglesworth, secretary of the Manifesto Group of the PLP and vice-chairman of the PLP finance and economic group, was elected in February, 1974. Director of Galleon World Travel Association Ltd (formerly Workers Travel Association); divisional director of Smiths Industries Ltd; parliamentary adviser to Civil and Public Services Association. B December 1939; ed Stockton Grammar School, Stockton-Billingham Technical College and College of St Mark and St John, Chelsea. Chairman, Labour Economic, Finance and Taxation Association; member, Select Committee on European Secondary Legislation. NUJ.

Mr John Jeffreys, manager with British Steel Corporation, covering all shipping operations in NE England. B 1930; ed Charterhouse. Chairman, Appeal Tribunals' National Dock Labour Board for the ports of Hartlepool and Middlesbrough. Member, Tees Pilotage Authority. President, Teesside and District Chamber of Commerce and Industry, 1972-74. Vice-chairman Cleveland county campaign, 1972.

Mr Nicholas Patmore, aged 30, is a computer programmer.

THANET, East

Electorate 48,989   1974: 47 941

*Aitken, J. W. P. (C)	20,367
Killberry, I. D. (Lab)	10,128
Hesketh, B. C. J. (L)	4,755
Dobing, B. (Nat Front)	376
C majority	10,239

No Change

	1974		1979
Total votes	34,303		35,626
Turnout	71·6%		72·7%
C	15,813	46·1%	57·2%
Lab	11,310	33·0%	28·4%
L	6,472	18·9%	13·3%
Nat Front	708	2·1%	1·1%
C maj	4,503	13·1%	28·8%
Swing		−2·1%	+7·8%

Mr Jonathan Aitken, journalist, was elected in February, 1974; contested Meriden, 1966. B August, 1942; ed Eton and Christ Church, Oxford. Chairman, British-Saudi Arabian Parliamentary Group. Former secretary, Conservative Broadcasting and Communications Committee.

Mr Ian Killberry, is a teacher. B February, 1947; ed Portsmouth Southern Grammar School and Oxford University. Dover district councillor since 1973. NUT.

Mr Barry Hesketh, managing director of an economic consultancy firm. B May, 1942; ed Chatham House Grammar School and Oxford, London, and Australian universities.

THANET, West

Electorate 45,694   1974: 43,901

*Rees-Davies, W. R. (C)	18,122
Little, J. F. (Lab & Co-op)	8,576
Payne, D. (L)	6,017
C majority	9,546

No Change

	1974		1979
Total votes	30,353		32,715
Turnout	69·1%		71·6%
C	13,763	45·3%	55·4%
Lab	8,655	28·5%	26·2%
L	7,935	26·1%	18·4%
C maj	5,108	16·8%	29·2%
Swing		−4·7%	+6·2%

Mr William Rees-Davies, QC, was elected in February, 1974; represented Isle of Thanet, 1953-74; contested Nottingham, South, 1950 and 1951. Barrister (Inner Temple, 1939). B November, 1916; ed Eton and Trinity College, Cambridge (cricket blue). Chairman, British Greek parliamentary group since 1976; chairman, All-Party Tourist Committee, 1970-74; served on select committees on anti-discrimination and on violence in marriage.

Mr James Little, transport manager, contested Lewes, in February and October, 1974. Member, Kent County Council; deputy leader, Labour group. Former member, Swanscombe Urban District Council, Northfleet Urban District Council, Gravesend Borough Council, Gravesend District Council and Gravesham Borough Council. Member, TSSA; General Secretary, Bermondsey Trades Council. Holder of the TUC silver medal. B October 1927; ed St Mary's Christian Brothers School, Belfast.

Mr Dennis Payne, aged 54, is a retail furnishing manager.

THIRSK AND MALTON

Electorate 71,905   1974: 63,856

*Spence, J. D. (C)	32,520
Roberts, E. J. (Lab)	11,924
North, R. (L)	10,533
C majority	20,596

No Change

	1974		1979
Total votes	46,538		54,977
Turnout	72·9%		76·5%
C	24,779	53·2%	59·2%
L	10,917	23·5%	19·2%
Lab	10,842	23·3%	21·7%
C maj	13,862	29·7%	37·5%
Swing		−1·3%	+3·8%

Mr John Spence, a member of the Speakers's panel of chairmen, and secretary of the Yorkshire group of Conservative MPs since 1972, was returned for this seat in February, 1974, having represented Sheffield, Heeley, 1970-74. Contested that seat 1966, and Wakefield, 1964. Civil engineering contractor having his own construction business for 20 years. B December, 1920; ed Queen's University, Belfast. Member, Select Committee on Nationalized Industries since 1974.

Mr Eric Roberts, journalist. B April 1947; ed King James's Grammar School, Huddersfield. National negotiator, branch chairman, NUJ.

Mr Rex North, is a British Rail clerical officer. B April, 1944; ed Watford Grammar School TSSA.

THURROCK

Electorate 91,712   1974: 89,440

*McDonald, Miss O. A. (Lab)	33,449
Baldry, A. (C)	27,030
Crowson, M. (L)	6,445
Burdett, E. (Nat Front)	1,358
Chattaway, B. (Ind)	365
Daly, M. (WRP)	242
Lab majority	6,419

No Change

	1974		1979
Total votes	61,307		68,889
Turnout	68·5%		75·1%
Lab	34,066	55·6%	48·6%
C	14,986	24·4%	39·2%
L	12,255	20·0%	9·4%
Nat Front	—	—	2·0%
Ind	—	—	0·5%
WRP	—	—	0·4%
Lab maj	19,080	31·2%	9·4%
Swing		−2·3%	+10·9%

1976 by-election: Total vote 49,034. Lab, 22,191 (45.3%); C, 17,352 (35.4%); L, 5,977 (12.2%); Nat Front, 3,255 (6.63%); others 259 (0.5%); Lab majority 4,839 (9.9%).

Miss Oonagh McDonald was elected at a by-election in 1976; contested Gloucestershire, South, February and October, 1974. B February, 1938; ed Roan School for Girls, Greenwich; East Barnet Grammar School, and King's College, London. Lecturer in philosophy, Bristol University, 1965-76. Member, Commons Expenditure Committee, 1977. ASTMS.

Mr Anthony Baldry, barrister (Lincoln's Inn, 1975), company director, and publisher. B July 1950; ed Leighton Park and Sussex University. Personal aide to Mrs Margaret Thatcher in October, 1974, election. Served in Leader of the Opposition's office, March-October 1975. Member, Executive Committee of the European Union of Conservative and Christian Democrat Students, 1971-72; National Executive Committee of the British Council of the European Movement, 1973-74; National Council of the Conservative Group for Europe since 1973. Founder member, Students for a United Europe. First national chairman of the Young European Democrats, 1974. European vice-president of the Young European Federalists.

Mr Michael Crowson, a teacher, contested Edmonton, West, in the Canadian Federal Elections, 1972, and Stony Plain in the Alberta provincial elections, 1970. B October, 1940; ed Bridlington Grammar School; Oastler College, Huddersfield and University of Alberta, Edmonton. NAS.

Mr Michael Daly, a staff nurse, has been a shop steward with COHSE since 1976 and branch chairman for 18 months. Branch delegate to Thurrock Trades Council. Ed Thames Polytechnic.

TIVERTON

Electorate 74,370   1974: 69,884

*Maxwell-Hyslop, R. J. (C)	33,444
Morrish, D. (L)	17,215
Cook, A. W. F. (Lab)	8,281
C majority	16,229

No Change

	1974		1979
Total votes	54,122		58,940
Turnout	77·4%		79·3%
C	25,265	46·7%	56·7%
L	19,911	36·8%	29·2%
Lab	8,946	16·5%	14·0%
C maj	5,354	9·9%	27·5%
Swing		−1·5%	+6·2%

Mr Robin Maxwell-Hyslop was elected in the 1960 by-election. Contested Derby, North, 1959. Former personal assistant to director of Sales and Service, Rolls Royce Aero Engine Division, following graduate apprenticeship and two years in export sales department. B June, 1931; ed Stowe and Christ Church, Oxford. Joint Secretary, Conservative parliamentary aviation committee since 1972. Member, trade, and industry subcommittee of Public Expenditure Committee, Standing Orders Committee; Procedure Committee; vice-chairman, Anglo-Brazilian Parliamentary Group.

Mr **David Morrish** contested the seat twice in 1974, and in 1970. College lecturer. B May, 1931, ed Sutton High School, Plymouth, Exeter University, and Wisconsin University. Member, Exeter City Council, 1961-74, and Devon County Council since 1973 (leader of Liberal group.) Chairman, Devon Liberal Party; member, Society of Friends (Quakers); Court of Exeter University; Devon sea fisheries committee. NATFHE.

Mr **Anthony Cook,** editor and proprietor of local newspaper, a director of Bay City Radio Co Ltd and a shareholder in Norman Frizzell Co Ltd. B Feb, 1953; ed Beech Hall School, Macclesfield; Oundle School; Harrow College of Further Education, and Exeter University. NUJ.

TONBRIDGE AND MALLING

Electorate 68,122   1974: 65,589

*Stanley, J. P. (C)	29,534
Ackerley, R. C. (Lab)	13,282
Knopp, G. J. (L)	10,904
Burnett, G. L. (Nat Front)	429
C majority	16,252

No Change

	1974		1979
Total votes	49,534		54,149
Turnout	75·5%		79·5%
C	23,188,	46·8%	54·5%
Lab	14,579	29·4%	24·5%
L	11,767	23·8%	20·1%
Nat Front	—		0·8%
C maj	8,609	17·4%	30·0%
Swing		−0·7%	+6·3%

Mr **John Stanley,** was appointed Minister of State, Housing, in May, 1979. Former PPS to Mrs Thatcher. Consultant to RTZ Industries Ltd. Elected in February, 1974; contested Newton, 1970. B January, 1942; ed Repton School and Lincoln College, Oxford. Member, Select Committee on Nationalized Industries, 1974-76; Secretary, Conservative

industry committee, 1974-75, vice-chairman, 1975-76. Former research associate of the International Institute for Strategic Studies.

Mr **Roy Ackerley** is a principal lecturer in management. Leader, Labour group, Ashford Borough Council since 1976. B October 1940; ed Lancaster and Manchester universities. NATFHE.

Mr **Gregory Knopp,** marketing services manager. D June, 1940; ed Christ's Hospital.

TORBAY

Electorate 87,987   1974: 85,575

*Bennett, Sir F. (C)	36,099
Mitchell, M. N. (L)	15,231
Fear, Miss E. V. (Lab)	12,919
Abrahams, D. (Ecology)	1,161
Spry, Mrs J. G. (Nat Front)	647
C majority	20,868

No Change

	1974		1979
Total votes	62,419		66,057
Turnout	72·9%		75·1%
C	30,208	48·4%	54·6%
L	17,770	28·5%	23·1%
Lab	14,441	23·1%	19·6%
Ecology	—		1·8%
Nat Front	—		1·0%
C maj	12,438	19·9%	31·5%
Swing		−1·1%	+4·8%

Sir Frederic Bennett was chosen in April, 1979, to lead the Conservative delegation to the Council of Europe, having been a UK delegate to Council of Europe and WEU since 1974. Elected in February, 1974; MP for Torquay 1955-74 (by-election) and for Reading, North, 1951-55. Contested Birmingham, Ladywood, 1950, and Burslem, 1945. Barrister

(Lincoln's Inn 1946, Southern Rhodesian Bar, 1947). B December, 1918; ed Westminster School. Director various financial and industrial institutions in United Kingdom and abroad. Member, Public Expenditure Committee, since 1974.

Mr **Michael Mitchell,** teacher. B April, 1949; ed Barnstaple Boys' Secondary; North Devon Technical College; Rolle College of Education, Exmouth. Member, Exmouth District Council, 1971-74, East Devon District Council since 1973. NUT.

Miss **Elaine Fear** is a trade union official. B June, 1950; ed Rawlins Girls' School and Trent Polytechnic College. APEX.

Mr **David Abrahams,** aged 31, is an animal keeper for Paignton Zoological and Botanical Gardens. Member, World Wildlife Fund. Ed Cullompton Secondary School. NUAW.

TOTNES

Electorate 83,960   1974: 80,715

*Mawby, R. L. (C)	35,010
Rogers, A. H. (L)	24,445
Duffin, J. (Lab Co-op)	7,668
C majority	10,565

No Change

	1974		1979
Total votes	61,939		67,123
Turnout	76·7%		79·9%
C	27,987	45·2%	52·2%
L	21,586	34·9%	36·4%
Lab	12,366	20·0%	11·4%
C maj	6,401	10·3%	15·8%
Swing		−0·7%	+7·8%

Mr **Ray Mawby** was elected in 1955; Assistant Postmaster General, 1963-64. Former chairman, West Country group of Conservative MPs. B February, 1922; ed Long Lawford Council School. Electrician, former chairman and shop steward, Rugby Branch, EEPTU. Director, Beaverbrook Western Newspapers. First president, Conservative trade

unionists national advisory committee; former executive member, 1922 Committee, and former member, Public Expenditure Committee.

Mr **Anthony Rogers,** hotelier, contested the seat in February and October, 1974. B April, 1938; ed Kingsbridge Secondary Modern School. Former chairman, South Hams District Council and Kingsbridge urban and rural councils.

Mr **John Duffin** is a managing director. B February, 1936; ed secondary school. Contested Devon, West, in February and October, 1974.

TOWER HAMLETS, Bethnal Green and Bow

Electorate 51,436   1974: 53,763

*Mikardo, I. (Lab)	14,227
Flounders, E. (L)	6,673
Page, R. (C)	5,567
Webster, M. (Nat Front)	1,740
Colvill, W. (WRP)	183
Varnes, R. (Soc Unity)	153
Lab majority	7,554

No Change

	1974		1979
Total votes	28,516		28,543
Turnout	53·0%		55·5%
Lab	19,649	68·9%	49·8%
L	3,700	13·0%	23·4%
C	2,995	10·5%	19·5%
Nat Front	2,172	7·6%	6·1%
WRP	—	—	0·6%
Soc Unity	—	—	0·5%
Lab maj	15,949	55·9%	26·4%
Swing		−3·8%	+14·0%

Mr **Ian Mikardo,** elected for this seat, February, 1974; MP for Poplar, 1964-74; for Reading 1945-50; Reading, South, 1950-55, and Reading, 1955-59. Management consultant; managing director, Ian Mikardo and Co Ltd. B July, 1908; ed Portsmouth Southern Secondary School and Portsmouth Municipal College. Chairman of Labour Party, 1970-71; member, party national executive committee, 1950-59 and 1960-78. Chairman, Select Committee on Nationalized Industries, 1966-70; President, ASTMS, 1968-73; member, Committee of Privileges, since 1974; chairman of PLP and PLP Liaison Committee, 1974. Sponsored by ASTMS.

Mr **Robin Page,** author and journalist. B May, 1943; ed Cambridgeshire High School for Boys. Member, Cambridgeshire South District Council; Barton Parish Council; Council of the Cambridgeshire and Isle of Ely Naturalists' Trust; Cambridgeshire Conservative Association executive committee.

Mr **William Colvill,** actor and playwright. Resident playwright, Half Moon Theatre, Aldgate. Former Equity deputy representative at National Theatre.

TOWER HAMLETS, Stepney and Poplar

Electorate 58,637   1974: 60,458

*Shore, P. D. (Lab)	19,576
Hughes, R. (C)	6,561
Winfield, R. (L)	2,234
Clarke, V. (Nat Front)	1,571
Johns, E. (Ind Lab)	672
Halpin, K. (Comm)	413
Chappell, P. (WRP)	235
Lab majority	13,015

No Change

	1974		1979
Total votes	31,140		31,262
Turnout	51·5%		53·3%
Lab	24,159	77·6%	62·6%
C	3,183	10·2%	21·0%
L	3,181	10·2%	7·1%
Comm	617	2·0%	1·3%
Nat Front	—	—	5·0%
Ind Lab	—	—	2·1%
WRP	—	—	0·8%
Lab maj	20,976	67·4%	41·6%
Swing		−1·0%	+12·9%

Mr **Peter Shore,** Secretary of State for Environment, 1976-79; Secretary of State for Trade, 1974-76. Member, shadow Cabinet, 1971-74, when he was spokesman on European affairs; he also had responsibilities for prices and consumer protection. Elected for seat February, 1974; MP for Stepney, 1964-74; contested St Ives, 1950, and Halifax, 1959. B May, 1924; ed Quarry Bank High School, Liverpool, and King's College, Cambridge. Minister without Portfolio and Deputy Leader of the House, 1969-70; Secretary of State for Economic Affairs, 1967-69; Parliamentary Secretary, Ministry of Technology, 1966-67; PPS to Mr Harold Wilson, 1965-66. Political economist and head of Labour Party research department, 1959-64. Sponsored by TGWU.

Mr **Robert Hughes,** television news film editor, became chairman of the Young Conservatives in March, 1979. B 1951; ed Spring Grove Grammar School and Harrow College of Technology. Treasurer, Greater London Area Young Conservatives. Member NUJ; Institute of Incorporated Photographers, Association of Broadcasting Staffs.

Mr **Rif Winfield,** aged 32, is a computer programmer.

Mr **Kevin Halpin,** contested the seat in October and February, 1974. Aged 52. London Transport engineer and former Ford convenor. Vice-president, Tower Hamlets Trades Council; chairman, Liaison Committee for the Defence of Trade Unions. AUEW.

Mr **Peter Chappell,** aged 38, was organiser of the 'Free George Davis' campaign.

TRURO

Electorate 76,597   1974: 71,992

*Penhaligon, D. C. (L)	33,571
Brown, Mrs R. (C)	24,863
Tidy, B. M. (Lab)	4,689
Whetter, Dr J. C. A. (Cornish N)	227
Hedger, N. F. (Nat Front)	182
L majority	8,708

No Change

	1974		1979
Total votes	56,624		63,532
Turnout	78·7%		82·9%
L	22,549	39·8%	52·8%
C	22,085	39·0%	39·1%
Lab	11,606	20·5%	7·4%
Meb Kernow	384	0·7%	—
Nat Front	—	—	0·3%
Cornish N	—	—	0·4%
L maj	464	0·8%	13·7%

Mr David Penhaligon, Liberal spokesman on employment since July, 1976, won the seat in October, 1974; contested it, February, 1974, and Totnes, 1970. Party spokesman on health and social services, 1974-76. Chartered mechanical engineer. B June, 1944; ed Truro School and Cornwall Technical College. Member, Liberal Party Council, since 1968.

Mrs Rosemary Brown, a journalist, broadcaster, author and company director, contested Newham, North-West, October, 1974. Chairman, Kensington Conservative Association political centre committee, 1974-77. Chairman, research study group on small businesses.

Mr Bruce Tidy, employed in industrial relations, contested St Ives twice in 1974. Member, TGWU and a full-time officer, NUPE, 1974-77. B 1948; ed Cornwall Technical College and Exeter University.

TYNEMOUTH

Electorate 74,722   1974: 76,449

*Trotter, N. G. (C)	29,941
Cosgrove, P. J. (Lab)	22,377
Pinkney, R. (L)	5,736

C majority	7,564

No Change

	1974		1979
Total votes	56,794		58,054
Turnout	74·3%		77·7%
C	24,510	43·2%	51·6%
Lab	21,389	37·7%	38·5%
L	10,895	19·2%	9·9%
C maj	3,121	5·5%	13·1%
Swing		−2·5%	+3·8%

Mr Neville Trotter, chartered accountant, was elected in February, 1974; contested Consett, 1970. Vice-chairman, Conservative shipping and ship-building committee and joint secretary of aviation committee. B January, 1932; ed Shrewsbury School and King's College, Durham. Member, Newcastle City Council, 1966-75. Member, Public

Expenditure Committee and its trade and industry subcommittee since 1974. Northern Ecomomic Planning Council, 1968-74. Consultant, Thornton Baker and Co, chartered accountants.

Mr Patrick Cosgrove, is a barrister and former teacher. Member, North Tyneside Metropolitan Borough Council. B April, 1947; ed St Cuthbert's School, Newcastle, and Leeds University. TGWU, NUT.

Mr Robert Pinkney, is a senior lecturer in government. B May, 1937; ed Ewell Technical College, Regent Street Polytechnic, London School of Economics. NATFHE.

ULSTER, Mid

Electorate 81,457   1974: 81,689

*Dunlop, J. (UUUP)	29,249
Duffy, P. A. (SDLP)	19,266
Fahy, P. (IIP)	12,055
Lagan, Dr A. (Alliance)	3,481
Donnelly, Mrs F. (Rep Clubs)	1,414

UUUP majority	9,983

No Change

	1974		1979
Total votes	64,528		65,465
Turnout	79·0%		80·4%
UUUP	—		44·7%
UUUC	30,552	47·3%	—
SDLP	25,885	40·1%	29·4%
REPUB	8,091	12·5%	2·2%
IIP	—		18·4%
UUUC maj	4,667	7·2%	—
UUUP maj	—	—	15·3%

Mr John Dunlop, a hotelier and businessman, won the seat in February, 1974. Member of N.I. Assembly as Vanguard Unionist, resigning from that party in 1975. Party's spokesman on health and social security. Member, Orange and Black Institutions. B 1922.

Mr Paddy Duffy, solicitor and former treasurer of the SDLP. Represented Mid-Ulster in N.I. Assembly and N.I. Convention. Founder and chairman of Dungannon and District Housing Association; secretary, Northern Ireland Resurgence Trust. B 1934; ed Queen's University, Belfast.

Mr Patrick Fahy, solicitor. Former chairman, Omagh civil rights movement. B 1945; ed Christian Brothers' Grammar School, Omagh, and Queen's University Belfast.

Dr Aiden Lagan, a member of the Royal College of Surgeons. Foundation member, Omagh Peace Movement; member, Omagh District Council. Ed Trinity College Dublin.

Mrs Francis Donnelly, Republican Clubs representative on Magherafelt District Council. B 1931.

WAKEFIELD

Electorate 70,509   1974: 66,535

*Harrison, W. (Lab)	27,124
Sheard, J. (C)	19,571
Collins-Tooth, N. (L)	6,059
Cooper, A. (Nat Front)	530

Lab majority	7,553

No Change

	1974		1979
Total votes	46,730		53,284
Turnout	70·2%		75·6%
Lab	25,616	54·8%	50·9%
C	12,810	27·4%	36·7%
L	8,304	17·8%	11·4%
Nat Front	—		1·0%
Lab maj	12,806	27·4%	14·2%
Swing		−2·9%	+6·6%

Mr Walter Harrison, Treasurer of the Household and Government Deputy Chief Whip, 1974-79. Elected in 1964. Foreman electrician. B January, 1921; ed Dewsbury Technical College and School of Art. Opposition deputy Chief Whip, 1970-74; a Lord Commissioner of the Treasury (whip), 1968-70, and assistant Government whip, 1966-68. Member, West Riding County Council, 1958-64; Castleford Borough Council, 1952-66 (alderman 1959-66). Sponsored by EEPTU.

Mr John Sheard, director, Audio Fidelity Ltd. B September, 1936; ed Batley Grammar School, Huddersfield Polytechnic and Bradford Polytechnic. Member, BIM.

Mr Norman Collins-Tooth, computer education consultant. B February, 1948; ed Royal Liberty Grammar School, Essex. ASTMS.

WALLASEY

Electorate 69,211   1974: 70,095

*Chalker, Mrs L. (C)	26,548
Hodge, Miss H. C. (Lab)	21,167
Thomas, N. R. L. (L)	5,269
Fishwick, J. (Nat Front)	491

C majority	5,381

No Change

	1974		1979
Total votes	53,458		53,475
Turnout	76·3%		77·3%
C	23,499	44·0%	49·6%
Lab	21,529	40·3%	39·6%
L	7,643	14·3%	9·9%
Nat Front	787	1·5%	0·9%
C maj	1,970	3·7%	10·0%
Swing		−0·4%	+3·1%

Mrs Lynda Chalker was appointed Under Secretary of State for Health and Social Security, May, 1979. An Opposition spokesman on the social services 1976-79. Elected February, 1974. B April, 1942; ed Roedean School, Heidelberg University, Westfield College, London University and Central London Polytechnic. Statistician and former head of international division of Louis Harris International Ltd. Member, General Advisory Council of BBC. Parliamentary adviser, Market Research Society. Member, National Union Executive Committee; Conservative Political Centre National Advisory Committee; former member, Select Committee on Immigration and Race Relations. Part-time industrial adviser to a bank.

Miss Hilary Hodge, dentist and research fellow in dental epidemiology, contested Farnham, October and February, 1974. B November, 1945; ed Abbey School, Reading, and Guy's and London hospitals. International tennis player. Sponsored by NUPE.

Mr Neil Thomas contested Bebington and Ellesmere Port, October, 1974. Development Officer of national charity. B January, 1934; ed Wallasey Grammar School and Jesus College, Cambridge. Member, Wallasey Borough Council, 1971-74; Wirral District Council, 1973-78.

WALLSEND

Electorate 91,312   1974: 90,300

*Garrett, W. E. (Lab)	38,214
Johnstone, L. (C)	21,695
Ryan, P. (L)	8,514
Hunter, Mrs I. (Nat Front)	472
Flynn, K. (WRP)	412

Lab majority	16,519

No Change

	1974		1979
Total votes	63,979		69,307
Turnout	70·9%		75·9%
Lab	37,180	58·1%	55·1%
C	15,911	24·9%	31·3%
L	10,453	16·3%	12·3%
Nat Front	—	—	0·7%
WRP	435	0·7%	0·6%
Lab maj	21,269	33·2%	23·8%
Swing		−3·9%	+4·7%

Mr Edward Garrett was elected in 1964. Engineer. B March, 1920; ed elementary schools and London School of Economics. Contested Hexham, 1955; Doncaster, 1959. Parliamentary adviser, Machine Tools Trades Association. Chairman, British-Czech parliamentary group. Member, Select Committee on Expenditure; North-umberland County Council, for 18 years. Sponsored by AUEW engineering section.

Mr Liddell Johnston, chartered surveyor and planning consultant. B 1932; ed Whitley Bay Grammar School and College of Estate Management, Kensington. Member, Tynemouth Borough Council. Director of family business, retailing textiles and clothing.

Mr Peter Ryan, production controller. Aged 33; ed Wigan Technical.

Mr Kevin Flynn, slinger-cum-storeman, Swan Hunter Shipbuilders. GMWU convenor, Wallsend Slipway Fabrication Yard. Aged 29. Contested the seat, October, 1974.

WALSALL, North

Electorate 73,102   1974: 71,525

Winnick, D. (Lab)	26,913
*Hodgson, R. G. (C)	21,047
Bentley, A. (L)	3,778
Parker, C. (Nat Front)	1,098

Lab majority	5,866

Lab gain from C

	1974		1979
Total votes	47,637		52,836
Turnout	66·6%		72·3%
Lab & Co-op	28,340	59·5%	50·9%
C	12,455	26·1%	39·8%
L	6,377	13·4%	7·2%
Comm	465	1·0%	
Nat Front	—	—	2·1%
Lab/Co-op m	15,885	33·4%	11·1%
Swing		−2·3%	+11·1%

Mr David Winnick was MP for Croydon, South, 1966-70; contested Harwich, 1964; Croydon, Central, October, 1974, and Walsall, North, by-election, November, 1976. B June, 1933; ed secondary schools and London School of Economics. Administrative employee. Member, Select Committee on Race Relations and Immigration, 1969-70; Willesden Council, 1959-64; Brent Council 1964-66. APEX.

Mr Robin Hodgson, company director, was elected at a by-election in October, 1976; contested the seat, February and October, 1974. B April, 1942; ed Shrewsbury School, Oxford University, University of Pennsylvania. Secretary, conservative health and social services committee, 1977-78; member, urban affairs committee, 1976-78. Chairman, Birmingham Bow Group, 1972-73.

WALSALL, South

Electorate 57,709   1974: 59,241

*George, B. T. (Lab)	22,539
Hill, Mrs A. (C)	20,951
Parker, Mrs V. (Nat Front)	795
Lab majority	1,588

No Change

	1974		1979
Total votes	43,579		44,285
Turnout	73·6%		76·7%
Lab	20,917	48·0%	50·9%
C	16,255	37·3%	47·3%
L	5,031	11·5%	—
Nat Front	1,226	2·8%	1·8%
Pros Brit	150	0·3%	—
Lab maj	4,662	10·7%	3·6%
Swing		−3·7%	+3·5%

Mr Bruce George was elected for the constituency in February, 1974; contested Southport, 1970. B June, 1942; ed Mountain Ash Grammar School, University College, Swansea, and University of Warwick. Senior lecturer in politics, Birmingham Polytechnic, 1970-74. Member, Select Committee on Violence in the Family; former secretary, all-party parliamentary group on widows and one-parent families.

Mrs Alma Hill, housewife. B April, 1927; ed Holly Lodge High School for Girls and secretarial college. Member, West Midlands Area Conservative Council, since 1958, vice-chairman, 1969-72; West Midlands Area Local Government, Committee since 1972; National Women's Advisory Committee 1969-75; National Executive Committee, since 1969. Chairman, West Midlands Area Women's National Advisory Committee, 1969-72. Specialist speaker for the WRVS on drug abuse.

WALTHAM FOREST, Chingford

Electorate 56,061   1974: 56,984

*Tebbit, N. B. (C)	24,640
Gerrard, N. F. (Lab)	12,257
Nicholson, D. A. (L)	5,225
South, Mrs D. (Nat Front)	1,157
Lambert S. (Ecology)	649
C majority	12,383

No Change

	1974		1979
Total votes	41,837		43,928
Turnout	73·4%		78·4%
C	19,022	45·5%	56·1%
Lab	14,377	34·4%	27·9%
L	8,438	20·2%	11·9%
Nat Front	—	—	2·6%
Ecology	—	—	1·5%
C maj	4,645	11·1%	28·2%
Swing		−0·6%	+8·5%

Mr Norman Tebbit was appointed Under Secretary for Trade in May, 1979. Elected for the constituency, February, 1974; represented Epping, 1970-74. B March, 1931; ed Edmonton County Grammar School. Member, Select Committee on Science and Technology, Commons Standing Orders Committee; chairman, Conservative aviation committee. Former airline pilot. Assistant director of information, National Federation of Building Trades Employers. Member, BALPA (former elected official).

Mr Neil Gerrard, college lecturer. B July, 1942; ed Oxford University. Member, Waltham Forest Borough Council, since 1973. NATFHE.

Mr David Nicholson contested the seat twice in 1974 and the Cities of London and Westminster, 1970. Senior lecturer. B October, 1939; ed Edge Hill College, Oxford, and London University. NATFHE.

Mr Steven Lambert, aged 30, housing manager. London representative, Ecology Party NEC.

WALTHAM FOREST, Leyton

Electorate 59,176   1974: 64,341

*Magee, B (Lab)	21,095
Cordle, A. (C)	15,361
Kitson, C. (L)	3,425
Pomery-Rudd, P. (Nat Front)	1,179
Lab majority	5,734

No Change

	1974		1979
Total votes	40,323		41,060
Turnout	62·7%		69·4%
Lab	22,130	54·9%	51·4%
C	10,617	26·3%	37·4%
L	5,408	13·4%	8·3%
Nat Front	2,168	5·4%	2·9%
Lab maj	11,513	28·6%	14·0%
Swing		−3·6%	+7·3%

Mr Bryan Magee, writer and broadcaster. Elected for the constituency, February, 1974. B April, 1930; ed Christ's Hospital, Lycée Hoche (Versailles), Keble College, Oxford. (President of Union, 1953), Yale. Contested Mid Bedfordshire, 1959 and 1960 by-election.

Mr Anthony Cordle is a consultant and managing director. B 1939; ed Shrewsbury School; RMA, Sandhurst (senior under officer); London Business School.

Mr Clyde Kitson, a teacher. Aged 40.

WALTHAM FOREST, Walthamstow

Electorate 49,315   1974: 52,280

*Deakins, E. P. (Lab)	17,651
Eyres, S. (C)	13,248
O'Flanagan, M. P. (L)	3,117
Flaxton, G. (Nat Front)	1,119
Lab majority	4,403

No Change

	1974		1979
Total votes	34,622		35,135
Turnout	66.2%		71.2%
Lab	19,088	55.1%	50.2%
C	8,424	24.3%	37.7%
L	5,199	15.0%	8.9%
Nat Front	1,911	5.5%	3.2%
Lab maj	10,664	30.8%	12.5%
Swing		−4.2%	+9.1%

Mr Eric Deakins, Under Secretary of State, Department of Health and Social Security, 1976-79. Under Secretary for Trade, 1974-76. Elected for this seat, February, 1974; MP for Walthamstow, West, 1970-74. B October, 1932; ed Tottenham Grammar School and London School of Economics. Contested Finchley, 1959; Chigwell, 1966 and Walthamstow,

West, 1967. Member, Tottenham Borough Council, 1958-61, 1962-63. TGWU.

Mr Stephen Eyres, editor of The Free Nation, contested Fife, Central, February, 1974. B December, 1948; ed Portsmouth Northern Grammar School, University of St Andrews. Secretary, Selsdon group. Researcher for MPs.

Mr Mervyn O'Flanagan, a company director, contested the seat twice in 1974. B February, 1925; ed Downlands College, Toowoomba, and Rockhampton Polytechnic, Queensland.

WANDSWORTH, Battersea North

Electorate 41,435   1974: 44,799

*Jay, D. P. T. (Lab)	15,834
Phillips, P. (C)	9,358
Brown, W. (L)	2,021
Salt, M. (Nat Front)	772
Lavelle, A. (Workers Rev)	104
Clay, P. (WRP)	47
Harwell, J. (Community P)	30
Lab majority	6,476

No Change

	1974		1979
Total votes	27,580		28,166
Turnout	61.6%		68.0%
Lab	17,161	62.2%	56.2%
C	6,019	21.8%	33.2%
L	3,048	11.1%	7.2%
Nat Front	1,250	4.5%	2.7%
Marx Len	102	0.4%	—
WRP	—	—	0.4%
Workers P	—	—	0.2%
Community P	—	—	0.1%
Lab maj	11,142	40.4%	23.0%
Swing		−3.7%	+8.7%

Mr Douglas Jay was elected in July, 1946. President of the Board of Trade, 1964-67; Economic Secretary to the Treasury 1947-50 and Financial Secretary 1950-51. B March, 1907; ed Winchester and New College, Oxford; a Fellow of All Souls, 1930-37. Appointed chairman, Common Market Safeguards Campaign, 1970,

and London Motorway Action Group, 1968. Chairman, Select Committee on Wealth Tax, 1976. Director, trade union unit trust. Personal assistant to Mr Attlee as Prime Minister, 1945-46.

Mr Peter Phillips, assistant secretary at British Institute of Management. B 1946; ed Clayesmore School, Dorset, London College of Printing and the School of Accountancy and Business Studies. Member, Bow Group; Hammersmith Council for Community Relations. Vice-chairman, Fulham Conservative Association, 1969-71; Hammersmith North Conservative Association 1974-76.

Mr William Brown, a caterer. Age 35.

Mr Anthony Lavelle, unemployed building trade worker. Age 31. Former UCATT shop steward.

WANDSWORTH, Battersea South

Electorate 43,712   1974: 46,724

Dubs, A. (Lab)	13,984
Wallace, T. (C)	13,652
Ware, Mrs J. (L)	2,802
Perry, A. (Nat Front)	561
Lab majority	332

No Change

	1974		1979
Total votes	30,008		30,999
Turnout	64.2%		70.9%
Lab	14,334	47.8%	45.1%
C	11,483	38.3%	44.0%
L	4,021	13.4%	9.0%
Pros Brit	170	0.6%	—
Nat Front	—	—	1.8%
Lab maj	2,851	9.5%	1.1%
Swing		−2.4%	+4.2%

Mr **Alfred Dubs,** a local government officer, contested Cities of London and Westminster, 1970, and South Hertfordshire in both 1974 elections. B December, 1932; ed London School of Economics, Member, Westminster City Council, 1971-78; chairman, Westminster Community Relations Council 1972-77. Nalgo.

Mr **Theo Wallace,** barrister, contested Pontypool, February, 1974, and Battersea South, October, 1974. B 1938; ed Charterhouse and Christ Church, Oxford. Vice-chairman, Greater London CPC Committee. Member, Royal Institute of International Affairs and Conservative Group for Europe.

Mrs **Jennifer Ware,** contested the seat in October, 1974. Hotelier. B January, 1932; ed St Paul's Girls School, Hammersmith.

WANDSWORTH, Putney

Electorate 64,648   1974: 66,515

Mellor, D. (C)	23,040
*Jenkins, H. G. (Lab)	20,410
Couldrey, N. (L)	5,061
Webster, J. (Nat Front)	685

C majority	2,630

C gain from Lab

	1974		1979
Total votes	47,731		49,196
Turnout	71·8%		76·1%
Lab	21,611	45·3%	41·5%
C	18,836	39·5%	46·8%
L	7,159	15·0%	10·3%
Pros Brit	125	0·3%	—
Nat Front	—	—	1·4%
Lab maj	2,775	5·8%	—
C maj	—	—	5·3%
Swing		−1·6%	+5·5%

Mr **David Mellor,** barrister, (Inner Temple, 1972), contested West Bromwich, East, October, 1974. B 1949; ed Swanage Grammar School, Christ's College, Cambridge. Chairman, Cambridge University Conservative Association, 1970; Chelsea Conservative Political Committee, 1974-76. Vice-chairman, Chelsea Conservative Association.

Member Bow Group; secretary Bow Group home affairs study group since 1975. Member, Society of Conservative Lawyers.

Mr **Hugh Jenkins** was Under Secretary, Education and Science, with responsibility for the arts, 1974-76, and Opposition spokesman on the arts, 1973-74. Elected in 1964; contested Enfield, West, 1950. B July, 1908; ed Enfield Grammar School. Member, Public Accounts Committee; Estimates Committee, 1964-65. Chairman, PLP Arts and Amenities Group, 1977-78. Chairman, Theatres Advisory Council to 1974; assistant general secretary, Equity, 1957-64. ASTMS. Governor of National Theatre.

Mr **Nicholas Couldrey,** solicitor. B April 1951; ed Ampleforth and York University.

WANDSWORTH, Tooting

Electorate 50,962   1974: 53,793

*Cox, T. M. (Lab)	18,642
Ritchie, R. (C)	13,442
Fife, R. (L)	2,917
Berbridge, P. (Nat Front)	682
Lewis, L. (Comm)	233

Lab majority	5,200

No Change

	1974		1979
Total votes	34,117		35,916
Turnout	63·4%		70·5%
Lab	18,530	54·3%	51·9%
C	10,675	31·3%	37·4%
L	4,644	13·6%	8·1%
Comm	268	0·8%	0·6%
Nat Front	—	—	1·9%
Lab maj	7,855	23·0%	14·5%
Swing		−3·7%	+4·2%

Mr **Thomas Cox** was an assistant Government whip 1974-77; Lord Commissioner of the Treasury (whip) 1977-79. Elected February, 1974; represented Wandsworth, Central, 1970-74; contested Stroud, 1966. B 1930; ed state schools and London School of Economics. Electrician. Former alderman, Fulham Borough Council. Sponsored by EETPU.

Mr **Richard Ritchie** works for an oil company. Contested Houghton-le-Spring twice in 1974. B 1949; ed Harrow and Ealing School of Business and Social Studies. Member, Spelthorne Borough Council, 1973-76.

Mr **Richard Fife** is a barrister. B May, 1949; ed Glengyle School, Putney, St Paul's School, Wandsworth Technical College and Inns of Court School of Law.

WARLEY, East

Electorate 55,026   1974: 57,530

*Faulds, A. W. M. (Lab)	21,333
Jones, R. K. (C)	16,236
Worrall, J. (Nat Front)	1,204

Lab majority	5,097

No Change

	1974		1979
Total votes	38,617		38,773
Turnout	67·1%		70·5%
Lab	21,065	54·5%	55·0%
C	12,888	33·4%	41·9%
L	4,664	12·1%	—
Nat Front	—	—	3·1%
Lab maj	8,177	21·1%	13·1%
Swing		−1·6%	+4·0%

Mr **Andrew Faulds** was elected in February, 1974; MP for Smethwick, 1966-74. Opposition spokesman on the arts, 1970-73. Contested Stratford upon Avon, 1964 and 1963 by-election. B March, 1923; ed George  Watsons, Louth Grammar School, Daniel Stewart's Edinburgh, Stirling High School and Glasgow University. Actor. Member, Select Committee on House of Commons (Services). Member, Equity (council member, 1966-69). Chairman, all-party heritage group; British branch, Parliamentary Association for Euro-Arab Cooperation; member, Council of Europe (Consultative Assembly) and WEU.

Mr **Roger Jones,** solicitor, contested Ogmore, February and October 1974. B 1945; ed Newport High School, Bridgend Grammar School and Wadham College, Oxford. Former chairman, Ogmore Conservative CPC. Former treasurer, South Wales Group of Conservative Associations. Member, Solicitors' European Group.

WARLEY, West

Electorate 60,935   1974: 61,274

*Archer, P. K. (Lab)		25,175
Evans, R. K. (C)		15,074
Fisher, F. M. (L)		2,864

Lab majority		10,101

No Change

	1974		1979
Total votes	41,028		43,063
Turnout	67·0%		70·7%
Lab	24,761	60·4%	58·3%
C	9,904	24·1%	35·0%
L	6,363	15·5%	6·7%
Lab maj	14,857	36·3%	23·3%
Swing		-1·2%	+6·5%

Mr **Peter Archer,** QC, Solicitor General from March, 1974 to May, 1979. Elected February, 1974; represented Rowley Regis and Tipton, 1966-74; contested Brierley Hill, 1964, and Hendon South, 1959. B  November 1926; ed Wednesbury High School, London School of Economics and University College, London. Apex.

Mr **Roger Evans,** barrister, fought the seat in October, 1974. B March, 1947; ed City of Norwich School, Bristol Grammar School and Trinity Hall, Cambridge. Chairman, Cambridge University Conservative Association, 1969; President, Cambridge Union, 1970; Member, Society of Conservative Lawyers.

WARRINGTON

Electorate 43,921   1974: 46,549

*Williams, Sir T. (Lab and Co-op)		19,306
Povey, G. (C)		9,032
Browne, I. B. (L)		2,833
Campbell, C. (Soc Dem)		144

Lab and Co-op majority		10,274

No Change

	1974		1979
Total votes	31,661		31,315
Turnout	74·4%		71·3%
Lab & Co-op	19,882	62·8%	61·7%
C	7,621	24·1%	28·8%
L	4,158	13·1%	9·0%
Soc Dem	—	—	0·5%
Lab/Co-op m	12,261	38·7%	32·9%
Swing		-3·1%	+2·9%

Sir Thomas Williams, QC, was elected at a by-election in 1961; represented Barons Court, 1955-60, and Hammersmith, South, 1949-55. B September, 1915; ed Aberdare Grammar School, University College, Cardiff, St Catherine's, Oxford. Recorder of Birkenhead, 1969-71. Member, Chairmens Panel; Select Committee on  Parliamentary Commissioner; chairman, Select Committee on Procedure. Chairman, Co-operative group of MPs, 1969-70; consumer group of Labour Party, 1966-70. President, World Council, Inter-Parliamentary Union. Member, Lord Chancellor's Committee on public records. NUT.

Mr **George Povey** is a distribution manager. B 1923; ed Runcorn Secondary School and Runcorn Technical Institute. Former chairman of Runcorn Urban Council. Member of Runcorn and Warrington water boards.

Mr **Iain Brodie-Browne,** secretary general Age Concern, in St Helens. Aged 26; ed City of London Polytechnic.

WARWICK AND LEAMINGTON

Electorate 85,074   1974: 78,666

*Smith, D. G. (C)		35,925
Gray, C. J. (Lab)		19,367
Woodcock, D. (L)		9,905
Sizer, P. (Ecology)		905

C majority		16,558

No Change

	1974		1979
Total votes	58,822		66,102
Turnout	74·8%		77·7%
C	27,721	47·1%	54·3%
Lab	19,476	33·1%	29·3%
L	11,625	19·8%	15·0%
Ecology	—	—	1·4%
C maj	8,245	14·0%	25·0%
Swing		-1·9%	+5·5%

Mr **Dudley Smith,** Under Secretary for the Army, 1974; Under Secretary for Employment, 1970-74. Elected at by-election, 1968; represented Brentford and Chiswick, 1959-66. Vice-chairman, Select Committee on Race Relations and Immigration. B November, 1926; ed Chichester High School. Management consultant. Opposition whip, 1964-66. Contested Peckham, 1955. Member, Middlesex County Council, 1958-63.

Mr Charles Gray, university lecturer. B June, 1940; ed Birmingham University. Member, Birmingham City Council. AUT.

Mr David Woodcock, aged 41, is a lecturer.

Mr Peter Sizer is a university lecturer. Aged 47; ed Hull University. Ecology Party treasurer.

WATFORD

Electorate 55,079 1974: 56,010

Garel-Jones, T. (C)	21,320
Banks, A. (Lab)	18,030
Bodle, B. (L)	5,019
Cheetham, B. (Nat Front)	388

C majority	3,290

C gain from Lab

	1974		1979
Total votes	43,311		44,757
Turnout	77·3%		81·3%
Lab	19,177	44·3%	40·3%
C	15,220	35·1%	47·6%
L	8,243	19·0%	11·2%
Nat Front	671	1·5%	0·9%
Lab maj	3,957	9·2%	
C maj	—	—	7·3%
Swing		−1·6%	+8·2%

Mr Tristan Garel-Jones, company director and financial consultant, contested Caernarvon, February, 1974, and Watford, October, 1974. Executive member, Hemel Hempstead Conservative Association. B 1941; ed Llangennech Primary School and King's School, Canterbury.

Mr Anthony Banks, assistant general secretary of the Association of Broadcasting Staff, contested Newcastle upon tyne, North, October 1974, and East Grinstead, 1970. Former special adviser to Mrs Judith Hart when she was Minister for Overseas Development. B April, 1943; ed state school, York University, and LSE. Member, Greater London Council (chairman, general purposes committee, 1970-77). Former head of research, AUEW. Sponsored by TGWU.

Mr Bruce Bodle, aged 33, is a business development manager.

WELLINGBOROUGH

Electorate 89,022 1974: 85,288

*Fry, P. D. (C)	37,812
Forwood, D. A. (Lab)	25,278
Stringer, L. E. (L)	8,506
Wright, S. F. (Nat Front)	529
Garnett, Miss D. M. P. (Ind)	209

C majority	12,534

No Change

	1974		1979
Total votes	67,898		72,334
Turnout	79·6%		81·3%
C	29,078	42·8%	52·3%
Lab	27,320	40·2%	34·9%
L	11,500	16·9%	11·8%
Nat Front	—		0·7%
Ind	—	—	0·3%
C maj	1,758	2·6%	17·4%
Swing		−0·3%	+7·4%

Mr Peter Fry, a former Conservative spokesman on transport, won the seat at 1969 by-election. Insurance broker/consultant. B May, 1931; ed Royal Grammar School, High Wycombe; Worcester College, Oxford. Contested Nottingham, North, 1964, and Willesden, East, 1966. Vice chairman, Conservative Transport Industries Committee; joint chairman, all-

party roads study group, secretary, British Yugoslav parliamentary group. Member, Buckinghamshire County Council, 1961-67. Partner in Political Research and Communications International. Vice-president, British Yugoslav Society.

Mr Derek Forwood, insurance broker, contested Daventry, 1974; Chorley, 1970; Brierley, 1967; and Solihull, 1966. B June, 1927; ed Thames Valley Grammar School, Twickenham. Leader, Labour group, Warwickshire County Council. Member, Nuneaton Borough Council, 1969-74. NATFHE.

Mr Leslie Stringer, aged 51, adminstration manager and Wellingborough councillor. Ed Woolwich Polytechnic and London University.

WELLS

Electorate 74,717 1974: 69,658

*Boscawen, R. T. (C)	30,400
Dutt Phillp, A. A. 3. (L)	18,204
Murphy, P. P. (Lab)	10,025
Livings, G. (Ind)	421
Thynn, A. (Wessex Reg)	155

C majority	12,196

No Change

	1974		1979
Total votes	54,944		59,205
Turnout	78·9%		79·2%
C	23,979	43·6%	51·3%
L	16,278	29·6%	30·7%
Lab	13,909	25·3%	16·9%
UDP	778	1·4%	—
Ind	—	—	0·7%
Wessex Reg	—	—	0·3%
C maj	7701	14·0%	20·6%
Swing		−0·5%	+8·0%

231

Mr Robert Boscawen was appointed assistant Government whip in May, 1979. Former Lloyd's underwriter, was elected in 1970; contested Falmouth and Camborne, 1966 and 1964. B March, 1923; ed Eton and Trinity College, Cambridge. Former member, Select Committee on Expenditure, Employment and Social Services sub-

committee. Vice chairman, Conservative health and social security committee since 1976. Member, London Executive Council, National Health Service, 1956-65.

Mr Alan Butt Philip, a university lecturer, contested the seat twice in 1974. B August, 1945; ed Eton and St John's and Nuffield colleges, Oxford. His wife, Christina Baron, contested Bridgwater. Member, AUT. Former president, Oxford University Liberal Club.

Mr Paul Murphy, technical college lecturer. B November, 1948; ed St Francis RC School, Abersychan, West Monmouth School, Pontypool and Oriel College, Oxford. Member, Torfaen Borough Council since 1973. NATFHE and TGWU.

WELWYN AND HATFIELD

Electorate 69,957   1974: 67,149

Murphy, C. P. Y. (C)	28,892
*Hayman, Mrs H. V. (Lab)	25,418
Hurd, Mrs J. (L)	4,688
Ruddock, P. (Nat Front)	459
C majority	3,474

C gain from Lab

	1974		1979
Total votes	54,576		59,457
Turnout	81·3%		85·0%
Lab	23,339	42·8%	42·8%
C	22,819	41·8%	48·6%
L	8,418	15·4%	7·9%
Nat Front	—	—	0·8%
Lab maj	520	1·0%	—
C maj	—	—	5·8%
Swing		−1·8%	+3·4%

Mr Christopher Murphy contested Tower Hamlets, Bethnal Green and Bow, in February and October, 1974. Advertising and marketing director. B April, 1947; ed Devonport High School and Queen's College, Oxford. Former president, Oxford Conservative Association, former member, executive committee of the

Federation of Conservative Students and of executive committee of the National Association of Conservative Graduates.

Mrs Helen Hayman was elected in October, 1974 and contested Wolverhampton, South-West, February, 1974. Social adminstrator. B March, 1949; ed Wolverhampton High School, Newnham College, Cambridge (President of the Union, 1969). Member, Select Committee on Abortion (Amendment) Bill. Member, Labour Friends of Israel. TGWU.

Mrs Jane Hurd, aged 30, is a laboratory technician and local councillor.

WEST BROMWICH, East

Electorate 57,660   1974: 58,400

*Snape, P. C. (Lab)	19,279
Wright, J. (C)	17,308
Smith, M. (L)	3,228
Allsopp, C. (Nat Front)	1,175
Lab majority	1,971

No Change

	1974		1979
Total votes	39,489		40,990
Turnout	67·6%		71·1%
Lab	19,942	50·5%	47·0%
C	12,413	31·4%	42·2%
L	5,442	13·8%	7·9%
Nat Front	1,692	4·3%	2·9%
Lab maj	7,529	19·1%	4·8%
Swing		−3·3%	+7·1%

Mr Peter Snape, Lord Commissioner of the Treasury (whip) since 1977; Assistant whip, 1975-77. Elected, February, 1974. Clerical officer, British Rail. B February, 1942; ed St Joseph's School, Stockport. Member, Bredbury and Romiley UDC, 1971-74 (chairman, Finance Committee, leader of Labour group). Member,

Council of Europe, since January, 1976. Sponsored by NUR.

Mr John Wright, chartered accountant. B October, 1947; ed Lea House School, Kidderminster and King's School, Worcester. Member, National Advisory Committee, Young Conservatives and National Union Executive Committee.

WEST BROMWICH, West

Electorate 58,803   1974: 59,749

*Boothroyd, Miss B. (Lab)	23,791
Harrison, D. (C)	14,323
Churms, R. (Nat Front)	1,351
Lab majority	9,468

No Change

	1974		1979
Total votes	37,514		39,465
Turnout	62·8%		67·1%
Lab	23,336	62·2%	60·3%
C	8,537	22·8%	36·3%
L	3,619	9·6%	—
Nat Front	2,022	5·4%	3·4%
Lab maj	14,799	39·4%	24·0%
Swing		−2·9%	+7·7%

Miss Betty Boothroyd, assistant Government whip, 1974-76, was MP for West Bromwich, May, 1973, until February, 1974, when she was elected for the new constituency. Member, European Parliament, since 1975. Contested Rossendale 1970; Nelson and Colne by-election, June, 1960; Peterborough 1959; Leicester, South-East by-election, 1957. B

October, 1929; ed Dewsbury Technical College. Member, select committees on Public Accounts, on Abortion (Amendment) Bill and Sound Broadcasting. Sponsored by GMWU.

Mr Daniel Harrison is a driver for Allied Breweries (UK) Ltd., B June, 1948; ed St Mowden's School and Burton-on-Trent Technical College. British judo champion 1972. Member, East Staffordshire District Council and Branston Parish Council. Chairman, TGWU, West Midlands Group; chairman, West Midlands Area Conservative Trade Unionists. Member, national committee Conservative Trade Unionists and national committee of Central Council of Conservative National Union.

WESTBURY

Electorate 79,538   1974: 73,592

*Walters, D. M. (C)	29,929
Jackson, P. (L)	15,950
Atkins, P. R. (Lab)	12,532
Alexander, S. (Ind)	2,547
Thatcher, T. (Wessex Reg)	1,905
Rodwell, Mrs S. (Ecology)	554

C majority	13,979

No Change

	1974		1979
Total votes	57,914		63,417
Turnout	78·7%		79·7%
C	24,129	41·7%	47·2%
L	18,129	31·3%	25·2%
Lab	15,613	27·0%	19·8%
Ind	—	—	4·0%
Wessex Reg	—	—	3·0%
Ecology	—	—	0·9%
C maj	6,043	10·4%	22·0%
Swing		−0·7%	+6·3%

Mr Dennis Walters was elected in 1964; contested Blyth, 1959 and at the 1960 by-election. B November, 1928; ed Downside School and St Catharine's College, Cambridge. Founder-member, Bow Group. Chairman, Federation of University Conservative and Unionist Associations, 1949-50. Joint secretary, Conservative foreign affairs committe, 1965-71, and joint vice-chairman, foreign and Commonwealth affairs committee since 1974. Director, Unigulf Investments Co and other companies. Trustee, ANAF Foundation. Adviser to Canadian Finance company. Member, Kuwait Investment Advisory Committee.

Mr Peter Grayling Jackson, journalist, editor of TV Times. B August, 1930; ed Queen Elizabeth Grammar School, Tamworth. Director, Independent Television Publications Ltd. NUJ (chapel officer 1960-63).

Mr Peter Atkins is a postal worker and sponsored by the UPOW. B December, 1929; ed elementary school and night school.

Mrs Sally Rodwell, aged 30, works with a play group for young children. Member of the Soil Association.

WESTERN ISLES

Electorate 22,393   1974: 22,477

*Stewart, D. J. (Scot Nat)	7,941
Matheson, A. (Lab)	4,878
Morrison, M. (C)	1,600
MacLeod, N. (L)	700

Scot Nat majority	3,063

No Change

	1974		1979
Total votes	14,253		15,119
Turnout	63·4%		67·5%
Scot Nat	8,758	61·4%	52·5%
Lab	3,526	24·7%	32·3%
C	1,180	8·3%	10·6%
L	789	5·5%	4·6%
Scot Nat maj	5,232	36·7%	20·2%

Mr Donald Stewart, leader of the Scottish National Parliamentary Party since 1974, has represented the seat since 1970. Provost of Stornoway, 1958-64 and 1968-70; Hon Sheriff Substitute, 1960. Member, Council of "Get Britain Out" (of EEC) Campaign. B October, 1920; ed Nicolson Institute, Stornoway. Town and county councillor for 20 years.

Mr Alexander Matheson, pharmacist, was Provost of Stornoway, 1971-75 and Honorary Sheriff, 1971. B November, 1941; ed Nicolson Institute, Stornoway and Robert Gordons Institute of Technology, Aberdeen. Member, Western Isles Council for 11 years. USDAW.

Mr Murdo Morrison works for an oil company. Aged 41; ed Bragan Public School, Lewis, and Nicolson Institute, Stornoway. Became Harris Tweed weaver; Writer, Royal Navy; Young Unionist organizer for East of Scotland; constituency agent, Glasgow, Kelvingrove. Member, Motherwell District Council. Fluent Gaelic speaker.

Mr Neil MacLeod, teacher. B June, 1933; ed Nicolson Institute, Stornoway, and Aberdeen University. Member, Scottish Secondary Teachers' Association.

WESTHOUGHTON

Electorate 76,922   1974: 72,055

*Stott, R. (Lab)	29,685
Johnson, Mrs C. (C)	24,398
Pigott, J. (L)	7,544

Lab	majority
	5,287

No Change

	1974		1979
Total votes	56,097		61,627
Turnout	77·9%		80·1%
Lab	30,373	54·1%	48·2%
C	16,798	29·9%	39·6%
L	8,926	15·9%	12·2%
Lab maj	13,575	24·2%	8·6%
Swing		−1·5%	+7·8%

Mr **Roger Stott,** telephone engineer, was elected at 1973 by-election; contested Cheadle, 1970. B August, 1943; ed Rochdale College and Ruskin College. Appointed PPS to Secretary of State for Industry, June 1975, and to the Prime Minister, 1976. Rochdale councillor, 1970-74 (Chairman, Housing Committee.) Sponsored by POEU. Vice chairman, PLP North-West area group.

Mrs **Carolyn Johnson** is a barrister and lecturer in law. B 1952; Elmslie Girls School, Manchester University College of Law, London. Member Preston District Council. Former Secretary, Manchester University Conservative Association. Executive member, Young European Democrats, 1974-76.

Mr **John Pigott** is a production planning manager in the paint industry. B February, 1947; ed Lymm Grammar School, Cheshire and Hull and Lancaster universities. Parish council chairman.

WEST LOTHIAN

Electorate 85,645   1974: 77,526

*Dalyell, T. (Lab)	36,713
Wolfe, W. C. (Scot Nat)	16,631
Whyte, J. R. (C)	13,162
Sneddon, W. (Comm)	404

Lab majority	20,082

No Change

	1974		1979
Total votes	61,100		66,910
Turnout	79·8%		78·1%
Lab	27,687	45·3%	54·9%
Scot Nat	24,997	40·9%	24·9%
C	6,086	10·0%	19·7%
L	2,083	3·4%	—
Comm	247	0·4%	0·6%
Lab maj	2,690	4·4%	30·0%
Swing		−4·5%	0·0%

Mr **Tam Dalyell** was elected at June, 1962, by-election, contested Roxburgh, Selkirk and Peebles, 1959. Teacher. B August, 1932; ed Edinburgh Academy, Eton, and King's College, Cambridge. Member, European Parliament, since 1975. Member, Public Accounts Committee, 1963-65; Select Committee on Science and Technology, 1965-68; PLP Liaison Committee 1974-75. Vice-chairman, PLP, 1975-76. Member, Select Committee on European Secondary Legislation, 1974-75; Select Committee on Wealth Tax, 1974. Sponsored by NUR.

Mr **William Wolfe,** chairman of the Scottish National Party since 1969, contested the seat in February and October, 1974, 1970, 1966, 1964 and 1962; and Edinburgh, North, November, 1973 by-election. Chartered accountant and company manager. B February, 1924; ed Bathgate Academy and George Watson's College, Edinburgh. ASTMS.

Mr **John Whyte,** retail training officer. B 1946; ed Dundee High School and Dundee Kingsway Technical and Commercial colleges. Vice-president of Edinburgh, Leith and Edinburgh, West, Young Conservatives.

Mr **William Sneddon,** aged 51, an electrician. Secretary, Falkirk Trades Council, Central Region Trades Council, Kincardine Power Station Refurbishment Campaign. Member, Central Regions Manpower Services Commission, Scottish Committee of Communist Party.

WESTMORLAND

Electorate 59,956   1974: 55,880

*Jopling, J. M. (C)	25,274
Hulls, K. (L)	12,867
Potts, A. (Lab)	6,497

C majority	12,407

No Change

	1974		1979
Total votes	40,431		44,638
Turnout	72·4%		74·5%
C	20,559	50·8%	56·6%
L	12,844	31·8%	28·8%
Lab	7,028	17·4%	14·6%
C maj	7,715	19·0%	27·8%
Swing		−1·1%	+4·3%

Mr **Michael Jopling,** was appointed Parliamentary Secretary of the Treasury and Government Chief Whip in May 1979; an Opposition spokesman on agriculture since 1974 he was elected in 1964; contested Wakefield, 1959. Farmer. B December, 1930; ed Cheltenham College and King's College, Durham University. Former member, select committees on Science and Technology and on Agriculture. Member, NFU national council, 1962-64; Thirsk RDC, 1958-64. Joint secretary, Conservative agriculture committee, 1966-70.

Mr **Kenneth Hulls,** project manager. B April, 1944; ed London University. ASTMS.

Mr **Archibald Potts** is a lecturer in economics at a polytechnic. B January, 1932; ed Monkwearmouth Central School, Sunderland, Ruskin College and Oriel College, Oxford, universities of London and Durham. GMWU and NATFHE.

WESTON-SUPER-MARE

Electorate 92,096   1974: 84,088

*Wiggin, A. W. (C)	40,618
Morgan, R. (L)	16,305
Taylor, A. H. (Lab and Co-op)	14,420

C majority	24,313

No Change

	1974		1979
Total votes	63,550		71,343
Turnout	74·8%		77·5%
C	31,028	48·8%	56·9%
L	18,169	28·6%	22·9%
Lab & Co-op	14,057	22·1%	20·2%
UDP	296	0·5%	—
C maj	12,859	20·2%	34·0%
Swing		−1·7%	+5·0%

Mr Jerry Wiggin, vice-chairman of Conservative agriculture committee since 1975, was returned at a by-election in 1969; contested Montgomeryshire, 1964 and 1966. B February, 1937; ed Eton and Trinity College, Cambridge. Farmer. Joint secretary, Conservative defence committee, 1974-75; chairman, Conservative West Country MPs, 1978; general rapporteur, economic committee, North Atlantic Assembly since 1976. Adviser to Bloodstock and Racehorse Industries Confederation and Ship and Boat Builders National Federation. Member of Lloyd's.

Mr Rowland Morgan, a civil engineer and university teacher, contested Bedwellty in February and October 1974. B December, 1934; ed Tredegar Grammar School and University of Manchester. AUT.

Mr Alan Taylor, planning research officer. B May, 1946; ed Southampton University. NUPE.

WHITEHAVEN

Electorate 52,787   1974: 50,964

*Cunningham, J. A. (Lab)	22,626
Somers, J. (C)	17,171
Akister, E. (L)	2,559
Dixon, W. (Ind)	790
Lab majority	5,455

No Change

	1974		1979
Total votes	39,294		43,146
Turnout	77·1%		81·7%
Lab	21,832	55·6%	52·4%
C	11,899	30·3%	39·8%
L	5,563	14·2%	5·9%
Ind	—	—	1·8%
Lab maj	9,933	25·3%	12·6%
Swing		−3·3%	+6·3%

Mr John Cunningham, Under Secretary for Energy 1976-79; was elected in 1970. Research chemist. B August, 1939; ed Jarrow Grammar School and Bede College, Durham University. Member, Select Committee on Science and Technology, 1970-76. Full time officer, GMWU 1968-70. Member, Chester-le-Street District Council, 1969-74. Sponsored by GMWU.

Mr John Somers is a student at Manchester University. B 1955; ed Valley Comprehensive School and Manchester University where he was chairman of the Conservative Association, 1974-76. Chairman, North West Federation of Conservative Students, 1975-76; chairman Stockport Young Conservatives, 1976.

Mr Edward Akister, senior civil engineer manager and aviation administrative manager. B October, 1933; ed The Friends' School, Lancaster, and Owens College, Manchester. Vice-chairman (chairman designate) British Institute of Management, Shropshire and district. Former chairman, Ironbridge Coalbrookdale Civic Amenity Society.

WIDNES

Electorate 78,228   1974: 75,141

*Oakes, G. J. (Lab)	32,033
Holder, B. G. (C)	21,752
Self, Mrs L. A. (L)	4,290
Lab majority	10,281

No Change

	1974		1979
Total votes	53,260		58,075
Turnout	70·9%		74·2%
Lab	31,532	59·2%	55·2%
C	14,661	27·5%	37·5%
L	7,067	13·3%	7·4%
Lab maj	16,871	31·7%	17·7%
Swing		−0·8%	+7·0%

Mr Gordon Oakes, Minister of State for Education and Science, 1976-79; Under Secretary for Environment, 1974-76; Under Secretary for Energy, 1976. Elected at 1971 by-election; represented Bolton, West 1964-70; contested Bebington, 1959, and Manchester, Moss Side, by-election 1961. Member, Select Committee on Race Relations, 1968-70. Solicitor. B June, 1931; ed Wade Deacon School, Widnes, and Liverpool University. Member, Widnes Borough Council, 1952-66; Mayor, 1964-65. Sponsored by TGWU.

Mr Brian Holder, lecturer. B May, 1937; ed Holt High School, Liverpool; Liverpool and Leicester universities. Member Halewood Town Council since 1971. NATFHE.

Mrs Lesley Self, a housewife and part time lecturer. Age 33; ed Liverpool College of Art and Leeds University.

WIGAN

Electorate 59,024   1974: 56,915

*Fitch, E. A. (Lab)	26,144
Peet, T. (C)	13,149
Bruce, K. (L)	4,102
Smith, A. (WRP)	348
Lab majority	12,995

No Change

	1974		1979
Total votes	42,105		43,743
Turnout	74·0%		74·1%
Lab	27,692	65·8%	59·8%
C	8,865	21·1%	30·1%
L	5,548	13·2%	9·4%
WRP	—	—	0·8%
Lab maj	18,827	44·7%	29·7%
Swing		−1·1%	+7·5%

Mr Alan Fitch, a member of the European Parliament, was returned at a by-election, June, 1958. Opposition whip, 1970-71. Member, Speaker's panel of chairmen since 1971; Vice-Chamberlain, HM Household (whip), 1969-70, a Lord Commissioner of the Treasury (whip), 1966-69; an assistant Government whip, 1964-66. Mineworker. B March,

1915; ed Kingswood School, Bath. Member, Select Committee on Nationalised Industries, 1959-64. Chairman, North-West Regional Council of Labour Party. Sponsored by NUM.

Mr Thomas Peet is an assistant electrical engineer. B 1942; ed at a Wigan secondary modern school and Wigan and District Mining and Technical College. Chairman, Wigan Conservative Association; former vice-chairman, Colliery Overseers and Supervisors' Association; member, Association of Mining Electrical and Mechanical Engineers.

Mr Anthony Smith works for Staveleys Ltd, Allerton. Aged 21. Member, Boilermakers' Society.

WINCHESTER

Electorate 87,412   1974: 82,790

Browne, J. (C)	38,198
Allchin, Dr W. H. (Lab)	15,378
Morgan, J. (L)	14,228
Mahoney, M. (Wessex Reg)	395
C majority	22,820

No Change

	1974		1979
Total votes	62,275		68,199
Turnout	75·2%		78·0%
C	27,671	44·4%	56·0%
L	18,451	29·6%	20·9%
Lab	16,153	25·9%	22·5%
Wessex Reg	—		0·6%
C maj	9,220	14·8%	33·5%
Swing		−2·1%	+7·5%

Mr John Browne, a member of Westminster City Council, 1974-78. Banker. B October, 1938; ed Malvern College, Royal Military Academy, Sandhurst, Cranfield Institute of Technology, Harvard Business School. Served in Grenadier Guards, retired as captain 1967.

Dr William Allchin, a psychoterapist and lecturer, contested the seat twice in 1974. B March, 1921; ed Westminster, Oxford and London universities. Former consultant psychiatrist, NHS. Member, Socialist Medical Association. ASTMS.

Mr John Morgan owns his own company. Contested Newport twice in 1974. B February, 1929; ed Tredegar Grammar and Pembroke College, Cambridge.

WINDSOR AND MAIDENHEAD

Electorate 85,441   1974: 79,703

*Glyn, Dr A. (C)	38,451
Price, Mrs V. I. (Lab)	13,321
Farrand, J. (L)	11,496
Crowley, P. (Nat Front)	930
Bex, C. (Wessex Reg)	251
C majority	25,130

No Change

	1974		1979
Total votes	57,207		64,449
Turnout	71·8%		75·4%
C	28,013	49·0%	59·7%
Lab	15,172	26·5%	20·7%
L	14,022	24·5%	17·8%
Nat Front	—	—	1·4%
Wessex Reg	—	—	0·4%
C maj	12,841	22·5%	39·0%
Swing		−1·0%	+8·2%

Dr Alan Glyn was elected in February, 1974, having been MP for Windsor, 1970-74, and for Clapham, 1959-64. Barrister (Middle Temple, 1955) and medical practitioner. B September, 1918; ed Westminster School, Caius College, Cambridge, St Bartholomew's Hospital and St George's Hospital. Chairman, Conservative foreign affairs subcommittee, Far East; chairman, Danish, Swedish, Mongolian and Indonesian parliamentary groups of the Inter-Parliamentary Union. Member, executive committee of IPU.

Mrs Valerie Price is a part-time secretary. B June, 1940; ed St Albans Grammar School. Former member, Windsor Borough Council and Windsor and Maidenhead District Council. GMWU.

Mr John Farrand, schoolmaster and councillor. Age 38; ed Nottingham University.

WIRRAL

Electorate 97,033   1974: 93,135

*Hunt, D. (C)	44,519
Ryder, C. (Lab)	21,188
Barnett, R. (L)	9,769
C majority	23,331

No Change

	1974		1979
Total votes	70,267		75,476
Turnout	75·4%		77·8%
Speaker	35,705	50·8%	
C	—	—	59·0%
Lab	22,217	31·6%	28·1%
L	12,345	17·6%	12·9%
Speaker maj	13,488	19·2%	
C maj	—	—	30·9%

1976 by-election: Total vote 41,945 (55·5%)—C 34,675 (66·7%); Lab 10,563 (20·3%); L 5,914 (11·4%); others 773 (1·6%). C majority 24,112 (46·4%).

Mr David Hunt was elected in March, 1976. B May, 1942; ed Liverpool College, Montpelier University, Bristol University, Guildford College of Law. Solicitor of Supreme Court of Judicature, admitted 1968. Chairman, British Youth Council, 1971-74, National Young Conservatives, 1972-73. Vice-chairman, National Union of Conservative and Unionist Associations, 1974-76. Contested Bristol, South, 1970, and Kingswood, 1974. Member, South Western Economic Planning Council, 1972-76, Advisory Committee on Pop Festivals.

Mr Christopher Ryder, teacher. B August, 1947; ed Marple Hall Grammar School, University College, Aberystwyth, and School of Oriental and African Studies, London University. NUT.

Mr **Richard Barnett,** solicitor. Aged 28; ed London University.

WOKING

Electorate 72,670   1974: 67,916

*Onslow, C. G. D. (C)	31,719
Beard, C. N. (Lab)	13,327
Dunk, G. H. (L)	9,991
Gleave, P. A. (Nat Front)	564
C majority	18,392

No Change

	1974		1979
Total votes	49,531		55,601
Turnout	72·9%		76·5%
C	22,804	46·0%	57·0%
L	14,069	28·4%	18·0%
Lab	11,737	23·7%	24·0%
Nat Front	921	1·9%	1·0%
C maj	8,735	17·6%	33·0%
Swing		−1·4%	+5·3%

Mr **Cranley Onslow,** Under Secretary for Trade and Industry (Aerospace) 1972-74, was elected in 1964. Company director, business consultant and journalist. B June, 1926; ed Harrow School, Oriel College, Oxford, and Geneva University. Chairman, Conservative backbench aviation committee, 1970-72. Member, United Kingdom delegation to Council of Europe since 1977. Member, Dartford RDC, 1960-62; Kent County Council, 1961-64. Council member, Anglers' Cooperative Association, Salmon and Trout Association and National Rifle Association.

Mr **Nigel Beard,** director, London docklands development team. B October, 1936; ed Castleford Grammar School, University College, London University. Chief planner for strategy, Greater London Council, 1973-74. Nalgo.

Mr **George Dunk,** marine claims broker, contested Dartford, October 1974. B January, 1951; ed independent grammar school and technical college.

WOKINGHAM

Electorate 85,001   1974: 73,598

*van Straubenzee, W. R. (C)	36,194
Furley, A. E. (Lab)	17,448
Mullarky, P. (L)	12,120
Sanders, Mrs G. (Nat Front)	722
C majority	18,746

No Change

	1974		1979
Total votes	55,642		66,484
Turnout	75·6%		78·2%
C	24,009	43·1%	54·4%
Lab	16,304	29·3%	26·2%
L	15,329	27·5%	18·2%
Nat Front	—		1·1%
C maj	7,705	13·8%	28·2%
Swing		−2·2%	+7·2%

Mr **William van Strauben-zee** was Opposition spokesman on education and defence during 1974. Chairman, Select Committee on Assistance to Members, 1976. Minister of State, Northern Ireland, 1972-74, and Under-Secretary for Education and Science, 1970-72. Opposition spokesman on education 1969-70. Elected, 1959; contested

Wandsworth, Clapham, 1955. Solicitor. B January, 1924; ed Westminster School. Vice-chairman, Conservative Northern Ireland Committee. Church Commissioner. Member, House of Laity of the Church Assembly for the Diocese of Oxford, 1965-70.

Mr **Alan Furley,** civil engineer. B March, 1942; ed Bishop Wordsworth Grammar School, Salisbury, and Southampton University. Member, Berkshire County Council since 1973 (Labour group opposition leader since 1977). ASTMS.

Peter Mullarky is a deputy headmaster. B August, 1931; ed St Bede's Grammar School, Bradford; St Edward's College, Liverpool; Liverpool and London Universities. AMA.

WOLVERHAMPTON, North-East

Electorate 67,994   1974: 69,513

*Short, Mrs R. (Lab)	24,046
Evans, J. (C)	17,986
McLean, L. (L)	4,760
Cooper, G. (Nat Front)	1,283
Lab majority	6,060

No Change

	1974		1979
Total votes	46,007		48,075
Turnout	66·2%		70·7%
Lab	25,788	56·1%	50·0%
C	11,135	24·2%	37·4%
L	7,156	15·6%	9·9%
Nat Front	1,928	4·2%	2·7%
Lab maj	14,653	31·9%	12·6%
Swing		−3·0%	+9·6%

Mrs **Renee Short,** elected in 1964, contested Watford 1959 and St Albans 1955. B April, 1919; ed Notts County Secondary School and Manchester University. Member, Estimates Committee, 1964-70; Expenditure Committee since 1970 (chairman, social services and employment sub-committee). Vice-chairman, parliamentary East-West trade group since 1968; chairman, Anglo-GDR parliamentary group; secretary, Anglo-Soviet parliamentary group; president, British-Romanian Friendship Association. Member, Labour Party NEC, since 1970. National President, Nursery Schools Association. Chairman, Theatres' Advisory Council. Freelance journalist. Sponsored by TGWU. NUJ.

Mr **Jonathan Evans,** solicitor. B June, 1950; ed Howardian High School, Cardiff, and College of Law, Lancaster Gate. Contested Ebbw Vale, February and October, 1974. Chairman, East Wales CPC, and vice-chairman, Wales CPC. Former chairman, Cardiff Central and Cardiff North Young Conservatives.

Mr **Laurence McLean,** chartered accountant. B February, 1931; ed St Chad's College, Wolverhampton.

WOLVERHAMPTON, South-East

Electorate 53,764   1974: 55,382

*Edwards, R. (Lab and Co-op)	20,708
Chalkley, P. (C)	12,807
Parsley, M. (L)	2,499
Jones, G. (Nat Front)	1,139
Lab and Co-op majority	7,901

No Change

	1974		1979
Total votes	36,573		37,153
Turnout	66·0%		69·1%
Lab/Co-op	21,466	58·7%	55·7%
C	9,768	26·7%	34·5%
L	3,636	9·9%	6·7%
Nat Front	1,703	4·7%	3·1%
Lab/Co-op m	11,698	32·0%	21·2%
Swing		−2·3%	+5·4%

Mr **Robert Edwards,** a member of the European Parliament since 1977, was elected for the seat, February, 1974; represented Bilston, 1955-74; contested by-elections Newport, 1945, and Stretford 1939, and general election, Chorley, 1935. B January, 1906; ed council schools and technical college. Chairman, Industrial Common Ownership Group. General secretary, Chemical Workers' Union, 1947-71; national officer. TGWU, 1971-76. Member, Liverpool City Council 1929-32. Chairman, Corton Beach (Holdings) Ltd. President, Britain-Cyprus Committee. Fought in Spain with the Republicans during the Civil War.

Mr **Peter Chalkley,** company director and management consultant. B May, 1938; ed Harlow College, University College School. Freeman of the City of London.

Mr **Michael Parsley** is financial director of an engineering company. B November, 1940; ed Cambridge Grammar School for Boys.

WOLVERHAMPTON, South-West

Electorate 66,180   1974: 64,675

*Budgen, N. W. (C)	26,587
Geffen, I. E. (Lab)	15,827
Wernick, J (L)	6,939
Lees, Mrs J. (Nat Front)	912
Deary, J. (ACMFE)	401
C majority	10,760

No Change

	1974		1979
Total votes	47,196		50,666
Turnout	73·7%		76·6%
C	20,854	44·2%	52·5%
Lab	15,554	33·0%	31·2%
L	9,215	19·5%	13·7%
Nat Front	1,573	3·3%	1·8%
ACMFE	—	—	0·8%
C maj	5,300	11·2%	21·3%
Swing		−1·2%	+5·0%

Mr **Nicholas Budgen,** a barrister, was elected in February, 1974. Contested Birmingham, Small Heath, 1970. B November, 1937; ed St Edward's School, Oxford and Corpus Christi College, Cambridge. Chairman, Birmingham Bow Group, 1967-68.

Mr **Ivan Geffen,** solicitor, contested the seat in October, 1974; Hereford, February, 1974; Newcastle upon Tyne, North, 1951 and Thirsk and Malton, 1950. B March, 1920; ed Westminster School and London University. ASTMS. Former member, NUM and CAWU. Member, National Executive, NCCL.

Mr **Joseph Wernick,** company managing director, contested the seat in February and October, 1974. B August, 1920; ed Wolverhampton Municipal Grammar School and Wolverhampton Technical College.

WORCESTER

Electorate 78,026   1974: 74,844

*Walker, P. E. (C)	30,194
Sparks, D. (Lab)	18,605
Elliott, Mrs D. (L)	8,886
Davenport, J. (Ecology)	707
Stevens, K. (Nat Front)	450
C majority	11,589

No Change

	1974		1979
Total votes	55,265		58,842
Turnout	73·8%		75·4%
C	25,183	45·6%	51·3%
Lab	20,194	36·5%	31·6%
L	9,888	17·9%	15·1%
Ecology	—	—	1·2%
Nat Front	—	—	0·8%
C maj	4,989	9·1%	19·7%
Swing		−1·7%	+5·3%

Mr **Peter Walker** was appointed Minister of Agriculture, Fisheries and Food, May 1979. Opposition spokesman on defence until February, 1975, and on trade and industry during 1974. Secretary of State for Trade and Industry, 1972-74; Secretary of State for the Environment, 1970-72; Minister of Housing and Local Government, June to October, 1970. Elected at by-election in March, 1961. Contested Dartford, 1955 and 1959. B March, 1932; ed Latymer Upper School, Hammersmith. Former chairman, Lloyd's insurance brokers and director of other companies. Member, party national executive, until 1962.

Mr **David Sparks,** careers officer, contested North Fylde, February, 1974. B November, 1948; ed Fisher More Secondary School, and Wade Deacon Grammar School, Widnes; Lancaster University and Manchester Polytechnic. Member, West Midlands County Council, Birmingham Trades Council. Nalgo. GMWU.

Mrs **Doreen Elliot** contested the seat in October, 1974, and Lichfield and Tamworth, February, 1974. Personnel manager in engineering industry. B October, 1932; ed Ashington Secondary Girls' School. NUJ.

Mr John Davenport, aged 41, is a salesman. Ecology Party parish councillor.

WORCESTERSHIRE, South

Electorate 79,036   1974: 73,695

*Spicer, W. H. M. (C)	34,926
Phillips, D. (L)	14,272
Daniel, G. (Lab)	10,206
Woodford, G. (Ecology)	1,722
C majority	20,654

No Change

	1974		1979
Total votes	55,366		61,126
Turnout	75·1%		77·3%
C	26,790	48·4%	57·1%
L	17,738	32·0%	23·3%
Lab	10,838	19·6%	16·7%
Ecology	—		2·8%
C maj	9,052	16·4%	33·8%
Swing		−1·0%	+5·8%

Mr Michael Spicer, an economist, was elected in February, 1974, and contested Easington, 1966 and 1970. Member, Conservative Research Department, 1966-68; Deputy chairman computer sub-committee of Commons Services Committee. B January, 1943; ed Wellington College and Emmanuel College, Cambridge. Managing director, Economic Models Ltd.

Mr David Phillips, aged 46, is sales manager.

Mr Gareth Daniel is a social worker. B 1954. Member, Child Poverty Action Group, Ealing Community Relations Council, Nalgo.

Mr Guy Woodford, aged 43, is a lecturer. Ed Lancing College, Reading University. Member, National Council for the Protection of Ancient Buildings.

WORKINGTON

Electorate 55,030   1974: 53,114

Campbell-Savours, D. (Lab)	24,523
*Page, R. L. (C)	18,767
Blackshaw, N. (L)	2,819
Lab majority	5,756

Lab gain from C

	1974		1979
Total votes	40,255		46,109
Turnout	75·8%		83·8%
Lab	22,539	56·0%	53·2%
C	12,988	32·3%	40·7%
L	4,728	11·7%	6·1%
Lab maj	9,551	23·7%	12·5%
Swing		−2·2%	+5·6%

1976 by-election: Total vote 40,207 (74.2%)—C 19,396 (48.2%); Lab 18,331 (45.6%); L, 2,480 (6.2%). C majority 1,065 (2.6%). C gain from Lab.

Mr Dale Campbell-Savours, export and technical agent, contested Darwen, February and October, 1974. B August, 1943; ed Keswick School and the Sorbonne. Member, Ramsbottom UDC, 1972-74. TGWU.

Mr Richard Page was elected at the November, 1976 by-election having contested the seat in both 1974 elections. B February, 1941; ed Hurstpierpoint College and Luton Technical College. Mechanical engineer and company director. Joint secretary, Conservative committees on industry and small business. Member, Banstead UDC. 1969-72.

Mr Neil Blackshaw, local government officer. B July, 1948; ed Hyde Grammar School and Manchester and Cardiff universities. Nalgo.

WORTHING

Electorate 74,961   1974: 72,594

*Higgins, T. L. (C)	33,624
Sudbury, B. (L)	13,244
Underwood, K. (Lab)	7,163
Hough, A. (Nat Front)	893
C majority	20,380

No Change

	1974		1979
Total votes	51,617		54,924
Turnout	71·1%		73·3%
C	30,036	58·2%	61·2%
L	12,691	24·6%	24·1%
Lab	8,890	17·2%	13·0%
Nat Front	—		1·6%
C maj	17,345	33·6%	37·1%
Swing		−1·9%	+3·6%

Mr Terence Higgins, Opposition spokesman on trade, 1974-76, and a spokesman on Treasury and economic affairs during 1974. Financial Secretary to the Treasury, 1972-74, and Minister of State, Treasury, 1970-72. B January, 1928; ed Alleyn's School. Dulwich, Gonville and Caius College, Cambridge, and Yale. Opposition spokesman on Treasury and economic affairs, 1966-70. Director, Warne Wright and Rowland Group. Former Olympic and Commonwealth Games athlete.

Mr Brian Sudbury, management services engineer. B January, 1939; ed Hove County Grammar School. Chairman, Worthing Shelter group.

Mr Kerry Underwood, trainee solicitor. B June, 1956; ed Red Hill School, College of Law. TGWU.

WREKIN, The

Electorate 92,592   1974: 82,650

Hawksley, W. (C)	32,672
*Fowler, G. T. (Lab)	31,707
Yarnell, R. (L)	7,331
C majority	965

C gain from Lab

	1974		1979
Total votes	62,374		71,710
Turnout	75·5%		77·4%
Lab	30,385	48·7%	44·2%
C	23,547	37·8%	45·6%
L	8,442	13·5%	10·2%
Lab maj	6,838	10·9%	—
C maj	—	—	1·4%
Swing		−0·6%	+6·1%

Mr Philip Hawksley, bank clerk, contested Wolverhampton, North-East in February and October, 1974. B March, 1943; ed Mill Mead Shrewsbury, and Denstone College, Uttoxeter. Member, Shropshire County Council since 1970. Former member, Young Conservative National Advisory Council and of National Union Executive Committee.

Mr Gerald Fowler was Minister of State for Education and Science, October, 1969—June, 1970, March-October, 1974, and January-September, 1976. Minister of State, Privy Council Office, 1974-76. Elected February, 1974; represented the seat, 1966-70; contested Banbury, 1964. Joint Parliamentary Secretary, Ministry of Technology, 1967-69. B January, 1935; ed Northampton Grammar School, Lincoln College, Oxford, and Frankfurt University. Vice-chairman, all-party parliamentary youth lobby. Member, Oxford City Council, 1960-64, District of The Wrekin Council 1973-76 (Leader, 1973-76). Branch Secretary, ASTMS, 1960-63. AUT, Apex.

Mr Raymond Yarnell is a senior lecturer at Wolverhampton Polytechnic. B October, 1927; ed Warley College of Technology, Bolton Training College, Open University and Manchester and Birmingham universities. NATFHE.

WREXHAM

Electorate 78,771   1974: 76,105

*Ellis, R. T. (Lab)	30,405
Graham-Palmer, R. (C)	18,256
Thomas, M. (L)	11,389
Roberts, H. W. (Pl Cymru)	1,740
Lab majority	12,149

No Change

	1974		1979
Total votes	56,514		61,790
Turnout	74·3%		78·4%
Lab	28,885	51·1%	49·2%
L	12,519	22·2%	18·4%
C	12,251	21·7%	29·5%
Pl Cymru	2,859	5·1%	2·8%
Lab maj	16,366	28·9%	19·7%
Swing		−3·6%	+4·8%

Mr Tom Ellis, a member of the European Parliament, since 1975, was elected in February, 1974, and contested West Flintshire, 1966. Mining engineer. B March, 1924; ed Ruabon Grammar School and universities of Wales and Nottingham. Former president, Wrexham Fabian Society.

Mr Roger Graham-Palmer is a farmer and company director. B February, 1941; ed Radley College, Abingdon, and Emmanuel College, Cambridge. Former lecturer, Royal Agricultural College. Member, Wrexham Maelor Borough Council since 1973.

Mr Martin Thomas, aged 42 is a barrister. President of the Welsh Liberal Party.

Mr Hywell Roberts, a lecturer, contested the seat in February and October, 1974. Former chairman of Plaid Cymru's London branch. B September, 1938; ed Ysgol y Moelwyn, Blaenau Ffestiniog, and University College, Aberystwyth. NATFHE.

WYCOMBE

Electorate 85,843   1974: 78,832

*Whitney, R. (C)	38,171
Fowler, T. J. (Lab)	18,000
Lawson, A. (L)	9,615
Jones, Mrs S. (Nat Front)	833
C majority	20,171

No Change

	1974		1979
Total votes	58,565		66,619
Turnout	74·3%		77·6%
C	27,131	46·3%	57·3%
Lab	18,052	30·8%	27·0%
L	11,333	19·4%	14·4%
Nat Front	2,049	3·5%	1·3%
C maj	9,079	15·5%	30·3%
Swing		−0·6%	+7·4%

1978 by-election: Total vote 49,511. C 29,677 (60.0%), Lab 14,109 (28.5%), L 3,665 (7.4%), Nat Front 2,040 (4.1%)—C maj 15,558 (31.5%).

Mr Raymond Whitney, export consultant, was elected at the by-election in April, 1978. Former member diplomatic service; resigned as head of overseas information department, Foreign and Commonwealth˙ Office, February, 1978. B November, 1930; ed Wellingborough School, Sandhurst and London University. Head of  Political Section, British Embassy, Peking, 1966-68; Head of Chancery, British Embassy, Buenos Aires, 1969-72; Assistant Head, East African Department; Foreign and Commonwealth Office, 1972-73; Deputy High Commissioner and Economic Counsellor, Dacca, 1974-75; Head of Information Research Department, Foreign and Commonwealth Office, 1973-77, and head of Overseas Information Department, 1977-78.

Mr Trevor Fowler, a printer, B 1931; ed Mill End Road Senior Boys School. Secretary, High Wycombe Trades Council, 1959-67. Former research assistant, TUC. Member, NGA and area branch secretary since 1972. Former borough councillor, district councillor and county councillor.

Mr Alan Lawson, educationist, contested South Fylde February and October 1974. B May, 1930; ed Ormskirk Grammar School, King Alfred's College, Winchester and Liverpool, and London universities.

YARMOUTH

Electorate 72,154   1974: 70,802

*Fell, A. (C)	28,066
Hollis, Mrs P. (Lab)	20,838
Minett, E. (L)	6,112
Holmes, T. (Nat Front)	640
C majority	7,228

No Change

	1974		1979
Total votes	52,136		55,656
Turnout	73·6%		77·1%
C	22,573	43·3%	50·4%
Lab	20,313	39·0%	37·4%
L	9,250	17·7%	11·0%
Nat Front	—		1·1%
C maj	2,260	4·3%	13·0%
Swing		−2·2%	+4·3%

Mr Anthony Fell, regained the seat for his party in 1970. He won it from Labour in 1951 but lost it in 1966. Contested by-election at Brigg, 1948, and South Hammersmith, 1949 and 1950. B May, 1914; ed Bedford School and Tauranga High School, New Zealand; former member, AEU.

Mrs Patricia Hollis, university lecturer, contested the seat in February and October, 1974. B May, 1941; ed Plympton Grammar School, Girton College, Cambridge, Berkeley and Columbia universities. Member, Norwich City Council since 1968. AUT.

Mr Eric Minett, senior lecturer. B July, 1932; ed Great Yarmouth Grammar School and Open University. Member Great Yarmouth Borough Council since 1974: NATFHE.

YEOVIL

Electorate 80,646   1974: 75,159

*Peyton, J. W. W. (C)	31,321
Ashdown, J. J. D. (L)	19,939
Luder, I. D. (Lab)	14,098
C majority	11,382

No Change

	1974		1979
Total votes	59,669		65,358
Turnout	79·4%		81·0%
C	24,709	41·4%	47·9%
Lab	17,330	29·0%	21·6%
L	17,298	29·0%	30·5%
UDP	332	0·6%	—
C maj	7,379	12·4%	17·4%
Swing		−0·7%	+6·9%

Mr John Peyton was chief Opposition spokesman on agriculture 1976-79. Shadow Leader of Commons 1974-76. Minister of Transport, 1970, and Minister for Transport Industries within the Department of the Environment, 1970-74; Parliamentary Secretary, Ministry of Power, 1962-64; Opposition spokesman on power, 1964-66. Unsuccessfully contested leadership of the party, February 1975. Elected 1951; contested Bristol, Central, 1950. B February, 1919; ed Eton and Trinity College, Oxford. Barrister (Inner Temple, 1945).

Mr Jeremy Ashdown is a personnel officer. B February, 1941; ed Bedford School, Bedford. TASS.

Mr Ian Luder, chartered accountant. B April, 1951; ed Haberdashers' Aske's School and University College, London. Member, North Beds Council since 1976. GMWU.

YORK

Electorate 76,832   1974: 77,172

*Lyon, A. W. (Lab)	26,703
Tod, Dr E. D. M. (C)	25,453
Pemberton, M. (L)	6,752
Radcliffe, F. C. J. (CSA)	569
Spink, P. A. (Nat Front)	221
Lab majority	1,250

No Change

	1974		1979
Total votes	58,122		59,698
Turnout	75·3%		77·7%
Lab	26,983	46·4%	44·7%
C	23,294	40·1%	42·6%
L	7,370	12·7%	11·3%
Pros Brit	304	0·5%	—
Protest P	171	0·3%	—
CSA	—		1·0%
Nat Front	—		0·4%
Lab maj	3,689	6·3%	2·1%
Swing		−2·5%	+2·1%

Mr Alexander Lyon, a barrister was Minister of State, Home Office, 1974-76; Opposition spokesman on home affairs, 1972-74, and Commonwealth Affairs, 1970-72. Won the seat in 1966 and contested it in 1964. B October, 1931; ed West Leeds High School and University College, London. Member, Expenditure Committee. Joint chairman, PLP Home Affairs Group.

Dr Edward Tod, senior partner in a group medical practice, contested Kingston upon Hull, East, in February, 1974. B March, 1930; ed Hymers College, Hull, and Edinburgh University. Member, International Society for Psychosomatic Obstetrics and Gynaecology and of the British Medical Association. Consultant to the *Medical Digest* and former leader writer. Member, Wandsworth Borough Council, 1968-71; Roehampton District Management Team (NHS), 1974-77.

Mr Martin Pemberton is a company secretary. B February, 1941; ed Stowe School. Governor, Park Lane College, Leeds. Member, British Junior Chamber of Commerce (national commission director 1973-74).

Political party and trade union abbreviations

The following abbreviations have been used for political parties standing in this and the last election:—

ACMC—Anti-Common Market Conservative; ACMFE—Anti-Common Market Free Enterprise; ACMOAT—Anti-Common Market On Any Terms; ARPSWR—Air, Road, Public Safety, White Resident; APS—Anti-Party System; Anti-Carr—Anti-Corruption; BSEP—British Socialist Empire Party; Brit C—British Candidate; C—Conservative; CACM—Conservative Against the Common Market; CD—Christian Democrat; CFMPB—Campaign For More Prosperous Britain; CFPG—Child and Family Protection Group; CPPS—Committee for Prevention of Police State; CSA—Christian Stop Abortion; CSD—Christian Social Democrat; Chr Party—Christian Party; CPV—Citizen's Protest Vote; Comm—Communist; Comm Marx-L—Communist Party of England, Marxist-Leninist; Comm Ire, Marx-L—Communist Party of Ireland, Marxist-Leninist; Comm PE—Communist Party of England; Cornish N—Cornish Nationalist; DLP—Dog-Lovers' Party; Dem U—Democratic Unionist Party; DMPSWR—Democratic Monarchist Public Safety White Resident; Dem Lab—Democratic Labour; Derry Lab—Derry Labour and Trade Union Party; ELPF—East London People's Front; ENP—English National Party; Ecology—Ecology Party; Eng Nat—English Nationalist; FDP—Fancy Dress Party; FG—Fine Gael; FP—Fellowship Party; GLF—Gay Liberation Front; GTB—Go To Blazes Party; ICRA—Irish Civil Rights Association; IDP—Inter-Dependence Party; IIP—Irish Independence Party; IMG—International Marxist Group; INP—Irish National Party; Ind—Independent; Ind Brit Nat—Independent British Nationalist; Ind C—Independent Conservative; Ind Dem—Independent Democratic; Ind Dem Lab—Independent Democratic Labour; Ind England Nat—Independent English Nationalist; Ind Lab—Independent Labour; Ind L—Independent Liberal; Ind L Dem—Independent Liberal Democrat; Ind Rep—Independent Republican; Ind Soc—Independent Socialist; IUU—Independent Ulster Unionist; JHC—Jesus and His Cross; KBUP—Keep Britain United Party; L—Liberal; Lab; Labour; Lab AP—Labour Alliance Party; Lab and Co-op—Labour and Co-operative; Lab and Dem—Labour and Democrat; Lab Integ—Labour Integrationist; Lab and TU—Labour and Trade Union; LCCP—Labour, Conservative Coalition Party; LDL—Liberal Dog Lover; Mod Lab—Moderate Labour; MCP—Middle Class Party; Meb Kernow—Mebyon Kernow; Nat Front—National Front; NI Lab—Northern Ireland Labour; NB—New Britain; Off UU—Official Ulster Unionist Party; Ox Ecol—Oxford Ecology Movement; Pl Cymru—Plaid Cymru PAA—People and Agrarian; PD—Property Development; PP—People's Party; Peo Cand—People's Candidate; Peo Power—People's Power; Protest P—Protest Party; PTC—Providers Through Care; RF—Rhodesian Front; Rad L—Radical Liberal; Rep Clubs—Republican Clubs; Rev Ref—Revolutionary Reform; Roy—Royalist; SBE—Save Birmingham Education; SDLP—Social Democratic and Labour Party; SLAG—Save London Action Group; Scot Nat—Scottish National Party; SL—Severnside Libertarian; SPGB—Socialist Party of Great Britain; Scot Lab—Scottish Labour Party; Soc Credit—Social Credit; Soc Unity—Socialist Unity; Soc Wkrs—Socialist Workers' Party; Soc Dem—Social Democrat; TOI—Troops Out of Ireland; UCP—United Country Party; UDP—United Democratic Party; UKF—United Kingdom Front; ULP—United Labour Party; UP and Eng Nat—United Party and English Nationalist; UPNI—Unionist Party of Northern Ireland; UU—Ulster Unionist; UUU—United Ulster Unionist; VUPP—Vanguard Unionist Progressive Party; VPP—Volunteer Political Party; Wessex Reg—Wessex Regionalist; WRC—Women's Rights Campaign; WRP—Workers' Revolutionary Party.

The following abbreviations for trade unions and other bodies have been used:—

ABS—Association of Broadcasting Staff; ACTT—Association of Cinematograph, Television and Allied Technicians; AMA—Assistant Masters' Association; APEX—Association of Professional, Executive, Clerical and Computer Staff; ASB—Amalgamated Society of Boilermakers, etc.; ASLEF—Associated Society of Locomotive Engineers and Firemen; ASTMS—Association of Scientific, Technical and Managerial Staffs; ATCDE—Association of Teachers in Colleges and Departments of Education; ATTI—Association of Teachers in Technical Institutions; AUBTW—Amalgamated Union of Building Trade Workers; AUEW—Amalgamated Union of Engineering Workers (TASS—Technical and Supervisory Section); DATA—Draughtsmen's and Allied Technicians' Association.

BALPA—British Air Line Pilots' Association; BLA—British Legal Association; BMA—British Medical Association; COHSE—Confederation of Health Service Employees; EETPU—Electrical, Electronic Telecommunications and Plumbing Union; EIS—Education Institute of Scotland; EPEA—Electrical Power Engineers' Association; ETS—Electrodepositors' Technical Society; FTATU—Furniture and Allied Trades Union; GMWU—General and Municipal Workers' Union; IPCS—Institute of Professional Civil Servants; ISTC—Iron and Steel Trades Confederation; LSE—London School of Economics; MPU—Medical Practitioners' Union.

NACODS—National Association of Colliery Overmen, Deputies and Shotfirers; NALGO—National Association of Local Government Officers; NAS—National Association of Schoolmasters; NATFHE—National Association of Teachers in Further and Higher Education; NATSOPA—National Society of Operative Printers, Graphical and Media Personnel; NATTKE—National Association of Theatrical, Television and Kine Employees; NFU—National Farmers' Union; NGA—National Graphical Association; NUAAW—National Union of Agricultural and Allied Workers; NUBE—National Union of Bank Employees; NUJ—National Union of Journalists; NUM—National Union of Mineworkers; NUPE—National Union of Public Employees; NUR—National Union of Railwaymen; NUS—National Union of Students and National Union of Seamen; NUT—National Union of Teachers.

PEST—Pressure for Economic and Social Toryism; PLP—Parliamentary Labour Party; POEU—Post Office Engineering Union; SIMA—Steel Industry Management Association; SLADE—Society of Lithographic Artists, Designers, Engravers and Process Workers; SMWU—Sheet Metal Workers' Union; TGWU—Transport and General Workers' Union; TSSA—Transport Salaried Staffs' Association; UCATT—Union of Construction, Allied Trades and Technicians; UNICEF—United Nations Children's Fund; UPOW—Union of Post Office Workers; USDAW—Union of Shop, Distributive and Allied Workers; WEA—Workers' Educational Association; WEU—Western European Union.

Ministers in House of Lords

Lord Hailsham   **Lord Carrington**   **Lord Soames**   **Lady Young**

Lord Hailsham of St Marylebone, the Lord Chancellor, held the office, 1970–74. Made life peer, 1970. As Mr Quintin Hogg, QC, he was chief Opposition spokesman on home affairs, 1966–70. Renounced the Hailsham viscountcy on November 20, 1963, to return to Commons and was elected for St Marylebone, 1963. Became Secretary of State for Education & Science in April, 1964. B October, 1907; ed Eton and Christ Church, Oxord. MP for Oxford City, 1938–50 when he succeeded to the peerage. Under Secretary for Air, April-July, 1945; First Lord of the Admiralty, 1955–56; Minister of Education, 1957; Lord President of the Council, 1957; Lord Privy Seal and Minister for Science, 1959; Lord President of the Council and Minister for Science, 1960-64. Chairman, Conservative Party Organization, 1957-59.

Lord Carrington, Secretary of State for Foreign Affairs and Minister of Overseas Development. Leader of the Opposition, House of Lords 1974-79 and 1964-70. Chairman, Conservative Party Organization, 1972-74; Minister of Aviation Supply, 1971-74; Secretary of State for Energy, 1974; Secretary of State for Defence, 1970-74; Minister without Portfolio and Leader of the House of Lords, 1963-64; First Lord of the Admiralty, 1959-63; High Commissioner in Australia, 1956-59; Party Secretary, Ministry of Defence, 1954-56, and of Agriculture and Fisheries, 1951-54. B June, 1919; ed Eton College; RMC, Sandhurst.

Lord Soames, Lord President of the Council. Formerly Sir Christopher Soames; Vice President of the European Commission, 1973-77; Ambassador to France, 1968-72. B October, 1920; ed Eton and RMC, Sandhurst. MP for Bedford, 1950-66. Minister of Agriculture, Fisheries and Food, 1960-64; Secretary of State for War, 1958-60; Parliamentary and Financial Secretary, Admiralty, 1957-58; Parliamentary Under Secretary, Air Ministry, 1955-57.

Lady Young, Minister of State, Education & Science. Formerly Opposition spokesman on the environment; Under Secretary of State for the environment, 1973-74; Baroness-in-Waiting (Government whip), 1972-73. A vice-chairman, Conservative Party Organization. B October, 1926; ed Dragon School, Oxford; Headington School and in US. Former Leader, Conservative group, Oxford City Council.

Earl Ferrers, Minister of State, Ministry of Agriculture, Fisheries and Food. Joint Deputy Leader of the Opposition, House of Lords, 1976-79. Parliamentary Secretary, Ministry of Agriculture, 1974; Lord in Waiting, 1962-64. B June, 1929; ed Winchester College; Magdalene College, Cambridge. Member, Armitage Committee on political activities of civil servants.

Lord Strathcona and Mount Royal, Minister of State for Defence. Deputy Leader of the Opposition in the Lords, 1976-79. Lord-in-Waiting (Government whip), 1973-74; Under Secretary for the RAF, 1974. B November, 1923; ed Eton; Trinity College, Cambridge; McGill University, Montreal.

The Earl of Mansfield, Minister of State, Scottish Office. An Opposition spokesman in the Lords since 1975. Member, European Parliament, 1973-75. B July, 1930; ed Eton; Christ Church, Oxford. Barrister.

Lord Cockfield, Minister of State, Treasury. Chairman of the Price Commission, 1973-77. Advisor on taxation policy to Chancellor of the Exchequer, 1970-73. Former Commissioner of Inland Revenue. B September, 1916; ed Dover County; London School of Economics.

Viscount Trenchard, a Minister of State for Industry. B December, 1923; ed Eton. Son of first Viscount Trenchard, Marshal of the RAF.

The Earl of Gowrie, Minister of State, Employment. An Opposition spokesman on economic affairs, 1974-79. Lord-in-Waiting (Government whip), 1972-74; a Conservative whip, 1971-72. B November, 1939; ed Eton; Balliol College, Oxford.

Lord Denham, Government Chief Whip and Captain of the Honourable Corps of Gentleman at Arms. Opposition Chief Whip, House of Lords, 1978-79. Opposition Deputy Chief Whip, 1974-78. Captain of the Yeoman of the Guard, 1971-74. B October, 1927; ed Eton; King's College, Cambridge.

Lord Sandys, Deputy Chief Whip and Captain of the Body Guard of the Yeomen of the Guard. Opposition Whip, 1974-79. Former Lord-in-Waiting. Landowner. B July, 1931; ed Royal Naval College, Dartmouth.

Lord Elton, Under Secretary, Northern Ireland Office. An Opposition spokesman in the Lords, 1976-79; Conservative whip, 1974-76. B March, 1930, ed Eton; New College, Oxford. Publisher.

Lord Belstead, Under Secretary, Home Office. Under Secretary for Education and Science, 1970-73; for Northern Ireland Office, 1973-74. B September, 1932; ed Eton; Christ Church, Oxford.

Lord Bellwin, aged 56 was formerly Mr Irwin Bellow, was made a life peer in May, 1979, and appointed Under Secretary, Department of the Environment. Appointed vice-chairman of the Association of Metropolitan Authorities in 1978. Elected to Leeds CBC in 1965 and became Alderman in 1968; housing committee chairman, 1967–72. Chairman of Leeds City Council policy and finance committee and leader of the Council, 1975-79.

243

Lord Mowbray, Segrave and Stourton, a Lord-in-Waiting; spokesman on arts, transport, environment and ancient monuments. Deputy Chief Opposition Whip, Lords, 1978-79; Lord-in-Waiting (Govt whip) and spokesman on the environment, 1970-74; Conservative whip, 1967-70 and 1974-78. B March, 1923; ed Ampleforth; Christ Church, Oxford.

Viscount Long, Lord-in-Waiting; spokesman on defence, Northern Ireland, industry, agriculture and posts. B January, 1929; ed Harrow.

Lord Cullen of Ashbourne, Lord-in-Waiting; spokesman on health and social security, the environment, the Treasurery and Wales. B October, 1912; ed Eton.

Lord Trefgarne, Lord-in-Waiting; spokesman on trade, aid and industry. Opposition Whip in Lords, 1977-79. B March, 1941; ed Haileybury and in US.

Lord Lyell, Lord-in-Waiting; spokesman on Scotland and employment. B March, 1939; ed Eton; Christ Church, Oxford.

Labour lost seven seats in by-elections

Labour were unsuccessful in 17 of the 30 by-elections held since the last general election in October 1974. There were 13 Labour victories, 16 Conservative and one Liberal.

The Labour Party entered the 1979 election with 13 fewer seats than when it gained an overall majority at the previous election. Since October 1974 there had been three defections of Labour MPs to other parties and six seats lost to the Conservatives in by-elections and one to the Liberals. Mr George Thomas (Cardiff, West) also became Speaker. The Conservatives by contrast had increased their strength by six.

When the election campaign began there were four seats vacant – two Labour, caused by the deaths of Mr Tom Swain (*Derbyshire, North-East*) and Sir Alfred Broughton (*Batley and Morley*) and two Conservative, caused by the death of Mr Reginald Maudling (*Barnet, Chipping Barnet*) and the assassination of Mr Airey Neave (*Abingdon*).

The by-elections with winning MPs were:

1975
June 26

Greenwich, Woolwich, W – Mr Peter Bottomley	C gain

1976
March 4

Coventry, North West – Mr Geoffrey Robinson	Lab

March 11

Wirral – Mr David Hunt	C
Carshalton – Mr Nigel Forman	C

June 24

Rotherham – Mr Stanley Crowther	Lab

July 15

Thurrock – Miss Oonagh McDonald	Lab

November 4

Newcastle upon Tyne, Central – Mr Harry Cowans	Lab
Walsall, North – Mr Robin Hodgson	C gain
Workington – Mr Richard Page	C gain

December 2

Cambridge – Mr Robert Rhodes James	C

1977
February 25

Cities of London and Westminster, South – Mr Peter Brooke	C

March 31

Birmingham, Stechford – Mr Andrew Mackay	C gain

April 28

Ashfield – Mr Timothy Smith	C gain
Grimsby – Mr Austin Mitchell	Lab

July 7

Saffron Walden – Mr Alan Haselhurst	C

August 18

Birmingham, Ladywood – Mr John Sever	Lab

November 24

Bournemouth, East – Mr David Atkinson	C

1978
March 2

Redbridge, Ilford, North – Mr Vivian Bendall	C gain

April 13

Glasgow, Garscadden – Mr Donald Dewar	Lab

April 20

Lambeth, Central – Mr John Tilley	Lab

April 27

Wycombe – Mr Raymond Whitney	C
Epsom and Ewell – Mr Archibald Hamilton	C

May 31

Hamilton – Mr George Robertson	Lab

July 13

Penistone – Mr Allen McKay	Lab
Manchester, Moss Side – Mr George Morton	Lab

October 26

Pontefract and Castleford – Mr Geoffrey Lofthouse	Lab
Berwick and East Lothian – Mr John Robertson	Lab

1979
March 1

Clitheroe – Mr David Waddington	C
Knutsford – Mr John Bruce-Gardyne	C

March 29

Liverpool, Edge Hill – Mr David Alton	L gain

In the general election Labour recaptured Walsall, North; Workington; Birmingham, Stechford, and Ashfield.

How the Nation Voted — May 1979

	C	Lab	L	Scot Nat / Pl Cymru	Nat Front	Comm	Others	Total
ENGLAND: Electorate								34,209,087
Votes	12,255,344	9,526,838	3,876,504	—	189,137	6,622	118,520	25,972,965
MPs	306	203	7	—	—	—	—	516
% of vote/turnout	47·2	36·7	14·9	—	0·7	0·0	0·5	75·9
Candidates	516	516	506	—	297	18	221	2074
Swing								+5·8%
SCOTLAND: Electorate								3,795,865
Votes	916,155	1,211,445	255,095	504,259	104	5926	23,653	2,916,637
MPs	22	44	3	2	—	—	—	71
% of vote/turnout	31·4	41·5	8·7	17·3	0·0	0·2	0·8	76·8
Candidates	71	71	42	71	1	12	16	284
Swing								+0·7%
WALES: Electorate								2,061,108
Votes	526,254	768,458	173,725	132,544	2,465	4,310	29,032	1,636,788
MPs	11	21	1	2	—	—	1*	36
% of vote/turnout	32·2	46·9	10·6	8·1	0·2	0·3	1·8	79·4
Candidates	35	35	28	36	5	8	7	154
Swing								+5·4%
NORTHERN IRELAND: Electorate								1,027,204
Votes	—	—	—	—	—	—	695,889†	695,889
MPs	—	—	—	—	—	—	12	12
% of vote/turnout	—	—	—	—	—	—	100	67·7%
Candidates	—	—	—	—	—	—	64	64
Swing								
UNITED KINGDOM: Electorate								41,093,264
Votes	13,697,753	11,506,741	4,305,324	636,803	191,706	16,858	867,094	31,222,279
MPs	339	268	11	4	—	—	13*	635
% of vote/turnout	43·9	36·9	13·8	2·0	0·6	0·1	2·8	76·0
Candidates	622	622	576	107	303	38	308	2,576
Swing								+5·2%

*Including the Speaker   †Separate table on page 248.

How the Nation Voted—October 1974

	Lab	C	L	Scot Nat Pl Cymru	Nat Front	Comm	Others	Total
ENGLAND: Electorate								33,341,321
Votes	9,695,051	9,416,242	4,878,792	—	113,757	7,032	80,195	24,191,069
MPs	255	253*	8	—	—	—	—	516
% of vote/turnout	40·1	38·9	20·2	—	0·5	0·0	0·3	72·6
Candidates	516	516	515	—	89	17	113	1,766
SCOTLAND: Electorate								3,684,787
Votes	1,000,581	681,327	228,855	839,617	86	7,453	182	2,758,101
MPs	41	16	3	11	—	—	—	71
% of vote/turnout	36·3	24·7	8·3	30·4	0·0	0·3	0·0	74·9
Candidates	71	71	68	71	1	9	2	293
WALES: Electorate								2,008,294
Votes	761,447	367,230	239,057	166,321	—	2,941	844	1,537,840
MPs	23	8	2	3	—	—	—	36
% of vote/turnout	49·5	23·9	15·5	10·8	—	0·2	0·1	76·6
Candidates	36	36	36	36	—	3	3	150
NORTHERN IRELAND: Electorate								1,036,523
Votes	11,539	—	—	—	—	—	690,555	702,094
MPs	—	—	—	—	—	—	12	12
% of vote/turnout	1·6	—	—	—	—	—	98·4	67·7
Candidates	3	—	—	—	—	—	40	43
UNITED KINGDOM: Electorate								40,070,925
Votes	11,468,618	10,464,799	5,346,704	1,005,938	113,843	17,426	771,776	29,189,104
MPs	319	277*	13	14	—	—	12	635
% of vote/turnout	39·3	35·9	18·3	3·5	0·4	0·1	2·6	72·8
Candidates	626	623	619	107	90	29	158	2,252

*Including the Speaker.

How the Nation Voted—February 1974

	Lab	C	L	Scot Nat. Pl Cymru	Comm	Others	Total
ENGLAND: Electorate							33,076,587
Votes	9,842,468	10,508,977	5,574,934	—	13,379	201,860	26,141,618
MPs	237	268*	9	—	—	2	516
% of vote/turnout	37·7	40·2	21·3	—	0·0	0·8	79·0
Candidates	516	516	453	—	23	166 inc 54 Nat Front	1,674
SCOTLAND: Electorate							3,656,204
Votes	1,058,159	950,668	229,162	632,622	15,071	1,393	2,887,075
MPs	40	21	3	7	—	—	71
% of vote/turnout	36·7	32·9	7·9	21·9	0·5	0·0	79·0
Candidates	71	71	34	70	15	4	265
WALES: Electorate							1,993,426
Votes	745,547	412,535	255,423	171,374	4,293	4,671	1,593,843
MPs	24	8	2	2	—	—	36
% of vote/turnout	46·8	25·9	16·0	10·8	0·3	0·3	80·0
Candidates	36	36	31	36	6	3	148
NORTHERN IRELAND: Electorate							1,027,256
Votes	15,483	94,301	—	—	—	607,842	717,626
MPs	—	—	—	—	—	12	12
% of vote/turnout	2·2	13·1	—	—	—	84·7	69·9
Candidates	4	7	—	—	—	37	48
UNITED KINGDOM: Electorate							39,753,473
Votes	11,661,657	11,966,481	6,059,519	803,996	32,743	815,766	31,340,162
MPs	301	297*	14	9	—	14	635
% of vote/turnout	37·2	38·2	19·3	2·6	0·1	2·6	78·8
Candidates	627	630	518	106	44	210	2,135

*including the Speaker.
Votes shown as Conservative in Northern Ireland in 1974 relate to Unionist candidates who supported the Sunningdale Agreement.

How Northern Ireland Voted—1974 and 1979

	October 1974				May 1979			
	Total Votes	% Total Votes	MPs	Candi-dates	Total Votes	% Total Votes	MPs	Candi-dates
UUUC	407,778	58·1	10	12	—	—	—	—
Off UU	—	—	—	—	254,578	36·6	5	11
Dem U	—	—	—	—	70,975	10·2	3	5
SDLP	154,193	27·0	1	9	137,110	19·7	1	10
Ind	32,795	4·7	1	1	22,398	3·2	1	1
Alliance	44,644	6·4	—	5	82,892	11·9	—	12
IIP	—	—	—	—	23,086	3·3	—	4
Repub Clubs	21,633	3·1	—	5	12,100	1·7	—	7
UU	—	—	—	—	36,989	5·3	1	1
ULP	—	—	—	—	1,895	0·3	—	1
NI Lab	11,539	1·6	—	3	4,411	0·6	—	3
UPNI	14,417	2·1	—	1	8,021	1·2	—	3
Unionist	11,019	1·6	—	1	—	—	—	—
UUUP	—	—	—	—	39,856	5·7	1	2
Derry Lab	—	—	—	—	639	0·1	—	1
Lab Integ	—	—	—	—	692	0·1	—	1
Reform	—	—	—	—	31	0·0	—	1
IDP	—	—	—	—	216	0·0	—	1
VPP	2,690	0·4	—	1	—	—	—	—
Marx-Len	540	0·1	—	3	—	—	—	—
Lab and TU	846	0·1	—	1	—	—	—	—
Totals	702,094	100·0	12	42	695,889	100·0	12	64
Electorate	1,041,886		Turnout 67·4%		1,027,204		Turnout 67·7%	

The state of the parties 1974-79

	February 1974	October 1974	1979
Labour	301	319	268
Conservative	296	276	339
Liberal	14	13	11
Scottish Nationalist	7	11	2
Plaid Cymru	2	3	2
United Ulster Unionist Coalition	11	10	–
Official Ulster Unionist	–	–	5
Democratic Unionist	–	–	3
Others	3	2	4
The Speaker	1	1	1
Total	635	635	635
Electorate	39,748,531	40,083,286	41,093,264
Poll	31,333,226	29,188,606	31,222,279
Percentage	78·8	72·8	76·0

The Voting Surveyed

by Ivor Crewe

Director, British Election Study, Department of Government, University of Essex.

The 1979 election ended over five years of an occasionally minority and always precarious Labour government by producing a Conservative majority of 71 over Labour and of 44 over all opposition parties combined (excluding the Speaker)—easily sufficient to sustain a Conservative administration through the normal by-election losses and backbench defections of a full parliament. It was only the sixth out of eleven elections since the war to result in a clear-cut parliamentary majority.

The Conservatives won 339 seats, gaining 51 from Labour, three from the Liberals and seven from the Scottish National Party. They lost six to Labour, but of these five had only been Conservative through by-election victories or defections since the previous election. To these six 'gains', Labour added a further five, two from the SNP, two from the breakaway Scottish Labour Party, and one from Plaid Cymru, to end up with 268 MPs. The minor parties, outside Ulster, all lost strength. The Liberals declined from 14 (which included their by-election gain from Labour at Liverpool Edge Hill) to 11; more dramatically, the SNP was reduced from 11 to a rump of two. Plaid Cymru slipped from three to two, and the Scottish Labour Party, whose two MPs had been elected under Labour's banner, was eliminated from Westminster.

The Conservative victory was more impressive than their moderate parliamentary majority at first suggests. Their lead over Labour of 2.19 million votes—7.0 per cent of the poll— was the biggest enjoyed by one major party over the other since 1935; not even the Labour 'landslide' of 1945 or Macmillan's victory in 1959 was based on quite so big a gap in votes between the two parties.

But claims to an overwhelming, as opposed simply to a clear, Conservative mandate need to be qualified in two ways.

First, the Conservative victory owed more to an exceptionally low Labour vote than to an unusually high Conservative one. Labour's share of the poll dropped from 39·3 per cent in October 1974 to 36·9 per cent, its lowest ebb since its débâcle in 1931.

Only one other election since the war has resulted in a smaller number of Labour MPs (258 in 1959) or a smaller total Labour vote (40,000 less in October 1974, but on a lower turnout). This was the third successive election at which Labour's share of the vote failed to reach 40 per cent, thus completing its poorest decade since the 1930s.

On the other hand, the Conservative share of the vote, although up from 35·9 per cent to 43·9 per cent, was well below that obtained at their earlier post-war victories of 1970 (46·4 per cent), 1959 (49·3 per cent), 1955 (49·7 per cent) or 1951 (48·0 per cent). And their share of the electorate, at 33·0 per cent, was similarly below that secured in the 1950s (39·5 per cent in 1951, 37·9 per cent in 1955, 38·5 per cent in 1959) or even 1970 (33·2 per cent). In this sense, the 1979 result spoke more eloquently of the electorate's rejection of Labour than embrace of the Conservatives.

Second, the electoral mandate for the Conservatives was limited by the abnormal regional variations in the result—at least by post-war standards. The majority of seats in both Wales and Scotland went as usual to Labour. And in England the swing to the Conservatives was much stronger south of the Trent: 6·6 per cent in the South East (7·1 per cent in Inner London), 6·1 per cent in the South West (but 7·0 per cent in Devon and Cornwall) and 6·7 per cent in the Midlands; but only 3·9 per cent in the North East, 4·4 per cent in the North West and 4·3 per cent in Yorkshire and Humberside. In Scotland there was actually a small swing (0·7 per cent) to Labour.

This regional pattern, accompanied and partly reinforced by a stronger movement to the Conservatives outside than inside the conurbations (except for London), continues a fifteen year trend, so that Labour has gradually comes to predominate in Scotland and the North, especially the main cities, whereas the Conservatives have steadily tightened their monopoly over the South, in particular the suburbs and countries. As a result, the Conservative majority has been largely built on the prosperous commuting areas, small towns and countryside of the South and Midlands, but has little foundation in the industrial areas of the North and Scotland.

Only one Conservative MP will be sent to Westminster by each of Newcastle (4 seats), Sheffield (6 seats), Manchester (8 seats) and, most strikingly, Glasgow (13 seats); only two will be sent by Leeds (6 seats) and Liverpool (8 seats). A quarter of century ago the picture was very different: when the Conservatives obtained a similar majority in 1955 a third of their MPs—111 out of 334—represented Scotland and the North; in 1979 it was barely a fifth (75 out of 339).

Four types of constituency deviated from the regional swing. First, and in terms of the election result most important, Labour kept the swing down in its own marginals. A uniform 5·2 per cent national swing would have transferred 64 seats from Labour to the Conservatives; the actual number changing hands was only 55 because, although Labour lost 12 seats vulnerable to a swing of over 5·3 per cent, it saved as many as 21 vulnerable to a swing below.

Second, there were abnormally low swings in some constituencies containing substantial immigrant communities (especially of Asians), such as Birmingham Sparkbrook (0·3 per cent), Southall (0·3 per cent) and Brent South (0·5 per cent); indeed, in Bradford West and the Leicester South, both containing very large Asian settlements, there were deviant swings to Labour of 2·9 per cent and 0·8 per cent respectively. Apart from Leicester South, brown and black electors probably played an important part in forstalling the Conservative capture of Battersea South, Dulwich, Walsall South and Leicester East.

The Conservatives, on the other hand, obtained exceptionally high swings in two types of affluent working class areas. They gained against all expectations two 'car workers' seats—Birmingham Northfield (10·2 per cent) and Hornchurch (8·5 per cent)—and secured massive swings in Dagenham (13·4 per cent) and Barking (13·9 per cent), home of the October 1978 Ford strike. And they did unusually well in New Towns such as Harlow (12·9 per cent), Basildon (11·0 per cent) and Herford & Stevenage (8·1 per cent), where they toppled Labour's Secretary of State for Education and Science, Mrs Shirley Williams. Conservative success in both areas was probably owed to the feelings on the part of high wage-earners that living standards were threatened by high taxes, incomes policies, and possibly strikes by their own unions, although confirmation will have to await the analysis of election surveys.

Even within these four categories of seat, however, there were exceptions: large swings to the Conservatives in such immigrant areas as the three Hackney seats (10·3 per cent average) and three Islington seats (9·3 per cent average); below average swings in such New Towns as Hemel Hempstead (3·5 per cent) and Welwyn and Hatfield (3·4 per cent) and the car-worker seat of Oxford (2·2 per cent)—perhaps because all three were marginals. Thus the 1979 election continued the trend towards greater electoral heterogeneity and unpredictability in individual seats.

The increasing fluidity of allegiance amongst British electors in recent years was confirmed by the 1979 election. The overall national swing of 5·2 per cent—defined as the average of the change in the Conservative plus the change in the Labour share of the UK vote—was the highest since the war, exceeding the 3·1 per cent which brought Mr Wilson to office in 1964 and the 4·8 per cent which toppled him in 1970. Swing statistics are a misleading index of volatility, however, as they summarise the net, relative change of support for two parties, but not the gross total of movement to and from all parties (including abstentions), the precise magnitude of which can only be gauged by detailed analysis of survey data. But an indication of volatility can be found in the disaggregation of the change in the parties' overall vote share (excluding Northern Ireland): Conservatives up 8·4 per cent, Labour down 4·6 per cent, Liberals down 2·3 per cent, others down 1·5 per cent, total change 16·8 per cent. With the important exception of February 1974 (total change 25·8 per cent) this total surpasses that of any post-war election.

The growing volatility of the British electorate is also illustrated by some of the extraordinarily large swings in individual constituencies. In the February 1974 election, which itself produced the highest constituency swings since 1945, there were only 10 seats with swings of over 7 per cent, of which five were above 10 per cent. In 1979 13 constituencies recorded double-figure swings—enough to topple such hitherto solidly safe seats as Anglesey (12·5 per cent swing) and Birmingham Northfield (10·2 per cent) and fully 150 swung by over 7 per cent.

The retreat of the minor parties and the return to secure single-party government at first suggests a restoration of the two-party system which prevailed from 1945 to 1970. Closer inspection of the 1979 result leads to a more cautious interpretation. Although the share of the vote and number of MPs secured by the minor parties fell, both remained at their highest level, 1974 excepted, since the war. The slow but accelerating erosion of popular support for the two main parties since the 1950s was reversed—but only slightly. The combined Conservative and Labour share of the vote was 80·8 per cent, somewhat higher than in the two 1974 elections (75·4 per cent and 75·2 per cent respectively) but well below that for any other post-war election, when the average was 92·0 per cent.

A better indicator of support for the two major parties is the proportion of the *electorate* turning out to vote Labour or Conservative, and again the trend is one of very limited reversion. At 61·3 per cent it was a bit higher than in October or February 1974 (56·1 per cent and 60·7 per cent), but substantially lower than for any of the earlier post-war elections, when the average was 72·2 per cent. In this respect the 1979 election result is closer to those of 1974 than to any of the preceding elections.

Liberal fortunes have declined throughout the century in elections following a period of Labour government, and 1979 was no exception. The Liberal vote fell from 5·35 million (18·3 per cent) in October 1974 (having reached 6·06 million the preceding February) to 4·3 million (13·8 per cent) in 1979. Liberal candidates lost more deposits (304 as against 130 last time) and came runner up in fewer constituencies (81 as against 105). Their vote share fell in most of the seats in which they took a strong second place last time and there were no seats in which they came within 5 per cent of winning. They fell back particularly badly in two traditional areas of strength: the 'far West' of Devon and Cornwall (as opposed to the 'mid West' of Gloucestershire, Wiltshire, Somerset and Hampshire where they held on better) and such ex-suburban seats as Orpington, Sutton and Cheam, Cheadle and Hazel Grove.

Yet the Liberal decline was less serious, and their finishing position much stronger, than in 1970, the last occasion of a reverse under a Labour Government. In 1970 they lost six of their 12 MPs; this time they lost only three out of 14; in 1970 there were only 17 constituencies in which the Liberal vote topped 30 per cent; this time there was 32. In 1970 the 332 Liberal candidates obtained an average of vote of 14·2 per cent; in 1979 the 576 Liberal candidates—many of them inevitably competing on much stonier ground—got an average of 15·2 per cent, better than in any election between 1945 and 1970. Thus despite their reverses, the Liberals are in a better position from which to make a comeback than at any time since the war.

Much the same can be said of the Scottish Nationalists. They lost 10 of their 12 MPs, and their share of the Scottish vote fell from 30·4 per cent to 17·3 per cent. At the last election they lost no deposits and took second place in 42 of Scotland's 71 constituencies; this time they lost 29 deposits and only won second place in four constituencies they had not previously held. They were clearly demoted from second to third party in Scotland. Nonetheless, a vote of 504,000 and a 17·3 per cent share of the poll represents a substantial advance on the 307,000 votes and 11·4 per cent share of the poll obtained in 1970, the election which immediately preceded their breakthrough of 1973-74.

A similar story of retreat rather than surrender could not be told, however, of Plaid Cymru. The massive anti-devolution vote in the March referendum was reflected in Plaid Cymru's poor showing throughout Wales, save for their two northern seats of Merioneth and Caernarvon where their majorities were increased. Plaid's 8·1 per cent share of the Welsh vote was the lowest since they started contesting all Welsh constituencies in 1970. They failed to take second place anywhere (except in the seat lost by their leader, Carmarthen) and forfeited all but seven of their deposits. Indeed, Plaid Cymru appear to have made no real progress—apart from securing representation at Westminster—over the last twenty years: in 1959 the average vote share won by their twenty candidates (9·4 per cent) was actually higher than that obtained (8·1 per cent) in this election.

The election in Wales was marked by the spectacular (but continuing) advance of the Conservatives. In their best performance since 1874 they increased their share of the Welsh vote by 8·3 per cent to 32·2 per cent, capturing three additional seats (Montgomery from the Liberals, Brecon and Radnor and Anglesey from Labour) to bring their parliamentary strength to 11, the highest since 1874. Although Labour pulled back one seat (Carmarthen) their total of 22 seats and 46·9 per cent of the vote was the lowest since 1935.

The Conservative success appears to have been more at the expense of the Liberals and Plaid Cymru, whose vote shares fell by 4·9 per cent and 2·7 per cent respectively, than of Labour. Thus the Conservative advance was most dramatic in areas of traditional Liberal and Plaid Cymru strength such as rural and largely Welsh-speaking Wales. The Conservatives now hold five of the nine most agricultural constituencies on a 37·0 per cent vote—a sea change from 1966 when they held only one on a 27·0 per cent share (and Labour held seven). Class appears to have replaced chapel and language as the main source of partisan allegiance in rural Wales.

In Northern Ireland the division of both votes and seats between the two communities remained unaltered (10 Protestant, 2 Catholic), but there were changes in the combination of forces representing the Unionist cause. The Rev. Paisley's militantly loyalist Democratic Unionist Party captured two Belfast seats from the more moderate official Unionists to bring their own Westminster strength up to three; moreover in Parliament the two official Unionists unopposed by the Democratic Unionists can normally be counted upon to vote with them.

There were also signs of a shift to extremism within the Catholic community: the independent Republican and IRA sympathiser, Frank Maguire, easily fended off a challenge from the SDLP in Fermanagh and South Tyrone, and in predominantly Catholic Mid Ulster the extreme nationalist IIP took over a third (37 per cent) of the Catholic vote, throwing victory to the official Unionist. The non-sectarian Alliance Party still failed to win a single Westminster seat, but came within a thousand votes of doing so, nearer than ever before, in Belfast East.

A record number of candidates (2,576) and parties (109) contested the election. All the fringe parties did badly. The National Front did least poorly, securing a record number of votes (191,706) but only by fielding more candidates than ever before (303). Wherever they stood for a second time their support dropped. They failed to save a single deposit or even take third place in any constituency contested by the three main parties. Their best results, as in October 1974, were in Mosley's pre-war stamping ground of London's East End: Hackney South and Shoreditch (7·6 per cent), Newham South (6·2 per cent) and Tower Hamlets, Bethnal Green and Bow (6·1 per cent). But even here their support was under half that won in the GLC elections two years earlier. Outside London they failed to win more than 4 per cent, even in such formerly promising territory as Leicester or the West Midlands.

The 38 Communists candidates (9 more than last time) all lost their deposits, averaging 0·9 per cent of the vote where they stood. Their best result was at Rhondda (3·6 per cent). Of the 12 seats in which they competed against the National Front, they came behind in 10. Candidates yet further to the left did worse still. The Workers Revolutionary Party candidates always came bottom of the poll (unless an independent stood) never winning more than a few hundred votes. But this did not necessarily prevent them from having an impact on the constituency results: in Paddington, for example, the Conservative toppled the left-wing Labour incumbent by a majority (106 votes) that was smaller than the WRP vote (117).

The newest minor party, Ecology, averaged 1·2 per cent in the 54 seats it contested and lost all its deposits. Its two best performances were in the green and rural Worcestershire South (2·8 per cent) and the grey and urban St. Marylebone (2·8 per cent).

Independents and party rebels generally fared no better than the fringe parties. But Jim Sillars, the Labour backbencher who defected to Scottish Labour, only lost in his home constituency of South Ayrshire to the official Labour candidate by 1,521 votes; and Eddie Milne, standing again as an Independent Labour candidate in Blyth, the constituency he represented as official Labour MP until February 1974, took second place with 28·8 per cent of the vote. Two Democratic Labour candidates splintered enough of the Labour vote in Lincoln (1,743 votes, 4·1 per cent of the poll) and at Brigg and Scunthorpe (2,042 votes, 2·8 per cent of the poll) to allow the Conservatives to gain both seats with majorities of 602 and 486 respectively.

At 76·0 per cent the turnout was nominally higher than in October 1974 (72·8 per cent) or than the elections of 1966 and 1970. But this does not mean that public interest in the 1979 election was unusually strong. The record number of candidates and parties will have mobilised an extra percentage or two of erstwhile abstainers; more important, the election was fought on a younger and therefore more accurate register than last time. Adjusting the 1979 turnout for the age of the register* raises it to 78·6 per cent, almost identical to adjusted turnout in both 1974 elections (79·1 per cent and 78·7 per cent respectively), but still well below that for the period 1950-64 when the average was 84·8 per cent. The pattern of lower participation in Britain's more recent elections has therefore been maintained, although not accentuated.

Constituency turnout varied markedly, along the usual lines: higher in marginal

---

*The formula is: +3·4 per cent (not registered) −1·0 per cent (registered twice) −.15m per cent (effects of deaths) −0·67m per cent (effect of removals) where m=months from the date of the register's compilation.

than safe seats (79 per cent as against 75 per cent), greater in the rural areas despite the longer distances to the polling booths, than the inner city; slightly more pronounced in the South West (79·3 per cent) and Wales (79·4 per cent) than the other regions. The highest recorded turnouts were in constituencies which combined two or three of these features: Fermanagh and South Tyrone (87·1 per cent), Kingswood (86·2 per cent) and North Cornwall (86·1 per cent). Similarly, the lowest were in the inner-London safe Labour seats of Stepney and Poplar (53·3 per cent), City of London and Westminister South (55·1 per cent) and Newham North West (55·4 per cent), although in other inner areas of London, notably Lambeth, Islington and Hackney, there were exceptionally large turnout increases compared with October 1974.

Changes in turnout bore no obvious relationship to Conservative or Labour fortunes and, as usual, failed to support the conventional wisdom that high or increasing turnout disproportionately helped Labour. In the twenty constituencies with the largest turnout increases, the average swing was identical to the national mean of 5·2 per cent. These 20 constituencies produced some exceptionally heavy swings to the Conservatives, such as 10·5 per cent in Lambeth Vauxhall (turnout up 9·7 per cent), 10·7 per cent Islington Central (turnout up 8·3 per cent) and 9·7 per cent in Hackney North (turnout up 8·1 per cent), but also some unusually small ones as in the Manchester constituencies of Central (0·5 per cent), Ardwick (0·1 per cent) and Moss Side (− 0·3 per cent).

In certain types of seat there was clear evidence of 'tactical' voting—that is, voting for an alternative to the party one most prefers in order to punish the party one least prefers. Glaring examples occurred where the real contest was between Conservative and Liberal, and supporters of the also-ran Labour candidate (or the SNP candidate in Scotland) switched to the Liberal in order to keep or turn out the Conservative. Thus although the average decline in Labour's vote share in England was 3·4 per cent, it slumped by 6·7 per cent in the eight October 1974 Liberal seats, and by 6·1 per cent in the sixteen 'near misses' where the Liberal had come within 10 per cent of the winning Conservative.

The impact of such tactical voting on Liberal fortunes depended on the number of Labour voters available to vote tactically. As a general rule the larger the Labour rump left from October 1974 the better the Liberal did. Thus David Penhaligon, the Liberal MP for Truro, increased his majority from 464 to 8,708 by raiding the still substantial enclave of Labour supporters (20·5 per cent in October 1974), whereas John Pardoe, Liberal MP for the neighbouring North Cornwall, where the Labour vote had already been squeezed dry at 6·4 per cent, saw his majority of 3,856 easily overturned. Tactical voting allowed the Liberals to retain the Isle of Wight (Labour vote down from 13·0 per cent to a tiny 4·0 per cent), the Isle of Ely (down from 21·6 per cent to 12·5 per cent) and Berwick-upon-Tweed (down from 14 per cent to 7·3 per cent)—although in this last case there was also a swing from Conservative to Liberal.

A similar pattern of tactical voting also occurred in the Liberals' October 1974 'near misses': where the Labour vote had stayed above 20 per cent it slumped this time (by 8·1 per cent on average) allowing the Liberal vote to remain steady (+ 0·5 per cent); but where the Labour vote had already been depressed to below 20 per cent, it only fell by 4·6 per cent, and so the Liberal vote also dropped—by 5·6 per cent.

The electoral system, as usual, unfairly penalised the minor parties to the benefit of the Conservatives and, even more, Labour. The Conservatives won 53 per cent of the seats on 44 per cent of the vote; Labour 42 per cent of the seats on 37 per cent of the vote. In Scotland, more anomalously, Labour secure three-fifths of the seats with only two-fifths of the vote. Of the minor parties it was again the Liberals who, by spreading their support evenly but thinly, were hardest hit, winning 14 per cent of the vote but only 2 per cent of the seats. It took 391,393 votes to elect a Liberal, as against 42,935 a Labour candidate and 40,406 a Conservative.

In Scotland the SNP received particularly rough justice, winning only two of the twelve seats to which their 17·3 per cent of the vote 'entitled' them. But Plaid Cymru's two seats in Wales and the Catholic community's two MPs in Northern Ireland were more or less in due proportion to their vote.

Exact proportional representation, assuming identical votes had been cast, would have reduced the Conservatives to 279 (from the 339 they actually won) and Labour to 234 (from 268). The number of Liberal MPs would have increased eight-fold, from 11 to 88, and 'other party' representation would have doubled from 17 to 34—including 4 MPs for the National Front. Deprived of an overall majority, the Conservatives would have been forced to form a coalition with the Liberals as junior but weighty partners—weighty enough to be able to switch their support to Labour and form an alternative coalition majority.

In another sense, however, the electoral system worked against the Conservatives. Despite notching up its biggest vote lead over Labour since 1935, the Conservative party's overall parliamentary majority (43) fell below that of both 1955 (59) and 1959 (99). The larger number of minor party MPs elected in 1979 (27) than in 1955 (7) or 1959 (8) is part of the explanation—but only a small part. The main reason rests with the anti-Conservative bias of the 1979 constituency boundaries.

The constituency boundaries were last drawn up in the late 1960s. Since then movements of population from inner city to outer suburb, New Town or country have created enormous variations in constituency sizes, largely at the Conservatives' expense. For example, the five counties with the largest average constituency sizes in 1979—Suffolk, Buckinghamshire, Worcestershire, Cambridgeshire and Berkshire— are all strong Consrvative territory, whereas four of the five counties (all metropolitan) with the smallest average constituency sizes—Glasgow, Manchester, Edinburgh, Liverpool and Monmouth—are overwhelmingly Labour areas.

Excluding Northern Ireland, the average constituency size is 65,000, but by 1979 almost a third deviated by plus or minus 15,000. Of the 95 seats with electorates above 80,000—mainly semi-rural areas in the South and Midlands undergoing rapid suburbanisation—76 went Conservative, 18 Labour and one Liberal. But of the 92 seats with electorates below 50,000, 59 went Labour, 27 Conservative and six to the Nationalists or Liberals. Had the Boundary Commissioners added and subtracted constituencies such that their average size was 65,000 within *every* county in 1979, the Conservatives could have expected an additional 19 seats at Labour's expense.

Party Gains and Losses

	Gains	Losses
Conservative	61	6
Labour	11	51
Liberal	—	3
Scottish National Party	—	9
Plaid Cymru	—	1
Democratic Unionist .	2	—
Official Ulster Unionist	—	2

CONSERVATIVE GAINS FROM LABOUR

	C	Lab	L	Others	Maj	Swing
	%	%	%	%	%	
Aldridge-Brownhills	50·3	39·4	10·3	—	10·9	+ 8·0
1974	38·4	43·5	17·7	0·4	5·1	− 2·2
Anglesey	39·0	31·7	9·0	20·3	7·3	+12·5
1974	23·8	41·6	15·5	19·1	17·8	− 0·7
Basildon	46·9	40·5	11·5	1·1	6·4	+11·0
1974	32·2	47·9	19·0	0·9	15·7	− 0·7
Bebington and Ellesmere Port	43·9	43·2	12·9	—	0·7	+ 5·1
1974	37·9	47·5	14·6	—	9·6	− 1·7
Belper	44·4	42·9	12·0	0·8	1·5	+ 5·6
1974	37·3	47·1	15·5	—	9·8	− 3·2
Birmingham Northfield	45·4	45·1	8·1	1·4	0·3	+10·2
1974	32·0	52·1	14·9	1·0	20·1	− 2·5
Birmingham Selly Oak	48·7	38·6	11·4	1·2	10·1	+ 5·4
1974	40·3	41·1	18·6	—	0·8	− 3·5
Birmingham Yardley	47·6	44·8	5·9	1·8	2·8	+ 6·2
1974	38·6	48·3	10·5	2·7	9·7	− 2·8
Brecon and Radnor	47·2	40·9	9·7	2·1	6·3	+ 6·5
1974	35·3	42·1	17·4	5·2	6·8	− 0·9
Brigg and Scunthorpe	43·4	42·7	10·8	3·0	0·7	+ 5·6
1974	34·9	45·5	19·6	—	10·6	− 3·1
Brighouse and Spenborough	44·7	41·4	13·9	—	3·3	+ 3·8
1974	39·6	43·9	16·5	—	4·3	− 0·8
Bristol North-West	48·6	39·8	11·0	0·6	8·8	+ 5·0
1974	40·9	42·1	16·9	—	1·2	− 1·2
Chorley	46·8	43·0	9·6	0·6	3·8	+ 4·1
1974	39·7	44·1	15·9	0·3	4·1	− 1·9
Cities of London and Westminster Paddington	45·5	45·2	7·9	1·4	0·3	+ 3·3
1974	41·2	47·6	10·4	0·9	6·4	− 2·2
Coventry South-West	49·3	39·3	10·4	1·0	10·0	+ 6·9
1974	39·2	43·1	15·9	1·8	3·9	− 1·5
Dartford	45·9	42·9	9·5	1·7	3·0	+ 7·7
1974	35·1	47·6	15·1	2·1	12·5	− 2·4
Dudley, West	51·0	49·0	—	—	2·0	+ 8·5
1974	36·0	51·1	12·9	—	15·1	− 3·7
Ealing, North	46·0	43·6	8·6	1·8	2·4	+ 3·8
1974	39·7	45·0	15·3	—	5·3	− 0·6
Enfield, North	48·1	41·3	9·0	1·6	6·8	+ 8·4
1974	33·6	43·7	19·9	2·8	10·1	− 1·9
Gloucestershire, West	47·9	40·8	10·8	0·5	7·1	+ 3·9
1974	40·9	41·7	17·4	—	0·8	+ 1·0
Gravesend	52·0	39·0	8·2	0·8	13·0	+ 8·2
1974	39·7	43·1	14·9	2·2	3·4	− 0·6
Hammersmith, Fulham	46·7	43·2	8·9	1·2	3·5	+ 8·2
1974	37·0	49·9	11·1	2·1	12·9	− 2·6
Havering, Hornchurch	44·9	43·3	9·8	2·1	1·6	+ 8·5
1974	33·1	48·5	16·6	1·8	15·4	− 1·3
Hemel Hempstead	48·7	42·3	8·1	0·8	6·4	+ 3·5
1974	42·0	42·7	15·3	—	0·7	− 0·5
Hertford and Stevenage	45·1	43·2	10·9	0·8	1·9	+ 8·1
1974	32·7	47·1	18·2	2·0	14·4	− 1·2
Huddersfield, West	44·2	40·6	14·9	0·2	3·6	+ 3·5
1974	38·0	41·4	18·4	2·2	3·4	− 1·0
Kingswood	45·4	44·8	9·3	0·5	0·6	+ 3·0
1974	38·5	44·0	17·5	—	5·5	− 1·1
Lichfield and Tamworth	50·3	40·1	9·0	0·6	10·2	+ 5·3
1974	42·1	42·6	15·3	—	0·5	− 1·5
Lincoln	41·8	40·4	13·3	4·6	1·4	+ 5·1
1974	28·3	37·1	—	34·6	2·5	− 4·2
Liverpool, Garston	48·1	43·3	8·4	0·2	4·8	+ 5·2
1974	42·1	47·8	10·1	—	5·7	− 2·3
Loughborough	48·0	39·6	10·7	1·8	8·4	+ 6·3
1974	37·2	41·5	18·9	2·4	4·3	− 1·6
Luton, East	43·7	41·6	13·0	1·6	2·1	+ 5·7
1974	36·1	45·5	17·7	0·8	9·4	− 3·1
Luton, West	44·1	43·6	10·9	1·5	0·5	+ 7·6
1974	32·0	46·7	21·3	—	14·7	− 2·1
Meriden	48·8	43·3	6·5	1·4	5·5	+ 8·9
1974	35·1	47·4	17·5	—	12·3	− 3·3
Nelson and Colne	45·0	43·9	11·1	—	1·1	+ 1·4
1974	43·0	44·7	12·4	—	1·7	− 1·1
Newark	45·8	42·9	11·2	—	2·9	+ 6·6
1974	37·5	47·9	14·6	—	10·4	− 1·4
Northampton, North	48·2	36·1	14·7	1·0	12·1	+ 8·1
1974	39·7	43·8	16·5	—	4·1	− 0·8
Oxford	45·3	42·8	10·3	1·6	2·5	+ 2·2
1974	40·8	42·7	15·3	1·1	1·9	− 1·7
Peterborough	48·8	39·8	10·0	1·4	9·0	+ 6·3
1974	40·7	44·4	14·9	—	3·7	− 1·9
Portsmouth, North	48·6	44·4	6·2	0·8	4·2	+ 3·4
1974	43·3	45·9	9·8	1·0	2·6	− 1·0
Preston, North	46·3	46·2	6·7	0·8	0·1	+ 2·3
1974	41·3	45·8	12·6	0·4	4·5	− 2·0
Redbridge, Ilford, South	46·8	42·7	8·9	1·5	4·1	+ 4·3
1974	40·2	44·7	14·6	0·4	4·5	− 0·9
Rochester and Chatham	47·5	42·8	9·0	0·7	4·7	+ 4·4
1974	39·3	43·4	15·4	2·0	4·1	− 2·8
Rossendale	48·0	43·6	8·3	—	4·4	+ 2·4
1974	39·1	39·6	21·3	—	0·5	− 1·2
Rugby	47·3	42·0	9·6	1·1	5·3	+ 8·1
1974	37·3	48·2	14·2	0·3	10·9	+ 0·6
Southampton, Test	46·4	42·7	10·9	—	3·7	+ 2·3
1974	41·2	42·2	16·6	—	1·0	− 1·7
Sowerby	42·2	39·3	18·5	—	2·9	+ 2·3
1974	37·1	38·8	23·7	0·4	1·7	− 0·7
Wandsworth, Putney	46·8	41·5	10·3	1·4	5·3	+ 5·5
1974	39·5	45·3	15·0	0·3	5·8	− 1·6
Watford	47·6	40·3	11·2	0·9	7·3	+ 8·2
1974	35·1	44·3	19·0	1·5	9·2	− 1·6
Welwyn and Hatfield	48·6	42·8	7·9	0·8	5·8	+ 3·4
1974	41·8	42·8	15·4	—	1·0	− 1·8
Wrekin, The	45·6	44·2	10·2	—	1·4	+ 6·1
1974	37·8	48·7	13·5	—	10·9	− 0·6

CONSERVATIVE GAINS FROM SCOT NAT

	C	Lab	L	SNP	Others	Maj
	%	%	%	%	%	%
Aberdeenshire, East	42·8	15·8	—	41·4	—	1·4
1974	35·5	9·4	6·6	48·5	—	13·0
Angus, South	43·6	10·1	4·8	41·5	—	2·1
1974	39·1	10·5	6·5	43·8	—	4·7
Argyll	36·8	15·9	15·4	31·8	—	5·0
1974	36·7	13·6	—	49·7	—	13·0
Banffshire	44·6	14·2	—	41·2	—	3·4
1974	37·9	7·3	8·9	45·9	—	8·0

	C	Lab	L	SNP	Others	Maj
Galloway	45·8	8·5	8·5	37·1	—	8·7
1974	40·2	9·0	10·5	40·3	—	0·1
Moray and Nairn	40·1	8·7	12·3	38·9	—	1·2
1974	40·0	9·7	9·1	41·2	—	1·2
Perth and East Perthshire	41·9	13·4	9·2	35·5	—	6·4
1974	38·9	13·6	6·7	40·8	—	1·9

CONSERVATIVE GAINS FROM LIBERAL

	C	Lab	L	Others	Maj
	%	%	%	%	%
Cornwall, North	51·7	3·2	43·7	1·4	8·0
1974	42·0	6·4	51·3	0·4	9·3
Devon, North	50·1	11·2	36·7	1·9	13·4
1974	36·7	14·3	48·1	1·0	11·4
Montgomeryshire	40·3	16·3	34·9	8·5	5·4
1974	28·4	19·2	43·1	9·3	14·7

LABOUR GAINS FROM CONSERVATIVE

	C	Lab	L	Others	Maj
	%	%	%	%	%
Ashfield	40·4	52·8	6·2	0·6	12·4
April, 1977	43·1	42·5	9·6	4·8	0·6
1974	22·3	63·4	14·3	—	41·1
Birmingham, Stechford	44·6	48·4	5·4	1·6	3·8
February, 1977	43·4	38·0	8·0	10·6	5·4
1974	27·8	57·6	14·6	—	29·8
Glasgow, Cathcart	41·8	45·9	5·3	6·9	4·1
1974	42·7	38·1	2·8	16·5	4·6
Walsall, North	39·8	50·9	7·2	2·1	11·1
November, 1976	43·3	31·6	3·2	21·8	11·7
1974	26·1	59·5	13·4	1·0	33·4
Workington	40·7	53·2	6·1	—	12·5
November, 1976	48·2	45·6	6·2	—	2·6
1974	32·3	56·0	11·7	—	23·7

Newham, North-East, was a Labour gain from Conservative because during the preceding Parliament the sitting MP (Reginald Prentice) left the Labour Party and joined the Conservatives. Similarly, Ayrshire, South, and Paisley were Labour gains because during the preceding Parliament the sitting MPs left the Labour Party to form the Scottish Labour Party.

LABOUR GAIN FROM PL CYMRU

	C	Lab	L	Pl C	Others	Maj
	%	%	%	%	%	%
Carmarthen	23·6	35·8	8·0	32·0	0·5	3·8
1974	5·7	38·1	10·4	45·1	0·7	7·0

LABOUR GAINS FROM SCOT. NAT.

	C	Lab	L	SNP	Others	Maj
	%	%	%	%	%	%
Dunbartonshire, East	34·1	37·9	7·5	20·6	—	3·8
1974	31·2	30·3	7·3	31·2	—	0·0
Stirlingshire East and Clackmannan	18·0	41·9	—	40·1	—	1·8
1974	10·5	36·4	2·5	50·7	—	14·3

In Northern Ireland the Democratic Unionist Party gained Belfast, East, and Belfast, North, from the Official Unionist Party.

Liberal Party Spokesmen

Mr David Steel, the Liberal leader, announced on May 10, 1979, the tasks assigned to his colleagues as spokesmen for the party. These are:

Education and Chief Whip in the Commons—Mr Alan Beith; Foreign and Commonwealth—Mr Jo Grimond; Treasury—Mr Richard Wainwright; Industry and employment—Mr Cyril Smith; Defence and Northern Ireland—Mr Stephen Ross; Scotland—Mr Russell Johnston; Agriculture and Wales—Mr Geraint Howells; Energy and Transport—Mr David Penhaligon; Environment (housing and local government)—Mr David Alton; Broadcasting, arts and sports—Mr Clement Freud.

Leader of Liberal peers—Lord Byers. Social Services—Lord Banks. Trade, prices and consumer protection—Lady Seear. Community relations—Lord Avebury. Home Office, law and chief whip in the Lords—Lord Wigoder. Health—Lord Winstanley.

Other tasks for Commons spokesmen are: Fishing—Mr Grimond and Mr Beith; Small business and Self-employed—Mr Howells; Social Services—Mr Penhaligon; Civil aviation—Mr Ross; Foreign and Commonwealth—Lord Gladwyn; Scotland—Lord Mackie; Housing and Local Government—Lord Evans.

LARGE MAJORITIES

The biggest majority was again at Antrim, South, where Mr James Molyneaux, the Official Unionist MP, had a majority of 38,868. In October, 1974, his majority was 38,432. The biggest majority in England, Scotland, and Wales was in South Fylde where Mr Edward Gardner retained the seat for the Conservatives with a majority of 32,247. At Rother Valley, where in October, 1974, Mr Peter Hardy's Labour majority of 32,777 was the largest in England, the majority fell to 26,002. At Hemsworth Mr Alec Woodall (Labour) had a majority of 26,043, compared with 31,572 in October, 1974.

The Narrowest Margins

Fifteen MPs were elected with a majority of under 1·0 per cent—seven Conservatives, six Labour, one Liberal, and one Democratic Unionist. The smallest majority—0·1 per cent (29 votes) – was that of Mr R. J. Atkins, the Conservative, at Preston, North. Mr Frank White, the Labour victor at Bury and Radcliffe, also had a majority of 0·1 per cent (38 votes).

Mr Robert Cryer retained Keighley for Labour with a 0·2 per cent majority (78 votes). In Northern Ireland, Mr Peter Robinson won Belfast, East, for the Democratic Unionists with a 0·2 per cent majority (64 votes). The smallest Liberal majority was that of Mr Stephen Ross who retained the Isle of Wight with a 0·5 per cent majority (352 votes). Mr Samuel Silkin, the former Attorney General, held Southwark, Dulwich for Labour by only 122 votes.

Of the marginal seats (2,000 votes and under) listed in *The Times Guide to the House of Commons* after the October, 1974, election, Labour lost 19 out of 30 seats, the Conservatives only one (Glasgow, Cathcart), the Liberals one (Truro) and the Scottish National Party lost all six.

Marginal seats with majorities of 5 per cent and less are as follows:

CONSERVATIVE

	%	Votes
Atkins, R. J., *Preston, North* ..	0·1	29
Wheeler, J., *Cities of London and Westminster, Paddington*	0·3	106
Cadbury, J. B. L., *Birmingham Northfield*	0·3	204
Carlisle, J., *Luton, West*	0·5	246
Aspinwall, J. H., *Kingswood* ..	0·6	303
Porter, B., *Bebington and Ellesmere Port*	0·7	486
Brown, M., *Brigg and Scunthorpe*	0·7	486
Lee, J., *Nelson and Colne*	1·1	436
Pollock, A., *Moray and Nairn* .	1·2	420
McQuarrie, A., *Aberdeenshire, East*	1·4	558
Carlisle, K., *Lincoln*	1·4	602
Hawksley, W., *Wrekin, The* ...	1·4	965
Sproat, I. M., *Aberdeen, South*	1·5	772
Faith, Mrs S., *Belper*	1·5	882
Squire, R. C., *Havering, Hornchurch*	1·6	769
Wells, P., *Hertford and Stevenage*	1·9	1,296
Blackburn, J. G., *Dudley, West*	2·0	1,139
Bright, J. F. J., *Luton, East* ...	2·1	847
Fraser, P., *Angus, South*	2·1	963
Greenway, H., *Ealing, North* ..	2·4	1,480
Patten, J., *Oxford*	2·5	1,497
Rifkind, M. L., *Edinburgh, Pentlands*	2·7	1,198
Hill, S. J., *Southampton, Test* ..	2·7	2,123
Bevan, D. G., *Birmingham, Yardley*	2·8	1,164
Thompson, D., *Sowerby*	2·9	1,180
Alexander, R., *Newark*	2·9	1,751
Dunn, R., *Dartford*	3·0	1,392
Waller, G. P. A., *Brighouse and Spenborough*	3·3	1,734
Myles, D. J., *Banffshire*	3·4	799
Stevens, M., *Hammersmith, Fulham*	3·5	1,499
Dickens, G., *Huddersfield, West*	3·6	1,508
Dover, D., *Chorley*	3·8	2,579
Thorne, N. G., *Redbridge, Ilford, South*	4·1	1,688
Griffiths, P., *Portsmouth, North*	4·2	2.311
Trippier, D. A., *Rossendale* ...	4·4	1,873
Fenner, Mrs. P. E., *Rochester and Chatham*	4·7	2,688
Thornton, G. M., *Liverpool, Garston*	4·8	2,787
Mackay, J. J., *Argyll*	5·0	1,646

LABOUR

	%	Votes
White, F. R., *Bury and Radcliffe*	0·1	38
Cryer, G. R., *Keighley*	0·2	78
Silkin, S. C., *Southwark, Dulwich*	0·3	122
Whitehead, P., *Derby, North* ..	0·4	214
Bennett, A. F., *Stockport, North*	0·8	333
Williams, A. J., *Swansea, West* .	0·8	401
Dubs, A., *Wandsworth, Battersea, South*	1·1	332
Kilroy-Silk, R., *Ormskirk*	1·1	858
Rooker, J. W., *Birmingham, Perry Barr*	1·3	491
Taylor, Mrs. W. A., *Bolton, West*	1·5	600
Thorne, S. G., *Preston, South* .	1·5	621
Silverman, J., *Birmingham, Erdington*	1·6	680
O'Neill, M. J., *Stirlingshire, East and Clackmannan*	1·8	984
Callaghan, J., *Middleton and Prestwich*	1·8	1,098
Fletcher, E. J., *Darlington*	2·1	1,052
Lyon, A. W., *York*	2·1	1,250
Homewood, W. D., *Kettering* ..	2·1	1,478
Price, C., *Lewisham, West*	2·3	1,050
Summerskill, Dr Shirley, *Halifax*	2·5	1,234
Newens, A. S., *Harlow*	2·6	1,392
Mitchell, R. C., *Southampton, Itchen*	2·7	1,602
Lestor, Miss J., *Eton and Slough*	2·8	1,340
Owen, Dr D. A. L., *Plymouth, Devonport*	2·9	1,001
McNally, T., *Stockport, South* .	3·0	1,125
Moyle, R. D., *Lewisham, East* .	3·2	1,593
Garrett, J. L., *Norwich, South* .	3·3	1,198
Robertson, J. D. H., *Berwick and East Lothian*	3·3	1,673
Wedgwood Benn, A. N., *Bristol, South-East*	3·5	1,890
George, B. T., *Walsall, South* .	3·6	1,588
Barnett, J., *Heywood and Royton*	3·6	2,287
Foulkes, G., *Ayrshire, South* ..	3·8	1,521
Davis, T., *Birmingham, Stechford*	3·8	1,649
Thomas, Dr. R. G., *Carmarthen*	3·8	1,978
Marshall, J., *Leicester, South* ..	3·8	1,998
Hogg, N., *Dunbartonshire, East*	3·8	2,324
Young, D. W., *Bolton, East* ...	4·0	1,852
Maxton, J. A., *Glasgow, Cathcart*	4·1	1,600
English, M., *Nottingham, West* .	4·4	2,500
Graham, T. E., *Enfield, Edmonton*	4·5	1,900
Snape, P. C., *West Bromwich, East*	4·8	1,971

LIBERAL

	%	Votes
Ross, S. S., *Isle of Wight*	0·5	352
Wainwright, R. S., *Colne Valley*	4·5	2,352

SCOTTISH NATIONAL

	%	Votes
Wilson, R. G., *Dundee, East*	5·0	2,519

DEMOCRATIC UNIONIST

	%	Votes
Robinson, P., *Belfast, East*	0·2	64
McQuade, J., *Belfast, North* ...	2·3	995

Regional, metropolitan and city voting patterns

The Times has drawn up the following regional and metropolitan breakdown of England, largely based on the Central Office of Information's groupings, in order to enable voting comparisons to be made between the regions and between metropolitan areas.

The county boundaries were changed in 1974 and the new counties and the remaining old ones do not cut across the regional boundaries chosen. A few parliamentary seats do cut across and these have been given to the regions to which they most naturally belong.

England has been divided into 10 regions as follows:

Region	No seats	Counties
London	92	Greater London
South Eastern	40	Kent, Surrey, East Sussex, West Sussex.
Southern and Wessex	42	Berkshire, Buckinghamshire, Dorset, Hampshire, Isle of Wight, Oxfordshire, Wiltshire.
South Western	34	Avon, Cornwall, Devon, Gloucestershire, Somerset.
Eastern	45	Bedfordshire, Cambridgeshire, Essex, Hertfordshire, Norfolk, Suffolk
East Midland	40	Derbyshire, Leicestershire, Lincolnshire, Northamptonshire, Nottinghamshire.
Midland	56	Herefordshire and Worcestershire, Salop, Staffordshire, Warwickshire, West Midlands.
North Western	76	Cheshire, Greater Manchester, Lancashire, Merseyside.
Yorkshire and Humberside	54	Humberside, North Yorkshire, South Yorkshire, West Yorkshire
Northern	37	Cleveland, Cumbria, Durham, Northumberland, Tyne and Wear.

Total 516

In addition there is: Wales 36; Scotland 71; Northern Ireland 12. Total number of seats 635.

The constituencies in the 10 Regions are as follows:

London (92 seats) Barking Barking, Barking Dagenham, Barnet Chipping Barnet, Barnet Finchley, Barnet Hendon North, Barnet Hendon South, Bexley Bexleyheath, Bexley Erith and Crayford, Bexley Sidcup, Brent East, Brent North, Brent South, Bromley Beckenham, Bromley Chiselhurst, Bromley Orpington, Bromley Ravensbourne, Camden Hampstead, Camden Holborn & St. Pancras South, Camden St. Pancras North, Cities of London and Westminster City of London & Westminster South, Cities of London and Westminster Paddington, Cities of London and Westminster St. Marylebone, Croydon Central, Croydon North East, Croydon North West, Croydon South, Ealing Acton, Ealing North, Ealing Southall.

Enfield Edmonton, Enfield North, Enfield Southgate, Greenwich Greenwich, Greenwich Woolwich East, Greenwich Woolwich West, Hackney Central, Hackney North & Stoke Newington, Hackney South & Shoreditch, Hammersmith Fulham, Hammersmith North, Haringey Hornsey, Haringey Tottenham, Haringey Wood Green, Harrow Central, Harrow East, Harrow West, Havering Hornchurch, Havering Romford, Havering Upminster.

Hillingdon Hayes & Harlington, Hillingdon Ruislip—Northwood, Hillingdon Uxbridge, Hounslow Brentford & Isleworth, Hounslow Feltham and Heston, Islington Central, Islington North, Islington South and Finsbury, Kensington & Chelsea Chelsea, Kensington & Chelsea Kensington, Kingston upon Thames Kingston, Kingston upon Thames Surbiton.

Lambeth Central, Lambeth Norwood, Lambeth Streatham, Lambeth Vauxhall, Lewisham Deptford, Lewisham East, Lewisham West, Merton Mitcham and Morden, Merton Wimbledon, Newham North East, Newham North West, Newham South, Redbridge Ilford North, Redbridge Ilford South, Redbridge Wanstead and Woodford, Richmond upon Thames Richmond, Richmond upon Thames Twickenham, Southwark Bermondsey, Southwark Dulwich, Southwark Peckham, Sutton Sutton & Cheam, Sutton Carshalton, Tower Hamlets Bethnal Green and Bow, Tower Hamlets Stepney and Poplar, Waltham Forest Chingford, Waltham Forest Leyton, Waltham Forest Walthamstow, Wandsworth Battersea North, Wandsworth Battersea South, Wandsworth Putney, Wandsworth Tooting.

South Eastern (40 seats): Arundel, Ashford, Brighton Kemptown, Brighton Pavilion, Canterbury, Chertsey and Walton, Chichester, Dartford, Dorking, Dover and Deal, Eastbourne, East Grinstead, Epsom and Ewell, Esher, Farnham, Faversham, Folkestone and Hythe, Gillingham, Gravesend, Guildford, Hastings, Horsham and Crawley, Hove, Lewes, Maidstone, Reigate, Rochester and Chatham, Royal Tunbridge Wells, Rye, Sevenoaks, Shoreham, Spelthorne, Surrey East, Surrey North West, Sussex Mid, Thanet East, Thanet West, Tonbridge and Malling, Woking, Worthing.

258

Southern and Wessex (42 seats) Abingdon, Aldershot, Aylesbury, Banbury, Basingstoke, Beaconsfield, Bournemouth East, Bournemouth West, Buckingham, Chesham and Amersham, Chippenham, Christchurch and Lymington, Devizes, Dorset North, Dorset South, Dorset West, Eastleigh, Eton and Slough, Fareham, Gosport, Havant and Waterloo, Henley, Isle of Wight, Newbury, New Forest, Oxford, Oxon Mid, Petersfield, Poole, Portsmouth North, Portsmouth South, Reading North, Reading South, Salisbury, Southampton Itchen, Southampton Test, Swindon, Westbury, Winchester, Windsor and Maidenhead, Wokingham, Wycombe.

South Western (34 seats): Bath, Bodmin, Bridgwater, Bristol North East, Bristol North West, Bristol South, Bristol South East, Bristol West, Cheltenham, Cirencester and Tewkesbury, Cornwall North, Devon North, Devon West, Exeter, Falmouth and Camborne, Gloucester, Gloucestershire South, Gloucestershire West, Honiton, Kingswood, Plymouth Devonport, Plymouth Drake, Plymouth Sutton, St. Ives, Somerset North, Stroud, Taunton, Tiverton, Torbay, Totnes, Truro, Wells, Weston-super-Mare, Yeovil.

Eastern (45 seats): Basildon, Bedford, Bedfordshire Mid, Bedfordshire South, Braintree, Brentwood and Ongar, Bury St. Edmunds, Cambridge, Cambridgeshire, Chelmsford, Colchester, Epping Forest, Essex South East; Eye, Harlow, Harwich, Hemel Hempstead, Hertford and Stevenage, Hertfordshire East, Hertfordshire South, Hertfordshire South West, Hitchin, Huntingdonshire, Ipswich, Isle of Ely, Lowestoft, Luton East, Luton West, Maldon, Norfolk North, Norfolk North West, Norfolk South, Norfolk South West, Norwich North, Norwich South, Peterborough, Saffron Walden, St. Albans, Southend East, Southend West, Sudbury and Woodbridge, Thurrock, Watford, Welwyn and Hatfield, Yarmouth.

East Midland (40 seats): Ashfield, Bassetlaw, Beeston, Belper, Blaby, Bolsover, Bosworth, Carlton, Chesterfield, Daventry, Derby North, Derby South, Derbyshire North East, Derbyshire South East, Derbyshire West, Gainsborough, Grantham, Harborough, High Peak, Holland with Boston, Horncastle, Ilkeston, Kettering, Leicester East, Leicester South, Leicester West, Lincoln, Loughborough, Louth, Mansfield, Melton, Newark, Northampton North, Northampton South, Nottingham East, Nottingham North, Nottingham West, Rushcliffe, Rutland and Stamford, Wellingborough.

Midland (56 seats): Aldridge—Brownhills, Birmingham Edgbaston, Birmingham Erdington, Birmingham Hall Green, Birmingham Handsworth, Birmingham Ladywood, Birmingham Northfield, Birmingham Perry Barr, Birmingham Selly Oak, Birmingham Small Heath, Birmingham Sparkbrook, Birmingham Stetchford, Birmingham Yardley, Bromsgrove and Redditch, Burton, Cannock, Coventry North East, Coventry North West, Coventry South East, Coventry South West, Dudley East, Dudley West, Halesowen and Stourbridge, Hereford, Kidderminster, Leek, Leomins-

ter, Lichfield and Tamworth, Ludlow, Meriden, Newcastle-under-Lyme, Nuneaton, Oswestry, Rugby, Shrewsbury, Solihull, Stafford and Stone, Staffordshire South West, Stoke on Trent Central, Stoke on Trent North, Stoke on Trent South, Stratford on Avon, Sutton Coldfield, Walsall North, Walsall South, Warley East, Warley West, Warwick and Leamington, West Bromwich East, West Bromwich West, Wolverhampton North East, Wolverhampton South East, Wolverhampton South West, Worcester, Worcestershire South, Wrekin, The.

North Western (76 seats): Accrington, Altrincham and Sale, Ashton-under-Lyne, Bebington and Ellesmere Port, Birkenhead, Blackburn, Blackpool North, Blackpool South, Bolton East, Bolton West, Bootle, Burnley, Bury and Radcliffe, Cheadle, Chester City of, Chorley, Clitheroe, Crewe, Crosby, Darwen, Eccles, Farnworth, Hazel Grove, Heywood and Royton, Huyton, Ince, Knutsford, Leigh, Lancaster, Liverpool Edge Hill, Liverpool Garston, Liverpool Kirkdale, Liverpool Scotland Exchange, Liverpool Toxteth, Liverpool Walton, Liverpool Wavertree, Liverpool West Derby, Macclesfield, Manchester Ardwick, Manchester Blackley, Manchester Central, Manchester Gorton, Manchester Moss Side, Manchester Openshaw, Manchester Withington, Manchester Wythenshawe, Middleton and Prestwich, Nantwich, Nelson and Colne, Newton, North Fylde, Northwich, Oldham East, Oldham West, Ormskirk, Preston North, Preston South, Rochdale, Rossendale, Runcorn, St. Helens, Salford East, Salford West, South Fylde, Southport, Stalybridge and Hyde, Stockport North, Stockport South, Stretford, Wallasey, Warrington, Westhoughton, Westmorland, Widnes, Wigan, Wirral.

Yorkshire and Humberside (54 seats): Barkston Ash, Barnsley, Batley and Morley, Bradford North, Bradford South, Bradford West, Bridlington, Brigg and Scunthorpe, Brighouse and Spenborough, Colne Valley, Dearne Valley, Dewsbury, Doncaster, Don Valley, Goole, Grimsby, Halifax, Haltemprice, Harrogate, Hemsworth, Howden, Huddersfield East, Huddersfield West, Keighley, Kingston upon Hull Central, Kingston upon Hull East, Kingston upon Hull West, Leeds East, Leeds North East, Leeds North West, Leeds South, Leeds South East, Leeds West, Normanton, Penistone, Pontefract and Castleford, Pudsey, Richmond, Ripon, Rotherham, Rother Valley, Scarborough, Sheffield Attercliffe, Sheffield Brightside, Sheffield Hallam, Sheffield Heeley, Sheffield Hillsborough, Sheffield Park, Shipley, Skipton, Sowerby, Thirsk and Malton, Wakefield, York.

Northern Region (37 seats): Barrow-in-Furness, Berwick-upon-Tweed, Bishop Auckland, Blaydon, Blyth, Carlisle, Chester-le-Street, Cleveland and Whitby, Consett, Darlington, Durham, Durham North West, Easington, Gateshead East, Gateshead West, Hartlepool, Hexham, Houghton-le-Spring, Jarrow, Morecambe and Lonsdale, Morpeth, Newcastle upon Tyne Central, Newcastle upon Tyne East, Newcastle upon Tyne North, Newcastle upon Tyne West, Penrith and the Border, South Shields, Sunderland North, Sunderland South, Teesside Middlesborough, Teesside Redcar, Teesside Stockton, Teesside Thornaby, Tynemouth, Wallsend, Whitehaven, Workington.

Regional analysis

	October 1974				May 1979			
	Total Votes	% Total Votes	MPs	Candidates	Total Votes	% Total Votes	MPs	Candidates
LONDON								
C	1,310,546	37·4	41	92	1,693,587	46·0	50	92
Lab	1,540,451	43·9	51	92	1,459,085	39·6	42	92
L	594,749	17·0	—	92	438,021	11·9	—	92
Comm	2,665	0·1	—	6	2,558	0·1	—	7
Nat Front	51,122	1·5	—	35	71,934	2·0	—	88
Others	7,919	0·2	—	31	15,644	0·4	—	61
Totals	3,507,452	100·0	92	343	3,680,829	100·0	92	432
Electorate	5,274,767		Turnout 66·5%		5,147,135		Turnout 71·5%	
							Swing +6·4%	

Regional analysis (continued)

	October 1974				May 1979			
	Total Votes	% Total Votes	MPs	Candi-dates	Total Votes	% Total Votes	MPs	Candi-dates
SOUTH EAST								
C	979,443	48·4	37	40	1,240,520	57·2	40	40
Lab	550,068	27·2	3	40	521,043	24·0	—	40
L	482,898	23·9	—	40	383,291	17·7	—	40
Nat Front	9,321	0·5	—	9	16,258	0·7	—	29
Others	1,521	0·1	—	7	7,129	0·3	—	13
Totals	2,023,251	100·0	40	136	2,168,241	100·0	40	162
Electorate	2,733,620		Turnout 74·0%		2,833,591		Turnout 76·5% Swing+6·0%	
SOUTH AND WESSEX								
C	998,595	44·8	35	42	1,341,703	54·4	38	42
Lab	644,129	28·9	6	42	607,596	24·6	3	42
L	573,290	25·7	1	42	494,435	20·0	1	42
Nat Front	7,784	0·3	—	8	9,170	0·4	—	15
Others	4,198	0·2	—	9	14,120	0·6	—	20
Totals	2,227,996	100·0	42	143	2,467,024	100·0	42	161
Electorate	2,977,108		Turnout 74·8%		3,178,340		Turnout 77·6% Swing+6·9%	
SOUTH WESTERN								
C	752,684	42·9	24	34	962,449	51·0	29	34
Lab	520,800	29·7	7	34	483,076	25·6	4	34
L	471,961	26·9	3	34	418,206	22·2	1	34
Nat Front	1,570	0·1	—	2	6,058	0·3	—	19
Others	6,949	0·4	—	15	17,585	0·9	—	28
Totals	1,753,964	100·0	34	119	1,887,374	100·0	34	149
Electorate	2,273,306		Turnout 77·2%		2,381,148		Turnout 79·3% Swing+6·1%	
EASTERN								
C	1,035,696	42·1	31	45	1,395,268	51·5	39	45
Lab	891,711	36·2	13	45	864,797	31·9	5	45
L	531,468	21·6	1	45	428,222	15·8	1	45
Comm	—	—	—	—	213	0·0	—	2
Nat Front	1,903	0·1	—	2	19,422	0·7	—	28
Others	2,100	0·1	—	4	3,723	0·1	—	13
Totals	2,462,878	100·0	45	141	2,711,645	100·0	45	178
Electorate	3,242,999		Turnout 75·9%		3,446,494		Turnout 78·7% Swing+6·8%	
EAST MIDLANDS								
C	784,219	38·5	19	40	1,034,050	46·7	24	40
Lab	852,577	41·8	21	40	845,742	38·2	16	40
L	373,734	18·3	—	39	313,557	14·2	—	40
Comm	973	0·0	—	2	1,071	0·0	—	1
Nat Front	10,572	0·5	—	6	15,372	0·7	—	24
Others	16,154	0·8	—	7	4,022	0·2	—	10
Totals	2,038,229	100·0	40	134	2,213,814	100·0	40	155
Electorate	2,722,745		Turnout 74·9%		2,839,286		Turnout 78·0% Swing+5·9%	
MIDLANDS								
C	992,685	37·5	21	56	1,334,079	47·1	31	56
Lab	1,159,987	43·9	35	56	1,135,803	40·1	25	56
L	470,975	17·8	—	56	323,961	11·4	—	50
Comm	954	0·0	—	3	1,105	0·0	—	2
Nat Front	16,248	0·6	—	12	25,849	0·9	—	34
Others	3,225	0·1	—	14	9,590	0·3	—	20
Totals	2,644,074	100·0	56	197	2,830,387	100·0	56	218
Electorate	3,667,229		Turnout 72·1%		3,758,247		Turnout 75·3% Swing+6·7%	
NORTH-WEST								
C	1,273,366	37·0	24	76	1,577,534	43·8	30	76
Lab	1,533,166	44·6	51	76	1,530,862	42·5	44	76
L	621,120	18·1	1	76	471,953	13·1	2	72
Comm	1,720	0·0	—	4	963	0·0	—	3
Nat Front	9,403	0·3	—	8	14,001	0·4	—	31
Others	2,274	0·1	—	10	8,465	0·2	—	19
Totals	3,441,049	100·0	76	250	3,603,778	100·0	76	277
Electorate	4,706,301		Turnout 73·1%		4,739,379		Turnout 76·0% Swing+4·4%	

	October 1974				May 1979			
	Total Votes	% Total Votes	MPs	Candi-dates	Total Votes	% Total Votes	MPs	Candi-dates
YORKSHIRE AND HUMBERSIDE								
C	802,567	32·5	15	54	1,044,167	39·3	19	54
Lab	1,155,393	46·8	38	54	1,195,802	45·0	34	54
L	492,813	19·9	1	54	391,406	14·7	1	54
Comm	720	0·0	—	2	469	0·0	—	2
Nat Front	5,123	0·2	—	6	9,336	0·4	—	24
Others	14,056	0·6	—	12	13,551	0·5	—	27
Totals	2,470,672	100·0	54	182	2,654,731	100·0	54	215
Electorate	3,472,887		Turnout 71·1%		3,564,461		Turnout 74·5% Swing+4·3%	
NORTHERN								
C	486,441	30·0	6	37	631,787	36·0	6	37
Lab	846,769	52·2	30	37	883,032	50·3	30	37
L	265,784	16·4	1	37	213,452	12·2	1	37
Comm	—	—	—	—	243	0·0	—	1
Nat Front	711	0·0	—	1	1,737	0·1	—	5
Others	21,799	1·3	—	4	24,691	1·4	—	10
Totals	1,621,504	100·0	37	116	1,754,942	100·0	37	127
Electorate	2,270,359		Turnout 71·4%		2,321,006		Turnout 75·6% Swing+3·9%	

The Scotland, Wales and Northern Ireland details are in the 'How the Nation Voted' and 'How Northern Ireland Voted' tables.

Metropolitan analysis

A further basis for comparison between the areas of heaviest population has been obtained by using the six new metropolitan areas plus London, as follows:

Region	Metropolitan area	Seats
London	London*	92
Midland	West Midlands County	31
North-Western	Greater Manchester	32
	Merseyside	16
Yorkshire and Humberside	South Yorkshire	13
	West Yorkshire	23
Northern	Tyne and Wear	14

*Divided into two areas: Outer London (57 seats) and Inner London (35 seats).

Constituencies making up the metropolitan areas are:

Outer London (57 seats): Barking Barking, Barking Dagenham, Barnet Chipping Barnet, Barnet Finchley, Barnet Hendon North, Barnet Hendon South, Brent East, Brent North, Brent South, Ealing Acton, Ealing North, Ealing South, Enfield Edmonton, Enfield North, Enfield Southgate, Haringey Hornsey, Haringey Tottenham, Haringey Wood Green, Harrow Central, Harrow East, Harrow West, Havering Hornchurch, Havering Romford, Havering Upminster, Hillingdon Hayes & Harlington, Hillingdon Ruislip-Northwood, Hillingdon Uxbridge, Hounslow Brentford & Isleworth, Hounslow Feltham & Heston, Newham North East, Newham North West, Newham South, Redbridge Ilford North, Redbridge Ilford South, Redbridge Wanstead & Woodford, Waltham Forest Chingford, Waltham Forest Leyton, Waltham Forest Walthamstow, Bexley Bexleyheath, Bexley Erith & Crayford, Bexley Sidcup, Bromley Beckenham, Bromley Chislehurst, Bromley Orpington, Bromley Ravensbourne, Croydon Central, Croydon North East, Croydon North West, Croydon South, Kingston-upon-Thames Kingston, Kingston-upon-Thames Surbiton, Merton Mitcham & Morden, Merton Wimbledon, Richmond-upon-Thames Richmond, Richmond-upon-Thames Twickenham, Sutton Sutton & Cheam, Sutton Carshalton.

Inner London (35 seats): Camden Hampstead, Camden Holborn & St. Pancras South, Camden St. Pancras North, Cities of London & Westminster City of London & Westminster South, City of London & Westminster Paddington, City of London & Westminster St. Marylebone, Hackney Central, Hackney North & Stoke Newington, Hackney South & Shoreditch, Hammersmith Fulham, Hammersmith North, Islington Central, Islington North, Islington South & Finsbury, Kensington & Chelsea Chelsea, Kensington & Chelsea Kensington, Tower Hamlets Bethnal Green & Bow, Tower Hamlets Stepney & Poplar, Greenwich Greenwich, Greenwich Woolwich East, Greenwich Woolwich West, Lambeth Central, Lambeth Norwood, Lambeth Streatham, Lambeth Vauxhall, Lewisham Deptford, Lewisham East, Lewisham West, Southwark Bermondsey, Southwark Dulwich, Southwark Peckham, Wandsworth Battersea North, Wandsworth Battersea South, Wandsworth Putney, Wandsworth Tooting.

West Midlands County (31 seats): Aldridge-Brownhills, Birmingham Edgbaston, Birmingham Erdington, Birmingham Hall Green, Birmingham Handsworth, Birmingham Ladywood, Birmingham Northfield, Birmingham Perry Barr, Birmingham Selly Oak, Birmingham Small Heath, Birmingham Sparkbrook, Birmingham Stechford, Birmingham Yardley, Coventry North-East, Coventry North-West, Coventry South-East, Coventry South-West, Dudley East, Dudley West, Halesowen & Stourbridge, Solihull, Sutton Coldfield, Walsall North, Walsall South, Warley East, Warley West, West Bromwich East, West Bromwich West, Wolverhampton North-East, Wolverhampton South-East, Wolverhampton South-West.

Metropolitan analysis (continued)

Greater Manchester (32 seats): Altrincham & Sale, Ashton-under-Lyne, Bolton East, Bolton West, Bury & Radcliffe, Cheadle, Eccles, Farnworth, Hazel Grove, Heywood & Royton, Ince, Leigh, Manchester Ardwick, Manchester Blackley, Manchester Central, Manchester Gorton, Manchester Moss Side, Manchester Openshaw, Manchester Withington, Manchester Wythenshawe, Middleton & Prestwich, Oldham East, Oldham West, Rochdale, Salford East, Salford West, Stalybridge & Hyde, Stockport North, Stockport South, Stretford, Westhoughton, Wigan.

Merseyside (16 seats): Birkenhead, Bootle, Crosby, Huyton, Liverpool Edge Hill, Liverpool Garston, Liverpool Kirkdale, Liverpool Scotland Exchange, Liverpool Toxteth, Liverpool Walton, Liverpool Wavertree, Liverpool West Derby, St. Helens, Southport, Wallasay, Wirral.

South Yorkshire (13 seats): Barnsley, Dearne Valley, Doncaster, Don Valley, Penistone, Rotherham, Rother Valley, Sheffield Attercliffe, Sheffield Brightside, Sheffield Hallam, Sheffield Heeley, Sheffield Hillsborough, Sheffield Park.

West Yorkshire (23 seats): Batley & Morley, Bradford North, Bradford South, Bradford West, Brighouse & Spenborough, Colne Valley, Dewsbury, Halifax, Huddersfield East, Huddersfield West, Keighley, Leeds East, Leeds North-East, Leeds North-West, Leeds South, Leeds South-East, Leeds West, Normanton, Pontefract & Castleford, Pudsey, Shipley, Sowerby, Wakefield.

Tyne & Wear (14 seats): Blaydon, Gateshead East, Gateshead West, Houghton-le-Spring, Jarrow, Newcastle-upon-Tyne Central, Newcastle-upon-Tyne East, Newcastle-upon-Tyne North, Newcastle-upon-Tyne West, South Shields, Sunderland North, Sunderland South, Tynemouth, Wallsend.

Voting in the Metropolitan areas was as follows:

Metropolitan areas

	October 1974				May 1979			
	Total Votes	% Total Votes	MPs	Candi-dates	Total Votes	% Total Votes	MPs	Candi-dates
OUTER LONDON								
C	954,932	40·2	35	57	1,227,344	48·9	40	57
Lab	941,904	39·7	22	57	906,504	36·1	17	57
L	438,414	18·5	—	57	325,321	13·0	—	57
Comm	850	0·0	—	2	802	0·0	—	2
Nat Front	35,086	1·5	—	23	43,277	1·7	—	53
Others	4,221	0·2	—	14	7,608	0·3	—	27
Totals	2,375,407	100·0	57	210	2,510,856	100·0	57	253
Electorate	3,393,160		Turnout 70·0%		3,370,604		Turnout 74·5%	
							Swing +6·1%	
INNER LONDON								
C	355,614	31·4	6	35	466,243	39·9	10	35
Lab	598,547	52·9	29	35	552,581	47·2	25	35
L	156,335	13·8	—	35	112,700	9·6	—	35
Comm	1,815	0·2	—	4	1,756	0·2	—	5
Nat Front	16,036	1·4	—	12	28,657	2·4	—	35
Others	3,698	0·3	—	17	8,036	0·7	—	34
Totals	1,132,045	100·0	35	138	1,169,973	100·0	35	179
Electorate	1,881,607		Turnout 60·2%		1,776,531		Turnout 65·9%	
							Swing +7·1%	
WEST MIDLANDS								
C	459,520	34·7	6	31	630,178	45·4	12	31
Lab	638,896	48·2	25	31	625,627	45·1	19	31
L	207,728	15·7	—	31	108,481	7·8	—	25
Comm	954	0·1	—	3	1,105	0·1	—	2
Nat Front	16,243	1·2	—	12	18,902	1·4	—	24
Others	2,481	0·2	—	11	3,914	0·3	—	13
Totals	1,325,827	100·0	31	119	1,388,207	100·0	31	126
Electorate	1,912,203		Turnout 69·3%		1,905,137		Turnout 72·9%	
							Swing +6·9%	
GREATER MANCHESTER								
C	461,567	33·1	5	32	580,590	40·2	5	32
Lab	657,560	47·2	26	32	671,490	46·4	26	32
L	266,592	19·1	1	32	184,615	12·8	1	29
Comm	648	0·0	—	2	542	0·0	—	2
Nat Front	5,019	0·4	—	4	5,975	0·4	—	14
Others	1,035	0·1	—	5	2,638	0·2	—	7
Totals	1,392,421	100·0	32	107	1,445,850	100·0	32	116
Electorate	1,912,871		Turnout 72·8%		1,896,296		Turnout 76·2%	
							Swing +3·9%	

	October 1974				May 1979			
	Total Votes	% Total Votes	MPs	Candi-dates	Total Votes	% Total Votes	MPs	Candi-dates
MERSEYSIDE								
C	250,443	36·1	5	16	295,586	41·4	6	16
Lab	333,189	48·1	11	16	308,419	43·2	9	16
L	107,469	15·5	—	16	104,572	14·7	1	16
Comm	1,072	0·2	—	2	421	0·1	—	1
Nat Front	787	0·1	—	1	1,095	0·2	—	4
Others	365	0·1	—	1	3,705	0·5	—	7
Totals	693,330	100·0	16	52	713,798	100·0	16	60
Electorate	1,001,082		Turnout 69·3%		982,052		Turnout 72·7% Swing +5·1%	
SOUTH YORKSHIRE								
C	145,314	23·5	1	13	205,815	31·2	1	13
Lab	367,520	59·3	12	13	374,955	56·8	12	13
L	95,349	15·4	—	13	74,396	11·3	—	13
Comm	403	0·1	—	1	279	0·0	—	1
Nat Front	723	0·1	—	1	2,803	0·4	—	8
Others	10,182	1·6	—	1	2,215	0·3	—	5
Totals	619,491	100·0	13	42	660,463	100·0	13	53
Electorate	888,423		Turnout 69·7%		903,528		Turnout 73·1% Swing +5·1%	
WEST YORKSHIRE								
C	314,235	31·7	4	23	399,176	37·9	7	23
Lab	468,500	47·2	18	23	484,564	46·0	15	23
L	204,407	20·6	1	23	159,881	15·2	1	23
Comm	317	0·0	—	1	190	0·0	—	1
Nat Front	2,383	0·2	—	3	4,383	0·4	—	10
Others	2,514	0·3	—	7	5,017	0·5	—	14
Totals	992,356	100·0	23	80	1,053,211	100·0	23	94
Electorate	1,378,761		Turnout 72·0%		1,403,831		Turnout 75·0% Swing +3·7%	
TYNE AND WEAR								
C	159,159	27·2	2	14	210,992	34·0	2	14
Lab	331,444	56·6	12	14	341,605	55·1	12	14
L	94,012	16·0	—	14	63,286	10·2	—	14
Nat Front	711	0·1	—	1	658	0·1	—	2
Others	435	0·1	—	1	3,359	0·5	—	4
Totals	585,761	100·0	14	44	619,900	100·0	14	48
Electorate	846,216		Turnout 69·2%		845,434		Turnout 73·3% Swing +4·1%	
ENGLISH METROPOLITAN COUNTIES								
Total for Category								
C	3,100,789	34·0	64	221	4,015,924	42·0	83	221
Lab	4,337,560	47·6	155	221	4,265,745	44·6	135	221
L	1,570,306	17·2	2	221	1,133,252	11·9	3	212
Comm	6,059	0·1	—	15	5,095	0·1	—	14
Nat Front	76,993	0·8	—	57	105,750	1·1	—	150
Others	24,931	0·3	—	57	36,492	0·4	—	111
Totals	9,116,638	100·0	221	792	9,562,258	100·0	221	929
Electorate	13,214,323		Turnout 69·0%		13,083,413		Turnout 73·1% Swing +5·5%	

English Metropolitan Cities

Voting has also been analysed in the following Metropolitan cities and towns:

	October 1974				May 1979			
LONDON								
C	1,310,546	37·4	41	92	1,693,587	46·0	50	92
Lab	1,540,451	43·9	51	92	1,459,085	39·6	42	92
L	594,749	17·0	—	92	438,021	11·9	—	92
Comm	2,665	0·1	—	6	2,558	0·1	—	7
Nat Front	51,122	1·5	—	35	71,934	2·0	—	88
Others	7,919	0·2	—	31	15,644	0·4	—	61
Totals	3,507,452	100·0	92	348	3,680,829	100·0	92	432
Electorate	5,274,767		Turnout 66·5%		5,147,135		Turnout 71·5% Swing +6·4%	

English Metropolitan Cities (continued)

<table>
<thead>
<tr><th></th><th colspan="4">October 1974</th><th colspan="4">May 1979</th></tr>
<tr><th></th><th>Total Votes</th><th>% Total Votes</th><th>MPs</th><th>Candi-dates</th><th>Total Votes</th><th>% Total Votes</th><th>MPs</th><th>Candi-dates</th></tr>
</thead>
<tbody>
<tr><td colspan="9">BIRMINGHAM</td></tr>
<tr><td>C</td><td>160,967</td><td>34·7</td><td>2</td><td>12</td><td>214,207</td><td>44·6</td><td>5</td><td>12</td></tr>
<tr><td>Lab</td><td>231,141</td><td>49·8</td><td>10</td><td>12</td><td>222,487</td><td>46·4</td><td>7</td><td>12</td></tr>
<tr><td>L</td><td>66,202</td><td>14·3</td><td>—</td><td>12</td><td>35,445</td><td>7·4</td><td>—</td><td>10</td></tr>
<tr><td>Comm</td><td>180</td><td>0·0</td><td>—</td><td>1</td><td>715</td><td>0·1</td><td>—</td><td>1</td></tr>
<tr><td>Nat Front</td><td>4,111</td><td>0·9</td><td>—</td><td>4</td><td>4,836</td><td>1·0</td><td>—</td><td>8</td></tr>
<tr><td>Others</td><td>1,312</td><td>0·3</td><td>—</td><td>6</td><td>2,073</td><td>0·4</td><td>—</td><td>7</td></tr>
<tr><td>Totals</td><td>463,913</td><td>100·0</td><td>12</td><td>47</td><td>479,763</td><td>100·0</td><td>12</td><td>50</td></tr>
<tr><td>Electorate</td><td>704,470</td><td colspan="3">Turnout 65·9%</td><td>686,175</td><td colspan="3">Turnout 69·9%
Swing+6·6%</td></tr>
<tr><td colspan="9">BOLTON</td></tr>
<tr><td>C</td><td>33,565</td><td>39·3</td><td>—</td><td>2</td><td>37,325</td><td>43·5</td><td>—</td><td>2</td></tr>
<tr><td>Lab</td><td>38,536</td><td>45·2</td><td>2</td><td>2</td><td>39,777</td><td>46·3</td><td>2</td><td>2</td></tr>
<tr><td>L</td><td>10,919</td><td>12·8</td><td>—</td><td>2</td><td>7,995</td><td>9·5</td><td>—</td><td>2</td></tr>
<tr><td>Nat Front</td><td>2,178</td><td>2·6</td><td>—</td><td>2</td><td>805</td><td>0·9</td><td>—</td><td>2</td></tr>
<tr><td>Others</td><td>149</td><td></td><td>0</td><td>1</td><td>—</td><td></td><td></td><td>—</td></tr>
<tr><td>Totals</td><td>85,347</td><td>100·0</td><td>2</td><td>9</td><td>85,902</td><td>100·0</td><td>2</td><td>8</td></tr>
<tr><td>Electorate</td><td>110,959</td><td colspan="3">Turnout 76·9%</td><td>108,703</td><td colspan="3">Turnout 79·0%
Swing+1·5%</td></tr>
<tr><td colspan="9">BRADFORD</td></tr>
<tr><td>C</td><td>47,388</td><td>33·2</td><td>—</td><td>3</td><td>56,107</td><td>37·3</td><td>—</td><td>3</td></tr>
<tr><td>Lab</td><td>69,193</td><td>48·5</td><td>3</td><td>3</td><td>75,701</td><td>50·4</td><td>3</td><td>3</td></tr>
<tr><td>L</td><td>25,665</td><td>18·0</td><td>—</td><td>3</td><td>16,614</td><td>1·1</td><td>—</td><td>3</td></tr>
<tr><td>Nat Front</td><td>—</td><td>—</td><td>—</td><td>—</td><td>1,669</td><td>1·1</td><td>—</td><td>3</td></tr>
<tr><td>Others</td><td>339</td><td>0·2</td><td>—</td><td>1</td><td>158</td><td>0·1</td><td>—</td><td>1</td></tr>
<tr><td>Totals</td><td>142,585</td><td>100·0</td><td>3</td><td>10</td><td>150,249</td><td>100·0</td><td>3</td><td>13</td></tr>
<tr><td>Electorate</td><td>202,091</td><td colspan="3">Turnout 70·6%</td><td>210,290</td><td colspan="3">Turnout 71·4%
Swing+1·1%</td></tr>
<tr><td colspan="9">COVENTRY</td></tr>
<tr><td>C</td><td>51,992</td><td>30·6</td><td>—</td><td>4</td><td>72,001</td><td>40·4</td><td>1</td><td>4</td></tr>
<tr><td>Lab</td><td>89,690</td><td>52·8</td><td>4</td><td>4</td><td>88,327</td><td>49·6</td><td>3</td><td>4</td></tr>
<tr><td>L</td><td>26,175</td><td>15·4</td><td>—</td><td>4</td><td>14,609</td><td>8·2</td><td>—</td><td>4</td></tr>
<tr><td>Comm</td><td>309</td><td>0·2</td><td>—</td><td>1</td><td>390</td><td>0·2</td><td>—</td><td>1</td></tr>
<tr><td>Nat Front</td><td>822</td><td>0·5</td><td>—</td><td>1</td><td>1,900</td><td>1·1</td><td>—</td><td>4</td></tr>
<tr><td>Others</td><td>809</td><td>0·5</td><td>—</td><td>3</td><td>981</td><td>0·6</td><td>—</td><td>4</td></tr>
<tr><td>Totals</td><td>169,797</td><td>100·0</td><td>4</td><td>17</td><td>178,208</td><td>100·0</td><td>4</td><td>21</td></tr>
<tr><td>Electorate</td><td>231,511</td><td colspan="3">Turnout 73·3%</td><td>234,327</td><td colspan="3">Turnout 76·1%
Swing+6·5%</td></tr>
<tr><td colspan="9">DUDLEY</td></tr>
<tr><td>C</td><td>31,645</td><td>32·5</td><td>—</td><td>2</td><td>44,992</td><td>44·5</td><td>1</td><td>2</td></tr>
<tr><td>Lab</td><td>52,361</td><td>53·7</td><td>2</td><td>2</td><td>51,540</td><td>51·0</td><td>1</td><td>2</td></tr>
<tr><td>L</td><td>12,262</td><td>12·6</td><td>—</td><td>2</td><td>3,639</td><td>3·6</td><td>—</td><td>1</td></tr>
<tr><td>Nat Front</td><td>1,171</td><td>1·2</td><td>—</td><td>1</td><td>884</td><td>0·8</td><td>—</td><td>1</td></tr>
<tr><td>Others</td><td>—</td><td></td><td>—</td><td>—</td><td>—</td><td></td><td>—</td><td>—</td></tr>
<tr><td>Totals</td><td>97,439</td><td>100·0</td><td>2</td><td>7</td><td>101,015</td><td>100·0</td><td>2</td><td>6</td></tr>
<tr><td>Electorate</td><td>135,127</td><td colspan="3">Turnout 72·1%</td><td>137,186</td><td colspan="3">Turnout 73·6%
Swing+7·3%</td></tr>
<tr><td colspan="9">LEEDS</td></tr>
<tr><td>C</td><td>70,865</td><td>30·9</td><td>2</td><td>6</td><td>86,177</td><td>35·2</td><td>2</td><td>6</td></tr>
<tr><td>Lab</td><td>112,564</td><td>49·0</td><td>4</td><td>6</td><td>118,481</td><td>48·4</td><td>4</td><td>6</td></tr>
<tr><td>L</td><td>45,424</td><td>19·8</td><td>—</td><td>6</td><td>36,582</td><td>14·9</td><td>—</td><td>6</td></tr>
<tr><td>Comm</td><td>317</td><td>0·1</td><td>—</td><td>1</td><td>190</td><td>0·1</td><td>—</td><td>1</td></tr>
<tr><td>Nat Front</td><td>—</td><td>—</td><td>—</td><td>—</td><td>1,495</td><td>0·6</td><td>—</td><td>4</td></tr>
<tr><td>Others</td><td>327</td><td>0·1</td><td>—</td><td>1</td><td>2,072</td><td>0·8</td><td>—</td><td>5</td></tr>
<tr><td>Totals</td><td>229,497</td><td>100·0</td><td>6</td><td>20</td><td>244,997</td><td>100·0</td><td>6</td><td>28</td></tr>
<tr><td>Electorate</td><td>354,655</td><td colspan="3">Turnout 64·7%</td><td>347,252</td><td colspan="3">Turnout 70·6%
Swing+2·4%</td></tr>
<tr><td colspan="9">LIVERPOOL</td></tr>
<tr><td>C</td><td>89,388</td><td>32·6</td><td>1</td><td>8</td><td>100,290</td><td>35·9</td><td>2</td><td>8</td></tr>
<tr><td>Lab</td><td>149,780</td><td>54·6</td><td>7</td><td>8</td><td>137,202</td><td>49·1</td><td>5</td><td>8</td></tr>
<tr><td>L</td><td>34,374</td><td>12·5</td><td>—</td><td>8</td><td>40,504</td><td>14·5</td><td>1</td><td>8</td></tr>
<tr><td>Comm</td><td>556</td><td>0·2</td><td>—</td><td>1</td><td>421</td><td>0·2</td><td>—</td><td>1</td></tr>
<tr><td>Nat Front</td><td>—</td><td>—</td><td>—</td><td>—</td><td>604</td><td>0·2</td><td>—</td><td>3</td></tr>
<tr><td>Others</td><td>365</td><td>0·1</td><td>—</td><td>1</td><td>528</td><td>0·2</td><td>—</td><td>3</td></tr>
<tr><td>Totals</td><td>274,463</td><td>100·0</td><td>8</td><td>26</td><td>279,549</td><td>100·0</td><td>8</td><td>31</td></tr>
<tr><td>Electorate</td><td>418,950</td><td colspan="3">Turnout 65·5%</td><td>399,380</td><td colspan="3">Turnout 70·0%
Swing+4·4%</td></tr>
</tbody>
</table>

English Metropolitan Cities (continued)

	October 1974				May 1979			
	Total Votes	% Total Votes	MPs	Candi-dates	Total Votes	% Total Votes	MPs	Candi-dates
MANCHESTER								
C	85,918	31·5	1	8	103,025	36·9	1	8
Lab	144,097	52·9	7	8	151,225	54·1	7	8
L	40,850	15·0	—	8	22,942	8·2	—	7
Comm	300	0·1	—	1	174	0·1	—	1
Nat Front	914	0·3	—	1	1,456	0·5	—	4
Others	334	0·1	—	2	669	0·2	—	3
Totals	272,413	100·0	8	28	279,491	100·0	8	31
Electorate	415,930		Turnout 65·5%		382,267		Turnout 73·1%	
							Swing +2·1%	
NEWCASTLE-UPON-TYNE								
C	39,695	31·4	1	4	49,381	36·4	1	4
Lab	68,663	54·2	3	4	72,489	53·5	3	4
L	18,241	14·4	—	4	13,675	10·1	—	4
Totals	126,599	100·0	4	12	135,545	100·0	4	12
Electorate	188,015		Turnout 67·3%		190,625		Turnout 71·1%	
							Swing +2·8%	
SHEFFIELD								
C	68,610	26·7	1	6	90,224	33·9	1	6
Lab	138,939	54·0	5	6	144,533	54·3	5	6
L	38,433	14·9	—	6	29,014	10·9	—	6
Comm	403	0·2	—	1	279	0·1	—	1
Nat Front	723	0·3	—	1	2,013	0·8	—	6
Others	10,182	4·0	—	1	111	0·0	—	1
Totals	257,290	100·0	6	21	266,174	100·0	6	26
Electorate	380,113		Turnout 67·7%		373,602		Turnout 71·2%	
							Swing +3·4%	
SUNDERLAND								
C	29,540	28·8	—	2	37,313	35·2	—	2
Lab	58,241	56·7	2	2	58,616	55·2	2	2
L	14,905	14·5	—	2	10,222	9·6	—	2
Totals	102,686	100·0	2	6	106,151	100·0	2	6
Electorate	152,056		Turnout 67·5%		152,124		Turnout 69·8%	
							Swing +3·9%	
WALSALL								
C	28,710	31·5	—	2	41,998	43·2	—	2
Lab	49,257	54·0	2	2	49,452	50·9	2	2
L	11,408	12·5	—	2	3,778	3·9	—	1
Comm	465	0·5	—	1	—	—	—	—
Nat Front	1,226	1·3	—	1	1,893	1·9	—	2
Others	150	0·2	—	1	—	—	—	—
Totals	91,216	100·0	2	9	97,121	100·0	2	7
Electorate	130,766		Turnout 69·8%		130,811		Turnout 74·2%	
							Swing +7·4%	
WARLEY								
C	22,792	28·6	—	2	31,310	38·3	—	2
Lab	45,826	57·5	2	2	46,458	56·8	2	2
L	11,027	13·8	—	2	2,864	3·5	—	1
Totals	79,645	100·0	2	6	81,836	100·0	2	6
Electorate	118,804		Turnout 67·0%		115,961		Turnout 70·6%	
							Swing +5·2%	
WEST BROMWICH								
C	20,950	27·2	—	2	31,631	39·3	—	2
Lab	43,278	56·2	2	2	43,070	53·5	2	2
L	9,061	11·8	—	2	3,228	4·0	—	1
Nat Front	3,714	4·8	—	2	2,526	3·1	—	2
Totals	77,003	100·0	2	8	80,455	100·0	2	7
Electorate	118,149		Turnout 65·2%		116,463		Turnout 69·1%	
							Swing +7·4%	

	October 1974				May 1979			
	Total Votes	% Total Votes	MPs	Candi-dates	Total Votes	% Total Votes	MPs	Candi-dates
WOLVERHAMPTON								
C	41,757	32·2	1	3	57,380	42·2	1	3
Lab	62,808	48·4	2	3	60,581	44·6	2	3
L	20,007	15·4	—	3	14,198	10·4	—	3
Nat Front	5,204	4·0	—	3	3,334	2·5	—	3
Others	—	—	—	—	401	0·3	—	1
Totals	129,776	100·0	3	12	135,894	100·0	3	13
Electorate	188,970		Turnout 68·7%		187,938		Turnout 72·3%	
							Swing +6·9%	

ENGLISH CITIES AND TOWNS (METROPOLITAN)

Totals for Category

	Total Votes	% Total Votes	MPs	Candi-dates	Total Votes	% Total Votes	MPs	Candi-dates
C	2,134,328	34·9	50	158	2,746,948	43·0	65	158
Lab	2,894,825	47·4	108	158	2,819,024	44·2	92	158
L	979,702	16·0	—	158	693,330	10·9	1	151
Comm	5,195	0·1	—	13	4,727	0·1	—	13
Nat Front	71,185	1·2	—	51	96,513	1·5	—	131
Others	21,886	0·4	—	48	22,637	0·4	—	86
Totals	6,107,121	100·0	158	586	6,383,179	100·0	158	697
Electorate	9,125,333		Turnout 66·9%		8,920,239		Turnout 71·6%	
							Swing +5·6%	

Non-Metropolitan Cities

Voting in principal non-Metropolitan cities and towns was as follows:

	Total Votes	% Total Votes	MPs	Candi-dates	Total Votes	% Total Votes	MPs	Candi-dates
ABERDEEN								
C	23,600	24·2	1	2	28,477	29·6	1	2
Lab	41,240	42·3	1	2	46,819	48·6	1	2
L	8,718	8·9	—	2	10,788	11·2	—	2
Scot Nat	23,990	24·6	—	2	10,157	10·6	—	2
Totals	97,548	100·0	2	8	96,241	100·0	2	8
Electorate	133,471		Turnout 73·1%		129,837		Turnout 74·1%	
							Swing −0·5%	
BELFAST								
Dem U	—	—	—	—	31,400	18·1	2	3
Off UU	—	—	—	—	63,745	36·8	1	4
UUUC	107,597	54·9	3	4	—	—	—	—
SDLP	35,611	18·2	1	3	27,997	16·1	1	3
Alliance	15,522	7·9	—	2	32,955	19·0	—	4
UPNI	14,417	7·4	—	1	8,021	4·6	—	3
NI Lab	11,539	5·9	—	3	4,411	2·5	—	3
Unionist	4,982	2·5	—	1	—	—	—	—
Repub Clubs	3,547	1·8	—	1	4,191	2·4	—	2
VPP	2,690	1·4	—	1	—	—	—	—
Lab Integ	—	—	—	—	692	0·4	—	1
Marks-Len	203	0·1	—	1	—	—	—	—
Totals	196,108	100·0	4	17	173,412	100·0	4	23
Electorate	294,292		Turnout 66·6%		268,358		Turnout 64·6%	
BLACKPOOL								
C	37,850	46·1	2	2	44,971	52·6	2	2
Lab	27,162	33·1	—	2	25,894	30·3	—	2
L	17,077	20·8	—	2	13,184	15·4	—	2
Nat Front	—	—	—	—	1,467	1·7	—	2
Totals	82,089	100·0	2	6	85,516	100·0	2	8
Electorate	117,694		Turnout 69·7%		118,172		Turnout 72·4%	
							Swing +4·6%	

Non-Metropolitan cities (continued)

	October 1974				May 1979			
	Total Votes	% Total Votes	MPs	Candi-dates	Total Votes	% Total Votes	MPs	Candi-dates
BOURNEMOUTH								
C	42,084	51·2	2	2	51,681	61·2	2	2
Lab	18,988	23·1	—	2	16,800	19·9	—	2
L	20,295	24·7	—	2	14,415	17·1	—	2
Nat Front	828	1·0	—	1	438	0·5	—	1
Others	—	—	—	—	1,104	1·3	—	2
Totals	82,195	100·0	2	7	84,438	100·0	2	9
Electorate	118,221		Turnout 69·5%		117,741		Turnout 71·7%	
							Swing +6·6%	
BRIGHTON								
C	40,766	47·1	2	2	47,730	53·7	2	2
Lab	30,684	35·4	—	2	29,603	33·3	—	2
L	14,862	17·2	—	2	10,144	11·4	—	2
Nat Front	—	—	—	—	840	0·9	—	2
Others	327	0·4	—	3	638	0·7	—	1
Totals	86,639	100·0	2	9	88,955	100·0	2	9
Electorate	122,794		Turnout 70·6%		121,173		Turnout 73·4%	
							Swing +4·3%	
BRISTOL								
C	77,863	34·7	1	5	98,700	42·7	2	5
Lab	102,261	45·6	4	5	100,181	43·3	3	5
L	42,091	18·8	—	5	28,616	12·4	—	5
Nat Front	1,570	0·7	—	2	1,735	0·8	—	5
Others	536	0·2	—	2	1,990	0·9	—	6
Totals	224,321	100·0	5	19	231,222	100·0	5	26
Electorate	309,274		Turnout 72·5%		305,880		Turnout 75·6%	
							Swing +5·1%	
CARDIFF								
C	50,969	35·5	2	4	50,276	35·1	2	3
Lab	62,025	43·2	2	4	48,667	33·9	1	3
L	24,785	17·3	—	4	9,753	6·8	—	2
Comm	—	—	—	—	112	0·1	—	1
Pl Cymru	5,733	4·0	—	4	5,724	4·0	—	4
Nat Front	—	—	—	—	1,287	0·9	—	1
Others	75	0·1	—	1	27,542	19·2	1	3
Totals	143,587	100·0	4	17	143,361	100·0	4	17
Electorate	197,027		Turnout 72·9%		198,150		Turnout 72·3%	
							Swing +4·4%	
DERBY								
C	39,777	35·4	—	2	49,436	41·9	—	2
Lab	53,302	47·5	2	2	55,742	47·2	2	2
L	18,115	16·1	—	2	11,289	9·6	—	2
Nat Front	—	—	—	—	1,179	1·0	—	2
Others	1,035	0·9	—	2	384	0·3	—	3
Totals	112,229	100·0	2	8	118,030	100·0	2	11
Electorate	157,039		Turnout 71·5%		159,002		Turnout 74·2%	
							Swing +3·4%	
DUNDEE								
C	16,553	17·6	—	2	21,964	22·0	—	2
Lab	34,617	36·9	1	2	41,632	41·6	1	2
L	3,497	3·7	—	2	2,317	2·3	—	1
Comm	381	0·4	—	1	316	0·3	—	1
Scot Nat	38,798	41·3	1	2	33,694	33·7	1	2
Others	—	—	—	—	95	0·1	—	1
Totals	93,846	100·0	2	9	100,018	100·0	2	9
Electorate	127,068		Turnout 73·9%		128,213		Turnout 78·0%	
							Swing −0·2%	
EDINBURGH								
C	82,805	32·2	4	7	100,334	38·2	4	7
Lab	85,685	33·3	3	7	102,423	39·0	3	7
L	27,492	10·7	—	7	32,172	12·3	—	6
Comm	213	0·1	—	1	173	0·1	—	1
Scot Nat	62,806	23·7	—	7	26,647	10·1	—	7
Others	—	—	—	—	852	0·3	—	3
Totals	257,001	100·0	7	29	262,601	100·0	7	31
Electorate	348,716		Turnout 73·7%		349,655		Turnout 75·1%	
							Swing +0·1%	

Non-Metropolitan cities (continued)

	October 1974				May 1979			
	Total Votes	% Total Votes	MPs	Candidates	Total Votes	% Total Votes	MPs	Candidates
GLASGOW								
C	80,614	20·2	2	13	97,499	25·8	1	13
Lab	196,225	49·0	11	13	218,861	58·0	12	13
L	16,939	4·2	—	12	15,081	4·0	—	5
Comm	1,209	0·3	—	3	1,301	0·3	—	4
Scot Nat	104,955	26·2	—	13	43,094	11·4	—	13
Nat Front	86	0·0	—	1	104	0·0	—	1
Others	27	0·0	—	1	1,294	0·3	—	5
Totals	400,055	100·0	13	56	377,234	100·0	13	54
Electorate	581,986		\multicolumn{2}{}{Turnout 68·7%}		533,860		Turnout 70·7%	
							Swing −1·7%	
KINGSTON-UPON-HULL								
C	33,265	24·7	—	3	42,036	29·8	—	3
Lab	77,000	57·1	3	3	81,479	57·7	3	3
L	24,514	18·2	—	3	16,268	11·5	—	3
Nat Front	—	—	—	—	1,207	0·9	—	3
Others	—	—	—	—	274	0·2	—	1
Totals	134,779	100·0	3	9	141,264	100·0	3	13
Electorate	202,494		Turnout 66·6%		202,313		Turnout 69·8%	
							Swing +2·2%	
LEICESTER								
C	50,778	36·2	—	3	60,732	39·9	—	3
Lab	65,682	46·8	3	3	74,424	48·9	3	3
L	16,512	11·8	—	3	13,511	8·9	—	3
Nat Front	7,292	5·2	—	3	3,633	2·4	—	3
Others	136	0·1	—	1	—		—	—
Totals	140,400	100·0	3	13	152,300	100·0	3	12
Electorate	201,107		Turnout 69·8%		205,192		Turnout 74·2%	
							Swing +0·8%	
LUTON								
C	28,163	33·9	—	2	39,039	43·9	2	2
Lab	38,279	46·1	2	2	37,946	42·7	—	2
L	16,236	19·6	—	2	10,518	11·8	—	2
Comm	—	—	—	—	107	0·1	—	1
Nat Front	—	—	—	—	1,162	1·3	—	2
Others	299	0·4	—	1	106	0·1	—	2
Totals	82,977	100·0	2	7	88,878	100·0	2	11
Electorate	111,821		Turnout 74·2%		113,613		Turnout 78·2%	
							Swing +6·7%	
NOTTINGHAM								
C	46,535	33·6	—	3	57,956	41·3	—	3
Lab	68,597	49·5	3	3	66,762	47·5	3	3
L	21,510	15·5	—	3	12,667	9·0	—	3
Comm	525	0·4	—	1	1,071	0·8	—	1
Nat Front	792	0·6	—	1	1,598	1·1	—	3
Others	736	0·5	—	1	444	0·3	—	2
Totals	138,695	100·0	3	12	140,498	100·0	3	15
Electorate	207,987		Turnout 66·7%		203,989		Turnout 68·9%	
							Swing +4·8%	
PLYMOUTH								
C	52,883	42·5	2	3	66,195	50·7	2	3
Lab	49,920	40·1	1	3	51,665	39·6	1	3
L	21,438	17·2	—	3	12,038	9·2	—	3
Nat Front	—	—	—	—	522	0·4	—	2
Others	312	0·3	—	1	203	0·2	—	1
Totals	124,553	100·0	3	10	130,623	100·0	3	12
Electorate	166,668		Turnout 74·7%		172,463		Turnout 75·7%	
							Swing +4·3%	
PORTSMOUTH								
C	46,386	45·4	1	2	53,191	51·5	2	2
Lab	39,660	38·8	1	2	39,351	38·1	—	2
L	15,015	14·7	—	2	9,841	9·5	—	2
Nat Front	—	—	—	—	755	0·7	—	2
Others	1,139	1·1	—	2	122	0·1	—	1
Totals	102,200	100·0	2	8	103,260	100·0	2	9
Electorate	139,862		Turnout 73·1%		136,216		Turnout 75·8%	
							Swing +3·4%	

Non-Metropolitan cities (continued)

	October 1974				May 1979			
	Total Votes	% Total Votes	MPs	Candi- dates	Total Votes	% Total Votes	MPs	Candi- dates
SOUTHAMPTON								
C	42,623	38·2	—	2	53,632	45·0	1	2
Lab	50,948	45·6	2	2	53,111	44·5	1	2
L	18,065	16·2	—	2	12,525	10·5	—	2
Totals	111,636	100·0	2	6	119,268	100·0	2	6
Electorate	155,904		Turnout 71·6%		158,041		Turnout 75·5%	
							Swing + 3·9%	
SOUTHEND								
C	41,563	46·8	2	2	51,862	57·0	2	2
Lab	22,931	25·8	—	2	19,980	21·9	—	2
L	24,265	27·3	—	2	17,829	19·6	—	2
Totals	88,759	100·0	2	6	91,027	100·0	2	8
Electorate	124,733		Turnout 71·2%		123,995		Turnout 73·4%	
							Swing + 7·0%	
STOKE-ON-TRENT								
C	33,889	25·7	—	3	42,696	30·9	—	3
Lab	80,109	60·8	3	3	81,969	59·4	3	3
L	17,830	13·5	—	3	13,083	9·5	—	3
Nat Front	—	—	—	—	341	0·2	—	1
Totals	131,828	100·0	3	9	138,089	100·0	3	10
Electorate	193,745		Turnout 68·0%		193,088		Turnout 71·5%	
							Swing + 3·3%	
SWANSEA								
C	23,743	26·1	—	2	34,463	35·1	—	2
Lab	49,300	54·3	2	2	56,084	57·2	2	2
L	12,015	13·2	—	2	3,484	3·6	—	1
Comm	—	—	—	—	308	0·3	—	1
Pl Cymru	5,756	6·3	—	2	3,744	3·8	—	2
Totals	90,814	100·0	2	8	98,083	100·0	2	8
Electorate	124,005		Turnout 73·2%		126,222		Turnout 77·7%	
							Swing + 3·0%	
TEESSIDE								
C	57,728	31·4	—	4	72,743	35·7	—	4
Lab	101,087	54·9	4	4	108,856	53·5	4	4
L	24,529	13·3	—	4	18,577	9·1	—	4
Comm	—	—	—	—	243	0·1	—	1
Nat Front	—	—	—	—	635	0·3	—	2
Others	750	0·4	—	1	2,555	1·3	—	4
Totals	184,094	100·0	4	13	203,609	100·0	4	19
Electorate	270,473		Turnout 68·1		278,679		Turnout 73·1%	
							Swing + 2·8%	

CITIES AND TOWNS (NON-METROPOLITAN)

Totals for Category

	Total Votes	% Total Votes	MPs	Candi- dates	Total Votes	% Total Votes	MPs	Candi- dates
C	950,437	30·6	21	70	1,165,613	36·8	25	69
Lab	1,307,241	42·1	48	73	1,358,249	42·9	43	69
L	405,800	13·1	—	69	288,100	9·1	—	57
Comm	2,328	0·1	—	6	3,631	0·1	—	11
Scot Nat	228,549	7·4	1	24	113,592	3·6	1	24
Pl Cymru	11,189	0·4	—	6	9,468	0·3	—	6
Nat Front	10,568	0·3	—	8	18,259	0·6	—	34
Others	189,941	6·1	4	30	211,015	6·7	5	58
Totals	3,106,353	100·0	74	286	3,167,927	100·0	74	328
Electorate	4,404,850		Turnout 70·5%		4,343,852		Turnout 72·9%	
							Swing + 2·7%	

Rise and fall of the Parties 1945-70

The following table gives the state of the parties after each election from 1945 to 1970; it also shows the size of the electorate and the percentage who voted.

	1945	1950	1951	1955	1959	1964	1966	1970
Conservative	213	298	321	345	365	303	253	330
Labour	393	315	295	277	258	317	363	287
Liberal	12	9	6	6	6	9	12	6
Independent	14	—	—	—	—	1	—	—
Others	8	3	3	2	—	1 (the Speaker)	2*	7*
	—	—	—	—	—	—	—	—
Total	640	625	625	630	630	630	630	630
Electorate	32,836,419	34,269,764	34,622,891	34,852,179	35,397,304	35,894,054	35,957,245	39,342,013
Poll	24,978,949	28,769,477	28,602,323	28,759,729	27,862,652	27,657,148	27,264,747	28,344,798
Percentage	76·1	84	82·6	76·8	78·7	77·0	75·9	72·0

*Includes the Speaker.

Disappointment for the Liberal Party

For the Liberal Party the election turned out to be a disappointment, especially with the defeat of its deputy leader, Mr John Pardoe, in North Cornwall, and its defence spokesman, Mr Emlyn Hooson, in Montgomeryshire.

The Liberals entered the election with 14 MPs and emerged with 11. The third reverse was suffered at North Devon where their former leader, Mr Jeremy Thorpe, was defeated by the Conservative, Mr Antony Speller, with an 8,473 majority.

The Liberals went into the election flushed with the by-election success of Mr David Alton at Liverpool, Edge Hill. He comfortably retained that seat. The Liberal leader, Mr David Steel, increased his majority at Roxburgh, Selkirk and Peebles by more than 3,000 votes.

Liberals were runners-up in 81 seats, 79 of them Conservative-held. In October, 1974, they were runners-up in 105 seats. In only three of the seats in which they were second did the Liberals reduce the percentage majority of the winning candidate.

The party fielded 576 candidates compared with 619 in October, 1974. They polled 4,305,324 votes, which was 13.8 per cent of the United Kingdom total. In October, 1974, they polled 5,346,800 votes – 18.3 per cent of the total.

The following table shows the percentage by which Liberals lost in constituencies where they came second, with the equivalent figure for October, 1974. A dash indicates that the party was not second on that occasion.

CONSERVATIVE SEATS

Constituency	May 1979	Oct. 1974
Aberdeenshire, West	5·4	5·8
Montgomeryshire	5·4	—
Richmond upon Thames, Richmond	6·2	17·7
Chippenham	7·9	3·3
Cornwall, North	8·0	—
Chelmsford	8·0	6·3
Hereford	10·3	2·5
Louth	11·7	5·6
Leominster	12·3	1·7
Salisbury	12·5	8·9
Skipton	12·6	1·4
Southport	12·8	11·5
Devon, North	13·4	—
Gainsborough	13·8	8·6
Totnes	15·8	10·3
Pudsey	16·0	9·0
Newbury	16·1	1·8
Denbigh	16·8	9·4
Yeovil	17·4	—
Bath	18·4	4·3
Bodmin	19·7	1·4
Fife, East	20·0	—
Wells	20·6	14·0
Cheltenham	21·0	18·0
Shrewsbury	21·0	12·3
Ludlow	21·2	17·1
Westbury	22·0	10·4
Richmond upon Thames, Twickenham	22·3	—
Chertsey and Walton	22·8	—
Derbyshire, West	24·9	20·3
Hazel Grove	26·1	5·1
Horncastle	27·1	14·9
Tiverton	27·5	9·1
Westmorland	27·8	19·1
Saffron Walden	28·9	13·4
Bromley, Orpington	29·0	9·6
Cirencester and Tewkesbury	29·2	16·5
St Albans	29·3	—
Maidstone	29·4	15·7
Howden	30·7	11·5
Cheadle	31·1	13·6
Torbay	31·5	19·9
Sutton, Sutton and Cheam	31·6	11·1

Constituency	May 1979	Oct. 1974
Farnham	31·9	17·3
Haltemprice	32·2	20·4
Southend, West	33·1	14·3
Folkestone and Hythe	33·2	18·6
Shoreham	33·8	22·2
Worcestershire, South	33·8	16·3
Weston-super-Mare	34·0	20·2
Petersfield	34·9	15·8
Fareham	35·0	10·1
Devon, West	35·6	13·1
Aldershot	35·7	17·1
Henley	35·8	22·4
Harrogate	36·1	29·2
Dorset, North	36·2	15·1
Dorset, West	36·9	20·8
Worthing	37·1	33·6
Lewes	37·3	26·0
East Grinstead	37·6	22·4
Chesham and Amersham	38·4	22·2
Stratford-on-Avon	38·4	23·6
Ripon	38·6	22·1
New Forest	38·7	23·1
Sussex, Mid	39·2	25·7
Richmond, Yorks	40·3	33·5
Rye	40·7	29·2
Bromley, Ravensbourne	41·6	23·7
Honiton	41·6	23·9
Epsom and Ewell	41·7	27·4
Dorking	41·8	23·3
Chichester	42·7	22·1
Surrey, East	43·1	23·2
Croydon, South	43·9	31·9
Eastbourne	44·2	28·8
Esher	45·4	30·7
Arundel	45·5	30·9
Christchurch and Lymington	49·1	33·6

LABOUR SEATS

Constituency	May 1979	Oct. 1974
Greenock and Port Glasgow	24·8	—
Tower Hamlets, Bethnal Green and Bow	26·4	55·9

The Scottish National Party

For the Scottish National Party, the May 1979 election proved a disaster for they lost nine of their 11 seats, seven to the Conservatives and two to Labour.

The four seats they won in the October 1974 election all went. The SNP vote slumped from 30·4 per cent in October 1974 to 17·3 per cent this year, but the SNP still polled over 500,000 votes out of nearly three million who voted in Scotland.

Only the leader of the parliamentary party, Mr Donald Stewart, in the Western Isles, and the deputy leader, Mr Gordon Wilson, in Dundee, East, held their seats. In October 1974 SNP candidates took second place in 42 seats; this time they came second in 13.

These 13 seats are: Aberdeenshire East; Angus, North and Mearns; Angus, South; Argyll; Banff; Dundee, West; Galloway; Kinross and West Perthshire; Moray and Nairn; Perth and East Perthshire; Ross and Cromarty; Sterlingshire, East and Clackmannan; and West Lothian.

Plaid Cymru

Plaid Cymru lost one of the three seats they held when the election was called. That was Carmarthen, the seat which Mr Gwynfor Evans, leader of the party, won at the October 1974 election.

The Plaid Cymru share of the Welsh vote was 8·1 per cent, compared with 10·8 in October 1974, 10 per cent at the February 1974 election, and 11·5 per cent in 1970.

Labour's share of the Welsh vote was 46·9 per cent. Its share in October 1974 was 49·5 per cent, compared with 46·8 in February 1974. The Conservative share of the vote rose from 23·9 per cent in October 1974 to 32·2 per cent. The Liberal share fell from 15·5 per cent to 10·6.

Only Plaid Cymru and the National Front contested Cardiff, West where Mr George Thomas sought re-election as Speaker.

PLP elections

Mr James Callaghan and Mr Michael Foot were unopposed as Leader and Deputy Leader of the Opposition. In the Parliamentary Labour Party elections in May 1979, Mr Frederick Willey (Sunderland, North) was elected chairman, defeating Mr Norman Buchan (West Renfrewshire) by 151 votes to 87. Mr Michael Cocks (Bristol, South) was re-elected Labour's Chief Whip, defeating Mr Martin Flannery (Sheffield, Hillsborough) by 188 votes to 44.

In the House of Lords, Lord Peart of Workington is the Leader of the Opposition there, with Lord Goronwy-Roberts as Deputy Leader, Lady Llewellyn-Davies as Chief Whip and Lord Lee of Newton as the representative of the backbench Labour peers on the Opposition's parliamentary committee.

Lost deposits

One thousand and two candidates lost their deposits making a total sum of £150,300, more than twice as much as in October, 1974. The Liberal Party and the National Front were the biggest contributors, the former losing 304 deposits and the latter 303 Plaid Cymru and the Scottish National Party each lost 29 deposits. Labour lost 25 and the Conservatives three. All other candidates, excluding those in Northern Ireland, lost their deposits.

Mr du Cann is Chairman of 1922 Committee

Mr Edward du Cann (Taunton) was re-elected in May 1979 as chairman of the 1922 Committee of Conservative backbenchers, a position he has held since 1972. In the voting he defeated Sir Paul Bryan (Howden).

Mr John Osborn (Sheffield, Hallam) and Mr Victor Goodhew (St Albans) are joint secretaries and the 12 members of the new executive of the 1922 committee are:

*Mr Kenneth Baker (City of Westminster, St Marylebone); *Mr John Biggs-Davison (Epping Forest); *Sir Bernard Braine (Essex, South-East); *Mr Anthony Buck (Colchester); Mr Winston Churchill (Stretford); *Sir Nigel Fisher (Kingston upon Thames, Surbiton); *Mr Anthony Grant (Harrow); *Mr Peter Hordern (Horsham and Crawley); Mr Geoffrey Johnson Smith (East Grinstead); Mrs Jill Knight (Birmingham, Edgbaston); *Mr Nicholas Scott (Kensington and Chelsea, Chelsea); Mr William van Straubenzee (Wokingham).

*denotes re-elected.

Defeated Members

Sixty-five former MPs of the October, 1974, to April, 1979, Parliament lost their seats in this general election. They consisted of 45 Labour, five Conservative, nine Scottish National, three Liberal, one Official Ulster Unionist, one Scottish Labour and one Plaid Cymru—Mr Gwynfor Evans, leader of the Welsh nationalist party.

The only Cabinet minister to be defeated was Mrs Shirley Williams, Secretary of State for Education and Science, beaten at Hertford and Stevenage. She had been at Westminster since 1964, representing Hitchin for the first 10 years. She has been a member of the Labour Party national executive committee since 1970.

Her junior ministerial colleague at the DES, Miss Margaret Jackson, went out at Lincoln, while former education junior ministers beaten were Mr Gerald Fowler (The Wrekin) and Mr Hugh Jenkins (Wandsworth, Putney), the former Minister for the Arts.

While Dr David Owen, Secretary of State for Foreign and Commonwealth Affairs, was retaining his fairly marginal seat at Plymouth, Devonport, three of his junior ministerial colleagues were defeated—Mr Frank Judd, Minister of State; Mr Evan Luard and Mr John Tomlinson, Under Secretaries of State.

Other ministers beaten were Mr Edward Bishop, Minister of State for Agriculture, Fisheries and Food, and Mr William Price, Parliamentary Secretary, Privy Council Office.

The Liberal Party suffered the loss of its deputy leader and Treasury spokesman, Mr John Pardoe, as well as its former leader, Mr Jeremy Thorpe, and defence spokesman, Mr Emlyn Hooson, who lost Monmouth at the same time as his cousin, Mr Timothy Hooson (Conservative) captured Brecon and Radnor from Labour.

The chief Conservative spokesman on Scotland, Mr Edward Taylor, was beaten at Glasgow, Cathcart, and the four other defeated Conservatives were all victors at by-elections held during the last Parliament.

Those who failed to be re-elected were:

LABOUR

Atkins, R. H., *Preston North*
Bates, A., *Bebington and Ellesmere Port*
Bean, R. E., *Rochester and Chatham*
Bishop, E. S., *Newark*
Carter, R. J., *Birmingham, Northfield*
Clemitson, I. M., *Luton, East*
Colquhoun, Mrs M. M., *Northampton, North*
Corbett, R., *Hemel Hempstead*
Cronin, J. D., *Loughborough*
Davies, B., *Enfield, North*
Edge, G., *Aldridge-Brownhills*
Ellis, J., *Brigg and Scunthorpe*
Fowler, G. T., *Wrekin, The*
Gould, B. C., *Southampton Test*
Grocott, B. J., *Lichfield and Tamworth*
Hayman, Mrs H., *Welwyn and Hatfield*
Hoyle, E. D. H., *Nelson and Colne*
Irving, S., *Dartford*
Jackson, Miss M. M., *Lincoln*
Jenkins, H. G., *Wandsworth, Putney*
Judd, F. A., *Portsmouth, North*
Latham, A. C., *City of Westminster, Paddington*
Litterick, T., *Birmingham, Selly Oak*
Loyden, E., *Liverpool, Garston*
Luard, D. E. T., *Oxford*
MacFarquhar, R. L., *Belper*
Madden, M. F., *Sowerby*
Molloy, W. J., *Ealing, North*
Moonman, E., *Basildon*
Noble, M. A., *Rossendale*
Ovenden, J. F., *Gravesend*
Price, W. G., *Rugby*
Roderick, C. E., *Brecon and Radnor*
Rodgers, G. *Chorley*
Sedgmore, B. C. J., *Luton, West*
Shaw, A. J., *Redbridge, Ilford, South*
Thomas, R. R., *Bristol, North-West*
Tierney, S., *Birmingham, Yardley*
Tomlinson, J. E., *Meriden*
Walker, T. W., *Kingswood*
Ward, M. J., *Peterborough*
Watkinson, J. T., *Gloucestershire, West*
Williams, A. L., *Havering, Hornchurch*
Williams, Mrs S. V. T. B., *Hertford and Stevenage*
Wise, Mrs A., *Coventry, South-West*

Conservative

Hodgson, R. G., *Walsall, North*
Mackay, A., *Birmingham, Stechford*
Page, R. L., *Workington*
Smith, T., *Ashfield*
Taylor, E. M., *Glasgow, Cathcart*

Scottish National

Bain, Mrs M. A., *Dunbartonshire, East*
Crawford, G. D., *Perth and East Perthshire*
Ewing, Mrs W. M., *Moray and Nairn*
Henderson, D., *Aberdeenshire, East*
MacCormick, I., *Argyll*
Reid, G. N., *Stirlingshire, East and Clackmannan*
Thompson, G., *Galloway*
Watts, H., *Banffshire*
Welsh, A., *Angus, South*

Liberal

Hooson, H. E., *Montgomery*
Pardoe, J. W., *Cornwall, North*
Thorpe, J. J., *Devon, North*

Official Ulster Unionist

Craig, W., *Belfast, East*

Scottish Labour

Sillars, J., *Ayrshire, South*

Plaid Cymru

Evans, G., *Carmarthen*

Former Ministers among retiring MPs

A total of 61 MPs – 35 Labour, 24 Conservative, an Ulster Unionist and one Scottish Labour – did not seek re-election. One of the best known departures on the Labour side was Mrs Barbara Castle, Secretary of State for Social Services, from 1974 to 1976. Among her other posts were Minister of Transport, 1965–68 and Secretary of State for Employment and Productivity, 1968–70.

Other former Labour ministers who did not stand include Mr Michael Stewart, Foreign Secretary until the General Election of 1970, Mr Edmund Dell, Secretary of State for Trade, 1976–78, Mr William Ross, Secretary of State for Scotland, 1964–70 and 1974–76, and Mr Cledwyn Hughes, chairman of the Parliamentary Labour Party and a former Agriculture minister and Secretary of State for Wales.

On the Conservative side former ministers who did not stand included Mr Joseph Godber, Minister of Agriculture, 1972–74 and Minister of State for Foreign and Commonwealth Affairs, 1970–72, Mr Richard Wood, Minister for Overseas Development, 1970–74, and Sir David Renton, QC, Minister of State, Home Office, 1961–62.

Two occupants and one former occupant of the Speaker's Chair also stood down. They were Mr Oscar Murton (*Poole,* C) Deputy Speaker and Chairman of Ways and Means, Sir Myer Galpern (*Glasgow, Shettleston,* Lab), a Deputy Speaker and Deputy Chairman of Ways and Means together with Miss Harvie Anderson (*East Renfrewshire,* C) the first woman to occupy the Chair as Deputy Speaker and Deputy Chairman of Ways and Means, 1970–73.

One other House of Commons figure who departed was the Father of the House, Mr George Strauss (*Lambeth, Vauxhall*).

The full list is:

Labour

Mr Arthur Blenkinsop (*South Shields*), Mr Harold Boardman (*Leigh*), Mr James Boyden (*Bishop Auckland*), Mr Richard Buchanan (*Glasgow, Springburn,* Mrs Joyce Butler (*Haringey, Wood Green*), Mrs Barbara Castle (*Blackburn*), Sir Geoffrey de Frietas (*Kettering*), Mr Peter Doig (*Dundee, West*), Mr Edmund Dell (*Birkenhead*), Mr Alfred Evans (*Caephilly*), Mr Ernest Fernyhough (*Jarrow*), Sir Myer Galpern (*Glasgow, Shettleston*), Mr Cledwyn Hughes (*Anglesey*), Mr Adam Hunter (*Dunfermline*), Mr Colin Jackson (*Brighouse and Spenborough*), Mrs Lena Jeger (*Camden, Holborn and St Pancras, South*), Mr Richard Kelley (*Don Valley*), Mr John Lee (*Birmingham, Handsworth*), Mr Kenneth Lomas (*Huddersfield, West*), Mr Simon Mahon (*Bootle*), Mr J. P. W. Mallalieu (*Huddersfield, East*), Mr Ronald King Murray (*Edinburgh, Leith*), Mr Maurice Orbach (*Stockport, South*), Mr Walter Padley (*Ogmore*), Mr Ernest Perry (*Wandsworth, Battersea, South*), Mr Colin Phipps (*Dudley, West*), Mr Paul Rose (*Manchester, Blackley*), Mr William Ross (*Kilmarnock*), Mr Harry Selby (*Glasgow, Govan*), Mr Michael Stewart (*Hammersmith, Fulham*), Mr George Strauss (*Lambeth, Vauxhall*), Mr Frank Tomney (*Hammersmith, North*), Mr Raphael Tuck (*Watford*), Mr David Weitzman (*Hackney, North and Stoke Newington*), and Mr Robert Woof (*Blaydon*).

Conservative

Miss Harvie Anderson (*East Renfrewshire*), Mr Daniel Awdry (*Chippenham*), Dr Reginald Bennett (*Fareham*), Sir Edward Brown (*Bath*), Mr John Cockcroft (*Nantwich*), Mr Robert Cooke (*Bristol, West*), Mr Petre Crowder (*Hillingdon, Ruislip-Northwood*), Mr Burnaby Drayson (*Skipton*), Sir John Gilmour (*Fife, East*), Mr Joseph Godber (*Grantham*), Mr Alfred Hall-Davies (*Morecambe and Lonsdale*), Sir Harwood Harrison (*Eye*), Mr Michael Clark Hutchison (*Edinburgh, South*), Mr David James (*Dorset, North*), Mr Arthur Jones (*Daventry*), Mr Evelyn King (*Dorset, South*), Mr Jasper More (*Ludlow*), Rear Adm M. C. Morgan-Giles (*Winchester*), Mr Oscar Murton (*Poole*), Sir David Renton (*Huntingdonshire*), Sir John Rodgers (*Sevenoaks*), Mr James Scott-Hopkins (*Derbyshire, West*), Sir George Sinclair (*Dorking*), and Mr Richard Wood (*Bridlington*).

Ulster Unionist

Mr John Carson (*Belfast, North*).

Scottish Labour Party

Mr John Robertson (*Paisley*).

Sponsored Labour MPs

Trades unions and the Co-operative Party are sponsoring 148 Labour members in the new Parliament. Of 148 sponsored MPs who sought re-election 18 were defeated, but 18 of 36 sponsored candidates seeking to enter the House of Commons for the first time, were elected.

The largest group of union-sponsored MPs – 22 – are sponsored by the Transport and General Workers' Union. They are:

Sydney Bidwell (Ealing, Southall); Norman Buchan (Renfrewshire, West); Lewis Carter-Jones (Eccles); Joseph Crowther (Rotherham); James Dunn (Liverpool, Kirkdale); Raymond Fletcher (Ilkeston); Harry Gourlay (Kirkcaldy); John Horam (Gateshead, West); Leslie Huckfield (Nuneaton); Roy Hughes (Newport); Neil Kinnock (Bedwellty); Edward Loyden (Liverpool, Garston); Hugh McCartney (Dunbartonshire, Central); Gregor Mackenzie (Rutherglen); Kevin McNamara (Kingston upon Hull, Central); David Marshall (Glasgow, Shettleston); Robert Mellish (Southwark, Bermondsey); Gordon Oakes (Widnes); Robert Parry (Liverpool, Scotland Exchange); Peter Shore (Tower Hamlets, Stepney and Popular); Mrs Renee Short (Wolverhampton, North-East); John Silkin (Lewisham, Deptford).

The 16 MPs sponsored by the National Union of Mineworkers are:

Dennis Concannon (Mansfield); Lawrence Cunliffe (Leigh); Alexander Eadie (Midlothian); Ray Ellis (Derbyshire, North-East); Alan Fitch (Wigan); George Grant (Morpeth); Frank Haynes (Ashfield); Roy Mason (Barnsley); Michael McGuire (Ince); Eric Ogden (Liverpool, West Derby); Albert Roberts (Normanton); Dennis Skinner (Bolsover); Eric Varley (Chesterfield); Edwin Wainwright (Dearne Valley); Michael Welsh (Don Valley); Alec Woodall (Hemsworth).

Fifteen MPs are sponsored by the Amalgamated Union of Engineering Workers. They are:

Norman Atkinson (Haringey, Tottenham); Bernard Conlan (Gateshead, East); Joseph Dean (Leeds, West); John Evans (Newton); Benjamin Ford (Bradford; North); Edward Garrett (Wallsend); Robert Hughes (Aberdeen, North); Daniel Jones (Burnley); William McKelvey (Kilmarnock); Stanley Orme (Salford, West); George Park (Coventry, North-East); Ernest Roberts (Hackney, North and Stoke Newington); Albert Stallard (Camden, St Pancras North); Harold Walker (Doncaster), and David Watkins (Consett).

Joseph Ashton (Bassetlaw); Albert Booth (Barrow-in-Furness); James Lamond (Oldham, East) and Ernest Ross (Dundee, West) are sponsored by the AUEW (Technical and Supervisory Section), and James Hamilton (Bothwell) by the AUEW (Constructional Section).

The General and Municipal Workers' Union are sponsoring 14 MPs:

Jack Ashley (Stoke-on-Trent, South): Miss Betty Boothroyd (West Bromwich, West); Robert Brown (Newcastle upon Tyne, West); Neil Carmichael (Glasgow, Kelvingrove); Michael Cocks (Bristol, South); John Cunningham (Whitehaven); Donald Dixon (Jarrow); Patrick Duffy (Sheffield, Attercliffe); Michael English (Nottingham, West); James Johnson (Kingston upon Hull, West); Giles Radice (Chester-le-Street); George Robertson (Hamilton); William Rodgers (Teesside, Stockton); Frank White (Bury and Radcliffe).

Other unions and the MPs they sponsor are:

National Union of Railwaymen: Gordon Bagier (Sunderland, South); Robin Cook (Edinburgh, Central); Harry Cowans (Newcastle upon Tyne, Central); Tam Dalyell (West Lothian); Ronald Lewis (Carlisle); Thomas McMillan (Glasgow, Central); Michael O'Halloran (Islington, North); Peter Snape (West Bromwich, East); Leslie Spriggs (St Helens); Phillip Whitehead (Derby, North).

National Union of Public Employees: Arthur Bottomley (Teesside, Middlesbrough); David Clark (South Shields); Peter Hardy (Rother Valley); Edward Leadbitter (Hartlepool); Roland Moyle (Lewisham, East); Thomas Pendry (Stalybridge and Hyde); Reg Race (Haringey, Wood Green).

Association of Scientific Technical and Managerial Staffs: Terry Davis (Birmingham, Stechford); Russell Kerr (Hounslow, Feltham and Heston); Ian Mikardo (Tower Hamlets, Bethnal Green and Bow); Dr Maurice Miller (East Kilbride); Jeffrey Rooker (Birmingham, Perry Barr); Gavin Strang (Edinburgh, East); Stanley Thorne (Preston, South); Frederick Willey (Sunderland, North).

Association of Professional Executive Clerical and Computer Staff: Ifor Davies (Gower); Edward Fletcher (Darlington); Denis Howell (Birmingham, Small Heath); Bruce Millan (Glasgow, Craigton); Frederick Mulley (Sheffield, Park).

Electrical Electronic and Telecommunications and Plumbing Trades Union: Thomas Cox (Wandsworth, Tooting); John Grant (Islington, Central); Walter Harrison (Wakefield); David Stoddart (Swindon).

Confederation of Health Service Employees: William Hamilton (Fife, Central); Alec Jones (Rhondda); Michael Meacher (Oldham, West).

Post Office Engineering Union: John Golding (Newcastle-under-Lyme); John McWilliam (Blaydon); Roger Stott (Westhoughton).

Union of Post Office Workers: Harry Ewing (Stirling, Falkirk and Grangemouth); Charles Morris (Manchester, Openshaw).

Union of Construction Allied Trades and Technicians: Eric Heffer (Liverpool, Walton); Thomas Urwin (Houghton-le-Spring).

Iron and Steel Trades Confederation: Donald Coleman (Neath), William Homewood (Kettering).

Union of Shop Distributive and Allied Workers: John Cartwright (Greenwich, Woolwich, East), Harry Lamborn (Southwark, Peckham), Frank McElhone (Glasgow, Queen's Park); Ray Powell (Ogmore); Thomas Torney (Braford, South).

Transport Salaried Staffs Association: Tom Bradley (Leicester, East); Stanley Cohen (Leeds, South-East); Walter Johnson (Derby, South).

National Union of Agricultural and Allied Workers: Miss Joan Maynard (Sheffield, Brightside).

National Union of Blastfurnacemen: James Tinn (Teesside, Redcar).

Amalgamated Society of Boilermakers, Shipwrights, Blacksmiths and Structural Workers: John Smith (Lanarkshire, North).

Furniture Timber and Allied Trades Union: Ronald Brown (Hackney, South and Shoreditch).

National Union of Seamen: John Prescott (Kingston upon Hull, East).

Co-operative Party: James Craigen (Glasgow, Maryhill); Richard Douglas (Dunfermline); Robert Edwards (Wolverhampton, South-East); Ioan Evans (Aberdare); George Foulkes (Ayrshire, South); Edward Graham (Enfield, Edmonton); Dr Dickson Mabon (Greenock and Port Glasgow); Alfred Morris (Manchester, Wythenshawe); Stanley Newens (Harlow); Arthur Palmer (Bristol, North-East); Laurence Pavitt (Brent, South); John Roper (Farnworth); Barry Sheerman (Huddersfield, East); Mike Thomas (Newcastle upon Tyne, East); John Tilley (Lambeth, Central); Thomas Williams (Warrington); Ian Wrigglesworth (Teesside, Thornaby).

Women MPs

Ages, jobs and education

Although the result of the election led to Mrs Margaret Thatcher being the first woman Prime Minister, the fewest number of women MPs since 1951 were returned with her to the House of Commons.

In the October, 1974, general election 27 women were returned, four more than in the February election of that year. But in May, 1979, only 19 women were elected, comprising 11 Labour and eight Conservative MPs, Mrs Thatcher among them.

Three new women MPs were elected and two of them gained seats for the Conservatives at the expense of Labour. They were Mrs Sheila Faith (*Belper*), who unseated Mr Roderick MacFarquhar, and Mrs Peggy Fenner (*Rochester and Chatham*), the former MP for that constituency, who was unseated by Robert Bean in October, 1974. She first won the seat in 1970. Mrs Sheila Wright retained *Birmingham, Handsworth,* for Labour.

Mrs Shirley Williams, the former Secretary of State for Education and Science, lost *Hertford and Stevenage* for Labour, and Miss Margaret Jackson the former Under Secretary of State for Education, lost at *Lincoln.*

Other women Labour MPs who lost their seats were Mrs Audrey Wise (*Coventry, South-West*), Mrs Maureen Colquhoun (*Northampton, North*) and Mrs Helene Hayman (*Welwyn and Hatfield*). The two woman members of the Scottish National Party, Mrs Margaret Bain (*Dunbartonshire, East*) and Mrs Winifred Ewing (*Moray and Nairn*), both lost their seats.

Three Labour and one Conservative women MPs retired at the election. Women MPs are:

Conservative
Mrs Lynda Chalker (*Wallasey*); Mrs Sheila Faith (*Belper*); Mrs Peggy Fenner (*Rochester and Chatham*); Miss Janet Fookes (*Plymouth, Drake*); Mrs Elaine Kellet-Bowman (*Lancaster*); Mrs Jill Knight (*Birmingham, Edgbaston*); Mrs Salley Oppenheim (*Gloucester*); Mrs Margaret Thatcher (*Barnet, Finchley*).

Labour
Miss Betty Boothroyd (*West Bromwich, West*); Mrs Gwyneth Dunwoody (*Crewe*); Mrs Judith Hart (*Lanark*); Miss Joan Lestor (*Eton and Slough*); Miss Joan Maynard (*Sheffield, Brightside*); Miss Oonagh McDonald (*Thurrock*); Miss Josephine Richardson (*Barking*); Dr Shirley Summerskill (*Halifax*); Mrs Renee Short (*Wolverhampton, North-East*); Mrs Ann Taylor (*Bolton, West*); Mrs Sheila Wright (*Birmingham, Handsworth*).

Age	C	Lab	L	Other	Total
Over 70	3	8	—	1	12
66—70	10	12	—	2	24
61—65	25	23	2	—	50
56—60	34	40	—	3	77
51—55	55	51	3	2	111
46—50	72	53	2	3	130
41—45	56	26	1	2	85
36—40	52	41	—	3	96
31—35	24	13	2	1	40
30 and under	8	1	1	—	10
Total	339	268	11	17	635

	C	Lab	L	Other
Barristers and advocates .	54	21	–	1
Solicitors	16	10	–	1
Journalists and authors ..	31	19	1	1
Publishers	5	–	–	–
Public relations	2	–	–	–
Teachers, lecturers	14	53	3	4
Doctors, surgeons, dentists	3	5	–	–
Farmers, landowners	25	2	2	1
Company directors	82	1	2	–
Accountants	12	4	1	–
Underwriters and brokers	17	–	–	–
Managers, executives and administratives	52	33	–	2
Architects and surveyors .	5	1	1	–
Scientists	1	5	–	–
Economists	8	9	–	1
Banking	12	–	–	–
Diplomatic	2	1	–	–
Social workers	1	3	–	–
Civil servants	–	3	–	–
Local government	1	2	–	–
Clerical and technical	1	3	–	–
Engineers	8	30	1	–
Mineworkers	–	16	–	–
Rail workers	–	9	–	–
Other manual workers ..	–	7	–	2
Trade union officials	1	27	–	–
Party officials	12	5	–	–
Hoteliers and publicans ..	–	–	–	2
Other business and professions	10	5	–	–
Ministers of religion	–	–	–	2

Some MPs have two or three professions or occupations and others have ceased their business, professions or occupations. Members of the Government have resigned from the directorships they held up to the time of appointment.

	C	Lab	L	Other
Oxford	94	38	2	–
Cambridge	75	20	1	1
Other universities	87	107	2	6
	256	165	5	7
Service colleges	16	–	–	–
Technical, art, & commercial, teacher training, etc colleges	27	56	2	1
Eton	50	1	1	–
Harrow	9	–	–	–
Winchester	7	2	–	–
Other public schools	138	18	4	–
	204	21	5	–
Grammar and equivalent	90	108	4	5
Secondary and elementary	13	112	–	5
Ruskin College	–	15	–	–
NCCL and adult colleges	–	9	–	–

By-Elections

Constituency and date		Party	
MANCHESTER CENTRAL 27/9/79	R. LITHERLAND MAJ: 5,992	LAB HOLD	L: 7494 LIB: 1502 C: 1275 IND LAB: 187 ECO: 129 BONKS: 12
HERTFORDSHIRE SOUTH-WEST 13/12/79	R. PAGE MAJ. 6,772	CON HOLD	C. 17031 LAB: 10,259 LIB: 8752 ECO: 602 ANTI-VOC 288 SOTON RAC 143
SOUTHEND EAST 13/3/80	E. TAYLOR MAJ. 430	CON HOLD	C. 13117 LAB 12687 LIB 8939 N BRIT 532 A-VOC 207 IND LIB 132 BONKS 23
GLASGOW CENTRAL 26/6/80	R. McTAGGART MAJ. 2,780	LAB HOLD	LAB 6902 SNP 2122 C 707 NF 148 SYLIB 134 ECOL 45 SOC DEM 10
CROYDON N.W. 22/10/81	W. PITT. MAJ. 3,254	L-SDP WIN	L-SDP 13800 CON 10006 LAB 8967 SDP. 8118
CROSBY 26/11/81	MRS S. WILLIAMS MAJ. 5,289	L-SDP WIN	CON 22829 LAB 5,450 ECOL. 650 LOONIST 223 BONKS 36
GLASGOW HILLHEAD 25/3/82	R. JENKINS. MAJ. 2,038	L-SDP WIN	SDP. 10,106 CON 8068 LAB 7846 SNP 3,416 BONKS 5
SOUTHWARK BERMONDSEY 24/2/83	MR. S. HUGHES MAJ. 9,319	L-SDP WIN	L-SDP. 17017 LAB 7,698 REAL LAB 2243 CON 1631 (12 OTHERS CANDIDATES)

Constituency and date		Party	
O O'BRIEN. 24/3/83	DARLINGTON MAJ. 2,412	LAB HOLD	LAB 2C CON A SDP 12

Constituency and date		Party

Constituency and date		Party

Constituency and date		Party

*The General Election Manifestos

The Conservative Party

'The Conservative Manifesto 1979'

In a foreword to the Conservative Party manifesto, Mrs Margaret Thatcher wrote:

For me, the heart of politics is not political theory, it is people and how they want to live their lives.

No one who has lived in this country during the last five years can fail to be aware of how the balance of our society has been increasingly tilted in favour of the state at the expense of individual freedom.

This election may be the last chance we have to reverse that process, to restore the balance of power in favour of the people. It is therefore the most crucial election since the war.

Together with the threat to freedom there has been a feeling of helplessness, that we are a once great nation that has somehow fallen behind and that it is too late now to turn things round.

I don't accept that. I believe we not only can, we must. This manifesto points the way.

It contains no magic formula or lavish promises. It is not a recipe for an easy or a perfect life. But it sets out a broad framework for the recovery of our country, based not on dogma, but on reason, on common sense, above all on the liberty of the people under the law.

The things we have in common as a nation far outnumber those that set us apart.

It is in that spirit that I commend to you this manifesto.

Our five tasks

The manifesto stated:

This election is about the future of Britain – a great country which seems to have lost its way. It is a country rich in natural resources, in coal, oil, gas, and fertile farmlands. It is rich, too, in human resources, with professional and managerial skills of the highest calibre, with great industries and firms whose workers can be the equal of any in the world. We are the inheritors of a long tradition of parliamentary democracy and the rule of law.

Yet today, this country is faced with its most serious problems since the Second World War. What has happened to our country, to the values we used to share, to the success and prosperity we once took for granted?

During the industrial strife of last winter, confidence, self-respect, common sense, and even our sense of common humanity were shaken. At times this society seemed on the brink of disintegration.

Some of the reasons for our difficulties today are complex and go back many years. Others are more simple and more recent. We do not lay all the blame on the Labour Party: but Labour have been in power for most of the 15 years and cannot escape the major responsibility.

They have made things worse in three ways. First, by practising the politics of envy

---

*The Labour, Conservative and Liberal manifestos are published in full with extracts from the manifestos of other parties.

and by actively discouraging the creation of wealth, they have set one group against another in an often bitter struggle to gain a larger share of a weak economy.

Second, by enlarging the role of the State and diminishing the role of the individual, they have crippled the enterprise and effort on which a prosperous country with improving social services depends.

Third, by heaping privilege without responsibility on the trade unions, Labour have given a minority of extremists the power to abuse individual liberties and to thwart Britain's chances of success. One result is that the trade union movement, which sprang from a deep and genuine fellow-feeling for the brotherhood of man, is today more distrusted and feared than ever before.

It is not just that Labour have governed Britain badly. They have reached a dead-end. The very nature of their party now prevents them from governing successfully in a free society and mixed economy.

Divided against themselves; devoid of any policies except those which have led to and would worsen our present troubles; bound inescapably by ties of history, political dogma, and financial dependence to a single powerful interest group, Labour have demonstrated yet again that they cannot speak and dare not act for the nation as a whole.

Our country's relative decline is not inevitable. We in the Conservative Party think we can reverse it, *not* because we think we have all the answers but because we think we have the one answer that matters most. We want to work *with the grain* of human nature, helping people to help themselves – and others. This is the way to restore that self-reliance and self-confidence which are the basis of personal responsibility and national success.

Attempting to do too much, politicians have failed to do those things which *should* be done. This has damaged the country and the authority of government. We must concentrate on what should be priorities for *any* government. They are set out in this manifesto.

Those who look in these pages for lavish promises or detailed commitments on every subject will look in vain. We may be able to do more in the next five years than we indicate here. We believe we can. But the Conservative government's first job will be to rebuild our economy and reunite a divided and disillusioned people.

Our five tasks are:

1   To restore the health of our economic and social life, by controlling inflation and striking a fair balance between the rights and duties of the trade union movement.

2   To restore incentives so that hard work pays, success is rewarded and genuine new jobs are created in an expanding economy.

3   To uphold Parliament and the rule of law.

4   To support family life, by helping people to become home-owners, raising the standards of their children's education, and concentrating welfare services on the effective support of the old, the sick, the disabled, and those who are in real need.

5   To strengthen Britain's defences and work with our allies to protect our interests in an increasingly threatening world.

This is the strategy of the next Conservative government.

Restoring the Balance

Sound money and a fair balance between the rights and obligations of unions, management and the community in which they work are essential to economic recovery. They should provide the stable conditions in which pay bargaining can take place as responsibly in Britain as it does in other countries.

The Control of Inflation

Under Labour prices have risen faster than at any peacetime period in the three centuries in which records have been kept, and inflation is now accelerating again. The pound today is worth less than half its 1974 value. On present form it would be halved in value yet again within eight years. Inflation on this scale has come near to destroying our political and social stability.

To master inflation, proper monetary discipline is essential, with publicly stated targets for the rate of growth of the money supply. At the same time, a gradual reduction in the size of the Government's borrowing requirement is also vital. This Government's price controls have done nothing to prevent inflation, as is proved by the doubling of prices since they came to power. All the controls have achieved is a loss of jobs and a reduction in consumer choice.

The state takes too much of the nation's income; its share must be steadily reduced. When it spends and borrows too much, taxes, interest rates, prices and unemployment rise so that in the long run there is less wealth with which to improve our standard of living and our social services.

Better Value for Money

Any future government which sets out honestly to reduce inflation and taxation will have to make substantial economies, and there should be no doubt about our intention to do so. We do not pretend that every saving can be made without change or complaint; but if the Government does not economise the sacrifices required of ordinary people will be all the greater.

Important savings can be made in several ways. We will scrap expensive socialist programmes, such as the nationalization of building land. We shall reduce government intervention in industry and particularly that of the National Enterprise Board, whose borrowing powers are planned to reach £4,500m. We shall ensure that selective assistance to industry is not wasted, as it was in the case of Labour's assistance to certain oil platform yards, on which over £20m of public money was spent but no orders received.

The reduction of waste, bureaucracy and over-government will also yield substantial savings. For example, we shall look for economies in the cost (about £1,200m) of running our tax and social security systems. By comparison with private industry, local direct labour schemes waste an estimated £400m a year. Other examples of waste abound, such as the plan to spend £50m to build another town hall in Southwark.

Trade Union Reform

Free trade unions can only flourish in a free society. A strong and responsible trade union movement could play a big part in our economic recovery. We cannot go on, year after year, tearing ourselves apart in increasingly bitter and calamitous industrial disputes. In bringing about economic recovery, we should all be on the same side. Government and public, management and unions, employers and employees, all have a common interest in raising productivity and profits, thus increasing investment and employment, and improving real living standards for everyone in a high-productivity, high-wage, low-tax economy. Yet at the moment we have the reverse – an economy in which the Government has to hold wages down to try to make us competitive with other countries where higher real wages are paid for by higher output.

The crippling industrial disruption which hit Britain last winter had several causes: years with no growth in production; rigid pay control; high marginal rates of taxation; and the extension of trade union power and privileges. Between 1974 and 1976, Labour enacted a 'militants' charter' of trade union legislation. It tilted the balance of power in bargaining throughout industry away from responsible management and towards unions, and sometimes towards unofficial groups of workers acting in defiance of their official union leadership.

We propose three changes which must be made at once.

Although the Government refused our offer of support to carry them through the House of Commons last January, our proposals command general assent inside and outside the trade union movement.

Picketing

Workers involved in a dispute have a right to try *peacefully* to persuade others to support them by picketing, but we believe that right should be limited to those in dispute picketing at their own place of work. In the last few years some of the picketing we have witnessed has gone much too far. Violence, intimidation and obstruction cannot be tolerated. We shall ensure that the protection of the law is available to those not concerned in the dispute but who at present can suffer severely from secondary action (picketing, blacking, and blockading). This means an immediate review of the existing law on immunities in the light of recent decisions, followed by such amendment as may be appropriate of the 1976 legislation in this field. We shall also make any further changes that are necessary so that a citizen's right to work and go about his or her lawful business free from intimidation or obstruction is guaranteed.

The Closed Shop

Labour's strengthening of the closed shop has made picketing a more objectionable weapon. In some disputes, pickets have threatened other workers with the withdrawal of their union cards if they refused to cooperate. No union card can mean no job. So the law must be changed. People arbitrarily excluded or expelled from any union must be given the right of appeal to a court of law. Existing employees and those with personal conviction must be adequately protected, and if they lose their jobs as a result of a closed shop they must be entitled to ample compensation.

In addition, all agreements for a closed shop must be drawn up in line with the best practice followed at present and only if an overwhelming majority of the workers involved vote for it by secret ballot. We shall therefore propose a statutory code under Section 6 of the 1975 Employment Protection Act. We will not permit a closed shop in the non-industrial Civil Service and will resist further moves towards it in the newspaper industry. We are also committed to an inquiry into the activities of the Slade union, which have done so much to bring trade unionism into disrepute.

Wider Participation

Too often trade unions are dominated by a handful of extremists who do not reflect the commonsense views of most union members.

Wider use of secret ballots for decision-making throughout the trade union movement should be given every encouragement. We will therefore provide public funds for postal ballots for union elections and other important issues. Every trade unionist should be free to record his decisions as every voter has done for a hundred years in parliamentary elections, without others watching and taking note.

We welcome closer involvement of workers, whether trade unionists or not, in the decisions that affect them at their place of work. It would be wrong to impose by law a system of participation in every company. It would be equally wrong to use the pretext of encouraging genuine worker involvement in order simply to increase union power or facilitate union control of pension funds.

Too Many Strikes

Further changes may be needed to encourage people to behave responsibly and keep the bargains they make at work. Many deficiencies of British industrial relations are without foreign parallel. Strikes are too often a weapon of first rather than last resort. One cause is the financial treatment of strikers and their families. In reviewing the position, therefore, we shall ensure that unions bear their fair share of the cost of supporting those of their members who are on strike.

Labour claim that industrial relations in Britain cannot be improved by changing the law. We disagree. If the law can be used to confer privileges, it can and should also be used to establish obligations. We cannot allow a repetition of the behaviour that we saw outside too many of our factories and hospitals last winter.

Responsible Pay Bargaining

Labour's approach to industrial relations and their disastrous economic policies have made realistic and responsible pay bargaining almost impossible. After encouraging the 'social contract' chaos of 1974–5, they tried to impose responsibility by the prolonged and rigid control of incomes. This policy collapsed last winter as we warned that it would. The Labour Government then came full circle with the announcement of yet another 'social contract' with the unions. For five years now, the road to ruin has been paved with such exchanges of promises between the Labour Government and the unions.

To restore responsible pay bargaining, we must all start by recognizing that Britain is a low-paid country because we have steadily become less efficient, less productive, less reliable, and less competitive. Under this Government, we have more than doubled our pay but actually produced less in manufacturing industry. It will do yet further harm to go on printing money to pay ourselves more without first earning more. That would lead to even higher prices, fewer jobs, and falling living standards.

The return to responsibility will not be easy. It requires that people keep more of what they earn; that effort and skill earn larger rewards; and that the state leaves more resources for industry. There should also be more open and informed discussion of the Government's economic objectives (as happens, for example, in Germany and other countries) so that there is wider understanding of the consequences of unrealistic bargaining and industrial action.

Pay bargaining in the private sector should be left to the companies and workers concerned. At the end of the day, no one should or can protect them from the results of the agreements they make.

Different considerations apply to some extent to the public sector, of whose seven million workers the Government directly employs only a minority. In the great public corporations, pay bargaining should be governed, as in private ones, by what each can afford. There can be no question of subsidizing excessive pay deals.

Pay bargaining in central and local government, and other services such as health and education, must take place within the limits of what the taxpayer and ratepayer can afford. It is conducted under a variety of arrangements, some of long standing, such as pay research. In consultation with the unions, we will reconcile these with the cash limits used to control public spending, and seek to conclude no-strike agreements in a few essential services. Bargaining must also be put on a sounder economic footing, so that public sector wage settlements take full account of supply and demand and differences between regions, manning levels, job security and pension arrangements.

A More Prosperous Country

Labour have gone to great lengths to try to conceal the damage they have done to the economy and to our prospects of economic expansion. Even in the depression of the 1930s the British economy progressed more than it has under this Labour Government. Their favourite but totally false excuse is that their appalling record is all due to the oil crisis and the world-wide economic depression. Yet since the oil crisis, despite our coal, and gas, and oil from the North Sea, prices and unemployment in Britain have risen by more than in almost any other major industrial country. And output has risen by less. With much poorer energy supplies than Britain, the others have nonetheless done much better – because they have not had a Labour Government or suffered from Labour's mistakes.

To become more prosperous, Britain must become more productive and the British people must be given more incentive.

Cutting Income Tax

We shall cut income tax at all levels to reward hard work, responsibility and success; tackle the poverty trap; encourage saving and the wider ownership of property; simplify taxes – like VAT; and reduce tax bureaucracy.

It is especially important to cut the absurdly high marginal rates of tax both at the bottom and top of the income scale. It must pay a man or woman significantly more to be in, rather than out of, work. Raising tax thresholds will let the low-aid out of the tax net altogether, and unemployment and short-term sickness benefit must be brought into the computation of annual income.

The top rate of income tax should be cut to the European average and the higher tax bands widened. To encourage saving we will reduce the burden of the investment income surcharge. This will greatly help those pensioners who pay this additional tax on the income from their life-time savings, and who suffer so badly by comparison with members of occupational or inflation-proofed pension schemes.

Growing North Sea oil revenues and reductions in Labour's public spending plans will not be enough to pay for the income tax cuts the country needs. We must therefore be prepared to switch to some extent from taxes on earnings to taxes on spending. Value Added Tax does not apply, and will not be extended, to necessities like food, fuel, housing, and transport. Moreover the levels of state pensions and other benefits take price rises into account.

Labour's extravagance and incompetence have once again imposed a heavy burden on ratepayers this year. But cutting income tax must take priority for the time being over abolition of the domestic rating system.

A Property-Owning Democracy

Unlike Labour, we want more people to have the security and satisfaction of owning property. Our proposals for encouraging home ownership appear later.

We reject Labour's plan for a wealth tax. We shall deal with the most damaging features of the capital transfer and capital gains taxes, and propose a simpler and less oppressive system of capital taxation in the longer term. We will expand and build on existing schemes for encouraging employee share-ownership and our tax policies generally will provide incentive to save and build up capital.

Industry, Commerce, and Jobs

Lower taxes on earnings and savings will encourage economic growth. But on their own they will not be enough to secure it.

Profits are the foundation of a free enterprise economy. In Britain profits are still dangerously low. Price controls can prevent them from reaching a level adequate for the investment we need. In order to ensure effective competition and fair pricing policies, we will review the working of the Monopolies Commission, the Office of Fair Trading, and the Price Commission, with the legislation which governs their activities.

Too much emphasis has been placed on attempts to preserve existing jobs. We need to concentrate more on the creation of conditions in which new, more modern, more secure, better paid jobs come into existence. This is the best way of helping the unemployed and those threatened with the loss of their jobs in the future.

Government strategies and plans cannot produce revival, nor can subsidies. Where it is in the national interest to help a firm in difficulties, such help must be temporary and tapered.

We all hope that those firms which are at present being helped by the taxpayer will soon be able to succeed by themselves; but success or failure lies in their own hands.

Of course, government can help to ease industrial change in those regions dependent on older, declining industries. We do not propose sudden, sharp changes in the measures now in force. However, there is a strong case for relating government assistance to projects more closely to the number of jobs they create.

Nationalization

The British people strongly oppose Labour's plans to nationalize yet more firms and industries such as building, banking, insurance, pharmaceuticals, and road haulage. More nationalization would further impoverish us and further undermine our freedom. We will offer to sell back to private ownership the recently nationalized aerospace and shipbuilding concerns, giving their employees the opportunity to purchase shares.

We aim to sell shares in the National Freight Corporation to the general public in order to achieve substantial private investment in it. We will also relax the Traffic Commissioner licensing regulations to enable new bus and other services to develop – particularly in rural areas – and we will encourage new private operators.

Even where Labour have not nationalized they interfere too much. We shall therefore amend the 1975 Industry Act and restrict the powers of the National Enterprise Board solely to the administration of the Government's temporary shareholdings, to be sold off as circumstances permit. We want to see those industries that remain nationalized running more successfully and we will therefore interfere less with their management and set them a clearer financial discipline in which to work.

High productivity is the key to the future of industries like British Rail, where improvements would benefit both the work force and passengers who have faced unprecedented fare increases over the last five years.

Fair Trade

Just as we reject nationalization, so we are opposed to the other socialist panacea – import controls. They would restrict consumer choice, raise prices, and invite damaging retaliation against British goods overseas. We will vigorously oppose all kinds of dumping and other unfair foreign trade practices that undermine jobs at home.

We fully support the renegotiated Multi-fibre Arrangement for textiles and will insist that it is monitored effectively and speedily. We also believe in a revised 'safeguard' clause under GATT, to give us a better defence against sudden and massive surges of imports that destroy jobs.

Small Businesses

The creation of new jobs depends to a great extent on the success of smaller businesses. They have been especially hard hit under Labour. Our cuts in direct and capital taxation, the simplification of VAT and our general economic and industrial relations policies are the key to their future. We shall make planning restraints less rigid; reduce the number of official forms and make them simpler; provide safeguards against unfair competition from direct labour; review the new 714 certificate system for subcontractors and review with representatives of the self-employed their national insurance and pension position. We shall amend laws such as the Employment Protection Act where they damage smaller businesses – and larger ones too – and actually prevent the creation of jobs.

We shall also undertake a thorough review of the enforcement procedures of Customs and Excise and the Inland Revenue, and introduce an easier régime for small firms in respect of company law and the disclosure of their affairs.

Energy

The development of our energy resources provides a challenge for both our nationalized industries and the private sector. Nowhere has private enterprise been more successful in creating jobs and wealth for the nation than in bringing North Sea oil and gas ashore. These benefits will be short-lived unless we pursue a vigorous policy for energy saving. Labour's interference has discouraged investment and could cost Britain billions of pounds in lost revenue. We shall undertake a complete review of all the activities of the British National Oil Corporation as soon as we take office. We shall ensure that our oil tax and licensing policies encourage new production.

We believe that a competitive and efficient coal industry has an important role in meeting energy demand, together with a proper contribution from nuclear power. All energy developments raise important environmental issues, and we shall ensure the fullest public participation in major new decisions.

Agriculture

Our agricultural and food industries are as important and as efficient as any that we have. They make an immense contribution to our balance of payments; they provide jobs for millions of people and they sustain the economy of the countryside. Labour have seriously undermined the profitability of these industries, without protecting consumers against rising food prices which have more than doubled during their term of office. We must ensure that these industries have the means to keep abreast of those in other countries.

We believe that radical changes in the operation of the common agricultural policy (CAP) are necessary. We would, in particular, aim to devalue the green pound within the normal lifetime of a Parliament to a point which would enable our producers to compete on level terms with those in the rest of the Community. We will insist on a freeze in CAP prices for products in structural surplus. This should be maintained until the surpluses are eliminated. We could not entertain discriminatory proposals such as those which the Commission recently put forward for milk production.

The uplands are an important part of our agriculture. Those who live and work there should enjoy a reasonable standard of life.

Fishing

The Government's failure to negotiate with our Community partners proper arrangements for fishing has left the industry in a state of uncertainty. The general adoption of 200-mile limits has fundamentally altered the situation which existed when the Treaty of Accession was negotiated. We would work for an agreement which recognized: first, that United Kingdom waters contained more fish than those of the rest of the Community countries put together; secondly, the loss of fishing opportunities experienced by our fishermen; thirdly, the rights of inshore fishermen; last, and perhaps most important of all, the need for effective measures to conserve fish stocks which would be policed by individual coastal states. In the absence of agreement, we would not hesitate to take the necessary measures on our own, but of course on a non-discriminatory basis.

Animal Welfare

The welfare of animals is an issue that concerns us all. There are problems in certain areas and we will act immediately where it is necessary. More specifically, we will give full support to the EEC proposals on the transportation of animals. We shall update the Brambell report, the codes of welfare for farm animals, and the legislation on experiments on live animals. We shall also re-examine the rules and enforcement applying to the export of live animals and shall halt the export of cows and ewes recently calved and lambed.

The Rule of Law

The most disturbing threat to our freedom and security is the growing disrespect for the rule of law. In government as in opposition, Labour have undermined it. Yet respect for the rule of law is the basis of a free and civilized life. We will restore it, re-establishing the supremacy of Parliament and giving the right priority to the fight against crime.

The Fight Against Crime

The number of crimes in England and Wales is nearly half as much again as it was in 1973. The next Conservative Government will spend more on fighting crime even while we economize elsewhere.

Britain needs strong, efficient police forces with high morale. Improved pay and conditions will help chief constables to recruit up to necessary establishment levels. We will therefore implement in full the recommendations of the Edmund Davies Committee. The police need more time to detect crime. So we will ease the weight of traffic supervision duties and review cumbersome court procedures which waste police time. We will also review the traffic laws, including the totting-up procedure.

Deterring the Criminal

Surer detection means surer deterrence. We also need better crime prevention measures and more flexible, more effective sentencing. For violent criminals and thugs really tough sentences are essential. But in other cases long prison terms are not always the best deterrent. So we want to see a wider variety of sentences available to the courts. We will therefore amend the 1961 Criminal Justice Act which limits prison sentences on young adult offenders, and revise the Children and Young Persons Act, 1969, to give magistrates the power to make residential and secure care orders on juveniles.

We need more compulsory attendance centres for hooligans at junior and senior levels. In certain detention centres we will experiment with a tougher regime as a short, sharp shock for young criminals. For certain types of offenders, we also support the greater use of community service orders, intermediate treatment and attendance centres. Unpaid fines and compensation orders are ineffective. Fines should be assessed to punish the offender within his means and then be backed by effective sanctions for non-payment.

Many people advocate capital punishment for murder. This must remain a matter of conscience for Members of Parliament. But we will give the new House of Commons an early opportunity for a free vote on this issue.

Immigration and Race Relations

The rights of all British citizens legally settled here are equal before the law whatever their race, colour or creed. And their opportunities ought to be equal too. The ethnic minorities have already made a valuable contribution to the life of our nation. But firm immigration control for the future is essential if we are to achieve good community relations. It will end persistent fears about levels of immigration and will remove from those settled, and in many cases born here, the label of 'immigrant'.

(i) We shall introduce a new British Nationality Act to define entitlement to British citizenship and to the right of abode in this country. It will not adversely affect the right of anyone now permanently settled here.

(ii) We shall end the practice of allowing permanent settlement for those who come here for a temporary stay.

(iii) We shall limit entry of parents, grandparents, and children over 18 to a small number of urgent compassionate cases.

(iv) We shall end the concession introduced by the Labour Government in 1974 to husbands and male fiancés.

(v) We shall severely restrict the issue of work permits.

(vi) We shall introduce a register of those Commonwealth wives and children entitled to entry for settlement under the 1971 Immigration Act.

(vii) We shall then introduce a quota system, covering everyone outside the European Community, to control all entry for settlement.

(viii) We shall take firm action against illegal immigrants and overstayers and help those immigrants who genuinely wish to leave this country – but there can be no question of compulsory repatriation.

We will encourage the improvement of language training in schools and factories and of training facilities for the young unemployed in the ethnic communities. But these measures will achieve little without the effective control of immigration. That is essential for racial harmony in Britain today.

The Supremacy of Parliament

In recent years, Parliament has been weakened in two ways. First, outside groups have been allowed to usurp some of its democratic functions. Last winter, the Government permitted strike committees and pickets to take on powers and responsibilities which should have been discharged by Parliament and the police. Second, the traditional role of our legislature has suffered badly from the growth of government over the last quarter of a century.

We will see that Parliament and no other body stands at the centre of the nation's life and decisions, and we will seek to make it effective in its job of controlling the Executive.

We sympathize with the approach of the all-party parliamentary committees which put forward proposals last year for improving the way the House of Commons legislates and scrutinises public spending and the work of government departments. We will give the new House of Commons an early chance of coming to a decision on these proposals.

The public has rightly grown anxious about many constitutional matters in the last few years – partly because our opponents have proposed major constitutional changes for party political advantage. Now Labour want not merely to abolish the House of Lords but to put nothing in its place. This would be a most dangerous step. A strong second chamber is necessary not only to revise legislation but also to guarantee our constitution and liberties.

It is not only the future of the second chamber which is at issue. We are committed to discussions about the future government of Scotland, and have put forward proposals for improved parliamentary control of administration in Wales. There are other important matters, such as a possible Bill of Rights, the use of referendums, and the relationship between Members of the European Parliament and Westminster, which we shall wish to discuss with all parties.

Northern Ireland

We shall maintain the Union of Great Britain and Northern Ireland in accordance with the wish of the majority in the Province. Its future still depends on the defeat of terrorism and the restoration of law and order. We shall continue – with the help of the courage, resolution and restraint of the security forces – to give it the highest priority. There will be no amnesty for convicted terrorists.

In the absence of devolved government, we will seek to establish one or more elected regional councils with a wide range of powers over local services. We recognize that Northern Ireland's industry will continue to require government support.

Helping the Family
Homes of Our Own

To most people ownership means first and foremost a home of their own.

Many find it difficult today to raise the deposit for a mortgage. Our tax cuts will help them. We shall encourage shared purchase schemes which will enable people to buy a house or flat on mortgage, on the basis initially of a part-payment which they complete later when their incomes are high enough. We should like in time to improve on existing legislation with a realistic grants scheme to assist first-time buyers of cheaper homes. As it costs about three times as much to subsidize a new council house as it does to give tax relief to a home buyer, there could well be a substantial saving to the tax and ratepayer.

The prospect of very high mortgage interest rates deters some people from buying their homes and the reality can cause acute difficulties to those who have done so. Mortgage rates have risen steeply because of the Government's financial mismanagement. Our plans for cutting government spending and borrowing will lower them.

The Sale of Council Houses

Many families who live on council estates and in new towns would like to buy their own homes but either cannot afford to or are prevented by the local authority or the Labour Government. The time has come to end these restrictions. In the first session of the next Parliament we shall therefore give council and new town tenants the legal right to buy their homes, while recognizing the special circumstances of rural areas and sheltered housing for the elderly. Subject to safeguards over resale, the terms we propose would allow a discount on market values reflecting the fact that council tenants effectively have security of tenure. Our discounts will range from 33 per cent after three years, rising with length of tenancy to a maximum of 50 per cent after 20 years. We shall also ensure that 100 per cent mortgages are available for the purchase of council and new town houses. We shall introduce a right for these tenants to obtain limited term options on their homes so that they know in advance the price at which they can buy, while they save the money to do so.

As far as possible, we will extend these rights to housing association tenants. At the very least, we shall give these associations the power to sell to their tenants.

Those council house tenants who do not wish to buy their homes will be given new rights and responsibilities under our tenants' charter.

Reviving the Private Rented Sector

As well as giving new impetus to the movement towards home ownership, we must make better use of our existing stock of houses. Between 1973 and 1977 no fewer than 400,000 dwellings were withdrawn from private rental. There are now hundreds of thousands of empty properties in Britain which are not let because the owners are deterred by legislation. We intend to introduce a new system of shorthold tenure which will allow short fixed-term lettings of these properties free of the most discouraging conditions of the present law. This provision will not, of course, affect the position of existing tenants. There should also be more flexible arrangements covering accommodation for students. At the same time, we must try to achieve a greater take-up in rent allowances for poorer tenants.

Protecting the Environment

The quality of our environment is a vital concern to all of us. The last Conservative Government had a proud record of achievement in reducing pollution, and protecting our heritage and countryside. We shall continue to give these issues a proper priority. Subject to the availability of resources we shall pay particular attention to the improvement and restoration of derelict land, the disposal and recycling of dangerous and other wastes, and reducing pollution of our rivers and canals.

We attach particular importance to measures to reduce fuel consumption by improving insulation.

Standards in Education

The Labour Party is still obsessed with the structure of the schools system, paying too little regard to the quality of education. As a result we have a system which in the view of many of our parents and teachers all too often fails – at a cost of over £8,000m a year – even to provide pupils with the means of communication and understanding. We must restore to every child, regardless of background, the chance to progress as far as his or her abilities allow.

We will halt the Labour Government's policies which have led to the destruction of good schools; keep those of proven worth; and repeal those sections of the 1976 Education Act which compel local authorities to reorganize along comprehensive lines and restrict their freedom to take up places at independent schools.

We shall promote higher standards of achievement in basic skills. The Government's Assessment of Performance Unit will set national standards in reading, writing, and arithmetic, monitored by tests worked out with teachers and others and applied locally by education authorities. The Inspectorate will be strengthened. In teacher training there must be more emphasis on practical skills and on maintaining discipline.

Much of our higher education in Britain has a world-wide reputation for its quality. We shall seek to ensure that this excellence is maintained. We are aware of the special problems associated with the need to increase the number of high-quality entrants to the engineering professions. We shall review the relationship between school, further education, and training to see how better use can be made of existing resources.

We recognize the valuable work done by the Youth Service and will continue to give help to those voluntary bodies which make such a considerable contribution in this field.

Parents' Rights and Responsibilities

Extending parents' rights and responsibilities, including their right of choice, will also help raise standards by giving them greater influence over education. Our parents' charter will place a clear duty on government and local authorities to take account of parents' wishes when allocating children to schools, with a local appeals system for those dissatisfied. Schools will be required to publish prospectuses giving details of their examination and other results.

The direct grant schools, abolished by Labour, gave wider opportunities for bright children from modest backgrounds. The direct grant principle will therefore be restored with an assisted places scheme. Less well-off parents will be able to claim part or all of the fees at certain schools from a special government fund.

The Arts

Economic failure and socialist policies have placed the arts under threat. Lightening the burden of tax should in time enable the private sponsor to flourish again and the reform of capital taxation will lessen the threat to our heritage. We will strengthen the existing provision whereby relief from CTT is available on assets placed in a maintenance fund for the support of heritage property. We favour the establishment of a national heritage fund to help preserve historic buildings and artistic treasures for the nation. We will continue to give as generous support to Britain's cultural and artistic life as the country can afford.

Sport and recreation have also been hit by inflation and high taxation. We will continue to support the Sports Councils in the encouragement of recreation and international sporting achievement.

Health and Welfare

The welfare of the old, the sick, the handicapped and the deprived has also suffered under Labour. The lack of money to improve our social services and assist those in need can only be overcome by restoring the nation's prosperity. But some improvements can be made now by spending what we do have more sensibly.

In our national health service standards are falling; there is a crisis of morale; too often patients' needs do not come first. It is not our intention to reduce spending on the health service; indeed, we intend to make better use of what resources are available. So we will simplify and decentralize the service and cut back bureaucracy.

When resources are so tightly stretched it is folly to turn good money away from the NHS and to discourage people from doing more for themselves. We shall therefore allow pay-beds to be provided where there is a demand for them; end Labour's vendetta against the private health sector; and restore tax relief on employer-employee medical insurance schemes. The Royal Commission on the Health Service is studying the financing of health care, and any examination of possible longer term changes – for example greater reliance for NHS funding on the insurance principle – must await their report.

In the community, we must do more to help people to help themselves, and families to look after their own. We must also encourage the voluntary movement and self-help groups working in partnership with the statutory services.

Making Sense of Social Security

Our social security system is now so complicated that even some ministry officials do not understand it. Income tax starts at such a low level that many poor people are being taxed to pay for their own benefits. All too often they are little or no better off at work than they are on social security.

This was one of our principal reasons for proposing a tax credit scheme. Child benefits are a step in the right direction. Further progress will be very difficult in the next few years, both for reasons of cost and because of technical problems involved in the switch to computers. We shall wish to move towards the fulfilment of our original tax credit objectives as and when resources become available. Meanwhile we shall do all we can to find other ways to simplify the system, restore the incentive to work, reduce the poverty trap and bring more effective help to those in greatest need.

Restoring the will to work means, above all, cutting income tax. It also involves bring unemployment and short-term sickness benefit within the tax system – an objective fully shared by Labour ministers. The rules about the unemployed accepting available jobs will be reinforced and we shall act more vigorously against fraud and abuse.

We welcomed the new child benefit as the first stage of our tax credit scheme. One-parent families face much hardship so we will maintain the special addition for them.

292

The Elderly and the Disabled

We will honour the increases in retirement pensions which were promised just before the election.

However, like others, pensioners have suffered from the high taxes and catastrophic inflation of Labour's years.

It is wrong to discourage people who wish to work after retirement age, and we will phase out the 'earnings rule' during the next Parliament. The Christmas bonus, which the last Conservative government started in 1972, will continue. We will exempt war widows' pensions from tax and provide a pension for pre-1950 widows of 'other ranks' who do not receive one at present.

Much has been done in recent years to help the disabled, but there is still a long way to go. Our aim is to provide a coherent system of cash benefits to meet the costs of disability, so that more disabled people can support themselves and live normal lives. We shall work towards this as swiftly as the strength of the economy allows.

A Strong Britain in a Free World

Improving our Defences

During the past five years the military threat to the West has grown steadily as the Communist block has established virtual parity in strategic nuclear weapons and a substantial superiority in conventional weapons. Yet Labour have cut down our forces, weakened our defences, and reduced our contribution to Nato. And the Left are pressing for still more reductions.

We shall only be able to decide on the proper level of defence spending after consultation in government with the Chiefs of Staff and our allies. But it is already obvious that significant increases will be necessary. The Salt discussions increase the importance of ensuring the continuing effectiveness of Britain's nuclear deterrent.

In recent times our armed forces have had to deal with a wide variety of national emergencies. They have responded magnificently despite government neglect and a severe shortage of manpower and equipment. We will give our Servicemen decent living conditions, bring their pay up to full comparability with their civilian counterparts immediately and keep it there. In addition, we must maintain the efficiency of our reserve forces. We will improve their equipment, too, and hope to increase their strength.

The European Community

If we wish to play our full part in shaping world events over the next few critical years, we must also work honestly and genuinely with our partners in the European Community. There is much that we can achieve together, much more than we can achieve alone.

There are some Community policies which need to be changed since they do not suit Britain's – or Europe's – best interests. But it is wrong to argue, as Labour do, that Europe has failed us. What has happened is that under Labour our country has been prevented from taking advantage of the opportunities which membership offers.

Labour's economic policies have blunted our competitive edge and made it more difficult for our companies to sell in our partners' markets. What is more, the frequently obstructive and malevolent attitude of Labour ministers has weakened the Community as a whole and Britain's bargaining power within it.

By forfeiting the trust of our partners, Labour have made it much more difficult to persuade them to agree to the changes that are necessary in such important areas as the common agricultural policy, the Community budget, and the proposed common fisheries policy.

The next Conservative Government will restore Britain's influence by convincing our partners of our commitment to the Community's success. This will enable us to protect British interests and to play a leading and constructive role in the Community's efforts to tackle the many problems which it faces.

We shall work for a commonsense Community which resists excessive bureaucracy and unnecessary harmonization proposals, holding to the principles of free enterprise which inspired its original founders.

Our policies for the reform of the CAP would reduce the burden which the Community budget places upon the British taxpayer. We shall also strive to cut out waste in other Community spending programmes.

National payments into the budget should be more closely related to ability to pay. Spending from the budget should be concentrated more strictly on policies and projects on which it makes sense for the Community rather than nation states to take the lead.

We attach particular importance to the coordination of member states' foreign policies. In a world dominated by the super-powers, Britain and her partners are best able to protect their international interests and to contribute to world peace and stability when they speak with a single voice.

Africa and the Middle East

In Africa and the Middle East, there is an increasing threat from the Soviet Union and its Cuban allies. That threat must be countered, not only through collaboration with our European and American allies but also by the people and governments in Africa and the Middle East whose independence is threatened.

We shall do all we can to build on the Egyptian/Israeli peace treaty, to seek a comprehensive settlement which will bring peace to the whole region.

Rhodesia

The Conservative Party will aim to achieve a lasting settlement to the Rhodesia problem based on the democratic wishes of the people of that country. If the Six Principles, which all British governments have supported for the last 15 years, are fully satisfied following the present Rhodesian election, the next government will have the duty to return Rhodesia to a state of legality, move to lift sanctions, and do its utmost to ensure that the new independent state gains international recognition.

Trade, Aid, and the Commonwealth

Like other industrial countries, Britain has a vital interest in bringing prosperity to poorer nations which provide us with a growing market and supply many of the raw materials upon which we depend. The next Conservative Government will help them through national and international programmes of aid and technical cooperation and by the encouragement of voluntary work. But we also attach particular importance to the development of trade and private investment through such instruments as the European Community's Lomé Convention. In particular, we will foster all our Commonwealth links and seek to harness to greater effect the collective influence of the Commonwealth in world affairs.

A New Beginning

In this manifesto we have not sought to understate the difficulties which face us – the economic and social problems at home, the threats to the freedom of the West abroad. Yet success and security *are* attainable if we have the courage and confidence to seize the opportunities which are open to us.

We make no lavish promises. The repeated disappointment of rising expectations has led to a marked loss of faith in politicians' promises. Too much has gone wrong in Britain for us to hope to put it all right in a year or so. Many things will simply have to wait until the economy has been revived and we are once again creating the wealth on which so much else depends.

Most people, in their hearts, know that Britain has to come to terms with reality. They no longer have any time for politicians who try to gloss over the harsh facts of life. Most poeple want to be told the truth, and to be given a clear lead towards the action needed for recovery.

The years of make-believe and false optimism are over. It is time for a new beginning.

The Labour Party:

'The Labour Way is the Better Way'

In the foreword to the Labour manifesto, Mr James Callaghan said:

Now, more than ever, we need Labour's traditional values of cooperation, social justice, and fairness. This manifesto restates these Labour principles in an action programme with a strong sense of the future. They appeal to all our people – young and old.

The world is changing rapidly. New industrial nations are rising to challenge our key industries on which British jobs and living standards depend.

The Labour Government is taking firm action to equip Britain to adapt to these changes and to seize new opportunities. And we will take great care to protect working people and their families from the hardships of change.

But although the 1980s will present a tough challenge, this country will have many things in our favour. North Sea oil offers a golden prospect as do our reserves of natural gas and coal. We must use these resources wisely to plan our future to create new wealth, new jobs, and to look after the family, the elderly, and those in need.

Too much is at stake to let the Conservatives frustrate the hopes of the coming decade by turning back the clock to the policies that they tried in the early seventies and that failed so badly before.

The Government's industrial strategy is about how to create more wealth and more jobs through a constructive national partnership with unions and management. The Conservaties will not admit that nowadays governments must step in to help create employment, to limit prices rises, to assist industry to modernize itself. They are ready to gamble the people's future on a return to the nineteenth century 'free market' – despite its pitiless social consequences. They are as dangerously out of their time as a penny farthing on the motorway.

Together the people and the Labour Government, even without a parliamentary majority, have achieved much these past five years, as the manifesto shows. In an uncertain world suffering the worst economic trouble for 40 years we have pointed the way forward.

But nobody who cares about Britain can rest satisfied until far, far more has been accomplished. As long as there are men and women struggling with low pay, mothers stretching the household budget to make ends meet, youngsters in search of a job, children learning in out of date classrooms, patients queueing for a hospital bed or families without a decent home – then there is work for a Labour Government.

Our purpose is to overcome the evils of inequality, poverty, racial bigotry, and make Britain truly one nation.

For these we need a Labour majority in Parliament. This manifesto sets out our aims for the next five years. Here are five of our priorities.

1. We must keep a curb on inflation and prices. Inflation is our enemy because rising prices hit most hardly at the pensioner, the low paid and the housewife, and inflation causes loss of jobs. Labour has brought inflation down from the alarming level caused by the Conservatives' failure to control the supply of money.

Now we set ourselves the task of bringing inflation down to 5 per cent in three years. It is an ambitious target. We need the assistance of everyone. And everyone will be better off if we succeed.

2. We will carry forward the task of putting into practice the new framework to improve industrial relations that we have hammered out with the TUC. The first step has been the creation of a new standing pay commission which will prevent the disruption of services to the public in future.

Next, each year there will be three-way talks between ministers, management and unions to consider the best way forward for our country's economy. Germany's Social Democratic Government under Willy Brandt and Helmut Schmidt has proved that this is a good way to reach agreement on how to expand output, incomes and living standards.

I am realistic enough to know that there are bound to be set backs. But experience reinforces what all of us know in our hearts – there is no sound alternative to working together.

A Conservative free-for-all in pay and prices would mean endless pitched battles that would be fatal to the interests of all of us. The Labour way is the better way.

3. We give a high priority to working for a return to full employment. A good job is a basic human right. During the last five years we have responded to the worldwide unemployment crisis by helping more than one million people to take up new jobs or new training.

Now we will concentrate special attention on more jobs and training for the regions, the young and the long-term unemployed, and give them hope for the future.

4. We are deeply concerned to enlarge people's freedom. Our policy will be to tilt the balance of power back to the individual and the neighbourhood, and away from the bureaucrats of town hall, company board room, the health service and Whitehall.

Industrial democracy – giving working men and women a voice in the decisions which affect their jobs – is an idea whose time has come. Council tenants will have more freedom from bureaucratic control in their own homes. Parents and teachers will have a greater freedom to influence the running of their children's schools. Whitehall will devolve power, in an acceptable form to Scotland. Local services will be handed back to local authorities closer to the people. These are practical ways to set the people free.

5. We will use Britain's influence to strengthen world peace and defeat world poverty. Europe has been at peace for over 30 years but ours is still a dangerous world with more armaments than ever before. Labour will keep Britain strong but we will also work hard for disarmament. It cannot be right that 15 million children in poorer countries die before they are five – yet the world spends so much on the means of destruction. There is a compelling moral need to raise the standard of life of all the world's citizens – no matter where they live.

We are ready and willing to work with our European partners in closer unity. But we must record that in some aspects of its work the Common Market lacks common sense.

Above all the agricultural policy is wasteful and expensive. In standing squarely against the discredited aspects of the dear-food policy, we are in fact defending the interests of European families just as much as British families. A nonsense is a nonsense in any language.

The Labour Government will give a strong lead in the decade ahead. But no government can do it all. Our purpose is to deepen the sense of unity and kinship and community feeling that has always marked out our fellow countrymen and women. No nation can succeed by accepting benefits without responsibilities. I ask everybody who shares our ideals and our faith in Britain to join with us in securing the return of a government that dares to turn the dream of a caring society into practical action. And then work with us to complete the building of a Britain offering hope, social justice, and fairness to all.

The manifesto stated:

This election is about the Britain of tomorrow – the kind of country we want to live in, the kind of community we wish for our children. In choosing their government, the people will be deciding what values and ideals will guide the nation in the critical years ahead. In this manifesto, Labour puts forward its policies for the future. The Labour Party is a democratic socialist party and proud of it. Labour seeks to build a stronger and more prosperous Britain – and we are determined to see that all our people share fully in that prosperity. We want a Britain which is open and democratic and which puts fair earnings for working people and the needs of the under-privileged before the demands of private profit.

Over the past five years, the Labour Government have laid the foundations of a stronger economy.

When Labour came to govern, in March, 1974, Britain was facing the most dangerous crisis since the war. The Tory programme of confrontation and social injustice had brought the country almost to its knees. Unlit streets, unheated homes, shut-down factories – these were the fruits of the Tory three-day week. We were

£1,000m in deficit in our national balance of payments, even before the rising oil prices. Prices were soaring month by month. Industry was enfeebled by years of under-investment. To top it all, Britain then had to contend with the four-fold rises in oil prices and the worldwide inflation and unemployment.

Our inheritance was a Britain in crisis. The new Labour Government sought cooperation in place of confrontation. Instead of division, we offered social justice. In place of compulsion, we worked to win consent for the tough economic measures we knew were needed. We forged a new partnership between the Labour Government and working people.

Our country has come a long way since then. The rate of inflation has been brought under control. It has become possible to improve living standards, to cut taxation and increase child benefit, pensions and benefits to the disabled to rates which more than overtake costs and inflation.

And over the past year, unemployment has at last begun to fall.

Now we offer a programme to carry Britain through the 1980s.

The Fight against Rising Prices

Nothing so undermines a nation as inflation. Not only does it make the family's task of budgeting more difficult, it is a threat to jobs and a standing invitation to our overseas competitors to invade our markets.

Now, with the renewed cooperation of the trade union movement, Labour will continue the battle against rising prices. With the wholehearted backing of the TUC, we have set ourselves a new target, to get inflation down to 5 per cent by 1982.

Our approach will be threefold:

Firstly, Labour will strengthen the Price Commission, giving it greater powers to initiate investigations and reduce prices, in contrast to the Tories who threaten its abolition. We will expand its powers to combine its functions with those of the Monopolies and Mergers Commission to ensure that consumers are not exploited by monopoly producers or unfair practices. We will further strengthen and extend consumer protection, in both the public and private sectors.

Secondly, Labour will seek radical reform of the Common Market's common agricultural policy, and will oppose any further increases in common prices until food surpluses have disappeared.

Thirdly, in contrast to the Tories' savage free-for-all which leads to soaring inflation and industrial chaos, the Labour Government will work with the TUC to achieve our agreed inflation target of 5 per cent in 1982. The Labour Government and the TUC have jointly agreed to set up a standing commission on comparability which will ensure that public sector workers, including those who are low-paid, receive fair wages that are in line with those paid in the private sector.

For the private sector, we declare our aim to be a high wage, high productivity, low unit cost economy. To this end, we pledge ourselves to make a reality of fair deal collective bargaining, in keeping with the criteria set down in the joint statement.

This agreement is a far better way of achieving industrial peace, prosperity and more stable prices than confrontation with the trade union movement.

Here is an agreement which can deliver industrial peace, fair wages, and greater price stability.

Jobs and Prosperity

In the major industrial nations of Europe and America, 17 million people are out of work. In Britain alone we have to find jobs for 170,000 new workers every year.

The Labour Government will pursue policies which give a high priority to the return to full employment. This must go hand-in-hand with keeping down inflation. We therefore aim at a rate of growth of 3 per cent or more.

Our North Sea oil gives us an advantage in securing full employment and a rise in living standards. The new technologies also hold out the prospect of faster growth and a better quality of life for all. This is particularly true of microtechnologies (the silicon chip) which will have a major impact on the lives of everybody. Only a Labour Government can ensure that our people as a whole derive the benefit.

In order to take full advantage of these opportunities, we must improve our industrial competitiveness at home and abroad – and that means making sure our industries adapt to new markets and technological changes. It also means easing the costs of rapid industrial change for working people. The use of crude market forces advocated by the Tories will not and cannot achieve these changes in a way that is acceptable to the British people. What we need is a firm industrial and employment strategy from a Labour Government aimed at increasing productivity, adding to investment, and creating new jobs.

We shall expand and improve programmes of training and retraining in skills.

We shall expand the work and finance of the National Enterprise Board, using public ownership to sustain and create new jobs, and ensure that we get an adequate return on our investment.

We shall continue our strong policy of regional incentives.

We shall expand the work of the Welsh and the Scottish Development Agencies. The Labour Government will create similar development agencies in the English regions suffering similar problems.

To ensure that private industry plays its full part in the drive for prosperity and full employment, we shall conclude planning agreements with the major industrial companies, with the necessary back-up statutory powers to do so. We shall establish within Government the necessary arrangements to make this effective.

We reaffirm the policy that we have pursued that wherever we give direct aid to a company out of public funds, we shall reserve the right to take a proportionate share of the ownership of the company; and wherever possible, this public support will be channelled through the planning agreement system.

Labour will continue with major aids to investment, including the selective investment scheme which has already supported projects in excess of £1,000m.

Labour will develop the work and funding of the Cooperative Development Agency in expanding cooperative enterprise.

This is a positive strategy for industry, based on cooperation between Government, trade unions, and management. The new agreement between the Government and the TUC, which includes provision for an agreed annual assessment of the nation's economic prospects, lays the foundation for working together in the 1980s.

Labour will work for an international agreement under which all countries are helped and encouraged to expand their economies to the limit of their productive capacity and so stimulate world trade. This will help British exports to increase still faster. But to do this, Britain needs a healthy and expanding economy.

We also need a programme to protect employment while the necessary changes and modernization of our industry takes place. We will not allow our industries to be wiped out by excessive imports before they have had a chance to recover their strength. The Labour Government will ensure that imports enter our market only within acceptable limits.

Under the Labour Government, we shall continue with programmes like the short-time working compensation scheme, the job release scheme, the small firms employment subsidy, and job creation programmes which have already created and saved over one million jobs.

We do not accept that individuals whose jobs have disappeared should remain unemployed for periods of time which demoralise them and improverish their families. We pledge ourselves to the progressive introduction of a scheme which will ensure within the lifetime of the next Parliament that no one shall be unemployed for more than 12 months without receiving either the offer of a job or of retraining.

Labour will also promote an expansion in housing, the health service, education and other social services which have such a crucial part to play in providing jobs as well as in meeting vital social needs.

If full employment is to be achieved, longer holidays, time off for study, earlier voluntary retirement, and a progressive move to a 35-hour working week, must play an increasing role during the 1980s. But these changes in the pattern of employment are not only necessary to keep jobs, but also to improve the quality of living for working people, to give them more leisure and the means to enjoy it to which their work and modern technology entitles them.

Labour must ensure that the financial institutions of this country play their part in our programme for the revival of industry. We acknowledge the many successes of the financial sector, and we are also concerned that the lure of short-term profit can outweigh the social gains to be had from industrial investment.

The banking sector would benefit from increased competition. We therefore intend to bring about a major development in the Girobank so that it will compete on equal terms with the big four clearing banks and improve standards of service to small savers. The National Savings Bank has a valuable role to play in providing a unique service and in making a significant contribution to financing the Government's operations, thus reducing our reliance on the City. By developing the Girobank and the National Savings Bank to their full potential, a Labour Government will ensure for the country a vigorous public banking sector.

Agriculture and Fishing

Agriculture has always flourished best under Labour Governments. We have already taken many steps to encourage production, while giving consumers and workers in the industry the best possible deal. Agricultural workers in tied cottages have been given security of tenure in England and Wales; we intend to do the same for Scotland.

Elsewhere we give our proposals to reform the EEC's common agricultural policy. There must also be a vigorous expansion of agriculture at home. Labour will:

Develop measures of special assistance to farmers on hill and marginal land.
Consider in the light of the official enquiry we have set up into agricultural land, protection for farmers against the intrustion of financial institutions into this field.
Continue to demand a common fisheries policy that gives preference in our own waters to a strong British fishing industry – betrayed by the last Tory Government – with a secure future. We will continue to take, and enforce, national measures to conserve stocks. We shall complete the process of decasualisation in the industry.

Energy

The world energy situation is deteriorating. Energy policy is vitally important to our survival. We shall strengthen the democratic planning of the long-term developments of Britain's own energy sources, backed by the necessary powers, under full parliamentary control.

Britain is almost alone among major industrial nations in achieving energy self-sufficiency; our resources have been developed, thanks to the skills of our scientists and of the workers. The Tories handed over our oil wealth to the multinationals. We changed that and will ensure that this energy wealth is developed wisely for industrial regeneration and public provision, and its fruits distributed fairly.

We will continue to support 'Plan for Coal' for the mining industry, which has a key role to play in our energy future.
In any programme for nuclear power, safety must continue to be the dominant factor. Any such development would have to take place within the public sector. We shall maintain strict safeguards over the disposal of nuclear waste. We have not decided whether to build a commercial fast breeder reactor. A major study and public inquiry would be held before any decision were to be taken.
We shall progressively increase the national stake in the North Sea, to safeguard the British people and regenerate British industry.
We have initiated and will continue a major programme of alternative energy, energy saving, through insulation grants, advice to industry, the 'Save-It' campaign, and an energy-saving approach to transport.
We shall continue to help people to afford adequate light, heat, and power in their homes.

A Fairer Britain

Economic success is not an end in itself. For the Labour Party, prosperity and fairness march in hand on the road to a better Britain. During the next Parliament, we intend to continue our fight against all forms of social injustice.

The tax system must be fair and seen to be so. We will mount an all-out attack on tax evasion. Everybody must make their fair contribution to the country's finances. In the next Parliament, we shall introduce an annual wealth tax on the small minority of rich people whose total net personal wealth exceeds £150,000.

Labour will continue to reduce the burden of income tax, and raise the tax threshold below which people pay no income tax.

Despite the difficulties of the economic situation, Labour has kept its pledge to look after the poor and vulnerable in our society – pensioners, the sick or disabled people, and the unemployed. Pensions are up by 20 per cent in real terms on the Tory level. Labour's new child benefit gives £4 a week per child for every mother. Disabled people have new benefits: a non-contributory invalidity pension, an invalid car allowance, and a mobility allowance for people who cannot walk.

The Labour Government will build on our record of achievement. Labour will:

As a next step towards a married couple pension of half gross average earnings and a single person's pension of one-third gross average earnings, increase pensions in November to around £35 for a married couple and £22 for a single person. Widows', invalidity and other long-term benefits will be increased in line.

As a step towards meeting our objective that families get as much help for their children when working as they do on short-term benefits, increase child benefit to £4.50 in November as a next step towards further help.

Give further cash and other help to one-parent families.

Raise the burial grant to a more realistic level.

For disabled people, Labour will:

Work for the further implementation of Labour's Chronically Sick and Disabled Persons Act.

Increase the mobility allowance again next November and continue to pay the mobility allowance beyond pension age without an upper age limit.

Introduce a new disablement allowance to include the blind, varying according to the severity of disablement.

A Healthier Nation

The nation's health must have priority. We reject Tory plans to create two health services: one for the rich, financed by private insurance with a second-class service for the rest of us. Labour reaffirms its belief in a comprehensive national health service for all our people. We oppose Tory proposals for higher prescription charges and charges for seeing a doctor or being in hospital. Our aim is to abolish all charges in the NHS.

For all the talk of cuts, the truth is that the Labour Government are spending over £600m a year more on health in real terms than the Tories. Labour will devote a higher proportion of the nation's wealth to the health service and the personal social services.

Labour's health priorities include a renewed shift from hospital treatment to care in the community through family doctors and health centres with supporting social services; a comprehensive family planning service within the NHS; more emphasis on the prevention of illness and handicap; a fairer share of health funds across the country; more help for the frail elderly, the mentally ill, and handicapped; better training and opportunities for nurses and all workers in the health services; a new career structure for hospital doctors; and a greater recognition and reward to those consultants whose only professional commitment is to the NHS.

We will streamline the bureaucratic and costly structure the Tories created and give a bigger say in running the NHS to the public and staff.

We are phasing-out the remaining private beds in NHS hospitals. We shall stop queue-jumping.

Education

The Labour Party believes in equality of opportunity. Universal comprehensive education, which is central to our policy, must be completed in the 1980s. Already class sizes are the lowest ever recorded. The ratio of pupils to teachers is now only 23.6 in primary schools and 16.9 in secondary schools. Labour will continue to give high priority to reducing class sizes further.

Independent schools still represent a major obstacle to equality of opportunity. Labour's aim is to end, as soon as possible, free-paying in such schools, while safeguarding schools for the handicapped. Labour will end as soon as possible the remaining public subsidies and public support to independent schools.

The Under-fives

Under this Labour Government, the proportion of 3- and 4-year-olds in nursery classes and schools has doubled. Local authorities will be encouraged to do much more. Our aim is to provide nursery education for 90 per cent of our 4-year-olds and half of our 3-year-olds by the early 1980s.

The Needs of Youth

We will provide a universal scheme of education and training for all 16–19 year olds, if necessary backed by statute. We will remove the financial barriers which prevent many young people from low income families from continuing their education after 16.

We will reintroduce legislation for income-related mandatory awards to all 16–18 year olds on all full-time courses.

Further and Higher Education

Further education places have increased by 25,000 under Labour. Labour will substantially increase the opportunities for people from working-class backgrounds – particularly adults – to enter further and higher education. We want to see more workers given time off work for study. To this end, the places at the Open University have increased from 42,000 in 1974 to 80,000 in 1978. We propose to extend the present mandatory grant system. Labour supported the adult literacy scheme, and will ensure its continuation.

Youth

Britain has the best youth programme in Europe. We have the youth opportunities programme, which guarantees every school-leaver either a job or a training place or employment experience. We are supporting a great range of opportunities for young people. Labour will see the youth service expanded to meet the social and recreational needs of young people.

Sport

In a society where leisure is increasing year by year, Labour wants to make facilities for sport and leisure available to all. We will continue to put more money into these activities.

Homes for All

Over 1.5 million homes have been completed since Labour took office. A further one million sub-standard or near slum houses have been substantially improved with Government finance, under the 1974 Housing Act. The homeless have had a new deal. And yet too many of our people still live in unacceptable housing conditions. We will continue a substantial programme of housebuilding and home improvement.

Under our new system of housing investment programmes, local councils will continue to play a central part in meeting housing needs.

We reject the philosophy that tenants are second-class citizens. Labour has already published its new Housing Bill which will give a new deal to council tenants to give them security of tenure; the right to a written tenancy agreement; the right to improve the home; the right to take in lodgers; the right to be consulted on housing management decisions; easier residential qualifications; and a new national scheme to help tenants to move from one part of the country to another.

We will improve the quality of our less popular council estates, which will mean relaxing the rules under which improvements to estates less than 30 years old cannot attract Government subsidy.

Labour does not oppose the sale of council houses to sitting tenants of two years' standing who want to buy, so long as such sales are at a fair price and do not damage a local authority's ability to meet the demands for decent homes to rent. But Labour will continue to oppose the sales of council housing in areas of serious housing need.

Labour also seeks to widen choice, and we shall therefore continue to help those who wish to buy their own homes.

Labour will:

Carry through its new home loan plan to give saving bonuses and interest-free loans· of up to £600 to first-time buyers.

Examine ways of expanding the scheme under which building societies lend to home-buyers nominated by local councils, particularly for older, cheaper properties.

Introduce new ways of lowering the cost and speeding the process of house purchase. Labour has set up the Royal Commission on Legal Services, which will be reporting on conveyancing. Labour policy is to end the monopoly on house conveyancing now enjoyed by solicitors, and improve leasehold enfranchisement.

With the growth of home ownership and council housing, private renting has entered an irreversible decline. We stand by the principles of security of tenure and rent regulations, and will legislate to close loopholes in the Rent Acts. We shall continue to encourage socially-accountable landlords – local authorities, housing associations and housing cooperatives – to take over privately rented property except where an owner-occupier lets part of his own home.

Labour will give private tenants access to improvement grants on the same basis as owners. We shall make it easier for a tenant to force a landlord to do necessary repairs.

We will legislate to give further protection to those who live in mobile homes and to the owners of holiday caravans. We will set up a new housing tribunal to replace the present confusing jumble of courts, tribunals and committees dealing with rents, security of tenure, and other housing problems.

Labour will give new rights to everyone whose home is tied to their job.

Building and Our Future

A well-organized and efficient construction industry is essential to the achievement of many of our economic and social objectives. Labour will:

Plan and coordinate public sector demand on the industry, in order to help stabilize the industry's workload.

Press forward with plans for decasualization and job security in the industry, building on the work of the Construction Industry Manpower Board, and giving their proposed registration scheme statutory backing if necessary.

Encourage the development of building workers' cooperatives.

Expand local authority direct labour organizations, ensuring that they are efficiently run as separate municipal enterprises, publicly accountable for their performance.

Develop and strengthen existing building capacity in the public sector so as to establish pace-making public enterprise for large and medium sized construction projects.

Labour and The Land

At the heart of all planning policy is the problem of the land. Labour's Community Land Act provides the means to tackle land speculation through public ownership. We shall seek to clarify and amend the regulations surrounding land valuation, not least to ensure that land is valued very much more closely to its present use value. We shall use it to ensure that social criteria rather than maximum profit decides how land is to be used. We intend to set up a publicly accessible register of all land.

We will authorize local authorities to charge rates on land which is left unused. We have simplified planning procedures. We intend that in future planning permissions not acted upon after five years will not be automatically renewed.

The Inner City

Labour is committed to save our inner cities. With the inner city partnerships, the new Urban Area Act, and the increased urban programme, Labour has begun to breathe new life into our inner cities.

First, we must bring back more jobs to these areas. Our national industrial policy will be used to bring investment to the inner cities. We will mount a concerted effort to stimulate the development of small firms and worker cooperatives in these areas.

Secondly, we will bring about during the lifetime of the next Parliament a further increase in the expenditure earmarked for refurbishing our inner cities, for education, for housing, and for the social services.

Rural Areas

The Labour Government will take measures to arrest the decline in the quality of life in rural areas. We will increase the funds available to the Development Commission, and widen its scope. We will reestablish the Rural Development Boards in England and ensure that the Co-operative Development Agency, the NEB, the tourist boards and the Manpower Services Commission play an active role in rural job creation. We shall encourage new forms of agriculture – such as fish farming.

Recognizing the importance of an adequate integrated rural transport service, we will provide greater support for rural buses, encourage improvements in the frequency and timetabling of conventional services, and open freight rail lines to passenger services.

We will improve and increase public sector housing in rural areas and improve their educational facilities and personal social services.

Our Environment

Labour is proud of its record on environmental matters. Our Standing Royal Commission on Environmental Pollution has set the pace for advance. For the future, however, we will have to give still higher priority to this important issue.

Labour will:

Develop policies for resource conservation.

Use our campaign for a better environment to provide the basis of secured employment, eg in pollution control and in waste recycling.

Further reduce the lead content in petrol.

Provide an annual 'State of the Environment' report to Parliament.

Ensure that, before the inquiry stage of major development proposals – perhaps two or three a year – the environmental effects are subject to detailed analysis and the report published.

Introduce an extended clean-up campaign – 'Making Britain Clean and Green', and start a real drive by local authorities and voluntary groups to clear up derelict land, and use it to the benefit of the community.

Transport

The majority of our people still depend on public transport. Labour believes in maintaining and improving within an integrated transport system. We will encourage closer coordination at local level between road and rail.

Railways

Under Labour, there will never be another Beeching. We will maintain the present rail network and increase investment in the future. As much freight as possible must be carried by rail; and the scheme whereby companies receive grants for installing railway facilities will be extended.

Buses, especially in country areas, will continue to require a permanent and substantial amount of public support to meet social needs. In areas where free travel does not yet exist, Labour will bring in a nationwide, off-peak, half-fares scheme for OAPs, the blind and the disabled.

We will sort out the present confusion surrounding arrangements for children's fares, so that there are free fares up to the age of five, and reduced fares up to 16. Those benefiting from the present free travel to school schemes will not be affected.

For the motorist, we want to reduce bureaucracy and ensure fair treatment. The phased abolition of vehicle excise duty will remove one source of annoyance and irritation. Labour will press for major improvements for customers in motorway service areas and garage repairs generally.

Heavy lorries will be made to carry, through taxation, their full share of road costs, including environmental costs. We will take further measures to reduce noise and pollution. The National Freight Corporation must be enabled to provide the basis for expanding the public sector in the road haulage industry. The Labour Government will continue to oppose any proposals to increase the permitted maximum weight limit for heavy lorries, which are inconsistent with road safety and the needs of the environment.

The road building programme will remain at its present level – but we will adopt a more selective approach than in the past. More by-passes will be built. Highway inquiries will also be more open, wider in scope, and with inspectors clearly seen to be independent.

In the ports industry, we reaffirm our policy to bring commercial ports and cargo handling into public ownership.

A Wider, More Open Democracy

A central theme of our programme for the eighties is the protection and enhancement of our democracy.

Democracy at Work

The time has come to recognize the increasing desire of employees to have a larger say in the decisions which vitally affect their working lives and jobs. We also wish to harness their energies and experience in a positive partnership to improve our industrial relationships in a way which reduced conflict and increased cooperation. We therefore commit the Labour Government to a major extension of industrial democracy. Democratic practice and good industrial relations means single status in industry and a dignified respect for all workers, whatever their plant grading.

We recognize – as have other countries – that employees should be entitled to fall back on certain basic rights if agreement is not achieved. To this end, we will encourage recognized trade unions to establish joint representation committees in all companies

303

employing more than 500 people, and place a legal obligation on employers to discuss company plans with these committees. We will establish an industrial democracy commission to stimulate and monitor schemes of industrial democracy in the private sector and nationalised industries.

Devolution

In our 1974 manifesto, we promised to create elected assembles in Scotland and Wales as part of our programme of decentralization and devolution of power. Following the result of the referendum in Wales, it is clear that the majority there does not want an assembly, and we accept their decision. In Scotland, however, a majority voted for devolution.

We reaffirm our commitment to devolution for Scotland. We are therefore ready to discuss constructively with all concerned any changes which would make the scheme in the present Act more widely acceptable, so that we can establish a Scottish Assembly.

Law, Rights and the Community

The protection and enhancement of human rights and civil liberties is an indispensible part of a wider democracy. We will fight against crime and violence which affect all Western societies. We will continue to back the police with proper resources and manpower. The police are substantially better-paid and equipped today than they were under the Tories. At the same time, we shall attack the social deprivation which allows crime to flourish.

Our policies on fighting deprivation and social injustice, on arresting the decay of our inner cities, on youth employment and helping the family, will all contribute to a happier and more law-abiding society.

During the next Parliament, we will increase law centres providing legal help for the ordinary citizen; provide more resources for the prison and probation services; extend legal aid to certain tribunal hearings; bring together and coordinate the various offices of Ombudsmen; consider responsibility for the conduct of prosecutions in the light of the report of the Royal Commission on Criminal Procedures; and provide further help for the victims of crime.

Democracy at Westminster

In central government, we will:

Make major improvements in the legislative process, including new methods of considering Bills in committee, and of scrutinizing the work of government through select committees.

Establish a more powerful and professional system of audit.

Introduce a Freedom of Information Bill to provide a system of open government, and enact the proposals made by the Government in its White Paper to reform Section Two of the Official Secrets Act.

Bring forward proposals to reform the machinery of government and the structure of public administration to bring them into line with modern conditions.

Reexamine the procedures for appointment to governmental and quasi-governmental bodies, and to the boards of public enterprises, and for recommendations for honours.

No one can defend on any democratic grounds the House of Lords and the power and influence it exercises in our constitution. We propose, therefore, in the next Parliament, to abolish the delaying power and legislative veto of the House of Lords.

Local Democracy

Already, the central government pays 61 per cent of the cost of most local services. We shall continue through the rate support grant to provide national Exchequer assistance to ratepayers, particularly in areas of greatest need. We shall seek ways of making finance for local government fairer to ratepayers.

Labour will extend public involvement in local government, so damaged by the bureaucratic and costly local government system imposed by the Tories.

To this end, the Labour Government will:

Give back to large district councils in England responsibility for education, planning, social services, local libraries and other local services.

End the automatic disqualification of local government employees from standing for election.

Enable councils to co-opt employee representatives to their committees as non-voting members.

Equality for Women

Labour's Sex Discrimination Act, Equal Pay Act, the Employment Protection Act, and Social Security Pensions Act have already created a new deal for women.

Disabled housewives, single mothers, women looking after a dependent relative – all have received help from this Labour Government.

We have made a start towards equal citizenship by giving to British women, married to foreign husbands, the same rights as British men with foreign wives. We have changed the regulations to make it possible for children born abroad to British mothers to acquire British nationality.

We shall progressively eliminate the inequalities that still exist in the social security and tax systems. We shall introduce further reforms proposed by the Finer Committee on One-Parent Families. We have already protected the anonymity of women victims of rape. We shall bring in a fairer system of family law with new family courts. Labour will abolish the contributory conditions for maternity grant and raise the level of the grant.

One community

Labour has already strengthened the legislation protecting minorities. The next Labour Government will continue to protect the community against discrimination and racialism. We will:

Give a strong lead, by promoting equality of opportunities at work throughout the public sector.

Help those whose first language is not English.

Monitor all Government and local authority services to ensure that minorities are receiving fair treatment.

Consider what measures may be necessary to clarify the role of the Public Order Act and to strengthen and widen the scope of the Race Relations Act.

Review the 1824 Vagrancy Act, with a view to the repeal of Section 4.

Large-scale migration to this country is ending, but we still have some major commitments to fulfil. Labour will honour these. A quota would merely cause even longer delays for dependants.

Our whole immigration and citizenship law needs revision. Progress has already been made on this with the publication of a Government Green Paper.

Northern Ireland

For over four years, Labour has governed Northern Ireland direct from Westminster. During this period, considerable progress has been made on the security front and on the efforts to bring peace and stability to the Province. Detention has been ended, a special independent Police Complaints Board has been set up, and the police themselves are now more widely accepted in the community.

Unfortunately, in spite of all the attempts by the Labour Government, it has not been possible to find common agreement between the political parties on the best form of government for Northern Ireland.

For the present, direct rule remains the only viable alternative. Any change can be made only with the consent of the people of Northern Ireland. We will work to make it more accountable and democratic.

In the field of security, there is an essential role for the army in protecting the people of Northern Ireland, but we will continue our policy of extending the role of the police so as to involve all sections of the community.

We accept the recommendations of the Bennett Committee, and we will see that they are carried out as quickly as possible to make ill-treatment impossible.

Labour has saved thousands of jobs in Northern Ireland and attracted much investment and industry to the most under-developed areas. But at about twice the United Kingdom average, unemployment continues at an intolerably high level. The industrial policies set out earlier will be applied with full force and vigour to Northern Ireland.

The Arts and the Media

Both the arts and the media play an important role in enhancing the quality of our democracy.

Arts. Aid to the Arts Council is going up 25 per cent this year. We will ensure more money for the Arts in future. The Arts Council should include elected representatives.

A Labour Government will set up a British Film Authority, with a distribution arm, to stimulate investment in British film productions.

The media. Our aim is to safeguard freedom of expression; to encourage diversity; and to guard both against the dangers of government and of commercial control.

On broadcasting, the Labour Government will implement the proposals in its White Paper, including instituting an Open Broadcasting Authority. We will phase out the television licence fee for old age pensioners during the lifetime of the next Parliament.

Animal Welfare

Under Labour's new council of animal welfare, we will have stronger control on the export of live animals for slaughter, and conditions of factory farming, and experiments on living animals.

Legislation to end cruelty to animals will include the banning of hare coursing, stag and deer hunting. Angling and shooting will in no way be affected by our proposals.

European Community

At this election, Labour will, once again, be the only major political party to offer the British people the prospect of bringing about fundamental and much-needed reform to the EEC.

We are concerned to ensure that Greece, Portugal, and Spain receive an early welcome into the Community. This enlargement of the Community will provide an opportunity to create a wider and looser grouping of European states, thus reducing the dangers of an over-centralised and over-bureaucratic EEC.

We aim to develop a Europe which is democratic and socialist, and where the interests of the people are placed above the interests of national and multinational capitalist groups, but within which each country must be able to realize its own economic and social objectives, under the sovereignty of its own Parliament and people.

A Labour Government will oppose any move towards turning the Community into a federation.

Trade and Industry

Working with our socialist colleagues, we will defend the ability of each member state to determine its own industrial policies. Our policy is to encourage such measures as import ceilings and orderly marketing arrangements where they are necessary to protect vital national economic interests.

Member states must be able to control and plan their own energy policies while at the same time maximizing cooperation and seeking agreement on areas of mutual interest, such as research and development.

Food and Agriculture

Membership of the Community has compelled us to pay more for our food than otherwise would be the case. The CAP raises serious problems for British agriculture – distorting the balance of production; decreasing consumption through inflated prices in the shops; and stopping the industry from growing. That is why Labour seeks a fundamental reform of the CAP.

The Tories back a policy which would raise food prices by the equivalent of £90 a year on the average family budget.

Labour will seek to:

End the scandal of food surpluses – which cost £900m per year in storage alone.

Improve access for cheap food from countries outside the EEC.

Reduce EEC support prices; and press for more scope under the CAP for national support arrangements, such as our beef premiums.

A change in emphasis from price support to structural reform.

The reforms we are calling for are in the interests of consumers throughout every country in the Community. We will do our utmost to gain the cooperation of our EEC partners. However, if these reforms are not speedily implemented, we shall protect our interests – if necessary vetoing any further increase in food prices until surpluses have been eliminated.

Economy and Finance

We will retain the freedom to determine our own budgetary policy and to control our own currency. A Labour Government will retain the power to impose controls on capital movements and will continue to resist any upward harmonisation of VAT or any reduction in the existing range of zero-rated VAT items in Britain. A Labour Government would not join an economic and monetary union.

The Community Budget

Major reforms are needed to the Community Budget. Britain is now providing a net subsidy to some of the other EEC countries amounting to £900m a year. No country whose national income falls below the average for the Community as a whole should be required to make a net contribution to the Budget.

    We should reduce the proportion (75 per cent) of the Community Budget spent on agriculture, and the funds so released could be directed into social and regional development.

    The Labour Government will ensure that the Community Budget should promote a fairer distribution of resources within the EEC, and the convergence of economic performance of member states, to achieve faster growth, higher employment and lower rates of inflation.

Parliamentary Sovereignty

The Labour Government will legislate to ensure that British ministers are accountable to the House of Commons before making any commitment in the Council of Ministers. Enlargement of the Community will provide the opportunity for seeking changes in the Treaty of Rome, which would enable the House of Commons to strengthen its powers to amend or repeal EEC legislation. This would involve consequential amendments to the 1972 European Communities Act.

The Third World

The Labour Government will press for improvements in the Lomé Convention, for widening the scope of the EEC's aid to include the most needy areas of the world, and for the EEC to place emphasis on trade and the stabilization of the export prices of third world commodities.

Foreign Policy

The Labour Party's priority is to build a democratic socialist society in Britain and to create the conditions necessary to free the world from poverty, inequality and war. We condemn violations of human rights wherever they occur and whatever the political complexion of the Government concerned, and will further human rights in all international organizations.

    Crucial to our policy is the pursuit of peace, development and disarmament by strengthening the process of detente. We shall seek to improve relations with the USSR and the countries of Eastern Europe, as well as with China.

    We shall continue to work for the peaceful and just settlement of disputes and the strengthening of international cooperation. The Labour Government will, therefore, continue its policy of strengthening international organizations, particularly the United Nations, and the Commonwealth.

    We shall continue to work to bring about a just settlement of the problems of Cyprus.

    We shall work for a negotiated settlement of the Israeli-Arab conflict which would ensure the right of all parties to achieve national self-determination and to live in a homeland within secure and recognized borders.

    Labour is totally opposed to the system of apartheid, and will continue to support opponents of apartheid, giving humanitarian and other aid to liberation movements of southern Africa. Labour believes that it is not only wrong, but contrary to British long-term interests, to be closely tied economically to South Africa. We will take active steps to reduce our economic dependence on South Africa and discourage new investment in South Africa by British companies. Those already operating there will be expected to comply with a strengthened code of conduct governing conditions of employment.

We have refused to approve the Rhodesian internal settlement and we will continue to work for a settlement of the Rhodesia problem acceptable to the people of Rhodesia as a whole. Until such time as an agreement is arrived at, we will maintain and intensify sanctions against the illegal regime.

We will continue actively to support the United Nations settlement proposals for Namibia, including upholding the territorial integrity of the country.

In respect of those countries of Latin America with dictatorial regimes, particularly Chile and Argentina, the Labour Government will demand that these regimes pay promptly their due debts. The restoration of human and trade union rights will be a prior condition for the rescheduling of future debt payments.

We will continue to pursue our policy of aid to the poorest countries and the poorest people, with the emphasis on rural development. Under Labour, aid is increasing at 6 per cent a year.

We will seek to implement the United Nations target of 0.7 per cent of the gross national product for official aid as soon as economic circumstances permit.

Labour will take account of human rights considerations when giving aid.

Help will continue to be given to the victims of repressive regimes, including the provision of refugee programmes.

The Labour Government approach the North-South dialogue in a spirit of cooperation. It will actively participate in the UNCTAD 5 and other negotiations seeking to establish a more just world trading system which recognizes the needs of poorer countries.

Detente and Defence

While actively pursuing a policy of detente, the Labour Government will continue to press for the implementation of the human rights provisions of the Helsinki Final Act. The Labour Government will continue to work for the success of the Mutual Balanced Force Reduction Talks in Vienna, and will give full support to the work of the United Nations Committee on Disarmament. The Labour Government will work for the speedy conclusion of a Comprehensive Test Ban Treaty. We shall also give every encouragement to our American allies to achieve a successful conclusion to the vital Strategic Arms Limitation Talks. The Labour Government will maintain its support for Nato as an instrument of detente no less than of defence. The ultimate objective of a satisfactory relationship in Europe is the mutual and concurrent phasing-out of both Nato and the Warsaw Pact.

We shall continue with our plans to reduce the proportion of the nation's resources devoted to defence, so that the burden we bear will be brought into line with that carried by our main allies. A Labour Government would plan to ensure that savings in military expenditure did not lead to unemployment for those working in the defence industries. We shall give material support and encouragement to plans for industrial conversion so that the valuable resources of the defence industries can be used for the production of socially-needed goods.

In 1974, we renounced any intention of moving towards the production of a new generation of nuclear weapons or a successor to the Polaris nuclear force; we reiterate our belief that this is the best course for Britain. But many great issues affecting our allies and the world are involved, and a new round of strategic arms limitation negotiations will soon begin. We think it is essential that there must be a full and informed debate about these issues in the country before the necessary decision is taken.

Labour will give every encouragement to those working for the cause of international peace. We will consider establishing a peace research institute. We shall negotiate with our friends and allies, to prevent the supply of arms to countries where any such supply would increase the chances of international conflict or internal repression.

Into the Eighties

This election comes at a time of change.unparalleled since 1945. A generation has now grown up in a welfare state which remains the envy of the world in health care and education. We have demonstrated a capacity for skill and inventiveness which keeps us at the forefront of world technology. Those are no mean achievements.

A Tory Government would put all this at risk. At work, they would substitute confrontation for cooperation. The free market forces they support would mean soaring inflation, rising prices and growing unemployment. Their uncaring meanness would mean misery for millions of the most vulnerable in our community, for their policy of cutting public expenditure can only mean a drastic reduction in all our social services.

Against this reactionary prospect, Labour sets its vision for the future. We seek to bring about a fundamental change in the balance of power and wealth in favour of working people and their families. We reject the concept that there is a choice to be made between a prosperous and efficient Britain and a caring and compassionate society. As democratic socialists, we believe they complement each other.

That is the spirit of this manifesto. A strong, fair, and more just society is the prize within our grasp. It is the message of hope for the future, based on a record of promises kept, that Labour puts to the British people at this election.

The Liberal Party:

'The Real Fight is for Britain'

Mr David Steel, in an introduction to the Liberal manifesto said:

With your support this election could be about something more important than a change of government. It could be a chance to change a failed political system.

Britain is deadlocked and that deadlock has meant economic and social decline. There can be very few voters, even among the keenest adherents of the Conservative or Labour cause, who really believe that our problems can all be solved just by yet another change of government. Oppositions promise grandiosely to generate 'the white hot heat of technological revolution' or to 'roll back the frontiers of the state'. It takes at least a year or two of government for them to come to terms with reality and discard their doctrinaire programmes. Each time the country is weakened further.

We have tried confrontation politics for long enough. In 1964, in 1970, in 1974, incoming governments promised that they held the key to Britain's industrial and social problems, if only they could undo the achievements of their predecessors and push their own prescriptions through Parliament. The hopes they raised have all been cruelly disappointed. It is high time to try a different pattern of government, which is based upon the consent and support of the broad majority of the electorate. That alone can now provide the basis for the long term programme of reform which Britain so desperately needs.

The Liberal Party has taken the first step towards breaking the deadlock during the past Parliament, by proving that co-operation among different parties is possible, practical and good for Britain. Unavoidably in this first experiment in a new style of government, our achievements were relatively limited. Many of the reforms which we wish to see implemented have had to wait.

But during the 18 months of the Liberal Agreement with the Labour Government the stability and consistency provided by co-operation among parties which represented a clear majority of the electorate, and the requirement that the Labour Government respect the views of that majority, helped to bring down the annual rate of inflation to 8 per cent. The Tories had raised it from 5.9 per cent to 13.2 per cent. Labour raised it further to a peak of 26.9 per cent, now it is rising again. The Lib-Lab Agreement also reduced Interest Rates to 10 per cent (Minimum Lending Rate). The Tories left it at 12.5 per cent under Labour it reached a peak of 15 per cent in October 1976. It is now back up again.

Industrial confidence began to return during the agreement. The divisive policies promoted by Labour's lunatic left-wing were effectively held in check. On Liberal insistence the law was changed to encourage profit-sharing, to help bridge the gulf of mistrust between the two sides of industry – which has so far led 48 companies to adopt new profit-sharing schemes.

Sadly, much of what was achieved for Britain during those 18 months has been thrown away since last October, as Labour clung on to office without secure and agreed majority support. If either of the two establishment parties grabs an exclusive hold on office after this election, Britain will slip even deeper into industrial confrontation and economic decay. The truth is, the Labour and Conservatives parties share a vested interest in the preservation of Britain's divided society. The unrepresentative nature of our electoral system protects them from the full effects of public disillusionment. Continuing industrial and social confrontation reinforces their links with the opposing sides of industry. Britain's secretive and centralised structure of government protects them, turn and turn about, from Parliament and the public.

Many, on both front benches, would rather see Britain's economy drift further behind our continental neighbours, would rather accept another cycle of industrial conflict and popular discontent, than touch the pattern of adversary politics which supports their alternating hold on political power.

I appeal to you, as a voter concerned with what is best for Britain, to throw your support behind the fresh approach which the Liberal Party represents – and which we have now demonstrated can work for Britain. The effectiveness of whatever government emerges after this election, the whole style of British government, will depend less upon which big/dinosaur Party returns with the largest number of parliamentary seats than upon the size of the Liberal wedge in the House of Commons. A mass Liberal vote throughout the country and many more Liberal seats will call the final whistle on a discredited Tory/Labour game.

Part Two of this manifesto sets out the Liberal Party's detailed electoral programme. I want here to stress four underlying themes: our commitment to fundamental political and constitutional reform; our proposals for economic and industrial reform; our plans to change and to simplify our overburdened tax system and our concern to bring to bear an environmental perspective across the whole range of government policies.

Political reform is the starting point. Until we break the two-party stranglehold, until we get away from the adversary class politics which are embedded in our parliamentary structure, we cannot successfully tackle the problems of economic weakness and industrial mistrust, of misspent resources in housing, of uncertain management of the public sector and of mishandled relations with our neighbours abroad. Electoral reform is the key to the lock. A democratic electoral system would deprive the Conservative and Labour parties of their ability to maintain electoral support by frightening wavering voters with the spectre of a single, unacceptable alternative. It would force them to face up to their own internal contradictions: the unstable coalition within a weakened Labour Party between its nationalising left and its conservative centre; the tensions within the Conservative Party between moderate Tories and doctrinaire free-marketeers. A democratic electoral system is needed, too, to generate the popular consent which is essential to support a long-term programme of economic and social reform.

The reluctant and unsatisfactory compromises which recent governments have offered in response to demands for the reform of Parliament, for an end to official secrecy, above all for devolution and decentralisation, also demonstrate the need for more thorough-going change and the inability of the establishment front benches to meet that need. Privately, many MPs from both the Labour and Conservative parties accept the case for far-reaching changes, but they are unwilling publicly to challenge their own leadership. A powerful wedge of Liberal MPs in the next Parliament could start a chain reaction of political change.

Economic and industrial reform must accompany and follow from political reform. Hardly surprisingly, the owner party and the union party have resisted the extension of democracy to industry, seeing a transformation of the pattern of industrial relations as a threat to their entrenched interests. Labour's preferred approach would only strengthen the position of trade unions, which are already one of the most conservative forces in our society. They do not want to involve the workforce as a whole. The Conservative alternative of lightly-disguised confrontation is even more dangerous in 1979 than their Selsdon Park proposals were in 1970, and would no doubt lead again after a painful two years in office to another expensive U-turn.

We Liberals seek instead to alter fundamentally the framework within which economic policy is made, to bring the different sides of industry together to work constructively to increase the well being of Britain – not to battle destructively over each other's share of a dwindling national cake.

The two-party confrontation has also wrought havoc with our tax system. Successive governments have tacked on new additions to an already unwieldy structure. It is too complex for most taxpayers to understand or to be sure of their rights and obligations. Many changes have been rushed through Parliament without adequate debate or consideration of their implications, at the behest of some vested interest or in the service of some outdated ideology. As a result tax avoidance has become our fastest growing industry. Liberals are concerned to simplify the personal tax system and reduce its burden to create a tax structure which encourages initiative and promotes a wider distribution of wealth, and above all to establish principles for a stable tax system which can command the respect of the electorate as a whole: wealthy, poor and average earners.

Neither of the two established parties has paid any serious attention to the long-term conservation of Britain's environment and resources. The argument over North Sea oil has been conducted in terms of immediate benefits rather than long term needs. The necessity to grow more of our own food and the conservation of man's natural habitat, including its flora and fauna, have been wrongly regarded as low

311

priorities in politics. The debate over Britain's future dependence on nuclear power has hardly touched Parliament, conducted instead by environmental groups through the limited forum of the Windscale inquiry. Yet conservation and recycling of our limited and often finite resources is a vital issue for Britain's future, and an issue which concerns a growing section of our electorate. We Liberals have used our influence to force Parliament to pay more attention to the ecological perspective.

But Parliament as at present constructed does not find it easy to focus on questions like this, which do not fall conveniently into the categories established by the conventions of two-Party politics or the Left/Right dog-fight. Here is a key issue for Britain as the new Parliament takes us into the 1980s, too complicated for the current ritual of debate but too important to ignore.

It may seem paradoxical that Liberals call at once for more stable government and for radical change. Our concern is for long-term change, as opposed to the twists and turns of short-term policies which have characterised British government since the end of the Second World War. Worthwhile reforms for Britain's economy, for its industrial relations, its tax structure, its social services, its political system itself, can only be achieved after thorough examination and open debate – and can only be made to last if they command the respect and acceptance of the majority of the electorate.

That is why we are prepared to co-operate with other parties, even as we insist on the need for a fundamental break in Britain's political habits. Of course we want in time to see Britain led by a Liberal Government, implementing a coherent radical programme with the support of a clear majority of voters. But meanwhile we are prepared to co-operate with whichever party will go with us some way along the same road. It would, after all, be a profound and radical change for Britain to benefit from stability in economic policy, to gain a new consensus in pay policy and industrial relations, to achieve a wider agreement on the structure of taxation, or to open up a searching debat on the best use of Britain's limited resources.

It would be a radical change in itself for the next government to have to base its policies upon the support of the representatives of a genuine majority of the electorate. With your support, and the support of millions of voters like you, we can ensure that those changes take place.

The Liberal programme stated:

Economic and industrial recovery can only follow from a radical programme of political and social reform. In a liberal society in Britain, power and wealth will be distributed more widely, and government subjected to open democratic control. Participation and self-management will be encouraged, in government and in industry; public and private power will be, where possible, dispersed; individual initiative and independence will be rewarded; and a sense of partnership and community strengthened. But UK action alone cannot provide the stimulus for these major political and social changes. Many of our problems have to be tackled at the European level; action is also needed in the regions and nations of the United Kingdom, and within local communities through the efforts of voluntary bodies and community groups. But in an over-centralised Britain the process of reform is most urgently needed at the centre, in Westminster and Whitehall.

POLITICAL REFORM

Britain has a grossly undemocratic voting system, over-centralised government and an ineffective Parliament. Piecemeal changes have failed to introduce the necessary constitutional reforms. Bureaucracy and powerful organisations triumph at the expense of individuals who feel powerless to influence decisions that affect them. Liberals believe:

1 That electoral reform is the essential first step to representative parliament and government.
2 In open government accountable to a reformed parliament.
3 That decisions must be taken at the most local level practicable.
4 People and their communities must take part in decisions that affect them.

Reform of the Voting System

Our first priority is *electoral reform,* because Britain's voting system is a root cause of our troubles:

It damages living standards by preventing consistent economic and social policies.

It leads to governments claiming a false mandate in favour of policies which have been decisively rejected by a majority of the voters.

It encourages native voting, frustrates the intelligent elector and leads to increasing alienation from the whole political system.

It rewards parties based on class distinctions and reinforces class divisions.

Without reform our whole democracy is at risk.

Liberals demand proportional representation at all levels of government:

At Westminster, to give us representative parliaments and genuine majority government.

For future elections to the *European Parliament,* to avoid the disgrace of being the only member of the EEC not to use a fair voting system.

In *local government,* where the present system can often produce one-party dominance with its dangers of corruption.

The system adopted must ensure that every vote is of equal value and affects the result. It must also ensure that parties win roughly the same proportion of seats as their proportion of votes, allow voters a choice between candidates in each party, and reflect minority interest and viewpoints. Liberals believe that of available PR systems, the single transferable vote (STV) best achieves these results.

The main opposition to the overwhelming popular demand for electoral reform comes from political machines exercising unjustified privilege, and from those MP's who fear that if voters had a real choice they would not be re-elected. Liberals support the people in their fight against electoral privilege, and will give first priority in the new Parliament to obtaining a cast-iron commitment to the early introduction of electoral reform.

Reform of Parliament and Government

Parliament should take control of its own business out of the hands of Government, and set up powerful Select Committees, to assert vigorous democratic control over the Executive. Section 2 of the Official Secrets Act should be repealed. We would introduce a Freedom of Information Bill similar to that of the Liberal MP Clement Freud in the last Parliament. This would give a right of public access to all official information except for certain listed categories (e.g. defence, economic and commercially sensitive information, and individual records).

A National Efficiency Audit should be set up to scrutinise public expenditure plans and reduce waste.

We need fixed dates for parliamentary elections to avoid the uncertainty which Prime Ministerial privilege imposes on the country.

The House of Lords should be replaced by a new, democratically chosen, second chamber which includes representatives of the nations and regions of the United Kingdom, and UK members of the European Parliament.

Reform of the Constitution – a Federal Solution

Liberals supported the Scotland and Wales Acts, for all their defects, because we believed they offered a step in the right direction. These deficiencies – the weakness of the proposed Welsh Assembly and the constitutional contradictions in the Scotland Act – were exposed in the referendum debates and contributed to the results. This experience has reinforced our belief that the massive decentralisation of power from Westminster and Whitehall to Scotland, Wales and the major regions of England – for which we have long called must involve legislative, executive and fiscal powers taken together. It has also demonstrated the need for a federal approach, which will involve a written constitution and a Supreme Court, as the only approach which can achieve legislative devolution within a workable framework of government for the United Kingdom.

Whatever the outcome of the election, Liberals will press for the widest possible consultations among the parties on constitutional reform.

Local Government

The Tory reorganisation of *local government* proved an expensive disaster. In due course, the district and county councils must be replaced by one tier of multi-purpose authorities, whose boundaries match local needs and circumstances.

We support the establishment of parish councils in urban areas and the extension of the powers of existing parish councils. These councils should have a statutory right 'to be consulted' by local government and other bodies and a duty to stimulate local democracy.

NORTHERN IRELAND

Progress towards peace ought to come from within the Province but if outside help is required Great Britain must be prepared to contribute.

As an interim measure we propose that a 15 to 20 member Advisory Council be elected by the people of Northern Ireland using PR(STV). Such a council would be large enough to let every signficant viewpoint have a voice but small enough for all its members to have real discussion with each other as well as with the Secretary of State and other political representatives.

The Council would:

1 Represent the views of the people of Northern Ireland to the Secretary of State and advise him accordingly, and
2 discuss how a constitutional conference should be set up to consider the means by which a generally acceptable form of government for the Province should be developed.

There must be no capitulation to violence. Direct rule must continue for the time being. The civil power must be given military assistance for as long as required. Britain will not force Northern Ireland to unite with the Republic of Ireland. All elections, including those for Westminster, must be by PR(STV). Continuing emphasis must be placed on the achievement of full human rights.

REFORMS TO STRENGTHEN CITIZENS' RIGHTS

The liberty of the individual requires constant vigilance. Restrictions can only be justified if they protect the freedom of others. Liberals emphasise:
1 Legislation to protect individual rights.
2 A clear definition of citizenship.
3 Equal opportunities for men and women in all spheres, especially equal pay for work of equal value.
4 Protection for minority groups.

Individual Freedom

We need a Bill of Rights – as a first step, Britain should incorporate the European Convention of Human Rights into United Kingdom law. Individual rights protected by law should include:

The right to see, correct and add comments to one's personal records held by public and private bodies.

The right of individual privacy.

The right of free association with others, including the right to be represented through a Trade Union.

The right to work without having to be a member of a Trade Union and the right to cross a picket line without intimidation.

The rights of those in police custody, by means of revised Judges' Rules.

Reduction of Crime

The steady increase in crime can only be checked in the short run by:

Recruiting many more police, by improving working conditions.

Strengthening the links between the police and the communities that they serve.

Having the greatest practicable number of policemen 'on the beat' by day and night.

Making more resources and facilities (including secure accommodation) available to magistrates and others concerned with juvenile offenders, to curb juvenile crime and rehabilitate juvenile offenders.

Prisons must be modernised and further experiments made with non-custodial treatment, except for those whose imprisonment is necessary for the protection of society.

At the same time, we must realise that the long term solution is to attack vigorously the social, environmental and economic seedbeds of crime such as broken homes, bad schools, drink and drugs, decaying cities, bad housing, unemployment, and the boredom of mass production society.

Nationality and Entry to the UK

There should be only one class of citizenship for citizens of the UK and colonies. We would abolish the discrimination against non-patrials which creates second-class citizens. Citizens of the UK and colonies, including residents of Commonwealth countries who accepted the offer of remaining UK citizens when independence was granted, should have a right of entry. Spouses, children and other dependents of UK residents should be allowed to join their families in Britain and all children who have been born abroad of British mothers must have automatic right of citzenship.

Liberals deplore the Tory policy of inflaming people's fears about unrestricted immigration when the numbers of immigrants are actually falling. We should, wherever practicable, accept bona fide refugees.

Equal Opportunities for Women and Men

In order to ensure equal opportunities and rewards for women and men, we propose:
Changes in the patterns of work to allow for greater flexibility, part-time and weekend work, so that men and women can better meet their social and family needs.
Legislation to ensure that job evaluation schemes give adequate weight to factors found predominantly in work customarily done by women.
Removal of anomalies in National Insurance benefits which are based on outdated assumptions about the roles of men and women in contributing to family income.
Reshaping the Equal Opportunities Commission to create an effective instrument against discrimination.

Minority Rights

Britain is a diverse and multicultural society and Liberals rejoice in its richness, which owes much to the peoples of many different ethnic origins and cultures who have chosen to live here. We defend their right to maintain and develop their own traditions. Minority groups must be allowed to practise and advocate their beliefs, provided this does not reduce the freedom of others. We will protect and defend the rights of minorities by:
A comprehensive law out-lawing discrimination on grounds of race, sex or political belief with enforcement through a single Anti-Discrimination Board.
Providing a legal right for nomadic people to live according to their life-style so long as this does not harm others.
Removing all legal discrimination based on sexual orientation.

ECONOMIC AND INDUSTRIAL REFORM

The failures of our political system are reflected in our economic and industrial system. Confrontation is used instead of co-operation, resistance to change obstructs innovation, and frequent changes of government policy weaken our economy still further. Inflation has started to rise again, unemployment is unacceptably high and we are becoming increasingly uncompetitive in world markets. We have an unjust industrial society in which most workers are pitted against management and are denied any share in decision-taking or in profits.

We need a radical long-term programme of reforms to restore Britain's economy and industrial prosperity.

Liberals believe in:

1 Controlled and steady economic growth (in co-operation with our European partners), with greater attention to conservation of scarce resources, especially energy and land.
2 Harnessing the potential of all at work to improve enterprise and productivity.
3 Providing opportunities of useful work for all.
4 Protecting the citizen from inflation by reconciling rises in incomes with the real rate of growth of the economy.
5 Ensuring that the primary aim of government intervention in industry should be the promotion of viable market enterprises.

We see a revolution in attitudes amongst all at work through the introduction of *Democracy in Industry* as the key to reversing Britain's economic decline. This means employees sharing control and profits with shareholders. We would achieve this by giving all employees (irrespective of trade union membership) legal rights as individual members of their company; a direct vote in electing the board of directors jointly with the shareholders; rights to information about its plans and prospects; to participate in decisions through elected works councils; and to share in the profits. Liberals would encourage producer co-operatives by establishing a Cooperative Development Bank.

Efficient use of resources means reducing Britain's consumption of non-renewable raw materials, through government support (including tax incentives and penalties) for conservation, energy saving and recycling schemes. Whilst public expenditure already takes too large a share of our *present* national income, our health services, the schools and other essential public services cry out for more resources and the armed services remain underpaid. Economic recovery is essential to provide in the long run extra funds needed to continue the fight against poverty and deprivation. But in the immediate future, they can be found only by a relentless war against bureaucratic waste in central and local government.

More jobs in new industries, as well as in agriculture and in the service sector, must be created to replace those being lost through international competition and technological change. Further positive discrimination in favour of small businesses and producer co-operatives, through changes in the tax system and in planning controls, will help to provide the catalyst for industrial renewal. This will build upon the success of the Liberals in getting the Government to appoint a senior Cabinet minister for the small business field, which has already led to major tax concessions and other reliefs.

Employers, unions and public authorities must not be allowed to obstruct retraining. Liberals also challenge the belief in bigness for its own sake and concentration of control at the centre in both the private and public sectors. We aim at decentralisation, with greater autonomy for individual working units to encourage initiative and participation.

We would introduce a sustained *prices and incomes policy* based on wide consultation and enforceable at law. Our incomes policy would be supported by tax measures and a national minimum income. It would reward increases in value-added. We support attempts to synchronise annual wage settlements.

Liberal proposals for reducing personal taxation, introducing industrial democracy and profit-sharing are essential elements of an incomes policy since they would transform the industrial climate, restore incentive and reduce inflationary expectations.

The role of government is to provide a stable political and economic framework, not to dominate the economy. But it is dangerous to pretend that government can be taken out of economic and industrial planning, given the unavoidable importance of public spending and the active involvement of governments of competitor countries in supporting their industries and promoting their own economic interests. There is no case for further large-scale nationalisation in Britain; but attempts to denationalise at present would further disrupt the industries affected. The National Enterprise Board provides a valuable mechanism for assisting new industries and for aiding companies temporarily in difficulty, but it should disengage from them when they regain commercial viability.

The framework of government economic and industrial policy should be made more open and more subject to parliamentary control, by including Opposition parties on the National Economic Development Council and by establishing a Select Committee for Economic Affairs to consider its reports. Economic recovery is too vital to be subjected to all the twists and turns of partisan tactics, with Opposition parties glorying in their ignorance of facts which face government, and promising to reverse central decisions. Consistent economic policy requires a transformation of the way in which policies are debated and decided.

REFORM OF THE TAX SYSTEM

The British tax system frustrates initiative, inhibits new enterprises and discourages the wider spread of wealth. Penal rates of taxation encourage successful avoidance and evasion; whilst the poor and disadvantaged face a bewildering array of means tests and often fail to receive an adequate income.

Liberals believe in:
1   Providing an adequate minimum income for all.
2   Treating men and woman as equals for tax purposes, whether married or single.
3   Providing greater incentives for earning, productivity and enterprise.
4   Encouraging employees to build up a stake in their enterprise.
5   Widening the distribution and individual ownership of wealth.

The central reform needed is the introduction of *Credit Income Tax* which should:
Abolish the means test.

Introduce cash credits in place of personal allowances, social security payments and national insurance benefits.

Provide credits for students of all ages, for rate relief and housing.

We also need a major switch from taxes on income to taxes on wealth and expenditure and propose:

Income Tax starting at 20 per cent with a top rate of 50 per cent.

A substantial increase in the level of income at which people first pay income tax.

A gifts and legacies tax paid by the recipient in place of Capital Transfer Tax.

A wealth tax on very large capital accumulations in place of the Investment Income Surcharge which would be repealed.

Tax incentives for profit-sharing and employee share ownership.

Self assessment of tax liability with spot-checks by the Inland Revenue.

The changeover would be introduced over several years and be matched by indexation of taxes on drinks and tobacco, a single rate of VAT and the replacement of the employer's National Insurance contribution with a regionally varied payroll tax.

In a Federal Britain, regional and local government would have powers to raise the revenue they need for the services they provide. Income tax would be the main source of revenue at regional level with a tax on all land values (except agricultural land which would be zero-rated) being the main source of revenue for local government, which would also have powers to levy its own taxes. These would replace domestic rates.

A CARING SOCIETY

Liberals laid the foundations of the modern welfare state, but the original vision has been lost in a jungle of complex rules, means tests and decisions taken by remote officials. Those most in need often fail to get help or are caught by the poverty trap, whilst others fall through the gaps.

Liberals believe in:

1 Recreating services which recognise and respond to human needs, without excessive bureaucracy.
2 Making a reality of democratic control.
3 Providing greater choice for the individual.
4 Renewing inner city life.

The Change to Credit Income Tax

Tax credits would meet the needs of the unemployed, retired, disabled and disadvantaged, and provide for maternity, children and students of all ages. All income would be taxable and where tax liability exceeds cash credits, the difference would be paid as tax; where credits exceed tax, individuals would receive cash regularly.

It would take several years to introduce a full tax credit scheme and in the meantime, we would give priority to:

Further increases in child benefit and the progressive conversion of other allowances against income tax into positive cash credits.

The introduction of a supplementary pension for all pensioners not qualifying for a full earnings-related pension under the new state pension scheme, reducing the number of pensioners needing to apply for supplementary benefit.

The introduction of a disablement allowance to help offset the additional expenditure caused by disablement.

The early introduction of housing credits based on average local rents.

An increase in the mobility allowance and its extension to those over retirement age.

The implementation of the 'Finer' recommendations for one-parent families.

The removal of the anomalies affecting widows and others through the application of the rule about overlapping benefits.

Care in the Community

Liberals seek to make the welfare state more effective and democratic. Providers and receivers of care should participate in running the services. The elderly (especially the over 75s), single-parent families, the disabled, the mentally handicapped and the mentally ill should have priority for additional resources.

We propose to tackle the mushrooming bureaucracy created by the Tories' reorganisation of the health service by abolishing the area health authorities and bringing power back to the level of the local health district, and by placing the regional health authorities under the control of elected Scottish, Welsh and Regional assemblies.

We would give a greater role for voluntary organisations in partnership with official services. We oppose widespread closure of cottage hospitals and encourage the retention of local pharmacies.

Housing

Housing policy should retain existing communities and help build new ones. Priority must be given to improvement of existing houses instead of wholesale clearance and rebuilding. Everyone must have access to adequate housing with a wide choice of tenure and type of home – within the price they can afford. Private and council tenants should have reasonable security of tenure, and help control the management of housing and its immediate environment. We would introduce an Occupiers' and Owners' Charter which safeguards the rights of both tenants and owners of rented housing.

Housing co-operatives and smaller locally-based housing associations, which should be run democratically, should be encouraged. Councils should be required to build more homes for sale, and adequate resources should be provided for the full implementation of the Housing (Homeless Persons) Act, a measure introduced by Liberals.

Liberals would concentrate resources on inner cities by positive planning for community based jobs, schools, housing and entertainment.

Education and Training

We see education and training as a lifelong process that must be as widely available as possible to people of all ages. Secondary education must be non-selective with schools and colleges matched to local needs and working together to give maximum choice to students. Post-school education must be integrated with closer links between universities, polytechnics and further education.

We want to see:

Nursery education for all children whose parents want it.

The immediate right of rising-fives to enter primary school.

Use of successfully qualified teachers now unemployed to reduce class sizes and improve literacy and numeracy.

The involvement of all staff, parents and pupils in the running of schools through elected governing boards, and elected schools councils for secondary schools.

Improved links between schools and industry to ensure preparation for the world.

Expansion of adult education and a major expansion of training and retraining facilities in which Britain still lags far behind its industrial competitors.

Education for retirement from employment.

CONSERVATION OF RESOURCES AND ENVIRONMENT

The industrial world consumes far too much of the world's non-renewable resources and is becoming increasingly dependent on imports of energy. Many of man's activities threaten the natural environment. Few recognise that after the year 2,000, shortages of food, raw materials and energy will mean drastic changes to our lifestyles. The bonanza of North Sea oil must not blind us to the dangers facing us when the oil runs out. We must start to change our attitudes now. Liberals believe in:

1 Conservation and wiser use of scarce resources, especially land and energy.
2 War on waste and pollution.
3 The need to preserve the natural environment for future generations.
4 A re-ordering of our economic and social priorities to put them on a sound basis.

Energy and North Sea oil

Liberals have repeatedly expressed doubts about a massive commitment to nuclear power and questioned the decision to expand the Windscale reprocessing plant. We must spread the extraction of North Sea oil over a longer period and use the revenues for long term investment with high priority for widespread energy conservation and developing alternative energy sources. We must:

Substantially increase research and development on fusion, wave, solar and other sustainable sources of energy.

Make greater use of combined heat and power systems which use waste heat.

Promote maximum effiency in the production and use of coal and the use of primary fuels.

Set up a permanent Energy Commission to discuss in public future energy options.
Not build any more nuclear power stations, at least until the problems of safe and permanent disposal of radioactive waste have been solved.

Transport

We would legislate to improve the standards of public transport in both towns and rural areas by making it more responsive to local needs and subject to democratic control. We would:

Encourage self-help and other schemes which improve freight and personal mobility in rural areas.

Amend the licensing laws governing stage carriage services to encourage local operators.

Plan jobs and homes closer together, discourage the private motor-car in city centres and provide better facilities for pedestrians and cyclists.

Limit expenditure on new road-building to socially desirable projects.

Increase emphasis on road safety and therefore support the early introduction of tachographs in lorries.

Oppose further nationalisation of the ports and reject implementation of the Dock Work Regulations Scheme.

Retain the British Waters Board and increase expenditure on canal maintenance.

Retain the British Rail network – and, where necessary, treat it as a social service.

Support a rail-only Channel Tunnel financed with the aid of EEC finances.

Improve the international communications of the regions by dispersing more international air traffic outside London.

Food and Agriculture

Liberal policy aims at providing a fair return for the farmer and reasonably priced food for the consumer. We also need a co-ordinated approach to the needs of food production and conservation of natural wild life which recognises their interdependence. We therefore propose:

Fundamental reform of the Common Agricultural Policy to produce competitive prices, avoid structural food surpluses and encourage efficient farming; the creation of a Land Bank to help new entrants to farming, and the expansion of co-operatives.

More land for small-holdings.

To raise the guaranteed minimum earnings for farmworkers.

Radical reform of the Common Fisheries Policy, conservation of fish stocks and a fifty mile exclusive limit for each member state within the EEC.

Increase the number of abattoirs to EEC standards to discourage the export of live animals.

Safeguarding the Environment

Land is a finite resource and we need careful planning to ensure an adequate supply of land for housing without using valuable farm land. Resources should be concentrated on inner city renewal and rural regeneration so that all parts of Britain are fit to live in. We have a duty to preserve in trust for future generations that which we inherit from the past. We would:

Make polluters pay the cost of their pollution.

Drastically amend the Community Land Act.

Introduce taxation of the unimproved value of land, in its optimum permitted use (agricultural land to be zero-rated).

Introduced fiscal incentives for conservation, reclamation of industrial wasteland and recycling.

Encourage rurally based crafts and appropriate industries in rural areas.

Support the demand of the General Election Co-ordinating Committee for Animal Protection for a Royal Commission on Animal Welfare.

Ban the importation and manufacture of any product derived from any species whose survival is threatened, and work for a total ban on commercial whaling.

Expedite the work of the Commons Commissioners and legislate to implement the recommendations of the Royal Commission on Common Land with regard to access and management.

Preserve moors, scrub woodland, wetlands and other wildlife 'reservoirs'.

EUROPE AND THE WORLD

Liberals believe in:

1 Opposing all forms of aggression and imperialism.
2 Emphasising the protection of political and human rights as a basis for foreign policy.
3 Fostering closer co-operation within the European Community as the most constructive means of promoting Britain's best interests.
4 Supporting closer integration of defence, security and weapons procurement policies within the Atlantic Alliance as the most effective way of utilizing scarce resources.
5 Working for a more equitable distribution of power and wealth throughout the world. Liberals support positive co-operation with the developing countries.

Economic weakness and political failure have reduced Britain's standing and influence in the world and strained the friendship of our partners in Western Europe and beyond.

In Europe, we support a stronger and more democratic Community. Our long-term aim is a federal Europe based upon democratic institutions and an equitable sharing of economic and social burdens. This involves working towards economic and monetary union and more effective regional and social policies to overcome unemployment and deprivation. It also means commitment to the strengthening of the European Parliament. Only such a Parliament, elected by Proportional Representation, can provide democratic political solutions to Europe's problems and make nationalist solutions as irrelevant as they are dangerous.

Both Labour and Conservative Governments have been short-sighted and inward-looking in their attitudes to Europe. The Labour Government's nationalistic stance has harmed Britain's interests by blocking avenues for wider agreement. Britain's foreign policy should become increasingly concerted with our European partners, and our aim must therefore be the evolution of common European policies, not to pursue the nostalgic illusion of independent power.

Europe's foreign policies must include continued close relations with the United States. We firmly support a peaceful settlement of the Middle East conflict within the framework of the relevant United Nations Resolutions. In Southern Africa, Britain has a special historic responsibility, and we must continue to work with our allies and with the United Nations to promote peaceful change. We support the Anglo-American efforts being made to end bloodshed and to establish an independent Zimbabwe with a Government elected under international supervision. We believe that sanctions should not be lifted nor recognition accorded until such a government is established.

Europe's defence must be a common defence, based on integrated forces and an integrated command within the Atlantic Alliance. Co-operation in armaments should be accompanied by ending British arms sales except in the context of a treaty of mutual defence. The fundamental solution to the problem depends on the establishment of a credible system of international controls of arms sales under the aegis of the United Nations. Arms control negotiations with the Soviet Union and its allies should be vigorously pursued to promote a basis for the mutual and balanced reduction of forces and armaments.

It is one of the most important duties of Europe to help those peoples of the *Third World* who still lack effective influence in the international economy. In this context, Britain, because of our links with the Commonwealth, has a distinctive contribution to make. Liberals want to see reductions in the barriers to world trade, and support current negotiations to give the developing countries stable prices for their raw materials. UK official aid should be increased to achieve the targets agreed by the United Nations.

The work of the UN specialised agencies and of voluntary organisations should be generously supported. Aid should be directed wherever possible through multi-lateral channels, but there is no justice in assisting governments which systematically deny basic human rights to their own citizens.

CONCLUSION

The Liberal programme offers a coherent framework for a series of reforms which will need years of intensive effort. This requires for its success the support of an informed public, co-operation in industry, and a new spirit of mutual understanding among the democratic political parties. The vital choice at this election is whether Britain will start along this new path, or continue to shuffle down the slope of economic and political decline. The contents of the first Queen's Speech are less important than the membership, composition and spirit of the new Parliament. A stronger Liberal presence, backed by a powerful Liberal vote throughout the country, will ensure that the door is opened to fundamental change, not slammed shut again by the negative reactions of the old two-party game which has failed the nation.

The Scottish National Party

The full and detailed declaration of the principles and proposals on which the Scottish National Party campaigned was published in November 1978 and entitled *Return to Nationhood*. A supplementary manifesto for the general election said:

The devolution fiasco of the last four years shows that the only pressure which will bring back any equality of decision-making to Scotland is that from an increased vote for the Scottish National Party. The SNP does not stand for "the break up of the UK" as some of its opponents emotionally and wildly claim. It stands for a new relationship under the Crown, with the other nations of the United Kingdom.

Scotland's people have bolstered other nations, particularly England and certain Commonwealth countries for far too long and to too great an extent, because of the lack of equal opportunity here in Scotland.

Since World War II over a million and a half Scots have emigrated. We have been the only declining nation of the Western world. What other nation would accept a situation in which they were denied even a share in their own oil revenues?

Scotland's principal permanent natural resource – her land – has been sold up to foreigners on an unprecedented scale under Labour. The inequality of job opportunity, the inequality of income levels, and the inequality of prices for consumer goods, all put the Scottish worker and the Scottish shopper at a disadvantage.

For so long as we allow another nation's Parliament to run our lives, use our finances, consume our resources, we will be a declining subject people, not really a nation at all.

Return to Nationhood stated:

At least £1,000m of the oil and gas revenues from the Scottish sector of the North Sea should be invested in Scotland. Oil and gas Petroleum Revenue Tax should be increased from 45 to 75 per cent. A significant reduction should be made in the permitted rate of extraction to maximise the amount of oil and gas recovered over the longest possible period of time.

The SNP want greatly increased financial support for the Scottish Development Agency and the Highland and Islands Development Board.

When the SNP wins the majority of the Scottish seats in the UK Parliament, it will invite the other Scottish MPs to cooperate in negotiating the orderly transfer of power from Westminster to Scotland and the preparation of a constitution. This proposed constitution will then be submitted to the Scottish electroate in a referendum and, if approved, an election will take place for the new Parliament.

Plaid Cymru

The Plaid Cymru manifesto *A Future for Wales* said:

Plaid Cymru campaigns for full self-government for Wales. There are already over 50 countries whose populations are smaller than Wales, but who are represented as full members of the United Nations organisation. A self-governing Wales would retain free trade with the rest of the British Isles and would remain within the Commonwealth.

The failure of the Labour Party to produce adequate proposals to improve the government of Wales means that only Plaid Cymru can be relied upon to win any measure of self-government for our country.

Plaid Cymru will also fight for a stronger voice for Wales in the EEC Parliament and institutions while we remain part of the EEC. It is outrageous that Wales has only four members of the European Parliament while Ireland with an identical population has 15.

Plaid Cymru is determined to get action on Wales' chronic problems of unemployment and depopulation. The Welsh Development Agency – whose setting up was demanded by Plaid for 40 years before the Government acted on the suggestion – must be made more aggressive, willing to take greater risks and to take initiatives in area of need.

No colliery should be closed unless workable reserves are exhausted. Some profits from North Sea oil should be invested in major research programmes into more efficient recovery and utilization of coal.

Imports of steel must be reduced and limited to those types of steel not produced at home, even at the risk of unpopularity with other European Community interests. Steel prices must be realistically controlled. Manufacturing industry in the public sector should be directed to use products of the British steel industry where this is possible. In particular, Plaid Cymru calls for the establishment of a Welsh Steel Corporation.

A permanent Government body now needs to be established to replace the defunct and powerless Welsh Language Council. Within seven years all pupils throughout Wales must be able to pursue their education through the medium of Welsh, should they so desire.

The water industry should be organised on an all-Wales basis. A modern road, rail and air network is essential to replace our appalling transport facilities. These are the arteries without which economic regeneration is impossible. Most important of all, Wales must have an economic plan.

The National Front

The National Front manifesto entitled *It's our Country—Let's win it back* stated:

The National Front believes that Britain should be a democracy but it also believes that today we need to reorganise our political institutions if real democracy is to exist. National Front economic doctrine is a revolution against the whole thinking of the orthodox economists of both right and left.

It is resolved progressively to eliminate the control of the multinationals over British industry by arranging the purchase of foreign subsidiaries either by British firms direct or by the Government with a view mostly to resale later to British firms.

Our reforms in the laws governing industrial tribunals will give employers much firmer powers to dismiss workers for persistent absenteeism and slackness on the job.

We will change the system of social security benefits. Any unemployed person in receipt of social security payments who refuses to accept suitable jobs offered to them will be required to report daily to a daily municipal job centre where community tasks will be allocated to them and the performance of these tasks will be a condition for their continued receipt of benefit.

This country has got to become a tougher place to live in if it is to start once again paying its way in the world.

The policies that we have advocated for British economic revival are incompatible with continued British membership of the European Common Market. Britain must withdraw from the Market and recover her economic and political independence.

The policy of the National Front when coming to office will be to place all coloured immigrants and their offspring on a register of persons liable to be required eventually to leave this country.

With all persons of mixed race decisions as to liability for resettlement will be made on the merits of each individual case. Where coloured and white married couples are involved, the white partner would normally be expected to leave Britain with his or her spouse.

No person would be required to leave this country before an alternative homeland had been found for them. Once such a homeland had been found, the person to be resettled would be given six months' notice to leave Britain.

The Ecology Party

The Ecology Party manifesto *The Real Alternative* said:

We believe that we are on the brink of unprecedented economic and social upheaval. To say this does not make us prophets of doom. There is still time to do something about it. But we must start now.

Our programme rests on six fundamental changes.

1 A move towards a sustainable way of life, conserving the earth's "capital", learning to rely mainly on those resources which can be renewed or recycled.

2 A move towards a stable economy, ensuring basic material security and prosperity for all.

3 A move towards economic self-sufficiency in terms of the basic necessities of life, particularly food and energy.

4 A move towards a decentralized way of life, so that people become more responsible for themselves and for others.

5 A move towards seeing things in the long term, rather than settling for convenient short term measures.

6 A move towards a society which places less emphasis on material values and more on personal development and achievement.

Such a programme adds up to a new economics for man, a new sense of values, the chance of a new future.

That means an escape from the narrow minded confrontations of right and left.

The Ecology Party veers neither to the one nor the other and views conventional political rivalries as dangerously irrelevant, in that they obscure the nature and the urgency of the problems we have to face up to.

The Communist Party

The Communist Party manifesto entitled *People before Profit* said:

Britain is not in crisis because its working people live too well or get too much to say. On the contrary, they do not live well enough nor have enough say in how the great resources of our country are developed and used.

A few giant companies and multinational firms dominate the economy. Their decisions affect the lives and jobs of millions. But they are not democratically controlled or accountable to the people and they put their profits before the needs of the community.

Employed and unemployed need to join together now to campaign for urgent measures to tackle unemployment, including the expansion of the economy and the restoring of public spending cuts.

Pay and pensions should be raised to stimulate demand for goods. Free collective bargaining should be restored and there should be a minimum wage of £60 per week, with a 35 hour week, longer holidays, higher pensions and earlier retirement.

All Britain's children should be entitled to a first class education without financial barriers and the provision of wider educational opportunities.

Local authorities should carry through a crash programme of new building and modernisation and renovation. There should be no selling of council houses.

The law should be strengthened to prevent the pollution of the air, rivers, lakes and sea.

It should be illegal for employers to refuse trade union recognition and unions should be entitled to negotiate 100 per cent trade union membership.

The House of Lords should be abolished and proportional representation introduced in voting.

Democratic control over the police should be extended. The police should not be used for strike breaking and both the police, and the armed forces, should have full trade union rights.

Britain should work for the fulfilment of the Helsinki agreement, withdraw from Nato and work for the winding up of both Nato and the Warsaw Pact and their replacement by an all-inclusive European security system.

Referendums on devolution

The people of Scotland and Wales gave their verdict on the Government's devolution proposals when they voted in separate referendums on March 1 1979.

The referendums were conducted on the electoral register which came into operation on February 16, 1979. The number of electors of voting age in Scotland on March 1, 1979 was 3,787,312 from which, under provisions in the legislation, deductions were made of 26,400 for deaths, 2,000 for convicted persons in prison, and 11,800 for students and nurses registered at more than one address. The number entitled to vote was 3,747,112.

In Wales, the number of people of voting age was 2,056,349 and with deductions of 14,900 for deaths, 800 for convicted persons in prison, and 2,600 for students and nurses registered at more than one address, the total number entitled to vote was 2,038,049.

The Scotland Act, designed to give Scots a measure of devolved government with a legislative assembly in Edinburgh, received a 51.5 per cent 'Yes' verdict from those who went to the polls and voted, but the total 'Yes' vote fell well short of the 40 per cent of the electorate required under the Act before it could be put into effect automatically. This requirement, which caused controversy, had been inserted as the legislation passed through the Commons.

In Scotland 33 per cent of the electorate favoured the devolution proposals and 31 per cent were against. An Order to repeal the Act was laid before Parliament but the Government proposed inter-party talks. Events at Westminster surrounding devolution for Scotland played a large part in the Government's eventual defeat when the Opposition motion of 'No confidence' was carried by one vote. In Scotland 1,230,937 (32.85% of the adjusted electorate) voted 'Yes' and 1,153,502 (30.78%) voted 'No' – a 'Yes' majority of 77,435.

The Wales Act, proposing an assembly in Cardiff, was massively voted down, every county being against the plans. The total figures were 'Yes' 243,048 (11.9% of the adjusted electorate) and 'No' 956,330 (46.9%), a 'No' majority of 713,282. The Government admitted that this was a clear defeat for their Welsh devolution plans and, here again, an Order repealing the Act was laid.

How Scotland and Wales voted

REGIONS		YES	% of vote	NO	% of vote	REGISTERED ELECTORATE TURN-OUT	% YES*	% NO
BORDERS	NO	20,746	40·3	30,780	59·7	66·4	26·7(27·0)	39·7
CENTRAL	YES	71,296	54·7	59,105	45·3	65·9	36·1(36·4)	29·9
DUMFRIES & GALLOWAY	NO	27,162	40·3	40,239	59·7	64·1	25·8(26·1)	38·3
FIFE	YES	86,252	53·7	74,436	46·3	65·3	35·1(35·4)	30·3
GRAMPIAN	NO	94,944	48·3	101,485	51·6	57·2	27·6(27·9)	29·5
HIGHLAND	YES	44,973	51·0	43,274	49·0	64·7	33·0(33·3)	31·7
LOTHIAN	YES	187,221	50·1	186,421	49·9	65·9	33·0(33·3)	32·9
STRATHCLYDE	YES	596,519	54·0	508,599	46·0	62·5	33·7(34·0)	28·7
TAYSIDE	NO	91,482	49·5	93,323	50·5	63·0	31·2(31·5)	31·8
ORKNEY	NO	2,104	27·9	5,439	72·1	54·1	15·1(15·2)	39·0
SHETLAND	NO	2,020	27·0	5,466	73·0	50·3	13·6(13·7)	36·7
WESTERN ISLES	YES	6,218	55·8	4,933	44·2	49·9	27·8(28·1)	22·1
TOTAL	YES	1,230,937	51·6	1,153,500	48·3	62·9	32·5(32·85)	30·4

		YES	% of vote	NO	% of vote	REGISTERED ELECTORATE TURN-OUT	% YES*	% NO
CLWYD	NO	31,384	21·6	114,119	78·4	51·1	11·0(11·1)	40·1
DYFED	NO	44,849	28·1	114,947	71·9	64·6	18·1(18·3)	46·5
GWENT	NO	21,369	12·1	155,389	87·9	55·3	6·7(6·7)	48·7
GWYNEDD	NO	37,363	34·4	71,157	65·6	63·4	21·8(22·1)	41·6
MID-GLAMORGAN	NO	46,747	20·2	184,196	79·8	58·5	11·8(12·0)	46·7
POWYS	NO	9,843	18·5	43,502	81·5	66·0	12·2(12·3)	53·8
S. GLAMORGAN	NO	21,830	13·1	144,186	86·8	58·7	7·7(7·8)	51·0
W. GLAMORGAN	NO	29,663	18·7	128,834	81·3	57·5	10·8(10·8)	46·7
TOTAL	NO	243,048	20·3	956,330	79·7	58·3	11·8(11·9)	46·5

*Figures in brackets are % Yes of notionally adjusted electorate

Referendum vote to continue in EEC

By a two to one majority the people voted 'Yes' to continued membership of the European Economic Community in the United Kingdom's first national referendum on June 5, 1975. Out of 68 counties and regions, only Shetland and the Western Isles voted against.

Announcing the result outside 10 Downing Street, Sir Harold Wilson, the then Prime Minister, said it meant that '14 years of national argument are over'.

Out of an electorate of 41,079,269 there were 17,378,581 'Yes' votes (67.2 per cent) and 8,470,073 'No' votes (32.8 per cent), a majority of 8,908,508. The turnout was 63.2 per cent.

In England there were 14,918,009 'Yes' votes and 6,812,052 'No' votes, a majority of 8,105,957. In Scotland 1,332,186 voted 'Yes' and 948,039 voted 'No' a majority of 384,157. In Wales the figures were 869,135 'Yes' and 472,071 'No' a majority of 397,064; while in Northern Ireland 259,251 voted 'Yes' and 237,911 'No', a majority of 21,340.

The detailed voting was as follows:

ENGLAND	Approx. Electorate	YES		NO		Turnout
Avon	665,484	310,145	(67·8%)	147,024	(32·2%)	68·7%
Bedfordshire	326,566	154,338	(69·4%)	67,969	(30·6%)	67·9%
Berkshire	443,472	215,184	(72·6%)	81,221	(27·4%)	66·4%
Buckinghamshire	346,348	180,512	(74·3%)	62,578	(25·7%)	69·5%
Cambridgeshire	375,753	177,789	(74·1%)	62,143	(25·9%)	62·9%
Cheshire	633,614	290,714	(70·1%)	123,839	(29·9%)	65·5%
Cleveland	392,672	158,982	(67·3%)	77,079	(32·7%)	60·2%
Cornwall	298,706	137,828	(68·5%)	63,478	(31·5%)	66·8%
Cumbria	349,596	162,545	(71·9%)	63,564	(28·1%)	64·8%
Derbyshire	653,005	286,614	(68·6%)	131,452	(31·4%)	64·1%
Devon	676,378	334,244	(72·1%)	129,179	(27·9%)	68%
Dorset	429,752	217,432	(73·5%)	78,239	(26·5%)	68·3%
Durham	444,783	175,284	(64·2%)	97,724	(35·8%)	61·5%
Essex	1,010,317	463,505	(67·6%)	222,085	(32·4%)	67·7%
Gloucestershire	347,218	170,931	(71·7%)	67,465	(28·3%)	68·4%
Greater London	5,250,343	2,201,031	(66·7%)	1,100,185	(33·3%)	60·8%
Greater Manchester	1,932,717	797,316	(64·5%)	439,191	(35·5%)	64·1%
Hampshire	975,440	484,302	(71%)	197,761	(29%)	68%
Hereford & Worcester	419,866	203,128	(72·8%)	75,779	(27·2%)	66·4%
Hertfordshire	662,177	326,943	(70·4%)	137,266	(29·6%)	70·2%
Humberside	607,890	257,826	(67·8%)	122,199	(32·2%)	62·4%
Isles of Scilly	1,447	802	(74·5%)	275	(25·5%)	75%
Isle of Wight	86,381	40,837	(70·2%)	17,375	(29·8%)	67·5%
Kent	1,035,313	493,407	(70·4%)	207,358	(29·6%)	67·4%
Lancashire	1,000,755	455,170	(68·6%)	208,821	(31·4%)	66·4%
Leicestershire	590,780	291,500	(73·3%)	106,004	(26·7%)	67·2%
Lincolnshire	370,518	180,603	(74·7%)	61,011	(25·3%)	63·7%
Merseyside	1,147,920	465,625	(64·8%)	252,712	(35·2%)	62·7%
Norfolk	485,229	218,883	(70·1%)	93,198	(29·9%)	63·8%
Northamptonshire	351,653	162,803	(69·5%)	71,322	(30·5%)	66·1%
Northumberland	212,846	95,980	(69·2%)	42,645	(30·8%)	65%
Nottinghamshire	705,183	297,191	(66·8%)	147,461	(33·2%)	63·1%
Oxfordshire	355,977	179,938	(73·6%)	64,643	(26·4%)	67·7%
Salop	249,463	113,044	(72·3%)	43,329	(27·7%)	62%
Somerset	293,191	138,830	(69·6%)	60,631	(30·4%)	67·7%
Staffordshire	706,230	306,518	(67·4%)	148,252	(32·6%)	64·3%
Suffolk	397,626	187,484	(72·2%)	72,251	(27·8%)	64·9%
Surrey	720,440	386,369	(76·2%)	120,576	(23·8%)	70·1%
East Sussex	511,437	249,780	(74·3%)	86,198	(25·7%)	65·8%
West Sussex	464,396	242,890	(76·2%)	75,928	(23·8%)	68·6%
Tyne & Wear	872,253	344,069	(62·9%)	202,511	(37·1%)	62·7%
Warwickshire	327,967	156,303	(69·9%)	67,221	(30·1%)	68%
West Midlands	1,972,987	801,913	(65·1%)	429,207	(34·9%)	62·5%
Wiltshire	344,833	172,791	(71·7%)	68,113	(28·3%)	67·8%
North Yorkshire	468,998	234,040	(76·3%)	72,805	(23·7%)	64·3%
South Yorkshire	954,539	377,916	(63·4%)	217,792	(36·6%)	62·4%
West Yorkshire	1,485,749	616,730	(65·4%)	326,993	(34·6%)	63·6%

WALES

Clwyd	272,798	**123,980**	(69·1%)	55,424	(30·9%)	65·8%
Dyfed	241,415	**109,184**	(67·6%)	52,264	(32·4%)	67·5%
Mid Glamorgan	390,175	**147,348**	(56·9%)	111,672	(43·1%)	66·6%
South Glamorgan	275,324	**127,932**	(69·5%)	56,224	(30·5%)	66·7%
West Glamorgan	272,818	**112,989**	(61·6%)	70,316	(38·4%)	67·4%
Gwent	314,369	**132,557**	(62·1%)	80,992	(37·9%)	68·2%
Gwynedd	167,706	**76,421**	(70·6%)	31,807	(29·4%)	64·3%
Powys	76,531	**38,724**	(74·3%)	13,372	(25·7%)	67·9%

SCOTLAND

Borders	74,834	**34,092**	(72·3%)	13,053	(27·7%)	63·2%
Central	188,613	**71,986**	(59·7%)	48,568	(40·3%)	64·1%
Dumfries & Galloway	101,703	**42,608**	(68·2%)	19,856	(31·8%)	61·5%
Fife	235,166	**84,239**	(56·3%)	65,260	(43·7%)	63·3%
Grampian	321,140	**108,520**	(58·2%)	78,071	(41·8%)	57·4%
Highland	127,925	**40,802**	(54·6%)	33,979	(45·4%)	58·7%
Lothian	548,369	**208,133**	(59·5%)	141,456	(40·5%)	63·6%
Orkney	13,157	**3,911**	(61·8%)	2,419	(38·2%)	48·2%
Shetland	13,411	2,815	(43·7%)	**3,631**	(56·3%)	47·1%
Strathclyde	1,759,889	**625,959**	(57·7%)	459,073	(42·3%)	61·7%
Tayside	282,160	**105,728**	(58·6%)	74,567	(41·4%)	63·8%
Western Isles	22,432	3,393	(29·5%)	**8,106**	(70·5%)	50·1%

NORTHERN IRELAND

Northern Ireland	1,030,534	**259,251**	(52·1%)	237,911	(47·9%)	47·4%

Constituency Index

The parliamentary constituency analysis which begins on page 30 is in alphabetical order under the correct full title of each seat. The following abbreviated index is mainly of seats in the Greater London area which are grouped under their London boroughs. Outside London seats in the major cities or towns are grouped together under the name of the city or town.

Index to Candidates

Those elected are named in bold type

335